CONVERSION
COURSE COMPANION
FOR LAW

CONVERSION
COURSE COMPANION
FOR LAW

Core Legal Principles and Cases for CPE/GDL

Edited by

Rhona Smith
Lynne Murrell
Deborah Rook

PEARSON
Longman

Harlow, England • London • New York • Boston • San Francisco • Toronto
Sydney • Tokyo • Singapore • Hong Kong • Seoul • Taipei • New Delhi
Cape Town • Madrid • Mexico City • Amsterdam • Munich • Paris • Milan

Pearson Education Limited

Edinburgh Gate
Harlow
Essex CM20 2JE
England

and Associated Companies throughout the world

Visit us on the World Wide Web at:
www.pearsoned.co.uk

———————————————

First published 2008

© Pearson Education Limited 2008

ISBN: 978-0-4058-7315-4

British Library Cataloguing-in-Publication Data
A catalogue record for this book is available from the British Library

Library of Congress Cataloging-in-Publication Data
A catalog record for this book is available from the Library of Congress

ARP Impression 98

Typeset in 9/12.5 Interstate Light by 73
Printed in Great Britain by Clays Ltd, St Ives plc

The publisher's policy is to use paper manufactured from sustainable forests.

Til far, mor og Lorna,
nu er vi der igen
RKMS

Voor de Nederlander,
met liefde en dank
LM

For Ben,
my shining star
DR

Contents

Contributors   xiii
Introduction   xvii

1   **CRIMINAL LAW**   1

Murder and intent
R v. *Woollin* [1999] 1 AC 82   3

Gross negligence manslaughter
R v. *Adomako* [1994] 3 All ER 79   8

Non-fatal offences against the person
R v. *Ireland* and *R* v. *Burstow* [1997] 4 All ER 225   12

Theft and appropriation
R v. *Hinks* [2001] 2 AC 241   17

Inchoate offences – attempts, conspiracy and incitement
R v. *Shivpuri* [1987] AC 1   21

Provocation and diminished responsibility as defences to murder
R v. *Morgan James Smith* [2001] 1 AC 146, House of Lords   25

Criminal Damage – recklessness; reconsidering *Caldwell*
R v. *G and Another* [2003] 1 AC 1034   33

Intoxication defences
DPP v. *Majewski* [1977] AC 443   37

Consent and offences against the person
R v. *Brown* [1994] 1 AC 212   42

Joint enterprise
R v. *Powell and Daniels*; and *R* v. *English* [1999] 1 AC 1, House of Lords   47

2   **PUBLIC LAW**   55

Rule of law
Entick v. *Carrington* (1765) 19 State Tr 1029   57

Supremacy of Parliament
R (on the application of Jackson and Others) v. *Attorney-General*
[2005] UKHL 56, [2005] All ER (D) 136   63

Public authorities and the Human Rights Act
*Aston Cantlow and Wilmcote with Billesley Parochial Church
Council* v. *Wallbank and Another* [2003] UKHL 37, [2003]
3 All ER 1213   70

Official secrets legislation and the separation of powers
R v. *Ponting* [1985] Crim LR 318   76

Police powers and the rights of suspects
R v. *Lattimore and Others* (1976) 62 Cr App R 53   81

Preventing a breach of the peace (public order)
R (Laporte) v. *Chief Constable of Gloucestershire* [2006] UKHL 55   84

Freedom to demonstrate and public order offences
DPP v. *Jones (Margaret)* [1999] 2 AC 240   89

Judicial review of administrative action
Council of Civil Service Unions v. *Minister for the Civil Service*
[1984] 3 All ER 935   93

Standing (*locus standi*) for judicial review proceedings
Inland Revenue Commissioner v. *National Federation of
Self-Employed and Small Businesses Ltd* [1982] AC 617   98

Bias (judicial review)
R v. *Bow Street Metropolitan Stipendiary Magistrate ex parte
Pinochet Ugarte (No. 2)* [1999] 2 WLR 272 HL   104

3 EUROPEAN UNION: LAWS AND INSTITUTIONS   109

Overview
Case 26/62 *Van Gend en Loos* v. *Nederlandse Administratie der
Belastingen* [1963] ECR 1   111

***L'effet utile* (effective judicial protection)**
Cases 14/83 *Von Colson and Kamann* v. *Land Nordrhein-Westfalen*
[1984] ECR 1891; C-106/89 *Marleasing SA* v. *La Comercial
Internacional de Alimentación SA* [1990] ECR I-4135   116

Preliminary rulings under Article 234 EC
Case 283/81 *Srl CILFIT and Lanificio di Gavardo SpA* v. *Ministry
of Health* [1982] ECR 3415   122

State liability
Cases C-6 and 9/90 *Francovich* v. *Italy* [1991] ECR I-5357   127

Free movement of goods
Case 120/78 *Rewe-Zentral AG* v. *Bundesmonopolverwaltung für
Branntwein (Cassis de Dijon)* [1979] ECR 649   132

Free movement of workers
Case 66/85 *Deborah Lawrie-Blum* v. *Land Baden-Württemberg*
[1986] ECR 2121   140

Freedom to provide services
Case C-76/90 *Säger* v. *Dennemeyer* [1991] ECR I-4221   145

Social policy
Case 43/75 *Defrenne* v. *Société Anonyme Belge de Navigation Aerienne
(SABENA)* [1976] ECR 455, [1976] 2 CMLR 98 (*aka Defrenne II*)   151

Competition law: cartels (Article 81)
Cases 56/64 and 58/64 *Etablissements Consten SA and
Grundig-Verkaufs-GmbH* v. *EEC Commission* [1966] ECR 299,
[1966] CMLR 418   156

Competition: dominant position (Article 82)
Case 6/73 *Europemballage and Continental Can* v. *Commission*
[1973] ECR 215   161

4 CONTRACT LAW (OBLIGATIONS)   165

Offer and acceptance
Carlill v. *Carbolic Smoke Ball Company* [1893] QB 256   167

Consideration
Williams v. *Roffey Brothers & Nicholls (Contractors) Ltd*
[1991] 1 QB 1   172

Intention to create legal relations
Balfour v. *Balfour* [1919] 2 KB 571   179

Contract terms
Liverpool City Council v. *Irwin* [1977] AC 239   186

Exemption clauses
George Mitchell (Chesterhall) Ltd v. *Finney Lock Seeds*
[1983] All ER 737   192

Misrepresentation
Howard Marine & Dredging Co. Ltd v. *Ogden & Sons
(Excavation) Ltd* [1978] 2 All ER 1134   197

Illegality
Littlewoods Organisation Ltd v. *Harris* [1978] 1 All ER 1026   202

Discharge
Davis Contractors v. *Fareham UDC* [1956] AC 696   208

Remedies
Ruxley Electronics and Construction Ltd v. *Forsyth* [1996] AC 344   217

Contents

5 TORT LAW   223

Duty of care
Donoghue (or Mc'Alister) v. Stevenson [1932] AC 562   225

Negligently inflicted psychiatric injury
Alcock v. Chief Constable of South Yorkshire Police [1992] 1 AC 310   231

Negligently inflicted economic loss
Hedley Byrne & Co. v. Heller and Partners Ltd [1964] AC 465   236

Factual causation
*Barnett v. Chelsea and Kensington Hospital Management
Committee* [1969] 1 QB 428   242

Causation in law
Knightley v. Johns and Others [1982] All ER 851, [1982] 1 WLR 349   249

Remoteness of damage
*Overseas Tankship (UK) Ltd v. Morts Dock & Engineering
(The Wagon Mound (No. 1))* [1961] AC 388, [1961] 1 All ER 404   254

Defences to negligence
Owens v. Brimmell [1977] QB 859   259

Occupiers' liability
Roles v. Nathan [1963] 1 WLR 1117   264

Private nuisance
*Hunter and Others v. Canary Wharf Ltd; Hunter and Others v.
London Docklands Development Corporation* [1997] AC 655   268

6 EQUITY AND TRUSTS   273

Certainty of intention
Paul v. Constance [1977] 1 WLR 527   275

Certainty of objects
McPhail v. Doulton (in Re Baden's Deed Trusts) [1971] AC 424;
Re Baden's Deed Trusts No. 2 [1973] 3 WLR 250   279

Constitution
Pennington v. Waine [2002] EWCA Civ 227   285

Non-charitable purpose trusts
Re Endacott [1960] Ch 232   290

Common intention constructive trusts
Lloyds Bank Plc v. Rosset and Another [1991] 1 AC 107   296

Breach of fiduciary duty
Bristol and West Building Society v. Mothew [1998] Ch 1   303

Investment by trustees
Nestlé v. *National Westminster Bank* [1993] 1 WLR 1260,
[1994] 1 All ER 118   309

Tracing
Foskett v. *McKeown* [2001] 1 AC 102   316

Knowing receipt
*Bank of Credit and Commerce International (Overseas) Ltd and
International Credit and Investment Company (Overseas) Ltd* v.
Chief Labode Onadimaki Akindele [2001] Ch 437   321

7 LAND LAW (PROPERTY LAW)   **325**

Unregistered land
Kingsnorth Finance Co Ltd v. *Tizard* [1986] 1 WLR 783   327

Overreaching and overriding interests
Williams & Glyn's Bank Ltd v. *Boland* [1981] AC 487;
City of London Building Society v. *Flegg* [1988] AC 54   332

Registered title
Abbey National Building Society v. *Cann* [1990] 2 WLR 832   338

Co-ownership
Kinch v. *Bullard* [1999] 1 WLR 423   344

The lease/licence distinction
Street v. *Mountford* [1985] AC 809   349

Contractual licences
Ashburn Anstalt v. *Arnold and Another* [1988] 2 WLR 706   355

Leases – the remedy of forfeiture
Expert Clothing Service and Sales Ltd v. *Hillgate House Ltd*
[1986] Ch 340   359

Mortgages – undue influence
Royal Bank of Scotland v. *Etridge (No. 2)* [2002] 2 AC 773   364

Easements
Payne v. *Inwood* (1996) 74 P&CR 42   369

The enforceability of freehold covenants
Rhone v. *Stephens* [1994] 2 AC 310   374

Index   379

Contributors

Liane Atkin is a solicitor and senior lecturer in law at Northumbria University. She generally teaches commercial and employment law.

Patrick Bishop is a lecturer in law at Swansea University. He currently teaches property law to both CPE and LLB students.

Debra Brown is a solicitor and senior lecturer in law at De Montfort University. She has extensive experience of teaching and researching in commercial law areas as well as EU law.

Dr Nicole Busby is a senior lecturer in law at the University of Stirling. She has published widely in peer reviewed journals, co-authors a textbook and co-edits a statute book. She currently teaches labour law and European law across a variety of undergraduate and postgraduate programmes including LLB.

Dr Sarah Christie is a senior lecturer at The Robert Gordon University, Aberdeen. She has published widely in the fields of criminal law and medical law, and teaches both subjects to LLB students.

Jan Cookson is a solicitor and senior lecturer in law, specialising in land law. She currently teaches land law, and property law and practice at Northumbria University.

Alan Davenport is a senior lecturer in law at Northumbria University and has published widely in public law and civil liberties. He currently teaches public law across various programmes including CPE.

Gemma Davies is a practising barrister and senior lecturer in law at Northumbria University. She teaches criminal practice and procedure as well as advocacy to BVC students.

Karen Davies is programme director for the GDL/CPE offered at the School of Law at Swansea University. She currently teaches EU law on both the GDL and LLB programmes, together with employment law (LLB) and the English legal system (GDL).

Brian Dowrick is a senior lecturer in the law school at the University of Glamorgan and has published widely in pensions and property related matters. He has taught the law of obligations module on the CPE/GDL at Glamorgan for over ten years and is currently course director of the CPE.

Emma Duff spent time in practice specialising in conveyancing and probate before joining the property team at Northumbria University.

Bob Evans is a senior lecturer at Northumbria University specialising in trusts succession and tax. He is also a solicitor practising in those areas in a small three-partner (two-office) firm in County Durham.

Fiona Fletcher practised in commercial litigation. She is currently a senior lecturer in law at Northumbria University where she teaches contract law.

Ross Fletcher is a barrister and senior lecturer in law at Northumbria University. He teaches a variety of subjects on the bar vocational course as well as company law at undergraduate and masters level, and is programme leader for LLM commercial law (distance learning) and in charge of the law school's mooting programmes.

Professor David Grant is director of the legal services unit at Northumbria University. He teaches tort and has particular expertise in travel law. He is co-editor of the *International Travel Law Journal*.

Emmanuel Guinchard is lecturer in law at Northumbria University. He has a master 2 research in private international law from Paris-II University (Panthéon-Assas) in France. He teaches competition law, EU law and world trade organisation law to both LLB and LLM students.

Dr Andrew Harries is a senior lecturer in law at the University of Central Lancashire. He's currently course leader for the LLB programme, teaches obligations, public law, legal theory and regulation. He's taught CPE contract law and various masters-level courses. Dr Harries has published articles relating to public and private dimensions of contracting practice and carried out empirical research in the NHS and local government.

Lucinda Hudson, solicitor (England and Wales, Hong Kong) and part-time employment judge, is a lecturer at Northumbria University, where she teaches public law and English and European legal systems. As a litigator, she practised European and public law for the UK and Hong Kong governments.

Valerie Humphreys is acting head of the School of Law at Birmingham City University. She has experience of running both GDL/CPE and LLB programmes. She currently teaches contract and property law and has a particular interest in private/property law theory.

Dr Andrew Iwobi, barrister and solicitor (Nigeria), lectures in the School of Law, Swansea University where he is currently the module director for equity and trusts on the LLB and GDL programmes. He has taught various aspects of property law at undergraduate level and has published in the field of property law and also on various aspects of Nigerian law.

Adam Jackson, barrister and senior lecturer in law at Northumbria University, specialises in criminal law and evidence. He teaches and researches in both subjects.

Dr Mark James is a reader in law at the University of Salford and has published widely on the subject of sports law. He is associate head of School for Research and currently teaches tort law and sports law.

Eva Joyce, barrister and senior lecturer in law at Anglia Ruskin University, is the course director of the CPE. She teaches EU law to both CPE and LLB students and also has a particular interest in human rights issues. She has also published in criminal law.

Dr Simone Lamont-Black (née Schnitzer) is an *Assessorin* and CEDR accredited mediator. She qualified as a civil lawyer in Bavaria and practised in Germany as '*Rechtsanwältin*' but is now a senior lecturer in Law at Northumbria University. She has taught EU law, though now teaches primarily (private) international trade law and dispute resolution.

Richard Lee is a barrister and senior lecturer at Manchester Metropolitan University. He teaches criminal law on the CPE and evidence on the LLB in both the UK and Hong Kong. He has also published in the areas of criminal law and human rights.

Maureen Maksymiw, is a solicitor and senior lecturer in law at Nottingham Law School at Nottingham Trent University. She leads and teaches the contract law course on the GDL and teaches on other programmes including the LPC.

Rebecca Moosavian, solicitor and senior lecturer in law, currently oversees the open learning LLB (Hons) degree programme at Northumbria University. She normally teaches jurisprudence and intellectual property law.

Judith Puech, solicitor and senior lecturer in law, teaches equity and trusts at Northumbria University. She has a particular interest in the law of charities.

Richard Ramsay is a senior lecturer in law at Oxford Brookes University and a barrister whose pupillage was in public and construction law. He has taught contract and tort to GDL students for many years, and public, company and environmental law to undergraduates. He has interests in law and its relations to history and literature as well.

Christopher Rogers, barrister and senior lecturer in law at Northumbria University, currently teaches English legal systems and European Union law. His main research interest is canon law.

Deborah Rook, solicitor and principal lecturer in law at Northumbria University, specialises in land law (property). She presently teaches and publishes in both land law and animal law.

Dr Caroline Sawyer, solicitor and reader in law at Oxford Brookes University, has taught across the core syllabus, publishing in child law and immigration law as well as property law.

Dr Rhona Smith is professor in law at Northumbria University. She has experience of teaching business law and more extensive experience of EU law though at Northumbria teaches primarily public law and human rights.

Zena Smith is a senior lecturer in law at Northumbria University. Having worked in practice as a solicitor for some years she now teaches criminal litigation to both LLB and LPC students.

Alistair Speirs is a lecturer at Newcastle Law School. He has taught across a number of subjects and programmes in Newcastle University. He has particular expertise in equity and trusts, land law and tort.

Tony Storey is a senior lecturer in law at Northumbria University, specialising in EU law and criminal law. He has also published various textbooks on both EU law and criminal law.

Louise Tait worked as a graduate teaching assistant teaching public law, EU and English legal systems at Northumbria University. During this time, she also completed a postgraduate research thesis on human rights.

Meryl Thomas is a reader in law at Birmingham City University. She specialises in land law, trusts and the law relating to pensions. She teaches and publishes in all of those areas.

Ralph Tiernan is a senior lecturer in law at Northumbria University. He has over thirty years experience of teaching tort across a range of law programmes. He also teaches international trade.

Contributors

Susan Wolf is a principal lecturer in law at Northumbria University. She specialises in EU law, environmental law and environmental information law. She publishes mostly in environmental law.

Mick Woodley is an associate dean in the School of Law at Northumbria University. He mainly teaches company law and employment law.

Natalie Wortley is a barrister and a senior lecturer in Law at Northumbria University. She currently teaches criminal law, evidence and advocacy. She continues to practise at the Bar, specialising in criminal law.

INTRODUCTION

There are few legal texts focused primarily on the needs of students undertaking the Graduate Diploma in Law (also known as the Common Professional Examination). Achieving competency in the Foundations of Law in a year (or two for part-time students) is no mean feat. A plethora of textbooks and statute books and hundreds of cases must be read and digested to secure a pass. This particular book seeks to provide an insight into some of the principal cases encountered while studying those subjects compulsory for the academic stage of legal qualification. It is equally applicable to those studying for an LLB undergraduate degree, or indeed those simply with an interest in law.

The Solicitors' Regulatory Authority (regulating the Law Society) and Bar Council agree the Foundations of Legal Knowledge required for those seeking entry into the professions in England and Wales: contract (obligations); criminal law; equity and the law of trusts; European Union (law and institutions); land law (property); public law including constitutional law, administrative law and human rights; and tort (obligations). The object of this book is to provide a concise student guide to each of the foundations of legal knowledge. Key cases are analysed and their impact discussed. The GDL/CPE course is intensive thus many students find it difficult to adequately research all cases. This book is thus a useful tool for them to consult as they proceed through the year(s).

For each of the foundation areas, a maximum of ten key topics have been identified. For each of these topics, a case which either demonstrates the key principle or a major issue is used as a vehicle for examining the topic. Obviously there is scope for academic debate as to what these key areas should be and which cases should be selected. Our selection was drawn up in consultation with experts in the field and reflects areas commonly addressed in textbooks and law modules. This book started as an in-house project at Northumbria University but soon extended to include contributors from a range of law schools. The breadth of experience of the contributors and combined years of teaching on CPE/GDL and LLB programmes ensures the book is appropriate for all students.

When writing each entry, the contributors generally have adopted the approach they found most appropriate based on their experience of teaching the area. Thus sometimes, there are extensive extracts from the case, while in others, the area of law raised in the case is explained in a much wider context. Each entry is accompanied by a further reading list which incorporates the references from the entry and suggestions for developing your understanding of the topic. Further reading is divided into two sections: primary sources which includes the relevant cases and statutes; and secondary sources which includes books and articles. The intention is simply to indicate related reading, the lists are not exhaustive and recourse should be had to your course notes and/or additional texts for more detailed information.

Perhaps unfortunately, but inevitably, this book is not a substitute for reading cases, textbooks and articles. Rather it should help the reader understand the importance of the case in the context of the subject area concerned. In effect, each topic will be explained through the cases. We do not seek to provide full standalone case analyses, rather our contributors take an integrated approach to each case, contextualising it within the syllabus. Moreover, this book cannot contain the entire GDL/CPE syllabus within its covers (consider the combined mass of textbooks and primary sources the average law student is expected to read!). The book does, however, strive to introduce readers to the some of the key concepts and principles encountered during their legal studies. A wide range of books are now available covering each of the key areas of law. Those formally studying law will be directed towards the preferred texts by tutors. A range of study aids are also available to assist with the revision process and focus on the key elements of each subject.

Although this book may serve as an introduction to key areas and concepts, it is no substitute for thoroughly reading the relevant cases. In the twenty-first century, there are no excuses for law students not having access to cases. Modern cases are often available free on open websites such as **www.bailii.org**. In addition, all universities subscribe to a number of electronic sources which permit students to access cases online through citations, case names and keyword searches (Lexis Nexis Butterworths, Westlaw, Lawtel etc.). Access to additional articles discussing the cases is also available online. For those studying law, citation indexing (also available online) is another tool you must gain familiarity with: i.e., identifying subsequent cases which have cited, considered, reversed or applied the case in question. Developing familiarity with these tools will hone legal research skills and allow these case entries to be updated as and when required.

There are no comparable texts in the market so we welcome any comments readers may have. We express our sincere gratitude to the contributors for helping make the final book such an exciting overview of the foundations of law. Obviously, the views expressed in each entry are those of the identified contributor.

Inevitably, there are many people we owe a debt of gratitude to. Firstly, the contributors whose forbearance during what has been a protracted process is much appreciated. Secondly, the publishers, in particular Zoe Botterill. Thirdly, we have benefited greatly from the support of some of our colleagues at Northumbria University who have read submitted entries and given valuable comments - Dave Cowley, Tony Storey, Steve Wilson, Andrea O'Cain and Mick Woodley (who also wrote the Introduction to Contract Law (page 165)), in particular.

As far as possible, the law contained in this text is accurate as at 25 January 2008.

Rhona Smith, Lynne Murrell, Deborah Rook
Newcastle upon Tyne
January 2008

1 CRIMINAL LAW

Criminal law is probably the area of law which most people first think of when 'law' is mentioned. It falls within the broad sphere of 'public law' as it involves the relationship between the state and the individual. Although serious criminal offences fall within criminal law, there is a lot more than murder, theft, assault etc. to study. For many offences, it is necessary that the perpetrator intended to commit an offence. However, reckless actions can also attract criminal responsibility as will be seen and the mere fact the offence is committed can be sufficient for a prosecution. Consequently, concepts such as intention to commit an offence and of responsibility for criminal actions will also be addressed. Definition is a major issue in criminal law – generally people think they understand what criminal activity is but the action must fall clearly within statute or common law offences for the police to be able to act and for prosecutions to follow.

According to the official Home Office statistics for 2006-7 (England and Wales), based on police recorded crime during that year, there were 757 deaths originally recorded as homicides in 2006-7, 75% of which were male. There were 59 shooting victims, though the most common method of killing was with a sharp instrument (35% of the recorded homicides). As of November 2007, 86 of these deaths had resulted in conviction for murder, 62 for manslaughter, 23 were declassified (no longer considered homicide by the police) and the rest were pending. Obviously there is more to criminal law than homicides. Indeed, the most common types of crime were offences against property (burglary, vehicle theft, vandalism etc.). Overall, the police recorded some 5.4 million crimes in 2006-7. Not all of these will result in prosecutions or, indeed, be ultimately dealt with by the court system. However, it does indicate the scale of criminal law today.

The entries in this chapter range from murder and manslaughter through theft to attempted crimes (inchoates) and recklessness. Some common defences will also be examined, notably provocation, intoxication and consent.

CONTENTS FOR CRIMINAL LAW

Murder and intent
R v. *Woollin* [1999] 1 AC 82   3

Gross negligence manslaughter
R v. *Adomako* [1994] 3 All ER 79   8

Non-fatal offences against the person
R v. *Ireland* and R v. *Burstow* [1997] 4 All ER 225   12

Theft and appropriation
R v. *Hinks* [2001] 2 AC 241   17

Inchoate offences – attempts, conspiracy and incitement
R v. *Shivpuri* [1987] AC 1   21

Provocation and diminished responsibility as defences to murder
R v. *Morgan James Smith* [2001] 1 AC 146, House of Lords   25

Criminal Damage – recklessness; reconsidering *Caldwell*
R v. *G and Another* [2003] 1 AC 1034   33

Intoxication defences
DPP v. *Majewski* [1977] AC 443   37

Consent and offences against the person
R v. *Brown* [1994] 1 AC 212   42

Joint enterprise
R v. *Powell and Daniels*; and R v. *English* [1999] 1 AC 1, House of Lords   47

Murder and intent

R v. Woollin [1999] 1 AC 82

Richard Lee, Manchester Metropolitan University

Many offences within the criminal law require the defendant to 'intend' the consequences of his act in order to be found guilty of the offence, yet the courts have struggled for some 30 years to try and define exactly what is meant by the term 'intention'.

The difficulties in defining intention seem to have stemmed from the failure of the judiciary to be sufficiently clear or precise in their use of language in the course of their judgments. The issue has been further complicated as many of the cases involving intention have revolved around a charge of murder, which brings with it various emotive issues and the consequence of a mandatory life sentence for those found guilty. Such matters have doubtless impacted on the judges' decision-making process as they try to ensure that justice is done in each individual case. The case of *Woollin* is the latest in a long line of cases dealing with the concept of intention within murder, and it has gone some way towards clarifying the law and is the current leading authority on the *mens rea* (state of mind) required for murder.

The definition of intention in murder: direct versus oblique intent

The courts' focus on the concept of intention within murder means that any study of intention is best carried out in the context of murder case law.

The *mens rea* for murder is that the defendant must have intended either to kill the victim or to cause them serious injury (grievous bodily harm). This is also sometimes referred to as 'malice aforethought'.

At its simplest level it is said that if someone 'intends' a consequence, then that means that it is that person's aim or purpose to bring about that consequence. This is a matter for the jury to determine using their commonsense, as Lord Bridge stated in the case of *Moloney*, at page 926:

> The golden rule should be that, when directing a jury on the mental element necessary . . . the judge should avoid any elaboration or paraphrase of what is meant by intent, and leave it to the jury's good sense to decide whether the accused acted with the necessary intent.

Hence, if the jury determines that the defendant's aim or motive was to cause the victim to die or cause them serious injury, then the jury can safely conclude that the defendant is guilty of murder. Where a defendant has this specific aim or motive this is known as 'direct intent'.

Difficulty arises where, for example, a man places a bomb on a plane with the intention of blowing the plane up and claiming the insurance money on the cargo. Here it is the man's intention to blow the plane up for the insurance money and he has no intention regarding the pilots at all. Yet it is clear that in blowing up the plane the pilots will be killed. Should such a man also be guilty of the murder of those pilots? Morally speaking, the answer would appear to be yes, and the criminal law has accordingly developed to incorporate this notion. This is known as 'oblique intent', and occurs where a person's intentional act causes a secondary consequence to occur. In such a case it can be said that the person *obliquely* intended that secondary consequence, even if he did not *directly* intend such a consequence.

Oblique intent in murder – the 'natural consequences' test

The case of *Moloney* involved a son and his stepfather taking part in a drunken competition over who could load, draw and shoot a shotgun the fastest. In the course of this competition the son shot and killed his stepfather. After a misdirection by the trial judge the House of Lords took this opportunity to examine all aspects of intention in murder cases and considered what was meant by the term oblique intent.

In the rare cases where it was necessary for the judge to direct the jury on oblique intent Lord Bridge conceded that the jury would need further guidance. He states at page 929 that the jury need to consider two questions:

> First, was death or really serious injury in a murder case a natural consequence of the defendant's voluntary act? Secondly, did the defendant foresee that consequence as being a natural consequence of his act? The jury should then be told that if they answer yes to both questions it is a proper inference for them to draw that he intended that consequence.

This statement caused later confusion as it was not clear what the phrase 'natural consequences' meant as Lord Bridge did not make any direct reference to the level of probability required. Was a natural consequence something that would *probably* happen, or be *likely* to happen, or *might* happen? It appears that Lord Bridge actually intended that a 'natural consequence' would carry a much higher degree of probability, as earlier in his speech on page 929 he says: '[Natural] conveys the idea that in the ordinary course of events a certain act will lead to a certain consequence unless something unexpected supervenes to prevent it.' Hence, Lord Bridge seems to have intended 'natural consequences' to mean something akin to 'certain outcome'.

The 'natural consequences' test re-interpreted

Only one year later the House of Lords re-visited the test for oblique intent in murder. In the case of *Hancock and Shankland* two striking miners pushed a concrete block off a bridge over a motorway. The block hit a passing taxi taking other miners to work, killing the driver. The trial judge misdirected the jury and (unnecessarily) applied the 'natural consequences' test, and failed to adequately explain what the terms meant.

On appeal, Lord Scarman took it upon himself to define what was meant by 'natural consequences', and in doing so seems to ignore Lord Bridge and put forward his own thoughts. He claimed that Lord Bridge made insufficient reference to the level of probability required and that the term 'natural consequences' required further elaboration for the jury. He regarded the current guidelines as 'unsafe and misleading'. Lord Scarman proposed a new interpretation of the guidelines arguing at page 473 that: '. . . the greater the probability of a consequence the more likely that it is that the consequence was foreseen and that if the consequence was foreseen the greater the probability is that the consequence was also intended.'

In using this approach Lord Scarman seems to imply that the jury should be entitled to infer intent where the defendant foresees that there is a high probability that the secondary consequence would occur. This is clearly a lower standard than the test put forward by Lord Bridge in *Moloney* as he required the level of probability to be something like a certain outcome. For many academic commentators Lord Scarman's test moves too far towards a concept of recklessness in murder. While it can be said that it seems appropriate for a jury to decide that a defendant can be deemed to have intended a secondary consequence if he knew that such a consequence was a certain outcome of his action; it seems that to find someone guilty on the basis that they merely foresaw a high probability that a secondary consequence might occur is almost tantamount to saying that recklessness is sufficient *mens rea* for murder.

The conflict resolved

Given the very confused state in which the law was left after *Hancock and Shankland* it is not surprising that later that same year the Court of Appeal decided to try to resolve the conflicting *dicta* coming from the House of Lords. *Nedrick* concerned a man who had poured paraffin through the letterbox of the house of a woman against whom he had a grudge and ignited it. He claimed that he only intended to frighten the woman, but unfortunately a child was killed in the blaze.

Lord Lane CJ returned to a narrower definition of the level of foresight required for oblique intention in murder stating at page 1028:

> . . . if the Jury are satisfied that at the material time the defendant recognised that death or serious harm would be virtually certain (barring some unforeseen intervention) to result from his voluntary act, then that is a fact from which they may find it easy to infer that he intended to kill or do serious bodily harm, even though he may not have had any desire to achieve that result.

So the test for oblique intention became:

1. Was death or serious harm a virtually certain consequence of the defendant's action?
2. Did the defendant foresee that his act would be virtually certain to cause death or serious harm?

If the answer to both these questions is yes then the jury are entitled to *infer* the intention for murder. It should be noted at this point that the jury are not required to automatically find the intention existed. The foresight of a virtually certain consequence is not intention *per se*, but the level of foresight is evidence from which the jury may go on to infer intent. Therefore, a jury must be able to consider the level of foresight held by the defendant alongside all other evidence in the case.

Woollin

The case of *Woollin* involved a father who threw his three-month-old son across the room in the direction of his pram in frustration over the infant's crying. The baby suffered a fractured skull and died as a result of the injury. It was accepted at the trial that the father did not have the direct intention to kill or cause the baby serious injury, hence, it was an issue of oblique intent. The House of Lords confirmed that Lord Lane CJ's direction in *Nedrick* was a 'tried and tested formula' and ought to be used by trial judges.

Lord Steyn also took this opportunity to further clarify the direction for the jury and recast the *Nedrick* direction in the following terms (emphasis added):

> Where the charge is murder and in the rare cases where the simple direction is not enough, the jury should be directed that they are not entitled to *find* the necessary intention unless they feel sure that death or serious bodily harm was a virtual certainty (barring some unforeseen intervention) as a result of the defendant's action and that the defendant appreciated that such was the case.

This replacement of the word 'infer' (which was used in *Nedrick*) with 'find' may have clarified matters, however, it is suggested that Lord Steyn also had it in mind to try to move away from the concept that the virtual certainty test was merely an evidential rule used to infer intention, and his modified direction implied that where a defendant satisfies the 'virtual certainty test' he should be regarded as having the required intention.

This move has met some resistance in the Court of Appeal where Rix LJ in *Matthews* stated at para. 43 that: 'In our judgment, however, the law has not yet reached a definition of intent in murder in terms of appreciating virtual certainty.' The Court of Appeal seemed keen that the jury should retain their discretion to decide not to infer intent should they wish, even where the virtual certainty test is satisfied. It is submitted that this is the correct approach as there may be circumstances where a defendant commits an act that may be virtually certain to cause death or serious injury, yet the reason behind that act makes a finding of guilt to murder inappropriate. For example, a desperate mother might throw her baby from a high window in a burning building if she thought that was the only possible means of saving her child from dying in the blaze. If that baby were to die due to the injuries caused from the fall the virtual certainly test would be very likely satisfied, yet it would seem harsh that the mother be found guilty of murder in these circumstances.

Conclusion

Woollin is currently the leading authority on intention in murder cases and clearly states that the requisite level of foresight is virtual certainty. It should be stressed that Lord Steyn expressly limited his comments on the virtual certainty direction to the crime of murder. However, many academics would regard it a detrimental step if a similar approach were not adopted to the meaning of intention across all crimes that have intention as part of their *mens rea*. Hence, the ideas in *Woollin* have generally come to represent the meaning of intention in criminal law as a whole.

FURTHER READING

Primary sources

Hancock and Shankland [1986] AC 455

Matthews [2003] EWCA Crim 192

Moloney [1985] AC 905

Nedrick [1986] 1 WLR 1025

Secondary sources

Kugler, I. (2004) 'Conditional Oblique Intent' (2004) *Crim LR*, 284.

Lacey, N. (1993) 'A Clear Concept of Intention: Elusive or Illusory?' (1993) 56, *Modern Law Review*, 621.

Norrie, A. (1999) 'After *Woollin*' (1999) *Crim LR*, 532.

Williams, G. (1987) 'Oblique Intention' (1987) *Cambridge Law Journal*, 47, 417.

1

CRIMINAL LAW

Gross negligence manslaughter

R v. *Adomako* [1994] 3 All ER 79

Gemma Davies, Northumbria University

Of all crimes, manslaughter is in law one of the most difficult to define, as it concerns homicide in so many and varying conditions. It is often said that murder is based, although not exclusively, on the intention to kill and manslaughter, again not exclusively, on the absence of an intention to kill, but nevertheless has the presence of some element of unlawfulness, for example, unlawfully assaulting someone. It is what constitutes this 'unlawfulness' that has been the basis of debate in several cases.

It is useful to divide manslaughter broadly into two categories, that of voluntary manslaughter and that of involuntary manslaughter. The distinction broadly being that for voluntary manslaughter there is the presence of intention, or malice aforethought, but the presence of some legally defined mitigating circumstances makes the crime less serious, provocation being the primary example. Involuntary manslaughter on the other hand consists of homicides which are unlawful but are committed without malice aforethought. Of course, complications arise because the fault required on the part of a defendant takes on more than one form and there inevitably follows uncertainty as to the boundaries of the offence. Broadly speaking involuntary manslaughter falls into two categories, manslaughter by an unlawful and dangerous act, and manslaughter by gross negligence or recklessness. The House of Lords' decision in *R* v. *Adomako* concerns the latter category.

Prior to this case, the case of *R* v. *Seymour* decided that in cases of involuntary manslaughter, other than unlawful act manslaughter, the fault required was *Lawrence*, or objective recklessness. Under objective recklessness the defendant must perform an act which creates a serious risk that is obvious to a reasonably prudent man and either he recognises such a risk but nevertheless takes it, or he has not given any thought to the possibility of such a risk and the risk was obvious. *R* v. *Seymour* replaced the offence of gross negligence manslaughter, established in the case of *R* v. *Bateman*, with reckless manslaughter. Ultimately the House of Lords' decision in *Adomako* overruled *Seymour* and re-established manslaughter by gross negligence.

Facts

Adomako was an anaesthetist who failed to notice for six minutes that a tube that supplied oxygen to the patient had become disconnected from the ventilator. As a result the patient died. At his trial the judge directed the jury that the test to be applied was whether the Defendant had been guilty of gross negligence manslaughter. The case was ultimately sent to the House of Lords on a point of law of general public importance, namely: 'in cases of manslaughter by criminal negligence involving a breach of duty is it a sufficient direction to the jury to adopt the gross negligence test as set out in

R v. Bateman without reference to the test of objective recklessness as defined in *R v. Lawrence* or as adapted to the circumstance of the case?'

The House of Lords in a relatively brief judgment of some ten pages redefined the law of gross negligence manslaughter, reversing the decision of *R v. Seymour*. In cases of gross negligence manslaughter, also referred to as involuntary manslaughter by breach of duty, the ingredients which had to be proved were the existence of a duty of care, a breach of the duty which had caused death and gross negligence which the jury considered justified a criminal conviction.

When does a duty arise?

Lord Mackay of Clashfern LC quoting Lord Hewart CJ in *R v. Bateman* stated that the ordinary principle of the law of negligence applied to ascertain whether a duty arises. Although a detailed analysis is outside the scope of this chapter, broadly speaking you owe a duty of care to anyone that may be foreseeably harmed by your actions. The use of the meaning of duty of care in tort has recently been confirmed by the Court of Appeal in *R v. Wacker*. The courts have found a duty of care in a whole array of situations. For example, a doctor owes a duty of care to his patient and a driver owes a duty of care towards other road users. Further to this, if a person causes death by his criminally negligent omission (such as a failure to prescribe necessary medicine) and if it can be shown that the defendant was under a duty to act, he will be guilty of manslaughter.

Breach of duty

It must be shown that the defendant breached his or her duty of care to the victim and that the defendant's breach of duty caused the victim's death. This latter point involves the straightforward application of the rules of causation - the negligence must have been a substantial cause of the death. In deciding whether there is a breach of duty the test is an objective one. In *Adomako* the defendant was a doctor holding himself out as possessing a special skill and knowledge. He owes a duty to the patient to use diligence, care, knowledge, skill and caution in administering his treatment. The law requires a fair and reasonable standard of competence. If the death of a person is alleged to have been caused by incompetence on the part of another, that person is to be measured against the standard of a reasonably qualified person holding himself out as possessing a particular skill, whether it be a doctor, a mechanic, or an electrician.

It therefore follows that Adomako was to be judged against the standard of a reasonable anaesthetist. Arguments raised by the defendant; that he had only a few hours sleep between shifts, that he did not have the support he required and that he was not properly trained were irrelevant to the question of whether his conduct fell below the standard to be expected of a reasonable anaesthetist.

Gross negligence

The last question to be considered by the jury is whether that breach of duty should be characterised as gross negligence and therefore a crime. It was accepted by Lord MacKay that this inevitably involved some circularity as the jury had to decide whether the Defendant's conduct amounted to a crime. The judgment of *Adomako* was criticised by counsel in *R* v. *Misra* as leaving effectively a question of law to the jury. The House of Lords in *R* v. *Misra* disagreed and held that the question for the jury laid down in *R* v. *Adomako* was not whether the defendant's negligence was gross and whether, additionally it was a crime, but whether his behaviour was grossly negligent and consequently criminal.

The question of whether the defendant's breach of duty should be characterised as gross negligence and therefore a crime will depend 'on the seriousness of the breach of duty committed by the defendant in all the circumstances in which the defendant was placed when it occurred' (page 88). Lord MacKay in *Adomako* makes it clear that this is a question for the jury, who should ask themselves whether the defendant's acts or omissions were so bad as to deserve a criminal conviction. It is emphasised that there is a need for a high degree of negligence if the jury are to convict and this is where the offence largely departs from the parallels drawn with the tort of negligence.

Lord MacKay approved the judgment in the Court of Appeal which defined the ambit of gross negligence. Lord MacKay stated that

> the jury might properly find gross negligence on proof of indifference to an obvious risk of injury to health or an actual foresight of the risk coupled either with a determination nevertheless to run it or with an intention to avoid it but involving such a high degree of negligence in the attempt at avoidance as the jury considered justified conviction. (page 84)

Adomako leaves the jury a wide discretion to decide whether or not to convict the accused. The jury can take 'all the circumstances' into account and in this respect there is an element of subjectiveness in gross negligence manslaughter. There may be cases where the defendant's state of mind is relevant to the jury's considerations when assessing the grossness of his conduct. Evidence of a defendant's state of mind is not a prerequisite to a conviction of manslaughter as was affirmed in *Attorney General Reference (No. 2 of 1999)*. The *Adomako* test is objective, but questions such as: did the defendant foresee the risk of death?; were there any explanations for why the defendant acted as he did?; may help a jury to decide whether to characterise the act or omission as gross negligence.

Risk of death

The question arises as to whether a person should only be convicted of gross negligence manslaughter if the risk of death was foreseeable. In *Adomako* it was unclear as to whether Lord MacKay was stating that the offence required the risk of death to be foreseeable. He talks of 'having regard to the risk of death' at several points but also refers to 'risk of injury to health' and approves the dicta in the case of *Stone and Dobinson* and *R* v. *West London Coroner, ex parte Gray* which seem to suggest that risk to health and safety of a victim is sufficient. It would seem logical that in an offence of homicide by gross negligence the circumstances must be that the defendant would have foreseen a serious risk of death as opposed to injury, even serious injury. In *Singh (Gurphal)* the Court of Appeal approved the trial judge's direction that a risk of death would have to have been foreseeable by a reasonably prudent person. In the 2004 case of *R* v. *Misra* the Court of Appeal provided welcome clarification that only a risk of death, and not serious injury, will be sufficient for gross negligence manslaughter (page 52). It remains to be seen whether this will be challenged.

The use of the word reckless

In *Adomako*, Lord Mackay stated that he considered the use of the word 'reckless' in cases of involuntary manslaughter as appropriate 'in the ordinary connotation of that word' rather than the meaning of reckless associated with *R* v. *Lawrence*. It is worth noting that there is substantial overlap between recklessness and gross negligence. However, one of the traditional cases of gross negligence is the situation where the accused appreciates the risk and tries to avoid it, but fails because he uses grossly negligent means. This was the form of the offence committed by Adomako. He observed the problems the patient was having and tried to correct them but used means which were quite wrong. It could be argued Adomako would have been acquitted by a jury applying *Lawrence* recklessness. On the other side the *Lawrence* test clearly does not require the jury to be satisfied that the defendant's conduct was bad enough to be a crime. In that sense a *Lawrence* direction would deprive the defendant of the chance of acquittal based on the jury's conclusion that the conduct was not bad enough to amount to a crime.

1

CRIMINAL LAW

FURTHER READING

Primary sources

Attorney General Reference (No. 2 of 1999) [2000] 3 All ER 182

Moloney [1985] 1 All ER 1025

Prentice, Adomako and Holloway, CA 1993 4 All ER 935

R v. *Bateman* (1925) 94 LJKB 791

R v. *Lawrence* [1981] 1 All ER 974

R v. *Misra* [2004] EWCA Crim 2375

R v. *Seymour* [1983] 2 All ER 1058

R v. *Stone, R* v. *Dobinson* [1977] 2 All ER 341

R v. *Wacker* [2002] EWCA Crim 1944

R v. *West London Coroner, ex parte Gray* [1987] 2 All ER 129

Singh (Gurphal) [1999] Crim LR 582, CA

Secondary source

Legislating the Criminal Code: Involuntary Manslaughter, 1996, Law Commission Report No. 237, Pt IV. HC 171

R v. *Ireland* and R v. *Burstow* [1997] 4 All ER 225

Adam Jackson, Northumbria University

The cases of *R* v. *Ireland* and *R* v. *Burstow* (*Ireland* and *Burstow*) were appeals heard jointly by a five-member bench of the House of Lords concerning the application of the Offences Against the Person Act 1861 (OAPA 1861). The Offences Against the Person Act 1861, along with the common law offences of assault and battery, is the primary way in which the criminal law deals with 'non-fatal' offences against the person. Non-fatal offences against the person can range in seriousness from causing someone to fear immediate personal violence, for example by threatening them (an assault), to causing someone really serious harm, for example breaking a person's legs with a cricket bat (causing grievous bodily harm with intent).

The fact that a five-member bench heard the appeals serves to highlight the importance of these judgments in determining the application and relevance of a piece of legislation almost 150 years old but which is still in almost constant use today.

In the two separate appeals the question arose as to the ambit (scope) of section 47 and section 20 of the OAPA 1861. The appeals were brought by defendants convicted respectively under the two sections. The defendants sought to challenge their convictions on the basis that their actions did not constitute offences under the 1861 Act. The decisions in *Ireland* and *Burstow* modernised the application of the OAPA 1861 and clarified its continuing relevance as a piece of criminal legislation.

The two appeals before the House

In the first appeal, *Ireland*, the defendant was convicted, after a plea of guilty, on three counts of assault occasioning actual bodily harm under s.47 of the OAPA 1861 and was sentenced to three years in custody. The circumstances of the offences with which Ireland was convicted were that the defendant made repeated silent telephone calls (sometimes resorting to heavy breathing), mostly at night, to three women, causing them to suffer psychiatric injury.

Ireland subsequently appealed against the conviction on the grounds that psychiatric injury could not amount to 'bodily harm' and that silent telephone calls could not constitute an assault. He therefore submitted that he had not committed an offence under s.47 OAPA 1861. The Court of Appeal rejected the appeal and ruled that psychiatric injury could amount to bodily harm under s.47 (applying the Court of Appeal's earlier decision in *R* v. *Chan-Fook*) and holding that repeated telephone calls of a menacing nature could cause victims to apprehend immediate unlawful personal violence and therefore constitute an assault.

The second appeal was similar in nature to the first but the conduct of the defendant was more serious than in *Ireland*. In *Burstow* the Defendant carried out an eight-month campaign of harassment against one woman. This included Burstow making silent and abusive telephone calls to her, distributing offensive cards in the street where she lived, visiting her place of work and her home, taking photographs of her and her family, and sending her a note which was intended, and was understood to be, menacing. As a result of the defendant's conduct, the victim suffered a severe depressive illness.

The judge at first instance ruled that it was possible for the psychological harm caused to constitute an offence under s.20 of the OAPA 1861, namely inflicting grievous bodily harm (GBH), leading the defendant to change his plea to guilty. He was sentenced to three years in custody and had an appeal against his conviction dismissed by the Court of Appeal.

Both defendants appealed against their convictions to the House of Lords.

Three specific features of the problem

The questions facing the House of Lords were threefold:

1. Does the criminal law take into account 'mere' psychiatric injury?
2. Can psychiatric injury be 'inflicted' for the purposes of s.20 OAPA 1861?
3. Can an assault be committed over the telephone as opposed to a face-to-face threat of violence and could the caller potentially avoid the reach of the criminal law by remaining silent?

The problem that was facing the House of Lords was that they were attempting to apply a piece of legislation almost 150 years old to a very modern problem. At the time the Offences Against the Person Act 1861 was drafted both the telephone and the science of psychiatry were in their infancy.

The 'familiar trilogy'

Giving his judgment in both appeals, Lord Steyn refers to the 'familiar trilogy' of non-fatal offences under the Offences Against the Person Act 1861 (as amended), reproduced in the table below in descending order of seriousness.

Section of 1861 Act	Offence	*Actus reus*	*Mens rea*	Maximum sentence
18	Grievous bodily harm, caused with intent	Causing* grievous bodily harm	Intention to cause grievous bodily harm	Life
20	Grievous bodily harm, inflicted without intent	Inflicting* grievous bodily harm	Intention/subjective recklessness as to whether some harm is caused	Five years imprisonment
47	Assault occasioning actual bodily harm	Assault causing more than 'trivial' harm	Intention/subjective recklessness as to whether some harm is caused	Five years imprisonment

*See below. - Despite the use in the statute of 'cause' for the s.18 offence and 'inflict' for the s.20 offence there is no significant difference between the *actus reus* of the two offences and therefore the words cause and inflict are taken to be interchangeable. The offences are distinguished solely on *mens rea*.

Essentially the three offences listed above form the statutory basis of the criminal law in relation to what are commonly referred to as non-fatal offences against the person. Section 47 refers to an 'assault occasioning actual bodily harm', more serious than the common law offences of assault or battery, s.47 is applied where the assault or battery causes more than 'trivial' harm (see *R v. Chan-Fook*). A good example of a section 47 offence would be a punch resulting in a black eye. Sections 18 and 20 deal with the more serious offences of grievous bodily harm or 'GBH', the harm required being 'really serious harm' (see *DDP v. Smith*), usually broken bones or other serious injury. The distinguishing feature between the section 18 and 20 offences is that the more serious section 18 offence requires an intention to cause grievous bodily harm whereas section 20 only requires an intention (or recklessness) to cause some harm.

The three sections above comprise the relevant law on the area and the Court had to consider its application. Both appeals raised the question can 'mere' psychiatric illness amount to bodily harm. The appeal in *Ireland* dealt with whether or not an assault can be committed over the telephone and the appeal in *Burstow* looked at whether bodily harm been 'inflicted' for the purposes of s.20 OAPA 1861.

It is important to note that both of the appeals dealt only with questions relating to the *actus reus* of the offences under the 1861 act. For instance the question of whether an assault can be committed over the telephone is a question of whether it is possible to assault someone by threatening them over the telephone and whether such a threat would cause the victim to apprehend immediate unlawful personal violence. The question is also one of whether words alone (for example, words unaccompanied by gestures) can constitute an assault.

The question does not consider the *mens rea* of the offence of assault or whether the caller possessed the requisite *mens rea* as the appellants in both *Ireland* and *Burstow* admitted their conduct and appealed on the basis that their conduct did not amount to offences under the 1861 Act. For clarity it should be noted (as mentioned above) that to prove the *mens rea* of the s.18 offence it must be shown that the accused intended to cause grievous bodily harm. To prove the *mens rea* for the s.20 and s.47 offences it must be shown that the accused intended, or was reckless as to whether, some harm would be caused.

It is to the above offences which Lord Steyn turned his attention when deciding whether the law provides effective criminal sanctions for these types of cases.

Can psychiatric illness amount to bodily harm?

A common question posed by both appeals was whether psychiatric illness can amount to bodily harm in terms of sections 18, 20 and 47 of the 1861 Act. This question posed a problem for the court. By its own admission 'the processes of the human mind and the causes of its disorders and disturbances' could never be completely explained. However, Lord Steyn also acknowledged that significant progress has been made in the field since the drafting of the Offences Against the Person Act in 1861. Particularly important in the context of the appeals is our ability now to distinguish neurosis in the form of anxiety and depressive disorders from simple states of fear.

The court looked at the approach taken in the civil courts, helpfully explained by Lord Macmillan in *Bourhill* v. *Young* (at page 402). The civil law already recognised the possibility of bringing a claim for 'injury by shock sustained through the eye or the ear without direct contact'.

Next the court turned its attention to the decision of the Court of Appeal in *Chan-Fook*, which the Court of Appeal in *Ireland* and *Burstow* had applied in dismissing the appeals of both defendants. The Court of Appeal was bound by its earlier decision in *Chan-Fook* but as the Court of Appeal cannot bind the House of Lords it was left free to interpret the decision in any way it saw fit. In *Chan-Fook* the Court of Appeal had decided that actual bodily harm was capable of including psychiatric injury. Approving the decision in *Chan-Fook* the Lords looked at the judgment of Hobhouse LJ (at pages 558-559) in which he addressed the question of whether psychiatric illness could amount to bodily harm, concluding:

> The body of the victim includes all parts of his body, including his organs, his nervous system and his brain. Bodily injury therefore may include any of those parts of his body responsible for his mental and Other faculties

but qualifying the statement by emphasising

> it does not include mere emotions such as fear or distress or panic nor does it include, as such, states of mind that are not themselves evidence of some identifiable clinical condition.

The lawyers representing the appellants in the case had argued that *Chan-Fook* had been decided incorrectly. The Lords rejected this and decided that the Act should be read in light of our best current understanding of psychiatric injury. As a result the Court ruled that 'bodily harm' in sections 18, 20 and 47 included recognisable psychiatric illness.

The meaning of inflict in section 20 (*R* v. *Burstow*)

Having come to the conclusion that psychiatric injury could amount to 'bodily harm' the Court then turned its attention to the individual appeals. In *Burstow* the appellant argued that use of the word 'inflict' in the wording of the s.20 offence made the offence narrower in scope than the more serious s.18 offence of 'causing' GBH. The argument was based on the premise that the draftsman would have used 'cause' or 'inflict' for both the s.20 and the s.18 offences had he intended the meaning to be identical. Counsel for the appellant also argued that the word 'inflict' carries with it an inherent application of direct or indirect force.

The Court considered and rejected both of these points, deciding that although the words 'cause' and 'inflict' are not synonymous there is 'no radical divergence' between their meanings. On the second point that the word 'inflict' carries with it a requirement of assault the Court decided that this was no longer the case and that causing serious psychological harm could be sufficient to constitute 'inflicting' GBH. Although the Court did not expressly overrule it, it seems that an earlier House of Lords decision in *Clarence* is now no longer relevant. Consequently Burstow's appeal was quashed and his conviction was upheld.

R v. Ireland: was there an assault?

The Court then considered the appeal brought by Ireland. Ireland's conduct had not been as varied as Burstow's and had solely included making silent telephone calls, sometimes accompanied by heavy breathing. Initially the Court looked at the two forms assault can take. The first, battery, involving the unlawful application of force by the defendant upon the victim. The Court dismissed the idea that the meaning of battery could be extended to include a silent caller causing psychiatric injury. The Court therefore turned its attention to the second form of assault, causing a victim to apprehend an immediate application of force (usually prosecuted under s.47 where the assault led to the victim suffering bodily harm).

Having already decided that psychiatric injury could constitute bodily harm the Court then had to decide whether an assault had been committed in order for the defendant to be guilty of an offence under s.47. The answer to this question was given as 'Yes, depending on the facts'. The caller clearly intends by his silence to cause fear. He puts the idea in the victim's mind that he knows who and where she is and puts her in fear of the possibility of imminent personal violence. If this is the intention of the caller and the result is that the victim suffers a recognisable psychological disorder then the caller is guilty of an offence under s.47 OAPA 1861.

Both of the appeals in *Ireland* and *Burstow* were dismissed and their convictions upheld. The decision of the House of Lords in both cases provided a number of important points. Firstly, they clarified the position of the criminal law in relation to psychiatric injuries caused to victims. Secondly, they clarified the position of the courts and the criminal law in relation to silent callers seeking to intimidate victims over the telephone. On a wider note the House of Lords confirmed the Offences Against the Person Act 1861 as a relevant piece of legislation and highlighted that the courts are willing to take an informed and proactive stance when interpreting legislation in our ever changing society.

FURTHER READING

Primary sources

Bourhill v. *Young* [1942] All ER 396

Clarence (1888) 22 QBD 23

DPP v. *Smith* [1961] AC 290

R v. *Chan-Fook* [1994] 2 All ER 552

R v. *Savage and Parmenter* [1991] 4 All ER 698

Theft and appropriation

R v. Hinks [2001] 2 AC 241

Zena Smith, Northumbria University

The case of R v. Hinks is a useful vehicle for understanding the law governing the criminal offence of theft. Theft consists of four elements: firstly, a dishonest intention; secondly, an appropriation; thirdly, property belonging to another; and fourthly, there must be an intention of permanently depriving the other of it. The case looks, in particular, at the meaning of appropriation which is an important element of the *actus reus,* this being 'the appropriation of property belonging to another'. The elements of the *actus reus* are considered in the judgment of Hinks and are detailed below.

Property

The definition of property includes money, real property, personal property such as choses in possession, chattels or goods and wild creatures. Bank accounts which are choses in action can also be stolen if in credit or within an agreed overdraft limit, however, an overdrawn account cannot be stolen, see **Kohn**. The property must have been dealt with in such a way as to comply with the other elements of the offence for a theft to have been committed.

Belonging to another

It is a requirement that the property belongs to someone other than the accused. It is generally irrelevant who the 'other' is. A corporation owning choses in action, money or other property may be the 'other'.

Appropriation

An essential element to the offence of theft is the appropriation of the property. Appropriation is defined as the assumption of any of the rights of the owner. This includes the circumstances whereby an individual has come by the property innocently or not and later assumes any of the rights of the actual owner. For example, where a person finds a twenty-pound note on the path, picks it up and places it in his wallet, he has assumed a right of the owner by placing it in his wallet and has therefore appropriated the property. The case of Hinks went on to consider 'appropriation' in detail.

The facts

The appellant, Hinks, was a 38-year-old woman. She was friends with a 53-year-old man, John Dolphin, who was of low intelligence. The appellant described herself as the main carer for Mr Dolphin. Mr Dolphin's IQ was between 70 and 80 (the average being 90 to 110).

He was described by the doctor for the prosecution as 'naïve and trusting and having no idea of the value of his assets or the ability to calculate their value'. Over a period of eight months, April to November 1996, Mr Dolphin withdrew sums totalling approximately £60,000 from his building society account and this money was deposited into the appellant's account. By the time the incident was reported Mr Dolphin had lost most of his savings and moneys inherited from his father. This information was not in dispute. In 1997 the appellant was charged with six counts of theft. It was the prosecution case that the appellant had coerced Dolphin into withdrawing the funds from his account and depositing them into hers. The trial lasted five days and evidence included testimony from building society employees who confirmed that Mr Dolphin and the appellant attended the branch daily to affect the withdrawals with the appellant doing most of the talking. The defence argued that the money was a gift from Mr Dolphin and that the title in the money had passed to the appellant and there could therefore be no theft – this view was rejected by Judge Warner at first instance. He directed the jury on two aspects of theft. Firstly, the appropriation of property, in which he said that the acquiring of property by a straight-forward taking or transferring of it would amount to an appropriation. He went on to say that acquiring it by way of a gift can also amount to an appropriation. The second element he considered was that of dishonesty. Was Hinks dishonest in her actions in accepting the money from Mr Dolphin and did she realise that what she was doing was dishonest? The question left to the jury was 'whether Mr Dolphin was so mentally incapable that the appellant herself realised that ordinary and decent people would regard it as dishonest to accept a gift from him?'. Hinks was convicted on five counts of theft. She was sentenced to eighteen months custody for each count, to run concurrently. She appealed to the Court of Appeal.

The Court of Appeal dismissed the appeal following consideration of two House of Lords' cases regarding the definition of theft, *Lawrence* and *Gomez*. LJ Rose concluded that the jury should not have been asked to decide whether there had been a gift, valid or otherwise, but whether there had been an appropriation. He confirmed that a gift may be clear evidence of appropriation as the recipient of the gift will assume the rights of the owner when it is gifted to him. But that the jury should not have been asked to consider whether a gift had been validly made.

Hinks appealed to the House of Lords. Her appeal was dismissed and the convictions were upheld. In deciding *Hinks*, Lord Steyn suggested that the starting point would be to look at the wording of the Theft Act 1968 as interpreted by the House of Lords in its previous decisions. Three cases were particularly relevant.

The first case in the trilogy is *R v. Lawrence*. The defendant, a taxi-driver, had asked an Italian student for the fare of £6 for a journey for which the lawful fare was 10s 6d. The student did not object to paying the £6 fare, though it was clear that the defendant had not indicated the correct fare. The defendant appealed against his conviction for theft on the ground that the Italian had consented to pay the fare. The appeal was dismissed. The House of Lords considered whether Parliament had omitted the words 'without the consent of the owner' from the 1968 Act on purpose. They concluded that the words had been deliberately left out so as to relieve the prosecution of the burden of establishing that the taking was without the owner's consent. Lord Dilhorne went on to say that the belief that the Italian student gave implied consent to paying in excess of the correct fare was relevant to the issue of dishonesty and not to whether there had been appropriation. The appeal was dismissed.

The second case is *R* v. *Morris*. The defendant appealed against two convictions of theft occurring on separate days. The offences involved the defendant switching the price labels on goods in a supermarket. The result being that the price of the goods he was to purchase was lower than they should have been. In the first case the defendant's deception was detected at the checkout and in the second he paid the lower price at the checkout. He was convicted of theft on both counts. The House of Lords had been asked to consider whether there had been a 'dishonest appropriation' of the goods in question. In both instances the answer was in the affirmative. The court confirmed that there was a need for the act to be unauthorised as opposed to the decision in *Lawrence*. The convictions were upheld.

The third case is *R* v. *Gomez*. In *Gomez*, the assistant manager of a shop, Gomez (G), persuaded his manager to sell items worth £17,000 to G's accomplice, A, and to accept payment in the form of two stolen cheques that G and A knew were worthless. The manager agreed to the transaction. G and A were later convicted of theft and appealed. The Court of Appeal held that there was a voidable contract between the manager of the shop and the receiver of the goods. They confirmed that the transfer had occurred with the consent of the manager and that accordingly there was no appropriation. The Court of Appeal quashed the convictions following a guilty plea by Gomez and A. The matter was appealed to the House of Lords where the House confirmed that following *Lawrence*, an appropriation had taken place and that the act could be authorised and still amount to theft. In their judgment the majority went on to say that any act can be an appropriation irrespective of whether it was done with the consent or authorisation of the owner. The House of Lords was asked to consider whether in the circumstance where the entire proprietary interest passes there will be no appropriation. They rejected this argument. The judgment clearly ruled out the argument that an indefeasible gift, whereby the proprietary interest of the property will have passed in its entirety to the recipient, could not amount to an appropriation. The House of Lords concluded that the word 'appropriation' meant the assumption of *any* of the rights of an owner. The convictions were restored.

In *Hinks* the House of Lords was asked to consider the appellant's proposition that a person could not appropriate property unless the owner retains some proprietary interest or right to resume or recover some proprietary interest beyond the instant of the theft. Lord Steyn rejected this argument as being in direct contradiction to the judgments of *Lawrence* and *Gomez*. He went on to say that it was clear that the jury had found that Hinks had acted dishonestly by raiding the building society account of a vulnerable man who trusted her. His Lordship was satisfied that the convictions were safe and that in practice the mental requirements of theft were adequate protection against injustice. Lord Steyn was referring to the *mens rea* of the offence which the prosecution must prove beyond reasonable doubt, together with the *actus reus*, to secure a conviction.

1

Mens rea

The *mens rea* of theft is 'the dishonesty' and 'the intention to permanently deprive' another of their property. The House of Lords in *Hinks* did not consider the mental element of theft in great detail but nevertheless *mens rea* is briefly considered below.

The word 'dishonest' is not defined in the Theft Act 1968 and consequently a general definition has been provided by the Court of Appeal in *Ghosh*. However, section 2 of the 1968 Act does set out some important factors to be considered regarding the interpretation of 'dishonesty'. These factors are as follows:

If the accused has an honest belief that he has a legal right to the property he will not be acting dishonestly. If the accused believed that the owner would consent to the appropriation of the property had he known of the accused's intention to take it, the accused will not be acting dishonestly, nor so where he believes that the owner cannot be traced by taking reasonable steps.

In certain circumstances a person's appropriation of property belonging to another may be dishonest notwithstanding that he is willing to pay for the property (*Boggeln* v. *Williams*).

The Act also preserves the common law requirement that the intention to permanently deprive must be exactly that, a permanent deprivation. The intention to temporarily deprive the owner of the property, by returning the property at a later date is not stealing. However, section 6 of the Theft Act does provide some assistance when considering the intention to permanently deprive, but this section should be referred to in exceptional cases only (*Lloyd* and *Coffey*).

In conclusion, it is clear that *Hinks* has been extremely important in establishing the definition of the term 'appropriation' in the context of the offence of theft. The principles underpinned in the judgment in *Hinks* remain the position regarding theft to the present day.

FURTHER READING

Primary sources

Boggeln v. *Williams* [1978] 1 WLR 873

Lawrence v. *Metropolitan Police Commissioner* [1972] AC 626

R v. *Coffey* [1987] Crim LR 498

R v. *Ghosh* [1982] QB 1053

R v. *Gomez* [1993] AC 442

R v. *Hinks* [1998] Crim LR 904

R v. *Hinks* [2001] 2 AC 241

R v. *Kohn* [1979] 69 Cr App Rep 395

R v. *Lloyd* [1985] QB 829

R v. *Morris* [1984] AC 320

R v. *Robin* [1977] Crim LR 173

Inchoate offences – attempts, conspiracy and incitement

R v. *Shivpuri* [1987] AC 1

Sarah Christie, The Robert Gordon University

Inchoate crimes, and in particular attempted crimes, have long provided a field of controversy for both academics and the judiciary. The difficulty lies in the nature of inchoate liability – the acts of the defendant do not come to their intended fruition. Inchoate means incomplete, and since the crime which the defendant meant to commit has not come about, the full extent of the harm or danger which he would have caused has also not come to pass. However, although criminal law looks for the defendant to exhibit his dangerousness and cause a criminal harm, that is not to say that the defendant who 'simply' carries out an inchoate crime rather than the full crime causes *no* harm. The harm caused by an inchoate crime is necessarily less than that caused by the full crime, and in order to take account of this, the punishment is proportionally less.

The case of *R* v. *Shivpuri* focuses on the issue of impossible attempts, but also provides an overview of the law on attempts and the interpretation of the Criminal Attempts Act 1981 (hereafter CAA). The case concerned a defendant who had been found guilty of attempting to be knowingly concerned in dealing with and harbouring a controlled drug, in contravention of both section 1 (1) of the CAA and section 170 (1) (b) of the Customs and Excise Management Act 1979 (CEMA). He had been found in possession of a powder which he had confessed to believing was, and which he later admitted in a confession to have strongly suspected was, heroin. In fact, the substance was something similar to snuff. He then denied in evidence that he had believed it to be heroin. He was convicted at trial, appealed unsuccessfully to the Court of Appeal, and ultimately to the House of Lords. His appeal was based on his assertion that, since the substance in question was not, in fact, an illegal drug, he could not be guilty of an attempt to be knowingly concerned in dealing with and harbouring such a drug. This assertion is based on an objective interpretation of events, which had been applied in previous cases. An objective stance looks at events from an external point of view, without the colour supplied by the defendant's own interpretation of those same events. An objective interpretation of his acts simply acknowledges the truth of the matter; that the substance found on him and in his flat was an innocuous, snuff-like substance and, as such, could not form the basis of a charge. However, impossible attempts require the court to consider how to approach the interpretation of events. A subjective approach, in contrast to the above, requires an interpretation which acknowledges the defendant's own assessment of his actions.

1

CRIMINAL LAW

The subjective approach and the Criminal Attempts Act

This subjective approach can be seen here, in *Shivpuri*, and also, for example, in the Scottish case of *Docherty* v. *Brown*. In both these cases, the appeal courts looked, not simply at what the defendant objectively did, but also at what he thought he was doing (in Shivpuri's case, being in possession of heroin, and in Docherty's case, Ecstasy). Subjectivism, here, argues that the defendant's state of mind is as guilty when mistakenly importing snuff as it would be if importing heroin. Objectivism looks at the lack of actual danger in what he had done, and the need to avoid legislating against what we *think* we are doing. The objectivist approach is shown in the preceding case of *Haughton* v. *Smith*, where the defendant was found not guilty of attempting to handle stolen goods. Since the goods were in the hands of the police, who had allowed them to continue on their way in order to trap the handlers, the goods were not stolen, and therefore Smith could no longer attempt to handle *stolen* goods. This case focuses on the situation without acknowledging the defendant's state of mind - his mistaken belief about the goods and his intention to bring about a criminal result - and in doing so, allows a defence of impossibility. *Shivpuri* looks instead at the defendant's belief as to the nature of his actions and, in doing so, downplays the reality that he had imported something innocuous. The court are more concerned with the fact that he believes he is in possession of heroin and that he is prepared to cause the associated harm. A subjective approach acknowledges that, even though the offender is mistaken in believing that he is in the process of carrying out a criminal offence, he is nonetheless prepared to be so involved, and has thus shown his determination to cause criminal harm. Fortuitously, on this occasion, he will not succeed, but this relies on the fact that he has made a mistake and, if not sanctioned for this act, he will be better prepared next time to achieve his criminal purpose without mistakes. Fortuitous circumstances cannot be relied on, particularly when considering the prevention of danger and harm to the public. Thus, the subjective approach, which allows for conviction on the basis of his view of the nature of his acts, produces a deterrent effect. This is now enshrined in section 1 (2) of the CAA.

The CAA abolishes the common law crime of attempt in favour of its own principles. Section 1 (1) requires that the defendant carries out an act which is more than merely preparatory to the commission of the offence he aims to commit. The distinction to be drawn here is between conduct which is genuinely carried out simply in preparation for the offence in view, and conduct which amounts to the beginnings of the commission of that offence. To be able to say that the defendant has done something which is more than preparatory requires that he engages in some acts which are clearly referable to the intended offence. Where the line is drawn between preparation and something more than preparation is difficult to state as a general proposition, as it will necessarily depend heavily on the facts of each case. Two defendants could have formulated plans to murder their estranged spouses, one by buying a sawn-off shotgun from a known criminal, and the other by buying a sledgehammer from B&Q. The defendant approaching his estranged spouse's house, shotgun in hand, has clearly moved beyond preparation and into the realms of attempting to commit an offence. The defendant approaching the house with his sledgehammer could be about to carry out murder, or break up the old patio - he has not yet carried out an act which makes his intent clear, and indeed may not exhibit any criminal intent at all. Numerous theories have been put forward as to the appropriate point for determining the existence of the *actus reus* of an attempt, and in some sense, all acts but the very last are preparatory. The defendant entering the estranged spouse's house with the shotgun is still preparing for the commission of his crime, in the sense that he has not yet taken aim and fired, but leaving liability for attempted murder that late is nonsensical. It would be as well to wait until he had fired, and then prosecute him for murder instead of attempted murder. The point to draw the line can perhaps best be described as the point when the defendant is setting out to commit the offence, as opposed to amassing necessary information or material in order to allow him to commit it.

As regards *mens rea,* section 1 (1) makes it clear that intention is required, in the sense set out in *R* v. *Mohan*. The defendant must have exhibited '. . . a decision to bring about, so far as it lies within (his) power, the commission of the offence which it is alleged (he) attempted to commit, no matter whether (he) desired that consequence of his act or not' (see page 11). Where recklessness as to circumstances is sufficient *mens rea* for the complete offence, this will also suffice for the attempted crime. There is, however, an issue about incorporating notions of recklessness, even where restricted to circumstances, in the definition of the *mens rea* of an attempted crime. The defendant who attempts to carry out an offence tends to fit the profile of an intentional actor, rather than one exhibiting recklessness. However, liability for an attempt requires an intention to carry out a certain result. It does not necessarily require intention in respect of other surrounding circumstances. Thus, prior to the CAA, the defendant in *R* v. *Pigg* was convicted of attempted rape on the basis of his intention to have sexual intercourse with his victim, while being reckless as to whether she consented.

Other jurisdictions allow for a defence of withdrawal, which applies where the defendant has taken some steps towards the commission of the offence, but has had a change of heart, or an attack of cold feet, and has voluntarily abandoned his plan. English criminal law takes a more robust stance and ignores any acts by the defendant to try to extricate himself. Certainly, where the defendant desists because he becomes aware that, for example, a police car is approaching, there is little justification for allowing him to avoid liability. His desistence is purely motivated by self-preservation and is not 'voluntary'. It is arguable that more account should be taken of the defendant who has a genuine change of heart, particularly if he is still at a relatively early stage in his attempt.

Other inchoate offences

While attempted crimes are probably the most often reported inchoate offences, and certainly responsible for most academic interest, conspiracy and incitement complete the set of offences described as inchoate. The unifying feature is that of incompleteness. A conspiracy amounts to an agreement by a group of co-conspirators to carry out a criminal plan, which they all intend to come to fruition. So long as at least two persons have conspired together, it does not matter how many individuals are involved. However, it remains possible for a court to convict a single individual of a conspiracy where co-conspirators are acquitted. The central criterion is agreement, which is construed as a continuous event, allowing individual conspirators to join the agreement at different times. Conspiracy existed at common law until the Criminal Law Act 1977, s.5(1) abolished all common law conspiracies except for conspiracy to defraud and to corrupt public morals and outrage public decency. The 1977 Act also abolished the double inchoate offences - that is attempting or inciting a conspiracy. The rationale for criminalising conspiracy is that group activity is more dangerous than individual acts. The group who come together for a criminal purpose have shared expertise, can carry out something more involved which would be impossible for the individual, and can provide each other with mutual support and encouragement.

Incitement is charged against the defendant who never intended to commit the crime himself, but has encouraged another to commit it. The term 'incitement' covers acts of encouragement, instigation, or persuasion, done with the intent that the person so incited carries out the offence. In *Race Relations Board* v. *Applin* it was also held to include threatening and pressurising. The defendant must have intended that the crime be committed by the incitee, but he does not need to be shown to have the *mens rea* for the crime in question. It may be addressed to a single individual or a group. It does not matter whether the incitee acts on the incitement. The criminality is found in the fact of persuading that person to break the law, not in what may or may not ensue from it. If the incitement never reaches its intended recipient, there has still been an attempt to incite, although proof of this may prove difficult.

FURTHER READING

Primary sources

Criminal Attempts Act 1981

Criminal Law Act 1977 Part 1

Docherty v. *Brown* 1996 SLT 325

Haughton v. *Smith* [1975] AC 476

R v. *Mohan* [1976] QB 1

R v. *Pigg* [1982] 2 All ER 591

R v. *Shivpuri* [1987] AC 1

Race Relations Board v. *Applin* (1973) 1 QB 815

Secondary sources

Case comment, 'Attempts: impossibility - s.1 Criminal Attempts Act 1981' (1986) *Crim LR*, 536-542.

Williams, Glanville (1985) 'The Lords Achieve the Logically Impossible' (1985) *New Law Journal*, 135, 502-5.

Williams, Glanville (1986) 'The Lords and Impossible Attempts, or *Quis Custodiet Ipsos Custodes*?' (1986) *Cambridge Law Journal*, 45, 33-83.

Provocation and diminished responsibility as defences to murder

R v. *Morgan James Smith* [2001] 1 AC 146, House of Lords

Tony Storey, Northumbria University

One evening, the defendant, Morgan James Smith, fatally stabbed a friend of his after a drunken row over some (allegedly stolen) tools. Smith was charged with murder and did not deny killing his friend. Instead, he raised defences of diminished responsibility and provocation. Both defences are located in the Homicide Act 1957, sections 2 and 3 respectively. The former requires the defence to prove (on the balance of probabilities) that the accused was suffering an 'abnormality of mind' arising from one of various sources specified in the Act which 'substantially impaired' his or her 'mental responsibility'.

Provocation, meanwhile, simply requires the defence to adduce evidence (either by things said, done, or both together) that he or she was provoked to such an extent he or she suffered a 'sudden and temporary' loss of self-control. (If no such evidence is forthcoming the defence fails and should be withdrawn from the jury.) The onus is then on the prosecution to prove to the jury (beyond reasonable doubt) either that the accused did not suddenly lose self-control (the subjective test) or, if he did, that the 'reasonable man' would not have lost self-control and done as the accused did, under the same provocation (the objective test).

The law according to *Camplin* (1978-2000)

The law prior to *Morgan Smith* subdivided the objective test into two separate, albeit related, questions. First, how grave was the provocation to the accused? Second, what level of self-control could be expected of the accused? This distinction was first made in the landmark House of Lords case of *DPP* v. *Camplin*. The case involved a 15-year-old youth accused of murdering an older man who had buggered him and then taunted him about it. The judge directed the jury to consider the effect this provocation would have had on an ordinary *man*, as opposed to a *youth of 15*. The House of Lords decided that the jury should have been told to assess the impact of the provocation on a reasonable 15-year-old. Lord Diplock, giving a model direction with which the rest of the House concurred, concluded that:

> A proper direction to a jury . . . should state . . . that the 'reasonable man' . . . is a person having the power of self-control to be expected of an ordinary person of the sex and age of the accused, but in other respects sharing such of the accused's characteristics as they think would affect the gravity of the provocation to him; and that the question is not merely whether such a person would in like circumstances be provoked to lose his self-control but also whether he would react to the provocation as the accused did.

25

Seventeen years later, in *Morhall*, Lord Goff, with whom the rest of the House agreed, confirmed that *Camplin* correctly stated the law when he said that

> it would be entirely consistent with the law as stated in s.3 . . . to direct the jury simply with reference to a hypothetical person having the power of self-control to be expected of an ordinary person of the age and sex as the defendant, but in other respects sharing such of the defendant's characteristics as they think would affect the gravity of the provocation to him.

Thus, the law pre-*Morgan Smith* allowed that, as far as the objective test was concerned, certain characteristics of the accused could be attributed to the 'reasonable man' for the purposes of the jury's assessment of the 'gravity' of the provocation to the accused but, when deciding upon the level of self-control to be expected of the accused, no characteristics were attributable to the 'reasonable man' other than the accused's age and sex.

Examples of such characteristics being attributed to the reasonable man for the purposes of assessing the 'gravity' of provocation included Battered Woman Syndrome, a type of post-traumatic stress disorder, on the basis a battered woman might well perceive threats of violence more seriously than a woman who had never suffered physical violence (*Ahluwalia*); eccentricity and obsessiveness (*Dryden*); attention-seeking and immaturity (*Humphreys*); obsessive personality disorder (*Thornton (No. 2)*). In *Morhall*, the accused had been nagged about his glue-sniffing habit, before losing his self-control and stabbing the victim. The Court of Appeal agreed with the trial judge that a characteristic like an addiction to glue-sniffing could not be attributed to the 'reasonable man', not even for the purposes of assessing the gravity of the provocation. However, on further appeal, Lord Goff, giving the leading speech in the House of Lords, held that

> where the defendant is taunted with his addiction (for example, that he is an alcoholic, or a drug addict, or a glue-sniffer), or even with having been intoxicated (from any cause) on some previous occasion [then] however discreditable such condition may be, it may where relevant be taken into account as going to the gravity of the provocation.

Applying the law as it then was, therefore, the trial judge in *Morgan Smith* directed the jury not to take account of evidence of the accused's clinical depression and brain damage (which may have affected his ability to control himself), when deciding what level of self-control was to be expected of him. However, the jury was authorised to use the same evidence in assessing the gravity of the provocation to the accused. The jury rejected both Homicide Act defences and convicted the accused of murder.

On appeal, the Court of Appeal allowed the appeal and quashed the murder conviction, substituting one of manslaughter. The Crown appealed to the House of Lords which, by a 3:2 majority, dismissed the appeal. A majority of the Law Lords (Lords Hoffman, Clyde and Slynn) held that characteristics were attributable to the reasonable man both in assessing gravity of the provocation and in also assessing the level of self-control to be expected. The minority (Lords Hobhouse and Millett) held that *Camplin* was correctly decided and should be confirmed.

The reasoning of the majority in *Morgan Smith* (2000)

Lord Hoffman's speech in *Morgan Smith* illustrates best the thought processes behind the majority's decision to reject the subdivision of the objective test in *Camplin*. Lord Hoffman quoted two judges from an unreported New Zealand case (*Rongonui* (2000)) to the effect that the *Camplin* 'distinction' required the jury to undergo 'mental gymnastics', and that most trial judges post-*Camplin* had seen

> the glazed look in the jurors' eyes as, immediately after instructing them that it is open to them to have regard to the accused's alleged characteristic in assessing the gravity of the provocation, they are then advised that they must revert to the test of the ordinary person and disregard that characteristic when determining the sufficiency of the accused's loss of self-control.

Both Lord Hoffman and Lord Slynn went so far as to hold that references to the 'reasonable man' were no longer necessary (despite the fact that the term 'reasonable man' appears in s.3 of the Homicide Act itself). Summarising the new legal position, Lord Hoffman said (emphasis in original):

> Judges should not be required to describe the objective element in the provocation defence by reference to a 'reasonable man', with or without attribution of personal characteristics . . . The jury must think that the circumstances were such as to make the loss of self-control sufficiently *excusable* to reduce the gravity of the offence from murder to manslaughter . . . The general principle is that the same standards of behaviour are expected of everyone, regardless of their individual psychological make-up. In most cases, nothing more will need to be said. But the jury should in an appropriate case be told, in whatever language will best convey the distinction, that this is a principle and not a rigid rule. It may sometimes yield to a more important principle, which is to do justice in the particular case. So the jury may think that there is some characteristic of the accused, whether temporary or permanent, which affected the degree of control which society could reasonably have expected of *him* and which it would be unjust not to take into account. If the jury takes this view they are at liberty to give effect to it.

Lord Slynn said that s.3 requires the jury to consider 'what could reasonably be expected of a person with the accused's characteristics . . . It is thus not enough for the accused to say "I am a depressive, therefore I cannot be expected to exercise self-control". The jury must ask whether he has exercised the degree of self-control to be exercised by someone in his situation.'

The view of the dissenting minority in *Morgan Smith* (2000)

The minority in *Morgan Smith* were of the view that to allow psychological characteristics (such as depression) to be attributed to the reasonable man for the purposes of assessing the power of self-control to be expected undermined the objective character of the 'reasonable man' test, essentially turning it into a subjective test. It also risked creating a confusing overlap with the defence of diminished responsibility, which is based on the defendant having an 'abnormality of mind'. After all, since the decision of the Court of Criminal Appeal in *Byrne* to define 'abnormality of mind' as any state of mind which the reasonable man would term abnormal, the courts have readily accepted that depression is indeed an 'abnormality of mind' (*Seers; Gittens; Ahluwalia*).

The minority's view echoed the opinion of the majority of the Privy Council (Lord Steyn dissenting) four years earlier in *Luc Thiet Thuan v. R*. There, the decision was that mental infirmity was not a characteristic that could be taken into account in the context of the provocation defence if its only relevance was that it impaired D's power of self-control

1

CRIMINAL LAW

(as opposed to having an effect on the gravity of the provocation). Lord Goff, giving the majority opinion, stated that it was necessary to return to 'the authoritative statement in Lord Diplock's judgment' in *Camplin*. Lord Goff said that to take into consideration characteristics which reduce D's power of self-control below that to be expected of the ordinary person 'would be to incorporate the concept of diminished responsibility indirectly into the law of provocation'. Lord Goff thought that this was 'most unlikely' to have been Parliament's intention when enacting the Homicide Act 1957, given that diminished responsibility and provocation appear next to each other in the Act (sections 2 and 3 respectively). This was especially the case given 'the imposition of a special rule relating to the burden of proof, *viz.*, that the burden of establishing diminished responsibility should rest upon the defendant'.

After *Morgan Smith* (2000-2005)

In the years after *Morgan Smith*, the Court of Appeal dutifully followed the majority's decision in a number of appeals where the trials had taken place prior to *Morgan Smith* and defendants had been convicted of murder. For example, in *Weller*, the Court of Appeal heard an appeal against a murder conviction after the trial judge had directed the jury (using the *Camplin* distinction) that they could not take into account the accused's exceptional jealousy and possessiveness when deciding on the level of self-control to be expected. Although the Court of Appeal dismissed the appeal, Mantell LJ said that, according to the majority in *Morgan Smith*, 'the question whether the defendant should reasonably have controlled himself is to be answered by the jury *taking all matters into account*. That includes matters relating to the defendant, *the kind of man he is and his mental state*, as well as the circumstances in which the death occurred' (emphasis added).

In *Rowland*, there was medical evidence to the effect that D had certain 'personality traits [which] lowered his threshold for impulsive behaviour'. However, the trial judge, applying the *Camplin* distinction, had directed the jury to apply a purely objective assessment of the power of self-control. The Court of Appeal quashed D's murder conviction. Potter LJ said that the jury had been denied the opportunity to hear 'evidence as to the level of self-control which would be likely or could reasonably be expected in a man with [D's] additional characteristics'. Had the jury heard this evidence, it 'might well have influenced the jury's view of the level of self-control which he could have been expected to exercise in face of the provocation he encountered'.

Back to *Camplin*: the Privy Council in *Holley* (2005)

Despite the acceptance of *Morgan Smith* by the Court of Appeal, there was considerable academic criticism (see in particular the article by Macklem and Gardner). Perhaps inevitably, the issue came back before the Law Lords. In June 2005, this duly happened. However, it was not the House of Lords, but an unusually large nine-member Privy Council, giving judgment in *Attorney-General for Jersey v. Holley*. A majority of the Board (Lords Nicholls, Hope, Scott, Rodger and Walker and Baroness Hale; Lords Bingham, Hoffman and Carswell dissenting) disagreed with the majority in *Morgan Smith* and instead confirmed the decision in *Luc Thiet Thuan*. Giving the majority opinion in *Holley*, Lord Nicholls said that:

> This majority view [in *Morgan Smith*] . . . is one model which could be adopted in framing a law relating to provocation. But their Lordships consider there is one compelling, overriding reason why this view cannot be regarded as an accurate statement of English law . . . However much the contrary is asserted, the majority view does represent a departure from the law as declared in s.3 of the Homicide Act 1957. It involves a significant relaxation of the uniform, objective standard adopted by Parliament. Under the statute the sufficiency of the provocation ('whether the provocation was enough to make a reasonable man do as [the defendant] did') is to be judged by one standard, not a standard which varies from defendant to defendant. Whether the provocative act or words and the defendant's response met the 'ordinary person' standard prescribed by the statute is the question the jury must consider, not the altogether looser question of whether, having regard to all the circumstances, the jury consider the loss of self-control was sufficiently excusable. The statute does not leave each jury free to set whatever standard they consider appropriate in the circumstances by which to judge whether the defendant's conduct is 'excusable'. On this short ground their Lordships, respectfully but firmly, consider the majority view expressed in the *Morgan Smith* case is erroneous.

Court of Appeal cases subsequent to *Holley*

The *Holley* decision created a conflict in the authorities as, strictly-speaking, the Privy Council cannot overrule decisions of the House of Lords. However, in *Mohammed*, the Court of Appeal chose to follow *Holley* rather than *Morgan Smith*. On the precedent value of *Holley*, Baker LJ said that 'Although *Holley* is a decision of the Privy Council, and *Morgan Smith* a decision of the House of Lords, neither side has suggested that the law of England and Wales is other than as set out in the majority opinion given by Lord Nicholls in *Holley* and we have no difficulty in proceeding on that basis'. Seeking to clarify the law, he went on to say that

> the objective yardstick against which the effect of provocation falls to be measured has become tighter. Indeed the law is once again as it used to be before the decision in *Morgan Smith* . . . the standard of self-control to be expected of the reasonable man in s.3 is fixed and not variable. Lord Hoffman's test of excusability introduced an unwarranted development of the law by the courts.

Subsequently, in *James*, *Karimi*, a five-member Court of Appeal confirmed that the decision of the Privy Council in *Holley* had, in effect, overruled that of the House of Lords in *Morgan Smith*. Giving the judgment of the appeal court, Phillips LJ said that

> once one postulates that there are circumstances in which a decision of the Privy Council can take precedence over a decision of the House of Lords, it seems to us that this court must be bound in those circumstances to prefer the decision of the Privy Council to the prior decision of the House of Lords. That, so it seems to us, is the position that has been reached in the case of these appeals.

James, *Karimi* was followed in *Moses*. At his 1997 murder trial, D relied on provocation. Evidence that D was suffering clinical depression, had an 'over-controlled personality' and was 'particularly sensitive about his masculinity' had not been taken into account for the purposes of assessing the level of self-control to be expected, as the trial judge directed the jury in accordance with *Camplin* and *Morhall*. D was convicted of murder. After the decision in *Morgan Smith*, however, his case (like those in *James*, *Karimi*) was referred to the Court of Appeal by the Criminal Cases Review Commission. Unfortunately (for him), by the time his case came before the appeal court the law as it was in 1997 had not only been confirmed to be correct by the Privy Council in *Holley* but also by the Court of Appeal in *James*, *Karimi*. The Court of Appeal therefore rejected the appeal.

More on the 'gravity' question

Thus, through the combined efforts of the Privy Council and Court of Appeal, the *Camplin* 'separation' of the objective test into two questions has been restored to English criminal law. Only the defendant's age and sex are attributed to the 'reasonable man' for the purposes of assessing the power of self-control to be expected. Any other characteristics of the accused – whether psychological or physical – are potentially relevant only when assessing the 'gravity' of the provocation. There are two circumstances in which such characteristics may be relevant.

1. When the characteristics are the target of the provocation. In *Holley* itself, Lord Nicholls stated that 'mental infirmity of the defendant, if itself the subject of taunts by the deceased, may be taken into account as going to the gravity of the provocation'.

2. Where the characteristics are not the target of the provocation but their very existence exacerbates its gravity. In *Holley*, Lord Nicholls decided that the decisions in cases such as *Ahluwalia* were correct in allowing psychological characteristics (such as battered woman syndrome) to be attributed to the reasonable man (or woman) for the purposes of assessing gravity, even where those characteristics were not the subject of taunts. Referring to the 'battered woman syndrome' type of case, Lord Nicholls said that such evidence 'may be relevant on two issues: whether she lost her self-control, and the gravity of the provocation for her. The jury will then decide whether, having regard to the actual provocation and their view of its gravity . . . a woman of her age having ordinary power of self-control might have done what [she] did'.

A recent case demonstrates the application of this second point. In *Gregson*, characteristics of depression and epilepsy were held to be potentially relevant when assessing the 'gravity' of the provocation to the 'reasonable man' even though the provocative words had no (or no direct) connection to either characteristic. In *Gregson*, D had stabbed his stepfather, V, to death after years of 'sustained verbal abuse, insults and put-downs' had triggered a loss of self-control. At D's murder trial, the judge ruled that D's characteristics (epilepsy and depression) were irrelevant in assessing gravity, because V's abuse was targeted at D's unemployed status (V allegedly referred to D as a 'waste of space' and a 'loser'). D was convicted of murder. However, the Court of Appeal quashed D's murder conviction and substituted one of manslaughter, stating that D's characteristics were potentially relevant, even though D had not been taunted about them. The key point was that the reasonable man *with* depression and epilepsy might have perceived V's abusive behaviour as more provocative than the reasonable man *without* those characteristics. Smith LJ said that D's depression and epilepsy were potentially relevant because D may have had a 'heightened sense of grievance about the insults because he felt that, due to his depression and epilepsy, it was not his fault he was out of work'.

This means that the concerns expressed by Lord Goff in *Luc Thiet Thuan* are still pertinent – there is a potentially confusing overlap between the defences of provocation and diminished responsibility. Indeed, in *Holley*, Lord Nicholls did not deny this; if anything he seemed to embrace it. According to Lord Nicholls, the potential availability of diminished responsibility 'underlines the importance of not viewing the defence of provocation in isolation from the defence of diminished responsibility. These two defences must be read together to obtain an overall, balanced view of the law in this field'.

FURTHER READING

Primary sources

Attorney-General for Jersey v. *Holley* [2005] UKPC 23; [2005] 2 AC 580

DPP v. *Camplin* [1978] AC 705

Luc Thiet Thuan v. *R* [1997] AC 131

R v. *Ahluwalia* [1992] 4 All ER 869

R v. *Byrne* [1960] 2 QB 396

R v. *Dryden* [1995] 4 All ER 987

R v. *Gittens* [1984] QB 698

R v. *Gregson* [2006] EWCA Crim 3364

R v. *Humphreys* [1995] 4 All ER 1008

R v. *James, R* v. *Karimi* [2006] EWCA 14, [2006] QB 588

R v. *Mohammed* [2005] EWCA Crim 1880

R v. *Morhall* [1996] 1 AC 90

R v. *Moses* [2006] EWCA Crim 1721

R v. *Rowland* [2003] EWCA Crim 3636

R v. *Seers* (1984) 79 Cr App R 261

R v. *Thornton (No. 2)* [1996] 1 WLR 1174

R v. *Weller* [2003] EWCA 815; [2004] 1 Cr App R 1

Secondary sources

Law Commission (all available at lawcom.gov.uk)

   Report, '*Partial Defences to Murder*' (August 2004).

   Consultation Paper, '*A New Homicide Act for England & Wales*' (December 2005).

   Report, '*Murder, Manslaughter & Infanticide*' (November 2006).

Ashworth, A. (2005) 'Murder – Provocation' [2005] *Crim LR*, 966.

Chalmers, J. (2004) 'Merging Provocation and Diminished Responsibility: Some Reasons for Scepticism' [2004] *Crim LR*, 198.

Edwards, S. (2004) 'Abolishing Provocation and Reframing Self Defence – The Law Commission's Options for Reform' [2004] *Crim LR*, 181.

Edwards, S. (2007) 'Descent into Murder: Provocation's Stricture – The Prognosis For Women Who Kill Men Who Abuse Them' (2007) 71, *J Crim L*, 342.

Elvin. (2006) 'The Doctrine of Precedent and the Provocation Defence' (2006) 69, *MLR*, 819 .

Holton and Shute. (2007) 'Self-Control in the Modern Provocation Defence' (2007) 27, *OJLS*, 49.

Mackay, R. and Mitchell, B. (2003) 'Provoking Diminished Responsibility: Two Pleas Merging into One' [2003] *Crim LR*, 745.

Mackay, R. and Mitchell, B. (2005) 'But is this Provocation? Some Thoughts on the Law Commission's Report on Partial Defences to Murder' [2005] *Crim LR*, 44.

Macklem, T. and Gardner, J. (2001) 'Compassion Without Respect? Nine Fallacies in *R* v. *Smith*' [2001] *Crim LR*, 623.

Power. (2006) 'Provocation and Culture' [2006] *Crim LR*, 871.

Quick and Wells. (2006) 'Getting Tough with Defences' [2006] *Crim LR*, 514.

Taylor. (2007) 'The Nature of "Partial Defences" and the Coherence of (Second Degree) Murder' [2007] *Crim LR*, 345.

Wilson, W. (2005) 'The Structure of Criminal Defences' [2005] *Crim LR*, 108.

Criminal Damage – recklessness; reconsidering *Caldwell*

R v. *G and Another* [2003] 1 AC 1034

Sarah Christie, The Robert Gordon University

The definition of recklessness in cases of criminal damage had been long subject to criticism following the House of Lords' decision in *Caldwell*, handed down twenty years before *R* v. *G*. Although Lord Diplock in *Caldwell* had clearly intended that his re-definition of recklessness should have broad application, it had increasingly been restricted to criminal damage cases. The Criminal Damage Act 1971 section 1(1) specifies that any person who, without lawful excuse, damages or destroys another's property, either intending to do so, or being reckless as to whether they do so, is guilty of an offence. Under section 1(3) if that damage or destruction is brought about by setting fire to the property, the offence charged is arson and carries a sentence of life imprisonment (section 1(4)).

The facts

The facts of *R* v. *G* are as follows: the defendants (two boys aged 11 and 12) came across bundles of newspapers in the back yard of a shop one night and set fire to some of the papers. They then threw them under a large dustbin and left without attempting to put them out. The resulting fire spread to the dustbin itself, and thence to the shop and adjoining buildings, resulting in about £1m worth of damage. They were charged under section 1(1) above, on the grounds that they had set fire to property being reckless as to whether it was damaged or destroyed.

In their defence, they argued that they had not expected that the fire would spread, and had assumed that the flames would go out instead. At trial, the judge felt himself bound to follow precedent, namely *Caldwell*, and instruct the jury to find them guilty if they had carried out an act with an obvious associated risk of causing damage or destruction of the property and had carried out the act either without recognising this risk (*Caldwell*-type inadvertent recklessness), or done so anyway even though they had been aware of the risk (*Caldwell*-type advertent recklessness). In deciding whether there was an obvious risk that the act would lead to the damage or destruction of the property, the judge instructed the jury, again following *Caldwell*, that they should assess this by reference to the reasonable man, without regard to any characteristics of the defendants (in particular, their age). This follows a particularly strong objectivist approach, determining recklessness by reference to a restrictive reasonable man standard, regardless of subjective assessments based on attributes of the particular defendant. The many objections raised in academic literature against the decision in *Caldwell* derive from this stance. It adheres to a strong objectivist approach which, in this context, does not require that the individual is himself aware of the factors which constitute his recklessness. Here, objectivism does not require that the two boys are aware of the likelihood that the fire would spread and destroy property, so long as the reasonable man in their position would have been so aware. The alternative approach – and the one upheld in *R* v. *G* in the House of Lords – is one based on subjectivism, where the defendant would be required to have himself been aware of the circumstances surrounding his act and the likely consequences. Subjectivism dispenses with the need for the reasonable man and looks instead through the eyes of the defendant in order to assess whether they were aware of a risk and decided to ignore it. These two schools of thought are in direct opposition to each other and form the groundwork for sustained academic debate, but it is at the very least clear that the objectivist approach is significantly more stringent, blocking as it does any possibility for the defendant to argue that he should not be convicted because *he* was not aware of the risk. The subjectivist approach aligns itself with notions of fairness to the defendant but raises it own difficulties. Those jurisdictions and areas of law that reject the subjective approach often cite the difficulty in determining which of the defendant's characteristics to use: age, gender, physical disability, psychological profile – the list is potentially endless, and it is fair to say that while it might be appropriate to determine recklessness on the basis of the awareness of a reasonable person of the age of the defendant, it might not be appropriate to determine it on the basis of the reasonable person with, for example, the same tendency to fly into a rage as the defendant.

However, the doctrine of precedent held sway and the jury, following the judge's *Caldwell*-type direction, convicted the boys. This was upheld in the Court of Appeal, before it came to the House of Lords, where the issue of overruling *Caldwell* was considered. It is always difficult for a senior court to consider overruling a long-established precedent, and inevitably, the Law Lords were presented with argument from the Crown that the objective approach endorsed by *Caldwell* had been in existence for a considerable time, worked well and did not lead to unfair results. Beyond that, there had been plenty of opportunity for Parliament to revisit the issue had it wished to do so, and the fact that it had not suggested that it felt no pressing need to do so. In rejecting that argument, Lord Bingham noted the misinterpretation of 'recklessness' that had originated in *Caldwell*. That case had taken the traditional common law definition of recklessness (being aware of a particular risk but deciding to continue with the act in question regardless), and extended it so that it also included the defendant who was simply unaware of the risk. As previously mentioned, this moves the definition of recklessness from a more restrictive definition based on advertent recklessness to a much wider definition based on either advertent or inadvertent recklessness. The Law Commission had already discussed the issue of reforming the law on (at that time) malicious damage, prior to the passing of the 1971 Act, and in their proposals, it was assumed that the definition of the various states of *mens rea* would remain unchanged. When the 1971 Act was passed, it followed the Law Commission's recommendations. Thus, Lord Diplock in *Caldwell* had defined 'recklessness' away from that which was intended by Parliament, and that, coupled with the fact that it had led to an unfair result in both subsequent cases and in *R* v. *G*, was a ground on which the House of Lords was prepared to overrule *Caldwell*. It was also noted that, while knowingly acting in the face of a risk of causing harm, or deliberately closing one's mind to such a risk, was blameworthy conduct, the same could not be said where the defendant had not appreciated the risk at all. His conduct should rather be classified as either stupid or lacking in imagination, neither of which should bring with it liability for a serious crime (at page 1055). It is worth remembering here that the punishment imposed under the statute is life imprisonment, and it may very well be the severity of the potential punishment which is, at least in part, driving the court to a subjective approach, to ensure that only those defendants who exhibited advertent recklessness are caught. A further factor in their decision to move to a subjectivist approach is what they perceive as the obvious unfairness of the result at trial. The trial judge expresses sentiments in his judgment which make it clear that he did not want to instruct the jury as he did, but was bound to do so, and the jury themselves clearly had difficulty deciding the case, given that they returned for further clarification, and took a considerable time to come to their decision. The House of Lords were also clearly influenced by the sheer weight and consistency of academic criticism of *Caldwell*, and the force of the two dissenting opinions in that case.

Since *R v. G*, the courts have had the opportunity to consider that decision in *R v. Castle*, *R v. Brady* and *R (on the application of D) v. DPP*. In *Castle*, the defendant was convicted at trial of arson being reckless as to whether life was endangered. The trial took place before the decision was handed down in *R v. G*, and as such, the jury were directed following *Caldwell*, and convicted him on the basis that a reasonable man in his position would have been aware that the fire he started would create an obvious risk that anyone in the flats above would be endangered. In the Court of Appeal, his conviction was quashed, noting that the '. . . direction, entirely objective as it is, is no longer appropriate' (at para 8). Similarly, in *Brady*, the Appeal Court state that it is now undeniably the case that a trial judge cannot direct the jury as regards 'risk' without stating that the risk must be obvious and significant. *R (on the application of D) v. DPP* however, provides an interesting consideration of the level of foresight required under *R v. G*. The defendant had smashed a window in a fit of temper, and admitted having done so. He had been convicted by the Youth Court of criminal damage, notwithstanding evidence from a child psychiatrist that he did not always fully consider the consequences of his actions, particularly when agitated. The Youth Court had determined that this evidence did not show an inability to appreciate the risk he was running (of damaging the window), and therefore declined to follow *R v. G*. When the case was appealed (by way of a stated case), Justice Goldring noted that there was a need to approach the case with an element of common sense (at para. 7). Given that D was observed smashing the window in a fit of temper, he concluded that it was not surprising that the Youth Court had determined that there was foresight of risk on D's part. The evidence in the psychiatric report was not sufficient to conclude that he could not foresee that there would be at least some damage to the window, and given this, his appeal was rejected. Thus, it would seem that *R v. G* principles will only excuse a defendant where he can be shown to have had no awareness of the risk he was running. Being sufficiently young to believe that burning newspaper would simply extinguish itself rather than spread from one object to another and eventually burn down a building would establish a level of immaturity that could be used to prove that there was no awareness of the particular risk. It would seem then, that defendants will benefit from this subjective assessment of recklessness where intrinsic issues such as their age, or presumably

1

mental disability, prevent them from appreciating that which would be obvious to a 'reasonable' man. This accords with a general tendency to increased subjectivism in the criminal law, which is also played out, for example, in the area of impossible attempts, on which see the entry on *R v. Shivpuri*. Ironically, whereas a subjective approach was used to uphold Shivpuri's conviction, looking at how his situation appeared to him, in *R v. G*, that same approach was used to quash their convictions.

FURTHER READING

Primary sources

Criminal Damage Act 1971

Commissioner of Police of the Metropolis v. *Caldwell* [1982] AC 341

R v. *Brady* [2007] Crim LR 564

R v. *Castle* [2004] EWCA Crim 2758

R v. *G and Another* [2004] 1 AC 1034 - House of Lords judgment

R v. *Gemmell, R* v. *Richards* [2003] 1 Cr App R 23 - Court of Appeal decision of the same case

R (on the application of D) v. *DPP* [2006] EWHC 3017 (Admin)

Secondary sources

Kimmel, D. (2004) 'Inadvertent recklessness in criminal law' [2004] *Law Quarterly Review*, 548-554.

Metcalfe, N. and Ashworth, A. (2004) 'Arson: *mens rea* - recklessness whether property destroyed or damaged' [2004] *Crim LR*, 369-372.

Intoxication defences

DPP v. Majewski [1977] AC 443

Natalie Wortley, Northumbria University

It is a fundamental principle of criminal law that no person shall be convicted of a crime unless the prosecution have proved beyond reasonable doubt both that the defendant was responsible for the proscribed act (the *actus reus*), and that his state of mind when so acting was culpable (the *mens rea*). This principle causes unique problems in cases of voluntary intoxication. Should a person who consumes alcohol or drugs to the extent that he does not know what he is doing and therefore does not possess the necessary *mens rea*, be entitled to escape liability when he commits what would otherwise be a criminal offence?

Perhaps unsurprisingly, for reasons of social policy and public protection, the courts developed a substantive rule of law that self-induced intoxication was no defence to a crime of basic intent. The House of Lords unanimously confirmed this rule in the case of *DPP* v. *Majewski*.

Majewski was convicted of three counts of assault occasioning actual bodily harm and three counts of assaulting a police constable in the execution of his duty. The assaults were all committed while the defendant was so intoxicated as a result of a combination of drugs and alcohol that he did not know what he was doing and had no recollection of the incidents that had occurred.

The trial judge directed the jury that the issue of whether the defendant had taken drink or drugs was irrelevant. The Court of Appeal dismissed his appeal and asked the House of Lords to decide a point of general public importance, namely 'whether a defendant may properly be convicted of assault notwithstanding that, by reason of his self-induced intoxication, he did not intend to do the act alleged to constitute the assault'.

In a lengthy and reasoned judgment, their Lordships analysed the evolution of the law relating to voluntary intoxication and the policy behind it. The judgment acknowledged that there had been significant academic criticism of a rule that allows a defendant to be convicted even though he lacks the *mens rea* prescribed by law for the offence. Their Lordships conceded that the law on voluntary intoxication was not strictly logical but concluded that absolute logic in legal matters is not always necessary or desirable (page 484A).

This case is essential reading for any student of criminal law. It is both the leading case on intoxication and provides a fascinating demonstration of how public policy can shape the law.

1

CRIMINAL LAW

Intoxication as a defence

Intoxication is not a defence in and of itself. It is no defence for a person to say that he was so intoxicated as a result of drink or drugs that he behaved in a way in which he would never have behaved had he been sober. However, a defendant may rely on intoxication to show that he did not form the *mens rea* for the offence, for example, where he was so drunk that he was incapable of forming any intent. Thus, where a defendant relies on intoxication, he does so in order to show that he lacked *mens rea*.

The corollary of this principle is that an intoxicated defendant who has the *mens rea* for the offence at the time of committing the *actus reus* is guilty. Following the case of *R* v. *Sheehan and Moore*, it is often said that 'a drunken intent is still an intent'. This principle was endorsed in Majewski (page 481E).

Involuntary intoxication

The courts have long recognised that intoxication that is not self-induced gives rise to entirely different considerations. Where a defendant lacks *mens rea* as a result of involuntary intoxication, such as where his drink has been 'spiked' without his knowledge or consent, he is entitled to be acquitted. In *Majewski*, this was said to be because involuntary intoxication 'was not the man's fault' (page 498H).

This issue has been clarified further in subsequent cases. In *R* v. *Allen*, the Court of Appeal confirmed that involuntary intoxication should be narrowly defined. Where a defendant knew that he was consuming alcohol, he could not rely on involuntary intoxication merely because he did not know the nature and strength of the drink.

A more difficult issue arises where an involuntarily intoxicated defendant forms the *mens rea* for an offence solely because he is intoxicated. His guilt in such a case arises entirely from circumstances beyond his control. In *R* v. *Kingston*, the defendant, who had paedophiliac tendencies, was convicted of indecent assault on a fifteen-year-old boy. His defence was that he had been drugged by his co-defendant, who planned to photograph him in a compromising situation with the boy and blackmail him. It was accepted that, had he not been drugged, he would not have acted as he did and he had no recollection of having so acted. He argued that, given the absence of any moral fault, he should not be criminally liable for his acts.

The House of Lords accepted that there was some attraction in the proposition that criminal liability should not attach to acts that were outside the volition of the actor. However, their Lordships ultimately confirmed Kingston's conviction holding that the defence of involuntary intoxication is not available to a defendant who possesses the required *mens rea*.

Voluntary intoxication

As explained above, a defendant who is intoxicated and forms the *mens rea* for an offence has no defence, whether his intoxication is voluntary or involuntary. Where, however, a defendant lacks *mens rea* by reason of self-induced, voluntary intoxication, his criminal liability will depend on the type of offence with which he is charged. In *Majewski*, the House of Lords confirmed that a voluntarily intoxicated defendant who lacks *mens rea* is entitled to be acquitted of a crime requiring a specific intent but has no defence to a crime of basic intent. An understanding of the distinction between offences of specific intent and offences of basic intent is therefore crucial.

Specific and basic intent

Delivering the leading judgment in *Majewski*, Lord Elwyn-Jones LC suggested that a crime of basic intent was a crime that could be committed recklessly (pages 474H–475A). While this definition is a useful rule of thumb, not all crimes can be classified in this way. For example, there are many offences that require neither intention nor recklessness but some other form of *mens rea*. Moreover, in the recent case of *R v. Heard*, the Court of Appeal classified sexual assault contrary to section 3 of the Sexual Offences Act 2003 as a crime of basic intent, even though the offence requires 'intentional touching' and cannot be committed recklessly.

In the absence of any universally applicable definition, academics have tended to define crimes of basic intent as crimes for which voluntary intoxication is not a defence. This is obviously a circular definition, which is of little use in practice.

Perhaps the safest way to ascertain whether a crime is one of specific or basic intent is to look at the previous decisions of the courts. The courts have classified murder, robbery, theft, wounding with intent, causing grievous bodily harm with intent, burglary with intent to steal, handling stolen goods, and causing criminal damage with intent to cause damage or endanger life, as offences of specific intent. Crimes of basic intent include manslaughter, most lesser forms of assault, kidnapping, false imprisonment, and simple criminal damage.

It is significant that many offences of specific intent contain a lesser, basic intent offence. For example, where a defendant is charged with murder but lacks the specific intent for murder, he remains liable to be convicted of manslaughter. In *R v. Lipman*, a case considered in *Majewski*, the defendant consumed LSD. During the course of the resulting hallucinatory experience, he believed that he was being attacked by snakes and strangled his girlfriend. The Court of Appeal confirmed that self-induced intoxication was no defence to a charge of manslaughter.

Similarly, where a defendant wounds another person but lacks the specific intent to cause grievous bodily harm required by section 18 of the Offences Against the Person Act 1861, he is nonetheless liable to be convicted of unlawful wounding under section 20 of that Act.

Thus, intoxication sometimes operates as a partial defence by providing a potential defence to a crime of specific intent but exposing the defendant to conviction of a lesser basic intent crime. It is important to note, however, that some offences of specific intent, such as theft, have no alternative basic intent offence.

Public policy

The House of Lords in *Majewski* accepted that, logically speaking, a person who wounds another without knowing what he is doing should be acquitted not only of wounding with intent but also of the related basic intent offence of unlawful wounding, the *mens rea* being equally absent for both the section 18 offence and the section 20 offence. The basis for distinguishing between crimes of specific and basic intent is perhaps even more questionable

1

CRIMINAL LAW

following the decision in *R v. G*, which confirmed that recklessness is subjective. A defendant who fails to form the intent to commit an offence as a result of self-induced intoxication is equally likely to lack subjective awareness of the required risk.

Lord Salmon accepted that 'there is a degree of illogicality in the rule that intoxication may excuse or expunge one type of intention and not another' (page 483H). However, it is clear from *Majewski* that the decision that voluntary intoxication should not be allowed to negate *mens rea* in a crime of basic intent is essentially a judgment based on public policy rather than a decision based on strict logic.

Their Lordships' judgments are punctuated by observations about the known connection between alcohol and violence and the worrying increase in crime fuelled by drug abuse. Lord Elwyn-Jones regarded the control of violence as 'the prime purpose of the criminal law' (page 469F). Their Lordships were clearly concerned that the acceptance of intoxication as a general defence would have damaging consequences: 'If there were to be no penal sanction for any injury unlawfully inflicted under the complete mastery of drink or drugs, voluntarily taken, the social consequence could be appalling' (Lord Salmon, page 484B).

One justification put forward for the position adopted in *Majewski* is that a person who becomes intoxicated of his own volition is reckless in so becoming and thus the requirement of *mens rea* is satisfied by his becoming intoxicated (Lord Elwyn-Jones, page 474H). The difficulty with this argument is that the *actus reus* and *mens rea* of an offence must normally exist at the same time, yet the act of taking drink or drugs is not usually contemporaneous with the *actus reus* of the offence. Moreover, the moral blameworthiness involved in becoming intoxicated frequently bears no relation to the moral blameworthiness for the *mens rea* of the offence. We have also seen that not all crimes of basic intent are crimes for which recklessness suffices (*R v. Heard*).

Dangerous drugs

It seems that the taking of drink or drugs is now usually sufficient of itself to constitute *mens rea* for a crime of basic intent. In *R v. Richardson and Irwin* the Court of Appeal confirmed that where a defendant is charged with a crime of basic intent and admits taking alcohol or drugs, the only question the jury have to answer is whether the defendant would have recognised the risk had he been sober.

There is one caveat to the above in the case of voluntary intoxication by drugs. Where there is no evidence that the drugs taken by a defendant were known by the defendant to cause aggression or unpredictability, the ordinary *Majewski* principles do not apply. In *R v. Hardie*, the defendant consumed unprescribed valium, which is generally known as a soporific drug. The Court of Appeal held that the jury should have been directed to consider whether the taking of the valium was itself reckless.

Voluntary intoxication and mistake

A man who mistakenly believes that he is under attack is normally entitled to use reasonable force in self-defence. The courts have held that where this mistake is a result of self-induced intoxication, he cannot rely on self-defence (*R v. O'Grady*). This principle applies equally to crimes of basic intent and crimes of specific intent (*R v. Hatton*).

Conclusion

DPP v. *Majewski* remains the leading case on voluntary intoxication. The judgment reflects the extent to which the development of intoxication as a defence has been heavily influenced by public policy. Notwithstanding a significant degree of academic criticism, subsequent decisions have consistently upheld the rule that self-induced intoxication is no defence to a crime of basic intent.

FURTHER READING

Primary sources

R v. *Allen* [1988] Crim LR 698

R v. *G* [2003] UKHL 50

R v. *Hardie* [1985] 1 WLR 64

R v. *Hatton* [2005] EWCA Crim 2951

R v. *Heard (Lee)* [2008] QB 43; [2007] 3 WLR 475; [2007] Cr. App. R. 37

R v. *Kingston* [1994] 3 WLR 519

R v. *Lipman* [1969] 3 WLR 819

R v. *O'Grady* [1987] 1 QB 995

R v. *Richardson and Irwin* [1999] 1 Cr App R 392

R v. *Sheehan and Moore* (1960) 60 Cr App R 308

Secondary sources

Ashworth, A. (1980) 'Intoxication and General Defences' [1980] *Crim LR*, 556.

Dashwood, D. (1977) 'Logic and the Lords in Majewski' [1977] *Crim LR*, 532.

Gough, S. (2000) 'Surviving Without Majewski' [2000] *Crim LR*, 719.

1

CRIMINAL LAW

Consent and offences against the person

R v. Brown [1994] 1 AC 212

Mark James, Salford Law School

The ruling of the House of Lords in *Brown* brings into focus a number of the theories that underpin judicial reasoning and judicial lawmaking in the criminal law. Although outwardly its focus is on the limits that can be placed on consensual injury-causing activities, one of its main contributions to legal discussion has been to highlight the inconsistent and irrational manner in which the law can develop when the underlying reasoning of a case is grounded firmly in public policy.

The House was concerned with the question of whether it was possible for a group of sado-masochistic homosexual men to consent in law to the deliberate infliction on their persons of injuries amounting to actual bodily harm (ABH) for sexual gratification. The definition of assault, as discussed in *Savage; Parmenter* was not at issue. Instead, the House had to determine the boundaries of consent to offences against the person. In rejecting the ability of the defendants to consent to injuries caused by acts of sado-masochism by a 3–2 majority, the House discussed all aspects of the general rule of consent, the categories of activity exempted from the general rule and the reasons why the full, free and informed consent of a victim (V) can operate as a defence to some forms of deliberate violence but not others.

The definition of consent to injury

The first problem encountered by their Lordships was the lack of any formal legal definition of consent. There was, and to some extent still is, argument over whether absence of consent is an ingredient of the crime of assault or whether it operates as a true defence. Although the cases seem to point to consent operating as a defence, thus placing an initial evidential burden of proof on the defendant, in the final analysis it will always be incumbent upon the prosecution to disprove V's consent, in each case where it may be relevant, beyond reasonable doubt.

The House in *Brown* did not seek to provide a single definition for the concept of consent that would cover all situations. Instead, it examined the effectiveness of V's consent and the limitations that can be imposed upon such consent once it has been given. In later cases, this has been referred to as being whether the consent given was full, free and informed. This initial examination of the effectiveness of V's consent is supplemented with an analysis of whether there are any legal limitations on the consent as given and whether it should be allowed to extend to the particular activity in question.

Although there is little agreement among the five Law Lords in *Brown*, a general rule can be stated quite simply: V's consent to an act provides no defence for a defendant (D) where that act causes ABH or greater, unless one of the recognised exemptions applies. Validly given consent is, therefore, always a defence to a charge of common assault but can only be a defence to the more serious offences under sections 47, 20 and 18 Offences Against the Person Act 1861 if the act occurred during one of the exempted activities.

This general rule gives rise to two main problems. First, it sets the level of harm to which V can consent at such a low level, harm that is no more than merely trifling and transient, that exemptions are required to ensure that many ordinarily lawful activities, such as contact sports, surgery and piercing, remain legal. Secondly, because there is no agreement on which theories of consent should form the basis of the rule, there is no clear advance indication of whether an activity to which full, free and informed consent has been given will be declared to be lawful or not.

Despite these apparent problems, the general rule has remained unaltered since *Brown*. Instead the focus of the subsequent cases has been on the effectiveness and the validity of the consent given.

The effectiveness of the consent

There are three essential factors that must be addressed when analysing the effectiveness of V's consent: was the consent given full enough to encompass the injury-causing act? Was it given freely? And was it given on the basis of an informed decision?

Fully given consent includes not only the specific acts that V desires to occur (*Wilson*) but also includes acts that are foreseen as likely to occur in the normal course of events, such as breaking a leg during a tackle in a football match (*Barnes*). It does not extend to cover acts not foreseen or agreed upon at the outset.

Freely given consent is where V has not been forced to submit to the injury-causing act through coercion, fear or threat of force. Consent can be given expressly, or on your behalf, as is the case for planned surgery (*Re R*), or it can be implied from V's participation in a specific activity, such as consenting to be punched during a boxing contest (*Coney*). Consent can also be implied where V deliberately runs a risk that is inherent in an activity, such as when playing sport (*Barnes*). Alternatively, consent can be assumed, for example the consent to the touchings inherent in everyday life such as being jostled in a bus queue (*Collins*). Submission is not, however, the same as consent. For example, where V submits to sexual intercourse because she has been threatened with violence, this is not the same as consenting to sexual intercourse (*Olugboja*). The consent must be given freely without coercion.

Consent must also be given from an informed perspective. V must not only be aware of the nature of the act about to be performed on them, they must also be aware of any relevant qualities associated with the act or with D. In *Tabussum*, D performed intimate examinations on several Vs by claiming that he was conducting research into breast cancer. D was convicted of indecent assault as he was not qualified to perform such examinations and the Vs would not have consented to the examinations had they known this. Recently in *Konzani*, D was found guilty of assault contrary to section 20 of the Offences Against the Person Act 1861 by infecting V with the HIV virus. It was held that V did not consent to the infection being passed on to her, or the risk of its being passed on, as she was unaware that D was HIV+; without the full information of D's HIV+ status, V's consent was ineffective.

The exemptions to the general rule

There are a number of activities that are exempted from the operation of the general rule. In each of the following areas, the social utility of the act is considered to outweigh the risk of harm caused to V.

1. Surgery

This is possibly the least contentious of the exemptions. Medical procedures, whether for emergency, therapeutic or cosmetic reasons, can all be consented to by V (*Re R*). The injuries caused by the operation are not assaults as long as they are performed by a competent person with the consent of the patient. In certain circumstances, courts have even forced treatment on minors without their consent where it is for their benefit (*Re R*). Where a competent adult refuses their consent, however, the procedure must not be performed, even where it would be lifesaving (*Blaue*). If the medical team ignores the patient's refusal to consent and proceeds to surgery, an assault is committed. Note that at present, male circumcision is covered by this exemption but there is an absolute prohibition on female circumcision (Female Genital Mutilation Act 2003).

2. Boxing and fighting sports

Any injury caused by an act that is within the rules of boxing is consented to (*Coney*). This would even include the infliction of deliberate injury resulting in death. The only limit on this exemption would appear to be the legally grey area that covers recently imported martial arts, such as Thai boxing, and the more modern hybrid sports that fall under the Mixed Martial Arts banner. Although the Law Commission has cast doubt on the legality of these sports because of their being seemingly more violent and less regulated than traditionally British combat sports such as boxing and wrestling, there have not been any prosecutions for promoting or participating in events of this kind. Fighting for 'no good cause', for example to settle a dispute, does not fall within this exemption (*A-G's Reference No 6 of 1980*). It extends only to organised boxing bouts.

3. Contact sports

Where injury is caused in the course of playing non-combat sports, there are more factors to take into account. If the injury is caused by an act that is part of the normal playing of the game, then it is consented to (*Barnes*). This includes not only injuries arising from all acts that are within the rules of the game but also those occurring as a result of breaches of the playing rules that occur so frequently that they are considered by those who play the game to be part of its playing culture, for example tripping or pushing in football. Where the act is intended to cause injury, however, then an assault is committed and the fact that it is within either the rules or the playing culture of the game will afford no protection to the defendant (*Billinghurst*).

4. Body adornment

The tattooing, piercing and even the branding of another with their consent is lawful. Tattooing and piercing have deep seated cultural traditions in the UK and are therefore considered to be acceptable forms of personal expression. In *Wilson*, the Court of Appeal considered that the branding of a wife by her husband, at her insistence, was to be considered analogous to this exemption.

5. Horseplay

The horseplay exemption, appealing to the notion that 'boys will be boys' and that a bit of playground rough and tumble should not lead to criminal conviction, is somewhat of an anomalous situation when compared to the other exempted activities. The other exemptions cover situations where the victim is either aware of the risk of injury occurring from the activity, for example while playing a sport, or is aware that a specific injury will be inflicted upon them, for example as part of a medical procedure. The horseplay exemption covers situations where despite the absence of the consent of the victim, the injurious activity is protected by the law as its continuation is considered by the courts to be in the public good. Therefore, it is acceptable to set a fellow RAF officer alight with aircraft fuel as part of an initiation test (*Aitken*) and to give a fellow pupil the bumps on his birthday (*Jones*) despite the respective victims being caused 80% third degree burns and suffering a ruptured spleen and broken arm.

1

CRIMINAL LAW

Public policy or legal justification?

The House of Lords gave a variety of reasons for their rulings on consent. These included clear statements of legal moralism from Lord Lowry, 'The reason [given by the defendants for legalising sado-masochism is] that both those who will inflict and those who will suffer the injury wish to satisfy a perverted and depraved sexual desire [which] cannot be . . . conducive to the welfare of society' (page 255) and paternalism from Lord Templman, 'Wounds can easily become septic if not properly treated, the free flow of blood from a person who is HIV positive or who has AIDS can infect another and an inflicter who is carried away by sexual excitement or by drink or drugs could very easily inflict pain and injury beyond the level to which the receiver has consented' (page 246) both giving judgments for the majority. In contrast, Lord Mustill considered that legal moralism cannot be the basis of making acts illegal (page 273) while Lord Slynn held that only those acts causing serious bodily harm should be illegal (page 281). While the majority held that all acts that cause ABH or greater are illegal unless one of the exemptions applies, the minority considered that consent should always operate as a defence unless the act itself is specifically prohibited.

With so little agreement or coherence between the judgments, it is difficult to come to any hard and fast rules concerning the legality of injury-causing acts. The judgments in *Brown* and all of the cases concerning the exempted activities are all firmly rooted in public policy; an activity is legal if the House of Lords thinks it should be and not if it doesn't.

FURTHER READING

Primary soruces

Female Genital Mutilation Act 2003

Offences Against the Person Act 1861

A-G's Reference (No. 6 of 1980) [1981] QB 715

Collins v. *Willcock* [1984] 1 WLR 1172

R v. *Aitken* [1992] 1 WLR 1006

R v. *Barnes* [2004] EWCA Crim 3246

R v. *Billinghurst* [1978] Crim LR 553

R v. *Blaue* (1975) 61 Cr App R 271

R v. *Coney* (1881) 8 QBD 534

R v. *Heard* [2007] EWCA Crim 125; [2007] 3 WLR 475; [2007] 3 All ER 306

R v. *Jones* (1986) 83 Cr App R 375

R v. *Konzani* [2005] EWCA Crim 706

R v. *Olugboja* [1982] QB 320

R v. *Savage; R* v. *Parmenter* [1992] 1 AC 699

R v. *Tabassum* [2000] 2 Cr App R 328

R v. *Wilson* [1997] QB 47

Re R [1991] 3 WLR 592

Secondary sources

Herring, J. (2006) *Criminal Law Text, Cases and Material*, 2nd edn, OUP, Ch. 6.

Law Commission Consultation Paper No. 139 'Consent in the Criminal Law' (1995) HMSO, Part XII.

Simester, A.P. and Sullivan, G.R. (2007) *Criminal Law Theory and Doctrine*, 3rd edn, Hart Publishing, Ch. 21.

Joint enterprise

R v. *Powell and Daniels*; and R v. *English*
[1999] 1 AC 1, House of Lords

Tony Storey, Northumbria University

In these cases, the House of Lords considered two separate appeals against murder convictions. As the cases raised essentially the same point of law, dealing with the liability for murder of those who are involved in a 'joint enterprise', the House dealt with them together.

In the first case, Anthony Powell, Antonio Daniels and a third man, known as 'Mikey', went to the flat of David Edwards, a 'small-time drug dealer' in south London. One of the three shot and killed Edwards. 'Mikey' disappeared and was never caught, but Powell and Daniels were charged with Edwards' murder, based on joint enterprise. Although the Crown could not prove who had actually fired the gun, the prosecution case was that it was enough for a conviction of murder that each man knew that one of them was carrying a gun which he might use to kill with intent to do so or to cause serious harm to the victim. Moreover, liability could be imposed even though the defendants might not have intended that the act be carried out. Powell and Daniels were convicted and appealed, unsuccessfully, to the Court of Appeal. They appealed again to the House of Lords.

In the second case, Philip English and Paul Weddle had been convicted of the murder of a police sergeant, Bill Forth. Sergeant Forth and PC William Hay had been called to a disturbance at the home of Weddle's former girlfriend in Gateshead, Tyne & Wear. Weddle, aged 25, and English, aged 15, who had both been drinking, attacked Sergeant Forth with wooden fence posts. English had then run off, chased by PC Hay. The officer caught English and had placed him under arrest – in fact, handcuffed him – by the time Weddle, who was still fighting with Sergeant Forth, produced a small knife and stabbed Forth to death. At the murder trial, the judge directed the jury that, even if English did not know that Weddle had a knife, they still had to consider whether English realised that Weddle might cause serious injury to Sergeant Forth with the wooden post. After both defendants were convicted of murder they appealed, unsuccessfully, to the Court of Appeal. English appealed to the House of Lords, contending that, to support a murder conviction, he would have had to have foreseen an act of the type actually carried out and that the use of the knife was fundamentally different from the use of a wooden post.

The Law Lords dismissed the appeals of Powell and Daniels but allowed English's appeal. The Lords held that:

1. In a case of murder as part of a joint enterprise, in order to establish liability it must be proven that the secondary party contemplated that the principal might kill with malice aforethought. This was the case even though it meant imposing a lower level

of *mens rea* in relation to the secondary party (contemplation) than in relation to the principal (intention).

2. Where, as part of a joint enterprise, death is caused by a weapon, the secondary party is not liable for murder or even manslaughter if he neither knew about that weapon nor contemplated that an equally dangerous weapon might be in the possession of the principal.

What is joint enterprise?

Where two or more defendants (D1 and D2) embark on a criminal endeavour together, for example burglary or robbery, this is joint enterprise. Some academics – principally the late Professor Sir John Smith – argued that joint enterprise was really a specific manifestation of secondary liability (aiding, abetting, counselling or procuring). However, other academics – notably Professor Andrew Simester – argue that joint enterprise liability is different. There is judicial authority that supports Professor Simester's view. In *Stewart and Schofield*, for example, Hobhouse LJ gave the following guidance:

> The allegation that [D] took part in the execution of a crime as a joint enterprise is not the same as an allegation that he aided, abetted, counselled or procured the commission of that crime. A person who is a mere aider or abettor, etc., is truly a secondary party to the commission of whatever crime it is that the principal has committed . . . If the principal has committed the crime of murder, the liability of the secondary party can only be a liability for aiding and abetting murder. In contrast, where the allegation is joint enterprise, the allegation is that [D] participated in the criminal act of another. This is a different principle. It renders each of the parties to a joint enterprise criminally liable for the acts done in the course of carrying out that joint enterprise.

The 'scope' of the joint enterprise

Generally speaking, D1 and D2 are jointly liable for crimes committed by either of them – provided that what happens is within the 'scope' of the joint enterprise. Problems arise if, on such a joint endeavour, D1 does something unexpected, for example, fatally shoots or stabs the householder during a burglary. D1 is now potentially liable for murder (depending on his *mens rea*). But is D2 now liable for murder as well? The answer is 'possibly'. Ultimately, it depends on whether D2 foresaw a possibility that D1 might kill, with malice aforethought, but still participated in the joint enterprise. Several cases, including *Powell and Daniels*; *English* have examined this issue. In one of the earlier cases, *Anderson and Morris*, Lord Parker CJ in the Court of Criminal Appeal said that:

> Where two persons embark on a 'joint enterprise', each is liable for the acts done in pursuance of that 'joint enterprise' [and] that includes liability for unusual consequences if they arise from the execution of the agreed joint enterprise but (and this is the crux of the matter) that, if one of the adventurers goes beyond what had been tacitly agreed as part of the common enterprise, his co-adventurer is not liable for the consequences of that unauthorised act. Finally . . . it is for the jury in every case to decide whether what was done was part of the 'joint enterprise', or went beyond it and was in fact an act unauthorised by that 'joint enterprise'.

Hence, according to *Anderson and Morris*, in the burglary-gone-wrong scenario, D2 is not liable for anything other than burglary if D1 has acted outside the scope of the joint enterprise. The point that, in such a case, D2 is not liable for murder unless he foresaw that D1 might kill with malice aforethought, might be termed the 'contemplation principle'.

The 'contemplation principle'

In this area of law, two opinions given by the Privy Council, hearing appeals against murder convictions from the Court of Appeal of Hong Kong, have been very influential. In *Chan Wing-Siu and Others*, involving a robbery by three defendants which culminated in V being stabbed to death by at least one of them, Sir Robin Cooke said (emphasis added):

> A secondary party is criminally liable for acts by the primary offender of a type which the former foresees but does not necessarily intend. That there is such a principle is not in doubt. It turns on *contemplation* or, putting the same idea in other words, *authorisation*, which may be express or is more usually implied. It meets the case of a crime foreseen as a possible incident of the common unlawful enterprise. The criminal culpability lies in participating in the venture with that foresight.

The appeals were dismissed. In *Hui Chi-ming*, a gang including the appellant had killed an innocent man having mistaken him for someone else. The victim had been battered with a length of metal pipe and the principal offender was convicted of manslaughter. The appellant, however, was convicted of murder. The Privy Council rejected his appeal, following *Chan Wing-Siu*. Lord Lowry said that the references in *Chan Wing-sui* to authorisation served 'to emphasise the fact that mere foresight is not enough: the accessory, in order to be guilty, must have foreseen the relevant offence which the principal may commit *as a possible incident of the common unlawful enterprise* and must, with such foresight, still have participated in the enterprise' (emphasis added).

Hui Chi-ming is authority for the proposition that D2 might, in certain circumstances face greater liability (such as murder) than D1 (manslaughter). This serves to emphasise the point that joint enterprise is separate from secondary liability (aiding, abetting, etc.). In *Hui Chi-ming*, the court accepted that D2 had foreseen that D1 might commit murder. That was enough to establish D2's liability for the more serious offence.

Chan Wing-Siu was then relied upon in *Powell and Daniels*; *English*. Lord Hutton stated that:

> Where two parties embark on a 'joint enterprise' to commit a crime, and one party foresees that in the course of the enterprise the other party may carry out, with the requisite *mens rea*, an act constituting another crime, the former is liable for that crime if committed by the latter in the course of the enterprise . . . The secondary party is subject to criminal liability if he contemplated the act causing the death as a possible incident of the joint venture, unless the risk was so remote that the jury take the view that the secondary party genuinely dismissed it as altogether negligible.

A good example of the 'scope' of the joint enterprise is provided by the recent case of *Rafferty*. D and two others had attacked V on a beach near Swansea in south Wales. The attack involved punching and kicking. While the attack continued, D left the beach with V's debit card and tried, unsuccessfully, to withdraw cash from his bank account. In his

49

absence, the others stripped V, dragged him into the sea and drowned him. The two others were convicted of murdering V, but the Court of Appeal decided that D, despite his participation in the original joint enterprise to attack and rob V, was not liable in respect of V's death. Hooper LJ said that the deliberate drowning of V was so 'fundamentally different' in nature from the original assault on V (involving punching and kicking) that it went beyond the scope of the joint enterprise.

Is the 'contemplation principle' too harsh?

This aspect of the law of joint enterprise has been criticised for allowing D2 to face murder liability because of what he foresaw *might* happen (in other words, recklessness) whereas D1 can only be guilty of murder if he acted with malice aforethought (in other words, intent). This point was addressed in *Powell and Daniels; English*. Lord Steyn, for example, acknowledged that 'at first glance there is substance in the argument that it is anomalous that a lesser form of culpability is required in the case of a secondary party, *viz.* foresight of the possible commission of the greater offence, whereas in the case of the primary offender the law insists on proof of the specific intention'. However, he went on to adopt what could be described as a 'robust' approach. He said:

> The answer to this supposed anomaly is to be found in practical and policy considerations. If the law required proof of the specific intention on the part of a secondary party, the utility of the accessory principle would be gravely undermined. It is just that a secondary party who foresees that the primary offender might kill with the intent sufficient for murder, and assists and encourages the primary offender in the criminal enterprise on this basis, should be guilty of murder . . . The criminal justice system exists to control crime. A prime function of that system must be to deal justly but effectively with those who join with others in criminal enterprises. Experience has shown that joint criminal enterprises only too readily escalate into the commission of greater offences. In order to deal with this important social problem the accessory principle is needed and cannot be abolished or relaxed.

Similarly, Lord Hutton said that 'the rules of the common law are not based solely on logic but relate to practical concerns and, in relation to crimes committed in the course of joint enterprises, to the need to give effective protection to the public against criminals operating in gangs'. He concluded this point by stating that there are 'practical considerations of weight and importance related to considerations of public policy which justify [the contemplation principle] and which prevail over considerations of strict logic'.

D2's knowledge that D1 is armed

It is often crucial in joint enterprise cases – typically when D1 produces a gun or knife and uses it to kill V during a burglary – to establish whether or not D2 knew in advance that D1 was armed. If D2 did have this knowledge it is much easier for the prosecution to prove that D2 foresaw the possibility that D1 might commit murder. In *Chan Wing-Siu*, Sir Robin Cooke said that where D was involved in joint enterprise aware that 'potentially murderous weapons are to be carried, and in the event they are in fact used by his partner with an intent sufficient for murder, he should not escape the consequences'. Lord Hutton addressed this point in *Powell and Daniels; English*. He said that, while it was 'undesirable to seek to formulate a more precise answer to the question', he did offer some general guidance for future cases:

> [If] the weapon used by the primary party is different to, but as dangerous as, the weapon which the secondary party contemplated he might use, the secondary party should not escape liability for murder because of the difference in the weapon, for example, if he foresaw that the primary party might use a gun to kill and the latter used a knife to kill, or *vice versa*. There will be cases giving rise to a fine distinction as to whether or not the unforeseen use of a particular weapon or the manner in which a particular weapon is used will take a killing outside the scope of the joint venture, but this issue will be one of fact for the common sense of the jury to decide.

Subsequent cases in the Court of Appeal have expanded upon this issue, in particular *Uddin*, *Greatrex*, *O'Flaherty* and *Rahman and Others*. In *Greatrex*, for example, D2 participated in a gang attack on V outside the *Zone* nightclub in Walsall. D2 anticipated that the violence would involve kicking. However, during the attack, D1 produced a metal bar or spanner and delivered a fatal blow to V's skull. The Court of Appeal quashed D2's murder conviction. The court stated that 'foresight by the secondary party of the possible use of the fatal weapon is required in all cases of joint attack except those in which the use of a *different but equally dangerous weapon* is foreseen' (emphasis added). As D2 did not know about the metal bar or spanner, and nor had the jury been invited to decide whether, as a matter of fact, a shod foot was an 'equally dangerous weapon', the conviction was unsafe.

In *Uddin*, the Court of Appeal established seven 'principles' to be used in murder by joint enterprise cases. Space precludes a detailed analysis of all of them here, but attention is drawn to principle (ii), where the court stated that the use of a weapon is 'a significant factor. If the character of the weapon, for example its *propensity to cause death*, is different from any weapon used or contemplated by the others and if it is used with a specific intent to kill, the others are not responsible for the death unless it is proved that they knew or foresaw the likelihood of the use of such a weapon' (emphasis added). In principle (iii), the Court stated that 'If some or all of the others are using weapons which could be regarded as *equally likely to inflict fatal injury*, the mere fact that a different weapon was used is immaterial' (emphasis added).

O'Flaherty illustrates this point. D and a group of friends had attended a concert by So Solid Crew at *Atmospheres* nightclub in Luton. Also at the club were a number of young men from south-east London, the 'Peckham Boys', including an 18-year-old called Marcus Hall. At around 2a.m., after the concert had finished, violence erupted in the street outside between D's group of friends on one side and the Peckham Boys on the other. Various *ad hoc* weapons were used including a baseball bat, a cricket bat, a claw hammer and beer bottles. After a few minutes, the disturbance moved into a neighbouring street, Park Street West. There, Hall died from multiple stab wounds. D had followed the disturbance into Park Street West and was seen on CCTV holding a cricket bat. D was convicted of murder based on joint enterprise and appealed, unsuccessfully, to the Court of Appeal. The court held that the trial judge had properly directed the jury in accordance with *Powell and Daniels*; *English*. The jury had decided that D knew that the other participants in the joint enterprise were using weapons like baseball bats, beer bottles and claw hammers and the jury was entitled to find that the use of a knife was not outside of the scope of the joint enterprise.

1

CRIMINAL LAW

Withdrawal from a joint enterprise

Although not an issue in the cases of *Powell and Daniels*; *English*, one other area of joint enterprise law should be examined: withdrawal. The courts have held that it is possible to withdraw from a joint enterprise. The principles are essentially those that govern withdrawal from secondary liability. In *Becerra and Cooper*, D1 and D2 were jointly engaged in a burglary. They were disturbed by one of the occupants of the house. D2 knew that D1 was in possession of a knife which D1 subsequently used to stab to death the householder. D2 tried to avoid liability for murder by claiming that he had already withdrawn, by shouting 'let's go!' climbing out of the bedroom window and running away. The jury rejected this and the Court of Appeal agreed that it was inadequate. Roskill LJ adopted a statement of law from a Canadian case, *Whitehouse*, in which it had been stated that for an effective withdrawal there must be 'something more than a mere mental change of intention and physical change of place by those associates who wish to dissociate themselves'. What exactly must be done to withdraw 'must depend upon the circumstances', although there was 'one essential element [that] ought to be established':

> Where practicable and reasonable there must be timely communication of the intention to abandon the common purpose from those who wish to dissociate themselves from the contemplated crime to those who desire to continue in it. What is 'timely communication' must be determined by the facts of each case but where practicable and reasonable it ought to be such communication, verbal or otherwise, that will serve unequivocal notice upon the other party to the common unlawful cause that if he proceeds upon it he does so without the further aid and assistance of those who withdraw. The unlawful purpose of him who continues alone is then his own and not one in common with those who are no longer parties to it nor liable to its full and final consequences.

This was confirmed in *O'Flaherty*, where Mantell LJ said that 'a person who unequivocally withdraws from the joint enterprise before the moment of the actual commission of the crime by the principal, here murder, should not be liable for that crime'. Moreover, the courts have limited the above requirements to cases of pre-planned criminal behaviour (of which *Becerra and Cooper* was an example). In cases of spontaneous violence, the Court of Appeal decided in *Mitchell and King* that it might be sufficient for D2 to simply walk away from the joint enterprise. This was also confirmed in *O'Flaherty*, where Mantell LJ stated that 'in a case of spontaneous violence, in principle it is possible to withdraw by ceasing to fight, throwing down one's weapons and walking away'.

FURTHER READING

Primary sources

Chan Wing-Siu and Others v. *R* [1985] AC 168

Hui Chi-ming v. *R* [1992] 1 AC 34

R v. *Anderson*; *R* v. *Morris* [1966] 2 QB 110

R v. *Becerra and Cooper* (1976) 62 Cr App R 212

R v. *Davies* [1954] AC 378

R v. *Gamble* [1989] NI 268

R v. *Gilmour* [2000] 2 Cr App R 407

R v. *Greatrex* [1999] 1 Cr App R 126

R v. *Hyde and Others* [1991] 1 QB 134

R v. *Mitchell and King* [1999] Crim LR 496

R v. *O'Flaherty and Others* [2004] EWCA Crim 526, [2004] 2 Cr App R 20

R v. *Rafferty* [2007] EWCA Crim 1846

R v. *Rahman and Others* [2007] EWCA Crim 342; [2007] 1 WLR 2191

R v. *Reid* (1976) 62 Cr App R 109

R v. *Stewart and Schofield* [1995] 3 All ER 159

R v. *Uddin* [1999] QB 431

R v. *Whitehouse* [1941] 1 WWR 112

Secondary sources

Ormerod, D. (2007) 'Joint Enterprise' [2007] *Crim LR*, 721.

Simester, A.P. (2006) 'The Mental Element in Complicity' (2006) 122, *LQR*, 578.

Smith, J.C. (1997) 'Criminal Liability of Accessories: Law and Law Reform' (1997) 113, *LQR*, 453.

1

CRIMINAL LAW

2 PUBLIC LAW

Public law is often termed 'constitutional and administrative law': constitutional law refers to the institutions and mechanisms of government; administrative law addresses matters related to the administration of government. Public law shares a lot in common with politics and with other societal and governmental studies. It is in the news almost every day, whether regarding the passing of legislation, calls for a particular minister of state to answer questions or even to resign, legal claims for the protection of individual's human rights or challenges in the courts to decisions and actions or omissions of the government.

Constitutional law concerns the relationship between the state and the individual. Is it a unilateral obligation owed by the state to individuals or do we as citizens also owe duties and obligations to the state? The relationship between the individual and the state is a central notion addressed in discussions on the Human Rights Act and on police powers and public order issues.

This section of the book addresses key themes in public law. The concept of separation of powers (which requires checks and balances between the executive (government), legislative (Parliament) and judicial (courts) organs of the state) permeates public law. Here, entries focus on the extent to which the judiciary can challenge the legislative (supremacy of Parliament) and the extent to which the judiciary can review the executive (judicial review). Complexities in the review of ministerial activities in Parliament are addressed in part in *R* v. *Ponting* with the omnipresent use of official secrets legislation. The relationship between the state and the individual is rarely far from the news, be it in the context of human rights, police powers or public order. This chapter thus contains entries on preventing a breach of the peace and facilitating freedom to demonstrate.

CONTENTS FOR PUBLIC LAW

Rule of law
Entick v. Carrington (1765) 19 State Tr 1029   57

Supremacy of Parliament
R (on the application of Jackson and Others) v. Attorney-General [2005]
UKHL 56, [2005] All ER (D) 136   63

Public authorities and the Human Rights Act
Aston Cantlow and Wilmcote with Billesley Parochial Church Council v. Wallbank
and Another [2003] UKHL 37, [2003] 3 All ER 1213   70

Official secrets legislation and the separation of powers
R v. Ponting [1985] Crim LR 318   76

Police powers and the rights of suspects
R v. Lattimore and Others (1976) 62 Cr App R 53   81

Preventing a breach of the peace (public order)
R (Laporte) v. Chief Constable of Gloucestershire [2006] UKHL 55   84

Freedom to demonstrate and public order offences
DPP v. Jones (Margaret) [1999] 2 AC 240   89

Judicial review of administrative action
Council of Civil Service Unions v. Minister for the Civil Service [1984] 3 All ER 935   93

Standing (locus standi) for judicial review proceedings
Inland Revenue Commissioner v. National Federation of Self-Employed and Small
Businesses Ltd [1982] AC 617   98

Bias (judicial review)
R v. Bow Street Metropolitan Stipendiary Magistrate ex parte Pinochet Ugarte
(No. 2) [1999] 2 WLR 272 HL   104

Rule of law

Entick v. Carrington (1765) 19 State Tr 1029

Accessible via http://www.constitution.org/trials/entick/entick_v_carrington.htm

Rebecca Moosavian, Northumbria University

2

PUBLIC LAW

Despite being over 240 years old, the case of *Entick* v. *Carrington* remains firmly situated within accounts of the 'rule of law', a vital but nebulous concept that underlies the British Constitution. Though the origins of the rule of law are ancient, it is viewed as an essential feature of western liberal states. In essence, as Raz claims, the rule of law has come to mean, in a narrow sense, 'that the government shall be ruled by the law and subject to it' (*The Rule of Law and its Virtue*, page 196).

Entick is a frequently cited example of the courts upholding the rule of law. The judgment, delivered by Lord Chief Justice Camden, represents an early display of judicial robustness in the face of executive excess. It also demonstrates the essential judicial function of protecting individual rights in action.

The facts

The case involved a trespass action brought by a publisher, John Entick, against the defendants, four state officers (including one Nathan Carrington). These officers were acting according to a general warrant granted by George Montagu Dunk, the Earl of Halifax and Home Secretary. The earl suspected Entick of preparing seditious material containing 'gross and scandalous reflections and invectives upon his majesty's government'. The defendants raided Entick's home; they forced entry and rifled through his possessions for four hours. Doors and furniture were broken open, private papers and books were pried into and seized. However, no offending materials were found.

The plaintiff, Entick, argued that the Home Secretary did not have a legal right to grant the warrant, that he had therefore acted outside of the law and an unlawful trespass had occurred. The defendants argued that the Home Secretary had been acting within the ambit of the law when issuing the warrant. The defendants also argued that warrants of this sort were a matter of tradition and had been used previously without challenge. Camden CJ refused to accept the defendants' arguments, held that the warrant was illegal and awarded damages.

The rule of law

The roots of the rule of law can be traced through the Roman and medieval eras, but it gained prominence in Britain during the seventeenth century when the absolute power of the monarch began to wane in the face of parliamentary moves to apply legal limits to the king. In the centuries since, the rule of law has been put forward in various guises by numerous theorists, though it is generally taken to entail the limitation of governmental power and the protection of individual liberties.

The rule of law was most famously propounded by A.V. Dicey (1835–1922), whose contribution to British constitutional understanding has been immensely influential and enduring. Dicey's account, first published in 1885, viewed the rule of law along with parliamentary sovereignty as a distinguishing characteristic of the British constitution. Dicey's rule of law comprises three distinct yet overlapping requirements. Firstly, there must be an absence of arbitrary governmental power. Secondly, every man must be subject to the law. Finally, individual liberties must be protected by judicial decisions.

The rule of law in *Entick*

Despite pre-dating Dicey's writings, the judgment in *Entick* demonstrated each of his three principles in operation. In the fourth and final stage of his judgment, Camden CJ considered whether the warrant to seize Entick's papers was lawful. He claimed that the Home Secretary's power to grant warrants must be authorised by law, adding 'If it is law, it will be found in our books. If it is not to be found there, it is not law'. Camden was unable to pinpoint a legal rule that set out that particular power: 'Where is the written law that gives any magistrate such a power? I can safely answer, there is none; and therefore it is too much for us without such authority to pronounce a practice legal, which would be - subversive of all the comforts of society'. Camden concluded that the Home Secretary had no authority to issue the warrant. In doing so he demonstrated an unwillingness to create a power where no rule provided for one; to do so would create a power of broad and arbitrary scope.

The second Diceyan principle can also be detected in Camden's unwillingness to accept the defendant's arguments based on past practice and in his contention that if the warrant was not lawful then trespass had inevitably occurred: 'If [the Secretary of State] had no such jurisdiction, the law is clear, that the officers are as much responsible for the trespass as their superior'. This indicated that a defendant could be held liable for unlawful conduct irrespective of his status.

Dicey's third principle, concern for individual liberties, arguably occupies the most prominent role in the *Entick* judgment. Camden warned of potentially dangerous implications if the defendants' actions were viewed as legal: 'the secret cabinets and bureaus of every subject in this kingdom will be thrown open to the search and inspection of a messenger whenever the secretary of state shall think fit to charge, or even to suspect a person to be the author, printer, or publisher of a seditious libel' (page x). The judge argued that the power could be exercised honestly, but also oppressively against innocent men.

The rule of law in its Diceyan format has continued to play an influential supporting role in constitutional case law. It can be detected running through many cases from *Entick* to the present day.

The absence of arbitrary power

Dicey's rule of law opposes arbitrary governmental power. He claimed that the rule of law 'excludes the existence of arbitrariness . . . or even of wide discretionary authority on the part of the government. Englishmen are ruled by the law, and by the law alone' (*An Introduction to the Study of the Law of the Constitution*, page 202). This results in greater clarity and certainty; individuals will only be punished when they have clearly breached a law (page 188). Dicey was wary of allowing government too much discretionary power; this feature was present in many continental systems of which he was critical. Instead, the rule of law required the government (or executive) to govern according to law and to have legal authority for its acts.

A general respect for the first principle has influenced a number of prominent judgments. One such case is *Rossminster* which displays broad similarities with the *Entick* facts. Here tax officers searched suspects' homes under warrants that did not specify the suspected persons or offences. Lord Denning in the Court of Appeal referred to *Entick*, holding the warrants to be invalid as they were too wide and did not specify the particular offences. He warned of the dangers of broad powers (page 972):

> The trouble is that the legislation is drawn so widely that in some hands it might be an instrument of oppression. . . . Once great power is granted, there is a danger of it being abused. Rather than risk such abuse, it is . . . the duty of the courts so to construe the statute as to see that it encroaches as little as possible on the liberties of the people of England.

The House of Lords later reversed the Court of Appeal judgment, finding in favour of the Inland Revenue.

Another case, *Pierson*, concerned the Home Secretary's power to increase prison tariffs beyond the trial judge's original recommendation. The House of Lords held that the statutory power could not be accorded a wide-ranging interpretation which would permit the minister to increase tariffs retrospectively after they had been fixed. Lord Steyn claimed that the court could not assume that Parliament would have legislated to create such an extensive and unprecedented power; such a power must be created clearly and explicitly. He decided that the case should be approached in accordance with Dicey's rule of law, stating that 'Unless there is the clearest provision to the contrary, Parliament must be presumed not to legislate contrary to the rule of law. And the rule of law enforces minimum standards of fairness, both substantive and procedural' (page 591).

The principle against arbitrary power may seem of limited relevance in the present day where it is an accepted constitutional arrangement that government ministers exercise wide powers. Nevertheless, these cases illustrate instances where judges have resisted executive requests to interpret the meaning of legislation broadly in its favour.

Every man is subject to the ordinary law of the land

Dicey's second rule of law requirement states that 'no man is above the law . . . [and] that . . . every man, whatever be his rank or condition, is subject to the ordinary law of the realm and amenable to the jurisdiction of the ordinary tribunals' (page 193). Two features

2

PUBLIC LAW

of the rule of law can be drawn from this statement. Firstly, that all men, irrespective of status, including government officials, should abide by the laws of the land. According to Dicey, in England 'every official, from the Prime Minister down to a constable or collector of taxes, is under the same responsibility for every act done without legal justification as any other citizen' (page 193). Dicey specifically cited *Entick* as an example of this proposition. Secondly, Dicey's statement refers to 'ordinary' laws and courts. Unlike continental countries England did not have a distinct administrative court system to deal with officials. Dicey thought that the English common law was a superior system because it entailed 'the equal subjection of all classes to the ordinary law of the land administered by the ordinary law courts' (page 202). Despite this, recent decades have seen increased use of specialist administrative tribunals instead of the 'ordinary' courts that Dicey so revered.

Instances of the courts ruling against high-ranking officials have continued. For example, in *Re M* the House of Lords held that the Home Secretary whose department had breached a court order was not entitled to plead crown immunity from liability. The minister in his official capacity was found to be in contempt of court. Lord Templeman set out the 'dangers' of placing government ministers beyond the reach of legal enforcement: 'if upheld, [it would] establish the proposition that the executive obey the law as a matter of grace and not as a matter of necessity, a proposition which would reverse the result of the Civil War' (page 395).

In another case, *Bennett*, the House of Lords ruled in favour of a suspected criminal who had been forcibly moved from South Africa to England in breach of international laws and the usual extradition procedures. The Lords held that UK courts would take account of an illegal abduction by law enforcement agencies and as a result refused to try the defendant in this case. Lord Bridge stated that 'There is . . . no principle more basic to any proper system of law than the maintenance of the rule of law itself. . . . To hold that the court may turn a blind eye to executive lawlessness beyond the frontiers of its own jurisdiction is . . . an insular and unacceptable view' (page 67).

Liberties are protected by judicial decisions

The third component of Dicey's rule of law provides that 'the general principles of the constitution (. . . for example, the right to personal liberty . . .) are . . . the result of judicial decisions determining the rights of private persons in particular cases brought before the courts' (page 195). Dicey drew a clear link between the judge-made constitution and respect for individual freedoms, claiming that 'In England the right to individual liberty is part of the constitution, because it is secured by the decisions of the courts' (page 197). It is no coincidence that all of the cases involving the rule of law are ultimately concerned with individual freedoms in one way or another. For example, the principle permeates the *Rossminster* and *Pierson* judgments (above). Furthermore, the *Human Rights Act 1998* has arguably bolstered Dicey's third principle by putting individual liberties on a statutory footing, thus entrenching and strengthening them.

In one recent case, *A* v. *Secretary of State*, the House of Lords unanimously ruled that laws did not allow the use of evidence obtained by torture in foreign jurisdictions in terrorism cases. Such evidence must on principle, and in accordance with the rule of law, be excluded from hearings. Departure from such fundamental principle could only be made by express parliamentary enactment. Lord Hope eloquently outlined the dangers: 'The lesson of history is that, when the law is not there to keep watch over it, [torture] is always at risk of being resorted to in one form or another by the executive branch of government. The temptation to use it in times of emergency will be controlled by the law wherever the rule of law is allowed to operate' (page 623).

The influence of Dicey's third principle can also be observed in *R* v. *Parole Board*. Here a Parole Board review hearing effectively required the claimant to present his case without any knowledge as to the allegations against him. Though the House of Lords dismissed the claimant's appeal, Lords Bingham and Steyn dissented, both claiming that the arrangement was contrary to the rule of law. Bingham argued that courts must work from the 'presumption that Parliament does not intend to interfere with the exercise of fundamental rights', and that this presumption 'is not a lawyer's fiction but a practical reality' (pages 759–60). Lord Steyn's judgment was also laced with concern for individual rights. Drawing an analogy with Kafka's *The Trial* he claimed that 'phantom' parole hearings where the claimant did not know the evidence against him were contrary to the rule of law and 'emptie[d] the prisoner's fundamental right to an oral hearing of all meaningful content' (page 788).

The rule of law today

Dicey's ideas about the rule of law must be viewed in context. They were conceived in a Victorian era of minimal government, *laissez-faire* values and restricted voting rights. Some commentators have questioned the extent to which his views are compatible with the contemporary administrative requirements of a welfare state and an increasingly complex society to regulate. Nevertheless, the rule of law remains a live issue in constitutional and political discourse. For example, it has been used as a basis for criticising current controversial anti-terrorist legislation that provides government with wide powers. It is clear from the case law in this area that the rule of law forms a mutable yet resilient ideal underpinning our legal system. For centuries it has been utilised by judges in a range of cases where government actions and individual freedoms are at odds, and its influence is likely to continue.

FURTHER READING

Primary sources

A and Others v. *Secretary of State for the Home Department (No. 2)* [2006] 1 All ER 575 (HL)

Inland Revenue Commissioners v. *Rossminster* (1980) AC 952 (HL)

R v. *Horseferry Magistrates' Court, ex parte Bennett* (1994) 1 AC 42 (HL)

R v. *Secretary of State for the Home Department, ex parte Pierson* (1998) AC 539 (HL)

Re: M (1994) 1 AC 377 (HL)

Regina (Roberts) v. *Parole Board and Another* [2005] 2 AC 738 (HL)

2

PUBLIC LAW

Secondary sources

Barnett, H. (2004) *Constitutional and Administrative Law*, 5th edn, Cavendish, Chapter 4.

Bradley A.W. and Ewing, K.D. (2007) *Constitutional and Administrative Law*, 14th edn, Longman, Chapter 6.

Craig, P. (2003) 'Constitutional Foundations, the Rule of Law and Supremacy.' *Public Law*, 92.

Dicey, A.V. (1985) *An Introduction to the Study of the Law of the Constitution*, 10th edn, reprint, Chapters IV, V.

Jowell, J. (2007) 'The Rule of Law and its Underlying Values', in Jowell and Oliver (eds) *The Changing Constitution*, 6th edn, OUP.

Raz, J. (1977) 'The Rule of Law and its Virtue', *Law Quarterly Review*, Vol. 93, page 195.

Supremacy of Parliament

R (on the application of Jackson and Others) v. Attorney-General [2005] UKHL 56, [2005] All ER (D) 136

Christopher Rogers, Northumbria University

This case (referred to throughout as *'Jackson* v. *Attorney-General'*) demonstrates the importance of the doctrine of parliamentary supremacy, or sovereignty, in English law. It also highlights the legal aspects of the relationship between Parliament and the courts, between statutory law and that created by the judiciary. Understanding this relationship is partly an historical and political question as much as it is a question of legal construction of the case law (see the opinion of Lord Steyn *Jackson* v. *Attorney-General* at paras 99 and 102, and Lord Hope of Craighead at para. 120). It demonstrates the legal relationship between the relative parts of the legislature, the House of Commons, the House of Lords, and the Queen, and how this has developed during the course of the twentieth century, and is now being re-interpreted in the twenty-first.

Jackson v. *Attorney-General* was a challenge to the Hunting Act 2004 on the main ground that it was not a valid Act of Parliament. The traditional understanding of an Act of Parliament for lawyers is that it is validly passed by the Commons, the Lords and the Monarch. This was the understanding at common law, and was to remain the understanding until the beginning of the twentieth century when the power of the House of Lords to veto a bill passed by the Commons was removed.

The argument of the applicants in the case also relied on the principle in public law that a power which has been delegated by one authority cannot be subsequently delegated to another authority, as this would be outside the scope of the original authority. Exceptionally in this case it was the power to make legislation, primary legislation, under the terms of the Parliament Acts 1911 and 1949. The rule on delegation applies equally, however, to secondary legislation which is made under the authority of a parent statute.

Jackson v. *Attorney-General* was a bold challenge to the authority of Parliament, although primarily to the House of Commons. As will be seen, it was decided on a very orthodox public law understanding of the proper relationship between the branches of government (legislature, executive, and judiciary), and of the meaning of Parliamentary Supremacy.

The supremacy of Parliament

The doctrine of the supremacy emerged from the struggles between King and Parliament which took place in the seventeenth century (see Tomkins and Chapter 4 of Bradley and Ewing). The modern statement of this doctrine regarding the relationship

2

PUBLIC LAW

between Parliament and the courts can be found in Article 9 of the Bill of Rights 1689 which prohibits the courts from enquiring into or questioning, any Act of Parliament. This new understanding of the authority of Parliament had emerged from the greater influence which Parliament had begun to assume during the course of the sixteenth century when representation was improved, and Parliament was used by the King or Queen to gain greater authority for acts of government. In particular this was true of the reformation Parliaments which conferred legitimacy on the religious settlement initiated by Henry VIII and Elizabeth I.

The modern theory of parliamentary supremacy is even wider than this political and historical settlement might suggest. It was classically expressed in the course of the nineteenth century by A.V. Dicey in his *Law of the Constitution*. This re-stated the doctrine contained in Article 9 that the courts could not question the authority of an Act of Parliament, but extended the theoretical understanding of the doctrine to deny any limits on Parliament's legal competency. As stated by the judges in their opinion: 'The bedrock of the British constitution is . . . the supremacy of the Crown in Parliament . . . the Crown in Parliament [is] unconstrained by any entrenched or codified constitution. It [can] make or unmake any law it [wishes].' (Lord Bingham of Cornhill at para. 9).

This competency, and particularly the tyrannical power which it may be seen to bestow on Parliament, was to be questioned through the course of the twentieth century and academics have continued to speculate on the possibility of when Parliament may actually limit its powers. In recent times judges such as Lord Woolf have asked when the courts may be able to question a statute because it infringes a fundamental law or natural right, now that these are protected by the Human Rights Act 1998. There have now been recent cases where the courts have held that Parliamentary legislation is incompatible with Convention rights (for example, *Ghaidan* v. *Godon-Mendoza*).

Recent constitutional statutes demonstrating the authority of Parliament to alter the constitution itself are the Scotland Act 1998 which delegated certain powers to a new Assembly for Scotland, and the House of Lords Act 1999 which removed the vast majority of the hereditary peers. The issues in *Jackson* v. *Attorney-General* concerned the nature of a parliamentary statute, and the relationship between the House of Commons and the House of Lords under the Parliament Acts 1911 and 1949.

Limitations on parliamentary supremacy

There has always been debate about the extent to which parliamentary supremacy is limited. The contemporary limitations on parliamentary supremacy may be divided into traditional understandings, such as the enactment of retrospective legislation, the relationship between parliamentary and international law, the impact, if any, which natural law has on Parliament's competence, the question as to whether Parliament can bind its successors, and the doctrine of implied repeal, as opposed to the modern challenges in the development of European Law, and the enactment of the Human Rights Act 1998 (see *Aston Cantlow*).

One major consequence of Parliament's legislative supremacy is that it may pass legislation which has a retrospective effect. It is a general principle of the common law that Parliament will not do so, for the obvious reason that it may result in injustice to individuals adversely affected by such legislation, for example by making an act criminal which at the time it was undertaken was not an offence. The best examples of when Parliament has enacted retrospective legislation are in relation to governmental action taken during wartime, for example the War Charges Validity Act 1925, the War Damage Act 1965, and the Indemnity Act 1965. The War Damage Act was used to reverse the decision of the court in *Burmah Oil Co v. Lord Advocate* in which a claim for compensation arising from actions by the British Government in wartime had been allowed, and may have resulted in large compensation claims from many other parties.

In respect of international law the traditional approach of British jurisprudence has been that Parliament is not bound to observe principles of international law whether they are general principles which have evolved as a result of the practice of nations in dealing with one another over the centuries, or even where the Government has entered into a treaty with other states. The making of treaties is one of the bundle of powers collectively known as prerogatives of the Crown, but not automatically part of the domestic law unless specifically incorporated by Act of Parliament. An Act continues to be valid, therefore, even if it contradicts international law. Considered in the context of *Jackson v. Attorney-General*, it is perhaps not surprising as Parliament's powers extend to altering the nature of the British constitution itself. Similarly in regard to natural law it was once thought that Parliament could not enact laws which were repugnant to the general moral law. This is the understanding found in *Dr Bonham's Case*, and also is comparable to modern understandings of the Human Rights Act and the protection afforded to individuals from the Convention. There are certain natural laws which Parliament may not impugn. This does not accord with the understanding advocated by Dicey (see also Lord Hoe, para. 120).

Whether one Parliament can bind its successors is one of the most debated issues surrounding parliamentary supremacy, and has the most practical effect for lawyers in the classical doctrine of implied repeal. Under this doctrine a later statute which clearly contradicts an earlier statute can be taken as impliedly repealing the earlier statute to the extent to which the two are incompatible. This doctrine is very important as it highlights the fact that one Parliament cannot bind its successors to its will in other Parliaments. Some speculate as to whether there are legislative provisions which are entrenched, such as, for example, the Treaty and Act of Union which created the British Parliament in 1707 (Lord Hope, para. 106). It was considered in *Jackson v. Attorney-General* whether certain types of constitutional bill (for example, those affecting the prerogatives of the Crown or disestablishment of the Churches of England or Scotland) were excluded from the provisions of the Parliament Act 1911 as affecting the very basis of the constitution. This was undertaken as a historical exercise in which certain amendments proposed some classes of bills be excluded from the provisions of the Act. All of them were rejected.

The greatest modern challenge to parliamentary supremacy can be found in the incorporation of European Community law into domestic law under the European Communities

2

PUBLIC LAW

Act 1972. In one sense, and as expounded by the European Court of Justice, the Act has limited the competency of our Parliament to enact laws which are inconsistent with pro-visions of European law. A good example of this is the litigation concerning *Factortame*. Some European lawyers speculate as to whether the European Communities Act 1972 is an entrenched form of legislation, in the sense that it would be difficult to repeal, and that the European Court of Justice has held that provisions of English law subsequent to the Act are incompatible with the treaties. Such a question is more political than legal, how-ever, in so far as a government wishing to remain part of the European Union would have to ensure that its legislation complied, but this precludes the possibility of a government acting to withdraw the United Kingdom from the Union in circumstances where this would be considered to be a matter of policy.

The Human Rights Act 1998 has also been considered as a type of entrenched bill, although it has preserved the doctrine of parliamentary supremacy in so far as the courts are only enabled to declare legislation as incompatible with a Convention right and such a declaration does not affect the continuing operation or validity of the Act rule to be incompatible. As Bradley and Ewing (2007, pages 72-73) remark re the continu-ing nature of parliamentary supremacy, the fact that a government cannot bind its successors makes it very difficult for there to be an entrenched bill of rights in the United Kingdom. This is similar to the issue in *R (on the application of Jackson and Others)* where the House of Lords was considering the full effect of the Parliament Acts 1911 and 1949 and how far if at all these could be reviewed by the courts, in partic-ular the latter.

The Parliament Acts 1911 and 1949, *Jackson* v. *Attorney-General* and the question of whether Parliament can bind itself

The Parliament Act 1911 was enacted to remove the veto which the House of Lords had over the enactment of legislation at common law. In the common law for a valid Act of Parlia-ment it had to be stated on the face of the Act that it was passed by the Monarch, the House of Lords and the House of Commons. The enacting formula in most cases preserves this principle:

> Be it enacted by the Queen's Most Excellent Majesty with the advice and consent of the Lords Temporal and Lords Spiritual in this present Parliament assembled.

In the period 1906-1911 the House of Lords opposed reforms to the tax system which the then Liberal government had promised at the general election to support the establish-ment of the welfare state, and Other aspects of the Liberal party's legislative programme. As a result of this opposition the Prime Minister approached King George V to ask him whether he would be prepared to appoint enough Liberal peers to flood the House of Lords and consequently get the legislation passed. The King consented and the Lords backed down and passed the 1911 Act limiting their own powers.

The 1911 Act allowed the House of Lords to delay the passage of legislation through Parliament, but not to prevent it being passed at all. Under the original terms of the Act the House of Lords could only delay legislation for two years, or for three consecutive sessions of Parliament. In 1945 the then Labour government also came across stiff resistance in the House of Lords to its legislative programme. As a result it regarded the House of Lords' delaying power to be excessive, and that it should be curtailed to two parliamentary sessions with consequently only one year between the introduction of the legislation in the first session and that in the second. In order to do so they would have to have the consent of the Lords, on a strict view of the definition of an Act of Parliament at common law.

The Lords resisted the curtailment and consequently the Parliament Act 1911 was invoked to pass the Parliament Act 1949. No-one contested that the Parliament Act 1911 was valid, it having met the formal procedural requirements of passing both the House of Commons and the House of Lords and then being presented for Royal Assent. The question which arose in *Jackson* v. *Attorney-General* was whether the 1949 statute was validly passed given that the Lords had not consented. Counsel for the applicants argued that the procedure laid down in the 1911 Act delegated authority to the Commons to make legislation with Royal Assent in certain specified circumstances, but not an unlimited power. As described in the discussion above, Parliament cannot bind its successors, but whether the 1949 Act was actually an Act of Parliament without the consent of the Lords was the issue to be determined.

The court which first heard the application refused to make a ruling that the 1949 Act was not an Act of Parliament and consequently was of no legal effect, and that consequently the Hunting Act was not an Act of Parliament and consequently was of no legal effect. The appeal to the Court of Appeal was similarly dismissed, and ultimately the House of Lords was to reject the applicants' arguments on these points as well. The applicants were arguing that the 1949 Act was made under power delegated by the Parliament Act 1911 to the House of Commons and the Monarch, and under public law principles that such powers could not be modified or enlarged as had happened in the case of the 1949 Act.

The decisions all highlight the effect of parliamentary supremacy that the courts are reluctant to question an Act of Parliament. The appeal in the House of Lords, because of its constitutional significance was heard by nine of the Lords of Appeal in Ordinary. The first opinion stressed that the appeal had nothing to do with the merits or de-merits of the Hunting Act, but was rather a constitutional and procedural question about the validity of the 1949 Act as passed using the 1911 legislation (para. 1). Their lordships construed s.2(1) of the 1911 Act to mean that *any* act subsequently passed was valid and *that no Act was outside of the provisions of this section*, the words used being unambiguous (Lord Bingham at paras 24, 39–40).

Their lordships surveyed the constitutional history which had led up to the passing of the 1911 Act, and in particular the relationship which had developed in political terms between the House of Commons and the House of Lords. As stated, this meant that in most cases, particularly in relation to finance, the House of Lords would defer to the will of the democratically elected chamber (Hale at para. 156). This relationship was given statutory force by the 1911 Act, and did not preclude *any* Act being passed using the procedure, and becoming a full and valid Act of Parliament. The procedure did not create a new way of enacting a special kind of primary legislation, which was more akin to secondary legislation, but

2

PUBLIC LAW

was a wholly new way of enacting primary legislation which for the reasons given above would be recognised as valid, and be applied by the courts in the same way that they apply other primary legislation without questioning its validity.

No class of bill was exempted in the 1911 Act other than the Lords' amendment that bills purporting to extend the life of Parliament beyond five years should be excluded. There had been classes of bill proposed by the Lords in their amendments in 1911, but none of these were eventually included. Since the Act came into force several statutes have been passed using the procedure (for example, Government of Ireland Act 1914; Parliament Act 1949; War Crimes Act 1991; Sexual Offences (Amendment) Act 2000).

Conclusion

Jackson v. *Attorney-General* is one of most important recent cases in the jurisprudence of the British constitution. It is essentially a case about power, or authority within the constitution which is of interest not just to public lawyers, but to all who live and work in this country. It does not itself state any new principle in relation to public law. Indeed, as was commented in the introduction, if anything, it is the most orthodox statement of the continuing importance of parliamentary supremacy. It rejected the arguments put forward in relation to the delegation of power and restated that the courts could not and would not inquire into the validity of Acts of Parliament. Although the 1911 Act had been passed as a political compromise between the House of Lords, as then constituted, and the Liberal government returned to the Commons, it was not the courts' business to challenge this, or indeed the 1949 Parliament Act which had been passed using the procedure set out in the 1911 Act. The 1911 Act had in itself set no restrictions on the class of Act which may be passed using the procedure other than those dealt with above.

Whether the courts should have greater authority to challenge Acts of Parliament, either because there is a procedural irregularity or because the Act infringes a fundamental human right, is another question. The Human Rights Act 1998 has introduced a procedure where courts may declare Acts incompatible with the European Convention, but such declarations have for the time being, at least, been relatively rare. It may well be that a Supreme Court outside of the House of Lords may begin to flex its muscles more on constitutional issues, although this does not seem to be an approach that the Labour government in its reforms is keen to advocate.

The wider issue is where authority should reside in the British constitution, and whether as currently constructed ours does allow for a proper and balanced relationship between the three branches of government (Lord Hope at para. 125 citing *Pickin*). Most commentators would argue that the reliance which Britain has placed on the Parliamentary system as an adequate check on the government's power may be under threat, not least as a result of the contempt in which successive governments have held Parliament. In the longer term, however, it is for the British people to decide whether they would be happy for the development of a legal as opposed to political constitution where the judges play a more active role in challenging government decisions and ultimately statute law, which under our system may be unduly influenced by the government of the day.

FURTHER READING

Primary sources

Aston Cantlow and Wilmcote with Billesley Parochial Church Council v. *Wallbank and Another* [2003] UKHL 37, [2003] 3All ER 1213

Burmah Oil Co v. *Lord Advocate* [1965] AC 75

Dr Bonham's Case (1610) 8 Co rep 114a

Ghaidan v. *Godin-Mendoza* [2004] UKHL 30, [2004] 2 AC 557, [2004] 3 All ER 411

Madzimbamuto v. *Lardner Burke* [1969] 1 AC 723

Pickin v. *British Railways Board* [1974] AC 765

R (on the application of Jackson and Others) v. Attorney-General [2005] UKHL 56, [2005] All ER (D) 136 (Oct) (Approved judgment)

R v. *Secretary of State for Transport ex parte Factortame Ltd* [1990] 2 AC 85

R v. *Secretary of State for Transport ex parte Factortame Ltd (No. 2)* [1991] 1 AC 603

R v. *Secretary of State for Transport ex parte Factortame Ltd (No. 5)* [2000] 1 AC 524

The Bill of Rights 1689

House of Lords Act 1999

Human Rights Act 1998

Hunting Act 2004

The Parliament Acts 1911 and 1949

Scotland Act 1998

2

PUBLIC LAW

Secondary sources

Allan, T.R.S. (1997) 'Parliamentary Sovereignty: Law, Politics and Revolution' (1997), 113, *Law Quarterly Review*, 443.

Bradley, A.W. and Ewing, K.D. (2007) 'Parliamentary Supremacy' in *Constitutional and Administrative Law*, 14th edn, Longman, London.

Dicey, A.V. (1985) *An Introduction to the Study of the Law of the Constitution*, 10th edn, reprint.

Feldman, D. (2004) 'The impact of human rights on the UK legislative process' (2004) *Statute Law Review*, 91–115.

Gravells (1992) 'Effective Protection of Community Law Rights: Temporary Disapplication of an Act of Parliament' [1992] *Public Law*, 180.

McLean, I. and McMillan, A. (2007) 'Professor Dicey's contradictions' (2007) *Public Law*, 435–443.

Tomkins, Adam (2003) *Public Law*, Clarendon Press, Oxford.

Woolf, Lord [1995] *Public Law*, 57.

Young, A. (2006) 'Hunting sovereignty: *Jackson* v. *Her Majesty's Attorney-General*' (2006) *Public Law*, 187–196.

Public authorities and the Human Rights Act

Aston Cantlow and Wilmcote with Billesley Parochial Church Council v. Wallbank and Another
[2003] UKHL 37, [2003] 3 All ER 1213

Christopher Rogers, Northumbria University

The decision of the House of Lords in *Aston Cantlow and Wilmcote with Billesley Parochial Church Council v. Wallbank* (*'Aston Cantlow'*) has been one of the most important cases to consider the extent and effect of the Human Rights Act 1998. It is a leading case on the meaning of 'public authority' as introduced in the legislation. It highlights the problems faced by lawyers in determining the boundaries of the public and private domains in English law, addressing the question of what can be regarded as part of the state, as a body which is a public authority, carrying out a public function, and what other bodies may sometimes be encompassed within a wide definition of public functions, and consequently public authorities. The determination of these questions is one of the most difficult areas of modern legal interpretation in which the meaning of a concept can change over time. In fact, *Aston Cantlow* showed how what might once have been regarded as very much a public authority, i.e. the Church of England, may, by subsequent development of the law, not be so regarded. One of the judges described the specific law involved in the case as 'one of the more arcane and unsatisfactory areas of property law'. Lord Nicholls of Birkenhead made this statement, going on to say that the liability of a lay rector, or lay impropriator, was 'in its very language redolent of a society long disappeared. The anachronistic, even capricious, nature of this ancient liability was recognised . . . by the Law Commission'.

The Human Rights Act incorporated into the United Kingdom's domestic law the Convention on Human Rights drafted by the Council of Europe in 1950. (Note The Council of Europe is an entirely separate body from the institutions of the European Union, or the European Communities, as they have developed from the Treaty of Rome 1957.) The Convention had been ratified by the United Kingdom in 1951, when it was opened for signature. By virtue of the doctrine of parliamentary supremacy, however, it was not possible for individuals, whether natural or corporate persons, to rely on Convention rights in front of domestic courts. Human rights protection in the UK has traditionally been founded on the common law, the development of the right to freedom of the person by the Habeas Corpus Act, the right to freedom of assembly and expression developed in the course of eighteenth and nineteenth centuries, to the extent that this did not conflict with parliamentary supremacy. It was a rights culture vested in the political protection of rights through democratic institutions, not least in the Parliament at Westminster.

Such an approach has attracted criticism from leading lawyers, politicians and Other civil liberties groups, but was in accord with the principles developed by the constitutional settlement of the seventeenth century, and which was consolidated in the following two centuries, that Parliament is the supreme power within the realm and no-one may question its authority to pass law, including the courts (explored further in *R (on the application of Jackson and Others)*. There was no scope in our constitution for arguing that a law made by Parliament was incompatible with a fundamental human right. This is not to say that rights were not protected under English law, indeed many of the rights contained in the Convention were developed from English law.

The Human Rights Act was canvassed by the Labour government as a way of bringing rights home, of incorporating those fundamental rights drafted in the 1950s into the domestic law. In particular it created a mechanism by which the courts must, so far as it is possible to do so, interpret statutes compatibly with the Convention. If it cannot do so, then a court may order a declaration of incompatibility. This has led some to argue that it is a weak form of incorporation as it does not give the courts power to strike down legislation in the way that, for example, the American Supreme Court may.

This discussion will look at the issues that were raised in the *Aston Cantlow* case. The meaning of public authority within this and the wider context will be explored. It will also set the background for the statutory framework for the protection of human rights in England and Wales, and what substantive rights are protected by the Convention. It will compare and contrast the case law which has been brought so far.

The issues in *Aston Cantlow*

Aston Cantlow was a case which involved the Church of England in the form of a Parochial Church Council ('PCC'). The Wallbanks were private individuals, but also the lay rectors, of the glebe land attached to their local Church. As the lay rectors they had been assessed for liability to repair the chancel of the Church (at the East end towards the altar, generally where the choir performs). They contended that the liability was a 'tax' which interfered with their right to enjoyment of their property under Protocol 1 of the Convention on Human Rights. The primary issue before the courts was whether the PCC was a public authority under the 1998 Act. It would then need to go on to consider whether there was an actual infringement of their rights or not.

The High Court at first instance decided in favour of the PCC, the judge reasoning that the liability for the repair of the chancel was clear, and that the PCC acted under primary legislation to enforce the liability under the Chancel Repairs Act 1932. The two highest appeal courts in England and Wales came to contrary judgments in the case. The Court of Appeal held that it was a public authority, whereas the House of Lords decided that it was not. The case was unusual in so far as it involved in-depth consideration of the position of the Church of England as the Church established by law. (Note that the situation is different elsewhere: the Church of Scotland was guaranteed its rights and privileges by virtue of the Treaty of Union 1706 and Act of Union 1707; the Church of England was disestablished in Wales by virtue of the Welsh Church Act 1914 to become the Church in Wales; and there is not an established Church in Northern Ireland.)

2

PUBLIC LAW

71

The meaning of establishment was considered by the judges at the different levels of the hierarchy in which it was litigated. Historically, establishment has meant that the state recognises the Church of England as the official religion of the nation, in historical terms as preaching the true gospel of Christ. Until the latter half of the nineteenth century the maintenance of true religion by the state, its protection and promotion were considered to be an essential component of government, in effect a very public function. The question for the court to consider was whether, at the beginning of the twenty-first century, this could still be said to be the case. In order to understand better what the issues were, the meaning of public authority under the Act must be explored.

The meaning of public authority under the Human Rights Act 1998

The 1998 Act gives only a partial definition of what is meant by public authority. The first reference which is made in the Act to public authority comes in s.6(1) which provides that it is 'unlawful for a public authority to act in a way which is incompatible with a Convention right'. By virtue of s.6(3) public authority includes courts and tribunals and 'any person certain of whose functions are functions of a public nature'. The Act expressly excludes both Houses of Parliament from its provisions. It also allows that some functions carried out by an authority may be private in nature, and consequently not covered by the provisions of the Act. An example of the latter category is the relationship between employer and employee which is considered in public law to be wholly private.

Academic commentators have adopted the classification of pure, hybrid, and private authorities, an analysis employed by Lord Hope of Craighead in his leading opinion in *Aston Cantlow*. Pure public authorities are those clearly part of the machinery of central government such as ministers, the Civil Service, the police, the armed forces, the traditional authorities of the state and state power. These will be public authorities regardless of the capacity in which they act. Hybrid authorities are those which carry out certain actions which are public, and Others which are private. The example of the latter category given at the time that the Bill was making its way through Parliament was Railtrack. Railtrack was a private company owning the track on which the other rail companies ran their services, but also given additional powers and authority by statute which may affect other individuals and their rights. A private body could be an individual, natural person, or a corporation who has no functions which are public in nature. Examples would include a limited company, a firm of solicitors, newspapers, or a private individual.

The case law which developed before *Aston Cantlow* examined the nature and impact of public funding, and the fulfilment of statutory duties imposed on a body, in deciding whether or not it is a public authority, or carrying out a public function. In *Poplar* v. *Donoghue* the Court of Appeal held that the housing association in the case, a private company, was so closely associated with the local authority that it could be a public authority, but that there was not an incompatibility between the statutory provision, and the human right claimed to have been infringed. In *R* v. *Leonard Cheshire Foundation* the same court held that the charity which ran the care home in which the appellants lived was not a public authority, as the local authority which had delegated its powers in relation to the provision of care had not relieved itself of the duty imposed on it by statute.

In the latter case the court went on to state that the provision of funding by the local authority did not determine whether the functions were public.

The Convention rights

The question arising from the above discussion is what were the rights which Mr and Mrs Wallbank argued had been infringed by the PCC in enforcing the repair of the chancel? The simple answer to this question is that they relied on Article 1 of the First Protocol to the Convention which states:

> Every natural or legal person is entitled to the peaceful enjoyment of his possessions. No one shall be deprived of his possessions except in the public interest and subject to the conditions provided for by the law and by the general principles of international law.

This is not one of the original rights framed in the Convention, being contained in the first Protocol to the Convention (effectively an additional treaty for states to agree to). The original rights in the Convention were much more fundamental than this one, and it again highlights the change in the scope of rights protection afforded by the Convention.

The Convention protects fundamental human rights. The recognition of a fundamental human right by a society may vary over time, and of course depending on what society you ask. When the Convention was drafted back in 1950 many states in Europe criminalised homosexual acts between men. By the 1980s cases were brought to the European Court of Human Rights challenging such legislation on the basis that it infringed the applicant's right to privacy. Very few in the 1950s would have seen the Convention as a tool for this kind of challenge, so what it highlights is the developing nature of human rights protection and the way in which the Convention may grow to cover situations not originally envisaged by the framers. This is what the court at Strasbourg means when it says that the Convention is a living instrument.

The rights under the Convention vary from those which are absolute to those which may be infringed by the state in the pursuance of a legitimate aim. In the first category are the right to life under Article 2, the prohibition of torture under Article 3, and the prohibition of slavery and forced labour under Article 4. The Convention then guarantees the right to liberty and security, Article 5, the right to a fair trial, Article 6, and the prohibition of any criminal sanction without law, Article 7. The later articles deal with more widely applicable rights which may be described as civil, or liberal democratic in origin, developing as many of them did from the political upheavals associated with the French Revolution. Article 8, the right to respect for private and family life has already been mentioned as one which has been considered by the European Court on several occasions, and which has begun to have more universal implications since the 1950s. Other rights are those such as the right to freedom of thought, conscience and religion under Article 9, an article which was to form an important background influence on the way in which the House of Lords decided *Aston Cantlow*. The right to freedom of expression under Article 10, freedom of assembly and association under Article 11 and the right to marry under Article 12.

As stated the most fundamental of rights are not qualified, there is no circumstance in which the state, or the public authority in domestic law may infringe these. The latter civil

2

PUBLIC LAW

rights, however, may be infringed by the state, or the public authority, if the infringement is prescribed by law and necessary in a democratic society, and in pursuance of a legitimate aim. The legitimate aims prescribed in the Convention are: the interests of national security, territorial integrity or public safety, for the prevention of disorder and crime, for the protection of health or morals, for the protection of the reputation or rights of others, for preventing the disclosure of information to others. In *Aston Cantlow*, an important reason for the House of Lords' decision that the PCC, and by extension the Church of England, was not a public authority was that it could not then be a 'victim', for the purposes of the Act. As one of the major rights guaranteed by the Convention is the right to freedom of religion, the Church collectively could not claim that its rights would be abused by the Convention.

The previous enforcement of human rights protection

In order to enforce an individual's rights under the Convention it is necessary to exhaust all domestic remedies before resort may be had to the European Court of Human Rights in Strasbourg. However, before the 1998 Act was introduced by the Labour government the Courts of England and Wales were not required to have regard to the Convention as a matter of course, but only as persuasive authority in deciding the case before them. This was altered by the statutory framework contained in the 1998 legislation.

Conclusion

Aston Cantlow is one of the seminal cases on the Human Rights Act 1998 which overlaps with many different areas of law, public, property and conveyancing, and ecclesiastical. It shows the difficulties which the courts, and legal commentators, face in trying to define adequately the boundaries, or frontiers, of the state in relation to the new statutory concept of public authority. The courts have so far only given a partial definition of what public authority means in these different contexts, and it is still difficult to state with precision what bodies may be included within the definition in subsequent cases. It also demonstrates the unpredictable ways in which the Act has been used since coming into force. The first case to engage Convention rights was not a case of fundamental injustice, or the extreme abuse of human rights which motivated the drafters of the Convention after the Second World War, but was a consumer credit case (*Wilson* v. *First County Trust*). As remarked at the start of this discussion the importance of rights and their protection by the state, is often a matter of perception, and it may be a disservice to trivialise the example of consumer credit. This is not true of all decisions which have been made under the Act and in particular can be contrasted with the decision of the House of Lords in *Ghaidan* v. *Mendoza* to include same-sex partners within the definition of spouse for the purposes of the Rent Acts.

The Act does represent a re-dressing of the power relationship within the constitution of an executive-dominated legislative chamber and the judiciary. The Act in its interpretative effect has altered, if not abolished, the old constitutional rule that judges should depart in interpreting statute with the literal rule to reinforce the supremacy of Parliament.

FURTHER READING

Primary sources

Bellinger v. *Bellinger* [2003] 2 AC 467

Ghaidan v. *Mendoza* [2004] UKHL 30, [2004] 2 AC 557, [2004] 3 All ER 411

Poplar Housing and Regeneration Community Association Ltd v. *Donoghue* [2001] EWCA Civ 595, [2001] 3 WLR 183

R (on the application of Heather) v. *Leonard Cheshire Foundation* [2002] EWCA Civ 366, [2002] 2 All ER 936

R (on the application of Jackson and Others) v. *Attorney-General* [2005] UKHL 56, [2005] All ER (D) 136

R v. *Lambert* [2002] AC 545

Re: S, re: W (Care Orders) [2002] 2 AC 291

Wilson v. *First County Trust* [2001] 3 WLR 42

The European Convention on Human Rights

The Human Rights Act 1998, c.42, particularly sections 3, 6 and 10

Secondary sources

Bradley, A.W. and Ewing, K.D. (2003) 'The nature and protection of human rights' chapter 19 in *Constitutional and Administrative Law*, 13th edn, Longman, London.

Fenwick, H. and Phillipson, G. (2003) Part VI 'The Protection of Civil Liberties in the UK', chapter 1 'The Traditional Protection of Civil Liberties in Britain and the impact of the Human Rights Act 1998' in *Text, Cases and Materials on Public Law and Human Rights*, 2nd edn, Cavendish Publishing, London, 839–903.

Joint Committee on Human Rights, Seventh Report, *The Meaning of Public Authority under the Human Rights Act* (2003–04 HL 39; 2003–04 HC 382).

Landau, J. (2007) 'Functional public authorities after YL' [2007] *Public Law*, 630–639.

Oliver, D. (2000) 'The Frontiers of the State: Public Authorities and Public Functions under the Human Rights Act' [2000] *Public Law*, 476.

Oliver, D. (2004) 'Functions of a Public Nature under the Human Rights Act' [2004] *Public Law*, 329.

Quane, H. (2006) 'The Strasbourg jurisprudence and the meaning of a "public authority" under the Human Rights Act' [2006] *Public Law*, 106–123.

Tomkins, Adam (2003) *Public Law*, Clarendon Press, Oxford.

2

PUBLIC LAW

Official secrets legislation and the separation of powers

R v. *Ponting* [1985] Crim LR 318

Rebecca Moosavian, Northumbria University

The legal and symbolic significance of *R* v. *Ponting* is immense, despite the fact that it occupies a peripheral role in most public law syllabi and indeed was never fully reported. It broached recurring thorny issues within the field of constitutional law; namely governmental control of information, the meaning of 'interests of the state' and ministerial accountability to Parliament.

Underlying case law in this area is the 'separation of powers' doctrine first propounded by John Locke and Baron de Montesquieu in the seventeenth and eighteenth centuries. It divides state power into three distinct limbs: the legislature which enacts law, the executive which governs within law and the judiciary which adjudicates according to law. The doctrine states that in order to avoid potentially dangerous concentrations of power the three state limbs should be independent, their functions should remain separate and power should be balanced between them. The separation of powers forms part of the checks and balances operating within the English constitution and is reflected in the vital constitutional convention that executive ministers are responsible to Parliament for their conduct of government; this accountability takes the form of answering parliamentary questions and overall scrutiny by select committees. However, not all areas of government action are subject to the same degree of judicial or parliamentary scrutiny. One area that has traditionally been treated with caution, arguably for cogent reasons, is 'national security' and most case law discussed here involves this very issue. As shall be seen, the government's maintenance of 'national security' enjoys relative immunity from open, comprehensive examination. This arrangement remains intact despite recent legislation such as the Human Rights Act 1998 and the Freedom of Information Act 2000 which was introduced to remedy the perceived culture of secrecy operating within British government.

The *Ponting* case was decided under the Official Secrets Act 1911, a law rushed through Parliament in one afternoon in a climate of pre-war anxiety. The purpose of the 1911 Act was to prevent enemy espionage but its provisions were notoriously wide in application, creating over 2000 criminal acts that extended to the most mundane and minor of disclosures. Though the court in *Ponting* ruled that the defendant was clearly guilty of an OSA breach, the jury controversially acquitted him. Such an unexpected outcome adds another important dimension to this case; in a finding that resonated with a wider sense of justice, the *Ponting* jury demonstrated the constitutional importance of jury trials as a vital final safety-net in the layers of protection for individual liberties in Britain.

The facts

This case occurred against the political backdrop of the high-profile sinking of an Argentine vessel, *The Belgrano*, during the 1982 Falklands conflict. The defendant was Clive Ponting, a senior civil servant, who had been ordered to prepare a report of the incident. The defendant's report showed that earlier accounts of the incident given by the government had been incorrect. However, it was decided that this information should not be revealed to Parliament and that officials should refrain from providing certain answers which would disclose secret changes in strategy during the Falklands conflict.

The defendant provided opposition MP Tam Dalyell with two documents. The first was a reply he had drafted to Mr Dalyell's written parliamentary questions which had never been sent by the relevant minister. The second was a confidential Ministry of Defence minute recommending that the Falklands strategy changes should remain undisclosed. Subsequently, in Parliament Mr Dalyell posed questions on the basis of this information, prompting criticism and political embarrassment for the government of the day.

The defendant was identified as the source of the leak and charged with a criminal offence under the OSA 1911.

Official secrets legislation

Section 2(1) of the 1911 Act covered a broad range of individuals including any person 'who is or has been employed under a person who holds [His Majesty's] office', thus squarely covering civil servants in their public role. The provision stated that it was a criminal offence for any such person to have 'in his possession or control any . . . information' resulting from his position and to 'communicate [it] to any person, *other than* a person to whom he is authorised to communicate it, *or* to a person to whom it is in the interest of the state his duty to communicate it'.

The defendant fully admitted all but one element of s.2(1). It was agreed that he had possessed the information by virtue of his civil service position and that he had passed this information to 'another person', Mr Dalyell. However, s.2(1) set out circumstances where passing information to another person would *not* come within the provision: firstly, where the communication was to an authorised person, or secondly, where the individual had a duty in the interests of the state to make the communication. The defence admitted that Ponting's disclosure had not been authorised. Instead they sought to rely on the second 'exception', claiming that the defendant's actions had been 'in the interest of the state' (see below).

Following *R* v. *Ponting* the OSA was replaced. The *Official Secrets Act 1989* was intended to address some of the shortcomings of its predecessor, its preamble stating it was 'an Act to replace s.2 of the [1911 Act] by provisions protecting more limited classes of official information'. This new Act essentially repealed the old 'catch-all' section 2, and substituted it with distinct categories including 'security and intelligence', 'defence', 'international relations' and 'crime'.

Despite appearing to narrow the OSA ambit, it has been claimed that the 1989 Act still has the capacity to encompass and restrict a wide range of activities.

2

PUBLIC LAW

'Interest of the state' in *Ponting*

'Interest of the state' and its similar counterpart 'public interest' are terms that can be found running through a number of statutory and common law areas in constitutional law. They touch upon questions of central importance to constitutional law; what is the 'state' or 'public' and how are its 'interests' to be ascertained?

'The interest of the state' became the central issue upon which this case hinged. The defence argued that Ponting's actions had been in pursuance of the interest of the state because government and its policies were subject to constitutional conventions, one of which was ministerial accountability to Parliament. It was of the utmost importance that Parliament was able to hold government and ministers to account effectively without being misled. Ponting's disclosure to Tam Dalyell MP enabled these higher conventions to be upheld. This defence argument relied upon a wider, more flexible view of the term 'interest of the state' citing the judgments of Lords Reid and Hodson in *Chandler* v. *DPP*, a case that considered the meaning of the term featured elsewhere in the OSA 1911.

In *Chandler* Lord Reid denied that 'state' meant the government or executive, preferring 'the country or . . . the organised community'. He supplemented this definition with the statement that 'I do not subscribe to the view that the government or a minister must always or even as a general rule have the last word about [what is or is not in the public interest]' (page 146). Lord Hodson defined the term in a similarly broad style, claiming that 'the wording of the statute opens the way to the defence to show that the Crown was not necessarily right in its decision and that its dispositions might not be in the interests . . . of the state' (page 152).

Instead, trial judge McCowan J accepted the prosecution's narrower view of 'interest of the state', approving the definition put forward by Lords Devlin and Pearce in *Chandler*. Devlin, commenting on the vagueness of the term, argued that 'the more precise use of the word state', the use to be expected in a legal context and the one which I am quite satisfied . . . was intended in this statute, is to denote the organs of government' (page 156). He proceeded to comment that 'the statute is not concerned with what the interests of the state might be or ought to be but with what they actually are'. Similarly, Lord Pearce, stated that 'the interests of the state must . . . mean the interests of the state according to the policies laid down for it by its recognised organs of government and authority' (page 160). Applying such reasoning it was in the interest of the state that civil servants carry out the policies of the government of the day, irrespective of their own personal or political views.

Though 'the interests of the state' has proved to be a somewhat nebulous concept, there is a long-standing tradition of courts equating it with the interests of the government of the day, a rationale that *Ponting* unsurprisingly continued.

One underlying reason for this approach, aside from the alleged pro-executive bias of some parts of the judiciary, is the judiciary's traditional reluctance to encroach upon policy and national security issues which it views as restricted to the remit of government. Such caution accords with the separation of powers doctrine that seeks to ensure the independence and political neutrality of the judicial limb. However, commentators have often criticised the timidity of the judiciary when faced with national security and defence issues. Though restrictions on information in these areas are of fundamental importance, it is claimed that there may frequently be a genuine countervailing public interest in disclosures that publicise executive misdeeds. Thus there may be occasions when the interests of the government of the day and those of the nation or public appear to clearly conflict. Which view of 'state interest' should prevail?

MacCormick is particularly critical of Judge McCowan's findings of law in *Ponting*. He distinguishes *Ponting* from more typical OSA cases involving defence and national security issues because it was primarily concerned with 'the proper interrelationship of the organs of the state . . . the relationship between Parliament and Ministers of the Crown and . . . securing the full answerability of the latter to the former' (*Questioning Sovereignty*, page 39). That the judge's legal directions to the jury were offset by a 'perverse' (but morally correct) verdict does not mitigate its shortcomings.

Subsequent cases

Vitally, the 'interests of the state' defence which was potentially available under s.2 of the 1911 Act is no longer a defence under the 1989 Act. A proposed amendment to include a public interest defence in the Bill was discussed during its passage through Parliament but defeated. This narrowing of the available defences has been subject to criticism. Feldman has claimed 'the defences [under the 89 Act] do not protect the rights of subjects. They do not protect the public interest save in cases where the government's view of the public interest is the correct one.' (*Civil Liberties & Human Rights in England and Wales*, page 894). Despite this development, the common law 'public interest' defence remains.

The 'public interest' defence was considered in later cases such as *R* v. *Shayler* and the seminal *Spycatcher* (*AG* v. *Guardian Newspapers (No. 2)*). Both involved the disclosure of highly sensitive and politically embarrassing information by ex-members of the security services. They showed the courts taking a similarly executive-favoured approach when defining 'public interest'. In *Spycatcher* Lord Keith, adopting an earlier judgment by Mason J, considered two rival conceptions of 'public interest' which must be balanced. The first was the proposition that 'disclosure will itself serve the public interest in keeping the community informed and in promoting discussion of public affairs'. The second position, favouring restriction of information, rested on the premise that 'disclosure will be inimical to the public interest because national security . . . or the ordinary business of government will be prejudiced' (page 258). That publication of the *Spycatcher* material was ultimately permitted was primarily due to its widespread international availability rather than a balancing act that favoured the first principle.

In *Shayler*, the defendant claimed that his disclosures to the press regarding alleged inefficiency and illegal activities of MI5 were necessary in the public interest. He was charged with breach of Section 1(1) OSA 1989. In his judgment Lord Woolf accepted the general existence of a public interest defence, claiming that it was now 'buttressed' by the Human Rights Act 1998, though this could not apply to the 'special situation' of the security services. Thus Woolf upheld the earlier decision that s.1(1) prohibited a 'public interest' defence. In keeping with the conventional judicial approach to such issues Woolf concluded that 'In an area as sensitive as this it does appear to us appropriate to show a degree of deference to the [democratically elected] legislators' decision' (page 2233).

2

PUBLIC LAW

Impact of the Human Rights Act 1998

The introduction of the HRA had the potential to impact upon OSA legislation, particularly by virtue of Article 10 which states that 'everyone has the right to freedom of expression'. However, Article 10(2) sets out broad standard derogations under which the right can be restricted including where it is 'necessary in a democratic society, in the interests of national security . . . or for the preventing of disclosure of information received in confidence'.

Section 1(1) of the OSA 1989, for example, prohibits disclosure of security and intelligence information. Unlike other provisions in the 1989 Act it does not require any damage or likely damage to occur as a result of a disclosure by a member of the security or intelligence services, effectively placing a blanket ban on any communication of this sort. Additionally, the 'interest of the state' and 'public interest' defences, which allowed a court to take into account wider benefits that could potentially justify a disclosure, have been removed. Are such restrictions on freedom of expression necessary and proportionate or do they offend the HRA? This question was considered by the Court of Appeal in *Shayler*. Lord Woolf held that the OSA 89 was a justified interference with freedom of expression and thus compatible with Article 10.

The court found that the security services were now governed by statute, which provided numerous potential avenues of independent redress for the defendant's concerns had he chosen to use them. In light of such safeguards, of the importance of protecting national security and because the blanket ban only covered this relatively small class of personnel, s.1(1) was held to be proportionate.

Shayler demonstrates that the HRA has left official secrets legislation unscathed, entirely predictably bearing in mind the sensitive subject of the latter and the extensive derogations of the former. The efficacy of freedom of expression in a case such as *Ponting*, which involved higher constitutional principles, remains to be seen.

FURTHER READING

Primary sources

AG v. *Guardian Newspapers (No. 2)* [1990] 1 AC 109 HL

Chandler v. *DPP* [1962] AC 763

R v. *Shayler* [2001] 1 WLR 2206 CA

Human Rights Act 1998. Article 10, Section 12

Official Secrets Act 1989, Sections 1–4

Secondary sources

Austin, R. (2007) 'The Freedom of Information Act 2000 – A Sheep in Wolf's Clothing?' in Jowell, J. and Oliver, D. (2007) *The Changing Constitution*, 6th edn, OUP, Chapter 16.

Feldman, F. (2002) *Civil Liberties & Human Rights in England and Wales*, 2nd edn, Oxford, 15.3.

MacCormick, N. (1999) *Questioning Sovereignty*, Oxford, pages 29–40.

Scott, R. (1996) 'Ministerial Accountability' [1996] *Public Law*, 410–426.

Woodhouse, D. (1997) 'Ministerial Responsibility – Something Old, Something New' [1997] *Public Law*, 262.

Police powers and the rights of suspects

R v. Lattimore and Others (1976) 62 Cr App R 53

Alan Davenport, Northumbria University

The events surrounding the case of *R* v. *Lattimore and Others* (1976) 62 Cr App R 53 and the quashing of the appellants' convictions highlight some of the major concerns that existed prior to the enactment of the Police and Criminal Evidence Act 1984 (PACE) about the lack of protection for the rights of suspects. Although the Act came into force over ten years after the appeal was heard, several of the issues raised in the case clearly influenced the provisions of the Act. This entry will examine the salient elements of the case, it will then highlight the relevant sections of PACE and examine some of the subsequent case law to assess the impact of the changes on the rights of suspects.

Lattimore and Others

In the early hours of Saturday, 22 April 1972, the body of Maxwell Confait, a transvestite usually known as Michelle, was found in his room. The room had been set on fire sometime after Confait had been strangled with a ligature. Three young men, Colin Lattimore, Ronnie Leighton and Ahmet Salih were arrested in connection with the homicide. They were questioned at length in police custody without access to legal advice, with no independent adult present and at a time when interviews were not tape-recorded. It should be noted that Colin Lattimore was a juvenile and mentally disabled, Ronnie Leighton was a juvenile and Ahmet Salih was a juvenile who spoke English as a second language. The three youths were alleged to have made oral admissions to police officers admitting to various degrees of involvement with the death and the arson. They then repeated these admissions in front of their parents. It should be noted that Mrs Salih required the assistance of an interpreter at this encounter. The youths challenged the veracity of their admissions at their original trial but Lattimore was convicted of manslaughter on the grounds of diminished responsibility and arson, Leighton of murder and arson and Salih of arson. This was despite the fact that, as Lord Scarman acknowledged in the Court of Appeal, 'Nothing was found to connect any of the appellants with either the killing of Michelle or the fire' (at page 57). The alleged admissions went to the core of the convictions.

On 18 June 1975, the Home Secretary referred the convictions back to the Court of Appeal under s.17 (1)(a) Criminal Appeal Act 1968 as he was satisfied that fresh evidence had arisen casting doubt on the safety of the three youths' convictions. New scientific evidence showed that much of the substance of the alleged confessions could not have been true. The Crown's case became untenable and the convictions in respect of the homicide and arson were quashed. The case was the subject of a subsequent inquiry led by Sir Henry Fisher.

The salient issues raised by the appeal were:

1. The lengthy questioning of vulnerable people.

2. The lack of access to legal advice.

3. The lack of an independent record of alleged admissions made in police custody.

4. The lack of an independent adult presence to ensure that vulnerable people's rights were protected.

Police and Criminal Evidence Act (PACE)

PACE was the result of a number of concerns raised by the Royal Commission on Criminal Procedure. It is a comprehensive statute which codified and clarified many existing police powers. PACE attempts to balance the needs of the police with the liberty of the subject by requiring powers to be exercised on an objective basis and requiring comprehensive and accurate recording of the exercise of any coercive powers.

In respect of the issues raised by *Lattimore* the following reforms were introduced.

1. PACE created the role of custody officer (ss.36, 39). This is an officer of at least the rank of sergeant who must be completely independent of the investigation of the offence for which a suspect has been arrested. The custody officer's role is to ensure that PACE is complied with and that all suspects are treated in accordance with the statute and its accompanying Codes of Practice. To assist this role, PACE introduced the custody record which provides a record of everything happening while the suspect is in custody. PACE even provides a procedure to ensure that senior officers cannot override a custody officer in performing their duties (s.39(6)). The Act also provides for a system of regular independent reviews of detention to ensure that people are in custody only for as long as is absolutely necessary (s.40). Failure to adhere to these rules can result in tortious action (see *Roberts* v. *Chief Constable of Cheshire*). Suspects can only be held for a maximum of thirty-six hours before a court warrant is necessary to authorise further detention. While in custody, Code of Practice C sets out provisions for the maximum length of time for which a suspect can be questioned without having a break. It also provides for adequate rest and refreshments for a suspect. Clearly, a fatigued and hungry or thirsty suspect may not give as reliable evidence and this only serves to hamper the investigative process.

2. Under s.58 PACE suspects in police custody are entitled to free legal advice. The custody officer must inform the suspect of this right and the suspect must sign the custody record to say whether or not they require legal advice. This right can be exercised at any time while in police custody. While there were initially some police attempts to bypass this right (as evidenced by Sanders and Bridges), the courts have emphasised the importance of access to legal advice and have been prepared to exclude evidence gained after access has been wrongly denied (*R* v. *Samuel*). S.58(8) does provide for some instances where access to a legal advice can be delayed for up to thirty-six hours on the authority of a senior officer but such cases are few and far between. Clearly, the provision of legal advice

can be absolutely crucial, especially where defendants are vulnerable. Given the requirements of Article 6 ECHR and the police's duty as a public body under s.6 Human Rights Act, it is now highly unlikely that a request for legal advice will be refused.

3. One of the major reforms introduced by PACE was the introduction of tape-recording of interviews between suspects and police officers. This was a great step forward. The tape provides an independent record of what was said. This prevents suspects claiming that they haven't said things which are on the tape and prevents the possibility of fabrication of admissions. In addition, a tape recording can indicate the suspect's manner and tone of voice. This can provide essential context to the conversation that is taking place.

4. PACE requires that young people under the age of 17 and adults who are considered to be mentally vulnerable must have an 'Appropriate Adult' with them when they are interviewed by the police. This person, who cannot be the suspect's solicitor, provides an independent presence and should be able to ensure that the suspect's welfare is looked after. How effective this role is is a moot point (see Parry) but it does at least provide an extra level of support for a vulnerable person in custody.

Conclusions

PACE and its accompanying Codes of Practice have greatly improved protection for the rights of suspects in police custody. Clearer rules, the courts' insistence on their observance and strict record-keeping requirements should ensure that cases such as *Lattimore* are never repeated. The system, especially recording of confessions, has been welcomed by the police as it provides a workable set of rules for all to follow.

FURTHER READING

Primary sources

R v. Lattimore and Others (1976) 62 Cr App R 53

R v. Samuel [1988] 2 All ER 135

Roberts v. Chief Constable of Cheshire [1999] EWCA Civ 665

Secondary sources

Baxter, J. and Koffman, L. (eds) (1985) *Police: The Constitution and the Community.* Professional Books, Abingdon.

Parry, R. Gwynedd (2006) 'Protecting the Juvenile Suspect: What Exactly is the Appropriate Adult Supposed to Do?' (2006) *Child and Family Law Quarterly*, 18, 373.

Report of an Inquiry by the Hon. Sir Henry Fisher into the circumstances leading to the conviction of three persons on charges arising out of the death of Maxwell Confait and the fire at 27 Doggett Road, London SE6; HMSO HC 90 1977.

Report of the Royal Commission on Criminal Procedure; HMSO Cmnd 8092.

Sanders, A. and Bridges, L. (1990) 'Access to Legal Advice and Police Malpractice' [1990] *Criminal Law Review*, 494.

Stone, R. (2006) *Textbook on Civil Liberties & Human Rights*, 6th edn, OUP, Oxford, Chapters 3 and 4.

2

PUBLIC LAW

Preventing a breach of the peace (public order)

R (Laporte) v. Chief Constable of Gloucestershire
[2006] UKHL 55

Alan Davenport, Northumbria University

Breach of the peace is a common law concept that is rooted in the duty owed by all citizens to the monarch to preserve the peace in his or her state, although in the case of a citizen it was described by Lord Diplock in the House of Lords in *Albert* v. *Lavin* as being one of 'imperfect obligation' (at page 880). In Scotland breach of the peace exists as a criminal offence, whereas in England and Wales, it does not. A person arrested for breach of the peace in England and Wales will be taken before a Magistrates' Court and bound over to keep the peace but this is not in itself equivalent to a criminal conviction. However, as will be seen below, those breaching the peace may finds themselves committing other substantive criminal offences.

It is pertinent to note that in the case of *Steel and Lush* v. *United Kingdom* the UK government accepted before the European Court of Human Rights that breach of the peace amounted to a 'criminal offence' for the purposes of determining a claim under Article 5(1) of the Convention (see paragraph 46 of the judgment). Some commentators such as Professor Richard Stone have suggested that the concept has outlived its usefulness and should be abolished but it remains a useful tool for police officers attempting to deal with public disorder situations.

Definition

There has never been one universally accepted definition of breach of the peace. In two cases in 1981, the separate Divisions of the Court of Appeal were called upon to deal with breach of the peace in the context of a criminal appeal and a judicial review and gave two differing definitions. In *R* v. *Howell*, Watkins LJ in the Court of Criminal Appeal defined breach of the peace in the following terms: 'there is a breach of the peace whenever harm is actually done or is likely to be done to a person or in his presence to his property or a person is in fear of being so harmed through an assault, an affray, a riot, an unlawful assembly or other disturbance' (at page 389).

By way of contrast, Lord Denning MR in the Court of Appeal (Civil Division) in *R* v. *Chief Constable of Devon and Cornwall ex parte CEGB* took the view that: 'there is a breach of the peace whenever a person who is lawfully carrying out his work is unlawfully and physically prevented by another from doing it' (at page 832). While subsequent cases such as *Percy* v. *DPP* have favoured the definition given in *Howell*, the definition given in the *CEBG* case has never been overruled.

Power of arrest

Both the police and the citizen retain the power at common law to arrest somebody for breach of the peace. The Court of Appeal in *Howell* (at page 388) stated that the power of arrest for breach of the peace arises where

(1) a breach of the peace is committed in the presence of the person making the arrest, or (2) the arrestor reasonably believes that such a breach will be committed in the immediate future by the person arrested although he has not yet committed any breach, or (3) where a breach has been committed and it is reasonably believed that a renewal of it is threatened.

Action short of arrest

In addition to the power to arrest for breach of the peace, the police have also taken several different measures short of arrest to prevent a breach of the peace. The definition of breach of the peace formulated in *Howell* above includes harm being 'likely to be done' and a person 'being in fear of being so harmed'. Both of these terms suggest that in addition to a breach of the peace occurring, apprehension of a breach of the peace is relevant in law and it is police powers to deal with an *apprehended* rather than *actual* breach of the peace that will form the core of the rest of this discussion.

Prior to the coming into force of the Human Rights Act 1998, the courts were of the view that the police had a duty to prevent breaches of the peace and with this duty came a power to take any *reasonable* steps necessary to perform this duty. This may have included taking steps against people who at the time of the police action are acting lawfully but whom the police believed to be a real and potential threat to the peace. While the issue of what is a reasonable step is clearly to be decided on a case-by-case basis, the courts had accepted that a reasonable step might include the power to remove emblems from people's clothing (*Humphries* v. *Connor*), the power to enter private property and remain there while a perceived threat to the peace existed (*Thomas* v. *Sawkins*, as enshrined in s.17(6) Police and Criminal Evidence Act 1984) and the power to require a meeting to be held at a place specified by a police officer (*Duncan* v. *Jones*). Perhaps the most controversial use of the power prior to the Human Rights Act 1998 came in the case of *Moss* v. *McLachlan*. *Moss* arose out of the Miners' Strike 1984-85 when the police perceived that 'flying pickets', i.e. groups of miners from other pits travelling to a single pit in a show of strength and support, were a potential threat to the peace. In order to deal with this perceived threat to the peace, Nottinghamshire police set up a roadblock at junction 27 of the M1 motorway. This roadblock was a mile and a half away from the nearest pit. Motorists attempting to leave the motorway at junction 27 would be stopped and anybody whom the police reasonably believed to be a striking miner would not be permitted to pass the roadblock. Moss objected to the police action claiming it was unlawful and his refusal to abide by the police instructions led to him being arrested for the offence of 'wilfully obstructing a police officer in the lawful execution of his duty' and his subsequent conviction in the Magistrates' Court. On appeal to the Divisional Court, the central issue was whether or not the roadblock could be justified by reference to the police's common law powers to prevent a breach of the peace. If it could not, then the conviction would have to be quashed as the police would not have been acting 'in the lawful execution' of their duty

2

PUBLIC LAW

and an essential ingredient of the offence would have been absent. The Divisional Court ruled that in the peculiar circumstances of the case, the police action was reasonable as being necessary to prevent an imminent breach of the peace. The Court pointed to the evidence of disorder that had already occurred at the pits in question, the short distance by car between the roadblock and the pits and the reasonable belief that there would be a breach of the peace if the cars were allowed to continue on their way. Clearly, the police have the power to interfere with citizens who are acting lawfully where they have a reasonable belief that to do so will prevent an imminent threat to the peace. This decision must always be treated with some caution as it concerns a very particular episode in the history of the policing of public disorder. With the coming into force of the Human Rights Act 1998, the police are now under a statutory duty (s.6 Human Rights Act 1998) to act in a manner which is compatible with the rights contained in the European Convention on Human Rights. Of particular pertinence to this area of law are the rights to liberty (Article 5) freedom of expression (Article 10) and freedom of association (Article 11). In order for the police to be able to show that an interference with these rights is lawful, such interference must be shown to be both necessary and proportionate. The first real test of the legality of this type of action came in *R (Laporte)* v. *Chief Constable of Gloucestershire.*

The *Laporte* Case

There had been a number of demonstrations at an RAF airbase in Gloucestershire beginning in December 2002. The base had been used by US forces involved in the conflict in Iraq and was thus a target for anti-war protestors. On 22 March 2003, a demonstration was due to take place. The organisers of this demonstration had given the Gloucestershire Police notice of their intention to demonstrate as required by s.11 Public Order Act 1986. Police intelligence sources warned that a recognised anarchist group were planning to attend the demonstration. There was evidence that this group had been involved in several disorderly incidents prior to the date in question. As a preventive measure, an instruction had been issued under s.60 Criminal Justice and Public Order Act 1994 permitting the stopping and searching of coaches travelling to the airbase for 'dangerous instruments or offensive weapons.' Three coaches were stopped some 5km from the airbase and searched. After finding some items which might be used to cause criminal damage, the police arrested one person and allowed three people who were due to speak at the meeting to proceed. The remainder of the people on the coaches, including the applicant Jane Laporte, were required to re-board the coaches which were then taken back to London under police escort. No refreshment breaks were allowed on this journey. Jane Laporte, a peaceful protestor who had simply been caught up in this situation, applied for judicial review of the legality of the police's action both in terms of preventing the coaches proceeding to the demonstration and in providing a compulsory escort back to London. The Court of Appeal ruled that the police were entitled to prevent the coach proceeding to the demonstration but that the provision of the escort was a disproportionate interference with her rights under the Human Rights Act 1998. Both parties appealed to the House of Lords against these rulings. The crucial issue for the Lords was whether or not the actions of the police in this case could be deemed to be both necessary and proportionate, a different standard from that of reasonableness as adopted prior to the Human Rights Act 1998.

The Lords took the view that there was a distinction between action taken to prevent an imminent breach of the peace as in *Moss* v. *McLachlan* (above) and action taken to prevent a breach of the peace from becoming imminent. In this case, the action had been taken for the latter reason and was thus a disproportionate interference with the rights of those who merely wished to exercise their right to peaceful protest. This is a very delicate distinction and one which police officers making on the spot decisions will have to have very much in mind. The Lords did acknowledge, albeit with some reservations (see paragraph 118 of the judgment) that *Moss* remains good law but extends the power of the police as far as it is possible to go.

In summary police action to prevent a breach of the peace can include a number of actions short of arresting somebody. However, *Laporte* indicates that only very limited action is legitimate where the purpose of the police is to prevent a breach of the peace from becoming imminent rather than from preventing a breach of the peace which is imminent. Where it was necessary, the police could interfere with the actions of people who were acting lawfully but who might pose an imminent threat to the peace. In this case the threshold of imminence had not been crossed.

Developments since *Laporte*

The issue of the legitimacy of preventive action arose again late in 2007 in the case of *Austin and Saxby* v. *Commissioner MPC*. The background to this case was a May Day demonstration in London on 2 May 2001. Owing to the exceptional circumstances pertaining at the time, the police cordoned off Oxford Circus and prevented a crowd of some three thousand people from leaving Oxford Circus for over seven hours. Ms Austin was a speaker at the demonstration and Mr Saxby was a bystander unconnected to the demonstration who simply happened to be in Oxford Circus at the pertinent time. They both challenged the legality of the police action as being both a civil wrong and an interference with their human rights. The Civil Division of the Court of Appeal held that the police action in this case was lawful. The Court reiterated the principle in *Laporte* that action short of arrest might have to be taken to prevent a breach of the peace. In this case, the only possible action was the curtailment of the freedom of movement of a substantial number of people for a significant period of time. However, given the specific facts of the case, it was permissible.

In conclusion, the power of the police to interfere with lawful conduct where there is a reasonable belief in an imminent threat to the peace has survived the Human Rights Act 1998 but *Laporte* suggests that the extent of this power may not be as great as that enjoyed prior to the Act.

FURTHER READING

Primary sources

Albert v. *Lavin* [1981] 3 All ER 878

Austin and Saxby v. *Commissioner MPC* [2007] EWCA Civ 989

Duncan v. *Jones* [1936] 1 KB 218

Humphries v. *Connor* (1874) Ir CLR 1

Moss v. *McLachlan* [1985] IRLR 76

Percy v. *DPP* [1995] 3 All ER 123

R v. *Chief Constable of Devon and Cornwall ex parte CEGB* [1981] 3 All ER 826

R (Laporte) v. *Chief Constable of Gloucestershire* [2006] UKHL 55

R v. *Howell* [1981] 3 All ER 383

Steel and Lush v. *United Kingdom* judgment of the European Court of Human Rights 23 September 1998 28 EHRR 603

Thomas v. *Sawkins* [1935] 2 KB 249

Secondary sources

Davenport, A. (2005) Apprehended Breach of the Peace: Lawfulness and Proportionality of Preventive Action [2005] *Journal of Criminal Law*, 69, 109.

Davenport, A. (2007) Apprehended Breach of the Peace: Lawfulness and Proportionality of Action [2007] *Journal of Criminal Law*, 71, 211.

Feldman, D. (1988) 'The King's Peace, the Royal Prerogative and Public Order: The Roots and Early Development of Binding Overs' [1988] *Cambridge Law Journal*, 101.

Kerrigan, K. (1997) 'Breach of the Peace and Binding Over – Continuing Confusion' [1997] 2, *Journal of Civil Liberties*, 30.

Stone, R. (2001) 'Breach of the Peace: The Case for Abolition' [2001] *Web Journal of Current Legal Issues*, 2.

Freedom to demonstrate and public order offences

DPP v. Jones (Margaret) [1999] 2 AC 240

Rhona Smith, Northumbria University

The right to demonstrate is claimed as an ingrained civil liberty in England and Wales, rooted in traditional concepts of liberty and democracy. However, there was (arguably until the Human Rights Act entered into force) no actual right in law to peaceful protests. This contrasts with many other countries which have written constitutions enshrining the right to peaceful protest. However, peaceful processions were not in themselves unlawful (for example, *Beatty* v. *Gillbanks*) although the consequences of the procession could be subject to a variety of laws, including the torts of trespass and nuisance and criminal charges for obstructing the highway. *DPP* v. *Jones* was the first case in which peaceful assemblies were accepted as being a reasonable use of the highway.

There is, in effect, a right to demonstrate: any interference must be justified by the authorities. Obviously this has a human rights element as the European Convention on Human Rights to which further effect is given by the Human Rights Act 1998 enshrines freedom of assembly and association (Article 11) and freedom of expression (Article 10). Thus today the right to demonstrate is a fundamental human right, and indeed commonly regarded as an indicator of democratic development in the wider world. As a consequence, the police are obliged to facilitate demonstrations, thereby respecting and promoting the associated freedoms of all citizens. Even protests against the government and its policies should be facilitated, as should demonstrations in support of causes which do not enjoy majority support in this country. However, the freedom to demonstrate is not unfettered and the police have powers to restrict protesters when necessary to maintain public order (this is also compliant with human rights – see Articles 10(2) and 11(2) of the European Convention). The use of common law powers associated with breach of the peace is discussed in the entry on *Laporte* (see page 84) and obviously the police can act to prevent a breach of the peace. However, a range of statutory powers also enables the police to intervene to maintain public order. The case of *DPP* v. *Jones* concerns one such power – the power to arrest those involved in trespassory assemblies contrary to s.14A of the Public Order Act.

First, though, the case law outlining what constitutes a reasonable use of the highway will be outlined. Demonstrations are usually held in public and often on the road or pavement. The judgment in *DPP* v. *Jones* will then be considered to understand its impact on common law. Finally, the wider picture will be outlined, including attempts by Parliament to restrict protests and demonstrations in their vicinity.

2

PUBLIC LAW

What is a reasonable use of the highway?

To state the obvious, highways (roads) allow for passage. '[T]he right of the public upon a highway is that of passing and repassing over land the soil of which may be owned by a private person' (*Harrison* v. *Duke of Rutland* per Kay LJ at page 158). Harrison was a protester, using the Duke's road to run around scaring grouse away and preventing the Duke's grouse-shooting activities. Harrison's activities were regarded as trespass, going beyond the normal use of a highway (that is, the right of passage). Does this mean if you stop during a passage along the highway, you have potentially effected a trespass?

This case was followed by the Court of Appeal in *Hickman* v. *Maisey* at the turn of the last century. Trespass was alleged in respect of a 'racing tout' who walked up and down part of a highway observing the training of race horses on adjacent land. Judicial statements in *Harrison* were considered, with the judges in *Hickman* noting that a purpose test could be used, asking what the purpose of the actions were. In both *Harrison* and *Hickman*, the purpose of the individuals concerned went beyond normal usage of the highway and could be distinguished from incidental usage such as resting. Some commentators argue the decision in *Hickman* actually extends the principle in *Harrison*, as subsequent cases (including *DPP* v. *Jones*) demonstrate. In any event, the decision is one of 'degree', or to use the common legal expression, 'it depends on all the facts and circumstances of the case'.

Is then a demonstration a reasonable use of the highway? If the right to demonstrate is a fundamental liberty in this country, the issue is clearly important. A demonstration has the purpose of drawing attention to a cause but can be entirely peaceful. This was considered in *Hubbard* v. *Pitt*, the case arising from a demonstration outside an estate agency with some picketing with placards and leafleting. An interlocutory injunction was sought to prevent the demonstration. Forbes J. stated that 'a tired pedestrian may sit down and rest himself. A motorist may attempt to repair a minor breakdown. Because the highway is used also as a means of access to places abutting on the highway, it is permissible to queue for tickets at a theatre or other place of entertainment, or for a bus. But wherever a person is using a highway other than purely as a means of passage, he is only entitled to use it for a purpose which is reasonably incidental to the right of passage' (at pages 149-150). Moreover, a 'reasonable' test applies (at page 150):

> The tired pedestrian or the motorist with the breakdown can only rest for a reasonable while. Those who queue for theatre tickets or stop to watch window displays must do so reasonably and in such a way as not unduly to obstruct other users. If a use of a highway, though incidental to the right of passage, is unreasonable in extent, it goes beyond the purpose for which the highway was dedicated.

The injunction was granted as the picket was not in furtherance of an industrial dispute and went beyond a reasonable use of the highway. The appeal (on grounds of nuisance) was dismissed (the dicta of the appeal was not relevant to the topic under consideration here) with Lord Denning (dissenting) opining that using the highway for a picket was not unreasonable and did not constitute a public nuisance. In this case, again the emphasis appears to be on the purpose of the activity on the highway. Note that picketing in connection with industrial disputes is covered in more detail by the Trade Union and Labour Relations (Consolidation) Act 1992.

DPP v. *Jones*

This brings the law to *DPP* v. *Jones*. The pre-existing case law suggested that demonstrations may not be a reasonable use of the highway as they were not 'incidental' to passage. (The situation of processions, moving along the highway is different but not addressed in this entry.)

Jones and Others were convicted of trespassory offences under s.14B of the Public Order Act 1986 by taking part in a demonstration near Stonehenge. Section 14A allows the police to ban certain gatherings (called trespassory assemblies) – meetings of more than twenty people (note normal assemblies are two or more people) on land to which the public have no or limited access (can include highways as limited use) and the assembly exceeds any permission of the landowner and may disrupt the life of the community or damage the important (historically, archaeologically etc.) land, building or monument. Such a ban can only be imposed for a maximum of four days and across a maximum five mile radius from a specified point: a ban was in place around Stonehenge. Dr Jones and Others congregated on the grass verge between the highway and the Stonehenge boundary fence. They refused to disperse when the police explained that a s.14A order was in force and thus were arrested and convicted for knowingly taking part in a prohibited assembly. This grass verge was accepted as forming part of the highway. Therefore a key issue was whether or not a demonstration on that highway verge was a reasonable use of the highway.

In the House of Lords, Lord Irvine of Lairg reviewed the common law and concluded 'the law to be that the public highway is a public place which the public may enjoy for any reasonable purpose, provided the activity in question does not amount to a public or private nuisance and does not obstruct the highway by unreasonably impeding the primary right of the public to pass and repass: within these qualifications there is a public right of peaceful assembly on the highway' (at page 257). This seems to be in accordance with the foregoing common law cases. However, there was a lack of consensus in the judgments as to extent of the reasonableness test: whether it was broadly to be construed as being a reasonable and usual use of the highway (could include the demonstration, for example, Lord Clyde at page 281) or whether it was to be more narrowly construed as reasonable and related to passage along the highway and activities incidental to that passage (thus not a demonstration, for example, Lord Slynn of Hadley at page 264). The same cases were cited by judges from both schools of thought and all agreed that any reasonable use of the highway would not involve trespass although obstruction of the highway would clearly remain the subject of prosecution (s.137 of the Highways Act 1980). By a 3:2 majority, the convictions were overturned thereby affirming that demonstrations may fall within the reasonable use of the highway. The majority judgment is not without its critics. Phillipson and Fenwick note that police action in *DPP* v. *Jones* 'lends credence to the civil libertarian and leftist thesis that UK public order law places enormous discretion in the hands of the police which may be used to harass marginal groups' (at page 640, referencing additional books on the topic). Certainly from the standpoint of the common law, there remains room for discretion as to what constitutes reasonable use of a highway.

2

PUBLIC LAW

The wider picture

The powers of the police under the Public Order Act to temporarily ban assemblies is not the only statute which gives the police (and government) powers to ban demonstrations. The Serious Organised Crime and Police Act 2005 implemented a prior notice and authorisation regime. As a result, any demonstrations within 'designated' areas which have not been authorised are unlawful and those involved can be charged with a criminal offence. The area around Parliament was designated under this Act, hence the prosecution of a 'Stop the War' campaigner who read out a list of British soldiers killed in Iraq while standing at the entry to Downing Street (*Evans et al.*) and various attempts to remove Brian Haw from his permanent (since 2001) encampment in Parliament Square. This encampment was not an obstruction (*Westminster City Council*) but ultimately Haw had to comply with the new legislative regime (*R (on the application of Haw)*).

DPP v. *Jones* was decided on the cusp of the entry into force of the Human Rights Act. Their Lordships delivered a majority judgment which is in conformity with European jurisprudence: freedom of assembly must be understood to enable peaceful demonstrations rather than to prosecute offenders; police and public authority discretion to limit demonstrations must be exercised in accordance with human rights. However, at present, the threat allegedly posed by terrorism appears to be used to justify restrictions on anti-war protesters etc. with public order the principal justification – compliant perhaps with the letter of human rights provisions but arguably less so with the spirit.

FURTHER READING

Primary sources

Beatty v. *Gillbanks* (1882) 9 QBD 308

Evans et al. v. *DPP* [2006] EWHC 3209 (Admin)

Harrison v. *Duke of Rutland* [1893] 1QB 142

Hickman v. *Maisey* [1900] 1 QB 752

Hubbard v. *Pitt* [1976] QB 142

R (on the application of Haw) v. *Secretary of State for the Home Department* [2006] EWCA Civ 532

Westminster City Council v. *Haw* [2002] EWHC 2073

Secondary sources

Clayton, G. (2000) 'Reclaiming Public Ground: The Right to Peaceful Assembly' [2000] *Modern Law Review*, 63, 252.

Phillipson, G. and Fenwick, H. (2000) 'Public protest, the Human Rights Act and judicial responses to political expression' 2000 *Public Law*, 627.

Judicial review of administrative action

Council of Civil Service Unions v. Minister for the Civil Service [1984] 3 All ER 935

Louise Tait, Northumbria University

The *Council of Civil Service Unions* v. *Minister for the Civil Service* case (the CCSU case) delivers one of the pivotal judgments in the area of judicial review. The applicability of judicial review to a decision exercised under the royal prerogative had the effect of increasing the range of decisions open to review by the courts. Lord Diplock also redefined the grounds on which a judicial review claim may be brought, and proposed a further area of development, proportionality, the implications of which are still being debated more than 20 years after the landmark ruling.

Judicial review is the control of administrative action through the inherent supervisory jurisdiction of the court, by allowing a judicial examination of any decision made by a public body which affects the rights of an individual. It must be stressed that judicial review is to be distinguished from judicial appeal. The courts are not questioning the merits of the decision, but rather the process by which that decision was made: it 'is not an appeal from a decision, but a review of the manner in which the decision was made' (*Chief Constable of North Wales Police* v. *Evans*, Lord Roskill at page 414).

The CCSU case revolved around an instruction issued by the Minister for the Civil Service – Prime Minister Margaret Thatcher – which purported to vary the terms of employment for staff at Government Communications Head Quarters (GCHQ) to the effect that membership of trade unions was no longer permitted. This followed her election on a mandate to, among other things, control the trade unions and avoid disruptive industrial action. The instruction was issued without any prior consultation with the unions or staff, and the claimants alleged that this failure to consult those concerned amounted to a breach of the Minister's duty to act fairly. There existed a long established tradition of consultation in relation to any important alteration in the terms and conditions of employment of staff at GCHQ, which created a 'legitimate expectation' that this would continue (per Lord Diplock at page 408). The reason the Minister had not engaged in consultation with those concerned was to protect the interests of national security: she argued that prior consultation would have risked disruptive industrial action at GCHQ which, as a result of the work undertaken at GCHQ, may have jeopardised national security.

2

PUBLIC LAW

The royal prerogative

The authority to issue the instruction in question arose as a result of the royal prerogative. The royal prerogative is the name given to those residual discretionary powers, rights and immunities of the monarch which originate in the common law, as opposed to statute. The royal prerogative may be exercised by the monarch personally or, more usually, by the ministers of central government on the monarch's behalf (Dicey, Law of the Constitution at page 421). The minister argued that the instruction was immune from review by the courts on the basis that, as an emanation of the prerogative, it could be exercised at the discretion of the sovereign and the way in which prerogative powers are exercised is not open to review by the courts (page 397). Traditionally, UK courts held the opinion that they were not entitled to inquire into the exercise of decisions made under prerogative powers, which led Lord Fraser in the CCSU case to assume, without deciding, that the exercise of all prerogative powers are immune from challenge: 'the courts will inquire into whether a particular prerogative power exists or not, and, if it does exist, into its extent. But once the existence and extent of a power are established to the satisfaction of the court, the court cannot inquire into the propriety of its exercise.'

However, Lords Diplock and Roskill did not subscribe to this opinion. They could see no reason why a decision-making power should be immune from judicial review simply because it is a power derived from a common law source, the royal prerogative, as opposed to a statutory source: there is 'no logical reason why the fact that the source of the power is prerogative and not statute should today deprive the citizen of the right to review the manner of its exercise which he would possess were the source of the power statutory' (per Lord Roskill at page 417). Susceptibility to judicial review depends on the subject matter of the power, and not on its source: the issue must be justiciable. It must be liable to judicial consideration and intervention. National security, according to Diplock, is a non-justiciable matter, as 'the judicial process is totally inept to deal with the sort of problems which it involves' (page 412). However, if the matter is justiciable and liable to judicial consideration the courts may review the exercise of decision-making powers arising from either statute or prerogative.

The traditional grounds

Traditionally, if a public authority exceeded its decision-making power – acted in excess of its jurisdiction – the decision was susceptible to judicial review on the basis that the decision was *ultra vires*: out with the power conferred by statute. Further, if the decision maker abused its discretionary powers, the decision would be amenable to review.

The strict language of *ultra vires* causes problems in analysing the reviewability of the decision-making power in the *CCSU* case. *Ultra vires* could be used in the case of statutory powers to determine whether the decision maker had acted out with the power expressly conferred by the Act. The very nature of prerogative powers precludes such an assessment: how can the courts define the outer limits of a power which is discretionary, the exercisable boundaries of which cannot be readily determined? In an attempt to clarify the exact circumstances in which a judicial review action may be brought, Lord Diplock moved away from the traditional language of *ultra vires*, and excess or abuse of jurisdiction. He preferred to refer to the grounds for judicial review as: illegality, irrationality and procedural impropriety.

A reclassification: illegality, irrationality and procedural impropriety

By illegality, Lord Diplock meant that 'the decision maker must understand correctly the law that regulates his decision-making power and must give effect to it'. Consequently, if a decision maker purports to exercise powers it does not possess, this will be reviewable under illegality (*Attorney General v. Fulham Corporation*). If a decision is exercised by the wrong person, the resultant decision will be illegal; for example, a decision maker may be entitled to delegate his power to another person, who can then take the decision on his behalf. If that person further sub-delegates, without the power or authority to do so, the eventual decision could be illegal (*Allingham v. The Minister of Agriculture and Fisheries*). It may be the case that before a decision-making body can exercise its powers a particular state of affairs must first exist. If the powers are exercised in the absence of such a state of affairs having been achieved the decision will be illegal (*White and Collins v. Minister of Health*).

By 'irrationality' Diplock simply redefined what had come to be known as 'Wednesbury unreasonableness'. He thought a decision 'which is so outrageous in its defiance of logic or of accepted moral standards that no sensible person who had applied his mind to the question to be decided could have arrived at it' would be reviewable on grounds of irrationality. A decision maker is required to take into account all relevant considerations, and ignore any irrelevant matters, when exercising their power (*Wednesbury Corporation*). If relevant considerations have been ignored or irrelevant considerations taken into account, the resultant decision will be irrational (*R v. Somerset County Council ex parte Fewings*). A power exercised for an improper purpose or motive – which was unintended by the conferral of the power – may also be subject to judicial review on grounds of irrationality (*Congreve v. Home Office*).

Procedural impropriety, according to Diplock, encompasses both the failure to observe the rules of natural justice and to act with procedural fairness, and the failure to comply with express procedural rules laid down in the legislation conferring the decision-making power (page 411). The rules of natural justice are twofold: the rule against bias (*nemo iudex in causa sua*) and the right to a fair hearing (*audi alteram partem*). The test for bias is whether 'the fair minded and informed observer, having considered the facts, would conclude that there was a real possibility that the tribunal was biased' (Lord Hope in *Porter v. Magill*). To ensure that an individual is afforded a fair hearing, he or she should be given the opportunity to both know and to understand any allegations made, and to make representations to the decision maker to meet those allegations (Barnett, H. at page 765).

In the *CCSU* case, Lord Roskill suggested that the idea of natural justice should be replaced by the 'duty to act fairly', the extent of which would vary greatly from one case to the other (page 414). In this case, the existence of a legitimate expectation that consultation would take place meant that the failure to consult constituted, *prima facie*, a breach of the duty to act fairly and had national security considerations not been involved the court would have protected this legitimate expectation. Where there is an express procedural requirement of consultation, any failure to comply will invalidate the resultant decision. The consultation will be inadequate if the decision maker fails to approach it with an open mind, if insufficient notice has been given or insufficient information provided (*Aylesbury Mushrooms*).

The potential of proportionality

Proportionality, a concept developed and employed by the European Court of Justice and the European Court of Human Rights, was proposed by Lord Diplock as further potential ground on which to base a judicial review claim. It requires that any interference with a person's rights must be no more than is necessary to achieve the intended result. The courts were originally reluctant to extend the ambit of judicial review to include proportionality, and in *R* v. *Secretary of State for the Home Department, ex parte Brind* it was suggested that 'an inquiry into and a decision upon the merits cannot be avoided' if a proportionality test was adopted (Lord Ackner at page 735). As noted above, this is something which is specifically prohibited by judicial review.

However, following the Human Rights Act 1998, which incorporates the European Convention into domestic law, proportionality has gained increased support as a ground for judicial review. It requires an intensity of review which is somewhat greater than that of irrationality, and in *R (Daly)* v. *Secretary of State for the Home Department* it was suggested that the courts may no longer be satisfied simply that the decision under review was 'not capricious or absurd' (Lord Cooke at page 447). While proportionality is clearly applicable in cases involving human rights, the question remains whether the doctrine will come to pervade all aspects of judicial review in the future. Despite the concerns voiced in *Brind*, the judiciary have been at pains to stress that the adoption of the proportionality test does not mean a move to a merits review (Lord Steyn in *Daly* at page 447). However, many commentators would agree that the distinction between the power to make a decision and its merits has been eroded as the courts have attempted to regulate the manner in which a decision-making power is exercised. The expansion of proportionality as a ground for judicial review is likely to exacerbate this.

It is undeniable that the *CCSU* case has played a major part in the development and clarification of the law of judicial review. It expanded the law to allow the review of prerogative powers, and Diplock's grounds clearly defined the circumstances in which judicial review would be available, provided the subject is one which lends itself to judicial contemplation. In proposing the development of proportionality as a ground for review, Diplock displayed incredible foresight, as the full implications and extent of this principle have not yet been fully resolved. The ruling in the *CCSU* case continues to be one of the most authoritative in this field.

FURTHER READING

Primary sources

Agriculture Training Board v. *Aylesbury Mushrooms Ltd* [1972] 1 All ER 280

Allingham v. *The Minister of Agriculture and Fisheries* [1948] 1 All ER 780

Associated Provincial Picture Houses Ltd v. *Wednesbury Corporation* [1948] 1 KB 223

Attorney General v. *Fulham Corporation* [1921] 1 Ch 440

Chief Constable of North Wales Police v. *Evans* [1982] 1 WLR 1155

Congreve v. *Home Office* [1976] QB 629

Council of Civil Service Unions v. *Minister for the Civil Service* [1984] 3 All ER 935

Porter v. *Magill* [2002] 2 AC 357

R v. *Secretary of State for the Home Department ex parte Brind* [1991] 1 All ER 720

R v. *Somerset County Council ex parte Fewings* [1995] 3 All ER 20

R (Daly) v. *Secretary of State for the Home Department* [2001] 3 All ER 433

White and Collins v. *Minister of Health* [1939] 3 All ER 548

Secondary sources

Allen, M. and Thompson, B. (2005) *Cases and Materials on Constitutional and Administrative Law*, 8th edn, Oxford University Press, Oxford.

Barnett, H. (2004) *Constitutional and Administrative Law*, 5th edn, Cavendish Publishing.

Bradley, A.W. and Ewing, K.D. (2003) *Constitutional and Administrative Law*, 13th edn, Pearson Education Limited.

2

PUBLIC LAW

Standing (*locus standi*) for judicial review proceedings

Inland Revenue Commissioner v. *National Federation of Self-Employed and Small Businesses Ltd* [1982] AC 617

Rhona Smith, Northumbria University

(Note that this case is sometimes referred to as the 'Mickey Mouse' case or the 'Fleet Street Casuals' case.)

The *CCSU* case (see separate entry) explains the concept of judicial review. As with any legal proceeding, various factors determine the applicability of judicial review as a legal remedy:

1. The identity of the body which made the decision/omitted to act, against whom review is sought.

2. The nature of the decision/omission at issue – is it reviewable by the courts?

3. Whether there is an appropriate ground for complaint.

4. Whether the person has legal standing (*locus standi*) to challenge the decision.

5. Whether the necessary procedural requirements have been met – time limits, exhaustion of remedies, completion of salient forms etc.

The entry on *CCSU* addresses many of these issues. This entry focuses on item 4 above – the issue of *locus standi*. Clearly without standing, no judicial review action is competent. A wide construction of *locus standi* would thus help ensure that decision-making bodies are held to account in the courts. There is no automatic right to apply for judicial review; rather the individual must seek permission to apply for review from the courts. Accordingly, the courts wield some power over who can challenge decisions and thus who can seek a remedy in this manner. Judicial review is a time consuming and expensive process thus the concept of an interest group, non-governmental organisation (NGO) or 'campaigning group' (Harlow at page 1) supporting and funding an application has obvious advantages.

The test for *locus standi*

As Wade and Forsyth note (at page 678) '[t]he law starts from the position that remedies are correlative with rights, and that only those whose rights are at stake are eligible to be awarded remedies. No one else will have the necessary standing before the court'. This has resulted in a fairly restrictive approach to the issue of standing in private law. Such an approach is less tenable in the public sphere as it does not recognise the need for respect for public interest as will be explained here. Traditionally, the tests for standing were interpreted differently depending on the remedy being sought: stricter rules for injunctions and declarations (though note Denning in *Blackburn v. A-G*) than for certiorari and prohibition orders, for example. However, since 1977 when the modern procedure for judicial review was introduced, a single standing requirement developed.

That test for standing is found in the Supreme Court Act 1981, s.31(3) of which states 'No application for judicial review shall be made unless the leave of the High Court has been obtained in accordance with rules of court; and the court shall not grant leave to make such an application unless it considers that the applicant has a sufficient interest in the matter to which the application relates'. This is confirmed in the rules of court, presently Civil Procedure Rules 1998 part 54. Given that judicial review forms part of the mechanism by which the judiciary can overview the actions of the government and ensure an element of accountability, it is inevitable that cases would arise when the courts may be keen to hear the arguments and consider the merits but the issue of sufficiency of interest is rather more opaque and appears to bar judicial review.

The scope of the 'sufficient interest' test was considered at length in *Inland Revenue Commissioner v. National Federation of Self-Employed and Small Businesses Ltd*. The Inland Revenue estimated it lost around one million pounds a year through systematic tax evasion measures: many of the 6000 workers in Fleet Street gave false names and addresses when working on a casual basis, thus precluding collection of tax due. Following discussions with the relevant employers and unions, it was decided to implement a special arrangement, granting, in effect, an amnesty to the casual workers, and implementing new and effective prospective systems of tax calculation and collection. The respondents (the National Federation) instituted proceedings seeking an order of mandamus (now a mandatory order) compelling the Inland Revenue to collect outstanding taxes. However, the interest of the National Federation was simply that they represented ordinary taxpayers, who did not benefit from such an 'amnesty' arrangement.

Locus standi was treated as a preliminary matter in the Divisional Court and this was the sole matter for decision before the House of Lords. Their Lordships intimated that although '[t]here may be simple cases in which it can be seen at the earliest stage that the person applying for judicial review has no interest at all . . . in other cases this will not be so' (Lord Wilberforce at page 630). Accordingly, it will be necessary for the consideration of all the circumstances of the case, including who is bringing the action, against whom and on what grounds. Lord Diplock was the only judge in the *Inland Revenue Commission* case to uphold standing (in his opinion, the case failed on merits). Lords Wilberforce, Roskill and Fraser appeared in agreement that the question of *locus standi*, while a preliminary issue, had to be resolved in light of what was known of the merits of the claim. Lord Fraser emphasised that standing should logically precede any discussion on merits (if no standing, then any merits argument was redundant). No single statement embodied an explanation of the 'sufficient interest' test.

This element of discretion accorded to judges as to whether or not to permit any given judicial review application permits the court to accept those rare applications which 'public interest' demands should be considered (for example, *ex parte World Development*

Movement case) although, as discussed below, this remains controversial. With the National Federation of Self-Employed and Small Businesses, their 'interest' was considered to be the same as any other tax payer – their grievance based on the fact that the Fleet Street casual workers were effectively granted an amnesty for tax evasion while other taxpayers (including their members) were not. Indeed as Lord Scarman notes (at page 647), members of the National Federation had experienced a 'relentless pursuit' of allegedly unpaid taxes. As no single taxpayer can ask the court to investigate the tax affairs of another person or organisation, no aggregate of taxpayers could be treated differently. Furthermore, although the claim was based on the alleged discriminatory treatment of different groups of taxpayers, the federation had not shown 'reasonable grounds for believing that the failure to collect tax from the Fleet Street casuals was an abuse of the revenue's managerial discretion' or there was a case which required investigation by the court (Lord Scarman at page 655). Lord Scarman elected to consider the merits of the claim alongside standing, in contrast to his colleagues. Although the judges diverged in their approaches to the matter of standing, tax authorities were not deemed immune from challenge (see, for example, *Re the European Union and taxpayers, ex parte Smedley*).

Elaboration of the 'sufficient interest' test

Case law has considerably enhanced understanding of the 'sufficient interest' test, with judges creating a pragmatic approach to *locus standi*. As Lord Diplock noted, '[i]t would, in my view, be a grave lacuna in our system of public law if a pressure group, like the federation, or even a single public-spirited taxpayer, were prevented by outdated technical rules of *locus standi* from bringing the matter to the attention of the court to vindicate the rule of law and get the unlawful conduct stopped' (*Inland Revenue Commissioner* case at page 644).

Stretching 'sufficient interest' to a more general public interest, while in accordance with elements of democratic theories of accountability, is certainly controversial. There is unlikely to be a shortage of people and groups seeking to challenge government policy and decisions, especially in areas such as foreign policy (for example, *ex parte Lord Rees-Mogg*; *R (Campaign for Nuclear Disarmament)*). Thus in the *World Development Movement* case, a non-governmental organisation was able to raise proceedings against the government on its decision to support financially the building of the Pergau Dam in Malaysia with money taken from the Overseas Development Aid fund. There was no relevant individual directly affected but Rose LJ concluded there were five factors of significance which combined to demonstrate the organisation had sufficient interest (at page 395): the importance of vindicating the rule of law; the importance of the issue raised; the likely absence of any other responsible challenger; the nature of the breach of duty against which relief is sought; and the prominent role of these applicants in giving advice, guidance and assistance with regard to aid. Contrasting the position of the National Federation in the *Inland Revenue Commissioner* case, the World Development Movement did not *ipso facto* obviously have *no* interest. However, Harden *et al.* suggests judicial review of financial expenditure in such situations should be limited: '[t]he courts should allow standing to individuals to bring judicial review proceedings to test the legality

of central government expenditure under the *Pergau* principle only where accounting officers or the NAO (National Audit Office) have clearly misdirected themselves in law, or
where a minister has rejected their views' (at pages 680–681).

Evidently not all situations will result in a successful application for review. Famously, a
group who formed a trust company to preserve the remains of the Rose Theatre in London,
were denied standing. The Trust was seeking review of the Secretary of State's decision
not to include the newly uncovered remains of the Rose Theatre on the Schedule of monuments under s.1 of the Ancient Monuments and Archaeological Areas Act 1979. Having
perused the *Inland Revenue Commissioners* case, Schiemann J noted (*ex parte Rose
Theatre Trust* at page 520) the following salient points re standing:

1. Once leave has been given to move for judicial review, the court which hears the application ought still to examine whether the applicant has a sufficient interest. 2. Whether an
applicant has a sufficient interest is not purely a matter of discretion in the court. 3. Not
every member of the public can complain of every breach of statutory duty by a person
empowered to come to a decision by that statute. To rule otherwise would be to deprive
the phrase 'a sufficient interest' of all meaning. 4. However, a direct financial or legal interest is not required. 5. Where one is examining an alleged failure to perform a duty imposed
by statute it is useful to look at the statute and see whether it gives an applicant a right
enabling him to have that duty performed. 6. Merely to assert that one has an interest
does not give one an interest. 7. The fact that some thousands of people join together and
assert that they have an interest does not create an interest if the individuals did not have
an interest. 8. The fact that those without an interest incorporate themselves and give the
company in its memorandum power to pursue a particular object does not give the company an interest.

Applying those points to the case, he concluded that as no individual had standing, a company created by those individuals could not have standing either. This despite the fact that
many eminent archaeologists and actors were included in the ensemble. The decision to
schedule a monument was considered 'one of those governmental decisions in respect of
which the ordinary citizen does not have a sufficient interest to entitle him to obtain leave
to move for judicial review' (page 521). This suggests that certain government and local
authority actions will be beyond challenge. The court examines the relevant power (for
example, statute), the matter to which the complaint relates and decides whether an individual is impliedly or expressly given a right or expectation to seek review. In the instant
case, there was no such right thus no standing. However, the judge did consider the merits
of the case as unproven first – perhaps had his findings been to the contrary, then the
decision on merits may have reflected the strength of the case. This compares with the
Inland Revenue Commissioner case in which the issue of standing was not singled out as
a preliminary question but related to the purported merits of the case, so too in *World
Development Movement*.

In many instances, an individual with sufficient interest can be found to 'head' the action.
Thus in *ex parte Greenpeace*, the organisation successfully challenged a government
decision to allow testing at the THORP nuclear processing centre in Sellafield, Cumbria;
it could claim some 2500 supporters in the region thus justifying a personal interest in
the matter, alongside the general concern of Greenpeace. A similar scenario emerged in

2

PUBLIC LAW

ex parte Friends of the Earth (page 15), the Court noting that Friends of the Earth was a company of high repute recognised as having the relevant expertise although, in any event, the review proceedings also named Andrew Lees. Mr Lees lived in one of the areas whose water quality was the subject of the review proceedings thus sufficient interest could easily be demonstrated. Finding a suitable individual to name on an application is thus a useful tool for NGOs but can an individual act altruistically on behalf of others, or the wider population? It would appear that major contentious issues could be open to review by concerned citizens.

Note, however, that for complaints raised under the Human Rights Act, the question of standing is different – s.7(1) of the Act specifies that applicants must be 'victims' of the action or proposed action of the public authority which is incompatible with a convention right (s.6) – generally precluding the possibility of challenge by a concerned non-governmental organisation or interest group. Certainly the European Court of Human Rights does not permit interest group actions unless the group can claim to be a victim. However, as certain 'human rights' based challenges can be made under ordinary judicial review processes, potential for action remains, though note that the question of which test of standing applies is not always deemed relevant given the merits (for example, *ex parte Bulger*).

Conclusions

For judicial review proceedings, the 'sufficient interest' test remains for establishing a primary right to seek judicial review. It would appear that the courts are willing to afford a broad interpretation to it where justice so demands and thus an element of discretion enters the equation. Certainly, in the *Inland Revenue Commissioner* case, the judges (in spite of diverse reasonings) were unwilling to deny standing without at least considering an outline of the merits of the claim. Given the considerable cost to an individual of instituting an action to seek judicial review, there is a tendency for public interest groups, unions etc. to be involved, at least financially (for example, *Edwards*). Judicial review is an important mechanism for securing the separation of powers in the State – it permits the judiciary to review executive action.

Lord Denning MR (in *Blackburn*) provides an appropriate conclusion:

> it is a matter of high constitutional principle that if there is good ground for supposing that a government department or a public authority is transgressing the law, or is about to transgress it, in a way which offends or injures thousands of Her Majesty's subjects, then any one of those offended or injured can draw it to the attention of the court of law and seek to have the law enforced, and the courts in their discretion can grant whatever remedy is appropriate.

FURTHER READING

Primary sources

Blackburn v. *Attorney-General* [1971] WLR 1037

R (Campaign for Nuclear Disarmament) v. *Prime Minister* [2002] EWHC 2777

R (on the application of Edwards) v. *the Environment Agency* [2004] EWHC 736

R v. *Greater London Council, ex parte Blackburn* [1976] WLR 550

R v. *Her Majesty's Inspectorate of Pollution, ex parte Greenpeace Ltd (No. 2)* [1994] 4 All ER 329

R v. *H.M. Treasury, ex parte Smedley* [1985] 1 All ER 589

R v. *Secretary of State for the Environment, ex parte Rose Theatre Trust Co* [1990] QB 504

R v. *Secretary of State for the Environment, ex parte Friends of the Earth* [1995] Env LR 11

R v. *Secretary of State for Foreign and Commonwealth affairs, ex parte Lord Rees-Mogg* [1994] QB 552

R v. *Secretary of State for Foreign and Commonwealth Affairs, ex parte World Development Movement Ltd* [1995] WLR 386

R v. *Secretary of State for the Home Department, ex parte Bulger* [2001] EWHC Admin 119

R v. *Secretary of State for Social Services, ex parte Child Poverty Action Group* [1990] 2 QB 540

Secondary sources

Cornford, T. (2000) 'The New Rules of Procedure for Judicial Review' [2000] 5, *Web Journal of Current Legal Issues*, http://webjcli.ncl.ac.uk/2000/issue5/cornford5.html.

Harden, I. *et al.* (1996) 'Value for money and administrative law' [1996] *Public Law*, 661.

Harlow, C. (2002) 'Public Law and Popular Justice', *Modern Law Review*, 65, 1.

Leyland, P. and Anthony, G. (2005) *Textbook on Administrative Law*, 5th edn, OUP, Oxford.

Ligere, E. (2005) 'Locus standi and the public interest: a hotpotch of legal principles' (2005) *Journal of Planning and Environment Law*, 292.

Wade, H.W.R. and Forsyth, C.F. (2004) *Administrative Law*, 9th edn, OUP, Oxford.

2

PUBLIC LAW

Bias (judicial review)

R v. *Bow Street Metropolitan Stipendiary Magistrate ex parte Pinochet Ugarte (No. 2)* [1999] 2 WLR 272 HL

Lucinda Hudson, Northumbria University

A decision of a court or public body, such as a local planning authority, can be challenged by judicial review. There are various grounds on which an application for judicial review can be brought. One of these is that the decision maker was biased. But does an applicant have to prove that a decision maker was actually biased?

Before the Pinochet case it was thought that a judge would only be automatically disqualified from hearing a case (i.e. no facts tending to show a danger of bias had to be proved) if he had a pecuniary (monetary) or proprietary (property) interest in the outcome of the litigation. The Pinochet case clarified that a judge would also be automatically disqualified from hearing a case if the judge's decision would lead to the promotion of a cause in which the judge was involved together with one of the parties.

It is obviously essential, if the public is to have confidence in the judicial system, that a legal case should be decided by an unbiased judge. A rule developed hundreds of years ago (in *Dr Bonham's* case) that no one should be a judge in a case in which they had an interest: *nemo judex in causa sua*. There are, however, different types of 'interest'. Any direct pecuniary interest, however small, in the outcome of a case automatically disqualifies a judge from hearing it *(Dimes* v. *Proprietors of Grand Junction Canal).* A proprietary interest would also result in automatic disqualification. Other degrees of interest in the outcome of a case, would not automatically disqualify a judge from hearing that case.

Having a shareholding in the canal company which was a party to the action meant that the Lord Chancellor's decision in *Dimes* v. *Proprietors of Grand Junction Canal* was void for bias, even though it was not suggested that the Lord Chancellor had *actually* been influenced by this when hearing the case. The thinking behind this appeared to be that bias should be presumed in such cases and decisions set aside, so that the decision-making process was seen to be free from any perceived bias.

In addition, in cases which did not involve pecuniary or proprietary interest, nevertheless jurisprudence developed to preserve the integrity of the *nemo judex* rule. For example, the same party could not act as both accuser and judge *(R* v. *Barnsley Metropolitan Borough Council ex parte Hook).* It was also established that '. . . justice should not only be done, but should manifestly and undoubtedly be seen to be done'. *(R* v. *Sussex Justices ex parte McCarthy,* page 259).

The test of 'apparent bias'

By 1993, there was doubt as to the correct test in a case involving not actual bias or a monetary interest, but the third kind of bias which was called 'apparent bias'. One test was whether a reasonable and fair-minded person sitting in the court and knowing all the relevant facts would have had a reasonable suspicion that a fair trial was not possible because of bias on the part of the decision maker. The second was whether there was a real likelihood, or danger, of bias. In *R v. Gough*, (a case in which a juror was the defendant's brother's next door neighbour, but did not recognise the connection until after the verdict had been given) the House of Lords held that the second test was the correct one.

In *R v. Inner West London Coroner, ex parte Dallaglio*, the Coroner described applicants to resume an inquest as 'unhinged' and 'mentally unwell'. Had he unconsciously allowed himself to be influenced against the applicants by a feeling of hostility towards them and undervalued their case that the inquests should be resumed?

In that case, Bingham MR referred to *R v. Gough*, and set out the three classes of case in which bias might arise. *Dallaglio* was another case of the third category, 'apparent bias'. Bingham MR said that, 'the description "apparent bias" traditionally given to this head of bias is not entirely apt, for if despite the appearance of bias the court is able to examine all the relevant material and satisfy itself that there was no danger of the alleged bias having, in fact, caused injustice, the impugned decision will be allowed to stand.' The question was whether there was a real danger of bias on the part of HM Coroner for Inner West London in the sense that he might have unfairly regarded with disfavour the cases of the applicants as parties to an issue under consideration by him.

An issue which was still unclear to a certain extent, was when might circumstances of apparent bias arise? Should a judge recuse himself (withdraw from the case) if he had previously received a brief from one of the solicitors in the case before him? Could a party object to a judge because of her religion or previous party political associations? The Court of Appeal said not without more evidence of bias (*Locabail (UK) Ltd v. Bayfield Properties* at pages 77-78):

> . . . a judge's religion, ethnic or national origin, gender, age, class, means or sexual orientation cannot form a sound basis of an objection. 'Nor, at any rate ordinarily, could an objection be soundly based on the judge's social or educational or service or employment background or history, nor that of any member of the judge's family; or previous political associations; or membership of social or sporting or charitable bodies; or Masonic associations; or previous judicial decisions; or extra-curricular utterances (whether in textbooks, lectures, speeches, articles, interviews, reports or responses to consultation papers); or previous receipt of instructions to act for or against any party, solicitor or advocate engaged in a case before him; or membership of the same Inn, circuit, local Law Society or chambers. By contrast, a real danger of bias might well be thought to arise if there were personal friendship or animosity between the judge and any member of the public involved in the case . . .

2

PUBLIC LAW

Ex parte Pinochet - the facts

General Pinochet was the former Head of State of Chile. His extradition was sought by the government of Spain, so that he could be tried for various crimes against humanity, allegedly committed while he was Head of State. Amnesty International (AI) was granted leave to intervene in the proceedings. The appeal was allowed by a majority of three to two. Of the majority, Lord Nicholls and Lord Steyn each delivered speeches holding that Senator Pinochet was not entitled to immunity: Lord Hoffmann agreed with their speeches but did not give separate reasons for allowing the appeal. Lords Slynn and Lloyd dissented.

Subsequently, the General discovered that Lord Hoffman was a director and chairperson of Amnesty International Charity Ltd (AICL), which had been incorporated to carry out AI's charitable purposes, and that Lady Hoffman had been employed by AI as an administrator for many years. He petitioned the House to set aside its order.

The test for bias

In *Pinochet No. 2* the House of Lords held that the principle of automatic disqualification was not restricted to cases in which a judge had a pecuniary interest in the outcome, but also applied to cases where the judge's decision would lead to the promotion of a cause in which the judge was involved together with one of the parties.

Browne-Wilkinson LJ said that this was a most unusual case, where the outcome of the litigation did not lead to financial benefit to anyone. The interest of AI in the litigation was not financial; it was its interest in achieving the trial and possible conviction of Senator Pinochet for crimes against humanity. The litigation was criminal, rather than civil, AI was neither the prosecutor nor the accused, but an intervener. He saw no good reason to limit automatic disqualification to pecuniary interest, just because that tended to be the usual conflict which arose in civil litigation. If, as in this case, the matter was concerned with the promotion of a cause, the rationale disqualifying a judge applied just as much, if the judge's decision would lead to the promotion of a cause in which the judge was involved together with one of the parties. Having decided that if Lord Hoffmann had been a member of AI he would have been automatically disqualified because of his non-pecuniary interest in establishing that Senator Pinochet was not entitled to immunity, Browne-Wilkinson LJ went on to consider whether it could make any difference that, instead of being a direct member of AI, Lord Hoffmann was a director of AICL. AICL was a company wholly controlled by AI and carrying on much of its work. Browne-Wilkinson LJ found that AI and AICL were parts of an entity working towards the same goals. He decided that if the absolute impartiality of the judiciary were to be maintained, there must be a rule which automatically disqualified a judge who was involved, whether personally or as a director of a company, in promoting the same causes in the same organisation as was a party to the suit.

As the relationship between AI, AICL and Lord Hoffmann led to the automatic disqualification of Lord Hoffmann to sit on the hearing of the appeal, it was unnecessary to consider whether there was a real danger or reasonable suspicion of bias.

Nolan LJ agreed, stating that in any case where the impartiality of a judge was in question, the appearance of the matter was just as important as the reality. The petition was granted and the matter referred to another committee of the House for rehearing.

The impact of the Human Rights Act

In 1998 the Human Rights Act was passed, which meant that the European Convention for the Protection of Human Rights and Fundamental Freedoms of 1950 was given further effect in United Kingdom law, and that in making decisions on bias (and Other issues), UK courts would have to follow the jurisprudence of the European Court of Human Rights. Article 6 of the Convention provides for the right to a fair trial, and so there was European case law on this issue.

In 2000 the Court of Appeal considered the test for bias in another case of apparent bias. Here (*DG of Fair Trading* v. *Proprietary Association of GB Medicaments and Related Classes of Goods No. 2*) a lay member of a court had recently applied for a job with a consultancy, from which one of the key witnesses came. The Court of Appeal applied principles derived from the jurisprudence of the ECHR. It first ascertained all the circumstances which had a bearing on the suggestion that the tribunal was biased. It then asked whether those circumstances would lead a fair minded and informed observer to conclude that there was a real possibility, or a real danger, the two being the same, that the tribunal was biased. In considering the question of bias the Court of Appeal found that a fair minded observer would apprehend that there was a real danger that the lay member would be unable to make an objective and impartial appraisal of the expert evidence placed before the court and should have recused herself.

The 'real possibility' test was affirmed by the House of Lords in *Porter* v. *Magill*.

The employment of a tribunal member by the same organisation whose decision is being challenged, did not lead to automatic disqualification under the 'fair minded and informed observer' test (in *Gillies* v. *Secretary of State for Work and Pensions (Scotland)*). The medically qualified member of the three-person tribunal was a doctor who had been providing reports to the Benefits Agency in disability living allowance cases and incapacity benefits cases as an examining medical practitioner. The social security commissioners allowed the claimant's appeal, concluding that an objective bystander would have a reasonable apprehension of bias on the part of the doctor, even though they had no reason to think that she had been consciously biased. The House of Lords confirmed that the test was whether a fair minded and informed observer would conclude, having considered the facts, that there was a real possibility that the doctor would not evaluate reports by other doctors who acted as examining medical practitioners, objectively and impartially against the other evidence. It held that there was nothing in the doctor's outside activities or in the way in which she conducted herself to show that she was unable to fulfil the duty of every tribunal member to reach an independent judgment. Accordingly, the test for the doctor's disqualification on the ground of apparent bias had not been made out and the appeal would therefore be dismissed.

The Court of Appeal again followed the test in a case in which a High Court judge who had known a witness in the case for over 30 years, did not stand down (*AMG Group Ltd* v. *Morrison*). The Court said that the test for apparent bias had now been settled by a line of recent decisions of itself and the House of Lords, and held that the judge should have done so. He would have had the 'greatest difficulty where a challenge was to be made as to the truthfulness of [the witness's] evidence'.

The *Pinochet* case was a very high profile case, involving not only a Head of State, but one of the most senior appeal judges in the UK. It established a third ground on which a party might rely in arguing for the automatic disqualification of a judge, where the question of bias arose.

FURTHER READING

Primary sources

AMG Group Ltd v. *Morrison* [2006] 1 All ER 967 CA

DG of Fair Trading v. *Proprietary Association of GB Medicaments and Related Classes of Goods (No. 2)* [2000] All ER (D) 2425 CA (European Convention)

Dimes v. *Proprietors of Grand Junction Canal* (1852) 3 HL Cas 759

Dr Bonham's case (1610) 8 Co Rep 114

Gillies v. *Secretary of State for Work and Pensions (Scotland)* [2006] 1 All ER 731 HL

Locabail (UK) Ltd v. *Bayfield Properties* [2000] 1 All ER 65 CA

Porter v. *Magill* [2002] 2 AC 357

R v. *Barnsley Metropolitan Borough Council ex parte Hook* [1976] 3 All ER 452 CA

R v. *Bow Street Metropolitan Stipendiary Magistrate ex parte Pinochet Ugarte (No. 2)* [1999] 2 WLR 272 HL

R v. *Gough* [1993] 2 All ER 724

R v. *Inner West London Coroner, ex parte Dallaglio* [1994] 4 All ER 139 CA

R v. *Sussex Justices ex parte McCarthy* [1924] 1 KB 256

Secondary sources

Allen, M. and Thompson, B. (2005) *Cases and Materials on Constitutional and Administrative Law*, 8th edn, Oxford University Press, Oxford.

Barnett, H. (2006) *Constitutional and Administrative Law*, 6th edn, Cavendish Publishing.

Carroll, A. (2007) *Constitutional and Administrative Law*, 4th edn, Pearson Education Limited.

3 EUROPEAN UNION: LAWS AND INSTITUTIONS

The European Union was created over the decades following the peace treaties ending the Second World War in Europe in 1945. A Congress of Europe was held in 1948, a meeting of the powerful political leaders in Europe, determined to prevent a third world war from further decimating the region. Churchill spoke of a 'United States of Europe', a position his successors as UK Prime Minister have shrunk from. Various positive outcomes emerged from this meeting: the Council of Europe was established in 1949 (its principal claim to fame is probably the European Convention on Human Rights); the European Coal and Steel Community was established in 1951 to regulate coal and steel (the armaments of war) followed by the European Economic Community and European Atomic Energy Community (to rebuild the economies of the region) in 1957; and agreement was reached on advancing a pan-European defence force (still not realised). The three communities developed rapidly and form the basis of the European Union as it is today. Various treaties (international agreements) have altered the institutions, membership and functions of the EU. Now, attention is focused on the 2007 Treaty of Lisbon amending the Treaty on European Union and the Treaty Establishing the European Community. This 'reform' treaty is being considered throughout the member states in 2008 and if they all ratify it, then aspects of the Union will once again be changed.

Since the UK acceded to the relevant treaties in 1972, it has become almost impossible to avoid the impact of the European Union. Many laws enacted by the institutions of the Union have effect in the UK; hundreds of other national laws are, in fact, based on EU provisions. No lawyer can afford to ignore it.

The cases covered in this section of the book address the main elements of EU law. In effect, studying EU law means undertaking a study of a new legal system – 'supranational law' which is distinguishable from national and international law. Thus, the cases selected begin with looking at the constitutional and institutional framework of the Union, focusing on the implications for members states. Key substantive areas of EU law will then be discussed including competition law, social policy and free movement of goods, workers and services.

CONTENTS FOR EUROPEAN UNION: LAWS AND INSTITUTIONS

Overview
Case 26/62 *Van Gend en Loos* v. *Nederlandse Administratie der Belastingen*
[1963] ECR 1   111

L'effet utile (effective judicial protection)
Cases 14/83 *Von Colson and Kamann* v. *Land Nordrhein-Westfalen*
[1984] ECR 1891; C-106/89 *Marleasing SA* v. *La Comercial Internacional de
Alimentación SA* [1990] ECR I-4135   116

Preliminary rulings under Article 234 EC
Case 283/81 *Srl CILFIT and Lanificio di Gavardo SpA* v. *Ministry of Health*
[1982] ECR 3415   122

State liability
Cases C-6 and 9/90 *Francovich* v. *Italy* [1991] ECR I-5357   127

Free movement of goods
Case 120/78 *Rewe-Zentral AG* v. *Bundesmonopolverwaltung für Branntwein
(Cassis de Dijon)* [1979] ECR 649   132

Free movement of workers
Case 66/85 *Deborah Lawrie-Blum* v. *Land Baden-Württemberg* [1986] ECR 2121   140

Freedom to provide services
Case C-76/90 *Säger* v. *Dennemeyer* [1991] ECR I-4221   145

Social policy
Case 43/75 *Defrenne* v. *Société Anonyme Belge de Navigation
Aerienne (SABENA)* [1976] ECR 455, [1976] 2 CMLR 98 (*aka Defrenne II*)   151

Competition law: cartels (Article 81)
Cases 56/64 and 58/64 *Etablissements Consten SA and
Grundig-Verkaufs-GmbH* v. *EEC Commission* [1966] ECR 299,
[1966] CMLR 418   156

Competition: dominant position (Article 82)
Case 6/73 *Europemballage and Continental Can* v. *Commission* [1973] ECR 215   161

Case 26/62 *Van Gend en Loos* v. *Nederlandse Administratie der Belastingen* [1963] ECR 1

Rhona Smith, Northumbria University

Uniquely among European Court of Justice cases, the dicta in Van Gend en Loos provides a pocket guide to EU law. Constitutional law, the single market and even the very nature of EU law are discussed in this seminal case. It is probably one of the singularly most useful cases in the area – this analysis will demonstrate the breadth of the case and its importance to the evolution of EU law.

The ruling was one of the earliest given by the Court but far from taking a tentative approach, the Court fully embraced its remit and handed out a ruling the full impact of which was still emerging some thirty years later. No aberration on the part of the Court, this case encapsulates many of the fundamental concepts of EU law. The ruling is remarkably short, barely 30 paragraphs, but no law student should avoid a careful reading of it.

The case was referred to the European Court of Justice for a preliminary ruling on two questions: whether Article 12 of the treaty had direct application within the territory of a member state and if so whether the import duty imposed by the Netherlands on ureaformaldehyde was an unlawful increase in a customs duty and thus prohibited under Article 12. The Court ruled that Article 12 produced direct effect and creates individual rights which national courts must protect. Moreover, the reclassification of ureaformaldehyde into a higher tariff band was contrary to Article 12.

The nature of EU law – a federal Europe?

Initially both Belgium and the Netherlands challenged the jurisdiction of the Court to consider what they claimed was the application of the treaty in the context of the constitutional law of the Netherlands. The question of whether the treaty should prevail over national law was thus a matter for the national constitutional law.

Now termed by some 'supranational law', EU law has common features with both international and national law. The Commission had submitted written observations to the effect that the European treaties cannot be considered solely under public international law. For his part, the Advocate-General, Mr Roemer, noted that the proceedings raised 'the fundamental question of the relationship between Community law and national law' (page 20) and continued that some aspect of EU law was intended to modify and supplement national law. However, he also opined that many provisions of the treaty are couched in terms of member states' obligations (i.e. conventional international law) and appeared to favour a more traditional approach. The Court went considerably further, 'the Community constitutes a new legal order of international law for the benefit of which the states have limited their sovereign rights, albeit within limited fields, and the subjects of which comprise not only Member States but also their nationals' (page 12).

The nature of this new legal order has become increasingly apparent over the intervening years. Perhaps most importantly, the twin principles of direct effect and supremacy have emerged from these initial statements.

Supremacy of EU law

In many respects *Van Gend en Loos* represents the first tentative indication of the supremacy of EU law. Being effectively obiter in the case, many commentators failed to grasp the significance of this paragraph at the time. States remained the primary actors in international law and many assumed that the EEC, given it was created under international law, was a typical international organisation. Like the United Nations and the International Labour Organisation, states were bound in a consensual manner and could opt in and opt out at will. Unless a state has a monistic approach to international treaty law (many EU member states, though not the UK, do) then Community law is *prima facie* of no relevance in the domestic sphere. It is binding on the state at the international level alone. This view was supported by the Advocate-General who drew support from the enforcement mechanisms created under Articles 169 and 170 (now Articles 226 and 227) (at page 21).

The Court acknowledged that the institutions of the EEC enjoyed sovereign powers (page 12) and that the individual European citizens had also been called upon to cooperate in the functioning of the community.

However, a more overt statement on supremacy was delivered the following year in *Costa* v. *ENEL* which confirmed that the Community has 'real powers stemming from a limitation of sovereignty or a transfer of power from the States to the Community' (at page 593). Perhaps, more importantly, it is 'impossible for the States, as a corollary, to accord precedence to a unilateral and subsequent measure over a legal system accepted by them on a basis of reciprocity' (at pages 593–4). It appeared that treaty law (essentially international law) could not be overridden by national law without being deprived of its character as community law thereby calling into question the legal basis of the community.

It was a further eight years before the Court had the opportunity of giving an actual decision on supremacy (as opposed to a preliminary ruling). In *Commission* v. *Italy*, the Court stated that '[t]he attainment of the objectives of the Community requires that the rules of Community law established by the Treaty itself or arising from procedures which it has instituted are fully applicable at the same time and with identical effects over the whole territory of the Community without the member states being able to place any obstacles in the way' (at page 532). Subsequent case law has made clear this principle applies even when the state has not yet repealed the legislation, when the more recent law is national (*Simmenthal*) or when the legislation in unrepealable (constitutional law) (*Internationale*).

For the United Kingdom, the issue of supremacy and its effect on the courts was clarified in the case of *Factortame*.

Direct effect of EU law

Direct effect in many respects is a logical corollary to supremacy. If the Community can produce laws which have effect in member states, it is perhaps inevitable that at least some of these laws should be legally enforceable against the state. In the words of the Court in *Van Gend en Loos* (page 12),

> [i]ndependently of the legislation of Member States, community law therefore not only imposes obligations on individuals but is also intended to confer upon them rights which become part of their legal heritage. These rights arise not only where they are expressly granted by the treaty, but also by reason of obligations which the treaty imposes in a clearly defined way upon individuals as well as upon the member states and upon the institutions of the Community.

Not all elements of European law meet the threshold for direct effect. Consideration thus has to be given to the nature of the provision (page 13):

> [t]he wording of Article 12 contains a clear and unconditional prohibition which is not a positive but a negative obligation. This obligation, moreover, is not qualified by a reservation on the part of states which would make its implementation conditional upon a positive legislative measure enacted under national law. The very nature of this prohibition makes it ideally adapted to produce direct effects in the legal relationship between member states and their subjects.

In the instant case, these were satisfied thus Article 12 was held to produce direct effect, 'creating individual rights which national courts must protect' (page 13). Other articles of the treaty have been held to produce direct effect, most notably Article 141 (equal pay) upon which there has been considerable case law.

With the evolution of community law, this concept has been expanded to other types of community law. When the same criteria are met, then direct effect can be produced in secondary legislation. *Van Duyn* suggested that directives could produce direct effect, at least when invoked against the states. The definition of the state was expanded in *Marshall* to ensure as many citizens as possible enjoy the rights accorded to them under the treaty and associated legislation.

The three requirements for direct effect are thus that the measure is clear and unconditional, a negative obligation and it requires no further action on the part of the state. In other words, the measure must exhibit the characteristics of law.

Interestingly in *Van Gend en Loos* the Court argued that the vigilance of individuals concerned to protect their rights was effectively supervision of the states in fulfilment of their obligations under the treaty and complementary to (what are now) Articles 226 and 227 (the interstate and EU state mechanisms) (page 13).

The power of individuals to challenge states is complementary to the power of the commission and Other states to do likewise. Should the treaty limit monitoring to the other states and the commission, the court felt that this would remove 'all direct legal protection' of the individual rights from nationals (page 13). In some respects this may be viewed as an embryonic recognition of the now accepted concept of Union Citizenship. The European Court clearly considered that from the outset individuals were also the subjects of Community law and benefited from rights derived therefrom.

3

EUROPEAN UNION: LAWS AND INSTITUTIONS

The apex of this line of reasoning was reached in *Francovich* when the state was found to be under an obligation to compensate individuals for failure to comply with directives within the prescribed time limit.

Common market

'The objective of the EEC Treaty . . . is to establish a Common market' (page 12). In further-ance thereof customs tariffs were to be abolished as between member states in prepara-tion for the establishment of a common external customs wall surrounding the Community. In the early years, the focus was on freezing existing intra-EU tariffs and reducing the tariffs to zero. In *Van Gend en Loos*, the reclassification of the substance resulted in a higher tariff being applicable. The Court was asked whether this was equiva-lent to a new (and thus prohibited) customs charge. Essentially the Court stated that it did not matter why a higher tariff was applicable to the product, the important aspect was that the same product entering the same country was subjected to a higher rate of duty (at page 15). The actual application of the provision on customs tariff to ureaformaldehyde was left to the national courts.

Obviously the single internal market has superseded the customs union. However, the approach of the court has wavered little since this early case – a strict approach is inevitably taken to any method of circumventing Community law.

Preliminary rulings

Van Gend en Loos is possibly one of the most famous of all the preliminary rulings issued by the court. '[T]he object [of Article 177, now Article 234] is to secure the uniform inter-pretation of the Treaty by the national courts and tribunals' (page 12).

Preliminary rulings are likely to form the majority of the cases you will read for EU law. It is the major mechanism for reviewing the application of community law in member states and, as such represents a compromise between judicial sovereignty of member states and the need for uniform application of EU law throughout. However, it is not an appellate func-tion. The European Court determines the question of law presented to it, the national court applies the response to the facts of the case and renders judgment. As *Van Gend en Loos* aptly demonstrates, the Court uses the preliminary ruling function to develop community law, dynamically examining provisions of the treaty and teleologically interpreting them as the Community has evolved into the Union of today. Much of the formative work in EU law was carried out under the veil of preliminary rulings. Although rulings, rather than deci-sions, and although the final decision in the case is made by the national court in light of the 'advice' issued by the European Court, the importance of the procedure cannot be underestimated today. As the Community continues to enlarge the relevance of preliminary rulings will be undiminished, contributing significantly to the development of a uniform system of law.

No-one can afford to underestimate the importance of *Van Gend en Loos* to the devel-opment of EU law. There are few cases in any legal system which have exerted such a fundamental influence over the nature and scope of law. With hindsight, it is easy to overlook the importance of this ruling, delivered in a Community of just six states. That it is still so fundamental to EU law today is testament to the prescience of that first bench of judges of the new organisation.

FURTHER READING

Primary sources

Case 48/71 *Commission v. Italy (Italian Arts Treasures Case)* [1972] ECR 527

Case 6/64 *Costa v. ENEL* [1964] ECR 585

Case C-213/89 *R v. Secretary of State for Transport, ex parte Factortame* [1990] 3 WLR 818

Case C-6&9/90 *Francovich v. Italy* [1991] ECR I-5357

Case 11/70 *Internationale Handelsgesellschaft mbH* [1970] ECR 1125

Case C-106/89 *Marleasing* [1990] ECR I-4135

Case 152/84 *Marshall v. Southampton & South West Hampshire Area Health Authority (Teaching)* [1986] ECR 723

Case 106/77 *Simmenthal SpA* [1978] ECR 629

Case 41/74 *Van Duyn v. Home Office* [1974] ECR 1337

Case 14/83 *Von Colson v. Land Nordrhein-Westfalen* [1984] ECR 1891

3

EUROPEAN UNION: LAWS AND INSTITUTIONS

L'effet utile (effective judicial protection)

Cases 14/83 *Von Colson and Kamann* v. *Land Nordrhein-Westfalen* [1984] ECR 1891

C-106/89 *Marleasing SA* v. *La Comercial Internacional de Alimentación SA* [1990] ECR I-4135

Eva Joyce, Anglia Ruskin University

Introductory comments – the principle of effectiveness or l'effet utile

The repeated use by the Court of Justice of the European Communities (ECJ) of the idea of the effectiveness of Community law has led to the academic community constructing the 'principle of effectiveness'. It is to be borne in mind that EU law comprises a new legal order whose principles, constructs and vocabulary are still at the formation stage which means that there is no general agreement about the language to be used to describe its workings. It should also be remembered that all documents, laws and rulings from the courts have to be translated and that there is bound to be some slippage of language. From the beginning of the Community the predominant language of the ECJ was French. The idea of the effectiveness of Community law is also called 'l'effet utile' and, more helpfully, perhaps, 'effective judicial protection'. It is the meaning of this final phrase, the essence of which is that individuals who have been wronged must be provided with a remedy, which gives a clue to the focus of the thinking and reasoning of the ECJ. There is, however, a broader formulation of the principle under which the focus is on the effectiveness of the European Union itself and thus of Community law generally.

Under the umbrella of the principle of effectiveness, whichever meaning is intended, the ECJ has developed three mechanisms whose dual objective seems to be, on the one hand, to ensure that individuals have access to proper remedies and, on the other, to persuade member states to harmonise their laws as they are required to do, in particular, by directives. The three mechanisms are direct effect, indirect effect and state liability under *Francovich* and they were developed by the ECJ in that order.

The term 'indirect effect' is an academic construct, which is why the phrase tends to appear within inverted commas. Unlike the phrase 'direct effect' the ECJ has not as yet adopted the term. 'Indirect effect' has been to some extent overlooked academically because attention has been focused on the creation of direct effect although, arguably, the reach of 'indirect effect' is potentially greater. It has even been argued by the Advocate-General in the recent *Adeneler* case that the duty of harmonious interpretation ought to arise when a directive is published, that is, before its implementation date. The ECJ did not agree with the AG on this occasion. 'Indirect effect', within the English legal system might be called 'purposive construction'. It is also called: the duty of 'harmonious interpretation' or 'consistent interpretation'.

Von Colson and Marleasing - the rulings

In the case of *Von Colson and Kamann*, the relevant directive was 76/207, the Equal Treatment Directive, under which persons discriminated against on the ground of gender are required to be compensated. It was accepted by both sides and the court that the claimants had been discriminated against in not being offered jobs on the basis of gender. The three difficulties facing the German court were that the directive did not spell out the nature and extent of the compensation; that under German law the only compensation payable was reimbursement of expenses incurred in applying for the job, and, thirdly, that the claimants argued that the directive required a level of compensation that would act as a deterrent to the 'employer' not to discriminate again. The court referred a list of questions to the ECJ. In that court it was accepted that the directive was not precise and unconditional on the issue of compensation and therefore this part of it could not be directly effective. The ECJ also ruled that the compensation under German law (enacted as purported compliance with the directive) was not adequate and that it was for the national court to award proper compensation. In so doing the court had the obligation to interpret national law 'in the light of the wording and purpose of the directive' in order to make the substance of the directive 'binding as to the effect to be achieved' under Article 249 (ex 189).

For the purposes of the development of the new legal order, therefore, the principle of the interpretive obligation was first articulated in this important case. Three matters should be noted: the defendant in *Von Colson* was part of the state (the Land prison service); the reason that the particular provision of the directive did not have direct effect was that the individual right was not clearly delineated; that German law was enacted, albeit ruled to be ineffective compliance, to comply with the directive.

In *Marleasing*, by contrast, the directive could not have direct effect because the relevant litigant against whom it was pleaded, was an individual. The claimant company, the said individual, brought an action in an attempt to safeguard its financial position. The defendants included a number of individuals who/which had formed under Spanish law a new public limited company, namely, La Comercial. Marleasing was a creditor of Barviesa, one of the individuals that formed the new company, and part of the claim was that La Comercial had been formed with a view to putting Barviesa's assets beyond the reach of its creditors. The action was, *inter alia*, to ask the Spanish court to declare the formation of the company void under the Spanish Civil Code for 'lack of lawful cause'.

The defendants argued that the Spanish Civil Code, in this respect, was incompatible with Directive 68/151, which provided an exhaustive list of permitted grounds for nullity that did not include the reason pleaded. Spain had not implemented the relevant provisions into Spanish law. The relevant part of the Spanish Civil Code pre-dated Spain's accession to the European Community. This was the difference between *Von Colson* and *Marleasing* and thus the reason for the request for a preliminary ruling from the ECJ.

The essential question for the ECJ was therefore whether a Spanish court (and thus all national courts of the member states) ought to interpret pre-existing national law in conformity with the directive. The answer from the ECJ was in the affirmative: 'as far as

3

EUROPEAN UNION: LAWS AND INSTITUTIONS

possible' a national court must employ harmonious interpretation to pre-existing law as well as to law that is put in place in response to EU requirements.

Marleasing, an individual, was, if the Spanish court was indeed able to interpret the Spanish civil code harmoniously, remarkably unfortunate in finding itself unable to rely upon national law to defend its interests and being instead bound by a directive of international law of whose existence the company was unlikely to have been aware.

Von Colson and *Marleasing* are thus the two foundation cases for the interpretive obligation of the member states' national courts. Treaty Article 10 (ex 5) is crucial in the reasoning relied upon by the ECJ's as the basis for 'indirect effect'. Article 10 requires member states to take all appropriate measures to ensure the achievement of the objectives of the treaty. The court has spelled out in these cases that the obligation under the Article is not just that of the lawmaker (legislature) and the government (executive) but also of the courts (judiciary). Thus it is that judges in the national courts have the obligation to interpret national law, so far as possible, in conformity with Community law.

This idea that all organs of the state are involved in the proper functioning of the Community is sometimes expressed as the fidelity principle: the idea that each level of government must act to ensure the proper functioning of the whole. The basis of the fidelity principle is that it draws all relevant institutions, national as well as Community institutions, into the job of effectively sustaining Community policy and thus the functioning of the European Union. Elsewhere there is mention of the solidarity principle, which seems to encompass the same idea.

In later cases the ECJ has also relied upon the idea of 'loyal cooperation'. When the court uses this phrase it is addressing itself to the judges of the national courts to consolidate the idea that the Community is built upon, *inter alia*, a cooperation between national courts and the ECJ. Another aspect to this cooperation is the fact that the ECJ depends upon the national courts to refer questions to it so that it can develop Community law.

Critique of 'indirect effect'

'Indirect effect', the duty of all member states' national courts to interpret national law so that it is 'in tune with' Community law, was and is criticised academically as a step too far in the ECJ's endeavour to fashion the new legal order. The duty was labelled 'indirect effect' because the interpretive obligation was an indirect means whereby an unimplemented or mis-implemented directive could place a burden upon an individual. It will be remembered that direct effect was limited in the case of *Marshall* such that a directive could only be invoked by an individual in actions against the state – vertical direct effect. Thus Mrs Marshall, whose action was against an employer which (it was decided) was part of the state, could succeed but it was immediately noted by commentators that on the same facts another employee whose employer was a private company (another individual) could not have a remedy because of the limitation on the scope of direct effect.

From this angle, focusing on the right of individuals who have been caused loss by the inaction (failure to implement a directive) or improper action (flawed implementation of a directive) of a member state, indirect effect and state liability under *Francovich*, should be viewed in tandem. In their different ways, they provide a remedy for a wronged individual. But seen from the point of view of the other side in litigation, while it seems appropriate for a member state to pay out damages to a claimant who has suffered loss as a result of that member state's fault, it seems inappropriate for an individual to be made liable in circumstances where he is merely acting in conformity with existing national law. It is not inconceivable that a litigant who suffers harm in this way, like Marleasing itself, under an unimplemented or improperly implemented Community measure, of which it had no knowledge, might itself in turn sue the state for loss caused to it by that same failure, the failure to abide by the state's obligation under Article 10, which caused the litigant to rely upon unmodified national law. In terms of general principles, the most obvious effect of the *Marleasing* ruling is the attack on the principle of legal certainty.

Further aspects of 'indirect effect' - the cases after *Von Colson* and *Marleasing*

The ECJ's rulings in these cases are problematic at national level. One of the questions they raise is: to what extent should a national court go to comply with its duty as stated by the ECJ?

In the *Wagner-Miret* case the ECJ added that in interpreting national law, which has been made to implement a directive, the national court should presume that the state intended to fulfil its obligations fully in its implementation. It was accepted, however, that the national court was unable to comply with its interpretive obligation in the circumstances of this case. Thus, this is a limit to the interpretive obligation: a national court cannot interpret '*contra legem*'.

Purposive interpretation has been problematic for English courts too but since the House of Lords decision in the *Litster* case, in which it was prepared to read into an English regulation (Transfer of Undertakings [Protection of Employees] Regulations or TUPE) a number of extra words so that it complied with the relevant directive, it seems to have been generally accepted. In *Litster* the House of Lords was willing to depart from an English court's traditional common law approach to statutory interpretation and to embrace the gap-filling, purposive approach of the civilian tradition. In the more recent case of *White*, however, the House of Lords refused to apply the *Marleasing* rule because their lordships considered that to do so would be to overstretch it.

An answer to a litigant who fails to persuade a court with his argument for harmonious interpretation, therefore, is, instead, to sue the state under *Francovich*. This is unsatisfactory for a number of reasons among which is the fact that a separate action has to be brought and, in addition, the existence of the *Francovich/Factortame* requirements themselves which may cause a wronged individual to fail in his action against the state.

In *Kolpinghuis Nijmegen and Arcaro* the ECJ for the first time limited the interpretive obligation to non-criminal matters. The effect of these rulings is that an individual cannot become criminally liable under an unimplemented or improperly implemented directive. This seems to be a correct approach in the sense that it upholds the general principle of legitimate expectations.

Some commentators took the view that in *Arcaro* the ECJ was distancing itself from the approach laid down in earlier cases but this would seem to be a flawed perception as in a very recent ruling, *Pfeiffer and Others*, a case involving the Working Time directive, the ECJ re-stated the doctrine of indirect effect in strong terms.

A further question is the relationship between 'soft' law and the interpretation of national law by a judge. In the *Grimaldi* case the national court was told it had to take account of soft law, in this case a Commission recommendation, in interpreting national law.

Broadening its approach even further, the ECJ in *Pupino* ruled that although there is no equivalent to Article 10 EC in the Treaty on European Union (TEU) it would be difficult to carry out the tasks in Article 1 TEU if the principle of loyal cooperation did not also bind member states in the area of police and judicial cooperation in criminal matters. The national court was required to have regard to the content of Community framework decisions in interpreting national law. This ruling has the effect of drawing 'indirect effect' into the third pillar (Justice and Home Affairs) of the European Union. It seems there remains the possibility of further development of the concept of 'indirect effect'.

FURTHER READING

Primary sources

Case C-212/04 *Adeneler* v. *Ellinikos Organismos Galaktos* [2006] ECR I-6057

Case C-168/95 *Arcaro* [1996] ECR I-4705

Case C-63/01 *Evans* v. *Secretary of State for the Environment, Transport and the Regions and Motor Insurers' Bureau* [2004] 1 CMLR 47

Case C-6 and 9/90 *Francovich and Bonifaci* v. *Italy* [1991] ECR I-5357

Case C-322/88 *Grimaldi* v. *Fonds des Maladies Professionelles* [1989] ECR 4407

Case 80/86 *Kolpinghuis Nijmegen* [1987] ECR 3969

Case 152/84 *Marshall* v. *Southampton and South West Hampshire Area Health Authority (Teaching)* [1986] ECR 723

Case C-397-403/01 *Pfeiffer and Others* v. *Deutsches Rotes Kreuz* [2004] ECR I-8835

Case C-105/03 *Pupino* [2005] 2 CMLR

Case C-48/93 *R* v. *Secretary of State for Transport ex parte Factortame Ltd and Others (Factortame 3)* [1996] ECR I-1029

Case C-334/92 *Wagner-Miret* v. *Fondo de Garantia Salarial* [1993] ECR I-6911

Litster v. *Forth Dry Dock* [1990] 1 AC 546

White v. *White and Motor Insurers' Bureau* [2001] 2 CMLR 1

Secondary sources

Accetto, M. and Zlepting, S. (2005) 'The Principle of Effectiveness: Rethinking its Role in Community Law' (2005) 11, *European Public Law*, 375.

Amstutz, M. (2005) 'In-between Worlds: Marleasing and the Emergence of Interlegality in Legal Reasoning' (2005) 11, *European Law Journal*, 766.

Arnull, A. (1999) *The European Union and its Court of Justice*, OUP, Oxford.

Betlem, G. (2002) 'The Doctrine of Consistent Interpretation: Managing Legal Certainty' (2002) 22, *Oxford Journal of Legal Studies*, 397.

Drake, S. (2005) 'Twenty Years after Von Colson: the Impact of "Indirect Effect" on the Protection of the Individual's Community Rights' (2005) 30, *European Law Review*, 329.

de Witte B. (1999) 'Direct Effect, Supremacy, and the Nature of the Legal Order' in P. Craig and G. de Burca (eds), *The Evolution of EU Law*, OUP, Oxford, 196–8.

3

EUROPEAN UNION: LAWS AND INSTITUTIONS

Preliminary rulings under Article 234 EC

Case 283/81 *Srl CILFIT and Lanificio di Gavardo SpA* v. *Ministry of Health* [1982] ECR 3415

Debra Brown, De Montfort University

In terms of their importance or usefulness, textbooks on EU law often describe certain cases as being 'seminal', but we should not forget how most of them got to the European Court of Justice (the ECJ) in the first place. The relationship between the ECJ and the national courts is not an appellate one. Contrary to what many people believe, individuals cannot appeal their cases involving Community law 'all the way to Europe', for they have no right of appeal to the ECJ. However, such cases may reach the ECJ as the result of preliminary references by the national courts under Article 234 (ex 177) EC. Certainly many of the cases analysed in this text came to the ECJ as a result of the Article 234 procedure and most of the major principles of Community law were formulated by the ECJ in the context of a preliminary reference. Such principles include the supremacy and direct effect of Community law.

The case that provides the focus for this chapter, *Srl CILFIT and Lanificio di Gavardo SpA* v. *Ministry of Health* (case 283/81) was itself the subject of a preliminary reference to the ECJ. It came 20 years after the very first preliminary ruling in *de Geus en Uitdenbogerd* v. *Robert Bosch GmbH*, in which Advocate General Lagrange summarised the purpose of Article 234. He said:

> The progressive integration of the Treaty into the legal, social and economic life of the Member States must involve more and more frequently the application and, when the occasion arises, the interpretation of the Treaty in municipal litigation, whether public or private, and not only the provisions of the Treaty itself but also those of the Regulations adopted for its implementation will give rise to questions of interpretation and indeed of legality.

Thus, the primary purpose of Article 234 was to ensure the uniform interpretation and consistency of Community law so as not to imperil the fundamental aim of market integration.

The relationship between the ECJ and the national courts is of crucial importance and there is no doubt that the Article 234 procedure depends entirely for its success on mutual cooperation between them. This is because Article 234 allows the national courts to apply to the ECJ for a preliminary ruling; it therefore depends on the national courts knowing how and when to refer and the ECJ knowing when to accept and when to decline a reference!

The relationship pretends to be on a horizontal level because the two courts are supposed to work together, on an equal footing. However, by the 1980s it had become clear that the ECJ was no longer happy to accept each and every preliminary reference sent its way, arguably because of the increase in the number of cases it had to deal with. This has caused a number of writers to claim that the horizontal relationship has slipped more towards the vertical, with the ECJ placing itself in a superior position to the national courts. The case which appears to confirm this belief is *CILFIT*.

The *CILFIT* reference

The Italian Ministry for Health imposed a health inspection levy on the importation of wool from outside the Community. The claimants were wool importers who disputed the levy on the grounds that it breached Regulation (EEC) No 827/68. Article 2(2) of the Regulation prohibits member states from levying any charge having an effect equivalent to a customs duty on imported 'animal products'. The wool importers argued that wool is an animal product, but the Italian Ministry for Health disagreed. Furthermore, the ministry claimed that the interpretation of 'animal product' was 'so obvious as to rule out the possibility of there being any interpretative doubt' and that this therefore obviated the need to refer the matter to the ECJ for a preliminary ruling.

The matter came before the Corte Suprema di Cassazione: an Italian Supreme Court against whose decisions there is no judicial remedy under Italian law. The wool importers argued that because there was no appeal from the Corte Suprema, the latter could not, according to Article 234(3), escape the obligation to bring the matter before the ECJ.

Under Article 234(3), where a question 'is raised in a case pending before a court or tribunal of a member state, against whose decisions there is no judicial remedy under national law, that court or tribunal shall bring the matter before the Court of Justice'. Referral is discretionary for all other courts; they are covered by Article 234(2) which provides that 'any court or tribunal of a member state may, if it considers that a decision on the question is necessary to enable it to give judgment, request the Court of Justice to give a ruling thereon'.

The conflicting arguments of the wool importers and the Ministry for Health caused the Corte Suprema to make its preliminary reference to the ECJ. It asked just one question:

> Does the third paragraph of Article 177 of the EEC Treaty [now Article 234] . . . lay down an obligation so to submit the case which precludes the national court from determining whether the question raised is justified or does it, and if so within what limits, make that obligation conditional on the prior finding of a reasonable interpretative doubt?

In order to answer this question, the ECJ held (at paragraph 5) that it was necessary to take account of the system established by Article 234. It considered the following issues to be of relevance.

The purpose of the preliminary rulings procedure

The purpose of Article 234 as a whole has already been discussed above. In the *CILFIT* case the Court looked in particular at the purpose of Article 234(3) and held that it 'seeks to prevent the occurrence within the Community of divergences in judicial decisions on questions of Community law'. Thus, this purpose should be kept in mind when questions arise as to the obligation imposed by Article 234(3).

3

EUROPEAN UNION: LAWS AND INSTITUTIONS

The nature of the preliminary rulings procedure

Next, the ECJ considered the meaning of the words 'where any such question is raised', to be found in Article 234(2). The ECJ confirmed (at paragraph 9) that Article 234 'does not constitute a means of redress available to the parties to a case'. It held that 'the mere fact that a party contends that the dispute gives rise to a question concerning the interpretation of Community law does not mean that the Court or tribunal concerned is compelled to consider that a question has been raised within the meaning' of Article 234.

The ECJ was therefore sending out a clear reminder of the nature of the preliminary rulings procedure. The decision to refer lies with the national court, not with the parties to the case and certainly not with the ECJ.

The national court's discretion relating to the relevance of the question

Taken literally, the wording of Article 234(2) and (3) would appear to indicate that determining whether a decision on the question is 'necessary to enable it to give judgment' applies only to Article 234(2) and therefore only to the Court's discretionary jurisdiction. The ECJ in *CILFIT* quashed such an interpretation. It held (at paragraph 10) that:

> it follows from the relationship between the second and third paragraphs of [Article 234] that the courts or tribunals referred to in the third paragraph have the same discretion as any other national court or tribunal to ascertain whether a decision on a question of Community law is necessary to enable them to give judgment.

Having then confirmed that 'those courts or tribunals [referred to in Article 234] . . . are not obliged to refer to the Court of Justice a question concerning the interpretation of Community law raised before them if that question is not relevant, that is to say, if the answer to that question, regardless of what it may be, can in no way affect the outcome of the case', the ECJ turned its attention to the crucial question of when a decision would not be necessary. To answer this question, the ECJ had to decide if the obligation laid down by Article 234(3) might, none the less, be subject to certain restrictions.

When is an obligation not an obligation?

The ECJ concluded that the obligation to refer under Article 234(3) is subject to two restrictions.

The first is when 'the question raised is materially identical with a question which has already been the subject of a preliminary ruling in a similar case' (paragraph 13). This was confirmation of the ECJ's own judgment in *da Costa en Schaake NV v. Nederlandse belastingadministratie* which appeared to incorporate a system of precedent into the Article 234 procedure.

However, in *CILFIT* the ECJ went even further than in *da Costa*. It decided that in addition to the above, a decision would not be necessary where 'previous decisions of the court have already dealt with the point of law in question, irrespective of the nature of the proceedings which led to those decisions, even though the questions at issue are not strictly identical' (paragraph 14). This makes it clear that a previous ruling can be relied on even if the proceedings are of a different type to the previous case and even if the questions at issue are not strictly identical.

This was an important development. While the ECJ qualified the restriction by stating (at paragraph 15) that 'it must not be forgotten that in all such circumstances national courts and tribunals, including those referred to in the third paragraph of [Article 234], remain entirely at liberty to bring a matter before the Court of Justice if they consider it appropriate to do so', this was a clear message from the ECJ that the national courts should rely on its previous rulings. There is no doubt that this has affected the horizontal relationship supposed to be enjoyed by the ECJ and the national courts. If previous rulings of the ECJ are to be relied on by national courts, such rulings must place the ECJ in a superior position.

The second restriction is encountered when 'the correct application of Community law may be so obvious as to leave no scope for any reasonable doubt as to the manner in which the question raised is to be resolved' (paragraph 16).

Both restrictions relieve the national court of its obligation to refer under Article 234(3), and have caused considerable debate. Many writers claim that the ECJ had introduced the doctrine of *acte clair* into Community law. This doctrine was developed in French administrative law to relieve the French courts of the burden to refer to the government questions relating to the interpretation of treaty provisions where the meaning of the provisions was so 'clear' that no question of interpretation existed.

Some commentators have expressed grave concerns over this apparent endorsement by the ECJ of the *acte clair* doctrine. *Acte clair*, they say, will allow national courts to abuse Article 234(3) by using it as an excuse to avoid the obligation to refer. In addition, dangers are perceived to exist where national courts erroneously believe a provision to be clear, when it is not. The UK case of *R v. Henn* and the French case of *Shell-Berre* may be seen as evidence supporting these concerns.

By contrast, some writers have welcomed the *CILFIT* ruling, claiming that it has strengthened the relationship between the ECJ and the national courts. This is because the ECJ laid down strict guidelines for the operation of its second restriction. To begin with, it held (at paragraph 16) that before a national court concludes that there is no scope for any reasonable doubt, it must be 'convinced that the matter is equally obvious to the courts of the other member states and to the Court of Justice'. The impact of this guideline should not be underestimated, especially as there are now 27 member states.

Furthermore, the ECJ held that the national court must bear in mind the specific characteristics of Community law and the particular difficulties to which its interpretation gives rise (paragraphs 17-19), as well as the risk of divergences in judicial decisions within the Community (paragraph 20). Some writers have argued that these stringent conditions should induce the national courts to make proper use of the *acte clair* doctrine, thereby reducing the risk of divergent interpretations.

There is no doubt that *CILFIT* has changed the face of the Article 234 procedure but its guidelines have nonetheless provided valuable assistance to the national courts when deciding if a question of Community law is 'necessary'.

3

EUROPEAN UNION: LAWS AND INSTITUTIONS

FURTHER READING

Primary sources

Cases 28-30/62 *da Costa en Schaake NV* v. *Nederlandse belastingadministratie* [1963] ECR 61

Case 13/61 *de Geus en Uitdenbogerd* v. *Robert Bosch GmbH* [1962] ECR 89

Customs and Excise Commissioners v. *Samex* [1983] 1 All ER 1042

H P Bulmer Ltd v. *J Bollinger SA* [1974] Ch 401

R v. *Henn* [1981] AC 850

Re Société des Pétroles Shell-Berre [1964] CMLR 462

Secondary sources

Arnull, A. (1989) 'The Use and Abuse of Article 177 EEC' (1989) 52, *Modern Law Review*, 622.

Craig, P. and de Burca G. (2003) *EU Law: Text, Cases and Materials*, OUP, Oxford, Chapter 11.

Douglas-Scott, S. (2002) *Constitutional Law of the European Union*, Longman, Chapter 9.

Mancini, G.F. and Keeling, D.T. (1991) 'From CILFIT to ERT: The Constitutional Challenge Facing the European Court' (1991) 11, *Yearbook of European Law*, 1.

Rasmussen, H. (1984) 'The European Court's *Acte Clair* Strategy in CILFIT' (1984) 9, *European Law Review*, 242.

State liability

Cases C-6 and 9/90 *Francovich* v. *Italy* [1991] ECR I-5357

Susan Wolf, Northumbria University

When the Italian state failed to implement the provisions of Directive 80/987 it should have known that this would constitute a breach of its obligations under both Articles 249 and 10 of the EC treaty. However, despite the fact that the success of the Community legal order depended on member state compliance with Community law, the enforcement mechanisms enshrined in the treaty were essentially weak. A defaulting member state might have expected the Commission, as 'Guardian of the Treaty', to commence infringement proceedings against it under Article 226 (then 169). Prior to amendments made by the Treaty on European Union in 1992, the worst that a member state could expect to face (at least at the judicial level) was a requirement to take the necessary steps to comply with the Court's judgment. In light of this the Italian state was almost certainly not prepared for the consequences flowing from this particular breach. When two Italian companies went into insolvency, leaving Francovich and Bonifaci and 33 others with unpaid wages, the consequences were to reverberate throughout the Community legal order as a result of the landmark ruling that would be given by the Court of Justice in the joined cases of *Francovich and Bonifaci and Others* v. *Italy*.

The Italian state had failed to set up a scheme to guarantee employees a minimum level of wage protection in the event of the insolvency of their employer, as required by EC Directive 80/987, which should have been transposed into national law by 1983. The default on the part of the Italian state resulted in the Commission bringing successful infringement proceedings under Article 226 in *Commission* v. *Italy*. However, the Court's declaration that the failure constituted a breach of its Community law obligations did not directly help the respective workers who found themselves unable to claim payment of their unpaid wages. They therefore sought to obtain, from the Italian state, the guarantees provided for in the Directive or, in the alternative, compensation.

Limitations of direct effect

By 1990 it was already firmly established that Community law was capable of conferring rights on individuals; rights which became part of their legal heritage and which were enforceable in the national courts. Not only had the Court of Justice determined that treaty articles were capable of direct effect, it had also made it clear that it would be incompatible with the binding effect which Article 249 of the EC treaty ascribes to directives to exclude in principle the possibility that they too could be capable of direct effect. This was particularly so in cases where the Community authorities had, by means of a directive, placed member states under a duty to adopt a certain course of action, such as the establishment of a wage guarantee scheme in Directive 80/987. The effectiveness of such measures would be diminished if persons were prevented from relying upon the terms of a directive in proceedings before a national court.

However, the limitations to the doctrine of direct effect in relation to directives were also well rehearsed. Earlier cases, such as *Marshall* and *Becker* had established that an individual could rely upon the provisions of an unimplemented directive against the state (even, as in *Marshall*, where the state is acting as an employer). However, these cases turned on whether the particular provisions in the respective directives were sufficiently clear and precise to be applied directly by national courts in the absence of proper implementation by the state. Given the vagaries of drafting not all directives were capable of satisfying this threshold for direct effect. In any event, even where a directive was sufficiently precise and unconditional to be capable of direct effect, it could not be relied upon in proceedings against any one. In *Marshall* (and later confirmed in *Faccini Dori*) the Court held that any rights conferred by a directive could only be exercised as against the state or an emanation of the state. Notwithstanding the generous interpretation of which bodies fall within the definition of the state, it was clear that the lack of horizontal direct effect for directives would create a situation in which certain claimants would be denied their rights because they were litigating against a private body. Such an anomalous situation did not sit easily with the Court's determination to secure the effective protection of Community rights. Although the Court attempted to assist such litigants through the development of the principle of indirect effect, in *Von Colson* and then *Marleasing*, the principle was not without its own significant limitations.

It is against this legal landscape that Francovich and Bonifaci brought their claims against the Italian state and before the Italian courts. The two Italian courts (the Pretura di Vicenza and Preture di Bassano) referred identical questions to the Court of Justice. The first question concerned the direct effect of Directive 80/987 and the second, important question, concerned the issue of whether the state would be liable for the loss and damage sustained by the parties as a result of the state's breach of its Community law obligations.

On a close examination of the directive the Court ruled that although it was sufficiently clear in respect of the beneficiaries of the guarantee and the rights that it conferred, it nevertheless lacked sufficient clarity and precision as to who should provide the wage guarantee. Moreover, it was not a requirement of the directive that the state should be the guaranteeing institution. In short, the Court concluded that the directive was not capable of direct effect.

The innovation of the Court's ruling lay in the answer to the second question; that the claimants should be compensated for their loss notwithstanding that the directive was not capable of producing direct effect.

Establishing state liability

With remarkable assertiveness the Court stated that it 'is a principle of Community law that the member states are obliged to make good loss and damage caused to individuals by breaches of Community law for which they can be held responsible'. Since no such principle can be found anywhere in the treaty it is quite clear that the Court's decision was based firmly on its own case law. The logic of the Court is, given the constitutional significance of the principle, remarkably simple. National courts, whose task it is to apply the provisions of Community law, are obliged, in so far as they have jurisdiction to do so, to ensure the full effect of Community law. National courts must protect the rights that Community law confers on individuals. The full effectiveness of Community law would be impaired and the protection of the rights which it grants would be weakened if individuals were unable to obtain redress when their rights are infringed by a breach of Community law. This is even more essential where the full effectiveness of the Community rules is subject to some prior action on the part of the state (such as legal and practical implementation of directives) and where, as a consequence of the absence of such action, individuals are unable to enforce their rights. In addition to which the Court added a further justification for the principle of state liability when it reminded member states of their obligation, under Article 10 (then 5) of the EC treaty, to take all appropriate measures, whether general or particular, to ensure fulfilment of their obligations under Community law. This, according to the Court, included the obligation to nullify the unlawful consequences of any breach of Community law. In short the Court concluded that the principle of state liability is 'inherent in the system of the Treaty'.

The assertion of this principle may have been greeted with some surprise and consternation by the member states, but it was a logical step in the Court's jurisprudence. Since Community law confers rights on individuals, rights which should be upheld by the national courts, then a further way of guaranteeing the full effect of Community law is to hold states liable in damages. It should also be recalled that the Court had, in previous decisions (*Van Gend en Loos*), referred to the fact that the vigilance of individuals concerned to protect their rights would assist in the effective supervision of the state. As stated at the outset, the Italian state may have anticipated in 1990 that the worst that could happen as a result of its default was a declaratory judgment from the Court. It now found that it could be liable to pay compensation to those who had suffered loss as a result of this default. Undoubtedly the Court intended this to be a much more powerful deterrent for defaulting member states.

Criteria for state liability

In the *Francovich* case the Court laid down three criteria for state liability. First, the result required by the directive must include the conferral of rights for the benefit of individuals; second the content of these rights must be determined by reference to the provisions of the directive and finally there must be a causal link between the breach of the obligation of the state and the damage suffered by the person affected. One of the most innovative aspects of the judgment, which is often ignored by students of law, is that the claim for damages is independent of the principle of direct effect. In the *Francovich* case it was held that, providing the conditions for state liability were satisfied, the claimant should be awarded damages notwithstanding the fact that the directive was not capable of direct effect. It has been argued (Steiner, 1993) that the Court, in

3

EUROPEAN UNION: LAWS AND INSTITUTIONS

the *Francovich* case, could without difficulty have found the provisions of the directive to be sufficiently clear and precise so as to be directly effective, but that the Court chose not to do this because it wished to establish a remedy for member states' infringements of Community law.

Although the *Francovich* judgment was expressed in terms of the state's liability for non-implementation of a directive, it was questionable whether the case would be confined to its special facts or whether the decision pointed towards a more general principle of state liability in favour of individuals who have suffered loss because of the state's failure to implement Community obligations or violations of Community law. The Court of Justice was given the opportunity of addressing these questions three years later in the joined cases of *Brasserie du Pêcheur SA* v. *Germany* and *R* v. *Secretary of State for Transport, ex parte Factortame*. In both of these cases the claimants were seeking compensation for losses incurred as a result of legislative action taken by Germany and the UK respectively. In the UK the Spanish fishermen sought damages caused by the enactment of the Merchant Shipping Act 1988, a piece of primary legislation, which clearly breached the fishermen's rights of establishment under Article 43 of the EC treaty. The Court of Justice held that the principle of state liability was not confined to a failure to implement EC directives. The principle would apply to all breaches of Community law resulting from the acts or omissions of the member state.

The *Brasserie du Pêcheur* and *Factortame* cases also gave the Court the opportunity to revisit and refine the conditions for state liability. The Court recognised that not all breaches of Community law should warrant a successful claim for damages; that the imposition of such strict liability would hamper the administration of the member states when faced with making legislative choices. Accordingly the Court held that a member state would only be liable where three conditions were met. The conditions were that the rule of Community law infringed must be intended to confer rights on individuals; the breach must be sufficiently serious to justify imposing state liability; and there must be a causal link between the breach of the obligation imposed on the state and the damage actually suffered by the applicant. These new conditions would be used, by the national courts, to test all claims for damages under the principle of state liability. Clearly it was the introduction of the second condition, the sufficiently serious breach, that was the significant refinement of the Francovich conditions and which has received the greatest judicial attention in subsequent cases. For liability to arise the state institution concerned must have manifestly and gravely disregarded the limits of its discretion.

Inevitably the determination of whether a breach will be sufficiently serious will vary from case to case, and should be determined by the national court faced with the claim. However, further judicial guidance has been provided by the Court of Justice in a number of subsequent cases, but unfortunately this has not always been consistent. Significantly, in the context of directives, the Court held in *Dillenkofer* (1996) that a failure to implement a directive was in itself a sufficiently serious breach of Community law since the obligation to implement directives is absolute. However, where implementation of a directive is flawed then the national court should consider, among other things, the clarity of the rule breached and whether the breach is excusable (as in *R* v. *HM Treasury, ex parte British Telecommunications plc* and *Denkavit*).

The principle of state liability, established in *Francovich*, and developed further in subsequent cases, notably *Brasserie du Pêcheur* and *Factortame*, should be regarded as a powerful aid to the enforcement of Community law, particularly directives. The principle sends a clear message to the member states about the potential consequences of failing to comply with Community law, while at the same time enhancing the rights of individuals on Community law. What is clear is that the number of future claims will continue to provide further judicial interpretation – keeping law students occupied for many years to come.

FURTHER READING

Primary sources

Case 8/81 *Becker* v. *Finanzamt Münster-Innenstadt* [1982] ECR 53

Cases C-46 and 48/93 *Brasserie du Pêcheur SA* v. *Germany, and The Queen* v. *Secretary of State for Transport ex parte Factortame* [1996] ECR I-1029

Case 22/87 *Commission* v. *Italy* [1989] ECR 143

Cases C-283, 291 and 292/94 *Denkavit International BV Bundesamt für Finanzen* [1996] ECR I-5063

Cases C 178, 179, 188, 189 and 190/94 *Dillenkofer* v. *Germany* [1996] ECR I-4845

Case C-91/92 *Dori (Faccini)* v. *Recreb Srl* [1994] ECR I-3325

Case C-106/89 *Marleasing SA* v. *La Coomercial Internacional de Alimentación SA*, [1990] ECR I-4135

Case 152/84 *Marshall* v. *Southampton and South West Area Health Authority (Teaching)* [1986] ECR 723

Case 26/62 *NV Algemene Transport-ex Expeditie Onderneming Van Gend en Loos* v. *Nederlandse Administratie der Belastingen* [1963] ECR 1

Case C-392/93 *R* v. *HM Treasury, ex parte British Telecommunications plc* [1996] ECR I-1631

Case 14/83 *Von Colson* v. *Land Nordrhein-Westfalen* [1984] ECR 1891

Secondary sources

Steiner, J. (1993) 'From Direct Effects to Fracovich: shifting means of enforcement of Community Law' (1993) *EL Rev*, 18(1), 3–22.

Steiner, J. and Woods, L. (2006) *Textbook on EC Law*, 9th edn, OUP, Oxford.

3

EUROPEAN UNION: LAWS AND INSTITUTIONS

Free movement of goods

Case 120/78 *Rewe-Zentral AG* v. *Bundesmonopolverwaltung für Branntwein (Cassis de Dijon)* [1979] ECR 649

Simone Lamont-Black, Northumbria University

The decision of the European Court of Justice in *Cassis de Dijon* is one of the milestones in the free movement of goods in the European Union. The case concerned a preliminary ruling sought by the Hessische Finanzgericht mainly on the interpretation of Article 28 of the EC treaty (the then Article 30 of the EEC treaty) with respect to the fixing of a minimum alcohol content for alcoholic beverages. After 22 years of the coming into force of the provisions on the free movement of goods, the case started a new era, giving guidance as to the categorisation and justification of national rules on the marketing of goods within the national territory.

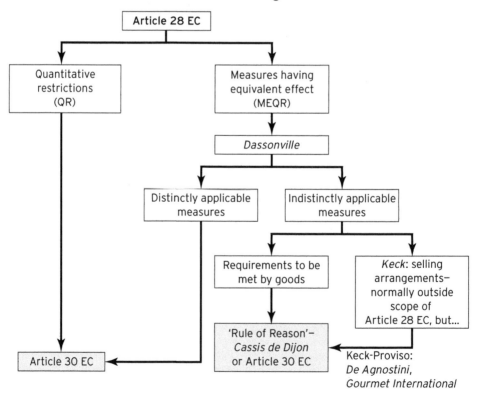

Free movement of goods

The facts

The plaintiff, Rewe-Zentral-AG, intended to import the French fruit-liqueur 'Cassis de Dijon' to the Federal Republic of Germany, and applied for authorisation from the relevant German authority, the Bundesmonopolverwaltung für Branntwein (the Federal Monopoly Administration for Spirits). The authority informed the plaintiff that, in accordance with section 100 (3) of the Branntweinmonopolgesetz (Spirits Monopoly Act) and relating regulations, 'Cassis de Dijon' could not be sold in Germany. In order to be lawfully marketed in Germany, a fruit liqueur must have a minimum level of alcohol of 25%. The product in question had only 15–20% of alcohol content so did not fulfil the requirements. The plaintiff argued that, as the law meant that well-known spirits from other EC member states could not be sold in Germany, it was a 'measure having equivalent effect to quantitative restrictions' and thus breached the free movement of goods as enshrined in Article 28 of the EC treaty. The issue was put to the European Court of Justice to give its opinion.

Article 28 EC treaty and MEQRs

Article 28 of the EC treaty states:

> Quantitative restrictions on imports and all measures having equivalent effect shall be prohibited between Member States.

Thus, Article 28 of the EC treaty effectively prohibits two different measures concerning goods by a member state:

- Quantitative restrictions, such as bans or quotas on imports; and

- Measures having equivalent effect to quantitative restrictions (MEQR).

(Article 29 of the EC treaty provides the mirror provision for exports, which is, however, not relevant here.)

Since the requirement of a minimum alcohol level for the marketing of liqueur did not directly create a 'quantitative restriction' on imports, the issue was firstly whether the law in question contained a MEQR instead and secondly whether such a measure could be justified.

The definition of MEQRs – also known as the Dassonville formula – is taken from Case 8/74 *Procureur du Roi* v. *Dassonville* (para. 5):

> All trading rules enacted by Member States which are capable of hindering, directly or indirectly, actually or potentially, intra-Community trade are to be considered as measures having an effect equivalent to quantitative restrictions.

Thus, it does not matter as such whether the law in question distinguishes between domestic and foreign products (distinctly applicable measure) or whether it is designed to treat all products in the same manner irrespective of their origin (indistinctly applicable measure). If the measure has the potential to hinder intra-Community trade, irrespective of whether it, in fact, happened or not, it is understood as a MEQR.

The law restricting the import of alcoholic beverages below a certain limit thus was a MEQR. German liqueurs would traditionally have been produced to the requirements of the

3

EUROPEAN UNION: LAWS AND INSTITUTIONS

German laws, whereas manufactures from other countries would find themselves in a peculiar situation. Having lawfully produced their product in their territory they found themselves locked out of the German market unless they changed their product to conform to German law.

The rule of reason in *Cassis*

Does this mean that national laws on the production and marketing of products are generally in breach of EC law? In *Cassis* the European Court of Justice explained that in the absence of common rules relating to the production and marketing of alcohol, the member states were free to regulate these matters themselves. The Court conceded that there could be rules that served an essential purpose in the general interest, and as such might take precedence over the free movement of goods. It established what was to be known as the 'Rule of Reason' (para. 8):

> Obstacles to movement within the Community resulting from disparities between the national laws relating to the marketing of the products in question must be accepted in so far as those provisions may be recognised as being necessary in order to satisfy mandatory requirements relating in particular to the effectiveness of fiscal supervision, the protection of public health, the fairness of commercial transactions and the defence of the consumer.

The court thus agreed that there is room for national measures which might have a negative effect on intra-community trade, as long as they are justified by overriding interests. The criteria that follow are that the rule of law must be:

(a) A MEQR, which is *indistinctly applicable*, thus equally regulating domestic and foreign goods (as confirmed in *Commission v. Ireland (Re Souvenir Jewellery)* - note *Commission v. Belgium (Walloon Waste)* which used environmental protection as a justification of a discriminatory measure is believed to be an exception to this rule).

(b) The measure must be intended to fulfil a *mandatory requirement*; mandatory requirements are those set out in the 'Rule of Reason' or, as indicated by the words 'in particular', any other requirement of overriding nature, for example environmental protection (see *Commission v. Denmark (Danish Bottles)*), the maintenance of social security systems (see *Decker*) or the protection of fundamental rights (see *Eugen Schmidberger v. Austria*).

(c) The measure must be *necessary* and *proportionate* to achieve the aim.

The derogations of Article 30 of the EC treaty

Previous to *Cassis de Dijon* a national measure prohibited by Article 28 EC treaty, whether a quantitative restrictions or a MEQR, could only be justified where the strict requirements of Article 30 of the EC treaty were met. Article 30 reads:

> The provisions of Articles 28 and 29 shall not preclude prohibitions or restrictions on imports, exports or goods in transit justified on grounds of public morality, public policy or

public security; the protection of health and life of humans, animals or plants; the protection of national treasures possessing artistic, historic or archeological value; or the protection of industrial and commercial property. Such prohibitions or restrictions shall not, however, constitute a means of arbitrary discrimination or a disguised restriction on trade between Member States.

In the first sentence the specific and exclusively listed grounds for justification are set out. Article 30 of the EC treaty is understood to be a closed list of derogations which cannot be expanded on (see *Commission* v. *Ireland (Re Souvenir Jewellery)* and *Leclerc* v. *Au Blé Vert*). In the second sentence, the principle of proportionality is invoked. As under the Rule of Reason, any measure must be necessary to achieve its purpose and must be proportionate in order to be justified. This is not fulfilled if there is a way to achieve the same objective by means which are less restrictive to intra-Community trade (see *De Peijper* and *ATRAL* for whether the justification is sought via Article 30 of the EC treaty or via *Cassis de Dijon*).

Thus, until the landmark decision of *Cassis de Dijon*, the few justifications enumerated in Article 30 of the EC treaty were the only ones available and they were interpreted restrictively due to the requirement of proportionality. More than 20 years after the coming into force of the free movement of goods provisions, *Cassis* has opened up the possibility to keep up with the requirements of modern life, enabling the member states to defend non-discriminatory laws by showing that they were essential to fulfil mandatory or overriding requirements. However, these grounds need to be well founded, since as a general rule, fundamental freedoms enshrined in the treaty, such as the free movement of goods, are interpreted widely, whereas any derogation from these freedoms is interpreted narrowly to best achieve the aims of Community law.

The derogations as argued in *Cassis*

In *Cassis* the German government claimed that the provisions relating to the minimum alcohol content were necessary in order to safeguard public health by avoiding the proliferation of alcoholic beverages as well as to protect the consumer against unfair commercial practices. The European Court of Justice did not give much weight to these defences. It opined that the German market contained alcoholic beverages of an extremely wide range and that highly alcoholic drinks could be consumed in diluted form, thus the consideration of public health did not necessitate the measure. Transparency of commercial transactions could easily be achieved by making sure that sufficient information is provided to the consumer, for example by indicting the origin and alcohol content on the packaging of the products.

Thus, despite the fact that consumer protection was now accepted as a mandatory requirement, its conditions were not met, as there were less restrictive measures available to secure the stated aims. Similarly in *Walter Rau* v. *De Smedt* the European Court of Justice suggested that labeling margarine and butter was sufficient to help the consumer distinguish the different products; specific rules on packaging were not necessary.

Mutual recognition - *Cassis* II

In *Cassis* the Court went on to create the principle of mutual recognition by stating (para. 14):

> There is therefore no valid reason why, provided that they have been lawfully produced and marketed in one of the Member States, alcoholic beverages should not be introduced into any other Member State.

The effect of this principle is that a member state that wishes to adopt stricter laws on product requirements than those used in other member states can do so only if it can prove that these higher standards are essential to cater for specific national characteristics. For example, laws banning certain ingredients from foodstuffs or drinks were acceptable, but only where specific national nutritional habits could be established (see *Ministère Public* v. *Muller* with respect to the ban of E475 in French pastry products and *Commission* v. *Germany (Beer Purity)* which questions the German Bier-Reinheitsgebot from 1516 which limited beer ingredients to malted barley, hops, yeast and water only.)

Thus the rule of mutual recognition is a presumption which can be rebutted, but the burden of proof is on the member state wishing to adhere to stricter rules than its counterparts. In *Cassis* this test was not fulfilled.

The Ruling in *Cassis*

In conclusion, the European Court of Justice decided:

> The concept of 'measures having an effect equivalent to quantitative restrictions on imports' contained in Article 30 of the EEC treaty is to be understood to mean that the fixing of a minimum alcohol content for alcoholic beverages intended for human consumption by the legislation of a Member State also falls within the prohibition laid down in that provision where the importation of alcoholic beverages lawfully produced and marketed in another Member State is concerned.

This meant that a law, such as section 100 (3) Branntweinmonopolgesetz, was in breach of the free movement of goods. It created a barrier to intra-community trade without being justified by an overriding purpose in the general interest.

Selling arrangements

Worth mentioning here is another fundamental development of the law relating to the free movement of goods: the decision in *Keck and Mithouard*. In these two combined cases two supermarket managers were prosecuted for illegally selling goods below their purchase price. In their defence the accused agued that the law in question breached Article 28 of the EC treaty. This case prompted the ECJ to change course slightly and where indistinctly applicable MEQRs are concerned to ask for the impact of the measure.

After recalling its decision in **Cassis de Dijon**, that even indistinctly applicable rules laying down requirements to be met by goods could be in breach of Article 28 of the EC treaty, it stated (paras 16 and 17):

> By contrast, contrary to what had previously been decided, the application to products from other Member States of national provisions restricting or prohibiting certain selling arrangements is not such as to hinder, directly or indirectly, actually or potentially, trade between Member States within the meaning of *Dassonville* (Case 8/74) . . . provided that those provisions apply to all affected traders operating within the national territory and provided that they affect in the same manner, in law and fact, the marketing of domestic products and of those from other Member States. . . .

> Provided that those conditions are fulfilled, the application of such rules to the sale of products from another Member State meeting the requirements laid down by that State is not by nature such as to prevent their access to the market or to impede access any more than it impedes the access of domestic products. Such rules therefore fall outside the scope of Article 30 of the treaty (now article 28 of the EC treaty).

The result was that Article 28 of the EC treaty did not apply to a national measure imposing a general prohibition on resale at a loss, leaving Keck and Mithouard without a defence.

Thus, since **Keck and Mithouard**, where the measure was not designed to impinge on the product itself (the so-called requirements to be met by goods, for example by imposing certain ingredients, a particular size or form, or requiring a particular packaging or labeling of the product) but only constituted a selling arrangement (for example by regulating only which goods can be sold when, where or from whom), these measures had to be understood as to be outside the scope of Article 28 of the EC treaty.

The requirements are:

- an indistinctly applicable measure;
- which is a selling arrangement as opposed to a requirement to be met by the goods themselves; and
- providing it affects in the same manner, in law and in fact, domestic and foreign goods (the Keck-Proviso).

Measures understood to be selling arrangements outside the scope of Article 28 of the EC treaty include rules on shop opening hours (see **Tankstation 't Heukske and JBE Boermans**) and the sale through specific outlets (**Commission v. Greece (Processed Milk)**). In cases of advertising bans the European Court of Justice distinguished between partial bans which were held to be outside the scope of Article 28 of the EC treaty (see **Hünermund**, concerning legislation preventing pharmacists from advertising using certain mass media, and **Leclerc-Siplec** involving the prohibition of TV advertising by the distribution sector) and total bans, where the Court considered that a total ban might affect foreign goods more seriously and, thus, the Keck-Proviso needed to be applied (see

3

EUROPEAN UNION: LAWS AND INSTITUTIONS

De Agnostini and TV-Shop involving an outright advertising ban aimed at minors and *Gourmet International Products* concerning an absolute ban on advertising of alcohol). Where it could be shown that the foreign goods suffered a substantial disadvantage the measure was covered by Article 28 of the EC treaty, but still justifiable either under the 'Rule of Reason' or under Article 30 of the EC treaty.

FURTHER READING

Primary sources

Case C 158/04 *Alfa Vita Vissilopoulos AE* v. *Greece* [2006] ECR I-8135

Case C-441/04 *A-Punkt Schmuckhandels GmbH* v. *Schmidt* [2006] ECR I-2093

Case C-14/02 *ATRAL* [2003] ECR I-4431

Case C-2/90 *Commission* v. *Belgium (Walloon Waste)* [1992] ECR I-4431

Case 302/86 *Commission* v. *Denmark (Danish Bottles)* [1988] ECR 4607

Case 178/84 *Commission* v. *Germany (Beer Purity)* [1987] ECR 1227

Case C-391/92 *Commission* v. *Greece (Processed Milk)* [1995] ECR I-1621

Case 113/80 *Commission* v. *Ireland (Re Souvenir Jewellery)* [1981] ECR 1625

Cases C-34 to 36/95 *De Agnostini and TV-Shop* [1997] ECR I-3843

Case C-120/95 *Decker* [1998] ECR I-1831

Case 104/75 *De Peijper* [1976] ECR 613

Case C-112/00 *Eugen Schmidberger* v. *Austria* [2003] ECR I-5659

Case C-405/98 *Gourmet International Products* [2001] ECR I-1795

Case C-292/92 *Hünermund* [1993] ECR I-6787

Cases C-267 and 268/91 *Keck and Mithouard* [1993] ECR I-6097

Case 229/83 *Leclerc* v. *Au Blé Vert* [1985] ECR 1

Case C-412/93 *Leclerc-Siplec* [1995] ECR I-179

Case 304/84 *Ministère Public* v. *Muller* [1986] ECR 1511

Case C-416/00 *Morellato* v. *Comune di Padova* [2003] ECR I-9343

Case C-20/03 *Openbaar Ministerie* v. *Burmanjer* [2005] ECR I-4133

Case 8/74 *Procureur du Roi* v. *Dassonville* [1974] ECR 837

Case 120/78 *Rewe-Zentral AG* v. *Bundesmonopolverwaltung für Branntwein (Cassis de Dijon)* [1979] ECR 649

Cases C-401 and 402/94 *Tankstation 't Heukske and JBE Boermans* [1994] ECR I-2199

Case 261/81 *Walter Rau* v. *De Smedt* [1982] ECR 3961

Secondary sources

Oliver, P. (1982) 'Measures of Equivalent Effect: a Reappraisal' (1982) 19, *Common Market Law Review*, 217.

Oliver, P. (1999) 'Some Further Reflections on the Scope of Articles 28-30 (ex Articles 30-36) EC' (1999) 36, *Common Market Law Review*, 783.

Oliver, P. and Enchelmaier, S. (2007) 'Free Movement of Goods: recent developments in the case law' (2007) 44, *Common Market Law Review*, 649.

Storey, T. and Turner, C. (2005) *Unlocking EU Law*, Hodder Arnold, London, Chapter 13.

Weatherill, S. (1996) 'After Keck: Some Thoughts on how to Clarify the Clarification' (1996) 33, *Common Market Law Review*, 885.

Weatherill, S. (2006) 'Current Developments: European Law, Free Movement of Goods' (2006) 55, *International and Comparative Law Quarterly*, 457.

Weatherill, S. (2006) 'Recent developments in the law governing the free movements of goods in the EC's internal market' (2006) 2, *Common Market Law Review*, 90.

3

EUROPEAN UNION: LAWS AND INSTITUTIONS

Case 66/85 *Deborah Lawrie-Blum* v. *Land Baden-Württemberg* [1986] ECR 2121

Tony Storey, Northumbria University

The *Lawrie-Blum* case is arguably the leading case involving the free movement of workers in EU law. The case was decided by the European Court of Justice (ECJ), on a reference from the Federal Administrative Court in West Germany (as it was then). There were essentially two issues. The first was the interpretation to be given to the word 'worker', which appears in Article 39 of the EC treaty (previously Article 48 of the EEC treaty, prior to that treaty's re-naming and renumbering). The second was the scope to be given to the concept of 'public service' employment, which also appears in Article 39 EC.

The facts were as follows. Mrs Deborah Lawrie-Blum, a British national residing in Germany, was refused entry to the *vorbereitungsdienst*, a two-year teacher training course, purely on grounds of her nationality. Completion of the training course was a pre-requisite for teaching both in state and private schools in Germany. Under German law, persons admitted onto the training course are classed as a 'trainee teacher' and, in addition, given the status of 'temporary civil servant'. The problem for Mrs Lawrie-Blum was that, under the law of Baden-Württemberg, German nationality was essential for classification as a 'civil servant'.

Mrs Lawrie-Blum brought an action against the Land, contesting that the refusal to admit her onto the *vorbereitungsdienst* constituted a breach of Article 39(2) EC and/or Article 1 of Regulation 1612/68/EEC. The former provides that 'freedom of movement [of workers] shall entail the abolition of any discrimination based on nationality between workers of the member states as regards employment'.

Both the first-instance and appeal courts in Baden-Württemberg rejected her claim, on the basis that Article 39(4) excludes the application of Article 39(2) to 'employment in the public service'. On further appeal, to the Federal Administrative Court, the case was referred to the ECJ under the preliminary rulings procedure (Article 234 EC, formerly Article 177 EEC).

Definition of 'worker'

The first issue for the Court was whether Mrs Lawrie-Blum could be regarded as a 'worker'. Although the function of the ECJ under Article 234 EC is to deal purely with questions of interpretation, it is pertinent to point out that, if Mrs Lawrie-Blum were to be admitted to the *vorbereitungsdienst*, she would have received a salary and would (during the second year at least) have been required to teach up to eleven hours of classes per week, initially under supervision and later independently.

The Court held that Mrs Lawrie-Blum's putative status as a 'trainee teacher' did not prevent her from being regarded as a 'worker' for the purposes of Article 39 EC. The Court ruled that the word 'worker' 'must be given a community definition' (para. 14). The Court went on to define a 'worker' as 'a person who is obliged to provide services to another in return for monetary reward and who is subject to the direction or control of the other person as regards the way in which the work is done' (ibid.).

The reference to a 'worker' being 'obliged to provide services to another' and being 'subject to the direction or control of the other person as regards the way in which the work is done' is designed to draw a distinction between workers and the self-employed. The latter are protected by EU law, but not by Article 39 EC. Rather, their rights are contained in Articles 43 (freedom of establishment) and 49 (freedom to provide services) of the EC treaty.

The reference to 'monetary reward' should be viewed with caution. Three paragraphs later, the Court adopted a slightly different test, holding that 'the essential feature of an employment relationship is that for a certain period of time a person performs services for and under the direction of another in return for which he receives remuneration' (para. 17). The fact that 'monetary reward' is not actually a prerequisite has been confirmed in subsequent cases, most notably *Steymann* and *Trojani*.

The latter case involved a French national living in a Belgian Salvation Army hostel where he did various odd jobs for 'about 30 hours a week', in return for board and lodging and 'some pocket money', as part of a 'personal socio-occupational reintegration programme'. An issue arose regarding his status in Belgium and various questions were referred to the ECJ, including whether he was a 'worker'. The Court held that 'neither the *sui generis* nature of the employment relationship under national law, nor the level of productivity of the person concerned, the origin of the funds from which the remuneration is paid or the limited amount of the remuneration can have any consequence in regard to whether or not the person is a worker for the purposes of Community law'.

Even before *Lawrie-Blum* the ECJ had ruled that part-time and/or low paid employment still qualifies as 'work' provided the activities in question can be described as 'effective and genuine' as opposed to 'marginal and ancillary' (*Levin*). The fact that a worker has to supplement his or her income in order to subsist has also been held to be irrelevant. In *Kempf*, the ECJ held that 'A person in effective and genuine part-time employment cannot be excluded from [Article 39 EC] merely because the remuneration he derives from it is below the level of the minimum means of subsistence and he seeks to supplement it by other lawful means of subsistence'.

Although the ECJ in *Lawrie-Blum* refers to 'a certain period of time' as one of the 'essential features', the Court has consistently refused to impose any form of minimum working time period (either calculated on a daily, weekly or monthly basis). In *Ninni-Orasche* the ECJ explicitly refused to hold that the fact that an Italian national had been employed for 2½ months over a period of three years in Austria automatically excluded her from the scope of Article 39 EC. Ultimately, whether or not she was a 'worker' was a question of fact for the national court, applying the 'effective and genuine' activities test.

3

EUROPEAN UNION: LAWS AND INSTITUTIONS

1. Trainees as workers

As far as Mrs Lawrie-Blum being a 'trainee teacher', the Court held that this was irrelevant. The Court held that 'The fact that teachers' preparatory service, like apprenticeships in other occupations, may be regarded as practical preparation directly related to the actual pursuit of the occupation in point is not a bar to the application of [Article 39 EC]' (para. 19). *Lawrie-Blum* was followed on this point in *Bernini*, where the ECJ stated that such a conclusion 'cannot be invalidated by the fact that the trainee's productivity is low, that he works only a small number of hours per week and, consequently, receives limited remuneration'. The Court did impose a proviso in *Bernini*, holding that 'the national court is entitled, when assessing the genuine and effective nature of the services in question, to examine whether in all the circumstances the person concerned has completed a sufficient number of hours in order to familiarize himself with the work.'

More recently, in *Kranemann* (which involved the inverse of *Lawrie-Blum*, with the complainant, a German national, undergoing training – specifically legal training – in the UK), the ECJ confirmed again that a trainee could satisfy the status of 'worker'. The Court observed that trainee lawyers are 'required to apply in practice the legal knowledge acquired during their course of study and thus make a contribution, under the guidance of the employer providing them with training, to that employer's activities and trainees receive payment in the form of a maintenance allowance for the duration of their training'. The Court actually concluded that because 'trainee lawyers carry out genuine and effective activity as an employed person they must be considered to be workers'. This is a relatively unusual step for the ECJ which normally contents itself with laying down abstract guidance and then inviting the national courts to apply it to the facts of the case.

2. Public service derogation

A worker employed in the 'public service' is not covered by the freedom to work provisions in the EC treaty (Article 39(4) EC). Given that member states could exploit this derogation in order to limit the freedom of immigrant workers to undertake employment, it has therefore been restrictively interpreted by the ECJ. First, it only applies to *access to* employment, not *conditions of* employment after access had been granted (*Sotgiu* v. *Deutsche Bundespost*).

More significantly, the ECJ has held that Article 39(4) EC does not apply to *all* employment in the public service, only 'certain activities' involving the exercise of official authority. In *Commission* v. *Belgium*, the ECJ stated that in disputed cases it was necessary to identify 'whether or not the posts in question are typical of the specific activities of the public service in so far as the exercise of powers conferred by public law and responsibility for safeguarding the general interests of the State are vested in it'.

Further guidance was given in *Lawrie-Blum*. The Land had argued that teachers were employed in the 'public service', asserting that specific activities such as lesson preparation, awarding marks to pupils, and deciding whether or not pupils should progress to a higher class, all required 'the exercise of powers conferred by public law'. It was further argued by the Land that education, the general activity of teaching itself, helped to 'safeguard the general interests of the State'.

The ECJ held first that Article 39(4) EC 'must be construed in such a way as to limit its scope to what is strictly necessary for safeguarding the interests which that provision allows the Member States to protect'. The Court expressly ruled out any possibility that simply classifying 'trainee teachers' as 'civil servants' allowed the Member States to invoke Article 39(4). Citing earlier authority (*Commission v. France*, where the Court had held that nurses were not employed in the 'public service'), the Court held that 'to make the application of [Article 39(4)] dependent on the legal nature of the relationship between the employee and the administration would enable the Member States to determine at will the posts covered by the exception laid down in that provision'.

The Court repeated its test from *Commission v. Belgium*, adding that 'public service' posts also required 'a special relationship of allegiance to the State on the part of persons occupying them and reciprocity of rights and duties which form the foundation of the bond of nationality'. Applying its own test, the Court held that 'trainee teachers' did not operate in the 'public service'.

This narrow reading of Article 39(4) has been confirmed subsequently. In *Colegio de Oficiales de la Marina Mercante Española*, involving a Spanish legal prohibition of foreign nationals holding positions as ship's captain, the ECJ held that it was possible that such a post did fall within Article 39(4), given the range of powers and duties exercised. However, the Court said that it was 'necessary that such rights are in fact exercised on a regular basis by those holders and do not represent a very minor part of their activities'. The Court added that the scope of the Article 39(4) EC derogation 'must be limited to what is strictly necessary for safeguarding the general interests of the Member State concerned, which cannot be imperilled if rights under powers conferred by public law are exercised only sporadically, even exceptionally, by nationals of other Member States'.

The role of EU citizenship

Cases involving Article 39 EC and the definition of the word 'worker' continue to reach the ECJ – at the time of writing, *Rockler* and *Öberg*. However, there is a parallel development which does somewhat undermine the significance of *Lawrie-Blum* and the other 'worker' cases: EU citizenship.

The concept of EU citizenship was only introduced in November 1993, when several new provisions were inserted into the EC treaty, including Articles 17 and 18 EC, by the Treaty on European Union. Article 17 EC provides that 'Citizenship of the Union is hereby established. Every person holding the nationality of a Member State shall be a citizen of the Union. Citizenship of the Union shall complement and not replace national citizenship.' Moreover, Article 18(1) EC states that 'Every citizen of the Union shall have the right to move and reside freely within the territory of the Member States, subject to the limitations and conditions laid down in the Treaty and by the measures adopted to give it effect'.

In case *Baumbast and R v. Home Secretary*, the ECJ held that Article 18 EC was directly effective, that is, it could be relied upon by EU citizens, to claim a rights of residence in other EU member states. Although Article 18 EC was subject to certain 'limitations and conditions', the Court held that this did not deprive it of direct effect. The ECJ held that the competent authorities of the member state and, where necessary, national courts, must ensure that those limitations and conditions were applied in compliance with the general principles of EU law and, in particular, the principle of proportionality.

3

EUROPEAN UNION: LAWS AND INSTITUTIONS

Moreover, the Court has also held that EU citizens lawfully resident in a state other than their own could invoke Article 12 EC – the general prohibition of discrimination on grounds of nationality. This has allowed, for example, unemployed Spanish nationals resident in Germany to bring challenges to allegedly discriminatory provisions of German law (*Martínez Sala*) and French students lawfully resident in Belgium and the UK respectively to challenge allegedly discriminatory national legal rules (*Grzelczyk* and *Bidar*).

A twenty-first century Deborah Lawrie-Blum would not, strictly speaking, need to establish 'worker' status given that, as a British national she is simultaneously a citizen of the EU (Article 17), entitled to reside in Germany (Article 18) and, finally, entitled not to be discriminated against by virtue of her nationality (Article 12).

FURTHER READING

Primary sources

Case C-413/99 *Baumbast and R* v. *Home Secretary* [2002] ECR 1-7091

Case C-209/03 *Bidar* [2005] ECR I-2119

Case C-405/01 *Colegio de Oficiales de la Marina Mercante Española* [2003] ECR I-10391

Case 149/79 *Commission* v. *Belgium* [1980] ECR 3881

Case 307/84 *Commission* v. *France* [1986] ECR 1725

Case C-184/99 *Grzelczyk* [2001] ECR I-6193

Case 139/85 *Kempf* [1986] ECR 1741

Case C-109/04 *Kranemann* [2005] ECR I-2421

Case 53/81 *Levin* [1982] ECR 1035

Case C-85/96 *Martínez Sala* [1998] ECR I-2691

Case C-413/01 *Ninni-Orasche* [2003] ECR I-13187

Case C-185/04 *Öberg* [2006] ECR I-1453

Case C-137/04 *Rockler* [2006] ECR I-1441

Case 152/73 *Sotgiu* v. *Deutsche Bundespost* [1974] ECR 153

Case 196/87 *Steymann* [1988] ECR 6159

Case C-456/02 *Trojani* [2004] ECR I-7573

Secondary sources

Castro-Oliviera (2002) 'Workers & Other Persons: Step-by-step from Movement to Citizenship – Case law 1995–2001' (2002) 39, *CML Rev*, 77.

Handoll (1988) 'Article 48(4) and Non-national Access to Public Employment' (1988) 13, *EL Rev*, 223.

Mather (2005) 'The Court of Justice and the Union Citizen' (2005) 11, *ELJ*, 722.

Morris, Fredman and Hayes (1990) 'Free Movement and the Public Sector' (1990) 19, *ILJ*, 20.

White (2005) 'Free Movement, Equal Treatment, and Citizenship of the Union' (2005) 54, *ICLQ*, 885.

Freedom to provide services

Case C-76/90 *Säger* v. *Dennemeyer* [1991] ECR I-4221

Eva Joyce, Anglia Ruskin University

The freedom to provide services was initially seen as the least important of the fundamental freedoms under the treaty but there have been an increasing number of cases before the ECJ involving this freedom. This is not perhaps surprising given that, according to the Commission, around 70% of GDP in many member states is accounted for by the service industry. The cases cover a very broad range of circumstances including tourism, medical, financial and business services, the transmission of television programmes, the provision of workers by employment agencies, gambling, transport, bank loans, insurance and sports.

The free movement rights for individuals including legal individuals is granted by the EC treaty to workers, the self-employed and companies in Articles 39 (ex 48), 43 (ex 52) and 49 (ex 59) and the ECJ has stated, for example in *Gebhard*, that the freedoms granted under the three Articles are mutually exclusive. In particular, Article 49, the main concern of this chapter, necessarily excludes the freedom of establishment by its wording. The freedom to provide services includes, under Article 50 (ex 60), activities of an industrial and/commercial character and the activities of professionals and craftsmen.

The freedom of establishment and the freedom to provide services have much in common in terms of the issues that have exercised the court. One of these is about qualification requirements for professionals. On the other hand, it is suggested by many, including Francis Jacobs, who was the advocate general in *Säger* itself, that the freedom to provide services is, or should be, sensibly seen as analogous to the free movement of goods under Article 28 (ex 30) as described in the *Cassis de Dijon* line of cases because of the similarities in the reasoning and approach of the ECJ. The case law has developed along similar lines in respect of indistinctly applicable national measures.

In terms of national professional regulations, which is the focus of this chapter, AG Jacobs distinguishes between a person who is established in a member state, who ought, not unreasonably, to comply with the law of that member state in respect of the commercial activity that he undertakes and a person established in one member state who provides services in another member state or states. If the provider of services were to be made to comply with the rules of all the member states in which he provides services then the idea of the single market as a reality becomes untenable. This fits with the ECJ's reasoning that the basis of the free movement of goods ought to be trust, such that the receiving member state ought to presume that a good that has been lawfully produced and thus is lawfully marketed in one member state can thereafter be freely marketed in the host state without any need for compliance with further

EUROPEAN UNION: LAWS AND INSTITUTIONS

3

national regulations. The principle of free movement in services, however, gives rise to more complex issues than the free movement of goods because the service industry is more varied than the marketing of physical goods.

Very early on in the development of this case law, the ECJ ruled that a necessary corollary of the freedom to provide services is the freedom to receive services. Furthermore, the requirement that there has to be an inter-state effect before the jurisdiction of the ECJ is to be invoked has been weakened so that many cases are concerned with issues that, in another context, might have been ruled to be purely internal matters. Finally, as with the free movement of goods, an important issue under this heading too is that of access to markets.

Säger v. *Dennemeyer*

This case is important because the ECJ sets out and explains the general principles that are to be applied to the freedom to provide services and the general approach that a national court should take where there is a dispute. More specifically the court in this case addressed the issue of whether Article 49 applied to national measures which were not discriminatory.

The problem that individuals have met in the establishment and services cases resides in the national differences between professional rules of conduct, ethics and/or qualifications for professionals. Qualification and training rules are likely to be the most disparate. (Professional rules of conduct and qualification rules could also affect migrant workers but the context for the case law has generally been the self-employed and companies.) Most professions in the member states are controlled by a professional body which lays down the rules of practice. While such rules are likely to have some similarities they nevertheless will have been formulated within a particular culture and tradition which is likely to result in differences.

Taking the example of a lawyer, which admittedly is an extreme case (there are fewer differences of qualification/training for an architect, doctor, nurse, plumber, hairdresser), the salient question to ask is: to what extent should an advocate, for example, qualified as such in Greece, say, be made subject to qualification requirements when she wishes to practise as a rechtsanwalt in Germany? This was one of the issues in *Vlassopoulou*, an establishment case. The qualification question is particularly important for lawyers because the laws and legal systems of the member states are different.

The rules at issue in *Säger* v. *Dennemeyer*, however, were the German requirements for patent agents. Säger, a qualified patent agent working as such in Munich, brought an action in a German court seeking an injunction to prevent Dennemeyer, an English company, from providing services in Germany. The company provided a patent renewal service, that is, it stored information about its clients' patents and informed such clients when the annual renewal fees were due. For some clients who requested it, Dennemeyer also paid the fees on their behalf. One reason for the action by Säger was that Dennemeyer's commission payable for the service was lower than the fees generally charged by German patent agents who provided the same service. Thus, one of the pleadings in Säger's action was that Dennemeyer was involved in unfair competition.

Under German law the position seemed to be (there was some uncertainty about the meaning and effect of the provisions) that only a lawyer, a patent agent or the holder of a licence issued pursuant to the German law could provide such services. Further, under German law a licence could only be issued to a human individual not to a company and therefore Dennemeyer could not obtain one and the particular activity in which Dennemeyer was engaged could only be carried out by patent agents – in effect patent agents had a monopoly on the service in Germany.

The questions asked of the ECJ were interpreted by that court to amount to a request for interpretation of Article 49 (ex 59): whether the licensing requirement was prohibited by it. Specifically, Article 49 prohibits restrictions on the freedom to provide services in respect of nationals who are established in a member state other than that of the person for whom the service is provided. Thus there is no clear indication in the treaty as to what kind of restrictions are to be prohibited or whether there is to be any possibility of justifying restrictions.

First, the court said in para. 13 of *Säger* that if a person wanting to provide services in another member state had to comply with all the regulations in place in the host member state (where the service is provided) then Article 49 would be deprived of all practical effect. In other words there would be no difference between establishment and the provision of services, no point in having two separate treaty articles.

Having been informed that an earlier case in a German court had established that German law reserved the payment of patent fees to a patent agent, the ECJ had to address the question of whether such reservation was prohibited by Article 49. The words of Article 49, it should be noted, are in wide terms that restrictions to the freedom shall be prohibited. Without going into any details and without citing any authority, the Court stated that the Article prohibited non-discriminatory measures if they impeded or were likely to impede the free movement of services. This was an issue at this time: whether Article 49 was designed to catch discriminatory measures only or was it also to prohibit measures that, as in this case, were indistinctly applicable.

It will be remembered that it was in *Cassis de Dijon* that the ECJ ruled, in the context of the free movement of goods, that indistinctly applicable national measures were prohibited by Article 28 of the treaty if they actually or potentially had an adverse affect on inter-state trade. The court in *Säger* took the same approach.

The limitation, in effect to reserve the activity to the person who had the prescribed qualifications, was a restriction within Article 49 because it prevented economic operators outside of Germany from providing the services: it prevented access to that market by non-German patent service providers. In addition, it prevented patent holders in Germany from freely choosing by whom their patent renewal was to be monitored.

Some imposition of rules by the host member state may not be incompatible with the treaty, said the ECJ in *Säger*, if such rules were justified by 'imperative requirements relating to the public interest'. Again, in this aspect of the ruling the link with the *Cassis* approach is clearly discernible. There is no mention of a public interest justification in the treaty in the chapter on goods, nor in that on services but the ECJ has filled the gaps.

3

EUROPEAN UNION: LAWS AND INSTITUTIONS

It will be recalled that the head of justification in *Cassis* itself for indistinctly applicable national measures was called (or translated as) 'mandatory requirements'. Whichever of these two phrases is used, they mean the same thing. The question is: does the public interest require the imposition of a limitation to a fundamental treaty freedom? The answer is that such a limitation will only be imperative/mandatory if the interest is not already adequately protected in the member state in which the service provider is established.

The Court went on to say that the limitation to the freedom must be objectively necessary and the proportionality principle was to be applied. The fundamental freedom is broadly construed by the Court whereas the limitation on that freedom is to be narrowly construed. The ECJ then applied the principles to the facts. The Court does not have jurisdiction to do this under the Article 234 (ex 177) reference procedure but it was no doubt helpful to the referring court. The ECJ made clear that the aim of the German measures was to protect recipients of services from being given legal advice by unqualified persons. But Dennemeyer were not giving legal advice. The ECJ said that whereas the public interest did indeed justify the limitation on the giving of advice by non-qualified persons, the German measures in place to protect that public interest were disproportionate.

Thus, the general rule is that non-discriminatory rules may be justified as long as they are not disproportionate. In more detail, this is to say that where there is already regulation in the state where the service provider is established and by which, therefore, he is bound, the host state may impose further regulation only if such further regulation is justified by imperative reasons in the public interest which are not already protected by the state of establishment and if the objective of such regulation cannot be achieved by less restrictive means.

Other issues within the freedom to provide services

As is clear from the cases under Article 49 (ex 59), for example, *Gebhard*, a provider of services may temporarily reside in the member state where the services are provided or could, as in the *Säger* case, conduct its activities by post, telecommunications, including the internet. Dennemeyer did not go to Germany on behalf of its clients but nevertheless those activities had effects in Germany when the company paid fees for its clients.

In these days of 'virtual' communications, many services cases in fact have involved a scenario where the service moves while the provider stays at home. This could be by fax or telephone, by email, via the internet or through cable, as in cable TV. An early case in point was that of *Bond* which involved the transmission of advertisements (and programmes) into the Netherlands from Luxembourg. Advertising is a very important aspect of the formation of the single market because it is arguably the easiest way for a company to penetrate another member state. Some services, by contrast, involve a movement by both service provider and the user of the service as for example is involved in air transport. Although the focus of this chapter has been a professional regulatory scheme that apparently protected a national monopoly, it should be noted that many of the barriers that exist between member states are the result of the sheer volume of regulatory systems which are not necessarily the result of protectionism. The rules also tend to be more complex than the rules that may affect the free movement of goods.

The interpretation of Article 49 is seen by many as the pivot for market liberalisation. It is argued that this approach, the breaking down of barriers by the ECJ's rulings, enters into new arenas, rules of private sporting bodies, for example, and thus goes too far. Not only is there the risk that it ignores cultural signifiers but also, it is suggested, the Treaty was never intended to apply to rules governing private associations. One context for such critique is sport. Another difficult area has been where the issue of public morality was in play as in the Irish cases concerning the provision of abortion services and the British case involving *in vitro* fertilisation (**Blood**).

A further issue is that of 'healthcare tourism' where a patient obtains medical treatment in a member state which is not his own. Should a member state pay for medical or health services received in another member state when the home state provides the same services? The national regulation that has been challenged by a number of recipients of health care who have failed to receive reimbursement when they returned home is the requirement to obtain national authorisation before receiving the treatment elsewhere. The ECJ's approach is that Article 49 applies to services that are provided for remuneration and therefore the prior authorisation rule has been held to be contrary to the treaty. The uncertainty that remains is the line between publicly and privately funded health services.

Qualification, mutual recognition and the Services Directive

The *Säger* case was not directly concerned with qualifications although in essence the practice of a patent agent was limited under German law by the possession of the relevant qualifications.

The approach advocated by the UK, intervening, in *Säger* was to wait for sectoral directives for such freedoms. The ECJ rejected the argument. For many professions there were, at the time, specific sectoral directives to spell out the circumstances for the mutual recognition of qualifications both for establishment and for the provision of services. The general approach has been that if a person has a qualification in one member state that qualification ought normally to be recognised in another member state. All the sectoral directives, except for the two for lawyers, have since been replaced by Directive 2005/36 which consolidates the mutual recognition of professional qualifications.

The other significant change since *Säger* is the adoption of Directive 2006/123 which, controversially, provides for the general liberalisation of service provision within the Community which aims, among other things, to simplify procedural obstacles to this fundamental freedom.

FURTHER READING

Primary sources

Case C-384/93 *Alpine Investments BV* v. *Minister van Financiën* [1995] ECR I-1141

Case 352/85 *Bond van Adverteerders and Others* v. *Netherlands* [1988] ECR 2085

Case C-422/01 *Försäkringsaktiebolaget Skandia* v. *Riksskatterverket* [2003] ECR I-68817

Case C-55/94 *Gebhard* v. *Consiglio dell'Ordine degli Avvocati e Procuratori di Milano* [1995] I-4165

R v. *Human Fertilisation and Embryology Authority ex parte Blood* [1997] 2 CMLR 591

Case C-158/96 *Kohll* [1998] ECR I-1931

Case C-405/98 *Konsumenombudsmannen* v. *Gourmet International Products* [2001] ECR I-1795

Case 120/78 *Rewe-Zentrale AG* v. *Bundesmonopolverwaltung für Branntwein (Cassis de Dijon)* [1979] ECR 649

Case C-76/90 *Säger* v. *Dennemeyer* [1991] ECR I-4221

Case C-275/92 *Schindler* [1994] ECR I-1039

Case C-159/90 *SPUC* v. *Grogan and Others* [1991] ECR I-4685

Case 33/74 *van Binsbergen* v. *Bestuur van de Bedrijfsvereniging voor de Metaalnijverheid* [1974] ECR 1229

Case C-340/89 *Vlassopoulou* v. *Ministrium fur Justiz* [1993] 2 CMLR 221

Case 36/74 *Walrave and Koch* v. *Association Union Cycliste Internationale* [1974] ECR 1405

Case C-372/04 *Watts* v. *Bedford Primary Care Trust* [2006] ECR I-4325

Secondary sources

Art, J. (1992) 'Legislative Lacunae: the Court of Justice and Freedom to Provide Services' in Curtin, D. and O'Keeffe, D. (eds) *Constitutional Adjudication in European Community Law and National Law*, Butterworths, Ireland.

Commission (2002) 'The State of the Internal Market for Services', COM, 441.

Daniele, L. (1997) 'Non-Discriminatory Restrictions to the Free Movement of Persons' (1997) 22, *European Law Review*, 191.

Davies, G. (2002) 'Welfare as a Service' [2002] *LIEI*, 27.

Hatzopoulos, V. and Do, T. (2006) 'The Case Law of the ECJ Concerning the Free Provision of Services 2000–2005' (2006) 43, *Common Market Law Review*, 923.

Jones, C. (1999, 2000) 'Television Without Frontiers', YEL, 299.

O'Leary, S. and Fernández-Martin, J. (2002) 'Judicially Created Exceptions to Free Provision of Services' in Andenas, M. and Roth, W.H. (eds) *Services and Free Movement in EU Law*, Oxford.

Roth, W. (2002) 'The European Court of Justice's Case Law on Freedom to Provide Services: is Keck relevant?' in Andenas, M. and Roth, W. (eds) *Services and Free Movement in EU Law*, Oxford.

Steyger, E. (2002) 'National Health Systems Under Fire (but not too heavily)' (2002) 29, *LIEI* 97, 106.

Van der Woude, M. and Meade, P. (1998) 'Free Movement of the Tourist in Community Law' (1998) 25, *Common Market Law Review*, 117.

Van Nuffel, P. (2005) 'Patients' Free Movement Rights and Cross Border Access to Healthcare' (2005) 12(3), *MJ*, 253.

Weatherill, S. (2000) 'The Helsinki Report of Sport' (2000) 25, *European Law Review*, 282.

Case 43/75 *Defrenne* v. *Société Anonyme Belge de Navigation Aerienne (SABENA)*
[1976] ECR 455, [1976] 2 CMLR 98 (*aka Defrenne II*)

Nicole Busby, University of Stirling

The principle of equality between the sexes is now recognised as a cornerstone of EC law and there are numerous legislative instruments and a plethora of case law to support its application. However, despite the reference to 'equal pay for equal work' in Article 119 (now 141) of the Treaty of Rome, the impact of European law on the further-ance of social as well as economic objectives was not widely acknowledged in the early days of European integration.

In the early 1970s a Belgian air hostess commenced proceedings against her employers which resulted in three early references for preliminary rulings under the Article 177 EC (now Article 234) procedure. Gabrielle Defrenne's litigation was based on the various forms of discrimination she had been subjected to on the grounds of her sex and the most celebrated of the cases, referred to widely as *Defrenne II*, concerns her equal pay claim.

The European Court of Justice's ruling in this case is interesting in three important respects: it added to the developing jurisprudence on the direct effect of treaty provi-sions; it dealt with the difficult policy issue of retroactivity in claims for damages; and, perhaps most importantly, it laid the foundations for the future development of EC sex equality law and formed the basis of the European Court of Justice's relationship with what has become known as 'the social dimension'.

The facts were as follows. Gabrielle Defrenne, an air hostess, brought an action for compensation against the airline that employed her on the grounds of discrimination in pay. From February 1963 until February 1966, she had been paid less than men who were doing the same job. Her employers did not dispute that the work performed by male air stewards and female air hostesses was the same or that there was discrimina-tion in the rates of pay applicable to men and women. As there was no remedy avail-able under Belgian law for gender-based pay discrimination, Ms Defrenne sought to rely on Article 119 (now 141). Article 119 set out the principle that men and women 'should receive equal pay for equal work'. The Belgian appeal court, the Cour du Tra-vail, referred the case to the European Court of Justice for a preliminary ruling under Article 234 (ex 177) on two counts. First, whether Article 119 of the Treaty of Rome was directly effective, in other words, whether its inclusion in the treaty introduced the principle of equal pay for equal work directly into the national law of each member state, thereby entitling workers to institute proceedings before national courts to ensure its observance and, if so, from which date. Second, the Cour du Travail asked if

Article 119 was directly applicable in member states or whether its application depended on it being adopted by national law.

The application of Article 119 to the Defrenne case was in relation to obligations which fall on individuals (i.e. employer and employee). This is known as horizontal direct effect. Vertical direct effect arises where a treaty obligation falls on a member state itself and reflects the relationship between the individual and the state (Van Duyn). Ms Defrenne's reliance on Article 119 arose due to the Belgian legislature's reluctance to implement the principle of equal pay into national law. Belgium was not alone in failing to fulfil its obligation in this way. Article 119 was intended to be implemented by member states by the end of the transitional period (December 1961). Although this deadline was moved to the end of 1964, it had still not been met at that date by several member states. The Commission had threatened to bring infringement proceedings against member states not complying by July 1973, but this threat was never carried out. In February 1975 the Council issued the Equal Pay Directive (75/117/EC) for implementation in states by July 1976.

The aim of Article 119

In considering the objectives set out in the Treaty of Rome, the Court identified the underlying rationale for the inclusion of Article 119 (now 141) thus:

> Article 119 [now 141] pursues a double aim. First, in the light of the different states of the development of social legislation in the various Member States, the aim of Article 119 is to avoid a situation in which undertakings established in States which have actually implemented the principle of equal pay suffer a competitive disadvantage in intra-Community competition as compared with undertakings established in States which have not yet eliminated discrimination against women workers as regards pay.

> Secondly, this provision forms part of the social objectives of the Community, which is not merely an economic union, but is at the same time intended, by common action, to ensure social progress and seek the constant development of the living and working conditions of their peoples . . . This double aim which is at once economic and social, shows that the principle of equal pay forms part of the foundations of the community.

In its clear recognition of the existence of the social as well as economic objectives of Community law, the Court can be said to have refocused the scope of the founding treaty and, thus, assured the future development of European Community sex discrimination law. This aspect was highly controversial at the time of the ruling. The newly established European Economic Community was viewed primarily as a vehicle for the avoidance of future armed conflict in Europe which, it was envisaged would best be achieved through the attainment of economic prosperity and market integration. The remainder of the social provisions within the treaty are drafted in a manner which appears aspirational rather than likely to give rise to specific legal rights. The Court's interpretation of Article 119 as being capable of giving individually enforceable rights has been central to its subsequent jurisprudence on sex equality and has also served as an important foundation for the establishment of a European social dimension to the law-making capacity of the EC institutions.

Equal pay as a 'principle'

In its ruling, the European Court stated that the fact that Article 119 referred to equal pay as a 'principle' gave it a specific status within the European legal order which made it 'impossible to put forward an argument against its direct effect' (para. 28). The subjective nature of Article 119's wording meant that the scope of 'equal pay' and 'equal work' would have to be determined by the Court. On the issue of the horizontal application of Article 119, the Court found that the Article was directly effective and not limited to public authorities but also covered the relationship between individuals as 'the fact that certain provisions of the treaty are formally addressed to the member states does not prevent rights from being conferred at the same time on any individual who has an interest in the duties thus laid down' (para. 31). This means that the rights bestowed by Article 119 apply directly to individuals and do not require implementation by member states. The Article can, thus, be utilised against employers in both the public and private sectors without the need for equivalent rights under domestic legislation. In such cases, applicants must rely on the precise wording of the Article which becomes part of domestic law. It follows that in cases of conflict between the provisions of domestic law and Article 119, the latter must prevail.

On the issue of legal certainty, although Article 119 was found to be 'sufficiently precise' to be capable of having direct effect, the Court drew a distinction between 'direct and overt discrimination' and 'indirect and disguised discrimination' in the pay of men and women. The former, the Court held, is prohibited by Article 119 which is directly effective in this respect as it can be identified by national courts 'solely with the aid of the criteria based on equal work and equal pay referred to by the Article'. However, the prohibition of the latter by Article 119 lacked sufficient precision to be directly effective as it could be identified only by 'reference to more explicit implementing provisions of a Community or national character' (page 143). This distinction has been set aside over the intervening years so that Article 141 has been held to have direct effect in certain circumstances in which a finding of indirect rather than direct sex discrimination has been made – most notably in relation to inequalities of pay between part-time and full-time workers – see *Bilka-Kaufhaus*.

The temporal limitation

Retroactive application of the ruling was not allowed and a temporal limitation was imposed so that the judgment was only effective for the future. This meant that, with the exception of claims already submitted at the date of the ruling, back pay could not be claimed in respect of inequalities of pay relating to periods of service prior to that time. The Court was clear that limitations of the temporal effect of a ruling is an exceptional measure which should only be imposed on the grounds of legal certainty if the effects of the ruling would have a seriously disruptive effect – in this case the large numbers of back-dated claims that would otherwise have been submitted would have had serious financial consequences for many organisations. Nevertheless, the imposition of such a limitation has been criticised as a blatant example of judicial law-making by which the furtherance of social objectives are subordinated to the economic imperative. For a subsequent use of the imposition of a temporal limitation see *Barber* and, more recently, *Preston* on the application of Article 141 to occupational pension schemes.

Developments since *Defrenne II*

In giving its ruling, the Court isolated the stated principle of Article 119 - equal pay for equal work - and sidestepped consideration of the more complex, and wide-reaching, question of equal value. This is reflective of the conditions of the time in which blatant sex-based inequalities in pay of the kind identified in the *Defrenne* litigation were common-place. Equal value, as a concept on which claims could be based, was very much in its infancy. In the intervening years, equal value has emerged as the most progressive provision on which to base claims and is now widely utilised. As the Court's jurisprudence since *Defrenne II* has demonstrated, the ruling certainly has application in claims relating to work of equal value as well as work which is the same or broadly similar to that performed by a suitable comparator as it is the core principle of Article 119 which was considered to be sufficiently precise rather than the effect of its application in what might be considered less precise circumstances. Furthermore, subsequent legislative developments have seen the principle expanded, in part to take account of jurisprudential factors.

Although Article 141 (ex 119) provided the only specific reference to equal treatment contained in the Treaty of Rome, it has served as a basis on which the principle of non-discrimination has been expanded beyond the originally narrow confines of equal pay. The Treaty of Amsterdam made some important amendments in this respect, most notably by pronouncing 'equality between men and women' as one of the goals outlined in Article 2. Article 141 has itself been expanded to provide explicitly for the application of equal pay for 'work of equal value' in addition to the original reference to 'equal work' and also refers to the principle of equal treatment in respect of action to promote equality.

In making its ruling in *Defrenne II*, the Court's primary concerns were that member states should not be able to escape obligations imposed by European law simply by refusing to transpose key principles into national law and that tardiness on the part of Community institutions should not be able to hamper the development of the Community's aims. This was particularly important in the social context as the institutions of the time lacked the political will to prise open the window of opportunity presented by the Treaty's inclusion of Article 119. Instead this was left to the European Court of Justice which, in its recognition of the EEC as a social as well as economic Community, laid the foundations for future development. In this respect, *Defrenne II* should be acknowledged as a pivotal case which helped to create an appropriate environment for the Court's involvement in the birth of social action.

FURTHER READING

Primary sources

Case 262/88 *Barber* v. *Guardian Royal Exchange* [1990] ECR 1944

Case 170/84 *Bilka-Kaufhaus GmBH* v. *Weber con Hartz* [1986] ECR 1607

Case 109/88 *Danfoss* [1989] ECR 3100

Case 96/80 *Jenkins* v. *Kingsgate (Clothing Productions) Ltd* [1981] 2 CMLR 241

Case C-78/98 *Preston and Fletcher* v. *Wolverhampton NHS Healthcare Trust* [2000] ECR I-3201

Case 41/74 *Van Duyn* v. *Home Office* [1974] ECR 1337

Secondary sources

Busby, N. (2001) 'Only a Matter of Time' (2001) 64, *Modern Law Review*, 489.

Craig, P. and de Búrca, G. (1998) *EU Law: Text, Cases and Materials*, OUP, Oxford, 172-173.

Fredman, S. (1992) 'European Community discrimination law: a critique' (1992) 21, *Industrial Law Journal*, 119.

McCrudden, C. (1993) 'The Effectiveness of European Equality Law: National Mechanisms for Enforcing Gender Equality Laws in the Light of European Requirements' (1993) 13, *Oxford Journal of Legal Studies*, 320.

Szyszczak, E. (2000) *EC Labour Law*, Longman.

3

EUROPEAN UNION: LAWS AND INSTITUTIONS

Competition law: cartels (Article 81)

Cases 56/64 and 58/64 *Etablissements Consten SA and Grundig-Verkaufs-GmbH* v. *EEC Commission* [1966] ECR 299, [1966] CMLR 418

(hereafter references will be made to the CMLR version)

Emmanuel Guinchard, Northumbria University

Competition law is known in Germany as 'Kartellrecht'. This name reflects the import-ance of the provisions that deal with the combinations of undertakings which agree to restrict competition and which are commonly known as cartels. In the European Com-munity the relevant provision is Article 81 of the EC Treaty (ex-Article 85). With the *Grundig* case the ECJ had one of its first opportunities to rule on Article 81.

The facts were quite straightforward. Grundig, a then well-known German manufacturer of electrical goods, had concluded a sole distribution agreement with Consten, a French company. Specifically, Grundig granted Consten the exclusive right to sell its products in France and to register its trademark GINT (Grundig International) there. In addition, it imposed on all its other distributors a prohibition on exports outside their contract terri-tory (and therefore to France). In return, Consten undertook not to sell like-products in France or to deliver Grundig products abroad. Consten was thus secured the full French market for Grundig's products. Consten also agreed to buy a minimum number of prod-ucts, promote them and offer customers appropriate service (for example, repairs).

For several reasons this agreement came to the knowledge of the European Commis-sion who decided that it infringed Article 81(1), which prohibits various cartels, and was therefore automatically void and null under Article 81(2) since it could not be exempted under Article 81(3). Consten and Grundig challenged this decision before the ECJ. In its judgment the Court established a number of principles on the application of Article 81, including its place among EC objectives.

The prohibition in Article 81(1)

According to Article 81(1) 'all agreements between undertakings, decisions by associations of undertakings and concerted practices which may affect trade between member states and which have as their object or effect the prevention, restriction or distortion of compe-tition within the common market' are prohibited. This is followed by a non-exhaustive list of examples of anti-competitive practices such as price fixing and market sharing.

There is no definition of an 'undertaking' given in the EC treaty. The ECJ has, however, construed this term widely. It held that the legal form of the entity in question is not an issue for the purposes of EC competition rules (*Höfner and Elser* v. *Macroton GmbH*).

Moreover, the way in which the entity is financed, and therefore the fact that it may not be profit-making, is irrelevant. As Advocate-General Jacobs put it, 'the basic test is whether the entity in question is engaged in an activity which could, at least in principle, be carried on by a private undertaking in order to make profits' (*Albany International BV v. SBT*, paragraph 311). This is to be contrasted with, for example, the exercise of official authority such as 'the exercise of powers relating to the control and supervision of air space' (*SAT Fluggesellschaft v. Eurocontrol*, para. 30).

In the *Grundig* case, Consten and Grundig were without any doubt undertakings within the meaning of Article 81(1). They had concluded a written agreement and thus clearly colluded. This saved the Commission the sometimes difficult task of ascertaining the existence of an agreement since the wide interpretation given to this term by the ECJ is not without limit and requires some form of consent between the parties (CFI, 26 October 2003, case T-41/96, *Bayer AG v. Commission*, upheld by the ECJ, 6 January 2004, case C-2 and 3/01). Two undertakings agreed but did this behaviour affect trade between member states?

1. Article 81(1) applies to agreements affecting trade positively or negatively

Article 81(1), i.e. EC law, only applies to agreements affecting trade between member states. Otherwise, national competition law applies exclusively. This was especially important at a time when most member states did not have any competition law or lacked a competition culture: the non-application of EC competition law potentially led to the non-application of any competition law. Today, with the influence of EC competition law on national competition laws, such a sharp distinction no longer exists.

The agreement must affect trade between member states (and the impact must not be insignificant except in the case of hardcore restrictions). This is clearly the case where trade is restricted because of the prevention of competition. What if the effect on trade is positive? The argument was that in the absence of the agreement with Consten, Grundig products would probably not have been sold in France at all. The answer, as established by the ECJ in its *Grundig* decision, is that EC law applies. This may seem strange but it is necessary to distinguish the scope of application of Article 81 from the assessment of the agreement under its substantive rules.

Do those substantive rules apply to a vertical agreement? If so, do they prohibit a vertical agreement such as the one in *Grundig*?

2. Article 81(1) applies to vertical as well as to horizontal agreements

Two parties at different levels in the economic process, for example a producer and a distributor, do not compete with each other. As a consequence, an agreement between them, a so-called vertical agreement as opposed to a horizontal agreement concluded between undertakings operating at the same level of the market such as two distributors, cannot *prima facie* restrict competition. Nevertheless, the ECJ decided in the *Grundig* case that the prohibition in Article 81 applies to vertical as well as to horizontal agreements. The rationale is that a vertical agreement may prevent competition between one of the parties and third parties. In the *Consten* case between, for example, *Consten* and Another company that would like to sell Grundig products in France.

3

EUROPEAN UNION: LAWS AND INSTITUTIONS

Furthermore, the letter of Article 81 does not distinguish between undertakings on the basis of their position in the economic process. Therefore, according to a principle of legal interpretation, *Ubi lex non distinguit, nec nos distinguere debemus*, i.e. no distinction should be made where the law, here the treaty, does not make any distinction, the prohibition in Article 81 applies to vertical as well as to horizontal agreements.

Last but not least, the Court referred to the very rationale for EEC competition law: 'an agreement between producer and distributor which might tend to restore the national divisions in trade between member states could be such as to thwart the most basic objects of the Community' (page 471), notably the establishment of a common market (today, the protection of the single internal market). The undertakings should not be allowed to do what member states are prohibited from doing (i.e. maintain the internal barriers to trade within Europe). This is a very important point: EC competition law aims not only to protect competition but to contribute to market integration. Where the two objectives conflict the second broader one often supersedes the first one. This is specific to EC competition law.

3. Article 81(1) prohibits a vertical agreement such as the one in *Grundig*

According to the ECJ, Article 81(1) protects competition between producers or inter-brand competition as well as competition between distributors of the same branded product or intra-brand competition. The fact that an agreement restricting the latter increases the former is insufficient to avoid the prohibition in Article 81(1). This has been subject to criticism, especially if an exemption under Article 81(3) is unavailable (see below).

However, *Grundig* was a major producer of electric products and the ECJ probably feared that inter-brand competition was not sufficient and therefore that intra-brand competition was a necessity. Besides, competition is only one of the policies of the European Community and in some circumstances it has to give way to other policies such as the protection of the common/internal market. The ECJ thus emphasised and condemned the 'insulation of the French market' (page 474) that it saw as the object of the agreement (note that an agreement may be condemned without a full market analysis of its actual effects where the object of the agreement is to restrict competition).

In the *Grundig* case trademarks assisted this insulation of the French market.

4. Trademark rights may not be enforced where their use partitions the market

Consten was the only company permitted by Grundig to register the trademark GINT (Grundig International) which was carried on all Grundig products in France. Consten was therefore able legally to oppose any parallel import of a Grundig product under French Intellectual Property Rights (IPR) law ('*action en contrefaçon*'). In other words it enjoyed absolute territorial protection. As a result competition was restricted. The difficulty was that IPR law is traditionally outside the scope of EC competences. However, the ECJ referred to the principle of effectiveness of EC law and considered the fact that 'the prohibition [in Article 81] would be fruitless if Consten could continue to use the trademark with the same aim as that contained in the agreement recognised as unlawful' (page 476). The Court reached a balance by introducing a distinction between the existence and the exercise of the IPR: the existence of an IPR resorts to national law but its exercise can be assessed under EC law (here Article 81) and any abuse condemned. Despite some criticisms this distinction is still used today and one of the most topical debates is the impact of competition law on IPR.

Nullity under Article 81(2)

As soon as an anti-competitive agreement is prohibited under Article 81(1), and provided it is not exempted under Article 81(3), it is automatically null and void under Article 81(2). This is normally not the only sanction: fines are also imposed under the enforcement regulation (Regulation 17/62 until 1 May 2004, Regulation 1/2003 since).

However, only those parts of the agreement that restrict competition should be prohibited under Article 81(1) and therefore made null and void under Article 81(2). The only exception is where those parts are not severable from the agreement itself. In the *Grundig* case the Commission failed to show that it is necessary to condemn the whole agreement and the ECJ annulled its decision in that respect, 'in so far as it extended the nullity of Article 81(2) to all the clauses of the agreement' (page 475). This was the only argument of *Consten* and *Grundig* that was accepted by the ECJ in this case.

The exemption in Article 81(3)

An agreement may restrict competition, and therefore fall under Article 81(1), but still have more advantages than disadvantages. For example, an exclusive distribution agreement might be necessary in order for the distributor to pay off its costs relating to the introduction or promotion of the producer's products in its allocated territory. Without absolute territorial protection the distributor may not recover its costs and therefore decide not to sell the producer's products thus decreasing competition with other brands and lessening consumer choice (one brand less on the market).

An agreement restricting competition therefore needs in certain circumstances to be exempted from the prohibition in Article 81(1) and this is the rationale for Article 81(3). Two positive conditions must be met. First, the agreement must improve the production or distribution of goods or promote technical or economic progress. Second, it must allow 'consumers a fair share of the resulting benefit'. In addition, the restrictions on competition must be indispensable (Article 81(3)(a)) and not such as to allow the cartel members to substantially eliminate competition (Article 81(3)(b)). These conditions are cumulative. A classic example is the *Grundig* case itself where the ECJ decided that the agreement did not fulfil the condition set out in Article 81(3)(a) and therefore considered that it was 'superfluous to examine the grounds relating to the other conditions for exemption' (page 480).

The ECJ thus upheld the decision of the Commission not to grant an exemption for the parts of the agreement that restricted competition. At that time, and until the entry into force of Regulation 1/ 2003, the Commission had the exclusive right to grant an individual exemption under Article 81(3) and the undertakings had the duty to notify the Commission. This led to a huge workload for the Commission and block exemption regulations (BER) soon became available. They still exist today even if their format has significantly

3

EUROPEAN UNION: LAWS AND INSTITUTIONS

evolved. A typical BER of the new generation is the one on vertical restraints (Regulation 2790/99) with its market share threshold (a company with a market share above 30% will not benefit from the block exemption) and its blacklist (listing hardcore restrictions that are prohibited in order to qualify for the block exemption).

FURTHER READING

Primary sources

Case C-67/96 *Albany International BV* v. *SBT* [1999] ECR I-5751

Case C-2 and 3/01 *Bayer AG* v. *Commission* [2004] ECR I-23

Case T-41/96 *Bayer AG* v. *Commission* [2000] ECR II-3383

Case C-41/90 *Höfner and Elser* v. *Macroton GmbH* [1991] ECR I-1979

Case C-364/92 *SAT Fluggesellschaft* v. *Eurocontrol* [1994] ECR I-43

Secondary source

Whish, R. (2000) 'Regulation 2790/99: The Commission's 'New Style' Block Exemption for Vertical Agreements' (2000) 37, *CML Rev*, 887.

Competition: dominant position (Article 82)

Case 6/73 *Europemballage and Continental Can* v. *Commission* [1973] ECR 215

Karen Davies, Swansea University

It is helpful to remind ourselves that the primary aim of the European Community has been economic integration between the member states, through the creation of a common market (Article 2 EC). This has meant that the task of removing the barriers to trade, which exist between the states, has been of paramount importance to the Community as a whole. The member states have had a significant part to play in achieving this aim and are required to ensure, among other things, that national laws do not create unnecessary barriers to trade within Europe (Articles 28 and 29 EC). However, the member states are not the only group required to play a part in economic integration and undertakings – that is, individuals and businesses, from sole traders to multinational corporations – also have an obligation in relation to the achievement of this central Community aim.

Article 3 EC sets out the activities of the Community and it is evident from even the most cursory examination of Articles 2 and 3 that achieving strong and fair competition between undertakings is seen as complementary to the rules on free movement and central to the aim of economic integration. The treaty rules on competition are also recognised as having benefits beyond those of integration. Consumers, for example, may enjoy increased choice, lower prices and improved quality as a result of strong competition, while the Community as a whole may benefit from increased efficiency, in matters such as the more effective use of raw materials. Undertakings themselves also profit in a healthy, competitive market, where small and medium-sized enterprises, as well as large corporations, are afforded equal opportunities to prosper.

The prohibition of anti-competitive behaviour

The prohibitions contained in Articles 81 and 82 EC, based on the USA's Sherman Acts, lie at the heart of European competition law. As we have seen, in basic terms, Article 81 EC prohibits *agreements* between undertakings that have the ability to distort or restrict competition within the Community. On the other hand Article 82 outlaws the abuse of a dominant market position, which can occur in both the supply and purchase of goods and services.

In the case of **Continental Can**, the ECJ made it clear that Articles 81 and 82 EC 'seek to achieve the same aim on different levels, that is the maintenance of effective competition within the common market' (page 11). It is, however, the second of these treaty Articles that we are concerned with here, in order to glean some indication as to how Article 82 EC has been interpreted and applied by the ECJ.

The *Continental Can* case

The Commission enjoys extensive enforcement powers in relation to ensuring that effective competition within the Community is maintained. These powers were, until relatively recently, largely bestowed on the Commission by Regulation 17/62/EEC.

As part of its role, the Commission issued a Decision (OJ 1972, L7), which provided that the Continental Can Company had infringed Article 82 EC (then Article 86 EC). The Commission argued that Continental Can had abused its dominant market position by acquiring, though its subsidiary Europemballage Corporation, an 80% share in a third undertaking, known as TDV. Continental Can subsequently sought the annulment of the Commission's Decision, by the ECJ, alleging that the Decision, among other things, was 'based on an erroneous interpretation of Article 86' (page 19).

The judgment of the Court in the *Continental Can* case can be seen as being instructive in a number of ways. Firstly, the judgment demonstrates the importance of correctly isolating the relevant market in goods or services, in which an undertaking is claimed to be dominant and, secondly, it provides guidance on how the relevant market may be isolated. Thirdly, it considers the issue of what may, or may not, amount to 'abuse' of such a dominant position. Consequently, each of these issues will be considered in turn.

The 'relevant product market'

It is clear that dominance itself is not prohibited by Article 82 EC: it is the abuse of such a market position that the Treaty seeks to outlaw. However, an undertaking must be proven to be dominant in a *particular* market before the matter of abuse becomes relevant and, consequently, the first step must be to isolate the relevant product or service market in which the undertaking or, on occasion undertakings, are claimed to be dominant.

In *Continental Can*, the ECJ provided that 'the definition of the relevant market is of essential significance, for the possibilities of competition can only be judged in relation to those characteristics of the products in question by virtue of which those products are particularly apt to satisfy an inelastic need and are only to a limited extent interchangeable with other products' (page 14).

The Court then went on to explain that 'In order to be regarded as constituting a distinct market, the products in question must be individualized . . . by particular characteristics or production which make them specifically suitable for this purpose.' In other words consideration must be given to the product – or service – supplied or produced, including not only products that are identical to those produced by the undertaking but also those that can be seen to be interchangeable or substitutable (that is, other products which a consumer may switch to) with the original product, in economic terms, the cross-elasticity of supply.

In the *Continental Can* case, where the company manufactured light metal containers for meat and fish, it was consequently necessary to consider the market share of other producers of the *same* product (light metal containers) and also producers of products which were *interchangeable* or easily substitutable with such containers. Such competitors can therefore be seen possibly to include producers of metal containers for vegetables – or even producers of glass or plastic containers – provided that it could be shown that such producers could easily adapt their products, allowing them to enter the market and thereby create 'a serious counterweight' (page 15) to the market share of Continental Can.

Dominance in the relevant product market

Once the relevant product market has been isolated, it then becomes necessary to calculate the share of the market which such producers or service providers enjoy, in order to ascertain whether or not they are dominant in that market.

The issue of what amounts to dominance was not central to the *Continental Can* case but the Court did make clear that the location of competitors (which has become known as the 'relevant geographical market') could also prove relevant when assessing dominance, as goods produced by 'manufacturers . . . located too far away from most . . . consumers to enable the latter to decide to use them as a permanent source of supply' (page 35) need not be considered.

'Abuse' of a dominant market position

Article 82 EC contains a list of abuses that may amount to a breach of EU law but, as the ECJ explained in *Continental Can*, the list merely gives examples and, importantly, is 'not an exhaustive enumeration of the abuses of a dominant position prohibited by the Treaty'. The Court went on to explain that 'abuse may . . . occur if an undertaking in a dominant position strengthens such a position in such a way that the degree of dominance reached substantially fetters competition . . .' (page 12).

'Abuse' is an objective concept and there is no requirement that the undertaking intended to distort competition. In considering whether the acquisition by Continental Can of shares in TDV, once its competitor, amounted to such an abuse, the Court provided that it was necessary to 'go back to the spirit, general scheme and wording of Article 86, as well as to the system and objectives of the Treaty' (page 22). The ECJ further provided that if competition in the Common Market is not to be distorted as required by Articles 2 and 3 EC then, logically, behaviour that amounts to elimination of competition must be considered to be an abuse under Article 82 EC, and is consequently prohibited.

Furthermore, the Court concluded that behaviour which strengthened the position of a dominant undertaking 'may be an abuse and prohibited under Article 86 of the treaty, regardless of the means and procedure by which it is achieved' (page 24).

The conclusions of the ECJ

Importantly, the ECJ in its judgment accepted that the behaviour of Continental Can, in its agreement to merge with TVD, enabled the undertaking to achieve absolute dominance in the relevant product market and *could*, consequently, amount to a breach of Article 86 EC. However, the Court came to the conclusion that the Commission's Decision should be annulled, as the Commission had failed to isolate the correct product market in which to assess Continental Can's dominance.

This judgment therefore clearly illustrates the continuing importance of correctly isolating the relevant product market *before* moving on to consider whether dominance, in fact,

3

EUROPEAN UNION: LAWS AND INSTITUTIONS

exists in that market and, finally, whether any such a dominant position had been abused by the undertaking(s) in question.

Furthermore, this case remains an important illustration of the broad manner in which the ECJ has interpreted Article 82 EC (ex-Article 86 EC) and continues to provide practical advice on isolating the relevant product market in which abuse is alleged to have occurred and also what may amount to abuse of a dominant market position.

The present position

The purchase of shares in TDV by Continental Can effected a merger of the two undertakings. Mergers can have a significant effect on competition – both positive and negative – but neither Articles 81 or 82 EC specifically refer to either mergers or takeovers.

It is consequently relevant to note that the control of mergers which have a 'European dimension' are now regulated by Council Regulation No. 139/2004 EC. While the behaviour outlined in *Continental Can* would probably now not be considered to be a breach of Article 82 EC but instead be subject to this Regulation, the principles discussed above are *still* relevant to the control of abusive and anti-competitive behaviour in the Community by undertakings.

FURTHER READING

Primary source

Council Regulation No. 139/2004 EC

Secondary sources

Craig, P. and De Burca, G. (2002) Chapters 12 to 25, *EU Law Text, Cases and Materials*, 3rd edn, Oxford.

Turnbull, S. (1996) Barriers to Entry, Article 86 EC and the Abuse of a Dominant Position. An Economic Critique of European Competition Law (1996) *ECLR*, 96.

Whish, R. (2003) *Competition Law*, 5th edn, LexisNexis Butterworths.

4 CONTRACT LAW (OBLIGATIONS)

All of us are subject to legal obligations. As citizens of the state we are obliged not to enter into criminal activity, otherwise we face potential penalties. As individuals we are also required not to conduct ourselves in such a way that our acts or omissions cause loss to others. Such civil wrongs may be classified as torts, obligations which are not willingly entered into but which are imposed upon us, or as contracts, obligations which generally we do willingly enter into. On occasions, of course, a set of facts may involve more than one type of obligation.

Contracts are made daily by all of us, although we rarely think in legal terms when boarding the bus, buying a newspaper or purchasing a drink from the ubiquitous coffee shop. It may cross our minds that certain rights and duties arise when we book our holidays or enter a lease for accommodation but even then few of us will analyse such agreements in formal terms. Contract law is based on both the common law and legislation. It facilitates exchanges by (*inter alia*) providing a set of rules that reduce transaction costs between parties (nobody consults their lawyer before entering the daily agreements noted above) and by allowing for remedial action should anything go wrong. In truth only a very small percentage of the contracts that we make ever give rise to legal disputes and only a small proportion of those disputes ever result in legal action. In part that is due to the skill of the lawyers who drafted the contract in the first place. In so doing they will be aware of the essential elements of a legally enforceable agreement that are discussed in the cases that follow: an agreement, consisting of an offer and an acceptance, consideration and an intention to be legally bound. The lawyers will also know that in addition to the express terms that are agreed to, orally or in writing, certain other terms may be implied into the contract. The process of negotiation between the contracting parties may result in statements being made that do not form part of the contract but which may, if they falsely represent the position, give rise to legal liabilities. In drafting the terms of the agreement attempts may, in fact, be made to limit or even exclude liability or to restrain the activities of one of the parties to the agreement once it has run its course. On occasions in fact an agreement may not run its course either because events occur which prevent that or because one of the parties acts in breach of the agreement leaving the innocent party to seek a remedy for any loss resulting from the breach. Understanding how these various 'rules' interact enables the good lawyer to draft contracts that meet the client's needs.

CONTENTS FOR CONTRACT LAW (OBLIGATIONS)

Offer and acceptance
Carlill v. Carbolic Smoke Ball Company [1893] QB 256   167

Consideration
Williams v. Roffey Brothers & Nicholls (Contractors) Ltd [1991] 1 QB 1   172

Intention to create legal relations
Balfour v. Balfour [1919] 2 KB 571   179

Contract terms
Liverpool City Council v. Irwin [1977] AC 239   186

Exemption clauses
George Mitchell (Chesterhall) Ltd v. Finney Lock Seeds [1983] All ER 737   192

Misrepresentation
Howard Marine & Dredging Co. Ltd v. Ogden & Sons (Excavation) Ltd
[1978] 2 All ER 1134   197

Illegality
Littlewoods Organisation Ltd v. Harris [1978] 1 All ER 1026   202

Discharge
Davis Contractors v. Fareham UDC [1956] AC 696   208

Remedies
Ruxley Electronics and Construction Ltd v. Forsyth [1996] AC 344   217

Offer and acceptance

Carlill v. Carbolic Smoke Ball Company [1893] QB 256

Rhona Smith, Northumbria University

Lord Wilberforce commented that English law has a schematic and technical doctrine of contract but a practical approach of allotting everything into offer, acceptance and consideration (*NZ Shipping Co. Ltd* v. *AM Salterthwaite & Co.*). These are the three essential features of every contract:

OFFER + ACCEPTANCE = AGREEMENT

However, as with so many aspects of the law, it is not quite as simple as it first appears: it is necessary to ensure the offer and acceptance is of exactly the same thing and that the resultant agreement includes all relevant (material) terms. More importantly, in the current context, it is necessary to define what is meant by 'offer' and by 'acceptance'. Under English law, an element of CONSIDERATION must exist (i.e. there must be an exchange between the parties – L gives something to G and G gives something to L in turn).

OFFER + ACCEPTANCE (with CONSIDERATION) = CONTRACT

Consideration is discussed in more detail in the entry on *Williams* v. *Roffey*. This entry will focus on 'offer' and 'acceptance', the extent of which was explained by the Court of Appeal in the famous case of *Carlill* v. *Carbolic Smoke Ball Company*. Although a very old case, it remains a relevant authority today (e.g., see *Bowerman* v. *ABTA*).

In sum, an offer is a willingness to contract on certain specified terms made with the intention that a binding agreement will exist once the offer is validly accepted. In the case of *Carlill*, the defendent inserted an advertisement into the *Pall Mall Gazette* for their Carbolic Smoke Balls. This advert stated that £100 would be paid to any person contracting influenza and related illnesses after having used the carbolic smoke ball thrice daily for a fortnight in accordance with the printed directions supplied with the ball. £1000 was stated as being deposited in a specified London bank to demonstrate the company's 'sincerity in the matter'. The plaintiff, Mrs Carlill, bought a smoke ball and used it as directed for a period of almost two months, but despite this contracted influenza. She sued for £100 and the court at first instance supported her claim. Was the advertisement indeed an offer which could form the basis for a contract and did Carlill's actions suffice for an acceptance of that offer, even though she had not written notifying the company that she was accepting their terms?

4

CONTRACT LAW (OBLIGATIONS)

Offer

As Atiyah (1995) notes, 'an offer is, in effect, a promise by the offeror to do or abstain from doing something, provided that the offeree will accept the offer and pay or promise to pay the 'price' of the offer' (*An Introduction to the Law of Contract* at page 56). Offers should be made with the intention that, if validly accepted, a binding contract is formed. A distinction must thus be drawn between an offer as a precursor to legally binding obligations and an 'invitation to treat', thus in *Boots Cash Chemists*, a self-service style shop where one paid at the checkout was examined by the Court of Appeal. The Court held that the goods on display were an 'invitation to treat' rather than an offer. This meant that the shop was simply 'advertising' available goods and indicating they would be willing to receive offers for them. The offer (in the legal sense) was made by the putative customer at the checkout and accepted by the cashier. The cashier could, technically, decide whether or not to accept the offer. In the case of *Boots Cash Chemists*, this was a vital point, as a pharmacist was present to oversee the sale of certain medicines at the checkout: Parliament enacted the Pharmacy and Poisons Act 1933 to ensure that 'poisons' (certain drugs) should not be sold without supervision; the pharmacist could intervene to prevent the sale of any medicines at the checkout. Lord Goddard draws on an analogy with bookshops:

> In most bookshops customers are invited to go in and pick up books and look at them even if they do not actually buy them. There is no contract by the shopkeeper to sell until the customer has taken the book to the shopkeeper or his assistant and said 'I want to buy this book' and the shopkeeper says 'Yes'. That would not prevent the shopkeeper, seeing the book picked up, saying: 'I am sorry I cannot let you have that book; it is the only copy I have got and I have already promised it to another customer'.

(at page 802).

Note that this means shopkeepers are not legally bound under contract law to sell a product at the price marked (although there may be problems for the shopkeeper under consumer protection legislation in such a case)!

Offers should be distinguished from mere 'puffs' which are advertising or marketing statements and devoid of legal meaning (for example, a laundry liquid will make your whites 'whiter than white'). Finally, offers must be distinguished from requests for information: thus, if you ask a car company what the best price is for a particular car, their reply is a response to a request for information and does not make a binding contract (see *Harvey* v. *Facey*). In *Carlill*, the deposit of money removed it from being a puff (Bowen LJ at page 268).

For an offer to be made, it must obviously be communicated, the offer being made when the offeree receives the offer. This causes potential problems for Carlill as the offer was not made to a named individual but communicated to the readership of the newspaper at large. However, Lindley LJ viewed the Carbolic Smoke Ball Company's offer as being an open offer extended to 'anyone who performs the conditions named in the advertisement' (at page 262). Early authorities were advanced in support of this (*Williams* v. *Carwardine*). Strength was garnered from the fact that the Company had deposited a thousand pounds in a bank. This was considered to demonstrate the intention to create legal obligations as the contract terms were specific enough. A similar idea underpins the idea of a cheque guarantee card (fast being replaced by 'chip and pin' technology). The card stipulates the maximum amount the bank will guarantee a cheque for – i.e. it offers the world to accept a cheque from the holder, safe in the knowledge that the bank will pay up to the specified maximum should the payee have insufficient funds in his/her account.

More recently in *Bowerman*, a notice displayed in ABTA offices outlining the ABTA scheme of protection applicable to all customers was held by a majority of the Court of Appeal to amount to a contractual offer, even though at first instance the judge had held that the notice was issued to the public at large with the principal intention of providing informa-tion on the ABTA protection scheme and the information was too 'equivocal and vague' (at page 454) to be contractual. A majority of judges in the Court of Appeal held that the notice was intended to be read (being displayed prominently in every ABTA travel agency) and contained an offer of a promise which was accepted by a customer booking in the agency. They considered it clear enough to attract legal consequences. The concept of an offer to the world, expounded in *Carlill* is still good law today.

An offer must be clear, be intended to create legal obligations and capable of acceptance, thus communicated.

Acceptance

An acceptance is a final unqualified assent to all the terms of the offer. In the commercial context, this can lead to a 'battle of the forms' as offers and counter-offers are mooted and rejected with further counter-offers. Ultimately, the material terms will be acceptable to both parties. For an agreement to emerge, the offer must be accepted. That is to say, the exact terms of the latest offer must be accepted as proposed. Obviously, if any terms are rejected, then the purported acceptance is in fact merely a counter-offer and negotia-tions must continue, or the discussions be terminated without securing a contract.

The mode of acceptance is usually specified by the offeror and acceptance must be com-municated (*Entores* v. *Miles Far East Corp*). Tacit acceptance is not recognised but note the existence of the postal acceptance rule whereby posting your valid acceptance, correctly stamped and addressed, into a postbox constitutes an acceptance irrespective of whether the letter arrives (*Brinkibon Ltd* v. *Stahag Stahl und Stahlwaren handelsde-sellschagt*) – no similar exception operates in civil law jurisdictions. This explains why many companies specify the offer is accepted on receipt of the letter. The situation in an age of electronic communications is rather more complicated with technological advances permitting instantaneous transactions and international electronic communications. Often the parties themselves may agree the fundamentals of formation of their contract but if a dispute ensues, it is the court which will be the final arbiter (see for example, articles by Connerty and by Deveci).

Generally, an acceptance would have to be communicated to the offeror in order to prove agreement with the terms proposed. For example, when making a purchase in a shop, there is a clear offer, acceptance and exchange of money (consideration) to seal the deal. A product is being bought by the purchaser from the seller for a specified amount of money. Detailed contract terms are not usually considered in these common, every day contracts, and actions effectively 'speak louder than words' in creating the contract at a person to person level. In *Carlill*, the court decided that acceptance need not be communicated directly as the company clearly intended for acceptance by performance. After all the advertisement contained very precise instructions on the required use of the smoke ball. Just as with cheque guarantee cards, the offer is open to anyone who elects to act in accordance with it (for cheque cards, that would mean the person who accepts the cheque from the payee for goods, services etc. on the underlying understanding the bank will honour the cheque to the specified amount). The exception in *Carlill* applies when it is clear that performance/action will constitute an acceptance of the terms of the offer. Had Mrs Carlill not followed the exact instructions as to the use of the smoke ball for a fortnight, there would have been no acceptance of the offer in the newspaper. She would have required the agreement of the company to vary the terms of the offer to her chosen usage of the smoke balls. Bowen LJ draws an analogy with an advertisement to the world that his dog is lost and money will be paid to anyone returning it – clearly the proposal can be accepted by the action of anyone looking for the dog, without them having to sit down and write a letter to that effect (at page 270). Performance of the condition specified in the advertisement can constitute a valid acceptance in these circumstances.

If there is no acceptance of the terms of the offer, a contract cannot be formed and legal obligations do not arise. Establishing the existence of a contract in law thus demands proof of the terms of the offer and acceptance absolutely and explicitly (by words or action) of those offer terms.

Agreement

Should a valid offer and acceptance be proven, then in England (unlike Scotland) that is not sufficient for a contract to be formed. Consideration is essential in English law, the inconvenience that the plaintiff was put to was considered to suffice for this. As Lindley LJ noted, 'there is a distinct inconvenience, not to say a detriment, to any person who [in accordance with the directions] uses the smoke ball' (*Carlill* at page 265). The resultant agreement is sometimes referred to as *consensus in idem* – literally agreement of the same. Both parties to the contract thus have the same understanding of the terms of the contract – the offer and acceptance match and are materially of the same thing.

It must be possible to identify the terms of the agreement, however few or many there may be. The absence of agreement of all the terms is not always fatal, as examples drawn from commercial law illustrate. Contracts for future performance can require some terms to be agreed as the contract evolves and the court will strive to uphold bargains agreed by the parties: '[b]usiness men often record the most important agreements in crude and summary fashion; modes of expression sufficient and clear to them on the course of their business appear to those unfamiliar with the business far from complete or precise. It is accordingly the duty of the court to construe such documents fairly and broadly, without being too astute or subtle in finding defects . . . ' (per Lord Wright in *Hillas & Co.* at page 503). Complexities of reality often obscure the contract and care must be taken to identify and define the material terms of the offer and acceptance to demonstrate the existence of an agreement.

In sum, an enforceable contract requires there to be an offer, an acceptance of that offer (i.e. the same exact terms) and agreement sealed with consideration of some description.

That this is perhaps a simplification will become apparent as the other entries on contract law discuss potential problems and difficulties.

FURTHER READING

Primary sources

Bowerman v. *ABTA Ltd* 1996 CLC 451

Brinkibon Ltd v. *Stahag Stahl und Stahlwaren handelsdesellschagt* [1983] 2 AC 34

Entores v. *Miles Far East Corp* [1955] 2QB 327

Harvey v. *Facey* [1893] AC 552

Hillas & Co. v. *Arcos Ltd* [1932] All ER 494

NZ Shipping Co Ltd v. *AM Salterthwaite & Co.* [1975] AC 154

Pharmaceutical Society of Great Britain v. *Boots Cash Chemists (Southern) Ltd* [1952] 2 QB 795

Williams v. *Carwardine* 4 B&Ald 621

Williams v. *Roffey Bros & Nicholls (Contractors) Ltd* [1944] 2 All ER 261

Secondary sources

Atiyah, P. (1995) *An Introduction to the Law of Contract*, 5th edn, Clarendon, Oxford.

Brownsword, R. (2006) *Contract Law – themes for the twenty-first century*, 2nd edn, OUP, Oxford.

Connerty, A. (1999) 'Electronic commerce: a United Kingdom view' (1999) *International Company and Commercial Law Review*, 65.

Deveci, H. (2007) 'Consent in online contracts: old wine in new bottles' (2007) *Computer and Telecommunications Law Review*, 223.

McMeel, G. (1997) 'Contractual Intention: the smoke ball strikes back' (1997) 113, *Law Quarterly Review*, 47.

4

CONTRACT LAW (OBLIGATIONS)

Consideration

Williams v. *Roffey Brothers & Nicholls (Contractors) Ltd*
[1991] 1 QB 1

Mick Woodley, Northumbria University

Not all agreements will be made with a view to their having legal effect if one of the parties does not comply with the terms of the agreement. Arranging to meet friends for a drink but then 'standing them up' may quickly lose you your friends but will not give rise to any legal obligations. Some way must therefore be found to distinguish between those agreements that do give rise to a legally binding contract and those that do not. For this the courts look in part to the intention of the parties, imposing certain presumptions depending in part on the relationship between the parties (see the case entry for *Balfour* v. *Balfour*). In some legal jurisdictions once it is established that the parties intended that their agreement should give rise to a legally binding relationship, then all that is necessary for a contract to be legally enforceable is present. But this is not the position for English law which, unless the contract is in the form of a deed, requires a further element, namely consideration.

There are several classic statements defining consideration. In **Thomas** v. **Thomas** Patteson J stated: 'Consideration means something which is of value in the eye of the law, moving from the plaintiff: it may be some detriment to the plaintiff or some benefit to the defendant, but at all events it must be moving from the plaintiff'. Subsequently Lush J declared that '. . . a valuable consideration in the sense of the law may consist either in some right, interest, profit or benefit accruing to the one party of some forebearance, detriment, loss or responsibility given, suffered or undertaken by the other' (*Currie* v. *Misa*). Pollock in his text on Contract, on the other hand, preferred to define consideration as follows: 'An act or forebearance of one party, or the promise thereof, is the price for which the promise of the other is bought, and the price thus given for value is enforceable' (see further **Dunlop** v. **Selfridge**). But such language is a product of its day and, with due respect, arcane to the puzzled student in the twenty-first century. In fact, what students examine as the consideration for the agreement is no more than one of the terms of the contract (i.e. the offer and the acceptance), albeit perhaps the principal one. What consideration brings to the parties' agreement is the exchange of promises, the element of 'bargain' (even if there may be no real choice over the particular deal that is made). Thus, the student who wishes not to upset her lecturer by being late boards the bus and hands over the requested fare in exchange for the ride into the university, a payment in return for a service. In order to be wide awake she purchases a cup of coffee, another exchange, this time a sum of money in return for goods. On each occasion the student may suffer a loss - she has reduced her income and dug into her student loan - but she has had the benefit of the bus ride and the restorative impact of the cup of coffee. A similar analysis may be made of the losses and benefits for the bus company and the coffee vendor.

Further examination of the cases and the textbooks informs us that consideration must be sufficient or real (i.e. it must have value in the eyes of the law) but it need not be adequate. Unless the promise is to provide or to do something otherwise deemed unlawful, the courts do not seek to interfere with the bargain made by the parties to a contract, even if they make a poor bargain. The latter approach is, of course, based on the apparent underpinning principle of contract law, namely 'freedom of contract'. Hence, property may be let at peppercorn rents (*Thomas* v. *Thomas*) or items provided in exchange for chocolate bar wrappers (*Chappel & Co. Ltd* v. *Nestle Co. Ltd*) without a judicial eyebrow being raised. Another basic tenet in relation to consideration is that past consideration is no consideration. A student volunteers to help at a university open day. The day is a great success and she is later told that she will be paid for her work. However, she cannot enforce the promised payment as the promise to pay her was made after the contribution to the open day was performed. However unjust this may seem, her help was not provided in exchange for the promise of a payment; it was gratuitous (see *Re McArdle*). On the other hand, where a party can show that there was a prior understanding, whether express or implied, that a payment was to be made for services but no specific sum had been mentioned, a later promise to pay a specific amount will be enforceable (see *Re Casey's Patents*). It will be easier to demonstrate such an understanding where the parties deal at arm's length as part of a commercial relationship rather than in social or domestic agreements.

Although the courts will not examine the adequacy of the bargain made, the sufficiency of the consideration will be scrutinised where party A fulfils a duty that A is already legally bound to fulfil but does so in response to a further promise from party B. In fact, this question has been analysed by the courts in three distinct circumstances: (a) where a public duty is imposed on A to do the act that B has promised to pay him for; (b) where A is bound by an existing contractual duty owed to C to do the act that B has promised to pay him for; (c) where A is bound by an existing contractual duty to B to do the act that B has made a further promise to pay him for. Unless A goes beyond his pre-existing public duty (see *Glasbrook Brothers Ltd* v. *Glamorgan County Council*), his performance of the duty does not provide sufficient consideration for B's additional promise (see *Collins* v. *Godefroy*). On the other hand, the courts have been prepared to find good consideration in the second situation (b), where a third party, C, is involved (see *Shadwell* v. *Shadwell* (1860) 9 CBNS 159 and *New Zealand Shipping Co.* v. *A M Satterthwaite & Co.* [1975] AC 154). Here, B obtains a benefit, namely the direct right to enforce the agreement with A, rather than relying upon C to do so, while A faces the prospect of an action from B if he does not fulfil his bargain with C even though he might have reached a compromise with C himself. The answer to the final permutation (c) seemed to depend upon a long-established principle laid down in the case of *Stilk* v. *Myrick* which stated that the performance of an existing duty already owed to B cannot amount to consideration for a further promise from B. However, that principle found itself subject to challenge in *Williams* v. *Roffey Brothers & Nicholls (Contractors) Ltd*.

The facts of the case have no doubt been repeated in many a construction and engineering contract where the main contractor subcontracts work to another firm. Here, the

4

CONTRACT LAW (OBLIGATIONS)

plaintiff, Williams, had been brought in to carry out the carpentry work on a block of flats which were being renovated by the main contractor for a housing association. Unfortunately the low price of Williams's original tender was compounded by his poor supervision of his workforce and, with the plaintiff facing financial difficulties, the work slipped behind schedule. The main contractors, who had their own pressures in the form of a time penalty clause in the contract with their client, became concerned that the plaintiff would not complete on time and agreed to pay a further sum as each flat was completed. Williams and his men had carried out substantial work on a further eight flats without completing any of them when they walked off the site. In order to finish the work the defendants were forced to engage other carpenters.

At first sight these facts seemed to fall full-square within the principle set out in *Stilk* v. *Myrick*. Williams had provided no consideration for the extra payments promised to him because he was already bound by his original agreement to do the work (even if he had perhaps miscalculated the price originally). But this was not the view taken either at first instance or in the Court of Appeal, where all three judges took the view that the main contractors had received consideration for their promise, although their Lordships were not in agreement as to the precise form of that consideration. The key question that the Court was faced with in *Williams* v. *Roffey* was the distinction between consideration in fact and consideration in law. The former emphasises the actual benefit received, while in law there is no consideration for a further promise if the promisee does no more than he is already bound to do. So what practical benefits did their Lordships identify that amounted to consideration for the promise of extra payments. For Glidewell LJ these were to be found in the fact that Williams and his men continued to work, replacement carpenters did not have to be engaged and the penalty clause was not invoked. In rejecting the argument that these practical benefits could not constitute consideration, his Lordship pointed to the earlier Court of Appeal decisions in *Ward* v. *Byham* and *Williams* v. *Williams* in both of which practical advantages had also been identified. In fact, Halson argues that the promises made in *Ward* and in *Williams* involved acts over and above the original promise and could thus amount to consideration in law and not just in fact. Nonetheless, Glidewell LJ believed that, while his approach refined and limited the principle in *Stilk* v. *Myrick*, it left the principle unscathed. Russell LJ and Purchase LJ also identified benefits accruing to the defendants, albeit on slightly different terms. But the law had moved on from the days when Lord Ellenborough rejected the demands of Stilk and his fellow sailors for the promised extra wages for 'want of consideration'. As Lord Justice Russell emphasised:

> In the late twentieth century I do not believe that the rigid approach to the concept of consideration to be found in *Stilk* v. *Myrick* is either necessary or desirable. Consideration there must still be but, in my judgment, the courts nowadays should be more ready to find its existence so as to reflect the intention of the parties to the contract where the bargaining powers are not unequal and where the finding of consideration reflects the true intention of the parties.

Whereas for Lord Justice Purchase:

> ... the modern approach to the question of consideration would be that where there were benefits derived by each party to a contract of variation even though one party did not suffer a detriment this would not be fatal to the establishing of sufficient consideration to

support the agreement. If both parties benefit from an agreement it is not necessary that each also suffers a detriment.

A further issue touched on, if only briefly, by the Court was the concept of economic duress. The defendants did not attempt to claim that Williams was prevented from enforcing his 'bonus' because of any unlawful threat. Indeed the initiative for the extra payments had come from the defendants, making such a claim untenable. But the Court recognised that economic duress had a part to play and various commentators have welcomed this development. Halson claims that the Court adopted an approach which involved 'a subtle but significant change in the law relating to modification of contract'. A factual benefit should be easier to identify than a legal benefit where there has been a modification to an existing contract and that modification would be enforceable if the benefit constitutes valid consideration, unless there has been the use of duress. Indeed Halson advocates going still further by abandoning the pretence of searching for even a factual benefit. Support for Halson's arguments that the doctrine of economic duress better fits the needs of the commercial world comes from Phang. But both Phang and Adams and Brownsword caution that, in turning to economic duress, there is a risk of replacing one set of problems for another.

A recent summary of the principles relating to duress was provided by Dyson J in *Carillion Construction v. Felix (UK) Ltd*.

> The ingredients of actionable duress are that there must be pressure, (a) whose practical effect is that there is compulsion on, or lack of practical choice for, the victim, (b) which is illegitimate, and (c) which is a significant cause inducing the claimant to enter into the contract . . . In determining whether there has been illegitimate pressure, the court takes into account a range of factors. These include whether there has been an actual or threatened breach of contract; whether the person allegedly exerting the pressure has acted in good or bad faith; whether the victim had any realistic practical alternative but to submit to the pressure; whether the victim protested at the time; and whether he confirmed and sought to rely on the contract. These are all relevant factors. Illegitimate pressure must be distinguished from the rough and tumble of the pressure of normal commercial bargaining.

Adam Opel GmbH v. Mitras Automotive UK Ltd provides a good example of how the focus on the enforceability of a renegotiated contract has swung from consideration to economic duress. The deputy high court judge, hearing the case, cited Dyson J and found that the defendant supplier's actions had gone beyond such 'rough and tumble' and amounted to illegitimate pressure which had caused the claimants to agree to pay a higher price than previously specified under an existing contract. If the matter had turned purely on the issue of consideration, the judge would have felt bound, albeit reluctantly, to follow the decision in *Williams v. Roffey*. However, as he remarked: 'The law of consideration is no longer to be used to protect a participant in such a variation. That role has passed to the law of economic duress, which provides a more refined control mechanism, and renders the contract voidable rather than void.'

This may answer one of the problems raised by the decision in *Williams v. Roffey* but it does not address another, namely its relationship with the line of cases that stems from *Pinnel's Case*. These establish that part payment of an existing debt by debtor A cannot constitute good consideration for a promise by creditor B to accept that part payment as satisfying the full amount owed by A and not to sue for the balance. Only if, at the request of B, A's part payment is made before the debt is due or if payment is made fully or partly in kind will fresh consideration be found. *Pinnel's Case* was subsequently approved by the House of Lords in *Foakes v. Beer* and thus is not easily ignored. Yet, perhaps surprisingly, it was not considered by the Court of Appeal in *Williams v. Roffey* even though it is the reverse side of the situation arising in that case. Thus assume the main contractors had run into difficulties with the penalty clause in their own contract for the renovation of the flats and were behind in payments for the carpentry work that Williams had done. Recognising this and anxious to secure at least some payment Williams says to the main contractors 'I won't insist on full payment but pay me in part and I will forgo the balance'. Assume further that Williams had agreed to this because he reasoned that payment of the smaller sum would at least cover his material costs and pay his suppliers, thereby allowing him to continue to trade and giving him peace of mind. Would the Court have found good consideration for the promise to accept part payment? (See further *D & C Builders v. Rees*). In two subsequent Court of Appeal decisions the opportunity to extend the reasoning in *Williams v. Roffey* to part payment of a debt was declined (see *Re Selectmove Ltd* [1995] 1 WLR 474 and *Re C (A Debtor)* unreported). As Peter Gibson LJ put it in *Re Selectmove*:

> When a creditor and a debtor who are at arm's length reach agreement on the payment of the debt by instalments to accommodate the debtor, the creditor will no doubt always see a practical benefit to himself in so doing. In the absence of authority there would be much to be said for the enforceability of such a contract. But, that was a matter expressly considered in *Foakes v. Beer*, yet held not to constitute good consideration in law. *Foakes v. Beer* was not even referred to in the *Williams* case, and it is in my judgment impossible, consistently with doctrine of precedent, for this court to extend the principle of the *Williams* case to any circumstances governed by the principle of *Foakes v. Beer*.

His Lordship went on to state that any extension of the law to cover part payment of a debt should come, at least from the House of Lords, and preferably from Parliament.

If the Court in *Williams v. Roffey* was silent on the issue of part payment, it did not delve much deeper into the question of promissory estoppel. This doctrine has been specifically developed by the courts (notably by Denning J, as he then was, in *Central London Property Trust v. High Trees House Ltd*) to cover a situation where reliance is placed upon a promise unsupported by consideration. As an equitable remedy the claimant seeking to rely upon it must not be acting in an unmeritorious fashion (see *D & C Builders v. Rees*). One reason for the reluctance of the plaintiff and the Court to look further into this doctrine may have been the rule which states that promissory estoppel may be used 'as shield but not a sword', that is that it may be used to defend a claim against a party but not itself create a right of action (see *Combe v. Combe*). (For an analysis of why the extension of the doctrine of promissory estoppel in *Williams v. Roffey* would have been preferable to the re-working of *Stilk v. Myrick*, see Blair and Hird. A recent example of the relationship between promissory estoppel and the rule in *Pinnel's Case* is provided by *Collier v. P & MJ Wright (Holdings) Ltd*).

It is often argued that the decision in *Stilk v. Myrick* was prompted by public policy grounds as much as by the apparent want of consideration provided by the unfortunate mariners who did not receive the extra payments they had been promised for sailing the ship back to port while short-handed. The prospects of sailors holding ships' masters to ransom hundreds or thousands of miles from home was for the courts too much to contemplate. (This was perhaps particularly true for the judge in the case, Lord Ellenborough, whose first cousin Fletcher Christian had led the mutiny on the HMS Bounty.) At the time the judgment in *Williams* v. *Roffey* was handed down, it was heralded as a welcome release from the straitjacket that *Stilk* had imposed and prompted much academic debate about the continuing existence of the concept of consideration. Does it still have a role to play and, if so, what should that role be? There has certainly been no judicial rush to follow the Court of Appeal's lead. Indeed, in *South Caribbean Trading Ltd* v. *Trafigura BV* Colman J. was quite scathing of the Court's reasoning. It seems that in relation to renegotiated contracts between commercial parties the courts are developing a more refined instrument in the form of economic duress and it might be speculated that this, alongside the doctrine of promissory estoppel and the requirement for intention to create legal relations, will eventually supplant the need for consideration at all. In the meantime students of contract law can continue to ride to their lectures on the bus and drink their cups of coffee, while contemplating what consideration has passed between them and their suppliers.

4

CONTRACT LAW (OBLIGATIONS)

FURTHER READING

Primary sources

Adam Opel GmbH v. *Mitras Automotive UK Ltd* [2007] All ER (D) 272

Carillion Construction v. *Felix (UK) Ltd* [2001] BLR 1

Central London Property Trust v. *High Trees House Ltd* [1947] KB 130

Chappel & Co Ltd v. *Nestle Co Ltd* [1960] AC 87

Collier v. *P & MJ Wright (Holdings) Ltd* [2007] All ER (D) 233, [2007] EWCA 1329

Collins v. *Godefroy* (1831) 1 B & Ald 950

Combe v. *Combe* [1951] 2 KB 215

Currie v. *Misa* (1875) LR Ex 153

D & C Builders v. *Rees* [1966] 2 QB 617

Dunlop v. *Selfridge* [1895] AC 847

Foakes v. *Beer* (1884) 9 App Cas 605

Glasbrook Brothers Ltd v. *Glamorgan County Council* [1925] AC 270

New Zealand Shipping Co v. *A M Satterthwaite & Co* [1975] AC 154

Pinnel's Case (1602) 5 Co Rep 117a

Re Casey's Patents [1892] 1 Ch 104

Re McArdle [1951] Ch 669

Re Selectmove Ltd [1995] 1 WLR 474

Shadwell v. *Shadwell* (1860) 9 CBNS 159

South Caribbean Trading Ltd v. *Trafigura BV* [2005] 1 Lloyd's Rep 128

Stilk v. *Myrick* (1809) 2 Camp 317, 6 Esp 129

Thomas v. *Thomas* (1842) 2 QB 852

Ward v. *Byham* [1956] 1 WLR 496

Williams v. *Williams* [1957] 1 WLR 148

Secondary sources

Adams and Brownsword (1990) 'Contract, Consideration and the Critical Path' (1990) 53, *MLR*, 536.

Blair and Hird (1996) 'Minding Your Own Business – *Williams* v. *Roffey* Re-visited: Consideration Re-considered' [1996] *JBL*, 254.

Halson (1990) 'Sailors, Sub-Contractors and Consideration' (1990) 106, *LQR*, 183.

Phang (1991) 'Consideration at the Crossroads' (1991) 107, *LQR*, 21.

Intention to create legal relations

Balfour v. *Balfour* [1919] 2 KB 571

Andrew Harries, University of Central Lancashire

Balfour v. *Balfour* is the first English case which gave recognition to a test for enforcing agreements based on broad legal presumptions of policy. The test looks for evidence that, when parties made their promises, they did so with an 'intention that they were to be legally binding'. The description for the test is usually known as a test of 'intention to create legal relations'. It stands alongside 'agreement' and 'consideration' as the one of the three key tests the judiciary use to identify when a legally binding contractual agreement exists. In effect, the test makes sweeping value judgments about what types of agreements should be enforced and which should not: the demarcation line is drawn between commercial contexts, where all promises are assumed to be made with an intention that they are legally binding, and social and domestic contexts where it is presumed promises are made without an intention to make them legally binding.

In asking whether the parties' minds were directed towards legal consequences when they made their promises it would seem that the parties' actual intentions are key in applying this test. However, the test is not premised on such an assumption. Rather, the test is objective and is based upon what as a matter of legal policy the courts' believe the parties *typically* presume when making promissory arrangements. The test is legal rather than factual in application. The legal assumptions are based on the different contexts within which promises are made. The application of the presumptions involves a legal value judgement about what types of promises the courts feel are best suited to legal protection and those promises made in different contexts may be more suited to extra-legal protection. The effect is that contracts are kept in their rightful place: in the market and away from domestic/social contexts.

The test of intention, then, requires courts to consider the reasons why promises are made, assess the context within which they are made and evaluate whether legal remedies are suitable instruments for regulating the typical relationships within that context. The short answer seems to be that the more a context creates relationships of discrete, calculable exchange, seen in market transactions, the more likely it is that legal remedies will be presumed to be the most relevant and suitable.

The legal significance of *Balfour*

The judgment itself is very short but its significance lies in expressing a number of broad assumptions regarding the boundary between enforceable and unenforceable agreements which in turn hinges on a number of value judgments as to which type of agreements merit legal protection and which do not.

The case concerned a domestic agreement between husband and wife where the husband promised to pay his wife a monthly allowance but then stopped paying it leading his wife to pursue a legal action for compensation based upon breach of contract. The legal issue was whether the courts recognise 'agreements' made within a non-commercial context, but having financial payments as their objective, as legally binding agreements giving rise to contractual liability. The case is significant because even where there is an agreement supported by consideration, there may not be a contractual agreement if the promises forming the agreement were not made with a *presumed* intention that should they be broken they would be enforced in court.

The intention principle in **Balfour** was once described by the eminent legal scholar Otto Kahn-Freund as '. . . one of those wise decisions in which the courts allow the realities of life to determine the legal norms which they formulate'. The decision reflects the different rules and assumptions which distinguish agreements made in different contexts. Unger recognised this quality in the decision when he suggested that 'The family circle differs from the market place in that it is not the setting for bargaining but for an exchange of gifts and gratuitous services.' However, these sentiments are not shared by all judges and commentators who believe there is insufficient sensitivity to the reality of contracts made at the border between commercial and non-commercial promises. But, the presumptions can always be rebutted by suitably strong evidence of a counter-intention. Critics also suggest that the rebuttal requirements are perhaps too tightly drawn in some instances.

The case

1. The facts

Mr and Mrs Balfour had lived in Ceylon (now Sri Lanka) for 15 years where Mr Balfour worked as a civil engineer for the government of Ceylon. They both returned to England between November 1915 and August 1916 while Mr Balfour was on extended leave. When he was due to return to Ceylon, his wife's doctor advised her to remain in England for a further three months to recuperate from the effects of rheumatic arthritis. Prior to his sailing, Mrs Balfour claimed her husband gave her a cheque to cover expenses until the end of August and promised to pay maintenance of £30 per month thereafter. Although her husband promised to return to England, he did not and later informed his wife that it would be best if they remained apart. Mr Balfour stopped the maintenance payments. The marriage was dissolved formally on 30 July 1918 and Mrs Balfour obtained an order for alimony in December 1918.

2. The dispute and proceedings

Mrs Balfour claimed that when her husband stopped the maintenance payments he was in breach of contract. She sued him to gain compensation for the money she never received. At first instance Justice Sargant held that Mr Balfour had breached an oral undertaking made on 8 August 1916 that he would pay maintenance to his wife of £30 per month. The terms were clear and his wife's agreement to be supported financially in this way was sufficient consideration to pay for her husband's promise to pay her £30 per month.

The law relating to husband–wife relations reflected the values of the period. A husband was under a legal duty to financially maintain his wife. In effect, Mrs Balfour's consideration was a forebearance: she had a legal right to pledge her husband's credit to buy the 'necessities' required for maintaining the household but she was willing to forgo this in exchange for payment of £30 per month out of which she would have to maintain herself. Mr Balfour claimed the arrangement was a purely domestic expedient designed to bridge any financial gap while they were temporarily separated. Counsel for Mr Balfour also claimed the arrangement 'was not intended to have a contractual operation' (page 573).

The judgments

All three judges rather pithily rejected Justice's Sargant's first instance decision. The grounds for their decisions were slightly different in each case: Warrington LJ focused on trying to imply an agreement; Duke LJ, on the absence of any real consideration for the husband's promise; and Atkin LJ, on a presumed intention to enter legal relations when a legally binding agreement is recognised.

1. Lord Justice Warrington

Lord Justice Warrington could find no evidence of an express bargain and suggested that a contract was impossible to find even by implication. He alluded to policy factors which perhaps explain his decision. He suggested that, taken to its logical conclusion, it would trivialise the law to find a contract in the instant case because *any* promise made by a husband to his wife while still married would be actionable as a contract and this was not in the public interest. He supports this contention by stating that the Balfours 'never intended to make a bargain which could be enforced in law' (page 575) and that the husband's promise was binding in 'honour' only.

2. Lord Justice Duke

Lord Justice Duke suggested there was an inherent quality associated with a commercial contract which is missing in relations between husband and wife. It is only when they formally separate that promises are given legal effect. Otherwise, given that marriage contains a steady stream of commitments made between husband and wife every day, it could lead to a very 'fruitful source of dissension and quarrelling' creating 'unlimited litigation in a relationship which should be obviously as far as possible protected from possibilities of that kind' (page 577).

3. Lord Justice Atkin

Lord Justice Atkin's speech is one of the most quoted in contract law and is the key speech from which the broad idea of 'intention' as a test for denying contractual liability is formed. He starts his speech by suggesting that there are myriad types of agreement in the world but only a small proportion are recognised as giving rise to liability in contract law. The law of contract is only concerned with specific types of agreements which satisfy certain rules on the process of their creation and the substance of their form. He provides some typical examples of 'social' agreements which are not recognised as contracts-in-law

4

CONTRACT LAW (OBLIGATIONS)

(agreements to receive hospitality or to go for a walk, for example). Atkin LJ suggests that agreements between husband and wife fall into the same category as these 'social' agreements. He further suggests that even when there is an apparent agreement supported by sufficient consideration there still may not be a binding contract. He then states: '. . . they are not contracts because the parties did not intend that they be attended by legal consequences' (page 579).

It is clear that Atkin LJ was introducing a further requirement for proving the existence of a binding agreement: evidence of an intention to create a legal relationship (i.e., you intend your relationships to be governed by legal rules and remedies when disputes arise). His justification for adding a further legal test for the creation of a contractual duty rests on a consideration of policy. First, in agreement with Duke LJ, Atkin LJ believed that legal recognition of such agreements as binding arrangements would lead to an unacceptable escalation in the number of comparatively trivial claims being made in court because of the sheer volume of daily communications between husband and wife which comprise an exchange of promises: '. . . the small Courts of this country would have to be multiplied one hundredfold if these arrangements were held to result in legal obligations' (page 579).

Second, the reason such arrangements should not be subjected to the litigation process is because '. . . in the inception of the arrangement [they] never intended that they should be sued upon' (page 579). They are agreements 'outside the realm of contracts' not because the parties choose this course but because the courts presume it should be the case in view of concerns of broad legal policy.

Third, Atkin LJ suggests that relations between husband and wife are different, qualitatively, from typical commercial relations and this also justifies non-enforcement in the courts: 'The consideration that really obtains for them is that natural love and affection which counts for so little in these cold courts' (page 579). Legal doctrines and concepts sit uneasily with the language of domestic relations which do not work in accordance with the cut throat competitiveness of the market. Cooperation not competition is what distinguishes the rationale for the relationship in each case. Given these assumptions, Atkin LJ concludes that as a matter of judicial policy the courts should not extend their reach into affairs pertinent to domestic relationships because to do so would destroy the very values which make domestic relationships work: '. . . each house is a domain into which the King's writ does not seek to run, and to which his officers do not seek to be admitted' (page 579).

Applying these assumptions to the facts in *Balfour*, Atkin LJ concluded that he could find no evidence that the Balfours objectively contemplated that breach of their oral agreement would draw legal consequences.

Implications and importance of the judgment

Although the judges in *Balfour* articulate their reasons in support of the parties 'actual' intentions, this is a legal fiction. The objective test of intention is a presumption of legal policy only and emphasises what judges think, with a large dose of hindsight, the parties contemplated when forming their agreement. The question is fictitious because the parties in all probability (if we assessed their subjective views after the fact) did not consider the questions at the time; and, even if they did, how do the courts know for sure that denying a remedy in say a domestic agreement between husband and wife always supports the parties intentions even if it causes injustice. In some domestic cases the courts have presumed a legal intention to protect parties who've exposed themselves to large financial risks through detrimental reliance on another's word (*Parker* v. *Clark*).

Lord Justice Atkin's speech was in essence articulating broad standards of legal policy for justifying why, in Stephen Headley's view, contracts need to be kept in their place: keep them within a commercial sphere and keep them out of the domestic/social sphere. Atkin LJ suggests three reasons why this value judgment is justified. First, he assumed that contractualisation of relationships is not always a good thing because it could destroy what is valuable in a relationship by reducing it to a calculable transaction only. Morality and social convention create their own system of expectations enforced by their own regime of sanctions which can work as effectively as legal sanctions and enforcement processes. The legal 'capture' of the private sphere (what sociologists call 'juridification') is not necessarily a good thing. However, where domestic relationships between, say, husband and wife have broken down, the courts have been willing to ascribe a positive intention to contract based on the necessity of distributing assets. When you squeeze the love, affection, trust and loyalty from what once were very close relationships, all you are left with is an arms-length relationship akin to that found in the market. This new context justifies the change in presumption (see *Merritt* v. *Merritt*). Second, Atkin LJ wanted to avoid what is known as the 'floodgates' problem: extending the realm of contractual liability into contexts where numerous 'promises' are made every day, but not necessarily with commercial objectives and financial gain in mind. The courts could be over-burdened with trivial disputes that would be best dealt with outside the legal system.

Finally, the objective presumptions regarding intention assume an implicit value judgment that commercial exchange should be encouraged and supported – where the mechanisms of trust based on familiar ties and relations seen in domestic and family relationships are missing – in trade between relative strangers. These relationships are also productive and, through wealth creation brought about by exchange, make us all better off in the long term and should be encouraged.

The development of the presumptive tests

McKendrick suggests the *presumptions* tend to be based on rules of law or policy while the assessment of whether a presumption is *rebutted* rests on the parties' intentions. Two broad assumptions are now clear from the case law: those based on social/domestic relations and those based on commercial relations.

1. Social and domestic relationships

Promises made within social and domestic relationships – between family members or friends and relatives – are presumed *not* to give rise to liability in law so long as there is a close tie of love, affection and friendship between the parties. Where a 'close tie' nexus breaks down irreconcilably the courts are more willing to treat the promises in the same way as commercial promises (*Merritt* v. *Merritt*), but not always (see

Jones v. *Padavatton*), the resultant agreement having to pass all the other tests of certainty required of legally binding agreements. Rebutting the presumption is never easy with intention cases. However, the courts have shown in cases such as *Parker* v. *Clark* that the greater the detrimental reliance experienced by those in social relationships the more likely it is that legal consequences can be reasonably inferred to protect against the effect of such risks.

2. Commercial relationships
Whenever agreements or promises are made within a clear commercial context the courts presume the parties intend such promises to be legally binding. The presumption can be rebutted by the insertion of an 'honour' clause (*Rose and Frank* v. *Crompton*) which makes the agreement binding in 'honour' not law.

Has the intention test a future?

Some judges and commentators have suggested the test of intention serves no real purpose given that 'intention' tests are applied in other areas of contract law, notably agreement and construction of terms, where the rules are clearer and can be more effectively applied. Ascribing an intention as a legal rule always runs the risk of undermining the parties' actual intentions rather than supporting them.

Others, such as Freeman, suggest the assumptions underpinning *Balfour* were a product of their time – Victorian ideas of marriage and relationships which prioritise status and duty above individual autonomy and choice, values more pertinent to the basis of many relationships today.

FURTHER READING

Primary sources

Albert v. *Motor Insurers Bureau* [1972] AC 301

ERDC Group v. *Brunel University* [2006] EWHC 687 (TCC)

Ermogenous v. *Greek Orthodox Community of SA Inc* (2002) 209 CLR 95

Esso Petroleum Ltd v. *Commissioners of Customs and Excise* [1976] 1 WLR 1

Hadley v. *Kemp* [1999] EMLR 589

Jones v. *Padavatton* [1969] 1 WLR 328

Merritt v. *Merritt* [1970] 1 WLR 1211

Parker v. *Clark* [1960] 1 All ER 93

Rose and Frank Co v. *J R Crompton and Bros Ltd* [1923] AC 445

Simpkins v. *Pays* [1955] 1 WLR 975

Secondary sources

Freeman, M. (1996) 'Contracting in the Haven: *Balfour* v. *Balfour* Revisited', in Halson, R. (ed.) *Exploring the Boundaries of Contract*, Elgar, 68.

Hedley, S. (1985) 'Keeping Contract in its Place – *Balfour* v. *Balfour* and the Enforceability of Informal Agreements' (1985) 5, *Oxford Journal of Legal Studies*, 391.

Hepple, B. (1970) 'Intention to Create Legal Relations' (1970) 28, *Cambridge Law Journal*, 122.

Treitel, G. (1953) 'The Deserted Wife's Right to Pledge her Husband's Credit for Necessaries' (1953) 16, *Modern Law Review*, 221.

Unger, J. (1956) 'Intent to Create Legal Relations, Mutuality and Consideration' (1956) 19, *Modern Law Review*, 96.

4

CONTRACT LAW (OBLIGATIONS)

Contract terms

Liverpool City Council v. *Irwin* [1977] AC 239

Mick Woodley, Northumbria University

There are different ways of classifying the terms of an agreement. One way is to distinguish between terms according to the remedy available, should that term be breached. Hence towards the end of most contract modules students study the distinction between conditions, warranties and innominate terms with respect to the right of the innocent party to repudiate the contract and/or to sue for damages for breach of contract. Another classification would be into express terms and implied terms. The *express* terms of an agreement are those terms discussed and negotiated by the parties themselves. Express terms may be written or oral. Indeed they may be a combination of both, the only real distinction between them being the evidential one of proof. *Implied* terms, by way of contrast, are not discussed by the parties or, if they are, no conclusion is reached and they do not seemingly form part of the offer. Implied terms are those terms introduced into an agreement from an outside source. Traditionally those sources are stated to be the Courts (common law implied terms) and Parliament (statutory implied terms). At this point the astute should be asking themselves two questions. Firstly, how, if the parties have not discussed and agreed upon a term, can a term become part of the offer – certain specified terms upon which the parties are agreed? Secondly, how, if the courts espouse the principle of freedom of contract and a reluctance to interfere in the bargain that the parties make, can the courts imply terms into a contract? The answers to these questions are not easy and require an analysis of the basis upon which the courts are willing to imply terms into a contract. In the case of statutory implied terms the position is more straightforward. Parliament, unencumbered with contract law's underpinning doctrine, can determine on policy grounds that it may be necessary to impose obligations on the parties to a contract in order to resolve any actual or perceived imbalance in their respective bargaining strengths. An example of such an obligation is the implied term (a *condition*, the breach of which allows the consumer to repudiate the contract) that goods supplied under a consumer contract are of 'satisfactory quality', see s.14 Sale of Goods Act 1979 (as amended). But, as will be seen, the courts are also not averse to implication of a term on policy grounds, even if they are not always ready to admit it openly.

The issue of how terms are to be implied into a contract lay at the heart of the case of *Liverpool City Council* v. *Irwin*. In the early 1970s a group of tenants in Liverpool, fed up with lifts that did not work, rubbish chutes that were blocked, overflowing lavatory cisterns and unlit stairwells, undertook a rent strike in protest. Their landlord, the local corporation which had endeavoured, despite vandalism and non-cooperation from tenants, to maintain the common parts such as lifts and stairwells, commenced proceedings for possession of the premises. The tenants counterclaimed (*inter alia*) on the basis that the corporation was obliged to keep the common parts under repair even though the terms of the tenancy apparently imposed no obligations on the landlord. Indeed such documentary evidence as there was (it not being the practice, at least in those days, to have a formal tenancy agreement for council lettings) seemed to impose many obligations on the tenants who were required to sign to accept the tenancy but none were specified on the landlord. Lord Wilberforce in the House of Lords observed that this amounted to 'a contract which [was] partly, but not wholly, stated in writing'. As such regard needed to be given, according to his Lordship, to the actions of the parties and the surrounding circumstances.

When the case came before the county court judge he expressed himself to be appalled by the general conditions of the property, finding several defects in the common parts involving non-functioning lifts and rubbish chutes, a lack of lighting on staircases and stairwells and dangerous holes giving access to the rubbish chutes. Not all these defects were believed to be caused by vandalism. Nonetheless the judge granted possession to the landlord, while at the same time awarding the nominal damages sought by the tenants on their counterclaim. With respect to the latter it was held that there was to be implied a covenant by the corporation to keep the common parts in repair. However, on appeal to the Court of Appeal that implied covenant (term) was rejected, albeit on differing grounds by the members of the court.

Roskill and Ormerod LJJ asserted what, in their view, was the well-established basis upon which a term would be implied into a contract by the courts, namely that of necessity. Lord Justice Ormerod relied upon a passage from Lord Goddard CJ in *R* v. *Paddington and St Marylebone Rent Tribunal* where it was stated that no term should ever be implied into a contract 'unless there [was] such a necessary implication that the court [could] have no doubt what covenant or undertaking they ought to write into the agreement' (at page 17).

Lord Denning MR, not for the first time, nor the last, was prepared to be more adventurous than his fellow judges. His Lordship rehearsed the standard bases on which a term would normally be implied into a contract. First, such would occur when it was 'reasonable and necessary to do so in order to give business efficacy to [a] transaction: see *The Moorcock*'. Second, a term would be implied when it was so obviously intended by the contracting parties to be a part of their agreement that, if an officious bystander had asked the parties whether there was to be such a term, they would both have testily suppressed the bystander with a common: 'Oh, of course. It was so obvious that we did not bother to mention it' (see *Shirlaw* v. *Southern Foundries (1926) Ltd*).

Lord Denning believed that, in fact, the cases showed that the courts went further than this and 'implied a term according to whether or not it was reasonable in all the circumstances to do so'. His Lordship stated that he was strengthened in his approach by the fact that a Law Commission Report on the Obligations of Landlords and Tenants had recommended that some term imposing a duty on landlords to keep common parts under repair

4

CONTRACT LAW (OBLIGATIONS)

should be imposed by statute. However, he did not believe that the courts should wait for Parliament to act. Rather, in his opinion, judges had a constructive role to play in the development of the law and should not allow litigants to have their cases 'decided by the dead hand of the past'. The only issue for Lord Denning was the extent of the duty to be implied. This, he determined, should not be an absolute duty but one to 'take reasonable care to keep the lifts, staircase, etc safe and fit for use by the tenants and their families and visitors'. However, unfortunately for the tenants, on the facts of the case he believed that the corporation had fulfilled this obligation. Its efforts had simply been defeated by the vandalism.

Roskill and Ormerod LJJ were unwilling to follow Lord Denning's lead. While accepting the hardships on tenants that might arise from the absence of the postulated implied term, they pointed to the fact that 'millions of tenancy agreements' had been entered into on the basis that there was no such term and that injustice might befall landlords subjected to 'unduly onerous or unreasonable obligations'. In their view such significant changes were for Parliament to introduce, not the courts.

On this last point Lord Wilberforce in the House of Lords agreed with the majority in the Court of Appeal that it was not for the courts 'to introduce into contracts any terms they think reasonable or to anticipate legislative recommendations of the Law Commission' (at page 257). On the other hand, Lord Salmon, in common with Lord Denning, believed that 'the law should not be condemned to sterility and that the judges should take care not to abdicate their traditional role of developing the law' (at page 263).

On the main issue in the case the opinions of their Lordships were equally divided, at least as to the basis for implication of any term, if not the outcome in the dispute. Having related the facts and the decisions of the lower courts, Lord Wilberforce (with whom Lord Fraser agreed) reviewed the basis for the implication of terms in a contract and high-lighted the fact that a term might be added because of established usage. Such might be the position in mercantile contracts where the term to be implied was well known to the parties and to which they would, if asked, readily concur. Or it might be that a term would be incorporated because without it the contract was unworkable – the business efficacy test. However, Lord Wilberforce rejected Lord Denning's third approach to implication, namely one based on the addition of reasonable terms. This he categorised as '[extend-ing] a long, and undesirable, way beyond sound authority' (at page 254). However, his Lordship stated that there was a further point on a continuous spectrum by which the court established what the parties intended their contract to contain. This required the court to read into the contract such terms as the nature of the contract itself demanded. Thus a term might be implied because it was a 'legal incident' of a particular relationship (see *Lister v. Romford Ice and Cold Storage Co. Ltd*) rather than one based on business efficacy. On the facts of the present case it was necessary, given the nature of the rela-tionship between the tenants and the landlord (a high rise block of flats with multi-occupation), that there should be some contractual obligation on the latter with respect to common parts. Having established the basis upon which a duty might be imposed upon the corporation, Lord Wilberforce proceeded to agree with Lord Denning that the extent of any duty was to take reasonable care to keep the premises in reasonable repair, and not the absolute duty for which the tenants had contended at first instance. Indeed, his

Lordship noted that he had reached the same result as Lord Denning but 'by a less dangerous route'.

Lord Cross agreed with Lord Wilberforce that on occasions the courts implied terms in all contracts of a certain type as a legal incident and postulated that Lord Denning in trying to 'kill off' the officious bystander test must have overlooked the authority of *Lister* v. *Romford Ice*. However, in Lord Cross's opinion the basis for implying such a term was not one of necessity as it had been for Lord Wilberforce but whether 'the term in question would be one which it would be reasonable to insert' (at page 258). On the other hand his Lordship agreed with both the Court of Appeal and the House of Lords that the duty to be implied was 'not an absolute one but only a duty to use reasonable care' (at page 259).

Lord Salmon viewed the tenancy agreement as being an all too common, one-sided document that spelled out the details of the tenants' obligations but expressed none of those owed by the landlord. But, as his Lordship pointed out, terms could be implied from all the surrounding circumstances, as well as being expressed. While agreeing with Lord Denning that the judiciary had a role to play in developing the law, he was not prepared to accept that a term could be implied into a contract 'merely because it seems reasonable to do so' (at page 262). Indeed, Lord Salmon's approach was akin to that of Roskill and Ormerod LJJ, namely that a term should only be implied if it was necessary to do so. However, his Lordship disagreed with the majority view in the Court of Appeal on the facts. He believed that it would be 'difficult to think of any term which it would be more necessary to imply than one without which the whole transaction would become futile, inefficacious and absurd', namely that the landlords on the facts owed a duty to exercise reasonable care with respect to the lifts and the staircases. Having said that Lord Salmon then declined to rule that the council had failed in this duty because that failure had not been pleaded at the outset, rather it had been claimed that the council had owed an absolute duty. The council had thus not had the opportunity to defend itself against a claim based upon lack of reasonable care.

Lord Edmund-Davies would also have agreed with the majority of the Court of Appeal that the basis for implication of a term into a contract was to be found in identifying the presumed intention of the parties. This was to be done according to the authority of cases such as *The Moorcock* and the dicta therein of Bowen LJ rather than on the basis which had commended itself to Lord Denning. But, his Lordship observed, an alternative, more attractive approach had been raised before the House, namely the implication of a term as a legal incident of a particular kind of contract as in *Lister* v. *Romford Ice*. The standard of duty to be achieved was one of reasonable care. However, on the issue of whether the council had reached that standard, Lord Edmund-Davies noted that the county court judge had not been asked to make a finding and that it would thus be wrong to do so at the appeal stage.

Overall their Lordships (or at least four of them) were prepared to find that the nature of the relationship, a tenancy in a high rise block of flats, required as a legal incident the implication of an implied duty on the landlord to take reasonable care to maintain the staircases and lifts so that they could be used by tenants to access their flats. This, of course, proved to be a somewhat hollow 'victory' given that the House ruled the duty not

4

CONTRACT LAW (OBLIGATIONS)

to be an absolute one but an obligation to use reasonable care, which the council was either held to have achieved or not to have had the opportunity to have established. The wider significance of the case, however, is the House's confirmation of the distinction between terms implied *in fact* and terms implied *in law*. The test for the former is still taken to be that of business efficacy or the officious bystander, while the latter arises as a legal incident of a particular relationship.

The admission of this distinction between fact and law and the acceptance of the latter arguably sowed the seeds for the subsequent development of implied duties, notably in relation to employment contracts in the context of constructive unfair dismissal. Here the overarching duty on the employer to treat its employees with mutual trust and respect has played a central role in balancing managerial prerogative in the workplace (see *Malik* v. *BCCI*). In *Johnson* v. *Unisys Ltd* Lord Hoffmann explained these developments as the common law adapting to recognise a new social reality. Not that every development has been as far reaching. In *Scally* v. *Southern Health and Social Services Board* Lord Bridge (with whom the rest of the House agreed) implied a term into the contracts of employment of a number of junior doctors that their employer was obliged to notify them of an opportunity to improve their pension provision. In so doing Lord Bridge preferred to found such a term as a necessary legal incident of a definable category of contractual relationship rather than on the basis of necessity to give the contract efficacy. However, having apparently introduced a term with a potentially wide ambit, his Lordship restricted its scope by closely defining the circumstances in which such a term would be applied. It is arguable that by limiting the application of the term with such precision the House has placed its decision somewhere between the term implied in fact and that implied in law (see further *Spring* v. *Guardian Assurance plc*). What these cases do illustrate is the apparently overlapping use of the term 'necessary' in relation to both types of term.

More recently the Court of Appeal has rejected 'the proposition that there is to be implied into the contract of employment a general duty on the part of the employer that he will take reasonable care of the economic well-being of his employees' (see *Crossley* v. *Faithful & Gould Holdings Ltd*, per Dyson LJ at page 460). In refusing the implication of this term his Lordship, after reviewing the case law developments post *Liverpool City Council* v. *Irwin*, noted that the House in the cases above had declined to take such a 'big leap', that such a term would impose 'an unfair and unreasonable burden on employers' and that there were no obvious policy reasons to do so.

Andrew Phang, who has written extensively on the question of the implication of terms, has argued that the implication of terms in law is a fiction which would best be replaced by accepting that there is in practice no difference between terms implied in fact and those implied in law, both depending ultimately upon 'an ad hoc value choice by the courts concerned' (see Phang, 'Implied Terms Revisited' at page 412). Phang criticises the use of the implication of terms as a weapon in the judicial armoury. He believes that such usage undermines the very predictability which the doctrine of freedom of contract seeks to protect and which commercial lawyers value because the parties to an agreement can be sure that the courts will not interfere with the bargain that they have reached. However, notwithstanding the caution recently displayed by the Court of Appeal in *Crossley*, the genie is very much out of the bottle and unlikely to go away.

FURTHER READING

Primary sources

Crossley v. *Faithful & Gould Holdings Ltd* [2004] 4 All ER 447

Johnson v. *Unisys Ltd* [2003] 1 AC 519

Lister v. *Romford Ice and Cold Storage Co. Ltd* [1957] AC 555

Malik v. *BCCI* [1998] AC 20

R v. *Paddington and St Marylebone Rent Tribunal* [1947] 2 All ER 15

Scally v. *Southern Health and Social Services Board* [1992] 1 AC 294

Shirlaw v. *Southern Foundries (1926) Ltd* [1939] 2 KB 206

Spring v. *Guardian Assurance plc* [1995] 2 AC 296

The Moorcock (1889) 14 PD 64

Secondary sources

Phang, A. (1990) 'Implied Terms Revisited' [1990] *Journal of Business Law*, 394.

Phang, A. (1993) 'Implied Terms in English Law: Some Recent Developments' [1993] *JBL*, 242.

Phang, A. (1998) 'Implied Terms, Business Efficacy and the Officious Bystander – A Modern History' [1998] *JBL*, 1.

4

CONTRACT LAW (OBLIGATIONS)

Exemption clauses

George Mitchell (Chesterhall) Ltd v. *Finney Lock Seeds*
[1983] All ER 737

Liane Atkin, Northumbria University

George Mitchell is an important case when considering exemption clauses and their enforceability in contract law. An exemption clause is a contractual clause which seeks to exclude or limit a party's liability for breach of the contract. Three conditions must be met before an exemption clause can be enforced:

1. The clause must be incorporated into the contract.
2. The clause must, on its usual meaning, cover the breach which has occurred.
3. The clause must be enforceable in light of the Unfair Contract Terms Act 1977 ('UCTA').

George Mitchell is most important in relation to the third condition as the case offered the first opportunity for the House of Lords to consider the impact of the definition of 'reasonableness' in UCTA and its approach has been of vital importance to cases decided since. The other two conditions were also considered in *George Mitchell* in the context of previous case law and these two conditions will be considered briefly before analysing *George Mitchell*'s approach to establishing 'reasonableness' as defined in UCTA.

1. The clause must be incorporated into the contract

In relation to the first condition, the *George Mitchell* case simply confirmed previous case law which had established that in order to rely on an exemption clause a party must show that it has been effectively incorporated into the contract.

In a situation where the document is not signed by the parties then it will be incorporated into the contract only if reasonable notice of the term was given (*Parker* v. *Southern Railway Co.*). In *George Mitchell* this issue was considered briefly in the Court of Appeal judgment. The claimants (who were farmers) had ordered a particular variety of cabbage seed orally from the defendant's representative. The claimants then received an invoice which contained conditions of sale on the reverse, including a clause limiting the defendant's liability. The cabbage ultimately supplied was of the wrong variety and was defective. As Lord Denning noted in the Court of Appeal judgment 'The farmers were aware that the sale was subject to some conditions of sale. All seed merchants have conditions of sale. They were on the back of the catalogue. They were also on the back of the invoice each year'. While Lord Denning commented that the conditions were not negotiated by any representatives, previous case law (*Thompson* v. *LMSR Co.* and *E'Estrange* v. *F Graucob Ltd*) reinforced the reluctant finding that where an exemption clause was expressed in clear words, albeit in small print, it would be effectively incorporated into the contract.

2. The clause must cover the breach

George Mitchell also confirmed previous case law which held that, provided the wording of the exemption clause was clear and unambiguous, it would effectively cover the breach and should not be 'twisted' to enable judges to find that clearly drafted exemption clauses should not be enforced. This arose from the Court's consideration of the second condition which must be fulfilled in order to rely on an exemption clause; that its words must effectively cover the breach.

The *contra preferentem* principle says that if there is any doubt or ambiguity in the meaning of the words then this should be interpreted against the party who is seeking to rely upon the clause. Before UCTA came into force in the UK (and before *George Mitchell*), the Courts had often sought to use this principle in order to ensure that apparently 'unfair' exemption clauses could not be enforced. This unfortunately resulted in judges at times giving what Lord Diplock in *George Mitchell* called a 'tortured meaning' to plain words in order to 'avoid giving effect to an exclusion or liability' which seemed unfair. An example of such a case is that of *Hollier* v. *Ramblers Motors (AMC) Ltd* in which it was decided that a clear term which held that 'the company is not responsible for damage caused by fire to customer's cars on the premises' was not plain enough to exclude liability for damage caused by a fire which resulted from the defendant's negligence. Also, in attempts to narrowly construe exemption clauses, the Courts had held in several cases that exemption clauses could not be used to restrict or exclude liability following 'fundamental breach' of the contract (a very serious breach going to the heart of the contract). However, two cases decided in the House of Lords shortly before *George Mitchell* and known as '*The Securicor*' *cases*, cautioned against giving limitation clauses such an artificial construction. The first of these cases was *Photo Production Ltd* v. *Securicor Transport Ltd* in which it was held that it was not good law to say that exemption clauses were no longer effective following termination by fundamental breach (and so effectively abolishing the 'doctrine of fundamental breach' in this context). The second of the Securicor cases, *Ailsa Craig Fishing Co. Ltd* v. *Malvern Fishing Co. Ltd*, argued that 'one must not strive to create ambiguities . . . the relevant words must be given their natural, plain meaning'.

In *George Mitchell* the House of Lords confirmed *The Securicor cases* and recognised that there could no longer be a 'doctrine of fundamental breach' nor should exemption clauses be given a strained construction. This decision overruled the earlier decision of the Court of Appeal in *George Mitchell* in which it was found that the clause did not cover the breach on its construction. Lord Denning dissented from this view in the Court of Appeal and argued that this approach was not available as the clause in its natural meaning was effective to cover the breach following the decisions of the House of Lords in the Securicor cases. The House of Lords agreed with Lord Denning and commented that the judgment of the Court of Appeal had 'come dangerously close to re-introducing by the

4

CONTRACT LAW (OBLIGATIONS)

back door the doctrine of "fundamental breach"'. They also pointed out that the limitation clause in *George Mitchell* referred to 'seeds' and the defective seeds were indeed seeds (albeit of the wrong variety) so there was no ambiguity of construction. The Lords concluded that they knew of no principle of construction which could be applied to prevent the limitation clause being enforceable, confirming **The Securicor cases** and making it clear that judges should not endeavour to give strained and 'hostile' constructions to clearly worded exemption clauses. In addition, the Lords rejected the concept of 'fundamental breach' as being effective to end the enforceability of exemption clauses, again clarifying the law following uncertainty reintroduced by the Court of Appeal's decision.

3. The clause must be enforceable in the light of UCTA

George Mitchell was the first case to analyse the definition of reasonableness in UCTA and, while each case will depend on its own particular facts, its approach provides a useful reference when considering the reasonableness of exemption clauses. In addition *George Mitchell* recognised that each case would need to be dealt with on its particular facts and confirmed that higher courts should not interfere with lower court's decisions unless they were clearly wrong on the facts.

UCTA contains statutory provisions which impact upon the enforceability of certain contract terms, including exemption clauses. Several of the Act's provisions state that a party may not rely upon an exclusion or limitation of liability except in so far as the exemption is 'reasonable'. In particular, section 6 of UCTA prevents limitation or exclusion of liability for breach of the terms implied into sale of goods contracts by ss.13, 14(2) and (3) and 15 of the Sale of Goods Act 1979 ('SOGA') (which respectively provide that goods should correspond with their description, be of satisfactory quality, be fit for purpose and correspond with any sample) as against businesses except where the term is 'reasonable'. Any attempted exclusion of these implied terms as against 'consumers' as defined in UCTA will be void.

Whether a contractual term is reasonable will always be dependant on the particular circumstances of the case. In relation to exemption of liability under sections 6 and 7 (which relates to exclusion of terms implied by the Supply of Goods and Services Act 1982 similar to those implied by the SOGA) of UCTA, courts are required to consider whether it was reasonable to include the clause at the time the contract was made in light of the guidelines set out in Schedule 2 to the Act. These guidelines contain a non-exhaustive list of factors which should be taken into account including:

(i) the relative strength of the bargaining powers of the parties;

(ii) whether the customer had any opportunity of buying the goods without the clause from any source;

(iii) whether the customer knew or ought to have known of the existence of the term;

(iv) whether it was reasonable at the time of the contract to expect compliance with the exempted condition would be practicable; and

(v) whether the goods were manufactured or processed to the special order of the customer.

Before *George Mitchell*, the courts had, in the case of *R W Green Ltd* v. *Cade Bros Farm*, considered the reasonableness test under the Supply of Goods (Implied Terms) Act 1973 which was similar to the test later set out in UCTA. In *Green* (which also involved the sale of seeds) Griffiths J considered the fact that the parties were of equal bargaining power (the terms in question had been negotiated by trade bodies), that the parties had contracted on the same terms for five or six years and that the farmer had chosen not to purchase seed which had been certified as healthy for a higher price. On the circumstances of this case the court held that the clause (which limited liability for defective seeds to the cost of the seeds) was fair and reasonable. However, *George Mitchell* was the first opportunity for the House of Lords to consider the definition of reasonableness within UCTA and, as remarked by Lord Bridge, 'this is the first time your Lordships' House has had the opportunity to consider a modern statutory provision giving the Court power to override contractual terms excluding or restricting liability, which depends on the Court's view of what is "fair and reasonable"'. The Lords considered the factors set out in Schedule 2 of UCTA. In favour of the defendants they concluded that the claimants had known of the relevant clause and that they were claiming a significant sum of damages by contrast to the price of the seeds. However, when considering the bargaining power of the parties they highlighted the fact that the terms had not been negotiated by representative bodies and that this was linked with the lack of opportunity to buy seeds without a limitation of liability. There was also factual evidence from witnesses on behalf of the defendants which stated that their practice was to negotiate settlement of farmer's claims where they believed the claims were justified. This evidence indicated a clear recognition that reliance on the limitation of liability would not be reasonable in all cases. Finally, the Lords considered the fact that the defendant could easily have insured against the risk of supplying defective seeds without a significant increase in the seeds' price. The Lords accordingly concluded that it would be unreasonable to allow reliance on the clause. An important aspect of the Lords' approach was that it effectively recognised that each case should be dealt with on its own facts and, significantly, Lord Bridge also provided guidance on how a decision on what is 'fair and reasonable' should be approached by an appeal court. He indicated that there will 'sometimes be room for a legitimate difference in judicial opinion' and that, in his view, an appeal court should avoid interference with the original court's decision unless it was clearly wrong.

The approach of the Lords to the issue of reasonableness in *George Mitchell* has been followed and referred to in many cases subsequently although, of course, by the very nature of the definition of reasonableness each case must ultimately be dealt with on its own particular facts. In the case of *St Albans City and District Council* v. *International Computers Ltd* the Court of Appeal considered the various factors set out in Schedule 2 of UCTA and particularly considered the fact that the defendant was in a very strong bargaining position and had insurance cover far in excess of the limitation of liability. Nourse LJ stated in this case that he did not see any grounds to overturn the decision of the trial judge, citing the non-interventionary approach espoused by Lord Bridge in *George Mitchell*. This approach has been endorsed in other cases including *Expo Fabric UK Ltd* v. *Naughty Clothing Co* and *Overseas Medical Supplies Ltd* v. *Orient Transport Services*.

4

CONTRACT LAW (OBLIGATIONS)

The decision in the important and relatively recent case of *Watford Electronics Ltd* v. *Sanderson CFL Ltd* decided on its particular facts that the original judge had been wrong in principle in deciding a clause was unreasonable. This case concerned two parties of equal bargaining power who had individually negotiated the contract. It was held in this case that when experienced businessmen negotiate a contract they should be taken to be the 'best judge on whether the terms of the agreement are reasonable'. While this does not mean that the courts will never interfere in such an agreement it suggests an increasing reluctance of the courts to become involved in individually negotiated commercial contracts.

In conclusion it is clear that *George Mitchell* has been extremely important to the development of the law in relation to exemption clauses. The decision not only usefully considered each of the requirements which must be fulfilled when seeking to rely on an exemption clause but also provided us with the first detailed consideration of the reasonableness test within UCTA which has been referred to in subsequent cases. It is for this reason that the case remains greatly significant and relevant today.

FURTHER READING

Primary sources

Supply of Goods (Implied Terms) Act 1973

The Sale of Goods Act 1979

The Unfair Contract Terms Act 1977

Ailsa Craig Fishing Co Ltd v. *Malvern Fishing Co. Ltd* [1983] 1 All ER 101

E'Estrange v. *F Graucob Ltd* (1934) 2 KB 394

Expo Fabric UK Ltd v. *Naughty Clothing Co.* [2003] EWCA Civ 1165

George Mitchell (Chesterhall) Ltd v. *Finney Lock Seeds* [1983] 2 All ER 108 (CA)

Hollier v. *Ramblers Motors (AMC) Ltd* [1972] CA

Overland Shoes Ltd v. *Schenkers Ltd* [1998] 1 Lloyds Rep 498

Overseas Medical Supplies Ltd v. *Orient Transport Services* [1999] 2 Lloyds Rep 273

Parker v. *Southern Railway Co.* (1877) CR 2CPD 416

Photo Production Ltd v. *Securicor Transport Ltd* [1980] 1 All ER 556

R W Green Ltd v. *Cade Bros Farm* [1978] 1 Lloyds Rep 602

St Albans City and District Council v. *International Computers Ltd* [1996] 4 All ER 481

Thompson v. *LMSR Co.* (1930) 1 KB 41 CA

Watford Electronics Ltd v. *Sanderson CFL Ltd* [2001] EWCA Civ 317

Secondary sources

Barker, D. (2001) 'A Return to Freedom of Contract' (2001) *New Law Journal*, vol. 151, no. 6974, 344.

Lawson, R. (1999) 'The Reasonableness Test, Recent Case Law under the Unfair Contract Terms Act 1977' (1999) *TRL*, vol. 18, no. 1, 18.

Misrepresentation

Howard Marine & Dredging Co. Ltd v. *Ogden & Sons (Excavation) Ltd* [1978] 2 All ER 1134

Maureen Maksymiw, Nottingham University

When parties negotiate prior to entering into a contract, numerous statements or representations are made. Some will become terms of the contract, others will not. The contract, for example, may later be put in writing but it may not include all the statements that were made during the negotiations. It does not mean that the person to whom the statements were made is without a remedy if it turns out one of those statements was false.

Such a person may have an action for misrepresentation if they can show that a false statement of fact had been made which induced him to enter into the contract. The representee, that is the person to whom the misrepresentation is made, can sue the maker of the statement, the representor, even if what had been said does not amount to a term of the contract. Different types of actionable misrepresentation have been established. Prior to 1964 there were only two types of actionable misrepresentation, fraudulent and innocent. The courts take any allegation of fraud very seriously and thus fraudulent misrepresentation is difficult to prove. One has to show not only that the statement was false but also that it was made with a dishonest intention. The action is one in the tort of deceit. If the claimant succeeds he can claim both rescission (setting the contract aside) and damages (money compensation). All other misrepresentations that are not made with a dishonest intention, for example, where the maker believes the statement to be true whether reasonably or not, were termed innocent for which there is only one main remedy, rescission. Damages cannot be awarded.

In 1962 the Law Reform Committee in its tenth Report recommended that a claimant should be entitled to damages for negligent misrepresentation. Its report was not acted on quickly and in 1963 a case on misrepresentation was heard by the House of Lords, *Hedley Byrne & Co. Ltd* v. *Heller & Partners Ltd*. The court decided that damages could be awarded in certain circumstances even if the misrepresentation had not been made fraudulently. The court did so by expanding the tort of negligence to cover misrepresentations made negligently. The liability depends on a duty of care arising from a 'special relationship' between the parties. Thus another type of misrepresentation was established. The scope of the decision is uncertain but it was made clear in 1976 in *Esso* v. *Mardon Petroleum Co. Ltd* that it extended to negligent misrepresentations that induced the representee to enter into a contract.

After *Hedley Byrne* had been decided the Misrepresentation Act 1967 was passed. This implemented the recommendations made in 1962 by the Law Reform Committee.

This report, of course, predated the decision of *Hedley Byrne*. The Misrepresentation Act 1967, s.2(1) states that

> where a person has entered into a contract after a misrepresentation has been made to him by another party thereto and as a result thereof he has suffered loss, then, if the person making the misrepresentation would be liable to damages in respect thereof had the misrepresentation been made fraudulently, that person shall be so liable notwithstanding that the misrepresentation was not made fraudulently, unless he proves that he had reasonable ground to believe and did believe up to the time the contract was made that the facts represented were true.

So, within a few years two further types of misrepresentation had been added to that of innocent and fraudulent for which damages could be awarded. One had been developed by the courts, often called negligent misstatement at common law, and the other introduced by statute. It was not clear what the differences between the two were.

Howard Marine & Dredging Co. Ltd v. Ogden & Sons (Excavation) Ltd

Another decade passed before the Court of Appeal heard the case of *Howard Marine*. It is an important case as the court considered both negligent misstatement at common law and misrepresentation under s.2(1) Misrepresentation Act 1967. By looking at the case in detail the differences between the two recently established types of misrepresentation can be considered.

The facts

The defendant, Ogden & Sons (Excavation) Ltd, was negotiating with a water authority over a contract to excavate and dispose of earth so that the water authority could construct some sewage works. The defendant wanted to hire two barges to carry the excavated earth out to sea and dump it there. It entered into negotiations with the plaintiff, Howard Marine & Dredging Co. Ltd, which owned some barges. In order to work out how long it would take to carry out the work and thus the price it would charge the water authority, the defendant needed to know the amount of earth each barge could transport. This was known as the payload of the barges. The plaintiff's representative, Mr O'Loughlin, stated that the payload of each barge was 1600 tonnes. This was wrong. The correct figure was, in fact, 1055 tonnes. In order to calculate the payload figure various deductions, such as the weight of the fuel and crew, had to be made from the barge's deadweight. He gave the wrong figure because he calculated it on the basis of an inaccurate entry in Lloyd's Register for the deadweight capacity of the barges. The correct figure for the deadweight was contained in the manufacturer's specification that the plaintiff had in its possession but which Mr O'Loughlin failed to check. When the error came to light the defendant realised it would take longer to excavate and dump the earth. It refused to pay the hire charges and so the plaintiff withdrew the barges from the contract and sued the defendant for the hire charges. The defendant counterclaimed and alleged that the plaintiff had wrongly stated the capacity of the barges and was therefore liable in damages.

The issues

The trial before the first instance judge, Bristow J, in the Commercial Court was on liability only, that is whether the plaintiff was liable for its false statement. There was no argument as to how much it should be paid if it were liable. The trial still took over two weeks to hear.

Three main arguments were put to Bristow J as to why the plaintiff was liable for the false statement:

(i)   that it had breached a term of the contract as to the carrying capacity of the barges,

(ii) that the plaintiff owed a duty to exercise reasonable care to be accurate in making such statements, following *Hedley Byrne*, and that duty had been breached,

(iii) that it was liable under s.2, Misrepresentation Act 1967.

At first instance the defendant failed in all its arguments and accordingly Bristow J ordered it to pay the hire charges owed to the plaintiff.

The appeal

The defendant appealed to the Court of Appeal. The plaintiff, although it had won at first instance, also served a notice of appeal stating that Bristow J's decision was correct on a further ground, that there was a term of the written contract that excluded any liability of the plaintiff. This was a further issue the Court of Appeal had to consider.

All three judges in the Court of Appeal gave judgments and their views on the arguments mentioned above. It is helpful to show their conclusions in the table below before looking at their reasoning.

Issue	Denning MR	Bridge LJ	Shaw LJ	Majority decision
1. Was it a term?	No	No	No	No
2. Was the plaintiff liable under *Hedley Byrne*?	No	Doubtful	Yes	No
3. Was the plaintiff liable under the Misrepresentation Act 1967?	No	Yes	Yes	Yes
4. Was any such liability excluded under the contract?	Yes	No	No	No

The defendant, therefore, succeeded in its appeal and the plaintiff was liable for the false statement under s.2(1), Misrepresentation Act 1967. The judges were divided in their views on the last three issues so one needs to look at their judgments on these issues in detail. One can see that if the defendant had relied solely on the *Hedley Byrne* principle it was unlikely to have succeeded and therefore the Misrepresentation Act 1967 was essential to its success. One must analyse why this was the case to understand the importance of the decision.

1. Was it a term?

It had been argued that the statement as to the barges' capacity was a contractual promise, a warranty, that the figures were accurate. All three judges agreed with the first

4

CONTRACT LAW (OBLIGATIONS)

199

instance judge that no such promise had been made. There was nothing in the circumstances to indicate the statement was made with the intention that it would amount to a contractual term.

2. Was the plaintiff liable under the *Hedley Byrne* principle?

Denning MR concluded that this was not a situation that gave rise to a duty of care. In order for a duty to arise under the *Hedley Byrne* principle the representee has to make clear to the representor the gravity of the inquiry and that he is seeking considered advice. Denning MR looked at the casual nature of the statement; it was given orally, in an offhand manner and was only the best answer Mr O'Loughlin could give from memory. No duty of care arose. Shaw LJ agreed that the gravity of the inquiry and the importance attached to the answer had to be made known. He felt, however, that in light of the fact that the purpose for which the barges were to be used was made known and a specific fact had been asked for from information within the knowledge of the representor, a duty of care did arise and it had been breached. Bridge LJ did not express a concluded view on negligence but did say he doubted the circumstances were such to impose a duty of care for the accuracy of the statement and doubted if the evidence established a breach of any such duty.

3. Was the plaintiff liable under s.2(1) Misrepresentation Act 1967?

One might think that the use of the words 'unless he has reasonable ground to believe' in s.2(1) imposes a duty on the representor equivalent to the duty of care under *Hedley Byrne* but Bridge and Shaw LJJ stated that even if the plaintiff did not owe a duty of care it was liable under s.2(1) of the Misrepresentation Act 1967. The plaintiff could not escape liability by disproving negligence but had to prove positively that it had reasonable grounds for its belief. An honest belief in what had been said was not enough. They concluded that the plaintiff did not have such reasonable grounds. Mr O'Loughlin had been aware of the existence of the accurate figures in the documents in the plaintiff's possession and could have consulted them. He could not explain why he did not consult them. He had, therefore, no objective reasonable grounds to use the incorrect figures in Lloyd's Register in preference to the correct ones. They concluded this even though the Lloyd's Register was a well-trusted and authoritative publication in the shipping industry and was usually an extremely reliable source of information.

Bridge LJ stated that under the Act there was 'an absolute obligation not to state facts which the representor cannot prove he has reasonable grounds to believe'. Relying on an authoritative document such as Lloyd's Register was not enough when the correct figures were in the plaintiff's possession. It is clear therefore that the burden to show one has reasonable grounds is a heavy one.

Denning MR dissented and took the view that Mr O'Loughlin had reasonable grounds for his belief as he had relied on an authoritative source, Lloyd's Register, that was described as the 'bible' in the industry.

4. Was any such liability excluded under the contract?

There was a term in the written contract that stated 'the acceptance of handing over the vessel shall be conclusive evidence that [the vessel] . . . is in all respects fit for the intended and contemplated use by [the defendant] and in every other way satisfactory to them'.

The plaintiff argued that even if it was liable to the defendant this term excluded any such liability. Under s.3 of the Misrepresentation Act 1967 at that time such a term could only be relied upon by the plaintiff if it was fair and reasonable in the circumstances of the case. The exact wording of s.3 has since been amended. Bridge LJ said that the clause had to be construed narrowly. It could only be relied on as conclusive evidence of the defendant's satisfaction in relation to attributes of the barges, which would be apparent on an ordinary inspection of them. The deadweight and payload capacity of the barges were not things that could be seen from inspecting the barges. They could only be established by calculation and inspection of the barges' documents. The clause did not, therefore, exclude the plaintiff's liability. Shaw LJ said very little about this term. He merely said that his judgment was not affected by the clause, as it did not absolve the plaintiff from the consequences of its negligence and that he agreed with Bridge LJ as to the effect of the relevant provisions of the Misrepresentation Act.

Denning MR dissented and thought that reliance on the term was fair and reasonable as the parties were commercial organisations of equal bargaining power, it was a clause common to contracts of this kind, and the defendant had had an opportunity to verify the figures when the barges were inspected by their surveyors.

Conclusion

In *Howard Marine* the court did not consider how the damages under s.2 of the Misrepresentation Act 1967 should be assessed but subsequent cases such as *Royscot* v. *Rogerson* have. The court considered only whether the plaintiff was liable for its misrepresentation. It appears highly unlikely that the defendant would have succeeded in its action for negligent misstatement following *Hedley Byrne* but it succeeded under s.2(1) of the Misrepresentation Act. *Howard Marine* established that under the Act there is no need to establish a duty of care. An important difference between an action under the Act and action for negligent misstatement is that under s.2(1) the burden of proof is reversed. In an action for negligent misstatement the plaintiff has the burden of proving the existence of a special relationship. Under s.2(1), once the representee has established a false statement of fact had been made which induced him to enter the contract, the burden passes to the representor to prove he had objectively reasonable grounds for believing the statement was true. *Howard Marine* shows that it is a heavy burden to discharge.

FURTHER READING

Primary sources

Esso v. *Mardon Petroleum Co. Ltd* [1976] 2 All ER 5

Hedley Byrne & Co. Ltd v. *Heller & Partners Ltd* [1963] 2 All ER 575

Royscot Trust Ltd v. *Rogerson* [1991] 3 All ER 294

4

CONTRACT LAW (OBLIGATIONS)

Illegality

Littlewoods Organisation Ltd v. *Harris*
[1978] 1 All ER 1026

Mick Woodley, Northumbria University

The modern law relating to contracts in restraint of trade stems from the House of Lords' decision in *Nordenfeldt* v. *Maxim Nordenfeldt* where it was held that *prima facie* all such contracts were void and unenforceable unless they were reasonable in the interests of the parties and reasonable in the interests of the public. Typically, restraint clauses are to be found in contracts for the sale of a business (*Nordenfeldt* itself) or in employment contracts. In the former the vendor of the business and its goodwill promises not to set up a similar business in competition with the purchaser. In the latter an employee agrees not to work for a competitor or to set up a rival enterprise. In relation to employment restraints an employer wishing to rely upon a restraint clause must not only prove that the restraint is reasonable but also that the employer has a proprietary interest to protect. Usually this has involved employers identifying either a trade secret or other confidential information worthy of protection, or establishing 'customer connections' that are likely to be influenced by a departing employee. It is only when either or both of these interests have been demonstrated that a court will proceed to examine the reasonableness of a restraint clause as between the parties. In determining this question the courts will take account of its duration, its geographical extent and its scope, considering each of these factors separately and then their collective effect (see, for example, *Forster & Sons Ltd* v. *Suggett*, *Fitch* v. *Dewes* and *Mason* v. *Provident Clothing & Supply Co. Ltd*).

Any restriction on trade is, of course, at first sight anti-competitive and thus contrary to the interests of the wider community. This may have particular significance where a business is being sold or where a manufacturer or distributor of goods or a service provider seeks to restrict an individual or organisation from supplying the goods or services of a competitor (see *Esso Petroleum Co. Ltd* v. *Harper's Garage (Stourport) Ltd*). In such cases there is a clear public interest in any restriction upon supply and the impact of that upon the price of goods or services. In employment contracts, however, less significance seems quite rightly to be placed upon the issue of whether a restraint is reasonable in the public interest. Even where an employment restraint has been held to be invalid on the ground of the public interest, it has seemed to be importing too much significance to the role of the restrained employee to rule that the community has been unreasonably deprived of his or her services (see *Wyatt* v. *Kreglinger and Fernau*).

In *Littlewoods Organisation Ltd* v. *Harris* the defendant had risen quickly through the plaintiff's retail chain store and mail order business until at the relevant time he occupied the position of executive director of the mail order business. The focus of the mail order business was its twice yearly catalogue which promoted a large range of goods and which was distributed to the company's agents. The latter would then publicise the available goods to family, friends and Other contacts.

After his latest promotion in August 1976 Harris was responsible for the planning and compilation of the spring/summer catalogue for 1977. He attended board meetings and was privy to policy making and confidential information about the company's business. At the same time, albeit unbeknown to his employer, he had been headhunted by Great Universal Stores Ltd (GUS), its major rival in the UK for mail order sales. Despite the defendant's apparent initial reluctance, he had eventually agreed a package with GUS in November 1976. In January 1977 he gave the company six months' notice, as required by his contract of employment, that he had accepted employment with GUS. It was pointed out to Harris that there was a term in his contract of employment specifically preventing him from working for GUS for twelve months after leaving the company. He was asked to provide an assurance that he would not infringe that term but the defendant indicated that he had taken legal advice and was unable to do so. As a consequence Harris was moved from mail order operations to the retail side of the company's business and thus worked out his notice in a position that would prevent access to confidential information. (In the equivalent circumstances in the present day an employee is likely to be put on 'garden leave'. Typically this would mean, as the term suggests, that the employee spends the relevant notice period at home with pay but with no work to do.) In the meantime Littlewoods sought an injunction to prevent Harris from breaking the restraint term in his contract. After an interim order was granted, Mr Justice Caufield refused to extend that to a full injunction but allowed the interim order to be extended until an appeal against his refusal had been heard. Thus the case came before the Court of Appeal.

Lord Denning MR pointed out that, while a restraint clause might protect trade secrets or other confidential information and preserve customer connections, an employer was unable to protect itself against competition from a former employee or his new employer (see *Herbert Morris* v. *Saxelby*). In other words a distinction was drawn between an employee's skill and experience gained from working in a particular trade or profession and the 'personal knowledge of and influence over the customers of his employer, or such an acquaintance with his employer's trade secrets as would enable him . . . to take advantage of his employer's trade connection or utilize information confidentially obtained' (per Lord Parker of Waddington, ibid. at page 709).

But, his Lordship noted, difficulties arose when it was not easy to say what was and what was not confidential information and any information possessed by an employee could be taken away in his or her head. In such cases the courts have acknowledged that the proper route for an employer was to draft a restraint clause restricting an employee's activities once the employment had been left (see *Printers and Finishers Ltd* v. *Holloway*). According to Littlewoods, this was just such a case.

On the facts before him the first instance judge found that the defendant had in his possession no confidential information or trade secret worthy of protection but the Court of

Appeal unanimously disagreed. Lord Justice Megaw believed that Caufield J had indeed alluded in his judgment to the very type of information which was capable of protection but had drawn an incorrect inference from the present facts. Certainly more recent cases make it clear that the information capable of protection by a restraint clause goes beyond secret formulae or the design of a machine to include the names of customers and the goods they buy (see dicta of Staughton LJ in *Lansing Linde* v. *Kerr*). Indeed, as Lord Justice Butler-Sloss remarked at page 88:

> ... we have moved into the age of multinational businesses and worldwide business interests. Information may be held by very senior executives which, in the hands of competitors, might cause significant harm to the companies employing them. 'Trade secrets' has, in my view, to be interpreted in the wider context of highly confidential information of a non-technical or non-scientific nature, which may come within the ambit of information the employer is entitled to have protected, albeit for a limited period.

See further, *Thomas* v. *Farr plc* [2007] IRLR 419.

While of one mind on this question, their Lordships were divided on the issue of whether the restraint was enforceable. Lord Justice Browne believed that an employer was entitled to rely only upon a 'proper' restraint by which he meant one that was no wider than was reasonably necessary for the protection of its trade secrets. This required a two part examination: firstly, was the relevant clause enforceable as it stood and, secondly, if not, could it be made enforceable either by construction or severance. On a literal reading of the clause, in his Lordship's view, it was too wide, restricting the defendant from working for GUS not only in its mail order business but in any of its many unrelated subsidiaries across the world. A similar clause had been ruled unreasonable and hence unenforceable by the Court of Appeal in *Commercial Plastics Ltd* v. *Vincent*.

Could the clause be cut down so as to make it workable? Lord Justice Browne thought not but in this he disagreed with his fellow judges. Lord Denning cited several cases in which the courts had been willing to construe wide words in such a way as to allow a clause to operate in the way the parties intended (see, for example, *Moenich* v. *Fenestre* and *Home Counties Dairies Ltd* v. *Skilton*). In so doing Lord Denning believed that the courts were preventing unskilful drafting from defeating the object of the clause. Lord Justice Megaw was of the same opinion. He noted that it was for the employer to show that a restraint was not too wide and that the courts would not re-write a clause simply by deleting or adding words in order to render it reasonable. The courts will, of course, sever a clause using what is often referred to as the 'blue pencil test'. Thus, where a restraint can be divided into several distinct promises, it is possible to remove those that are objectionable and to leave behind those that are reasonable (see *Goldsoll* v. *Goldman*). On the other hand, if an agreement is indivisible, despite containing several apparently separate promises, the courts will refuse to strike out the unwanted words (see *Attwood* v. *Lamont*). Needless to say the real issue for the potential litigants in a dispute over a restraint clause is to determine whether or not in their case the court will wield the blue pencil and to this there seems to be no easy answer.

However, on the facts in Littlewoods, this was not a case of severance, rather it came down to the issue of construction of the clause. In this Megaw LJ, relying on the same authorities as Lord Denning, held that the present clause should be construed to apply only to that confidential information which related to mail order business operating in the UK, even though on a literal interpretation it looked to cover all of GUS's many subsidiaries across the globe. How could this stance be reconciled with the Court's earlier decision in *Commercial Plastics*? The latter was distinguished on the ground that the cases dealing with construction of a clause had not been considered and thus it was not a decision that should be followed.

In *Commercial Plastics v. Vincent* Lord Justice Pearson, while ruling that the clause was too wide both geographically and with respect to its scope, stated that it was 'unfortunate that a home-made provision, offered and accepted in good faith between commercial men and not in the least intended to be oppressive, [had] to be ruled and declared void . . . for the lack of the necessary limiting words'.

This sentiment was clearly in the minds of the majority of the Court in the present case. If such an approach smacks of 'palm tree' justice, then readers will find little reassurance in the knowledge that subsequent case law is equally inconsistent. According to Lord Denning himself in *Greer v. Sketchley Ltd* the approach to restraint clauses varies from one generation to another. *Littlewoods* he described as a decision in which the court had not strained to hold a clause invalid but had sought to interpret it reasonably and to hold the restraint good because it was reasonable between the parties. Courts, he said, would not hold restraints 'unreasonable simply because one [could] find some far-fetched examples of how they might operate unreasonably'. In *Sketchley* itself the Court of Appeal, despite a generational gap of merely two years, declined to read limiting words into a clause that prevented a former director of a dry cleaning company from engaging 'in any business which is similar to any business involving such trade secrets and/or secret processes carried on by the Company'. Invited by counsel to write in the word 'competing' before that of business their Lordships declined to do so. The company's business was confined to certain areas of the UK only and by specifying protection across the UK the clause was geographically too wide and the plain language of the present clause could not be qualified 'except by distortion and deformation of the clause itself' (per Shaw LJ at page 448).

The reasoning behind any judicial reluctance to re-draft restraint clauses by sympathetic construction was succinctly expressed by Lord Justice Simon Brown in *J A Mont (UK) Ltd v. Mills* (at page 176):

> If the Court here were to construe this covenant as the plaintiffs desire, what possible reason would employers ever have to impose restraints in appropriately limited terms? It would always be said that the covenants were basically 'just and honest', and designed solely to protect the employers' legitimate interests in the confidentiality of their trade secrets rather than to prevent competition as such. And it would be no easier to refute that assertion in other cases than it is here. Thus would be perpetuated the long-recognised vice of ex-employees being left subject to apparently excessive restraints and yet quite unable, short of expensive litigation and at peril of substantial damages claims, to determine precisely what their rights may be.

4

CONTRACT LAW (OBLIGATIONS)

In the following year, by way of contrast, the Court of Appeal in *Hanover Insurance Brokers Ltd* v. *Schapiro* was willing to construe an otherwise wide clause in more limited terms. Distinguishing *Mont* v. *Mills* on its facts Lord Justice Nolan accepted that 'there [was] an apparent difference between the unsympathetic approach there adopted towards the construction of restrictive covenants of excessive width and the more flexible and supportive approach adopted [in Littlewoods]'.

In *Commercial Plastics* Lord Justice Pearson remarked that 'a good deal of legal "know-how" [was] required for the successful drafting of a restrictive covenant', an observation that remains as true today as it did then. The latter day draftsperson will approach the task with a greater sophistication than may once have been the case. The modern employment restraint clause will almost invariably be subdivided into separate restraints specifying non-solicitation, non-competition and confidentiality, allowing more readily for severance of any clause that might be adjudged excessive and reducing reliance on sympathetic judicial construction of the type to be found in *Littlewoods* v. *Harris*.

The operation of the restraint of trade doctrine is, of course, yet another example of a qualification of the principle of 'freedom of contract' which lies at the heart of the development of English contract law. By determining which restraints are reasonable and hence enforceable the courts inevitably interfere in the freedom of the parties to strike their own bargain for better or worse. In the development of the doctrine of restraint of trade in the context of employment one can see the courts endeavouring to balance the competing interests of employer and employee, the former seeking to protect their legitimate business interests and the latter to preserve their ability to exercise their skill and expertise with the employer of their choice. Whether by sympathetic construction of a clause or outright severance the courts, just as they utilise the implication of terms, seek to ensure that an agreement is, if at all possible, viable, while at the same time protecting the weaker party to the agreement from unfair bargains.

FURTHER READING

Primary sources

Attwood v. *Lamont* [1920] 3 KB 571

Commercial Plastics Ltd v. *Vincent* [1965] 1 QB 623

Esso Petroleum Co. Ltd v. *Harper's Garage (Stourport) Ltd* [1968] AC 269

Fitch v. *Dewes* [1921] 2 AC 158

Forster & Sons Ltd v. *Suggett* (1918) 35 TLR 87

Goldsoll v. *Goldman* [1915] 1 Ch 292

Greer v. *Sketchley Ltd* [1979] IRLR 445

Hanover Insurance Brokers Ltd v. *Schapiro* [1994] IRLR 82

Herbert Morris v. *Saxelby* [1916] 1 AC 688

Home Counties Dairies Ltd v. *Skilton* [1970] 1 All ER 1227

J A Mont (UK) Ltd v. *Mills* [1993] IRLR 172

Lansing Linde v. *Kerr* [1991] IRLR 80

Mason v. *Provident Clothing & Supply Co. Ltd* [1913] AC 724

Moenich v. *Fenestre* (1892) 61 LJCh 737

Nordenfeldt v. *Maxim Nordenfeldt* [1894] AC 535

Printers and Finishers Ltd v. *Holloway* [1964] 3 All ER 731

Thomas v. *Farr plc* [2007] IRLR 419

Wyatt v. *Kreglinger and Fernau* [1933] 1 KB 793

Discharge

Davis Contractors v. *Fareham UDC* [1956] AC 696

Andrew Harries, University of Central Lancashire

Frustration of contract

Davis v. *Fareham UDC* (*Davis*) is a leading case on how the risks of market trading should be allocated and the role of the court in identifying and apportioning the costs of such risks when interpreting an agreement. The case focuses on a particular type of contingency: the impact of highly unusual events (such as natural or man-made disasters) on the performance of the agreement. This type of risk is not usually contemplated in any detail at the agreement stage because the likelihood of these risks materialising is too remote: the additional costs, inconvenience and complexity involved in planning for such unlikely events is not, therefore, justifiable.

But what happens if that remote possibility does materialise when you are performing your agreement? The consequence will be that, despite your best efforts, performing as agreed is either impossible or requires you to do things never agreed or anticipated initially. In other words the event interferes with what you would like to do under the agreement and what is now possible under changed circumstances (lawyers describe these situations as examples of 'subsequent impossibility' caused by 'supervening' or 'intervening' events). So, because of the supervening event you now find yourself trading in a war zone; or trading with the enemy; or floods have ruined or destroyed your factory; or key personnel die or are incapacitated; or the law is changed making a previously lawful activity unlawful; or fluctuations in the price of raw materials make trade uneconomic; or supplies are delayed; or roads, sea lanes or air space closures or restrictions create severe inconvenience or make it impractical to deliver to agreed schedules; or an important event is cancelled, postponed or delayed.

These all illustrate how unforeseen events outside the parties' direct control can 'frustrate' their ability to perform their legal obligations despite their best efforts. The legal response to this type of situation is dealt with by an emerging body of rules and principles known collectively as 'Frustration of the contract' – although a more accurate, but less succinct, definition proposed by Lord Wright in *Joseph Constantine Steamship Line* is 'frustration of the adventure or of the commercial or practical purpose of the contract' (page 182). This more expansive conception covers both situations of genuine 'impossibility' and those where performance is still literally 'possible' but would create unfair and unreasonable consequences for the parties if they were required to perform within a context affected by the supervening event.

The traditional legal response to this type of event was to assess whether they had been expressly allocated under the agreement by using, for example, exemption terms such as *force majeure* (typically, 'Acts of God' type clauses seen in many buildings insurance contracts), hardship, and price escalation clauses and the like.

The legal rules on Frustration may be used by the courts to allocate these unplanned risks in very limited circumstances. In doing so, two important questions are raised: first, should the courts intervene ever (and, if so, when?) to support parties whenever their contracts are silent on the consequences of unusual risks impacting on their agreement; or, second, should they merely let the losses lie where they fall, the parties having to absorb the full risk? This practical imperative translates into two questions concerning legal policy, one normative (or justificatory), the other practical: (1) should the courts intervene and help parties or not under any circumstances; and (2) if so, how should the courts intervene and with what objective?

Anatomy of a leading case: the legal significance of *Davis* v. *Fareham UDC*

Davis is generally recognised as giving the clearest statement of principle in response to the two questions of legal policy set out above. The case articulates the modern position on frustration of contract and, as such, can be used to justify in law a bilateral termination of agreement without fault falling on either party; or, it can be raised as a defence to an action for repudiatory or anticipatory breach of contract. The principles articulated in *Davis* are still being used today, 40 years after the judgment was handed down.

Pre-history 1: the absolute obligations rule

The leading case which provides an answer to questions of who allocates the risk of market exchange, how and on what basis is *Paradine* v. *Jane*. In this case a landlord was successful in an action of debt based on a breach of promise (or covenant) by one of his tenants to pay rent on property despite the fact that the tenant was dispossessed from the property by an invading army during the English Civil Wars. Without the benefit of the property or an ability to earn an income the tenant was unable to pay the rent promised under the terms of the lease. He asked the court to excuse his non-payment because of circumstances outside his control.

The court rejected the tenant's plea to be excused from his strict liability. The court upheld the principle that once created, the law expected performance of promises to be 'absolute', affirming the principle of sanctity of contract. There was no legal exception permitted except where the parties themselves had agreed terms exempting liability whenever specified events occurred. There was no such exemption clause in *Paradine*. Underlying this decision are two fundamental assumptions: first, that the court's role is to respect the parties' allocation of risks and not interfere; second, that the agreement expresses the parties' intentions, in respect of risk allocation, clearly and completely and whatever distributive outcome materialises is fair and just.

However, some judges believed that upholding the absolute obligations rule literally in all instances does not necessarily reflect or support the parties' intentions. A legal rule allowing deviation from the doctrine may be justified if the court was convinced that such a flexible interpretation may better support and reflect their intentions.

Pre-history 2: the birth of frustration – *Taylor* v. *Caldwell*

Taylor v. *Caldwell* was the first case to recognise a lawful excuse for non-performance of agreed promises. Its novelty lies in providing a qualified answer to the question, 'Can parties be excused from their contractual obligations if they have not fully performed them?' In *Paradine* the answer was categorically 'no'. The answer to the same question in *Taylor* was a qualified 'yes'. As such, the case established for the first time a defence to what may *appear* to some as repudiatory or anticipatory breach of contract but is in fact an example of performance being frustrated by events out of the direct control of both parties.

In *Taylor* a promise to supply a music hall for holding a series of four evening concerts was discharged by the court when the music hall was destroyed by fire prior to the first performance. Taylor sued the owners of the music hall for his lost profit and wasted promotional expenditure caused by Caldwell failing to perform his 'absolute' obligation to supply a music hall for Taylor's purposes. There was no evidence the fire was the fault of either party so in this sense it was unforeseen. Fire was also a risk not expressly provided for in the terms of contract.

Taylor's claim would appear to fall foul of the absolute obligations principle in *Paradine* and should fail because his claim is not underpinned by a recognised legal cause of action – there being, at this time, no excuse for non-performance caused by supervening events outside the parties' immediate control. If the parties did not allocate the risk, the loss should lie where it fell: in this instance Taylor loses the benefit of his commercial venture (the concerts are cancelled) and Caldwell must find the costs of rebuilding his music hall as well as the loss of income caused by the destruction of his property. Yet, Justice Blackburn found in Caldwell's favour and he was not liable for Taylor's losses. His justification for such a remarkable *volte-face* was the start point for the development of an excuse doctrine for subsequent impossibility. The 'termination' of contract in this instance is a legal decision based on a particular reading of the parties' agreement and is not attributable to the fault of either party as would be the case for a normal breach of contract. For the first time there was now a lawful excuse for non-performance. The broader implications were stark: not all contractual obligations in law are 'absolute' and neither, for that matter, is the principle of sanctity of contract.

However, explaining the rationale for this excuse doctrine to anticipate *when* it may be used and *how* was harder to establish, not least because of the rather convoluted justification applied by Justice Blackburn in his judgment. He suggested a fundamental term could be implied into any agreement, the basis of which was the assumptions made by the parties (but implied by the courts) when contracting with one another. The judge takes the role of the 'officious bystander' who, in Lord Hailsham's view in *National Carriers* v. *Panalpina*, hypothetically 'intrudes' on the parties at their moment of agreement and asks *if* say (on the facts in *Taylor*) they knew there was a possibility the music hall could be destroyed by fire whether they would continue with the agreement, the answer would be a resounding 'of course not'. This response indicates the continued existence of the music hall for the duration of the contract is an essential condition of contract which induced the parties to contract with one another to begin with. So, if the object of the contract is destroyed by fire this will be treated as a breach of this implied assumption or 'condition' and breach of a condition – whether express or, as in this case, implied – in law allows the parties to terminate the contract immediately. Because neither party is at fault they both escape their contractual obligations without legal penalty (there is still the financial penalty of the losses caused by the frustrating event falling on both parties).

So by implying a condition into the contract in respect of a fundamental assumption, Justice Blackburn treats the contract as at an end – breach of condition in law automatically terminates the contract – but attributes this implied condition to the parties' intention: if they'd thought about it and talked about it expressly at the time of agreement they would have made this an express term of their agreement. The judge is in effect making express what the parties imply or assume in entering the contract. This *appears* to not breach one of the fundamental principles of the sanctity of contract because the courts are not writing the parties' contract. Rather, judges are merely facilitating the expression of the parties' latent intention. This can, however, lead to problems. If not all promises are absolute what is the test for those which are and those which are not? What are the implications for sanctity of contract?

Pre-history 3: the call for revision

Other problems arose, the most important of which was understanding and justifying when the doctrine should be applied and to what types of consequences. This question became particularly acute as the principles were applied to novel situations: destruction of the object of the contract (as in *Taylor*) is one thing, but termination for the effects of poor business planning or judgement (such as increased costs or inconvenience) can not be squared so easily with the rationale given for the physical destruction of property or the death of an individual. Opinion was certainly polarised between those who believed the case merely gave effect to the parties' intentions (Lord Loriburn in *Tamplin Steamship v. Anglo-Mexican Petroleum*) to those who believed that in upholding the 'implied term' theory, the courts were perpetuating a legal fiction which was unsustainable, unprincipled and, ultimately, dishonest.

Such revisionist thoughts were described by Lord Wright – one of its most important proponents – as 'heretical' to some judges. Judges such as Lord Sumner (see *Hirji Mulji v. Cheong Yue SS*) suggested that what was really happening in cases like *Taylor* was that courts were allocating risks in support of broader interests such as commercial fairness, something that was only very remotely related to the parties' actual intentions. Rather, the revisionists were articulating an 'objective' test on the same line of the 'officious bystander'. The key difference between the Blackburn and Sumner methods of implication was that the former approach was a subjective, factual test, while the latter was an objective, legal test.

What this line of critique suggests is that courts should, euphemistically, 'come clean' and state the real objectives behind their decisions – paternalistic intervention in the market to uphold the reasonable expectations of the fair and honest businessman. Clearly this approach is replete with value judgments which judges such as Lords Sumner and Wright thought should be expressed openly and clearly to help guide businesses in their legal

4

CONTRACT LAW (OBLIGATIONS)

planning. Only by making clear the true basis of frustration could, these judges assumed, the doctrine be put on a more principled footing as a justifiable, rational and fair exception to the principle of sanctity of contract. Lords Sumner and Wright's views cleared the ground in preparation for such a re-statement. The judgments in *Davis* can be read as a conversation with this ongoing argument, an argument that was settled by this landmark case.

The case

1. The facts

Fareham Urban District Council ('the council') invited tenders to build 78 houses. The council accepted Davis Contractor's ('Davis') fixed price bid of £92,425 to complete all building works within 8 months. A contract under seal was agreed on 9 July 1946 but the council transferred site control to Davis on 20 June 1946 to allow construction and site preparation work to start before legal formalities were completed.

Davis suffered severe shortages of raw materials and adequately skilled labour – not helped by a term of contract requiring them to employ a proportion of workers from the Fareham locality, where there was insufficient supply. The council accepted these problems were out of Davis's control and allowed work to continue rather than treat it as a breach of contract. The houses were finally completed on 14 May 1948, an overrun of 14 months. The final build cost was £115,233, an overspend of £22,808 on the agreed bid price. However, once *agreed* adjustments were taken into account, the council agreed to pay Davis £94,424, but not the £20,809 additional costs Davis incurred.

2. The dispute and proceedings

When the council did not reimburse Davis the additional £20,809 overspend, Davis started arbitration proceedings. The arbitrator found in Davis's favour at first instance, but on considering additional evidence reduced the quantum owed to £17,258. Eventually the Court of Appeal overturned the arbitrator's award. Davis was given leave to appeal to the House of Lords and they were asked to reconsider the legal basis of Davis's original claim.

3. The key elements of Davis's legal claim

Davis's argument to the House of Lords was based, in part, on a claim that the original contract was frustrated after the 8 month period elapsed owing to the shortages in labour and materials. If this was accepted, the costs of the 14 month overspend could be recouped in restitution on a *quantum meruit* basis: *viz.*, payment of a reasonable sum – equal in value to the overspend – should be awarded to prevent the council being 'unjustly enriched' by not paying the full price for benefits received (completed houses). However, the success of this claim hinged on proving the contract was frustrated.

The judgments

Their Lordships were unanimous in finding insufficient evidence to justify terminating the contract for frustration. The most important judgments are those given by Lords Reid and Radcliffe because they address the underlying theoretical justification for pleading frustration and also give a clear indication how this test should operate as an express legal rule in future.

1. Lord Reid

Lord Reid followed Lord Porter's suggestion in *Denny, Mott & Dickson* v. *Fraser* that the legal basis of frustration requires the court to (1) construe the true meaning of the contract, through (2) implication of common assumptions or conditions which explain, (3) whether the basic 'footing' upon which the contract was made has been totally undermined by the frustrating events.

Lord Reid then makes a direct attack on the approach first adopted by Justice Blackburn in *Taylor* and followed in *Tamplin Steamship*. He doubts whether the 'implied term theory' expounded by Justice Blackburn can explain fully all cases where frustration was found. He suggested that the correct justification and method is one that construes the parties' intentions in light of the contract as a whole and the context within which the contract was made. The courts then assess these assumptions in view of the changed circumstances and ask whether the parties intended to be bound to one another under these changed circumstances. The test is to construe the terms in such a way that they can encompass the new situation: if they can not, the contract is ended.

Applying this method to the facts in *Davis*, Lord Reid took the view that although Davis was subject to the inconvenience of delay and increased costs, his performance, despite these problems, was not of a fundamentally different nature from the one anticipated and intended when the contract was formed (page 723). The extra costs should be borne by Davis as a consequence.

2. Lord Radcliffe

Lord Radcliffe's speech is perhaps the most influential because it dismantles the assumptions underpinning *Taylor* v. *Caldwell*. Of particular concern was the assumption that the courts can (1) imply terms for parties about events they never thought about or foresaw; and even if a term could be implied (2) how can the courts be sure the parties would intend the contract to be ended under such circumstances?

These logical blind spots at the heart of *Taylor* justified, in Lord Radcliffe's view, an assessment of (1) the circumstances which justify raising frustration and (2) whether it applies in any given circumstance. Lord Radcliffe stated that the answer to both questions was a matter of law and could not be inferred from an assessment of the facts. The legal principles should, therefore, be stated more clearly to promote greater certainty (page 727). This was the key move which spelled the end of the implied term theory under *Taylor* – the test for frustration moving from a factual test of the actual subjective intentions of the parties to a legal test based on the objective intentions of the hypothetical reasonable and fair-minded businessman. The legal test was aligning itself with similar tests found when implying terms into a contract or construing a term as a condition to justify lawful repudiation.

Lord Radcliffe realised that what the courts were actually doing was applying an objective rule of law to the contractual obligations they imposed on themselves. The next step in his argument, having undermined the logical basis of the implied term theory, was to articulate (1) the true nature of the rule and its justification, and (2) explain how it operates in practice to frustrate the contract (a mixed question of fact and law).

4

CONTRACT LAW (OBLIGATIONS)

The true theoretical underpinning of the doctrine of frustration was based, then, on a number of assumptions such as (1) the parties not always thinking through all the consequences of their agreements; (2) absolute consequences do not necessarily follow absolute obligations; (3) judges should not always assume the parties' intentions can be found from a literal reading of the agreement; (4) the judge's role is to ensure just and fair exchange which reflects the needs and expectations of reasonably honest and fair-minded businessmen; (5) reasonably fair minded and honest businessmen contract with their agreements less than complete, the gaps being filled by a commercial sense of good faith 'give and take'.

These type of assumptions inform Lord Radcliffe's view that when construing the agreement the courts will identify its meaning from the objective perspective of what the reasonable businessman would have agreed in similar circumstances, the court being the 'spokesman' for the reasonable businessman. This is an approach to construction based on ascertaining the parties 'objective' intentions. As in other areas of contract law the test is legal not factual (i.e., it does not rely on the actual thoughts and aspirations of the parties concerned). Construction takes account of the language, nature and context within which the contract was made so an inference can be made about whether it depends for its existence on a certain state of affairs which are its base or foundation. If this fundamental base is radically altered – by destruction, delay, changes in the law etc. – then the courts can presume that the reasonable contractor would never have agreed to contract under those changed circumstances.

Lord Radcliffe then articulated what is generally agreed to be the modern legal test of frustration: '. . . frustration occurs when without default of either party a contractual obligation has become incapable of being performed because the circumstances in which performance is called for would render it a thing radically different from that which was undertaken by the contract. *Non haec in foedera veni*. It was not this that I promised to do' (page 729).

This is known as the 'radical alteration' theory – proof of a radical alteration in the fundamental basis of the contract coming after the court has applied the objective test of construction based on the reasonably fair minded and honest businessman. The key judgment is that the reasonable businessman would never agree to contract or continue to perform under circumstances of 'radical alteration' because it would be unreasonable (as a matter of fact and law) to hold him to an agreement he never intended performing or consenting to.

Having reformulated the juristic basis of frustration, Lord Radcliffe then explained how the legal test would operate in practice. He outlined three steps for assessing if a contract is frustrated: first, what do the terms require; second, what is required under the changed circumstances; third, apply a legal judgment as to whether there is a radical difference in expectation between the two which justifies terminating the agreement in the interests of fairness and reasonableness. The judgment phase is crucial because this recognises the judge's role in weighing up competing factors and balancing them against one another to arrive at a judgment which is driven by legal standards not the parties' actual wishes. Applying these principles to the facts in *Davis*, Lord Radcliffe concluded rather scathingly that this case was ' . . . a long way from a case of frustration'. (page 729). In his view the doctrine should be used very sparingly.

Implications and importance of the judgments in *Davis*

Frustration allows the courts to avoid some of the harsher effects of a literal application of the absolute obligations rule in the interests of justice. *Davis* recognises that when the parties' intentions in respect of unforeseen events runs out, judicial standards of reasonableness take over. Rather than applying a strained construction by hypothesising what the parties actually thought (when the courts can never know this with any certainty) the post-*Davis* approach asks whether the reasonable businessman would have made suitable provision for the contingency. The standards of fairness and reasonableness applied reflect the expectations of commerce not judges. *Davis* affirms the view that the parties' express terms do not always reflect their express or implied intentions and more flexible approaches to construing their intentions should be adopted in the interests of reasonable and just trading.

Lord Radcliffe's 'radical alteration' test of frustration has stood the test of time. A number of recent House of Lords decisions have confirmed that his approach is correct (*National Carriers* v. *Panalpina, The Nema, The Hannah Blumenthal*) and an important recent decision on common mistake in the Court of Appeal (*Great Peace Shipping* v. *Tsavliris*) has identified themes common to both common mistake and frustration (the doctrines covering initial and subsequent impossibility) and identified the rationale adopted by Lord Radcliffe in *Davis* as the underlying juristic basis for both doctrines.

Furthermore the technique of construction adopted in *Davis* – focusing on the 'root commercial basis' upon which the parties contract – is broadly similar to other approaches to construction used when assessing anticipatory or repudiatory breach of contract. It has also been suggested by some commentators that the rules underpinning frustration and withdrawal for breach show an 'alignment' of assumptions and approach. Further evidence of an even broader alignment can be found in *Great Peace Shipping* v. *Tsavliris* where Lord Philips suggested a theme common to frustration and common mistake based on the idea of 'impossibility of performance'.

Perhaps the only real difficulty which remains lies not in asking the question 'how can we justify terminating a contract for unforeseen events' but *how* is the test applied? This is always going to be a source of residual uncertainty, as any exception to a general rule is. Perhaps this is also one of the reasons frustration is used so sparingly by the courts and why it has always been kept within very tight limits. This sends a clear message to contractors: plan your agreements carefully, both for performance and the risk that things may not turn out as you expect.

FURTHER READING

Primary sources

Amalgamated Investment v. *John Walker* [1976] 2 All ER 509

Bank Line Ltd v. *Arthur Capel & Co.* [1919] AC 435

British Movietone News v. *London and District Cinemas* [1952] AC 166

CONTRACT LAW (OBLIGATIONS)

Crickelwood Property and Investment Trust Ltd v. *Leighton's Investment Trust Ltd* [1943] KB 493

Denny, Mott & Dickson Ltd v. *Fraser (James B) & Co. Ltd* [1944] AC 265

Great Peace Shipping v. *Tsavliris Salvage (International) Ltd* [2003] QB 679

Hirji Mulji v. *Cheong Yue SS Co. Ltd* [1926] AC 497

J Lauritzen AS v. *Wijsmuller BV (The Super Servant Two)* [1990] 1 Lloyd's Rep 1

Joseph Constantine Steamship Line v. *Imperial Smelting Corp Ltd* [1942] AC 154

Martime National Fish Co. v. *Ocean Trawlers* [1935] AC 524

Metropolitan Water Board v. *Dick Kerr & Co. Ltd* [1918] AC 119

National Carriers v. *Panalpina (Northern) Ltd* [1981] AC 675

Paarl Wilson and Co. v. *Partenreederei Hannah Blumenthal (The Hannah Blumenthal)* [1983] 1 AC 854

Paradine v. *Jane* (1647) Aleyn 26

Pioneer Shipping Ltd v. *BTP Tioxide Ltd (The Nema)* [1982] AC 724

Sir Lindsay Parkinson & Co. Ltd v. *Commissioners of Works* [1949] 2 KB 632

Tai Hing Cotton Mill Ltd v. *Liu Chong Hing Bank Ltd* [1986] AC 80

Tamplin [FA] Steamship Co. Ltd v. *Anglo-Mexican Petroleum Products Co. Ltd* [1916] 2 AC 397

Taylor v. *Caldwell* (1863) 3 B & S 826

Tsakiroglou & Co. Ltd v. *Noblee Thorl Gmbh* [1962] AC 93

Secondary sources

Beatson, J. (1991) 'Gap Filling and Risk Reversal' in Beatson, J. *The Uses and Abuses of Unjust Enrichment*, Oxford University Press.

Hall, C. (1984) 'Frustration and the Question of Foresight' (1984) 4, *Legal Studies*, 300.

Haycraft, A.M. and Waksman, D.M. (1984) 'Frustration and Restitution' (1984) *Journal of Business Law*, 207.

Kull, A. (1991) 'Mistake, Frustration and the Windfall Principle of Contract Remedies', (1991) 43, *Hastings Law Journal*, 1.

McKendrick, E. (ed.) (1994) *Force Majeure and Frustration of Contract*, 2nd edn, Lloyd's of London Press.

Posner, R. and Rosenfield, A. (1977) 'Impossibility and Related Doctrines in Contract Law: An Economic Analysis' (1977) 6, *Journal of Legal Studies*, 83.

Smith, S. (1994) 'Contract – Mistake, Frustration and Implied Terms' (1994) 110, *LQR*, 400.

Treitel, G. (2004) *Frustration and Force Majeure*, 2nd edn, Oxford University Press.

Remedies

Ruxley Electronics and Construction Ltd v. *Forsyth*
[1996] AC 344

Fiona Fletcher, Northumbria University

This is an interesting and unusual case on the law of damages for breach of contract. While the facts are not commonplace (see below), the legal issues which arise are of wider relevance to everyday contracts. The principal aim of damages for breach of contract is to put the claimant in the position he would have been in – in so far as money can – had the contract been performed (*Robinson* v. *Harman*). This is known as the claimant's performance interest. The purpose of such damages is to compensate the innocent party and not to punish the party who is in breach. The law has traditionally used two measures of assessing damages to satisfy the claimant's performance interest:

(i) difference in value; or
(ii) cost of cure/reinstatement i.e., what it would take to secure full performance.

These can generally be assessed in financial terms and may often be similar amounts. In cases concerning building contracts the general rule has been that reinstatement is the *prima facie* measure and difference in value is only used if cost of cure is inappropriate. The *Ruxley* case looks at the basis of awarding such damages to protect the performance interest.

Where losses for breach of contract are non-financial (for example, disappointment or distress), the law has generally refused to allow a party to recover damages for such losses as a result of breach of contract (*Addis* v. *Gramophone*). In recent years, however, the courts have begun to recognise certain limited categories where a claimant *can* recover damages for non-financial losses arising from a breach of contract. These exceptions to the *Addis* rule include, for example, where an important object of the contract was pleasure, relaxation or peace of mind. The House of Lords decision in *Ruxley* is important as it contains *obiter* comments which represent a further potential departure from the *Addis* rule that a party may not recover damages for losses arising on a breach of contract which are non-financial. These *obiter* comments have contributed substantially to the development of the law in this area.

The facts

The facts were simple, if out of the ordinary. Mr Forsyth (Forsyth) contracted with Ruxley Electronics and Construction Limited (Ruxley). Ruxley agreed to build a swimming pool in Forsyth's garden at a price of £17,797.40. It was an express oral term of the contract that the depth of the diving area of the pool was to be 7 feet 6 inches. When built, the diving area was in fact only 6 feet 9 inches. This had no adverse effect on Forsyth's use of the pool – he could still use it for diving. It had no effect on the market value of his property. The only practicable method of achieving the specified depth would be to demolish the pool and build a new one at a cost of £21,560. Forsyth refused to pay Ruxley the outstanding balance for building the pool.

The procedure

Ruxley sued Forsyth for the outstanding balance in respect of the cost of building the pool. Forsyth counterclaimed for damages. Originally he sought only small repair costs, but at trial, for the first time, he sought full reinstatement cost of £21,560. The trial judge gave judgment in favour of Ruxley, ordering Forsyth to pay the outstanding balance. He dismissed the counterclaim. He held that the cost of cure (reinstatement) was unreasonable, but he did award Forsyth damages of £2,500 for loss of amenity.

Forsyth then appealed to the Court of Appeal, which held by a majority (Strange and Mann LJJ, Dillon LJ dissenting) that the correct measure of damages was the amount required to place Forsyth in the same position he would have been in had the contract been performed. That was the cost of cure, the reinstatement cost of £21,560. Ruxley appealed to the House of Lords.

The arguments

Ruxley argued:

- That in order to recover the cost of cure, Forsyth had to show that the cost of reinstatement was reasonable. It was for the Court to consider what was reasonable in all the circumstances. Where the cost of cure is out of all proportion to the benefit which would accrue to the claimant, then the Court can adopt an alternative measure of difference in value of the works. The difference in value in this case was nil. Giving him the pool and £21,560 would overcompensate him which was not the purpose of contractual damages.

- No challenge was made to the loss of amenity award.

- That to claim cost of cure, Forsyth had to show that he actually intended to reinstate the pool.

Forsyth argued:

- That Ruxley's approach was at odds with the fundamental principle of contract law that where a party sustains loss by virtue of a breach of contract, he is – so far as money can do it – to be placed in the same position, with respect to damages, as if the contract had been performed (*Robinson* v. *Harman*). The objective of this contract, he argued, was the satisfaction of a purely personal preference which was not satisfied. He had not got the performance he expected under the contract. The trial judge had found that he had suffered a real loss, in the sense that he had received something of less value to him. This was caused by breach of contract by Ruxley. It was not too remote. He was therefore entitled to the cost of cure – reinstatement. Reasonableness was only relevant to mitigation.

■ Unusually, Forsyth challenged the loss of amenity award. He argued that the Court could only choose between two measures of damages – cost of cure and difference in value. The measure of the latter was nil. The trial judge had found that as a matter of fact, he had suffered a real loss. The Court could not then award nil. They therefore *had* to order cost of cure. There was no middle ground of loss of amenity and the trial judge had been wrong to order payment of £2,500 on those grounds.

■ Whether he reinstated the pool or not was irrelevant.

The decision

Ruxley's appeal was allowed and the award of £21,560 in the Court of Appeal was overturned. The House of Lords held:

■ That where the cost of cure expenditure was out of all proportion to the benefit to be obtained, the appropriate measure of damages was not the cost of cure (reinstatement) but the diminution in value of the work occasioned by the breach even if that resulted in a nominal award.

■ Ruxley had not challenged the decision of the trial judge to award £2,500, so that award still stood.

■ As they declined to award cost of cure damages, no finding was made on whether it was necessary that the claimant, in fact, intended to reinstate.

The House of Lords judgments

1. Cost of cure and difference in value

The Court upheld the principle of *Robinson* v. *Harman*, that damages are designed to put the party in the position they would have been in had the contract been performed: to compensate and not to punish. The judges all accepted that damages for breach of contract should relate to the loss which the claimant had suffered because he did not get what he bargained for. And yet, interestingly, while upholding this principle they refused to award him damages to enable him to build the pool he contracted for. This was because cost of cure, reinstatement was not reasonable. For Lord Bridge, the issue was simple: damages are designed to compensate for an established loss and not to provide a gratuitous benefit to the claimant. The reasonableness of the award is linked to the loss suffered. The cost of cure was unreasonable here as Forsyth had not suffered such a loss. He had no need to reinstate his pool – he had 'a perfectly serviceable pool' (page 355). The reinstatement cost did not represent his actual loss. The Court could therefore refuse cost of cure damages on the basis of the principle in *Robinson* v. *Harman*. Lord Lloyd also took the *Robinson* v. *Harman* principle as his starting point. For him, reasonableness in damages was not limited to mitigation of loss. Lord Lloyd made clear that where the cost of reinstatement is less than the difference in value, cost of reinstatement will invariably be the appropriate measure. If the claimant was allowed to claim difference in value in those circumstances he would have failed to mitigate his loss as cost of cure would be the cheaper option. All judges in the House of Lords agreed that for an award of reinstatement, it had to be shown that the measure was reasonable. This was an objective reasonableness test, i.e., it was the Court deciding what a bystander would consider reasonable, not what a claimant such as Forsyth would consider reasonable. If they had adopted a subjective reasonableness test this would have been similar to the concept of consumer surplus (below) in taking account of what the claimant considered reasonable. For Lord Bridge (page 355), personal preference was a factor of reasonableness in determining what the loss is but could not be determinative of what the loss is.

2. Only two measures of damage to protect performance interest?

The Court held it is not obliged to order cost of cure damages just because difference in value measure would provide no compensation. It is important to recall that Forsyth's barrister argued that the Court was only entitled to choose between two measures of damage – cost of cure or difference in value. If difference in value was nil, yet the Court found the claimant *had* suffered a loss (as was the case here) that meant cost of cure damages *had* to be awarded. The Court rejected this argument.

3. Damages for loss of amenity – a middle ground?

Not only did their Lordships reject the argument that they were restricted to choosing between cost of cure or difference in value, but some of the judges agreed with the decision of the trial judge to adopt a middle approach and award damages for loss of amenity. If the difference in value measure was nil, and cost of cure damages were not recoverable as disproportionate, the Court *should* nevertheless be able to award damages to compensate a party who had suffered a loss in as much as he did not get what he contracted for. Lord Mustill said that the only proper measure of loss was the true loss suffered by the promisee (page 357). This may be reinstatement or may be the difference in value but these remedies were not exhaustive. Remember that the House of Lords did not hear argument on the loss of amenity award. Ruxley did not challenge this award in the House of Lords – only the award of £21,560 by the Court of Appeal. The comments are therefore *obiter* but important nevertheless.

Lord Mustill (Lord Bridge concurring) agreed with the loss of amenity award. As a matter of principle, if it was true that there were only two measures of damage, and no middle ground, in a situation where a householder could not show that the market value of his house had depreciated as a result of defects, no damages could be awarded if rebuilding costs were disproportionate. Lord Mustill stated that such a conclusion was unacceptable to the average householder and unacceptable to him (page 356). He felt that the law had to cater for those occasions where the value of the promise to the promisee exceeded the financial enhancement of his position, i.e., the value of those inches to Forsyth as a personal preference, which only full performance would secure. He labelled this as the 'consumer surplus' – what the promise is worth to the promisee over and above mere financial value. This is 'incapable of precise valuation in terms of money exactly because it represents a personal, subjective and non-monetary gain' (page 357). Not only did he believe that there was no reason in principle why the Court should not be able to award damages of this kind, he thought that in some cases the power may be essential to enable the Court to do justice. He gives the following example (page 357):

> The lurid bathroom tiles . . . which may be so discordant with general taste that the builder may be said to do the employer a favour by failing to install them. But this is too narrow and materialistic a view of the transaction. No one had a right to substitute their preference for that of the contracting party. It would be unreasonable to deny some recovery for such a loss.

This introduces a subjective element to the award of damages which cannot be easily assessed in financial terms. Nevertheless, fairness demanded that it was recoverable in principle.

Lord Lloyd also agreed with the approach of the trial judge that damages *could* be awarded for loss of amenity. He characterised it as non-pecuniary loss and saw it as an adaptation of the pleasure exception to the *Addis* principle to a new situation. He thought that the award of £2,500 was on the high side but as Ruxley had not actually challenged it, the award stood. On the basis of his judgment, such damages would only be recoverable where pleasure/relaxation/enjoyment/peace of mind was an important object of the contract. Lord Mustill's concept of consumer surplus is much wider. It could potentially apply to any case where the market value is less than the consumer's own valuation of what full performance meant to him. The *obiter* comments of Mustill and Lloyd LJJ are important as they represent the first departure from the constraints of the case law in this area. They are, for example, a relaxation of the rule in *Watts* v. *Morrow* which had adhered to the *Addis* rule.

The future

The House of Lords decision in *Ruxley* clarifies that, in a building case, where the cost of reinstatement is unreasonable and not recoverable, the correct measure of damages is the difference in value. What is perhaps more interesting are their Lordships comments on the loss of amenity award, which was not actually the subject of debate before them. Lord Mustill's wide notion of the consumer surplus, if developed, could represent a significant departure from the recognised rule in *Addis*. Lord Lloyd's adaptation of the pleasure/relaxation exception would also result in an inroad to *Addis* – not as large as carved by Mustill LJ, but a substantial inroad nevertheless. Both approaches were approved in another, more recent, House of Lords case (*Farley* v. *Skinner*). While significant in principle, the practical impact of these approaches may be less significant – the House of Lords in *Ruxley* agreed that the award of £2,500 was high and this approach was later confirmed in *Farley*.

FURTHER READING

Primary sources

Addis v. *Gramophone Co. Ltd* (1909) AC 488

Farley v. *Skinner* (2001) UKHL 49

Robinson v. *Harman* (1848) 1 Ex 850

Watts v. *Morrow* (1991) 1 WLR 1421

Secondary sources

Capper, D. (2002) 'Damages for Distress and Disappointment – Problem Solved?' (2002) *LQR*, 193.

Phang, A. (2003) 'The crumbling edifice? The award of contractual damages for mental distress' (2003) *JBL*, 341.

5 TORT LAW

The word 'tort' is derived from the French word for wrong, though as a term of art it covers only part of what might loosely be referred to as the law of wrongs. The law of tort serves a variety of purposes and seeks to give protection to a wide range of interests; largely as a result of its historical development it remains a fragmentary and disorganised subject. Broadly speaking this branch of the law is principally concerned with providing a remedy to those who have been harmed by the conduct of others. While it is a not uncommonly held belief that whenever A suffers loss as a result of B's conduct he is entitled to redress, this is not the case. The rules of the law of tort determine whether redress will be granted in any particular case, and the main function of the law may be said to be the allocation, or in some cases the prevention, of losses which are bound to occur in society.

Each tort has particular elements which must be present in order for a claim to succeed. This chapter examines some of the principal elements, via selected case law. Particular attention has been given to the tort of negligence, which forms the basis of the majority of tort actions. Negligence consists of the breach of a legal duty of care by the defendant, causing consequential loss to the claimant. In addition to the entries on common law negligence, the chapter also considers occupier's liability (a statutory form of negligence) and private nuisance (which concerns unreasonable interference with the use or enjoyment of land).

CONTENTS FOR TORT LAW

Duty of care
Donoghue (or Mc'Alister) v. Stevenson [1932] AC 562   225

Negligently inflicted psychiatric injury
Alcock v. Chief Constable of South Yorkshire Police [1992] 1 AC 310   231

Negligently inflicted economic loss
Hedley Byrne & Co. v. Heller and Partners Ltd [1964] AC 465   236

Factual causation
Barnett v. Chelsea and Kensington Hospital Management Committee
[1969] 1 QB 428   242

Causation in law
Knightley v. Johns and Others [1982] All ER 851, [1982] 1 WLR 349   249

Remoteness of damage
Overseas Tankship (UK) Ltd v. Morts Dock & Engineering (The Wagon
Mound (No. 1)) [1961] AC 388, [1961] 1 All ER 404   254

Defences to negligence
Owens v. Brimmell [1977] QB 859   259

Occupiers' liability
Roles v. Nathan [1963] 1 WLR 1117   264

Private nuisance
Hunter and Others v. Canary Wharf Ltd; Hunter and Others v. London
Docklands Development Corporation [1997] AC 655   268

Duty of care

Donoghue (or Mc'Alister) v. Stevenson [1932] AC 562

Ross Fletcher, Northumbria University

The case of *Donoghue* v. *Stevenson* is, without question, the most important authority in the history of the tort of negligence in English law. While there have been subsequent cases (such as *Caparo Industries Plc* v. *Dickman*) that have modified the rules laid down by the House of Lords in 1932, none have altered them to any great extent. It is for these reasons that the case is frequently the first one that students are referred to in order to gain an understanding of the law of negligence.

The story behind the case is almost as celebrated as the case itself. It began in the Wellmeadow Café in Paisley, Scotland, which Mrs Frances Donoghue (*neé* Mc'Alister) and her friend visited in 1928. Mrs Donoghue's friend purchased for her a bottle (which was, significantly, made of opaque glass) of ginger beer which was poured out for her to drink. Upon consumption of the beverage Mrs Donoghue allegedly noticed the remains of a decomposed snail at the bottom of the bottle, causing her to suffer shock and develop gastroenteritis from the beverage that she had consumed. She sought to sue Stevenson (the manufacturer of the soft drink) for damages. He denied liability on the ground that there was no contract between himself and Mrs Donoghue. The case was appealed through all the Scottish courts and eventually ended up on appeal in the House of Lords.

For such an important case it is interesting to note how vague some of the facts are. It is unclear whether there was indeed a snail in the bottle (the case settled before this could be determined), whether the drink purchased was in fact ginger beer ('ginger' is a Scottish slang word for any soft drink) and who Mrs Donoghue's friend was.

Pre-*Donoghue*: the duty of care

Before *Donoghue* came before the House of Lords it was difficult to find an authoritative ruling as to what duty is owed to others to prevent harm occurring negligently. This was remarked upon by Lord Atkin in his leading speech and by his brother judges in the House of Lords also. A number of cases had been decided in which articles, buildings or vehicles had been manufactured in what turned out to be a negligent fashion which led to persons sustaining injury. In many cases the injured parties had sought to claim damages but had been denied relief on the ground that there was no contractual relationship between the manufacturer and the injured party. This was so in *Winterbottom* v. *Wright*, a case relied upon heavily by Lords Buckmaster and Tomlin in their dissenting speeches in *Donoghue*. The case involved a carriage which collapsed due to negligent manufacture causing injury to a passenger who sought to obtain damages for his injuries. His claim was rejected for several reasons; chief amongst them being that the defendant was able to be sued by his employer for his negligent work due to his breach of contract in improperly performing his duties. The point was also made that if the claimant were allowed to obtain relief for his injuries then it would allow all passengers in vehicles which were involved in an accident to sue for damages, which Lord Tomlin described in *Donoghue* as what would have been 'alarming consequences'.

A similar sort of claim was again dismissed in the Scottish case of *Mullen v. Barr & Co., McGowan v. Barr & Co.*, another case cited with approval by the dissenting judges in *Donoghue*. The case had very similar facts to *Donoghue* other than that it involved the claimant (or 'pursuer', to use the procedural term utilised in Scots civil litigation) consuming the remains of a decomposed mouse. Lord Anderson, who gave the judgment of the Second Division of the Scottish Court of Judicature stated that it would be 'outrageous' to impose potential liability upon the 'defenders' (to use the procedural term utilised in Scots civil litigation) in respect of every product leaving their works, the products being widely sold throughout Scotland. If such responsibility attached to the defenders, they could be faced with claims 'which they could not possibly investigate or answer'.

However, there were some such cases in which the courts had been prepared to look further than the strict confines of a contractual relationship in determining the parties who were owed a duty not to be injured. One such case was *Heaven v. Pender*. The facts of the case concerned a negligently erected stage at premises to which the claimant had been invited. In dicta relied upon by counsel for Mrs Donoghue, Brett MR stated that 'wherever one person is by circumstances placed in such a position with regard to another that everyone of ordinary sense who did think would at once recognise that if he did not use ordinary care and skill in his own conduct with regard to those circumstances he would cause danger of injury to the person or property of the other, a duty arises to use ordinary care to avoid such danger'. His Lordship drew particular reference to cases involving manufactured goods containing defects that could not be discovered by the person to whom they were supplied prior to their using them.

Brett MR's statement was regarded by the judges (particularly those dissenting) in *Donoghue* as expressing too broad a duty to expect of manufacturers, and it was pointed out that it had been qualified to an extent by that same judge in the subsequent case of *Le Lievre and Another v. Gould*. In this case a builder had a relationship with mortgagees whereby they advanced him money upon the provision of surveyors' certificates verifying that certain stages in his building work had been achieved. It transpired that the surveyor (who had no contractual relationship with the mortgagees) had made incorrect statements in the certificates due to his negligence and he was sued for damages. Lord Esher MR (as he had then become) explained that although *Heaven v. Pender* had established that 'under certain circumstances, one man may owe a duty to another, even though there is no contract between them', this principle operated where 'one man is near to another, or is near to the property of another'. He concluded that *Heaven v. Pender* had no bearing on the instant case and it was held that the surveyor owed no duty of care to the mortgagees.

226

The dissenting speeches

For the reasons discussed above, Lords Buckmaster and Tomlin were of the opinion that the appeal by Mrs Donoghue should be dismissed. Their Lordships shared the view that the cases where damages had been awarded to persons who had no contractual relationship with the persons who had injured them ought to be confined to their particular facts. They regarded Brett MR's attempt to draw up an all-encompassing principle based upon what 'everyone of ordinary sense' would regard as likely to result in injury by which to hold a tortfeasor liable as having no place in English or Scottish law. Lord Buckmaster made the point that to allow the pursuer relief in the instant case would be to go a step further than previous authorities had allowed and 'if one step, why not fifty?'

Their speeches were clearly based upon the facts of the instant case and an exceptionally declaratory approach to the rules of judicial precedent, and were influenced by the lack of decided cases in which manufacturers of foodstuffs had been successfully sued for damages by injured consumers of their products who had no contractual relationship with them (indeed, Lord Buckmaster's speech seems to suggest that even those who did have a contractual relationship with such defendants should be unable to obtain relief if there were too many of them). The judges were unprepared to take a step as bold as Brett MR had done and attempt to formulate a general principle by which to determine the circumstances in which negligence could sound in damages and were content to leave the law of tort in its fragmented state.

Lord Macmillan

Lord Macmillan was prepared to adopt a more flexible approach to interpreting the standards to which manufacturers of products should adhere. His Lordship stated that, should a manufacturer of products treat goods in such a way as to expose them to circumstances in which they might become dangerous to the members of the public who might use them then he ought to be held liable for any 'deleterious matter' that enters the product as a result of his negligence (but not for anything that might happen as a result of 'a mere accident'). His Lordship relied upon similar dicta by the eminent American judge Cardozo J in the US case of *McPherson* v. *Buick Motor Co.* In the most interesting passage of his speech, Lord Macmillan appears to criticise his fellow judges for their restrictive approach to the evolution of the common law, and remarks upon the many situations in the (then) modern age in which one person might cause injury or loss to another. He takes the view that the law ought to set the standard whereby such persons' conduct might be judged. His Lordship made the oft-quoted *bon mot* that 'The categories of negligence are never closed'. However, it is noteworthy that His Lordship was still unwilling to espouse such a general principle in the instant case and based his finding for the appellant on the unusual contention that it involved 'a special instance of negligence where the law exacts a degree of diligence so stringent as to amount practically to a guarantee of safety'.

The final noteworthy point about Lord Macmillan's speech is His Lordship's reference to *The Law of Torts* (13th edn) by Sir Frederick Pollock, in which the author criticised the courts' having 'a certain tendency to hold that facts which constitute a contract cannot

5

TORT LAW

227

have any other legal effect' as displayed in cases like *Winterbottom* v. *Wright*. Upon contrasting this with Lord Buckmaster's view that 'the law books give no assistance because the works of living authors, however deservedly eminent, cannot be used as authorities' it can be noted that the case illustrates something of a paradigm shift in the use by the courts of academic commentary to shed light on grey areas of the law.

Lord Thankerton

Lord Thankerton based his finding for the pursuer upon the contention that the manufacture of a product which could logically be consumed by her brought about a 'direct relationship' as a result of which the manufacturer was liable for her injuries. His Lordship drew an analogy with the case of *Gordon* v. *M'Hardy*, in which consumption of salmon from a tin which was dented when purchased led to the death of the pursuer's son. His Lordship was of the view that if the defendant grocer could not be held liable for the loss in question it would be unjust not to hold the manufacturer (who in the case could not be identified) so liable. Lord Thankerton gave the shortest speech of the judges in the majority as he largely agreed with the speech of Lord Atkin, but like Lord Macmillan was still careful to form his decision in terms of an analogy with contract law.

Lord Atkin

The longest and most influential speech in the House of Lords was by Lord Atkin. His Lordship began by criticising the 'elaborate classification of duties' made by the English courts into different categories of standards of care depending upon the particular nature of the relationship between the parties in each instant case and was alone among their Lordships in drawing assistance from Brett MR's dicta in *Heaven* v. *Pender*, of which His Lordship was of the view that 'with the necessary qualification of proximate relationship' as suggested in *Le Leivre* v. *Gould* it correctly 'expresses the law of England'.

His Lordship suggested that the pursuer's case was based upon the contention that if a product is manufactured in such a way as to be delivered to a consumer without the possibility of intermediate examination by that consumer the manufacturer should be liable for damages if the product causes the consumer injuries due to the manufacturer's negligence. This was acknowledged to be a sound viewpoint and that although 'it is said that the law of England and Scotland is that the poisoned consumer has no remedy against the negligent manufacturer . . . if this were the result of the authorities I should consider the result a grave defect in the law'.

However, His Lordship went further than introducing the test by which consumers of defective products could obtain relief and like Brett MR before him enumerated a general set of principles to be applied in cases of negligence through what has come to be known as 'the neighbour test'. This in its simplest form is based upon the Biblical doctrine that 'you must love your neighbour' which in law is to be interpreted as meaning that 'you must take reasonable care to avoid acts and omissions which you can reasonably foresee would be likely to injure your neighbour'. His Lordship went on to explain that in legal language one's neighbour is 'persons who are so closely and directly affected by my act that I ought reasonably to have them in contemplation as being so affected when I am directing my mind to the acts or omissions which are called into question'.

The neighbour principle finally disposed of the analogy between tort and contract law and remains the central criterion for establishing the existence of a duty of care. If there is no contractual relationship between the parties, then the application of the neighbour test allows the judge to determine whether on the facts of the instant case the injured party ought to obtain relief; if there was no reasonable foreseeability of loss resulting from the acts or omissions in question then the claim will not sound in damages.

A landmark decision

The decision of *Donoghue v. Stevenson* is a landmark decision for a number of reasons. Firstly, it sets out a general test to judge where a duty of care arises in cases not just of defective products but of all situations where negligence results in loss. Secondly, it shows a significant alteration in the way judges have interpreted case law in the marked contrast between the dissenting judges and Lord Atkin's speeches. Finally, there is the oft-overlooked but still important point with regard to the emphasis placed upon academic commentary in elucidating points of law which are not firmly decided by the courts. For all these reasons the case is one of the most important in the history of the common law system.

It should be noted that the test for establishing whether a duty of care is owed in the tort of negligence has been developed by numerous subsequent authorities. The most important of these include *Caparo Industries v. Dickman* (op cit) (in which the House of Lords held that in addition to foreseeability of damage, it must also be established that the relationship between the parties is one of 'proximity' and that it is fair, just and reasonable to impose a duty), *Murphy v. Brentwood* (in which it was held that if economic loss was the only loss sustained it would not be recoverable in tort) and *Hill v. Chief Constable of West Yorkshire* (where the appeal was dismissed on the grounds that it would be contrary to public policy to allow the claimant damages).

FURTHER READING

Primary sources

Caparo Industries Plc v. Dickman [1990] 2 AC 605

Donoghue (or Mc'Alister) v. Stevenson [1932] AC 562

Gordon v. M'Hardy (1903) 6F (Ct of Sess) 210

Heaven v. Pender (1883) 11 QBD 503

Hill v. Chief Constable of West Yorkshire [1989] AC 53

Le Lievre and Another v. Gould [1893] 1 QB 491

McPherson v. Buick Motor Co. (1916) 217 NY 382

Mullen v. Barr & Co, McGowan v. Barr & Co. [1929] SC 461

Murphy v. Brentwood [1991] 1 AC 398

Winterbottom v. Wright (1842) 10 M & W 109

5

TORT LAW

Secondary sources

Castle, R. [2003] 'Lord Atkin and the neighbour test: origins of the principles of negligence in *Donoghue* v. *Stevenson*' 7(33), *Ecc. LJ*, 210.

Hemraj (2002) 'The emergence of the foreseeability rule in England and Wales' 23 (7), *Comp. Law*, 205.

Heuston, R.F.V. (1957) '*Donoghue* v. *Stevenson* in retrospect' 20, *MLR*, 1.

Holbrook, J. (2007) 'The sliding snail' 157, *NLJ*, 168.

McBride, N.J. [2004] 'Duties of care: do they really exist?' *OJLS*, 24.

Morgan, J. [2006] 'The rise and fall of the general duty of care' 22(4), *PN*, 206.

Rodger, A. [1988] 'Mrs Donoghue and Alphenus Varus' *CLP*, 1.

Rodger, A. (1992) 'Lord Macmillan's speech in *Donoghue* v. *Stevenson*' 108, *LQR*, 236.

Negligently inflicted psychiatric injury

Alcock v. *Chief Constable of South Yorkshire Police*
[1992] 1 AC 310

Ralph Tiernan, Northumbria University

It should be noted at the start that this comment is concerned only with negligently inflicted psychiatric illness caused by 'shock' which, in the words of Lord Ackner in *Alcock*, 'involves the sudden appreciation by sight or sound of a horrifying event which violently agitates the mind'. It therefore has no bearing on liability in other types of case where such loss may arise, for example psychiatric illness induced by work-related stress or by the negligent communication of distressing news.

The law before *Alcock*

The law evolved to a point where the claimant would be owed a duty of care and could therefore succeed if:

(a) he was himself injured or reasonably feared that he might be (*Dulieu* v. *White*); or

(b) shock resulted from injury to his spouse or child (or perhaps other close relation involving similar ties of affection), or from the fear of such injury, and came about through the sight or hearing of the event (*Hambrook* v. *Stokes Bros*) or its immediate aftermath (*McLoughlin* v. *O'Brian*).

In addition to the above there was authority to suggest that rescuers formed a special category of claimant (see, for example, *Chadwick* v. *British Transport Commission*).

However, there were in all cases two prerequisites to the right of recovery. First, the claimant had to establish that he was suffering from a recognisable psychiatric illness, so that no damages could be awarded for the ordinary emotions of anxiety, fear or grief (see, for example, *Hinz* v. *Berry*), subject to a limited right to claim for bereavement introduced by the Administration of Justice Act 1982 (which created a new section 1A of the Fatal Accidents Act 1976). Secondly, unless the claimant's psychiatric illness was consequential upon physical injury, he had to prove that such illness was reasonably foreseeable (see, for example, *Hambrook* v. *Stokes Bros*), and, in applying the test of foreseeability, it was to be assumed that the claimant was a person of ordinary fortitude (*Bourhill* v. *Young*). The abnormally sensitive claimant would therefore fail unless a person of normal fortitude could have foreseeably sustained psychiatric illness in the circumstances, in which case the sensitive claimant was entitled to damages for the full extent of his injury even if exacerbated by a predisposition to such harm (*Brice* v. *Brown*). While the first prerequisite remains today, the claimant, as will be seen, will not in all cases have to prove foreseeability of psychiatric harm.

Alcock

The claims in *Alcock* arose out of alleged negligence by the police responsible for crowd control at a football match. The defendant had allowed an excessive number of intending spectators into a part of the stadium which was already full, with the result that 95 spectators were crushed to death and over four hundred injured. The events were broadcast live on television and later as a news item, and the disaster was also broadcast over the radio. In accordance with broadcasting guidelines the television coverage did not show the suffering or dying of recognisable individuals. Of the sixteen original claimants ten were successful at first instance, but the Court of Appeal allowed the defendant's appeal in respect of nine of them and dismissed the cross-appeals of the six who were unsuccessful. Ten of the fifteen appealed to the House of Lords. Two of them had been present at the match, though not in the danger area, while the others had watched the events either on live television or on later news bulletins. Their relationship to the immediate victims of the tragedy ranged from parents to brother, sister, brother-in-law, fiancée and grandfather.

In his judgment Lord Oliver drew attention for the first time to the distinction between two categories of potential claimant. On the one hand there were ' . . . those cases in which the injured plaintiff was involved, either mediately or immediately, as a participant . . . ' (primary victims), while on the other hand ' . . . those in which the plaintiff was no more than the passive and unwilling witness of injury caused to others' (secondary victims). Adopting the approach of Lord Wilberforce in *McLoughlin* v. *O'Brian* their Lordships unanimously held that, in order to succeed, a secondary victim would have to prove all of the following:

(a) that he had a close tie of love and affection to the immediate victim, such that it was reasonably foreseeable that he might suffer psychiatric illness;

(b) that he was spatially and temporally close to the accident or its 'immediate aftermath';

(c) that psychiatric illness was the result of seeing or hearing the event or its immediate aftermath.

With regard to (a) above their Lordships concluded that the class of persons to whom a duty might be owed was not limited by reference to particular relationships, and that as between spouses and in the parent-child relationship the required tie would be rebuttably presumed to exist (Lord Keith also thought that the presumption might arise in favour of engaged couples). With more remote relationships, however, the claimant would have to adduce evidence to prove the closeness of the tie, although according to Lords Keith, Ackner and Oliver a possible exception to this requirement was in the case of a particularly horrific accident, when even a bystander might be able to recover if a reasonably strong-nerved person would have been so affected.

As far as requirement (b) is concerned it was accepted that the accident included not only the event itself but also its 'immediate aftermath', a proposition first recognised in *McLoughlin* v. *O'Brian*. In that case the claimant's husband and three children were involved in an accident caused by the defendant's negligence. She was told of the accident an hour or so later and went immediately to the hospital where she found her family smothered in dirt and oil and in obvious pain and distress. In these circumstances she was held to have satisfied the spatial and temporal proximity requirement.

The final criterion for establishing a duty ruled out claims for psychiatric injury brought about by communication of the event by a third party, although their Lordships thought that there might be circumstances where the element of direct perception would be satisfied by witnessing the event on a simultaneous television broadcast.

The House of Lords dismissed all of the appeals on the ground that either (i) the appellants were not at the match but had seen the event on television or heard radio broadcasts and thus, in view of the broadcasting guidelines which did not allow the showing of recognisable individuals caught up in the tragedy, failed to satisfy the proximity requirement, or (ii) they had not established a sufficiently close tie of love and affection to the immediate victim.

Developments after *Alcock*

1. *Page* v. *Smith*

Although *Alcock* laid down the criteria for recovery by secondary victims it said little about primary victims, although in Lord Oliver's opinion this category included not only those exposed to the risk of physical injury (or who reasonably believed themselves to be at risk), but also rescuers and 'involuntary participants'. The latter were those who, as a result of the defendant's negligence, were put in the position of being, or of thinking that they were about to be or had been, the involuntary cause of another's death or injury and psychiatric illness was the product of the claimant's awareness of this supposed fact (see, for example, *Dooley* v. *Cammell Laird & Co. Ltd*). Whether the claimant believed himself to be at risk or that he was in some way responsible for what happened to another, the Court of Appeal held that such belief had to be reasonable (*McFarlane* v. *EE Caledonia Ltd*; *Hunter* v. *British Coal Corp.*).

In *Page* v. *Smith* the claimant was involved in a moderately severe car crash though he was physically unhurt. He had in the past suffered sporadically from ME which was in remission at the time of the accident but which, as a result of his experience recurred with chronic intensity. Allowing the defendant's appeal against the decision at first instance the Court of Appeal held that psychiatric illness was not reasonably foreseeable in a person of ordinary fortitude. A majority of the House of Lords reversed the Court of Appeal. In the case of a primary victim, defined by Lord Lloyd in terms of those who were 'directly involved in the accident' and 'well within the range of foreseeable physical injury', the test was whether personal injury, physical or psychiatric, was reasonably foreseeable by the defendant. If so, it was irrelevant that no physical injury, in fact, occurred or that psychiatric injury in the circumstances was unforeseeable, because the defendant had to take his victim as he found him. In reaching this decision their Lordships were clearly treating psychiatric illness and physical injury as damage of the same kind, so that no special rules applied to the primary victim.

2. *White* v. *Chief Constable of South Yorkshire Police*

This case involved claims by a number of police officers who had been present at, and some of whom had assisted at, the same event that had affected the claimants in *Alcock*. They claimed on the ground that they were to be regarded as being in the same position as employees of the defendant and were thus owed a duty by virtue of their employment status, or alternatively on the ground that they were rescuers. A majority of the House of Lords interpreted *Page* v. *Smith* as establishing that a claimant who was neither at risk of foreseeable physical harm, nor reasonably believed that he was, fell into the category of secondary victim to whom the *Alcock* criteria applied. It therefore followed that merely because the claimant was an employee or a rescuer did not entitle him to primary victim status. It also seems clear from the decision that, in order to qualify as a primary victim, the claimant need not be aware at the time that he is in physical danger nor, even if he is so aware, need he prove that psychiatric illness was caused by his perception of the danger rather than by the general horror of the event (see also *Young* v. *Charles Church (Southern) Ltd*).

Outstanding problems

It remains unclear whether it is necessary in all cases for the primary victim to be at risk of physical harm, or to reasonably believe that he is. Despite Lord Oliver's classification of the 'involuntary participant' as a primary victim, Lord Hoffmann in *White* v. *Chief Constable of South Yorkshire* was sceptical of such a view, although he conceded that there might be grounds for treating such cases as exceptional and therefore not subject to the *Alcock* criteria. Further, in *W* v. *Essex CC*, Lord Slynn thought that the categorisation of those claiming to be primary victims was not finally closed, but was 'a concept still to be developed in different factual circumstances'.

With regard to secondary victims, although there had been a suggestion in *Alcock* that there might be circumstances in which a bystander could recover, the Court of Appeal in *McFarlane* v. *EE Caledonia* rejected the possibility on the ground that to extend a duty of care in this way would be to base the test of liability on foreseeability alone, and this had been ruled out in *Alcock*. In addition, given that people's reactions to horrific events are variable and subjective, there would be significant problems in deciding which accidents were sufficiently horrific to justify such an extension. It is therefore very unlikely that a bystander could recover today, particularly in the absence of further authority in support of the proposition. More significantly, perhaps, it is not at all clear what will be held to constitute the 'immediate aftermath' of an event. In this respect *McLoughlin* v. *O'Brian* may be contrasted with *Alcock*, where a visit to a mortuary to identify a body some eight or nine hours after death did not qualify as the *immediate* aftermath. Lord Jauncey in *Alcock* further considered that the purpose for which the claimant attended the scene was also relevant in establishing proximity, and thought that attendance at a mortuary to identify a dead body was very different from the situation in *McLoughlin* where the claimant went within a short time of the accident to administer aid and comfort to her family. In *W* v. *Essex CC* Lord Slynn said that whether the aftermath test was satisfied had to be determined in the light of the particular facts. In that case the defendant placed a boy who was a known sexual abuser with a foster family without disclosing his history. The boy abused the children of the family during a four week period before the parents found out, and the House of Lords, refusing an application to have the claim struck out, held that further detailed investigation might justify the conclusion that the spatial and temporal limitations of *Alcock* were satisfied (see also *Farrell* v. *Merton, Sutton and Wandsworth Health Authority; Palmer* v. *Tees Health Authority*).

Conclusion

It seems clear that the *Alcock* control mechanisms applying to secondary victims are intended to restrict the number of potential claimants for fear of opening the floodgates to litigation, though it may also be that there still exists a judicial fear and scepticism of the genuineness of such claims. In many respects the law is in need of clarification with a view to creating a more coherent body of principle, but no doubt radical reform, as a number of judges have acknowledged, can only be achieved by Parliament (see, for example, Lords Slynn and Hoffmann in *White v. Chief Constable of South Yorkshire*). In view of the lack of response to the Law Commission's proposals for reform (see Liability For Psychiatric Illness, Law Com No. 249, 1998), parliamentary intervention seems most unlikely for the foreseeable future.

5

TORT LAW

FURTHER READING

Primary sources

Alcock v. Chief Constable of South Yorkshire Police [1992] 1 AC 310

Bourhill v. Young [1943] AC 92

Brice v. Brown [1984] 1 All ER 997

Chadwick v. British Transport Commission [1967] 2 All ER 945

Dooley v. Cammell Laird & Co. Ltd [1951] I Lloyd's Rep 271

Dulieu v. White [1901] 2 KB 669

Farrell v. Merton, Sutton and Wandsworth Health Authority (2000) 57 BMLR 158

Hambrook v. Stokes Bros [1925] 1 KB 141

Hinz v. Berry [1970] 2 QB 40)

Hunter v. British Coal Corp [1997] 2 All ER 97

McFarlane v. EE Caledonia Ltd [1994] 2 All ER 1

McLoughlin v. O'Brian [1983] 1 AC 410

Page v. Smith [1996] AC 155

Palmer v. Tees Health Authority [1999] Lloyd's Rep Med 351

W v. Essex CC [2001] 2 AC 592

White v. Chief Constable of South Yorkshire [1999] 2 AC 455

Young v. Charles Church (Southern) Ltd (1997) 39 BMLR 146

Administration of Justice Act 1982

Fatal Accidents Act 1976

Secondary source

Liability For Psychiatric Illness, Law Com No. 249, 1998.

Negligently inflicted economic loss

Hedley Byrne & Co. v. Heller and Partners Ltd
[1964] AC 465

Brian Dowrick, University of Glamorgan

Hedley Byrne v. *Heller* is one of the most fascinating and significant cases in the modern era developments of the duty of care in the tort of negligence. *Donoghue* v. *Stevenson* is a case that usually takes the plaudits, but it took *Hedley Byrne* (along arguably with *Dorset Yacht* v. *Home Office*) to point out its limits and, as it were, breathe life into it. *Candler* v. *Crane Christmas* is one example of the attempts to marginalise *Donoghue* (by the legal techniques of narrowing the ratio and/or distinguishing the case), in the years after its reporting.

At this stage, you will have probably been introduced to the tort of negligence and the concept of the duty of care. It can be frustrating to understand how all these ideas and concepts fit together. This is where the law creates a *legal relationship* or nexus between the parties (or as it is sometimes referred to, an obligation – from the Roman law, *vinculum iuris* or legal bond). Of course, in many instances of action (or sometimes inaction), causing loss to another, the question whether X owes Y a duty of care to avoid the injury is answered positively without too much trouble particularly in cases involving personal injury (consider the most common form of injury-causing activity, motoring). This is the combined result of cases like *Donoghue* and their precedent value. *Hedley Byrne*, however, took this development into new areas of loss creation, vitalising *Donoghue* by providing lawyers with a 'toolkit' of concepts with which to create or deny a duty of care; recognised as comprising *foreseeability of the type of loss*, (latterly) *proximity* (or *legal* closeness) between the parties and the rather open-ended idea of whether it is *fair, just and reasonable* (fairness) that the duty should exist (the so-called *Caparo* tripartite test: *Caparo Industries* v. *Dickman*). It has also become significant in addressing obligations (duties) for causing a variety of loss types. It is enough here to recognise that the courts in creating these 'tools' have vacillated over the importance, meaning and content of them. Just as it is possible to require a screwdriver for a particular task, it is equally possible to have the wrong type or size. In other words, for example, 'proximity' may be the selected tool, but it may be the wrong 'type' in a given situation. You should try to remember though that it is a function of English law methodology, that legal rules established through precedent evolve and it may be (as it was in the 1980s and 1990s), that a different composition of judges in the senior appellate courts see the role and function of these rules relating to liability in tort somewhat differently than their predecessors. As a result they may not necessarily be overruling earlier precedent (though, of course, this was the fate for a substantial part of *Anns* v. *Merton BC*), but may reshape, narrow or expand the ideas in them.

Before looking at the case, it is important to understand that while for teaching purposes, the duty of care is compartmentalised into duty/negligent statements/economic or pure economic loss/nervous shock etc., any boundaries between these concepts is not rigid. Really, the focus will be on the duty of care (or as we have put it, the existence of a tortious legal relationship), for different activity and loss types. For example, while you may be asked to think about the duty of care for pure economic loss, almost invariably, cases involving so-called negligent statements will have a complaint that the (negligent) statement has led to pure economic losses (as in *Hedley Byrne* itself). The point here then is that cases like *Hedley Byrne* tend to be treated as if they are relevant only to 'negligent statements'. Remember, this is not so.

The facts

The case in raw terms concerned the giving of references (concerning credit-worthiness) by a bank (Heller & Partners) about a company, Easipower, its own customer. Easipower was in a business relationship with the ultimate *recipient* of the references, Hedley Byrne. Heller provided two references. The first was provided orally and followed up in writing, the second by letter only. Nothing as such turns on whether the references were oral or in writing though in other cases it may be easier to evidence when they are written. Hedley Byrne required and used the reference to (it hoped), further its business relationship. The request for the references by Hedley Byrne was made via its own bank (National Provincial) as it was a feature of banking relations that requests for information/references about customers would be dealt with as a matter of professional courtesy – with at least a requirement that it be provided honestly. Hedley Byrne made no payment for the reference, thus raising no contractual claim. Heller provided references in general terms. The important parts of the references were statements to National Provincial (and confirmed in writing) that Easipower was a 'respectably constituted company and considered good for its ordinary business engagements'. Also important for the outcome of the case was the statement that the references were provided 'for private use and without responsibility'. These references were communicated to Hedley Byrne. Although they were in a pre-existing business relationship with Easipower, Hedley Byrne claimed that as a result of these statements, they engaged in extra expenditure on Easipower's behalf and when subsequently Easipower went into liquidation (meaning essentially that Hedley Byrne's chances of recovering any money was through the law of tort against Heller), they had incurred around £17,661 of losses.

Special relationships and assumptions of responsibility

It is worth considering the arguments of the parties as they are exemplar, well rehearsed and skilful arguments in this area of the law. For example, the appellants wanted the Lords to recognise that no duty of care in the giving of the reference would be 'an unfortunate gap' in the law and that the principles of *Donoghue* should apply to 'words as well as deeds'. The former point is reminiscent of 'policy' arguments (here legal 'policy') – sometimes under the rubric of the *fairness* part of the duty 'toolkit'. This is wide enough to consider these matters and is used extensively to create new or extend existing duties of care.

5

TORT LAW

Lord Goff in *White* v. *Jones*, uses the 'lacuna in the law argument' to close the 'gap' he identifies in the existing law, with a duty. Conversely, for the respondents, the point was that in giving the reference, they never had identified, nor had in mind Hedley Byrne (remember, the references were provided to Nat Pro). They were not 'neighbours' so famously identified by Lord Atkin in *Donoghue*. In other words, using our 'tools', they (Hedley Byrne) and the losses suffered were not *foreseeable* and neither were they *proximate* with Heller (Lord Morris gives the *foreseeability* point short shrift by saying 'the bank must have known that the enquiry was being made by someone contemplating doing business with Easipower and that their answer . . . would be passed on').

Additionally, the respondents powerfully argued that the law relating to statements caus-ing loss had recognised recovery only in specific circumstances, and in negligence this had been where the statement causes physical injury to the person or property of the claimant. To extend the law to create a general duty as Hedley Byrne was contending, would 'open the floodgates of litigation'. This latter point is a common argument where counsel and judges wish to limit or deny the existence of a duty of care and features heav-ily in cases involving pure economic loss (as was suffered by Hedley Byrne; this also fea-tures in the so-called nervous shock duty cases). Again, if we think of our 'toolkit', it can feature in, though it is by virtue of the lack of content to the concepts not limited to, the *fairness* concept ('it is not fair, just and reasonable to create a duty because it may open the floodgates to litigation'), or can feature in the general 'policy' arguments sometimes favoured by both judges and counsel. In other words, the judges are not limited to the spe-cific 'justice' or 'fairness' to the parties in the case. The respondents also used authority (said to be binding on the trial judge and the Court of Appeal), to argue that liability if it does exist, is for *fraudulent* representation (*Derry* v. *Peek*) or where there is *carelessness* (negligence), it can only arise in the absence of fraud in a contractual or fiduciary relation-ship (*Candler* v. *Crane Christmas*). Again these are common lawyerly tactics in painting a picture of the law that recognises a duty for specific activity or types of legal relationship. These parties were neither in a contractual nor fiduciary relationship; *ergo*, it was argued, there was no duty of care.

Essentially, the decisions of the five Law Lords, dismissing the appeal by Hedley Byrne could be summarised as saying that in *special relationships* or where one party *assumes responsibility to the other*, there can be a duty of care in negligence owed by A to B for losses which are purely economic arising out of statements made by A. This was not though, one of those situations. The parts of the references that 'disclaimed' responsibility, were effective in destroying any putative duty of care in negligence (other than a basic requirement of honesty), in the making of the statement and any resultant losses were irrecoverable by Hedley Byrne. This is not the end of the matter though and the importance of *Hedley Byrne* lies in its recognition of the contribution of *Donoghue* v. *Stevenson* (albeit with limits), the circumstances in which a duty of care for negligent (careless) statements may arise and the possibility of a duty of care in negligence for causing (pure) economic loss (contrary to the view that there is a general proposition precluding recovery of pure economic loss in tort). Clearly though, 'policy' issues weigh heavily with this type of loss (see, for example, Denning LJ in *Spartan Steel* v. *Martin*). Latterly, some of the ideas in the case have also been utilised for duties of care involving other types of loss (the assumption of responsibility point, below, has featured in many significant decisions not considering pure economic loss, for example *Barrett* v. *MOD* and *Phelps* v. *Hillingdon LBC*).

What the speeches demonstrate with regard to the tort of negligence, is that a party can be negligent (careless) and not be liable in tort (because there may not be a legal duty to take care) and neither is there a *general* duty in law to be careful in speech (nor in deed). These points should dissuade you from embracing some of the common misconceptions about the tort of negligence. Judges often warn of the dangers in thinking that duties of care exist in the abstract (it is common to hear students say 'a road user owes *all* other road users a duty of care', though if you do, you are in good company as Lord Morris was prepared to state this in *Hedley Byrne*!).

Lawyers tend to look to cases like *Hedley Byrne* to attempt to formulate some general or abstract principles which is why *Donoghue* attracts such reverence, and at times judges appear willing to do so, and at others, not. Compare how the judges in *Hedley Byrne* comment upon *Donoghue*. For Lord Reid, it 'is a very important decision, but I do not think it has any direct bearing on this case . . . ' and for Lord Pearce, '(it) cannot be read as if (it was) dealing with negligence in word causing economic damage'. Lord Hodson's speech is heavily influenced by the 'important' decision of *Donoghue* as it 'shows that the area of negligence is extensive'. Lord Devlin states 'the real value of (*Donoghue*) . . . is that it shows how the law can be developed to solve particular problems'. The point of this is not only to show the approval, but the caution of the judges in extending dramatically the duty situations. They were, however, it appears, happy to describe a duty existing, the basis for which was founded on two very general ideas. The key appears to be two closely related concepts: the *special relationship* and the *assumption of responsibility*. They do, however, pose more questions than they appear to answer.

The categorisation of the relationship said to evidence a duty of care as *special* is a rather open-ended idea. It *includes* contractual and fiduciary relationships (Lord Browne-Wilkinson in *White* v. *Jones* demonstrates this). For Lord Reid there was no logical reason why this categorisation should stop short of those relationships where it is plain that the party seeking information or advice was reasonably trusting the other to exercise a degree of care as required and where the other giving party knew or ought to have known he was being relied upon. It also features in Lord Hodson's speech (though in places he refers to a 'special duty'). Lord Devlin is plainly attracted by this idea as well as it appears to justify the recognition of a duty, first outside of the contractual/fiduciary relationships and second, as a means of providing for a (very) narrow duty. This latter point is important as it recognises the unease of judges in tort to open-ended and expansive liability (well for some types of loss anyway). Develop the law, but develop it cautiously and progressively (also the motivation behind the incremental development idea in *Murphy* v. *Brentwood DC*). He does however decide that where the relationship is 'equivalent to contract' there will be a duty of care. He expands upon this (in terms that echo the 'assumption' point) by stating, 'It is a responsibility that is voluntarily accepted or undertaken either generally where a general relationship is created, such as a solicitor and client . . . or specifically in relation to a particular transaction'. Whether this takes the matter forward is exceedingly moot and you may conclude that it is perhaps no more helpful or accurate than identifying when the parties are 'proximate' or are 'neighbours'. Whether the special relationship exists only when the advice or information is

5

TORT LAW

given by someone who has a special skill (in the sense of being a professional or expert in the matter) is to be doubted – the real point is that a duty may arise where someone holds themselves out as having the necessary qualities that can be relied upon by the other.

The 'special relationship' does not get us very far. The second and far more influential point has been the 'assumption of responsibility'. What appears vital is the deduction from the facts that a person can be said (objectively) to assume responsibility for the giving of the advice or information or for undertaking tasks for the other in circumstances where it is reasonable to place reliance upon them. Does this though require a different consideration to asking whether the losses are reasonably foreseeable and that the parties be proximate? Does it require the assumption to be deduced before a duty can be established or is it synonymous with a duty? These are difficult questions to answer but I suppose you may think that this is bound to happen when we are dealing with the 'empty vessels' provided by the judges. It is probably correct to view the assumption point as being synonymous with the existence of a duty – it would be unlikely to conclude that there is an assumption but no duty. Therefore, in a particularised way (because of the fear of extensive leaps in liability), the assumption point requires us to identify factors of the exchange that make it possible to identify the foreseeability of the loss etc., and you should consider the words of Lords Reid and Devlin above, again. In this way also, one party can be said to assume responsibility for the making of the statement. But you should remember that aside from the obvious foreseeability, proximity etc., points, the wider consequences of holding that a duty will exist will also be considered. A good example of this is the decision in *Watson* v. *British Boxing Board of Control*. The Court of Appeal considers the above points (concluding that the defendants had assumed responsibility to the claimant for the medical care at the boxing match), but also explicitly addresses the 'policy' issues (in that case, for example, the effects of a duty on the non-profit and uninsured sporting body).

Conclusion

I hope that from this brief consideration you will have realised that the ideas and concepts that we are asked to consider in the duty of care are very malleable. *Hedley Byrne* has provided us with a valuable contribution to the evolutionary process. The 'special relationship' and 'assumption' points are not necessarily answers to specific or abstract questions in themselves concerning the existence, meaning or content of the duty of care. Thus the formulation of the duty of care is evidently a complex combination of a number of factors: the specifics of the facts (to deduce the 'assumption') and the context in terms of the law's approach to the consequences of its decision to impose or not impose a duty.

FURTHER READING

Primary sources

Anns v. *Merton BC* [1978] AC 728

Barrett v. *MOD* [1995] 1 WLR 1217

Candler v. *Crane Christmas* [1951] 2 KB 16

Caparo Industries v. *Dickman* [1990] 2 AC 605

Derry v. *Peek* (1889) App Cas 337

Donoghue v. *Stevenson* [1932] AC 562

Dorset Yacht v. *Home Office* [1970] AC 1004

Hedley Byrne v. *Heller* [1964] AC 465

Murphy v. *Brentwood DC* [1990] 3 WLR 414

Phelps v. *Hillingdon LBC* [2001] 2 AC 619

Spartan Steel v. *Martin* [1973] QB 27

Watson v. *British Boxing Board of Control* [2001] QB 1134

White v. *Jones* [1995] 2 AC 207

Secondary sources

Barker (1993) 'Unreliable Assumptions in the Modern Law of Negligence' (1993) 109, *LQR*, 461.

Stapleton (1991) 'Duty of Care and Economic Loss: A Wider Agenda' (1991) 107, *LQR*, 249.

Witting (2000) 'Justifying Liability to Third Parties for Negligent Misstatement' (2000) 20, *OJLS*, 615.

Witting (2005) 'Duty of Care: An Analytical Approach' (2005) 25, *OJLS*, 615.

5

TORT LAW

Barnett v. *Chelsea and Kensington Hospital Management Committee* [1969] 1 QB 428

Richard Ramsay, Oxford Brookes University

It is trite law that a claimant must show on a balance of probabilities that the defendant was not merely negligent but that that negligence caused the claimant's injury. This is normally solved by the application of the 'but-for' test: it is more probable than not that but for the defendant's act or omission the claimant would not have suffered the alleged injury. There may be many different causes. If I invite you to have a drink with me at a certain pub and while you are waiting you fall over a defectively laid carpet, or you are beaten up by a group of yobs who have casually come in looking for trouble, you could say that 'but-for' my invitation you would not have been in that pub in the first place. It does not follow that I bear any legal liability. This may be because a new cause intervened (*novus actus interveniens*) or that my act is too remote from the damage you have sustained. Most tort textbooks contain a chapter entitled 'causation and remoteness'. This in turn is usually divided up between 'causation in fact' and remoteness or 'legal causation', the latter being more of a question of policy, as to how far the courts are prepared to hold defendants responsible for their actions when they are not proximate causes.

Barnett v. *Chelsea and Kensington Hospital Management Committee* rests on a mystery that might have baffled Sherlock Holmes.

The facts

William Barnett, the deceased, was a night-watchman at Chelsea College of Science and Technology. He was on duly on 31 December 1965 with two colleagues. They had a few drinks to celebrate the new year but it was not suggested that they were drunk. At about 4 o'clock in the morning of 1 January 1966 one of them, Frederick Whittall, was struck on the head with an iron bar by an intruder. He was taken to St Stephen's Hospital, under the management of the defendants, by the police. He was treated by a nurse and casualty officer and told to return in the morning. The deceased collected him from the hospital and they went back to the college. At about 5.00 am all three watchmen shared some tea, some from a flask and some freshly made in a pot. The deceased immediately complained of the heat in the room and after twenty minutes all three began to vomit. The vomiting persisted until 8.00 am when the day workers began to arrive at the college. All three went in the deceased's car, which he drove normally, to St Stephen's Hospital, where they were seen by a nurse but the casualty officer who also felt unwell, declined to see them. They all returned to the college where Barnett lay down and when the college's own doctor was called at

1.00 pm it was too late to do anything and he died on the way to the hospital at about 2.00 pm. The coroner returned a verdict of murder by person or persons unknown. Quite who had laced the night-watchmen's tea with arsenic has never been discovered.

The decision

Dismissing the claim in negligence by the widow as administratrix of the deceased's estate and her two dependent children, Neild J found that the hospital had been negligent because the nurse and the casualty officer had undertaken a duty of care once Barnett had presented himself for consultation and the casualty officer was negligent in not seeing him and treating him or having him treated. However, the claim failed as Barnett would inevitably have died of the poisoning even had he been admitted to the hospital wards when he first presented himself and had been treated with all care. The plaintiff had thus failed to establish on the balance of probabilities that the defendant's negligence had caused Barnett's death.

Barnett is thus clear on the point that there must be a causal connection between the alleged act of negligence and the damage which must thus be consequential. The simple 'but-for' test fails in *Barnett* because he would not have died but for the acts of the unknown poisoner, but one cannot say that but for the failure of the defendants to treat him properly or at all, he could have been saved.

Factual causation creates a problem where there are several causes at work simultaneously, and it cannot be unequivocally established which is operative. Thus in *Wilsher* v. *Essex Area Health Authority*, a child suffered blindness in one eye and partial blindness in the other from a condition called retrolental fibroplasia. He claimed that it had been caused when a doctor had negligently given him excess oxygen. The medical evidence showed that, apart from the excessive oxygen, there were six separate potential causes of his blindness that were derived from the plaintiff's premature birth. He could not show on the balance of probabilities that the excess oxygen was the 'guilty' one and it was impossible from the trial judge's notes to determine as a matter of fact, in the face of conflicting medical evidence, which it was. The cause in question need not be determined as the only one. The test developed in *Bonnington Castings Ltd* v. *Wardlaw* was that the defendant's breach of duty had materially contributed to the pursuer's harm. There the pursuer (the case originated in Scotland) developed pneumoconiosis after inhaling silicon dust when at work. The dust could have been produced by two sources, one tortious, the other not. The House of Lords unanimously found for the pursuer. Where the defendant has committed acts that are negligent and it can be shown that one materially contributed to the claimant's injury it is surely a just result that the claimant does not have to specify which act was the wrongful one, provided it was actually one of them rather than only *perhaps* being the one.

If causation could be established as unambiguously as night follows day, all would be easy. There are, however, two situations that have recently been aired in the House of Lords in which there have been considerable doubts. In *Gregg* v. *Scott* the issue was the loss of a chance. In 1994 the claimant went to his general practitioner with a lump under his arm but the defendant doctor misdiagnosed this as benign. Nine months later a different doctor referred him to a hospital where it was discovered that it was non-Hodgkin's lymphoma.

5

TORT LAW

By that time the disease had spread elsewhere. The claimant had treatment but then a relapse and a second relapse. Although the trial judge held the first doctor to be negligent, on the balance of possibilities, the claimant had less than a 50% chance of surviving more than ten years anyway. He was, of course, still alive at the time of the appeal to the Lords, although his good luck hardly affects his contention that his difficult treatment and impaired prospects of survival were the result of the negligence. Lord Nicholls of Birkenhead (dissenting with Lord Hope of Craighead) said (para. 6):

> The deterioration in Mr Gregg's condition reduced his prospects of disease-free survival for ten years from 42%, when he first consulted Dr Scott, to 25% at the date of the trial. The judge found that, if treated promptly, Mr Gregg's initial treatment would probably have achieved remission without an immediate need for high dose chemotherapy.

The trial judge nonetheless concluded that the claimant had a less than even chance (45%) of avoiding the deterioration in his condition and hence he was bound to follow the House of Lords decision in *Hotson* v. *East Berkshire Health Authority*. In that case the plaintiff was thirteen years old when he injured his hip in falling from a tree. He was treated by the defendant health authority where his injury was misdiagnosed. After much pain he returned to the hospital five days later when a correct diagnosis was reached but despite emergency treatment, he had sustained avascular necrosis causing deformity of the hip and reducing his mobility by the time he was twenty years old. The trial judge, Simon Brown J, found that there was a 25% chance that the plaintiff would have avoided the avascular necrosis had his injury been correctly diagnosed and he awarded 25% of the damages that he considered the plaintiff should have received for the condition in which he found himself. In other words, there was a 75% chance that the plaintiff would have developed the avascular necrosis as a result of the fall alone. The House of Lords upheld the defendant health authority's appeal, originally dismissed by the Court of Appeal. They held that it was for the plaintiff to establish on the balance of probabilities that the delay in treatment had at least materially contributed to the avascular necrosis but, in fact, the trial judge's findings were, again on the balance of probabilities, that the fall had been the sole cause of the condition. Hence, on the question of causation, the plaintiff failed and thus no issue of quantification arose. Lord Bridge of Harwich pointed out that had there been a more than even chance that the defendant had caused the plaintiff's injury, he would have been entitled to the full measure of damages. This view was echoed by Lord Ackner. Lord Mackay of Clashfern explicitly said that *Hotson* did not show that a plaintiff could never succeed in proving that there was a loss of a chance in a medical negligence case.

Gregg v. *Scott* was argued against this background. The majority of the House (Lord Hoffmann, Lord Phillips of Worth Matravers, and Baroness Hale of Richmond) held, dismissing the claimant's appeal, that a claim for damages in clinical negligence required proof on the civil standard that the negligence was the cause of the adverse consequences which were complained of, and that no exception could be made to provide for a percentage reduction in the claimant's prospects of a favourable outcome (in fact, from 42% to 25% chance of surviving more than ten years so that he was almost half as badly off because of the delay). Because the claimant could not show that the delay in treatment was the cause of his likely premature death and because there was a lack of remedy for the reduction in his chance of a cure, damages could not be awarded. One wonders what might have happened if the figures had been different: say, a 60% chance of survival if diagnosed immediately and only 40% if the delay occurred. According to Lord Nicholls he would be compensated (para. 46) while a person whose prognosis had deteriorated from 40% to nil would receive nothing. He commented in his powerful dissent, 'This is rough justice indeed'. Of course, in a situation like this it is the cancer that kills but the very reason for consulting a doctor is to detect early symptoms and hence increase one's chances of survival.

For Lord Hoffmann in the majority, the matter was better left to Parliament as he manifestly believed that things had a cause that could be determined and that the law had to use the means of proof as the only way of finding out what would otherwise be hypothetical matters. How could one tell if Mr Gregg were to be in the fortunate 42% who survived with the lymphoma for more than ten years, or would be in the unlucky 58%? Statistics are one thing but they do not and cannot tell us about Mr Gregg's personal chances of survival. As Baroness Hale commented, Mr Gregg's chances of survival were enhanced at every milestone he passed in the course of his disease.

The other problem with factual causation is what happens when a number of discrete defendants are all admittedly negligent but it cannot be shown because of lack of available evidence precisely which one caused the claimant's injury.

This was the issue addressed in *Fairchild v. Glenhaven Funeral Services Ltd.*

The facts

Fairchild concerned a set of conjoined appeals in which the original claimants had been employees who had developed mesothelioma by being negligently exposed to asbestos dust while at work. Each claimant had been exposed to the asbestos dust for different periods while working for different employers, all of whom were admittedly negligent in failing in their duty to protect their employees from the resulting disease. Mesothelioma was caused by exposure to a single fibre of asbestos and hence the claimants were not in a position to point, on the balance of probabilities, precisely to which of the defendants was the one whose breach of duty had caused their illness. Clearly, however, it was one of them but the principle of law that states that only the party responsible for the damage should be liable for it meant that the claimants were likely to be unsuccessful because it was impossible to trace the exact origin of the 'single fibre' that had caused their respective diseases.

The decision

The House of Lords held, allowing the appeals, that where an employee had been exposed by different defendants during different periods of employment, to the risk of inhaling asbestos dust in breach of each of the defendants' duty of care to protect employees from contracting mesothelioma, and where the disease had occurred but the current state of medical knowledge could not attribute its commencement to any particular exposure, there should be a modified approach to proof of causation. In the circumstances where each defendant had materially increased the risk of contracting the disease this sufficed to satisfy the causal requirement for liability.

5

TORT LAW

Lord Bingham of Cornhill, giving the leading speech, pointed out that the normal rule regarding causation still obtained but the question here was whether there should be any variation or relaxation of it. He cited the Australian case of *March v. E & M H Stramare Pty Ltd*, where Mason CJ had questioned the acceptability of the 'but-for' (which he also denominated the *causa sine qua non*) test when there were multiple defendants or causes because it could result in none of the causes being held responsible, contrary to common sense as Winfield and Jolowicz on Tort had already indicated. He said it lacked principle to insist on the application of a rule that appeared to produce unfair results.

The former leading case of *McGhee v. National Coal Board* was considered. There the pursuer claimed that he had contracted dermatitis as a result of working for a brief period in his employer's kilns where, in the heat, the dust and ashes of the kiln clung to the workmen's bodies and the defendants had failed to provide showers where they could wash themselves before going home at the end of the day. Despite some disagreement between the pursuer's and the defender's medical experts, the Lord Ordinary (Lord Kissen) said that at its best, the evidence only showed a material increase in the risk of contracting the disease and this was different from saying, as the pursuer's counsel argued, that the failure to provide showers for washing was a material contribution to contracting dermatitis. The material increase in risk only refers to possibilities and these cannot thus make a possibility into a probability. When that case reached the House of Lords, Lord Reid opined that he could see no difference in the distinction and that since the legal concept of causation was based neither on logic nor philosophy, it followed that from a practical point of view, materially increasing the risk of injury was the same as saying that the defender materially contributed to the injury. This view was supported by others in the House.

In his review of *McGhee* Lord Bingham drew certain conclusions. Firstly, that the House was deciding a matter of law, not of fact. Secondly, that the question of law was whether a pursuer who could not show that the defender's breach had probably caused the damage complained of might nevertheless succeed. Thirdly, the House could not draw a factual inference that the breach had probably caused the damage as this was contradicted by the medical experts for both parties but it was sufficient to show that the breach had increased his risk of contracting the disease. Fourthly, Lord Reid, Lord Simon and Lord Salmon had all expressly stated that there was, in the circumstances, no distinction between making a material contribution to causing the disease and materially increasing the risk of its being contracted. Thus the proposition expressly rejected by the Lord Ordinary, the Lord President and Lord Migdale was equally expressly accepted by the majority in the House of Lords. Fifthly, the House recognised that the pursuer faced insuperable difficulties of proof under the orthodox test for causation and hence the majority of the House adapted that test (see para. 21).

Fairchild marks a distinct step forward in the development of the simple but-for test. Nonetheless, it leaves unanswered the question of quantum: exactly how much should each tortfeasor pay? If they are all able should they pay in equal shares? This response gives a simple answer but it seems unfair if the claimant's exposure to the first defendant's negligence was brief but it was of greater duration in respect of the second defendant. Some sort of apportionment seems called for and this was discussed in the case of *Barker v. Corus UK Ltd*. This was another mesothelioma case with multiple claimants that came before the House of Lords. The case of Mr Barker, brought by his widow, concerned a man who contracted mesothelioma after exposure to asbestos dust when he had worked for a company that had become insolvent, then for the defendant company and, finally, when he was self-employed. In his case the trial judge held the defendant jointly and severally liable alongside the insolvent company but reduced the damages by 20% for the deceased's contributory negligence for the period while he was self-employed. The other appeals concerned claimants who had worked for several defendants, some of whom had become insolvent and their executors had made claims on the basis of joint and several liability against those employers who were still solvent. The defendant employers had appealed.

The House held first (Lord Rodger of Earlsferry dissenting) that where a number of defendants had materially increased the risk that the employee would contract mesothelioma, liability should be distributed according to each's contribution to the risk. Hence their liability was several only. Secondly, where not all the exposures to asbestos that could have caused the mesothelioma were the result of breaches of duty by the claimant's employers (whether the other exposure was tortious or not or derived from the employee himself), the exception to the usual rule about causation would apply. This was generally a blow for sufferers of the disease who protested vociferously when they found that they could not recover from an insolvent defendant and would hence recover only that proportion of their damages from the solvent defendant for which he was responsible.

As a result, section 3 of the Compensation Act 2006 was enacted specifically to reverse the effect of the *Barker* decision (the initial Bill was amended to include this provision). This provided that mesothelioma sufferers were entitled to joint and several damages from 'responsible persons' who had negligently or in breach of statutory duty exposed the claimant to asbestosis from which he had contracted mesothelioma and the state of knowledge rendered it impossible to identify the specific source. This seems to bring back the situation to the original *Fairchild* position where all those in breach of their duty were liable and the claimant could succeed against whomsoever he pleased. The Act specifically refers to sufferers from mesothelioma so it appears that anyone who suffers from a different disease that cannot be attributed to the fault of any one of a number of negligent defendants will still be bound by the *Barker* ruling.

This story of causation of disease cannot be concluded without reference to the most recent case of *Rothwell v. Chemical & Insulating Co. Ltd and Others*. Mr Rothwell and Other claimants suffered from a condition called pleural plaques. The case was decided in the House of Lords. These plaques resulted from exposure to asbestosis dust and the sufferers were at risk of developing one or more long-term asbestosis-related diseases. The pleural plaques themselves had caused no symptoms (they were detected in the course of routine X-rays), were neither painful nor visible lesions, did not increase susceptibility to any other asbestos-related diseases and did not shorten life expectancy. They were not, therefore, injuries that could give rise to a claim for damages in tort. They did, however, show that the claimants' lungs had been penetrated by asbestos fibres that might independently cause other fatal diseases. The risk of developing those other diseases, nor any potential anxiety about those diseases occurring were not actionable in tort either. Finally,

5

TORT LAW

their Lordships held that there was no principle of aggregation whereby the plaques could be connected to the risk of future asbestos-related disease, or the anxiety at such a prospect, no cause of action having ever existed.

FURTHER READING

Primary sources

Barker v. *Corus UK Ltd* [2006] 2 AC 572

Barnett v. *Chelsea and Kensington Hospital Management Committee* [1969] 1 QB 428

Bonnington Castings Ltd v. *Wardlaw* [1956] AC 613

Fairchild v. *Glenhaven Funeral Services Ltd* [2003] 1 AC 32

Gregg v. *Scott* [2005] 2 AC 176

Hotson v. *East Berkshire Health Authority* [1987] AC 750

March v. *E & M H Stramare Pty Ltd* (1991) 171 CLR 506

McGhee v. *National Coal Board* [1973] 1 WLR 1

Page v. *Smith* [1996] AC 115

Rothwell v. *Chemical & Insulating Co. Ltd*; *Grieves* v. *F T Everard & Sons Ltd* [2007] 3 WLR 876

Wilsher v. *Essex Area Health Authority* [1988] AC 1074

Compensation Act 2006

Secondary sources

Deakin, S., Johnston, A. and Markesinis, B. (2008) *Markesinis and Deakin's Tort Law*, 6th edn, Clarendon Press, Oxford, 244-280.

Khoury, L. (2008) 'Causation and Risk in the Highest Courts of Canada, England and France' (2008) *LQR*, 103.

Lunney, M. and Oliphant, K. (2008) *Tort Law. Text and Materials*, 3rd edn, Oxford University Press, 210-283.

Murphy, J. (2007) *Street on Torts*, 12th edn, Oxford University Press, 135-168.

Reece, H. (1996) 'Losses of Chances in the Law' (1996) *MLR*, 188.

Rogers, W. (2006) *Winfield and Jolowicz, Tort*, 17th edn, Sweet and Maxwell.

Stapleton, J. (1988) 'The Gist of Negligence. Part II' (1988) *LQR*, 389.

Stapleton, J. (2003) 'Cause-in-Fact and the Scope of Liability for Consequences' (2003) *LQR*, 388.

Knightley v. *Johns and Others*
[1982] All ER 851, [1982] 1 WLR 349

Adam Jackson, Northumbria University

The case of *Knightley* v. *Johns* looks at the tort of negligence, in particular the foresee-ability of any harm arising from a negligent act and the question of whether the chain of causation can be broken by an intervening act. Put another way was the harm caused to (A) a natural and probable consequence of the negligence of (B) or could intervening actions (*novus actus interveniens*) break the chain of causation and create a com-pletely new cause of action?

The facts of the case explain the proposition more clearly. The cause of action arose out of a road traffic accident described by Stephenson LJ, giving judgment in the case in the Court of Appeal, as unusual and unlucky. A member of the public, while driving his motor car in a negligent manner, overturned his vehicle in a one-way road tunnel. A police inspector who arrived on the scene forgot to close the road tunnel immediately to traffic, despite a police standing order to that effect being in place. As a result he ordered the claimant, a police officer, and Another officer, both of whom were riding motorcycles to go back and close the tunnel.

The two officers attempted to carry out the inspector's orders by riding back up the tunnel against the flow of traffic and round a blind bend. The inspector had no objection to them attempting to execute his orders in that manner. Each officer took a slightly dif-ferent approach to negotiating the tunnel, the first hugging the inside wall to give cars a better chance of avoiding him and the claimant hugging the outside wall to give him-self a better line of sight. Near to the entrance of the tunnel a car entering the tunnel swerved to avoid the first police officer and as a result struck the claimant's motorcycle and caused him to sustain injuries.

The decision at first instance

The claimant sued in the tort of negligence for the injuries that he sustained. He named four separate defendants in his cause of action. The first defendant was the driver of the car that caused the original accident in the tunnel causing him to have to go back and close the tunnel. The second defendant was the driver of the car that actually struck his motorcycle and caused him to sustain injuries. The third defendant was the chief con-stable of the police force and the fourth defendant was the inspector at the scene who had forgotten to close the road tunnel and had ordered him to go and shut it.

At first instance the judge took the view that neither the inspector nor the claimant had been negligent and that their actions did not constitute a *novus actus intervieniens*. Thus,

5

TORT LAW

he took the view that the first defendant's negligence was an 'operative cause of the [claimant's] injury' and that he was solely liable for the injuries sustained by the claimant. The first defendant appealed.

The appeal

The negligence of the first defendant was not an issue that the court had to spend a great deal of time deliberating as it had been accepted by the first defendant that he had been driving the car negligently as part of his evidence at the original hearing. It is straightforward to establish that the first defendant owed a duty of care in the circumstances (*Donoghue* v. *Stephenson*) and the admission by the first defendant that he was driving negligently meant the court did not have to investigate whether or not he was in breach of the duty. For guidance on the standard of care imposed on motorists see *Nettleship* v. *Weston*.

The appeal turned on the issue of whether the injury sustained by the claimant was a natural and probable result of the original negligence of the first defendant. In order to answer this question, the court had to assess the actions of the police inspector and the claimant, because, as Stephenson LJ explained, 'his [the first defendant's] liability depends on the nature of what they did'. Thus, the crux of the matter was whether the actions of the inspector or of the claimant himself broke the chain of causation between the first defendant's negligence and the injuries sustained by the claimant.

The chain of causation – defining *novus actus interveniens*

The usual test for factual causation is often referred to as the 'but-for' test; 'if the damage would not have happened but for a particular fault then that fault is the cause of the damage; if it would have happened just the same, fault or no fault, the fault is not the cause of the damage' (per Denning LJ *Cork* v. *Kirby Maclean Ltd*).

In *Knightley* v. *Johns* the question of whether the first defendant's negligent act caused the injuries sustained by the claimant would be answered by determining whether or not the actions of the police at the scene constituted a *novus actus interveniens* and therefore broke the chain of causation. A *novus actus interveniens* is essentially an intervening act that is so unforeseeable the damage sustained by the claimant can no longer be regarded in law as being caused by the original negligent act.

In the case of *Haynes* v. *Harwood*, Greer LJ examined the concept of a *novus actus interveniens* and when it might be applied:

> If what is relied upon as *novus actus interveniens* is the very kind of thing which is likely to happen if the want of care which is alleged takes place, the principle embodied in the maxim is no defence. The whole question is whether or not, to use the words of the leading case, *Hadley* v. *Baxendale*, the accident can be said to be 'the natural and probable result' of the breach of duty.

Another leading case in the area *Overseas Tankship (UK) Ltd* v. *Morts Dock & Engineering Co. Ltd (The Wagon Mound)* expanded the principle further joining the principle that the damage should be a 'natural and probable result' of the breach with a test of reasonable foreseeability. Stephenson LJ giving judgment in the present case referred to the fact that *The Wagon Mound* case affirms what is implicit in the judgment of Greer LJ in *Haynes* v. *Harwood* that a test of reasonable foreseeability applies to damage following acts intervening between tort and damage (*The Wagon Mound* at page 422):

> It is the principle of civil liability, subject only to qualifications which have no present relevance, that a man must be considered to be responsible for the probable consequences of his act. To demand more of him is too harsh a rule, to demand less is to ignore that civilised order requires the observance of a minimum standard of behaviour.

He continued (*The Wagon Mound* at page 426):

> But if it would be wrong that a man should be held liable for damage unpredictable by a reasonable man because it was 'direct' or 'natural,' equally it would be wrong that he should escape liability, however 'indirect' the damage, if he foresaw or could reasonably foresee the intervening events which led to its being done . . .

Therefore it can be established that *novus actus interveniens* will occur if it can be established that the intervening act is sufficiently unforeseeable as to create a new cause, breaking the chain rather than just constituting 'another link' in the chain of causation.

Did the actions of the police break the chain of causation?

Having reviewed pertinent authorities dealing with rescue attempts (including, *inter alia*, *Haynes* v. *Harwood*, *Baker* v. *Hopkins* and *Videan* v. *British Transport Commission*), Stephenson LJ concluded that the original tortfeasor whose negligence creates the danger that invites a rescue attempt, will be responsible for the natural and probable results of his wrongful act. However, notwithstanding the foreseeability of a rescue attempt, the court acknowledged that the chain of causation may be broken if the rescue attempt is unreasonable.

Thus, Stephenson LJ quoted from the judgment of Morris LJ in *Baker* v. *T.E. Hopkins & Son Ltd*: 'If a rescuer acts with a wanton disregard of his own safety it might be that in some circumstances it might be held that an injury to him was not the result of the negligence that caused the situation of danger'. He also cited Willmer LJ in the same case, who talked of acts 'so foolhardy as to amount to a total disregard for his own safety', such acts, amounting to wanton interference or disregard, clearly capable of amounting to a break in the chain of causation where other reasonable conduct would not.

Although it is possible for a rescuer's conduct to be considered sufficiently 'foolhardy' to break the chain of causation, such a finding is rare. Indeed, as *Baker* v. *Hopkins* demonstrates, it is uncommon that a rescuer, reacting instinctively to a dangerous situation, will be found to have been negligent. The court in *Knightley* decided that the claimant was not negligent in riding the wrong way down the tunnel or in deciding on the spur of the moment to ride his motorcycle close to the wall. As Stephenson LJ commented, the claimant 'disobeyed [the order] because he was ordered to do so by the inspector. I am not satisfied that he would have disobeyed it . . . unless he had been given the order'. Thus the actions of the claimant (the rescuer) did not break the chain of causation, and did not amount to contributory negligence.

In determining liability the Court of Appeal also had to decide whether the actions of the police inspector in ordering or allowing the claimant to drive the wrong way down the tunnel broke the chain of causation.

Stephenson LJ highlighted actions and omissions for which the claimant was not responsible, namely 'a series of acts of ineptitude on the part of the police.' These included failing to ascertain precisely where the collision occurred, failing to close the tunnel then having failed to close the tunnel sending the police officers back instead of ordering them to radio for more help (most of these acts contravening the police standing order set up to deal with a situation of this nature).

Stephenson LJ then went on to consider whether the whole sequence of events was a 'natural and probable consequence' of the first defendant's negligence and a 'reasonably foreseeable result of it'. In answering that question he argued that it would be 'helpful but not decisive' to determine which events were 'deliberate choices to do positive acts and which were mere omissions or failures to act; which . . . were innocent mistakes or miscalculations and which were negligent'.

He determined that negligence would be more likely to break the chain of causation than conduct which was not negligent and that positive acts would more easily constitute new causes of action. He indicated that a wrongdoer should not be able to escape responsibility for the consequences of their actions simply by referring to them as improbable or unforeseeable and that they should accept the 'risk of some unexpected mischances'.

However Stephenson LJ also indicated that each case should be decided according to the specific set of circumstances that arise on the facts and he decided that in this case the actions of the police inspector at the scene could be deemed negligent. He concluded that the negligent act of the inspector was not a 'concurrent cause running with the first defendant's negligence, but a new cause disturbing the sequence of events . . . interrupting the effect (of the first defendant's negligence)'. Thus, the negligent actions of the police inspector constituted a *novus actus interveniens*. Accordingly, the appeal was allowed and judgment against the first defendant was set aside.

Conclusion

The judgment in this case affirms the position that where an intervening act, or series of intervening acts occur between the first negligent act and the damage sustained by the victim, where the intervening act is so unforeseeable (perhaps due to the negligence of a third party) that it creates a new cause of action, the intervening act will constitute a *novus actus interveniens* and will break the original chain of causation.

FURTHER READING

Primary sources

Baker v. *T.E. Hopkins & Son Ltd* [1959] 1 WLR 966

Cork v. *Kirby Maclean Ltd* [1952] 2 All ER 402

Donoghue v. *Stephenson* [1932] AC 56

Hadley v. *Baxendale* (1854) 9 Exch. 341

Haynes v. *Harwood* [1935] 1 KB 146

Nettleship v. *Weston* [1971] 2 QB 691

Overseas Tankship (UK) Ltd v. *Morts Dock & Engineering Co. Ltd (The Wagon Mound)* [1961] AC 388 ('The Wagon Mound')

Videan v. *British Transport Commission* [1963] 2 All ER 860

Secondary sources

Cook, R. (1978) 'Remoteness of Damages and Judicial Discretion' [1978] *CLJ*, 288.

Stapleton, J. (2001) 'Unpacking Causation' in Cane, P. and Gardner, J. (eds) *Relating to Responsibility*, Hart Publishing.

5

TORT LAW

Remoteness of damage

Overseas Tankship (UK) Ltd v. Morts Dock & Engineering (The Wagon Mound (No. 1)) [1961] AC 388, [1961] 1 All ER 404

Ross Fletcher, Northumbria University

The case of *The Wagon Mound* is one of the most important, if not the most important, decisions in the law of negligence with regard to the principles it establishes in the law regarding remoteness of damage. The case was decided in the Privy Council on appeal from a decision of the Australian courts. Although the opinions of the judges of the Privy Council are not strictly speaking binding upon the courts of England and Wales, since the judges sitting as the Judicial Committee of the Privy Council are made up of senior House of Lords judges their opinions are accorded great importance by less eminent common law judges.

This was particularly the case in respect of *The Wagon Mound*, as the decision of the Privy Council to disapprove what had previously been the leading English case on the matter led to a new approach being adopted in determining causation in this area of the law. As with many landmark decisions, it is worthwhile examining the old law on this subject in order to help understand the reasons why the judges came to their decisions.

The problems with *Re Polemis*

Prior to *The Wagon Mound* the law on remoteness of damage was that which was established by the Court of Appeal in the case of *Re Polemis*. That case concerned a wooden plank that while being hoisted on board the claimants' ship by stevedores in the employ of the defendants was negligently dropped down a shaft resulting in sparks that in turn caused petrol fumes from the ship's engine room to ignite, ultimately destroying the ship.

The claimants successfully obtained damages on the grounds that if it could be established (as was conceded by the parties in the case) that some kind of damage was foreseeable as resulting from the defendants' negligence then in the words of Scrutton LJ 'The fact that they did directly produce an unexpected result, a spark in an atmosphere of petrol vapour which caused a fire, does not relieve the person who was negligent from the damage which his negligent act directly caused'. Accordingly, the case established that if some damage, however insignificant, was foreseeable, then liability should extend to any damage that was the direct result of the negligent act. The Court of Appeal appeared to base this view upon a dictum of Lord Sumner in the case of *Weld-Blundell* v. *Stephens* that foreseeability 'goes to culpability, not to compensation'.

Reliance was also placed on a number of older authorities, notably *Smith* v. *London & South Western Railway Co.* where Channell B had stated that 'when it has once been determined that there is evidence of negligence, the person guilty of it is equally liable for its consequences, whether he could have foreseen them or not'. It was noted by Viscount Simonds in *The Wagon Mound* that no authority was cited for this extremely broad proposition. Also, the point was made that when the case was decided the tort of negligence had only recently come to be recognised by the court as a means of obtaining legal relief and so it was unclear whether or not the judges in that case had fully realised what the implications of their decision might be.

A fragmented system

Like the law on duty of care prior to Lord Atkin's speech in *Donoghue* v. *Stevenson* the law on causation in negligence was in an extremely fragmented state prior to *The Wagon Mound* and in spite of the decision in *Re Polemis* it was unclear exactly what test ought to be employed in order to determine what should be compensatable damage as a result of a negligent act or omission. This was remarked upon by Viscount Simonds in *The Wagon Mound*, who pointed out that many judges in the lower courts had expressed problems with applying the test enumerated by the Court of Appeal. One such judge was Denning J (as he then was) in *Minister of Pensions* v. *Chennell*, who stated that *Re Polemis* was of very doubtful authority in the light of intervening cases such as *Donoghue* v. *Stevenson*, where much reliance had been placed upon the need for the damages claimed to be reasonably foreseeable in order for the relief pleaded to be claimed.

Several cases had also arisen prior to *Polemis* in which the notion that a tortfeasor should be held liable for the direct consequences of his actions, whether foreseeable or not was either not applied or disapproved entirely. This occurred in *Sharp* v. *Powell*, where the defendant was held not to be liable according to Bovill CJ, who held that 'one who commits a wrongful act . . . is not liable for damage which is not the natural or ordinary consequence of such an act, unless it be shown that he knows, or has reasonable means of knowing, that consequences not usually resulting from the act are, by reason of some existing cause, likely to intervene so as to occasion damage to a third person'. It was noted by Viscount Simonds in *The Wagon Mound* that at no point in *Sharp* v. *Powell* was it suggested that the defendant should be held liable for consequences that he did not foresee.

A further point made by Viscount Simonds was that many judges in negligence cases, as they appeared to be unaware of the exact nature of the claim that was being brought before the court, were likewise unaware of exactly what needed to be proven in order to establish a case of negligence. His Lordship referred to *Hadley* v. *Baxendale*, which established that in breach of contract cases 'damages naturally foreseeable as a result of the breach' ought to be recoverable and noted that a like position was adopted in tort cases, or at least it was prior to *Polemis*.

In all, Viscount Simonds made the excoriating point that judges in previous cases in this area 'were feeling their way to a coherent body of doctrine, and were at times in grave danger of being led astray by scholastic theories of causation and their ugly and barely intelligible jargon'.

The facts of *The Wagon Mound*

The basic facts of the case were that on 30 October 1951 the *Wagon Mound*, a ship char-
tered by the appellants, was anchored off Caltex Wharf in the Port of Sydney. Nearby Sheerlegs
Wharf was owned by the respondents, who used it to carry on the business of ship fitting
and repair work. Significantly for the purposes of the case, their work included welding with
oxyacetylene and torches. While the *Wagon Mound* was being refuelled a quantity of oil was
negligently spilt by the appellants' employees, causing it to disperse into the water off the
harbour and along the foreshore near Sheerlegs Wharf. The respondents' works manager
told the workmen on Sheerlegs Wharf not to continue working until further notice, whereupon he enquired as to whether or not the oil would be likely to ignite while in the open. He
was told, as he believed, that it would not and ordered his men to continue working. They did
so until two days later, when a fire broke out causing damage to the wharf.

The respondents sued for damages and evidence at the hearing before Kinsella J in the
Supreme Court of New South Wales in Admiralty disclosed that the fire had broken out not
solely because of the oil but because of a piece of smouldering cotton that was floating on
the oil which had ignited. Expert evidence was heard to verify that the appellants did not
and could not have been reasonably expected to know that the oil was capable of being
set on fire while in the water. However, it was held that the oil had caused some foreseeable damage, however insignificant (and in respect of which the respondents made no
claim for damages) through its spilling onto the wharf and interfering with the workmen's
performance of their duties. Accordingly, applying the principles in *Polemis*, the appellants were ordered to pay damages for the reasons that because as they ought to have
foreseen some damage resulting from the oil spill they ought to be held liable for the full
extent of the loss that was, in fact, caused by it. This decision was upheld by the Full Court
and was appealed to the Privy Council.

Viscount Simonds' opinion

Viscount Simonds expressed the reasoning of the Board. His Lordship accepted the '*cri de
coeur*' expressed by Manning J in the court below that the Privy Council ought to clarify
the considerable doubts that had arisen in the wake of *Re Polemis*. His Lordship did not
agree with counsel for the respondents' contention that *Polemis* was a decision of such
status that it should not be reviewed.

His Lordship's review of the decision in *Polemis* involved analysing other cases in the House
of Lords in which the rule in *Polemis* appeared to have been side-stepped or ignored entirely.
One such example was *Bourhill* v. *Young*, where no reference was made to Lord Sumner's
dictum in *Weld-Blundell* v. *Stevens* that there is 'one criteria for culpability, another for
compensation'. Likewise, in *Roe* v. *Minister of Health* Denning LJ said that foreseeability
was disregarded where negligence is the immediate or 'precipitating' cause of the damage.

His Lordship based his disapproval of *Polemis* upon policy arguments with regard to the
problems that might arise from the unworkable nature of the 'direct' consequences test,
which might lead to a never-ending series of claims. The view of Sir Frederick Pollock that
'the lawyer cannot afford to adventure himself with philosophers in the logical and meta-
physical controversies that beset the idea of cause' was referred to with regard to the law's

duty to limit liability to what might be reasonably foreseen as ensuing from a negligent incident. With regard to forseeability, His Lordship referred again to Manning J, who had stated that 'if the ordinary man in the street had been asked . . . to state the cause of the fire at Morts Dock, he would unhesitatingly have assigned such cause to spillage of oil by the appellants' employees'. In disapproving this reasoning, His Lordship made the important point that the law is not concerned so much with what assignation of blame is made after the event than with what ought to have been reasonably foreseen before the event took place. His Lordship pointed out that 'After the event even a fool is wise' and that 'it is not the hindsight of a fool, but the foresight of a reasonable man, which alone can determine responsibility'.

Accordingly, the appeal was allowed on the basis that the presence of the cotton which in fact caused the fire was not reasonably foreseeable, or in other words that the damage that resulted was not 'of such a kind as the reasonable man should have foreseen'.

The impact of *The Wagon Mound*

It has been doubted by some commentators whether or not the decision in *The Wagon Mound* made any practical difference, as some cases have came before the courts in its aftermath where the 'kind of damage' in question is argued as being not reasonably foreseeable, but damages have still been awarded because the category of 'the kind of damage' has been interpreted widely. For example, the test was interpreted liberally in the case of *Hughes* v. *Lord Advocate*, in which the defendant's employees were liable for injuries sustained by the claimant after he had dropped down a utility hole a paraffin lamp left unattended by the employees, and in *Jolley* v. *Sutton London Borough Council*, where the claimant injured himself attempting to repair a boat left unattended on land belonging to the defendant. Conversely, however, in *Tremain* v. *Pike* (where the defendant ran a rat-infested farm at which a worker contracted a rare disease caused by contact with rat urine) and *Doughty* v. *Turner Manufacturing Co.* (where cauldrons used by the defendants at their factory containing a chemical that emitted steam when at a certain temperature resulted in injury to the claimant when a cover fell into the cauldron, which then erupted) a narrower approach was adopted and the defendants were held not to be liable, as the damage was of 'a different kind' from that which was reasonably foreseeable.

The Wagon Mound is undoubtedly of great importance as the test that it introduces is one which makes much more practical sense than the unworkable test in *Re Polemis* and the case is of value through the practical approach adopted by the judges rather than the adherence to doubtful dogma deployed by the judges in *Polemis*. The case also illustrates the higher courts' willingness to cast doubt upon decisions of lower courts, however important they appear at first blush to be, an ability which they continue to utilise readily today.

FURTHER READING

Primary sources

Bourhill v. *Young* [1942] 2 All ER 396

Donoghue v. *Stevenson* [1932] AC 562

5

TORT LAW

Doughty v. *Turner Manufacturing Co.* [1964] 1 QB 518

Hadley v. *Baxendale* (1854) 9 Exch 341

Hughes v. *Lord Advocate* [1963] AC 837

In Re Polemis [1921] All ER Rep 40

Jolley v. *Sutton London Borough Council* [2000] 3 All ER 409

Ministry of Pensions v. *Chennell* [1947] KB 250

Roe v. *Minister of Health* [1954] 2 All ER 131

Sharp v. *Powell* (1872) LR 7 CP 253

Smith v. *London & South Western Railway Co.* (1870) LR 6 CP 14

Tremain v. *Pike* [1969] 3 All ER 1303

Weld-Blundell v. *Stephens* [1920] AC 983

Secondary sources

Davies, M. (1982) 'The road from Morocco: *Polemis* through *Donoghue* to no-fault' 45, *MLR*, 534.

Dias, R.M.W. [1962] 'Remoteness of liability and legal policy' *CLJ*, 178.

Goodhart, A.L. (1952) 'The imaginary necktie and the rule in *Re Polemis*' 68, *LQR*, 514.

Kidner, R. [1989] 'The duty-interest theory and the reinterpretation of *The Wagon Mound*' 9(1), *LS*, 1.

Stapleton, J. (2003) 'Cause in fact and the scope of liability for consequences' 119, *LQR*, 388.

Staunch, M. (2001) 'Risk and remoteness of damage in negligence' 64, *MLR*, 191.

Williams, R. (2001) 'Remoteness. Some unexpected mischief' 117, *LQR*, 30.

Defences to negligence

Owens v. *Brimmell* [1977] QB 859

David Grant, Northumbria University

Drinking and driving: there are stupider things, but it's a very short list.

(Anon.)

If a claimant in a case of negligence can establish the elements of the tort, i.e. that the defendant owed him a duty, that the duty had been breached and that damage was suffered as a consequence, the claimant will succeed unless the defendant can establish a defence. One such defence is contributory negligence. A generally accepted definition can be found in *Jones* v. *Livox Quarries Ltd*: A person is guilty of contributory negligence if he ought reasonably to have foreseen that, if he did not act as a reasonable, prudent man, he might be hurt himself and in his reckonings he must take into account the possibility of others being careless. (Denning LJ)

Owens v. *Brimmell*, a case on contributory negligence, is an ideal vehicle to explore the elements of that defence but is also a springboard for a discussion of two other major defences in tort – illegality and *volenti non fit injuria*.

The facts

The facts of the case are straightforward. In an age before the phrase 'binge drinking' had entered the popular lexicon the claimant and his friend, the defendant, went out drinking on a Saturday night as they had done previously on frequent occasions. They travelled in the defendant's car and the claimant fully expected to be driven home by the defendant. After drinking a considerable amount of alcohol each, about 8 or 9 pints of beer, they did indeed go home in the defendant's car. On this occasion, however, the defendant lost control of the vehicle after overtaking another car and collided with a lamp post. The claimant was thrown out of the car and suffered broken bones and severe brain damage.

Liability in negligence was admitted by the defendant but a plea of contributory negligence was entered. It was argued that the claimant was contributorily negligent on two counts. First, for failing to wear a seat belt, and secondly, for accepting a lift with a drunken driver.

On the issue of not wearing the seatbelt, Watkins J held, relying upon the Court of Appeal case, *Froom* v. *Butcher*, that failure to wear a seat belt amounted to contributory negligence. He cited the judgment of Lord Denning MR: 'Contributory negligence is a man's carelessness in looking after his own safety. He is guilty of contributory negligence if he ought reasonably to have foreseen that, if he did not act as a reasonable prudent man, he might be hurt himself'. He also referred to the judgment of Blackburn J in *Swan* v. *North British Australasian Co. Ltd*, where it was said that the essence of contributory negligence is that the plaintiff was negligent as regards himself.

However, he went on to say that it was not only necessary to show that the claimant had been careless with regard to his own safety, it must also be shown, on the balance of probabilities, that that carelessness had contributed to the damage, i.e. causation as well as breach had to be established for the defence to succeed. On the evidence available the defendant had not discharged the burden of proof. At first glance this seems a little odd: if a passenger is thrown out of a car and sustains head injuries causing brain damage the immediate conclusion that one is drawn to is that this was caused by some impact which could have been prevented by the wearing of the seat belt. However, the evidence was ambiguous. The injury might have been caused by the claimant striking the lamp post when he was thrown out of the car. Alternatively it could have occurred when his head, unrestrained by a seat belt, was thrown forward and struck the facia board of the car. Equally, however, it could have been caused by the facia board being driven back into his face when the car came to a sudden halt. There was also the possibility that the injury could have been caused by severe whiplash. Given this ambiguity the judge held that on the causation issue the defendant had failed to prove his case.

On the issue of accepting a lift with a drunken driver the defendant had more success. At the outset Watkins J admitted that as far as he and counsel were concerned this was a novel issue in English law. Between them they could find no case where a passenger had had damages reduced for contributory negligence for accepting a lift with a drunken driver. Reference was made to *Dann* v. *Hamilton*, a case in which the drunken defendant unsuccessfully pleaded *volenti*, but where contributory negligence had not been pleaded. Asquith J, who decided the case, subsequently commented that he had encouraged the defendant to raise the defence but the invitation had not been taken up. Working therefore from first principles but drawing heavily upon US and Commonwealth sources, Watkin J concluded that the claimant was contributorily negligent. This was put on two grounds:

> . . . it appears to me that there is widespread and weighty authority for the proposition that a passenger may be guilty of contributory negligence if he rides with the driver of a car whom *he knows* has consumed alcohol in such quantity as is likely to impair to a dangerous degree that driver's capacity to drive properly and safely. So, also, may a passenger be guilty of contributory negligence if he, knowing that he is going to be driven in a car by his companion later, accompanies him upon about of drinking which has the effect, eventually, *of robbing the passenger of clear thought and perception* and diminishes the driver's capacity to drive properly and carefully. [Emphasis added]

Thus, it is contributorily negligent to get into a car with someone you know is drunk and it is also contributorily negligent to go out drinking with someone who you know will be driving you home later – because you know the drink will diminish your capacity to make rational decisions and the driver's ability to drive competently. The judge preferred the latter reasoning but did not rule out the former.

Note that in each case there is a degree of knowledge required by the claimant before the defence can succeed. This leaves open the issue of the claimant who has no prior knowledge of the defendant's drunken state and who, when he accepts the lift is so drunk that he does not appreciate that the defendant is drunk. Would it be sufficient to say that if you choose to drink then you know that you might end up doing all kinds of foolish things, including accepting a lift from another drunk, and therefore drinking in itself amounts to contributory negligence as it disables a person, who knows or ought to know, that it will cause him to act carelessly with regard to his own safety? In *Booth v. White* the Court of Appeal held that it did not amount to contributory negligence if you were so drunk that you did not realise that the driver who offered you a lift was drunk if that driver was not obviously drunk. The clear implication was that if he had appeared drunk then it would have been contributorily negligent for the drunken passenger to accept the lift.

The effect of a finding of contributory negligence is that the claimant, by virtue of the Law Reform (Contributory Negligence) Act 1945 will have their damages reduced 'to such extent as the court thinks just and equitable having regard to the claimant's share in the responsibility for the damage . . .' (s.1(1)). Reductions for contributory negligence are notoriously difficult to calculate but some guidance is given in *Froom v. Butcher* where a rough and ready tariff was established: the reduction in damages for failure to wear a seat belt should be 25% for those injuries which would have been prevented by wearing a belt and 15% for those injuries which would have been less severe. There should be no reduction if the injuries would have been the same if a belt had been worn. Note that the reduction is only 25% because according to *Froom v. Butcher* the driver bears the greater responsibility because he caused the accident.

On the face of it *Owens v. Brimmell* also seems a potential candidate for the application of one of the other major defences – *volenti non fit injuria*. The scope of this defence was explained in *Letang v. Ottawa Electric Rly Co.*: 'If the defendants desire to succeed on the ground that the maxim volenti non fit injuria is applicable, they must obtain a finding of fact that the plaintiff freely and voluntarily, with full knowledge of the nature and extent of the risk he ran, impliedly agreed to incur it.'

In *Dann v. Hamilton*, mentioned above, Asquith J rejected the defence on the basis that although the claimant had knowledge that the driver had been drinking she did not impliedly consent to or absolve the driver from liability for any subsequent negligence on his part. He considered that it would only apply if: '. . . the drunkenness of the driver at the material time is so extreme and so glaring that to accept a lift from him is like engaging in an intrinsically and obviously dangerous occupation, intermeddling with an unexploded bomb or walking on the edge of an unfenced cliff.'

However, as far as road traffic cases are concerned the defence is now unavailable to drivers by virtue of s.149 Road Traffic Act 1988 (formerly s.148(3) of the Road Traffic Act 1972) which prevents the application of the *volenti* defence. Despite some doubts (Symmons) this was confirmed by the Court of Appeal in *Pitts v. Hunt*, a case in which a drunken

5

TORT LAW

motorcyclist, encouraged by his pillion passenger engaged in reckless driving, culminating in the death of the motorcyclist and severe injuries to the claimant passenger. The Court of Appeal was in little doubt that in the circumstances the defence would have applied if it had not been for the provisions of the Road Traffic Act.

Morris v. *Murray*, a case involving a drunken pilot and a drunken passenger, demonstrates that the defence is available in cases not covered by the Act. There, the Court of Appeal held that despite having been drinking all afternoon with the defendant pilot, who had had the equivalent of 17 whiskies, the claimant passenger was 'not so drunk as to be incapable of appreciating the risk or knowing really the state of intoxication of Mr Murray [the pilot].' This finding, which surely flies in the face of reality, neatly allows the court to avoid the dilemma posed by Stocker LJ in the case, namely that if the test for *volenti* is a subjective test then the position arises that if the claimant is sober when he accepts the flight he clearly knows the risk and will be met by the defence, but if he is too drunk to realise the danger the defence will be ineffective. Paradoxically it seems his drunkenness will be rewarded. Perhaps it would not seem so paradoxical if we start from the position that the pilot was not just negligent but reckless and that recklessness caused severe injuries to a person who was not in a state to take an informed rational decision for their own safety – and that if the claimant is to be penalised for his self-intoxication the defence of contributory negligence is available and more appropriate.

On the issue of whether the test is objective or subjective Stocker LJ did not commit himself, only going so far as saying, 'I do not, for my part, go so far as to say that the test is an objective one . . . ' but the very nature of the defence suggests that the test is subjective.

Again, although **Owens v. Brimmell** does not raise it, the defence of illegality (*ex turpi causa non oritur actio* to give it the name it formerly went by – paraphrased by Tony Weir as 'Bad people get less' (Weir, A., *Casebook on Tort*)) has been an issue in other drunkenness cases, in particular *Pitts v. Hunt* referred to above. It would be true to say that the full extent of this defence has still to be worked out but the classic exposition of it was given by Lord Asquith in **National Coal Board v. England**:

> If two burglars, A and B, agree to open a safe by means of explosives, and A so negligently handles the explosive charge as to injure B, B might find some difficulty in maintaining an action for negligence against A. But if A and B are proceeding to the premises which they intend burglariously to enter, and before they enter them, B picks A's pocket and steals his watch, I cannot prevail on myself to believe that A could not sue in tort . . . The theft is totally unconnected with the burglary.

The defence was examined at some length in **Pitts v. Hunt** and various reasons were given for denying the claimant compensation on the grounds of illegality. These included public policy, the fact that the claimant's injuries arose directly from a criminal act and the difficulty of setting a standard of care to be applied in such cases. The Law Commission has also investigated the defence in some depth (The Law Commission, Consultation Paper No. 160, 'The Illegality Defence in Tort') and discussed a variety of other rationales for the defence including the need to preserve the dignity and reputation of the courts and legal system; the need to deter unlawful or immoral conduct; the need to prevent a claimant profiting from his or her own wrongdoing; not condoning the illegal activity or encouraging others; and preserving the integrity of the legal system through the prevention of internal inconsistency.

Their views were summed up in the words of Professor Beale:

> The present rules on the effect of illegality on tort claims are unclear and difficult to predict, and there is the risk that they could be used in an arbitrary or disproportionate way. Our provisional proposals would allow a court to reach its decision on the facts of a particular case in the light of the policy rationales behind the illegality defence, and to take full account of factors such as the seriousness of the illegality involved.

FURTHER READING

Primary sources

Ashton v. *Turner* [1981] QB 137

Barrett v. *Ministry of Defence* [1995] 1 WLR 1217

Bennett v. *Tugwell* [1971] 2 QB 267

Booth v. *White* [2003] EWCA Civ 1708

Dann v. *Hamilton* [1939] 1 KB 509

Froom v. *Butcher* [1976] QB 286

Green v. *Bannister* [2003] EWCA Civ 1819

Insurance Commissioner v. *Joyce* 77 CLR 39

Jones v. *Livox* [1952] 2 QB 608

Letang v. *Ottowa Electric Rly Co.* [1926] AC 725

Malone v. *Rowan* [1984] 3 All ER 402

Morris v. *Murray* [1991] 2 QB 6

National Coal Board v. *England* [1954] AC 403

Owens v. *Brimmell* [1977] QB 859

Pitts v. *Hunt* [1991] 1 QB 24

Swan v. *North British Australasian Co. Ltd* (1863) 2 H. & C. 175

Secondary sources

Asquith (1953) 'Note' 69, *LQR*, 317.

Brazier, Margaret and Murphy, John (1999) *Street on Torts*, Butterworths.

Jones, Michael (2002) *Torts*, Oxford University Press, 8th edn.

Roberts, R. (2004) 'Riding with a Drunken Driver and Contributory Negligence Revisited' (2004) *JPIL*, 1, 21-27.

Rogers, W.V.H., *Winfield & Jolowicz on Tort*, Sweet & Maxwell.

Symmons, C. (1973) 'Volenti non. fit. injuria and Passenger Liability' 123, *NLJ*, 373.

Todd, S. (1989) 'Case Comment, The Reasonable Incompetent Driver' (1989) 105, *LQR*, 24-28.

The Law Commission (2001) Consultation Paper No. 160, 'The Illegality Defence in Tort'.

Williams, K. (1991) 'Defences for Drunken Drivers: Public Policy on the Roads and in the Air', 54, *MLR*, 745.

5

TORT LAW

Occupiers' liability

Roles v. Nathan [1963] 1 WLR 1117

Ross Fletcher, Northumbria University

The case of *Roles* v. *Nathan* was the first to be decided by the Court of Appeal under the Occupiers' Liability Act 1957. It is therefore a useful case to consult when considering the steps that occupiers of premises have to take in order to ensure that visitors are reasonably safe in using their premises. Prior to the Act's coming into force, the duties owed in such circumstances were governed by the common law. It is therefore useful to consider the common law position in order to understand the background to the then-new criteria that the Court of Appeal had to apply to the unfortunate circumstances of the case.

The old law

The position at common law was that various degrees of duty of care were owed by occupiers of premises towards people who happened to be on the premises, depending on whom they were. Trespassers were owed no duty at all, save in respect of intentionally or recklessly causing them injury. In respect of lawful visitors, a distinction was drawn between people visiting the premises in pursuance of a contractual undertaking for the use of the premises and for people on the premises for purposes which were ancillary to the performance of a contract. Visitors to premises for purposes otherwise than the performance of a contractual obligation were again divided into categories of the invitee (a person in whose presence the occupier had a material interest, for example, a business associate) and the licensee (persons present for social or other reasons), the latter category being afforded a lesser degree of protection than the former.

This cast of, as Lord Denning put it in the instant case, 'unpleasant characters', led to unnecessarily complicated litigation, as it was not always easy for judges to determine into which category the visitor in a particular case fell. Moreover, the common law position was established long before the landmark decision in *Donoghue* v. *Stevenson* wherein the House of Lords emphasised that a general duty of care is owed to all who might be reasonably expected to be affected by one's actions. Accordingly, the Occupiers' Liability Act 1957 introduced the sweeping reform of abolishing the common law rules and introducing one uniform class of 'visitor', to whom is owed 'the common duty of care'.

The 1957 Act reforms

The Act imposes liability on 'occupiers' of 'premises'. Neither of the terms are defined by the Act, but the common law rules suggest that an 'occupier' need not necessarily be the owner of premises, but only a person with a sufficient degree of control over the premises in question to warrant their having to fulfil the common duty of care. Indeed, if an owner of premises has acted in such a way as to vest control over the premises to another he may no longer be said to be an occupier within the meaning of the Act, as was the case in *Wheat* v. *E. Lacon & Co. Ltd*, where a landlord who let premises to a tenant was said no longer to be an occupier within the meaning of the Act. The term 'premises' is used in the legal sense, meaning any land whether with buildings upon it or not.

Occupiers must exercise a duty of care towards 'visitors'. Into such a category would fall everyone who would have been treated either as a contractual visitor, an invitee or a licensee under the common law. It should be borne in mind that invitations to a premises can be limited, and a person can be regarded as a visitor for a particular purpose, but a trespasser for others, or, in the words of Scrutton LJ 'When you invite a person to your house to use the staircase, you do not invite him to slide down the banisters' (*The Carlgarth*). Trespassers are not within the remit of the Act, but are afforded protection by the Occupiers' Liability Act 1984.

Section 2 of the Act provides that an occupier owes all visitors to his premises 'the common duty of care'. This is a duty to ensure, so far as is reasonable in the circumstances of each case, that a visitor is reasonably safe in using the premises for the purpose for which he is present. Although all visitors are afforded the same degree of protection, the matters to which the court must have regard in any case brought against the occupier include factors particular to the visitor. Some examples of such factors are given in s.2(3) as the special need to be aware that children may be less careful than adults and that 'a person, in the exercise of his calling, will appreciate and guard against any special risk ordinarily incident to it, so far as the occupier leaves him free to do so' (s.2(3)(b)). The meaning of this paragraph was the key issue for the Court of Appeal to determine in *Roles* v. *Nathan*.

The facts of the case

The premises in question were the Manchester Assembly Rooms, a building heated by a 30-year-old boiler in the basement which used coke as a fuel. The fumes from the fuel were carried away from the boiler by a system of flues, which involved a flue that ran along the floor before joining onto a vertical flue which led up a chimney. The horizontal flue contained an inspection chamber underneath a paving slab in the floor and the vertical flue a 'sweep hole' nine feet above the ground, into which chimney sweeps could climb in order to clean the chimney. The boiler was often difficult to ignite due to large quantities of smoke accumulating in the flues, which the occupiers were advised by builders who carried out repairs to the building in April 1958 could be remedied by lighting a fire at the foot of the flue to create a draught.

On 9 December 1958, Mr Corney, the son-in-law of the occupier (who was looking after the premises during his father-in-law's illness) called in two chimney sweeps, Donald and Joseph Roles, to clean the flues. They were warned of the dangers of carbon monoxide (a toxic gas given off by coke when burning) but took no notice. The boiler continued to be defective due to problems with fumes and smoke despite the sweeps cleaning out the flues, so an expert was called in. He advised that it was dangerous to remain in the building.

Again, the sweeps took no notice and had to be 'more or less drag[ged] out'. It was agreed that an induction fan would have to be installed in the base of the chimney in order to remedy the smoke, and that the inspection chamber and sweep hole should be sealed up. The expert advised everyone present, including the sweeps, that it could be possible to seal up the holes with the fire on, but that it would be dangerous to remain in the basement for any length of time.

On 12 December, the sweeps attempted to seal up the two holes but did not finish the work that evening. Mr Corney assumed that they would return to complete the job the following morning after the fire had gone out. However, the following morning the two sweeps were found dead from carbon monoxide poisoning, evidently having gone back later in the evening in an attempt to seal up the holes.

At trial, Elwes J held that the occupier was liable for causing the deaths of the two sweeps, but that they were contributorily negligent in 'the way they ignored explicit warnings, and showed complete indifference to the danger . . . and this strange indifference to the fact that the fire was alight, when Mr Collingwood had said it ought not to be, until the sweep hole had been sealed'. The occupier appealed, arguing that on the true construction of the 1957 Act, there was no negligence at all.

The decision of the Court of Appeal

Lord Denning MR gave the lead judgment of the Court. His Lordship focused upon the Act having retained the position established by *Christmas v. General Cleaning Contractors*, namely, that occupiers of premises are ill-suited to protect visitors to premises who are there for reasons particular to their occupation or contractual duty to protect them from dangers that they might expect to encounter as part of that duty and should therefore be expected to guard against. His Lordship drew a distinction between the situation in the instant case and a situation where the stairs leading down to the basement had given way, pointing out that the latter situation would be one for which the occupier might be responsible, but not 'those dangers which were special risks ordinarily incident to [the sweeps'] calling'.

His Lordship additionally referred to s.2(4)(a) of the Act, which provides that where damage is caused by a danger of which the visitor had been warned by the occupier, the occupier's duty may be discharged if the warning 'was enough to enable the visitor to be reasonably safe'. His Lordship illustrated the meaning of this provision by the example of premises accessible only by a bridge which was rotten and dangerous, stating that a warning as to the danger posed in accessing the bridge would not be adequate to discharge liability. However, if another, safe, bridge were also available, and the warning gave notification of both the dangerous footbridge and the safe bridge upstream, the occupier could escape liability because the warning would be sufficient to enable the visitor to be reasonably safe. His Lordship compared this with the instant case, in which the sweeps had been warned as to the danger posed by the fumes and the need to return the following morning after the fire had gone out before attempting to seal up the holes. As such, His Lordship held that the occupier had discharged his statutory duty and that the deaths of the sweeps were entirely their own fault.

Harman LJ was doubtful as to whether the occupier had done all he could to protect ordinary visitors from risks, given that he had lit the fire which was the ultimate cause of the sweeps' deaths. However, His Lordship agreed with the Master of the Rolls that they had 'deliberately chose[n] to assume the risk notwithstanding the advice given' and held that the warning was sufficient to discharge the duty. Pearson LJ dissented, holding that the risk of the poisoning was not 'ordinarily incident' to the sweeps' calling, and that the warning was not sufficient to enable the sweeps to be reasonably safe, as it was insufficient to remedy the risk created by the occupier.

The impact of the case

Not for the first, and certainly not the last, time, Lord Denning was seen to give a judgment that was somewhat at odds with the views of his fellow judges. However, His Lordship's judgment has proven to be the most insightful in terms of understanding how to interpret the 1957 Act. The judgment is useful for the student looking to understand the exact nature of the duty owed to particular types of visitors under the 1957 Act in terms of what ought to be done in order to discharge the duty incumbent on an occupier under the Act. It is also useful in general for those with an interest in learning how statutory duties develop out of common law principles and how judges apply common law principles to new statutory rules that may supplant or develop them.

5

TORT LAW

FURTHER READING

Primary sources

The Carlgarth [1923] P 93

Christmas v. *General Cleaning Contractors* [1952] 1 KB 141

Donoghue v. *Stevenson* [1932] AC 562

Wheat v. *E. Lacon & Co Ltd* [1966] 1 Q.B 335

Secondary sources

Allen, D. and Holyoak, J. 'Recent developments II: Occupiers' Liability' 134, *NLJ*, 347.

Barker, F.R. and Parry, N.D.M. (1995) 'Private property, public access and occupiers' liability' 15, *LS*, 335.

Bradbury, P.L. 'Knowledge and exemption in Occupiers' Liability' 119, *NLJ*, 520.

McMahon, B.M.E. (1975) 'Conclusions on judicial behaviour from a comparative study of Occupiers' Liability' 38, *MLR*, 39.

Odgers, F.J. [1957] 'Occupiers' Liability: a further comment' *CLJ*, 59.

Payne, D. (1958) 'The Occupiers' Liability Act' 21, *MLR*, 359.

Hunter and Others v. Canary Wharf Ltd; Hunter and Others v. London Docklands Development Corporation [1997] AC 655

Ross Fletcher, Northumbria University

The case (or, more accurately, cases) of *Hunter* v. *Canary Wharf* is the leading modern authority on private nuisance. The House of Lords, as in *Donoghue* v. *Stephenson* with the law of negligence, took the opportunity in determining the various appeals to clarify the considerable doubts that had arisen in this area after other then-recent cases and to set out some guiding principles to be adhered to when bringing claims in this tort.

The background

The background to these lengthy and costly proceedings arose from the seemingly minor problem of interference with television reception. The representative claimant, Patricia Hunter, was one of several hundred claimants, all of whom resided in the London Docklands area. They did not all own the property in which they resided: some of them were the spouses or children of the owners. They brought a claim in nuisance and/or negligence against Canary Wharf Ltd, a development company that had acted under the authority of the Isle of Dogs Designation Order 1982 to build Canary Wharf Tower, a tower some 250 metres high and over 50 metres square designated primarily for commercial use but also used for residential and Other purposes. Their claim was that, following the tower's construction in 1989, the 'shadow' cast by the metallic structure of the tower interrupted the signals transmitted to their televisions from the broadcast station at Crystal Palace in South London. They consequently sought damages for the loss of enjoyment of their television viewing and the diminution in value of the sum they had paid for their television licences.

Additionally, a claim was brought in nuisance against the London Docklands Development Corporation, a company authorised by the Local Government, Planning and Land Act 1980 to construct the Limehouse Link Road, a road linking central London with the Docklands developments. The claim was in relation to dust churned up by the Corporation's vehicles and building equipment during the construction of the road and deposited in substantial quantities on the property where the claimants resided.

Both claims were listed for preliminary hearings by Judge Richard Havery QC, sitting in the Official Referee's Court (now known as the Technology and Construction Court). The judge held *inter alia* that it was necessary for a person to have an interest in property in order to claim in private nuisance in respect of loss of enjoyment of that property, and also that such a person must have a right to exclusive possession of the property in question.

The first appeal

The claimants appealed to the Court of Appeal against these rulings. They argued that the case of *Malone* v. *Laskey*, upon which the judge had placed reliance, should be disapproved or distinguished. In that case, the wife of the manager of a company which owned the house in which she resided as a licensee was injured by a bracket that fell off a wall in the house due to vibrations from an engine operated by the defendant on the adjoining premises. The Court of Appeal dismissed her claim on the basis that 'no . . . principle of law [can] be formulated . . . to the effect that a person who has no interest in property . . . can maintain an action for a nuisance' (page 151 *per* Sir Gorell Barnes P).

The appellants argued that this case should be reviewed in the light of *Khorasandjian* v. *Bush*, a case reported shortly before the instant proceedings were heard by the judge. In *Khorasandjian*, a young woman had formed a friendship with an older man that subsequently broke down, resulting in violent and threatening behaviour including a series of abusive telephone calls directed at her. The Court of Appeal had to consider whether the Court had jurisdiction to grant an injunction in respect of the defendant's abusive telephone calls, given that as the claimant was a mere licensee at a house owned by her mother she would traditionally be regarded as having no claim in the tort of private nuisance. It was held that in such circumstances the Court did have the power to make such an injunction.

The appellants contended that a distinction should not be drawn between cases of deliberate interference with enjoyment of property (as in *Khorasandjian*) and negligent interference with such enjoyment (as in this case) and that the fact that some of the appellants did not own the property in question should not disentitle them to a remedy in nuisance.

The Court of Appeal accepted this reasoning. Pill LJ (who gave the only reasoned judgment, with which the other two judges concurred) was very sceptical about whether it was possible to bring a claim in respect of interference to one's television reception. His Lordship drew an analogy with cases like *Dalton* v. *Angus*, which established that it is not possible to sue for deprivation of a view in the absence of an agreement to confer that particular view on the claimant. However, His Lordship accepted the reasoning of the Court in *Khorasandjian* and held that it was not necessary to have a right to exclusive possession of land in order to sue in private nuisance, referring to *Sedleigh-Denfield* v. *O'Callaghan*, where Lord Wright stated that 'possession or occupation' of land is necessary in order to bring such a suit. The defendants appealed against this to the House of Lords, arguing that *Khorasandjian* should be overruled or, alternatively, 'regarded as *sui generis*' and establishing 'a new species of tort, related to, but not to be equated with, private nuisance'.

The House of Lords

The two questions for the House of Lords to consider were whether the claimants were entitled to claim damages for the interruption to their television viewing and, if so, whether the claimants who did not occupy the land on which they resided could claim in nuisance for either the interruption to their viewing or for the dust deposited on their land by the second defendant's servants or agents. In response to the first question,

Lord Goff of Chieveley accepted the important role played by television in the lives of many people, 'in particular . . . the aged, the lonely and the bedridden' (page 685) and acknowledged that in an appropriate case a claim in nuisance might lie against the interference with such an amenity.

However, Lord Goff stated that the claim in the instant case was barred by the 'more formidable obstacle' (page 686) that the interference in question was caused solely by the defendant's building. His Lordship accepted the reasoning of Pill LJ and held that in the absence of an easement to convey a right to receive a television signal (as with cases concerning a right to receive to enjoy light, a view or a flow of air) it was not possible to bring a claim in nuisance under this head. This view was accepted by the other Law Lords, with Lord Hope of Craighead highlighting the fact that, if the law were to recognise the existence of such an easement, a builder would find it difficult, if not impossible, to ascertain what rights to receive invisible signals were possessed by his neighbours. Accordingly, the claimants' appeal was dismissed.

Lord Cooke's speech

As to the defendants' appeal (or more appropriately, cross-appeal in the case of Canary Wharf), on the question of whether the claimants who were not owners of the land were entitled to sue in nuisance, Lord Cooke of Thorndon upheld the view of the Court of Appeal. His Lordship noted the distinction made in past cases (for example, *St Helen's Smelting Co.* v. *Tipping*) between claims in nuisance for physical damage (either to one's person or one's property) and claims in respect of distress, inconvenience or discomfort. The absence of any clear definition of the term 'occupier' in respect of land was additionally noted.

As to *Malone* v. *Laskey*, his Lordship noted that the views of the judges as to the status of the wife in respect of the matrimonial home were not in accordance with modern sensibilities (either those of the lay public or of Parliament in passing the Family Law Act 1996), Fletcher Moulton LJ in particular having described her as a person who was 'merely present' in the house when she was injured.

Additionally, His Lordship stated that, in order to give proper effect to the relevant provisions of the Convention on the Rights of the Child and Article 12 of the European Convention on Human Rights, it was necessary to regard children of homeowners as having the same right to enjoy occupation of that home as their parents. A number of United States cases, along with *Khorasandjian* v. *Bush*, were cited in support of this contention.

As to the vexed question of where a line should be drawn regarding persons resident in a house who ought not to be able to sue in nuisance, His Lordship referred to the examples given by other judges of 'the lodger' and 'the au pair girl'. However, His Lordship stated that it would be unjust to deprive spouses or children of homeowners of the law's protection for fear of setting a precedent that would allow a welter of unsustainable claims, and that instead the law should proceed on a case-by-case basis as 'normally there should not be any difficulty about sensible compromises with the author of the nuisance' (page 719).

The majority speeches

The other Law Lords did not concur with Lord Cooke's view. Lord Goff was of the view that the Court of Appeal in *Khorasandjian* had erred in law in applying the Canadian case of *Motherwell* v. *Motherwell*. In that case, persons with no interest in the property to which the harassing telephone calls were made were entitled to an injunction. Lord Goff held this to be based on a misapplication of the law on occupants who may sue in private nuisance, and accordingly undermined the reasoning behind *Khorasandjian*. His Lordship went further and held that as the tort in *Khorasandjian* was not in actuality directed at the claimant's enjoyment of land (the telephone calls could have been received by her anywhere) it was not really a claim in private nuisance at all, but in fact a 'tort of harassment' (page 693) created by the Court of Appeal, which had since been superseded by the Protection from Harassment Act 1997.

Accordingly, His Lordship restated the traditional position that a mere licensee on land does not have a right to sue in private nuisance in respect of loss of enjoyment of that land. His Lordship stated that adopting the extension suggested by the Court of Appeal would 'transform [private nuisance] from a tort to land into a tort to the person' (page 694), and that spouses of householders were already provided with ample protection by the Matrimonial Homes Act 1983 and the Family Law Act 1996. His Lordship stated that he did not reach the same conclusion arrived at by Lord Cooke following his consultation of the same authorities and that the defendants' appeal and cross-appeal should therefore be allowed.

Lord Lloyd of Berwick echoed these sentiments, and stated that to extend the tort of private nuisance to protect people with no interest in the land in question would 'bring about a fundamental change in the nature and the scope of a cause of action' (page 697). Lord Hoffman additionally emphasised that in cases where persons claim in nuisance for injury, annoyance or inconvenience, such claims are properly said to be *an aspect* of 'the injury to the amenity of the land' (page 706) rather than the converse situation (that such losses were *a consequence of* the loss of amenity) possibly envisaged by the Court of Appeal. His Lordship bluntly stated also that 'Nuisance is a tort against land' (page 703). Lord Hope of Craighead agreed also, emphasising that, unlike actions in negligence, nuisance is a tort for which a tortfeasor can be found strictly liable and to suggest that remedies may be given on a basis other than that of strict liability would be to introduce confusion into the law.

The importance of this case

Hunter v. *Canary Wharf* is an ideal starting point for a student looking to understand the law of private nuisance. The Law Lords' speeches survey the development of the tort over the 400 years in which it has been recognised and apply with care its principles to the modern-day situation of interference with television signals (Lord Goff's reference to 'the rapid spread of the availability of cable television' at page 688 prefigures the replacement of analogue television with digital transmission that would commence 10 years after the judgment). The case also illustrates the importance of exercising caution when departing from established precedent in favour of developing the law, as can be seen in comparing the rationale of the majority speeches with that of Lord Cooke. Finally, the case emphasises the key principles behind the tort of private nuisance and cautions against any extension in any way which, while *prima facie* just, may be militated against by considerations of policy.

5

TORT LAW

FURTHER READING

Primary sources

Dalton v. *Angus* (1881) 6 App. Cas. 740

Donoghue v. *Stephenson* [1932] AC 562

Khorasandjian v. *Bush* [1993] QB 727

Malone v. *Laskey* [1907] 2 KB 141

Motherwell v. *Motherwell* (1976) 73 DLR (3d) 62

Sedleigh-Denfield v. *O'Callaghan* [1940] AC 880

St Helen's Smelting Co. v. *Tipping* 11 HL Cas 642

Secondary sources

Cane, P. (1997) 'What a nuisance!' 113, *LQR*, 515.

Crawford, C. [1992] 'Public law rules over private law' *J.Env.L*, 251.

Davies, M. (1990) 'Private nuisance, fault and personal injuries' 20, *UWALR*, 129.

Gearty, C. [1989] 'The place of Private Nuisance in a modern law of torts' *CLJ*, 214.

Ghandi , P.R. [1998] 'Orthodoxy affirmed' *Conv*, 309.

Kidner, R. (1998) 'Nuisance and rights of property' 62, *Conv*, 267.

Lee, M. (2003) 'What is private nuisance?' 119, *LQR*, 298.

Newark, F.H. (1949) 'The Boundaries of Nuisance' 65, *LR*, 480.

Steele, J. [1997] 'Being there is not enough: the House of Lords puts the brakes on nuisance in the home' *J.Env.L*, 345.

6 EQUITY AND TRUSTS

The trust concept is flexible, making precise definition difficult. However, in essence a trust arises where one party (the trustee) owns property (the trust property) but is compelled to hold it not for his own benefit but for the benefit of someone else (the beneficiary). The trustee's conscience is bound so that he must respect the rights of the beneficiary and must act in the best interests of the beneficiary rather than in his own interests.

The trust concept originated centuries ago as an equitable response to a deficiency in the common law. While the common law recognised the transfer of property from A to B, it did not acknowledge any obligation on B to hold the property for the benefit of A. Consequently, even where B had undertaken to hold the property for A, the law treated B as being entitled to exercise full rights in relation to the land. Clearly, the common law position was unfair, and therefore the Chancellor began to intervene in this sort of situation to enforce the arrangement between A and B. This was achieved by recognising a separation of legal and equitable ownership, so that while B was acknowledged to be the legal owner, A was entitled to the benefit of the land. It was from these early ideas that the concept of a trust emerged.

This chapter deals with some of the principal cases concerning the law of equity and trusts. It covers aspects of the creation of express trusts (certainty and constitution), constructive trusts of the family home, trusts for non-charitable purposes, some of the duties of trustees (fiduciary duties and duties relating to investment), and the rules that govern the identification of the beneficiary's property in the hands of the trustee or a third party (tracing and knowing receipt). The intention is to help you develop your understanding of some of the important areas of trusts law, rather than to provide exhaustive coverage of your syllabus.

CONTENTS FOR EQUITY AND TRUSTS

Certainty of intention
Paul v. Constance [1977] 1 WLR 527   275

Certainty of objects
McPhail v. Doulton (in Re Baden's Deed Trusts) [1971] AC 424; *Re Baden's
Deed Trusts No. 2* [1973] 3 WLR 250   279

Constitution
Pennington v. Waine [2002] EWCA Civ 227   285

Non-charitable purpose trusts
Re Endacott [1960] Ch 232   290

Common intention constructive trusts
Lloyds Bank Plc v. Rosset and Another [1991] 1 AC 107   296

Breach of fiduciary duty
Bristol and West Building Society v. Mothew [1998] Ch 1   303

Investment by trustees
Nestlé v. National Westminster Bank [1993] 1 WLR 1260, [1994] 1 All ER 118   309

Tracing
Foskett v. McKeown [2001] 1 AC 102   316

Knowing receipt
*Bank of Credit and Commerce International (Overseas) Ltd v. Chief Labode
Onadimaki Akindele* [2001] Ch 437   321

Paul v. Constance [1977] 1 WLR 527

Emma Duff, Northumbria University

Paul v. Constance concerns the creation of express trusts, and specifically the intention to create a trust. In general terms, a trust will exist where there is a separation of the legal and equitable ownership of property – so that the trustee owns the property at law, but he holds the property for the benefit of the beneficiary. The beneficiary has the equitable (or beneficial) title to the property and thus the right to use and enjoy it.

For a valid express trust to be created, three certainties must be present: certainty of intention, certainty of subject matter and certainty of object. Thus, if Simon wishes to give £100 to Tim to hold on trust for Bertha, it must be clear, firstly, that Simon intended to create the trust, secondly, what the subject matter of the trust is to be (here £100) and, thirdly, who is to be the object or beneficiary of the trust (here Bertha).

Certainty of intention

It must be clear that the settlor (i.e. the person creating the trust) intended to create a trust. Trusts can be created in one of two ways, as set out in *Milroy v. Lord*:

(a) by the settlor declaring himself to be a trustee of the subject matter of the trust, or

(b) by the settlor transferring the subject matter of the trust to the trustee.

Paul v. Constance concerns a settlor declaring himself as trustee. For a trust to be created in this way, there must be a declaration of trust from which it is clear that the settlor intends the beneficiary to have a beneficial interest in the property that is to form the subject matter of the trust. This case gives useful guidance on what constitutes a valid declaration of trust.

The facts

Mr Dennis Constance had separated from his wife Mrs Bridget Constance in 1965, but the two remained married. In 1967 Mr Constance met and moved in with Mrs Doreen Paul and they lived as man and wife. In 1973 Mr Constance received £950 in damages. Following discussion with Mrs Paul, they decided to open a bank account with the money. Accordingly the two of them had an appointment with the bank manager. As they were not married, the bank manager suggested that the account should be in Mr Constance's name only, and Mr Constance agreed. Provision was, however, made for Mrs Paul to make withdrawals. On a number of occasions Mr Constance said to Mrs Paul 'This money is as much yours as mine'. Some joint bingo winnings were later paid into the account. One withdrawal was made, and the money was divided between them after some had been used for buying Christmas presents and food.

In 1974 Mr Constance died intestate (i.e. without a will) and accordingly his wife was entitled to his estate. Mrs Constance claimed to be entitled to the account on the grounds that it belonged beneficially to her husband at the time of his death. Mrs Paul claimed that Mr Constance had declared an express trust of the account for himself and Mrs Paul, and that therefore half the proceeds of the account belonged to her. The matter therefore turned on whether or not there had been a valid declaration of trust by Mr Constance. At trial the judge found the existence of an express trust; Mrs Constance appealed to the Court of Appeal.

The declaration of trust

In reviewing the relevant law, Scarman LJ established that there is no particular form of wording that must be used, but it must be clear from what is said or done by the settlor that he intended to create a trust. This is a question of fact in each case. The case of *Jones* v. *Lock* was considered. In this case Mr Jones put a cheque into the hand of his baby son saying 'Look you here, I give this to baby'. He then spoke to his solicitor about changing his will to provide for his son, but he died before he could do so. It was held that 'loose conversation' of this sort would not be enough to establish certainty of intention to create a trust. In this case what was intended was a gift of the cheque to the son, but the gift failed because the cheque had not been endorsed over to the baby.

The case of *Richards* v. *Delbridge* was also considered. Here Mr Richards attempted to gift his business to his grandson Edward by endorsing a note on the lease of the business premises to the effect that he gave the lease together with the stock to Edward. The gift failed because the necessary formalities for transfer had not been complied with. It was held that if what was intended was a gift, but the gift was imperfect, the intended transfer could not operate as a trust. Otherwise, every failed gift would be made effectual as a trust.

Turning now to the facts of *Paul* v. *Constance*, there was no suggestion that a gift was intended here. As mentioned above, there is no particular form of wording that must be used, nor is there is any necessity to use the word 'trust' when declaring oneself a trustee – indeed in this case it was unlikely that Mr Constance and Mrs Paul understood the concept of a trust. They would, however, have understood their own situation, and what they said and did should be considered in the context of their own background and circumstances. Scarman LJ agreed with the trial judge that when Mr Constance repeatedly told Mrs Paul 'This money is as much yours as mine', this clearly indicated that Mrs Paul was to have a beneficial interest in the property and thus was a valid declaration of trust. His Lordship considered that their conduct in relation to the bank account backed up this interpretation, in that joint winnings were paid into the account and the withdrawal of funds was divided between them. His Lordship conceded that it was difficult to pinpoint a particular moment of declaration, but in all the circumstances, the necessary declaration had been made. Mr Constance had therefore declared himself a trustee of the bank account for himself and Mrs Paul and so Mrs Paul was entitled to half the proceeds of the account.

It is clear from the judgment that there was no requirement for the declaration of trust to be in writing. It is important to note, however, that S.53(1)(b) Law of Property Act 1925 provides that a declaration of trust in respect of land or any interest therein must be manifested and proved by some writing.

Precatory words

The cases considered so far relate to the settlor declaring himself as trustee. In cases where the trust is created by the settlor transferring the subject matter of the trust to the trustee (see method (b) in *Milroy* v. *Lord* above) there can also be dispute as to whether the settlor had certainty of intention.

In *Re Adams and the Kensington Vestry* a testator left all his property to his wife Harriet Smith 'in full confidence that she will do what is right as to the disposal thereof between my children, either in her lifetime or by will after her decease'. This was held not to create a trust – no intention was present, but giving the words their ordinary meaning, the testator was merely expressing confidence that his wife would do what was right without imposing any obligation on her. (Words expressing a wish or hope are referred to as precatory words.)

In *Re Steele's Will Trusts* a provision in a will that certain jewellery was to be given to the testatrix Mrs Steele's son 'to go and be held as an heirloom by him and by his eldest son on his decease and to go and descend to the eldest son of such eldest son and so to the eldest son of his descendants as far as the rules of law and equity will permit (and I request my said son to do all in his power by his will or otherwise to give effect to this my wish)' was held to create a trust. Wynne-Parry J considered the authorities and in particular the case of *Shelley* v. *Shelley* as the words used in Mrs Steele's will were taken exactly from the will in *Shelley*, where the words were held to create a trust. In considering the suggestion that *Shelley* was no longer good authority, the judge did allow that cases since *Shelley* had tended to require mandatory words before a trust would be created. However, since the will had been professionally prepared and as it used the words from *Shelley*, it could be assumed that the drafter intended the words to have the same effect as in the earlier case. Perhaps the main conclusion to be drawn here is that those drafting wills should consider carefully whether or not a trust is intended and ensure that their drafting reflects this.

Constructive and resulting trusts

Although the facts of *Paul* v. *Constance* may give rise to a constructive or a resulting trust, discussion of such trusts was specifically excluded on the grounds that the case was argued by counsel on the basis of an express declaration of trust and thus could only be considered as such.

Later cases

Paul v. *Constance* was applied in the case of *Rowe* v. *Prance*. In this case Mr Prance and his mistress Mrs Rowe planned to spend two years sailing around the world; even though the yacht was registered in Mr Prance's name alone, he repeatedly referred to it as 'our yacht'. The effect of these repeated assertions, together with other conduct indicating that Mrs Rowe had an interest in the yacht was, following *Paul* v. *Constance*, that Mr Prance had declared himself a trustee of the boat. For a discussion of this case see 'Declarations of Trust and Unmarried Couples', *Fam Law*, 29 (721).

Conclusion

Whether or not a settlor intended to create an express trust is a question of fact. There are no formalities to be complied with and there is no requirement for a declaration of trust to be in writing (save for trusts of land), but what the settlor did and said must be considered against the background of his own situation. It must be clear that a trust was intended, rather than a gift or an expression of hope that the recipient would act in a particular way.

FURTHER READING

Primary sources

Jones v. *Lock* (1865) 1 Ch App 65

Milroy v. *Lord* (1862) All ER 783

Paul v. *Constance* (1977) 1 WLR 527

Re Adams and the Kensington Vestry (1884) 27 Ch D 394

Re Steele's Will Trusts (1948) 2 All ER 193

Richards v. *Delbridge* (1874) LR 18 Eq 11

Rowe v. *Prance* (1999) 2 FLR 787

Shelley v. *Shelley* (1868) LR 6 Eq 540

Secondary source

Pawlowski, M. and Everett, K. (1999) 'Declarations of Trust and Unmarried Couples', 29 *Fam Law* 721.

Certainty of objects

McPhail v. *Doulton (in Re Baden's Deed Trusts)*
[1971] AC 424
Re Baden's Deed Trusts No. 2 [1973] 3 WLR 250

Andrew Iwobi, Swansea University

In *Knight* v. *Knight*, Lord Langdale MR alluded to three certainties which must be present in order for a trust to be effectively declared. These are certainty of intention (or words), subject matter and objects. The essence of these three certainties has been neatly summed up by Watkin who indicates that they constitute 'a description of the require-ments for the creation of a trust; of the elements which a settlor has to make clear if he wishes the settlement to be enforced by the courts'. Over the years, the three certainties have been elevated to a position of such importance that Watkin has been prompted to remark that 'the concept has been reiterated in cases and textbooks as though it were an ultimate truth. In short, it has become a dogma, the criticism or negation of which is virtual heresy'. English trusts law is replete with instances in which the courts have been called upon to pronounce on the validity of trusts in circumstances where it is contended that the words employed in the relevant declaration do not evince a sufficient intention to create a trust; that the subject matter (i.e. property to be held on trust) or the interests to be taken by the beneficiaries have not been identified with sufficient clarity or precision; or that the declaration has not been framed in such terms that the objects of the trust (i.e. its intended beneficiaries or purposes) can be determined with sufficient certainty.

One of the more notable episodes in the recent history of English trusts law relates to what has aptly been described by Hopkins as 'the prolonged litigation which arose out of clause 9 of the [trust deed] of Bertram Baden'. The first phase of the Baden saga ultimately led to the landmark decision of the House of Lords in *McPhail* v. *Doulton* (otherwise known as *Re Baden No. 1*). The second phase of the litigation culminated in the decision of the Court of Appeal in *Re Baden's Deed Trusts (No. 2)*. The fundamental issues which the courts had to address in the course of this litigation revolved around the requirement of certainty of objects.

The essential facts of *Baden*

The deed which gave rise to the litigation in the two Baden cases had been executed by Mr Baden (the settlor) in 1941. At the time, he was the Chairman and Managing Director of Mathew Hall Ltd and the deed established a trust fund consisting of shares in this com-pany. Paragraph (a) of clause 9 declared that:

> The trustees shall apply the net income of the fund in making in their absolute discretion grants to or for the benefit of any of the officers and employees or ex-officers and

6

EQUITY AND TRUSTS

> ex-employees of the company or to any relatives or dependants of any such persons in such amounts, at such times and on such conditions (if any) as they think fit.

After the settlor's death in 1960, a dispute arose between the trustees and the executors of his will. The executors sought to contend that the declaration in clause 9(a) was uncertain in terms of its objects, that this rendered the trust void and that, accordingly, the part of the trust fund that had emanated from the settlor rightly belonged to his estate.

Trust or power? – The primary question in *McPhail* v. *Doulton*

In the ensuing litigation, the trial judge (Goff J), the Court of Appeal and the House of Lords were all preoccupied with seeking to determine whether the declaration under consideration had given rise to a trust or a mere power. As Lord Hodson put it in the House of Lords, the primary question in this case was 'whether on its true construction, the provisions of clause 9(a) . . . constitute[d] a trust binding the trustees to distribute income or . . . a mere power not imposing any such duty.' In order to appreciate the pivotal importance of this question, it is instructive to distinguish between trusts and powers and to highlight the significance of this distinction in the context of certainty of objects prior to the decision in *McPhail*.

As Pearce and Stevens emphasise, '[t]he trust is not the only mechanism which has been developed by equity to facilitate the management and allocation of property'. Instead of declaring a trust, a property owner may confer a power on another party (called the donee) authorising the latter to deal with such property. In particular, it is quite common for a property owner to grant a power of appointment which authorises the donee to decide how such property is to be distributed among the members of a designated class who constitute the objects of the power. The traditional distinction between the trust and the power was that the trust was imperative or obligatory; whereas a *mere power* (i.e. one not held in a fiduciary capacity) imposed no enforceable duty on the donee. From the outset, therefore, in the case of a trust, the trustee was duty-bound to allocate the benefits in accordance with the terms of the trust. If he failed to perform this duty, the court would do so at the behest of the objects of the trust whose proprietary interests equity recognised. By contrast, the donee of a power of appointment was under no obligation to distribute or even to consider whether to distribute the property while the objects of the power had no proprietary interest prior to distribution. This distinction was relatively easy to sustain in a bygone era when the norm was to create *fixed trusts* either in favour of individuals or a class of objects whose interests were determined at the outset by the settlor. By the nineteenth century however, it had become quite commonplace for property owners to enter into arrangements which sought to combine the obligatory dimension of the trust with the discretionary element of the power. The most notable manifestation of such 'trust powers', as they came to be known, was the *discretionary trust* under which the trustees are directed to hold the trust property or fund on trust for a designated class but are invested with the discretion to distribute it in whatever manner they see fit among the members of the class.

Whether one is dealing with a power of appointment or a trust in favour of a class, it is necessary to safeguard against the allocation of benefits to persons outside the designated class. Accordingly the courts have long insisted that the intended objects must be specified with sufficient clarity and certainty by the donor or settlor. In the case of trusts in favour of a class, unless all the members of the class were ascertainable, the trust was liable to fail for uncertainty of objects. Cases such as *IRC v. Broadway Cottages* and *Re Saxone Shoe Co. Ltd's Trust Deed*, established that this 'class ascertainability test' applied not only to fixed trusts in which the entire class would ordinarily be entitled to benefit from the trust, but also to discretionary trusts under which it was open to the trustees not to allocate the benefits among all the members. The justification proffered by the courts for extending this test to discretionary trusts was that if the trustees failed to exercise their discretion, it would be incumbent on the court to distribute the trust property. Unlike the trustees, the court would not possess sufficient knowledge to exercise discretion and would therefore have to order an equal division among all the members of the class. As the law then stood, if the courts in *McPhail* chose to construe clause 9(a) of the Baden deed as a discretionary trust, it would fail for uncertainty of objects since it would have been virtually impossible to ascertain all the relatives and dependants of the company's employees and ex-employees.

A less stringent test for certainty of objects was devised for powers of appointment. Elaborating on this test, Harman J stated in *Re Gestetner's Settlement*, that 'it was not necessary to know all the objects in order to appoint' and there was therefore no need for the person exercising the power 'to worry their heads surveying the world from China to Peru in order to ascertain how many objects there were'. In his view, '[i]n order for the power to be exercisable, all that was necessary was that it must be possible to ascertain whether any given [individual] was a member of the class of persons eligible to receive the settlor's bounty'. In *Re Gulbenkian's Settlement Trusts (No. 1)* which was decided not long before *McPhail v. Doulton* reached the House of Lords, their Lordships approved of *Re Gestetner* and affirmed that the 'individual ascertainability test' enunciated in that case was indeed the appropriate basis for assessing whether the requirement of certainty of objects had been satisfied in the context of powers.

The decision in *McPhail*

In *McPhail*, both the trial court and the Court of Appeal contrived to uphold the validity of clause 9(a) of the Baden deed on the basis that the objects specified therein were sufficiently certain by construing this clause as creating a power rather than a trust. On further appeal to the House of Lords, all five Law Lords took cognisance of the imperative terms in which clause 9(a) was framed and opined it constituted a discretionary trust and not a power. There was, however, a divergence of judicial opinion among their Lordships regarding the proper basis for determining whether the objects of this trust were sufficiently certain. Lord Hodson and Lord Guest endorsed the traditional approach espoused in *IRC v. Broadway Cottages*. This approach was, however, repudiated by the majority. Lord Wilberforce, with the concurrence of Lord Reid and Viscount Dilhorne held that the appropriate test for determining whether there was sufficient certainty of objects in the present case was not the class ascertainability test enunciated in *Broadway Cottages* but the test for powers propounded in *Re Gulbenkian*.

6

EQUITY AND TRUSTS

In arriving at this decision, Lord Wilberforce acknowledged that the decision in *Broadway Cottages* gave the authority of the Court of Appeal to the distinction between a power of selection and a trust for selection (i.e a discretionary trust). His Lordship reiterated that '[t]he basis for the *Broadway Cottages* principle is stated to be that a trust cannot be valid unless, if need be it can be executed by the court and . . . that the court can only execute it by ordering an equal distribution in which every beneficiary shares'. This proposition was called into question by Lord Wilberforce, who argued that:

> As a matter of reason, to hold that the principle of equal distribution applies to trusts such as the present is certainly paradoxical. Equal division is surely the last thing the Settlor ever intended; equal division among all may, probably would, produce a result beneficial to none. Why suppose that a court would lend itself to a whimsical execution? And as regards authority, I do not find that the nature of the trust, and of the court's powers over trusts, calls for any such rigid rule. Equal division may be sensible and has been decreed, in cases of family trusts for a limited class, here there is life in the maxim 'equality is equity', but the cases provide numerous examples where this has not been so, and a different type of execution has been ordered, appropriate to the circumstances . . .

Having thus reviewed the *Broadway Cottages* case, Lord Wilberforce concluded that 'the wide distinction between the validity test for powers and that for trust powers [i.e discretionary trusts] is unfortunate and wrong, that the rule recently fastened on the courts by the *Broadway Cottages* case ought to be discarded, and that the test for the validity of trust powers ought to be similar to that accepted by this House in *Re Gulbenkian* . . . for powers . . . '. This meant, in effect, that the Baden trust would be adjudged to be valid, if it could be said with sufficient certainty that any given individual was or was not a member of the class.

The resumption of hostilities in *Re Baden (No. 2)*

The appeal to the Lords did not mark the end of this protracted dispute since their Lordships remitted the case to the Chancery Division and then the Court of Appeal (under the name *Re Baden (No. 2)*) to decide whether the objects referred to in clause 9(a) of the deed were sufficiently certain under the individual ascertainability test. In pursuing this subsequent litigation, Mr Baden's executors contended that even if this less stringent test was adopted, the reference to 'relatives' in this clause meant that the trust would be bound to fail since 'it would be quite impracticable for the trustees to ascertain in many cases, whether a particular person was *not* a relative of an employee'. In addressing this crucial point, each of the three Court of Appeal judges approached the test from differing perspectives, thereby compounding the uncertainty that already prevailed in this area of law.

Stamp LJ adopted a stringent approach, insisting that the test would be satisfied only if it could be said affirmatively of *any* given individual that he was or was not within the designated class. This would have meant that a trust for relatives would ordinarily fail for uncertainty of objects if 'relatives' was construed in the broad sense of persons descended from a common ancestor in view of the difficulty of determining that any given person is *not* related to another. Stamp LJ circumvented this difficulty by construing 'relatives' in a manner that equated this term with narrower concepts such as 'next of kin' or 'nearest blood relations'. He concluded that that there was no difficulty in determining whether any given individual fell within or outside this more narrowly defined class.

Sachs LJ adopted a rather less dogmatic approach than Stamp LJ. He signified that a trust would not fail on account of *evidential uncertainty* under the individual ascertainability test which was more concerned with *conceptual uncertainty*. He signified that once the words used in defining the class were conceptually certain, it became a question of fact whether any given individual could be proved on inquiry to be within the defined class. In effect, the burden lay with any potential claimant to establish that he fell within the class. If he could not, the trustees were entitled to proceed on the assumption that he fell outside it, even if it could not definitely be said that he did so. Consequently, even if 'relatives' denoted all the descendants of a common ancestor, the term as thus employed was conceptually certain and the trust would thus be valid. Any person who could not prove such descent would be deemed not to be a relative even if it could not conclusively be stated that he was not.

For his part, Megaw LJ approached the matter from a different standpoint. He maintained that since the trustees under a discretionary trust were not obliged to distribute among the entire class, the individual ascertainability test would be satisfied so long as it could be said that a substantial number of persons definitely fell within the specified class, even if there was also a substantial number of other persons of whom it could not definitely be said whether or not they came within the class. According to this reasoning, the trust in this case would not fail for lack of certainty once it could be shown that a substantial number of persons were relatives of employees.

Conclusion

Writing several decades before Mr Baden's deed fell under the judicial spotlight, Glanville Williams asserted that '[w]hat is a sufficiently certain beneficiary or object is frequently a matter of great difficulty'. The complexity of the issues that fell to be determined in the two Baden cases and the divergences in judicial opinion that emerged as the dispute wended its way through the courts clearly bear out this assertion. In conclusion, it is perhaps apposite to leave the last word to Hopkins whose unflattering assessment is that '[t]he *Baden* litigation as a whole has many unsatisfactory features and a distressing degree of uncertainty remains after it'.

FURTHER READING

Primary sources

IRC v. Broadway Cottages [1955] AC 20

Knight v. Knight (1840) 3 Beav 148

McPhail v. Doulton (In Re Baden's Deed Trusts) [1971] AC 424

Re Baden's Deed Trusts No. 2 [1973] 3 WLR 250

Re Gestetner's Settlement [1953] Ch 672

Re Gulbenkian's Settlement Trusts (No. 1) [1970] AC 508

Re Saxone Shoe Co. Ltd's Trust Deed [1962] 1 WLR 943

Secondary sources

Harris, J. (1970) 'Discretionary Trusts – An End and a Beginning?' [1970] 33, *MLR*, 686.

Hopkins, J. (1971) 'Certain Uncertainties of Trusts and Powers' [1971] *CLJ*, 68.

Hopkins, J. (1973) 'Continuing Uncertainty as to Certainty of Objects of Trust Powers' [1973] *CLJ*, 36.

Pearce, R. and Stevens, J. (2006) *The Law of Trusts and Equitable Obligations*, 4th edn, Oxford, 120–131.

Watkin, T.G. (1979) 'Doubts and Uncertainties' [1979] 8, *Anglo-Am. L. Rev.*, 123.

Williams, G. (1940) 'The Three Certainties' [1940] *MLR*, 40.

Constitution

Pennington v. *Waine* [2002] EWCA Civ 227

Andrew Iwobi, Swansea University

The background to *Pennington* v. *Waine*

When a prospective donor or settlor evinces an intention to make an outright gift of his property or to pass such property to someone else to hold on trust, but vesting does not occur, the gift or trust is said to be incompletely constituted. This is the case where the donor or settlor has either taken no steps or failed in his attempt to transfer the property to the donee or trustee in the manner prescribed by law. The courts are frequently called upon to decide whether such an incompletely constituted gift or trust is enforceable by or on behalf of the intended donee or beneficiary. In the well-known case of *Milroy* v. *Lord*, the Court of Appeal made it abundantly clear that equity would not intervene to enforce an incompletely constituted trust or gift in favour of a volunteer (i.e a donee or beneficiary who has furnished no consideration). In *Milroy*, Thomas Medley, who owned shares in a bank executed a voluntary deed in which he declared that Samuel Lord was to hold these shares on trust for the benefit of his daughter. A deed of this nature was not the appropriate means of transferring shares. Rather, the mode of transfer stipulated in the Bank's constitution entailed the completion of a specified transfer form and the registration of the new owner in the Bank's books. Medley executed a power of attorney authorising Lord to act on his behalf. This would have enabled Lord to apply for registration but Medley died before Lord took any steps in this regard. This meant that the shares had not been effectively transferred to Lord in Medley's lifetime and devolved as part of Medley's estate. Proceedings were commenced to compel Medley's personal representatives to give effect to the intended trust in the beneficiary's favour. The Court of Appeal however, refused to enforce this trust on the footing that 'there is no equity in this court to perfect an imperfect gift'.

Equity's professed reluctance to enforce such imperfect gifts at the behest of volunteers has been subjected to intense judicial scrutiny in a host of subsequent cases. In particular, there are several cases of note, including *Re Rose*, *Mascall* v. *Mascall* and *Choithram* v. *Pagarani* in which the process of transferring property in dispute to the intended donee or to all the intended trustees had not been completed in the manner prescribed by law, but the courts nevertheless proceeded to circumvent the constraints imposed by *Milroy* v. *Lord* on the basis that the donor or settlor had done enough for the transfer to take effect in equity. *Pennington* v. *Waine* is the most recent decision in which an intended gift was enforced on this basis.

The facts of *Pennington*

In *Pennington*, as in *Milroy*, the subject matter of the intended gift consisted of shares. The donor, Ada Crampton, owned 75% of the issued share capital in Crampton Bros Ltd and was also a director of the company. In September 1998, she had intimated to Mr Pennington, a partner in the company's auditors that she wished to make her nephew, Harold, her co-director and intended to transfer 400 of her shares to him. Pennington sent Ada a share transfer form which she signed and returned to him. Ada then informed Harold that she wished to give him some of her shares and instructed Pennington to seek Harold's consent to act as a director. Harold received a letter from Pennington, notifying him that Ada had directed Pennington to arrange for the transfer of 400 shares to Harold and requesting Harold to sign the enclosed director's consent form (Form 288A) which Harold duly did. The letter asserted that the transfer required no further action on Harold's part. Pennington did not, therefore, deem it necessary to deliver the share transfer form signed by Ada, to Harold to enable him to apply for registration as the new owner of the shares. To compound matters, Pennington made no effort to initiate the registration process himself by lodging the share transfer form with the company but simply placed it in a file where it remained until Ada's death in November 1998. Ada's executors commenced proceedings with a view to determining whether Harold was entitled to the 400 shares or whether they formed part of her estate to be distributed in accordance with Ada's will.

The decision in *Pennington*

It was held at first instance, that even though the legal title to the 400 shares had not been transferred by Ada to Harold, the gift was effective in equity and operated to transfer her entire beneficial interest in the shares to him. On appeal, it fell to the Court of Appeal to clarify what was necessary in order for an equitable assignment of shares by way of gift to be valid. Arden LJ (whose judgment was adopted in its entirety by Schiemann LJ) began by declaring on the authority of *Milroy*, that 'where the transaction was purely voluntary [as in the present case], the principle that equity will not assist a volunteer must be applied and respected'. Her Ladyship observed that this principle 'at first sight looks like a hard-edged rule of law not permitting much argument and exception'; and that its operation had 'led to harsh and seemingly paradoxical results'. She, however, emphasised that in its desire to mitigate the harshness of this principle, equity had on more than one occasion and in more than one way 'tempered the wind to the shorn lamb (i.e. the donee)'.

Elaborating on this theme, Arden MR drew attention to an important exception to the principle in *Milroy*, which had emerged in cases such as *Re Rose* and *Mascall v. Mascall*. In *Re Rose*, the donor had duly completed a share transfer form which he handed over together with the share certificates to the donee which were then lodged with the company's secretary for purposes of registration. In *Mascall* the donor had completed a land transfer form which he left with the donee's solicitor. He also handed over his Land Certificate to the donee, which the donee's solicitor then sent to the Inland Revenue for stamp duty to be assessed prior to an application being made to the Lands Registry for the donee to be registered as the new proprietor. The Court of Appeal held in both cases that the donor had done everything which according to the nature of the property was necessary to be done by him to transfer the property and that the gift would be effective in equity even though the requirement of registration dictated that something further had to be done in order for the legal title to pass. Pending such registration, the donor would be obliged to hold the legal title on constructive trust for the donee. Having reviewed *Re Rose* and *Mascall*, Arden LJ stated that the decisions in these two cases were 'predicated on the basis that delivery of the transfer [documents] to the donee was necessary and had occurred'. In *Pennington*, by contrast, Ada had not done everything required of her to transfer her 400 shares since the share transfer form had neither been lodged with the company nor handed over to Harold, the donee, but remained with Mr Pennington, as Ada's agent. This effectively precluded Arden LJ from relying on the exception in *Re Rose* as the basis for holding that the gift in Harold's favour was enforceable in equity.

The case of *Choithram* v. *Pagarani* was also highlighted by Arden LJ as affording a further example of equity's efforts to mitigate the harshness of the principle in *Milroy*. In her determination to give effect to the intended gift in Harold's favour, her Ladyship seized upon a line of reasoning advanced by Lord Browne-Wilkinson in *Choithram*. In this case, Mr Pagarani had established a charitable foundation to be administered by himself and several other persons as trustees. He declared that he would give all his wealth to the foundation but died before transferring most of his assets into the joint names of himself and the other trustees. The enforceability of this trust fell to be determined by the Privy Council. Lord Browne-Wilkinson, who read the judgment of the Privy Council, asserted that 'although equity will not aid a volunteer, it will not strive officiously to defeat a gift'. Since Mr Pagarani had declared that he was giving property owned by him to a trust which he himself had established and of which he had appointed himself to be a trustee, Lord Browne-Wilkinson maintained that 'it would be unconscionable and contrary to the principles of equity to allow such a donor to resile from his gift'. He held in the light of this that the trust was enforceable in equity. This proposition that a gift would be enforceable in equity if it would be unconscionable for the donor to resile from it was endorsed by Arden LJ who declared in *Pennington* that 'a principle which animates the answer to the question whether an apparently incomplete gift is to be treated as completely constituted [and hence enforceable] is that a donor will not be permitted to change his or her mind if it would be unconscionable in the eyes of equity, *vis-à-vis* the donee'. Having regard to all that had transpired in the present case, Her Ladyship concluded that the stage had been reached when it would have been unconscionable for Ada to change her mind and resile from the gift and held on this basis that it was enforceable in equity even though there had been no delivery of the share transfer form as contemplated in *Re Rose* and *Mascall*. She accordingly dismissed the appeal.

Clarke LJ agreed with Arden LJ that the appeal should be dismissed. As he saw it, the crucial question in this case was whether the share transfer form signed by Ada could take effect as an equitable assignment of her shares to Harold without having been delivered either to Harold or to the company. He conceded that Ada could have done more in the circumstances – she could have delivered the transfer form to Harold or to the company or could indeed have applied to the company to enter Harold's name in its register by virtue of s.183(4) of the Companies Act 1985. This notwithstanding, he made it clear that unless there was binding authority to the contrary, he was inclined to hold that an equitable assignment of the shares had occurred and that the beneficial interest had accordingly passed to Harold. Counsel for the appellants submitted that such authority was to be found in the line of cases exemplified by *Re Rose*. In her judgment, Arden LJ had signified that the ratio of *Re Rose* was that delivery was necessary for the intended transfer to be enforceable in equity, but Clarke LJ did not subscribe to this view. According to him, 'the ratio of *Re Rose*, was that the gifts of the shares were completely constituted [in equity] by the crucial date, which was 10 April 1943, by which time the deeds had been executed and delivered to the donee. It does not, however, follow that the decision would have been different if no such delivery had taken place. The court did not have to decide that question'. Referring in particular to his reading of Evershed MR's judgment in *Re Rose*, Clarke LJ was left in no doubt that the Master of the Rolls would have held that Ada's beneficial interest in the 400 shares was transferred to Harold by virtue of her execution of the share transfer form even without delivery. He accordingly decided that Ada had made a valid equitable assignment in favour of Harold by signing the form in circumstances in which she had no intention of revoking it in the future. Clarke LJ went on to indicate that even if, contrary to this view, some further step was required on Ada's part, the gift would nevertheless have still been enforceable in equity in the manner contemplated by Arden LJ since it would have been unconscionable of Ada to assert that the beneficial interest in the shares had not passed to Harold and would equally be unconscionable for her executors to seek to resile from the transfer after her death when she has plainly intended Harold to own the shares.

Comment

It is discernible from the judgments of Arden LJ and Clarke LJ that even though Harold was a volunteer, the court was very favourably disposed towards him and was prepared to go to considerable lengths to give effect to what was arguably an imperfect gift. Tham suggests that 'it is difficult to disagree with the outcome of *Pennington* v. *Waine*'. This is echoed by Halliwell who states that 'One can . . . readily symphathise with the Court of Appeal in *Pennington* v. *Waine*. I am sure that everyone would agree that the outcome was fair'. There has, however, been considerably less sympathy in academic circles for the judicial reasoning through which this outcome was reached. Much of the academic criticism has centred on the manner in which Arden LJ, in her eagerness to ensure that the gift was effective in equity, introduced an exception to the exception in *Re Rose* by invoking the unconscionability principle. Particular disquiet has been expressed by Pearce and Stevens who, commenting on this development, argue that it 'dangerously undermines the well established principle that equity will not act to perfect an imperfect gift nor assist a volunteer . . . The effectiveness of alleged transfers of property should not be determined by the vagaries of whether the courts consider that it would be 'unconscionable' for the transferee to change his or her mind . . . It remains to be seen whether this new approach founded on unconscionability finds favour with the higher courts'. This is not a particularly satisfactory state of affairs, for as Halliwell points out, 'if we are left with a maxim that equity will not assist a volunteer unless it is unconscionable not to do so, then we are left with a very unruly beast indeed'.

FURTHER READING

Primary sources

Choithram v. *Pagarani* [2001] 1 WLR 1

Mascall v. *Mascall* (1985) 50 P & CR 119

Milroy v. *Lord* (1862) 4 De GF & J 264

Pennington v. *Waine* [2002] EWCA Civ 227

Re Rose [1952] 1 All ER 1217

Secondary sources

Halliwell, M. (2003) 'Perfecting Imperfect Gifts and Trusts: Have We Reached the End of the Chancellor's Foot?' [2003] *Conv*, 192.

Pearce, R. and Stevens, J. (2006) *The Law of Trusts and Equitable Obligations*, 4th edn, Oxford, 173–178.

Tham, C. (2006) 'Careless Share Giving' [2006] *Conv*, 411.

6

EQUITY AND TRUSTS

Non-charitable purpose trusts

Re Endacott [1960] Ch 232

Bob Evans, Northumbria University

What is wrong with wanting to provide for the upkeep of your dog or cat after your death, or seeking to ensure that your gravestone is kept in reasonable repair, or even trying to ensure that after your death some useful, if non-charitable, facility will be provided? The answer, of course, is nothing. Enforcement of such purposes does not cause the law the same difficulties as those purposes which are illegal. These latter type of arrangements will not be capable of enforcement however they are set up. This is because the law does not approve of the objectives that the parties are trying to attain.

In the case of the former type of arrangements there is nothing wrong with what it is intended to do, nevertheless, there are two issues arising which cause problems if it is intended to use a trust to attempt to carry out such purposes.

Issues relating to non-charitable purpose trusts

The first of these issues concerns the rule against perpetual trusts. This rule is not restricted to purpose trusts as it applies to all private, i.e. non-charitable trusts. It is a policy of the law that non-charitable trusts cannot continue indefinitely. The trust must come to an end no later than the end of the perpetuity period. The common law definition for the perpetuity period was life or lives in being plus twenty-one years, together with a period of gestation where that actually existed. Lives in being are simply anyone in existence at the date of the instrument setting up the trust. The lives might be those of beneficiaries or of anybody else. They simply mark out a period of time. Because of the difficulties of keeping track of ordinary people over relatively long time spans draftsmen tended to use royal lives to mark out the period if they were not content to use the lives of beneficiaries. To this could be added twenty-one years plus a period of pregnancy if that were required to get the interest to vest.

A trust might therefore be set up for the grandchildren of Ann born before the end of the perpetuity period. The perpetuity period for this could be the period marked out by the lifespan of the survivor of all the descendants of King George VI alive at the date of the settlement plus twenty-one years. In the unlikely event that at the end of that time A's daughter was pregnant but the child not yet born you would be allowed to add the extra period of gestation.

Various changes were brought about by the Perpetuity and Accumulations Act 1964, but these do not apply to purpose trusts. It is still therefore the case that such trusts must end within the common law perpetuity period and what is more, under the common law rules applicable it must be possible at the outset to say that there is no possibility, however remote, of contravening those rules otherwise the trust will be invalid from the start.

If, what you want to do is to maintain a cat or dog, it should be fairly easy to ensure that these rules are not contravened. Such animals generally do not live beyond twenty-one years. At least in the case of executory trusts, i.e. where the testator nominates a purpose and leaves the trustees to find the appropriate way of fulfilling it, the courts have tended to say that if you use an expression such as maintaining an animal etc. so far as the trustees could legally do so (*Re Hooper*), or 'for so long as the law for the time being permits' (*Pirbright* v. *Salwey*) that will satisfy the rule. In *Re Haines* the court even went so far as to take judicial notice that a cat would not live beyond twenty-one years and therefore a trust for its maintenance could not possibly offend the rule. In such situations, the trust would only be able to last twenty-one years because no lives in being were nominated.

If what you wanted to do was to have your tombstone maintained there could be more of a problem as such purposes could go on forever. In these instances more attention needs to be paid to the drafting to ensure that the perpetuity rules are not infringed.

The second, and more fundamental difficulty with trusts for purposes stems from the definition of a trust. There are many definitions available, but they all share at least one common aspect, which is that a trust is an obligation placed upon the trustee which can be enforced by the beneficiaries.

> A trust is an equitable obligation binding a person (called a trustee) to deal with property over which he has control (called the trust property) for the benefit of persons (called beneficiaries or cestui que trust) of whom he himself may be one and any of whom may enforce the obligation. (Underhill)

This concept is commonly encountered in the area of certainty of intention where the use of non-mandatory words will result in failure to set up a trust (*Lamb* v. *Eames*). It is equally relevant in the area of trusts for purposes because while a settlor may use all the mandatory words he/she likes, if there is no one capable of bringing an action to enforce then there is no effective obligation on the trustee. In consequence, where the settlor gave £10,000 to Alex on trust to maintain the settlor's cat, if Alex took the money and refused to look after the animal no action could be brought against him for breach of trust.

Historically, the courts have taken a different view, which to modern eyes may appear incongruous. In some cases they were prepared to accept that it was perfectly possible to have an unenforceable obligation if the person in the position of 'trustee' were to give an undertaking to the court to carry out the task in question. Alternatively, or more usually, in addition, there may be a remainderman who could apply to the court to have the funds paid to him if they were not used for the specified purposes (*Re Thompson*, *Pettingall* v. *Pettingall*).

In *Re Astor* these justifications were swept aside by Roxburgh J on the basis that such cases are anomalous. They offend the principle that stems from *Morice* v. *The Bishop of Durham* that a trust requires somebody capable of enforcing it, which is known as the beneficiary principle.

It could be argued that the same problem would arise in the case of a charitable trust where it exists for the achievement of a purpose rather than for the benefit of individuals. A trust to provide a recreation ground would undoubtedly be valid so long as it was available to the whole community despite the fact that it exists for a purpose. The solution in the case of charities is that the Crown, acting through the Attorney General can enforce them.

On this footing it has been argued that (Underhill and Hayton: Law of Trusts and Trustees) if a trust instrument were to appoint an enforcer, i.e. attempt to give *locus standi* to a person to enforce it then it should not be vulnerable to attack on the grounds of non-human beneficiaries. It remains to be seen how the English courts would view this as fitting in with the doctrine of **Saunders v. Vautier** where the beneficiaries acting in concert are able to bring a trust to an end regardless of the intentions of the settlor.

In **Re Endacott** the issue of purpose trusts and the beneficiary principle came before the Court of Appeal. A senior court thus had the opportunity to consider the impact of **Re Astor** on the area.

In this case the testator left his residuary estate to the North Tawton Devon Council 'for the purpose of providing some useful memorial to myself'. Various issues arose from this case, but having decided that it was not charitable, neither was it an outright gift to the Council, the court had to deal with it on the basis of an attempted purpose trust.

The court looked at the 'anomalous' exceptions to the beneficiary principle. It held that this was too uncertain to fall within any of them and must therefore fail. The judgments did not stop there, however. The Court upheld that there was generally a requirement of a human beneficiary in order for a private trust to be valid. It acknowledged, however, that there had been situations where this rule had not been followed as scrupulously as could have been the case and following the classification in Morris and Leach, The Rule Against Perpetuities accepted that there were five allowable exceptions to the beneficiary principle. These were trusts for graves and monuments, for specific animals, for the saying of masses, for unincorporated associations and a miscellaneous head.

While it is interesting discussing whether or not it is possible to have a valid trust for a purpose, the major impact of this area is in respect of unincorporated associations. An unincorporated association has been defined in **Conservative and Unionist Central Office v. Burrell** (Lawton LJ):

> Two or more persons bound together for one or more common purposes, not being business purposes, by mutual undertakings each having mutual duties and obligations, in an organisation which has rules which identify in whom control of it and its funds rests and on what terms, and which can be joined or left at will.

Unlike a company, an unincorporated association is not able to hold property in its own name. If its bank account is held in the name of the treasurer, it may be able to regulate this by means of a contract between the members and the treasurer. In this situation, any gift to the organisation would have to be treated as for the purposes of the association and held subject to the contract between the members while the association still exists

(*Re Recher*). Even here, where the assets are purely money, it is at least arguable that it is difficult to prevent a trust from arising given the *Quistclose* line of cases. Where the asset in question is land it will be impossible to argue that there is no trust because of the need to register title in the names of no more than four persons.

The problem is best highlighted in an example. If a generous donor wishes to give five acres of land to the local football club to be used as a playing field, who will become the registered transferee of that land? Plainly, the transferee cannot be the club if it is unincorporated. One obvious solution would be to incorporate the club, i.e. turn it into a company. It is not then necessary to use a trust and the problems caused by the beneficiary principle disappear.

If, for some reason, incorporation is not desired the registered title will have to be put into the names of persons to hold it as trustees. Assuming that the draftsperson remembers to avoid the issues of perpetuity by an appropriate clause, the question still arises as to what are the terms of the trust?

Clearly it could be held on trust for the persons who were members of the club at the time of the gift, but this would present serious difficulties. For example, this does not deal with the problem of a member who thereafter ceases to belong to the club. Under such a trust he would still own an equitable interest in the club property. Similarly it does not help the new member who subsequently joins the club as he would have no interest in its assets. Worst still, from the donor's point of view it would allow any of those members to sever their share and dispose of their interest in the property. This is likely to be the last thing that the donor wants. If he had intended the field to be used for property development he would probably have done this for himself and not given it away. What he wants is for it to be held for the purposes of playing football, but a trust 'for the purposes of playing football' immediately puts it into conflict with the beneficiary principle which would result in the trust being invalid.

These issues were discussed by Cross J in *Neville Esates v. Madden*. Cross J indicated that to be valid and to prevent the members from severing their share the trust could be to the existing members subject to their contractual rights. It is therefore better if all of the restrictions are contained in the contract and not the trust. Thus there should be a transfer to trustees who will hold on trust for the members of the club. The club constitution would exist as a contract between all the members. Apart from dealing with issues such as how the club is to be run, how the committee is elected etc. it would also contain terms to the effect that members may not sever their share; that on leaving the club they relinquish all claims on the club assets for no payment; that on joining, a new member gets a proportionate share of the assets. It may also make it difficult for the membership to exercise their rights as beneficiaries under the rule in *Saunders v. Vautier* to wind up the trust and divide the spoils between themselves by providing, for example, that the members may not decide to wind up the club and share its assets until a large majority, for example 75%, have voted to do so.

These restrictions will have the effect of keeping the assets for the use of the club, but as they are contained in a contract, the trust is still for the members, not for purposes and does not offend the beneficiary principle.

6

EQUITY AND TRUSTS

293

A recent example of this can be seen in the case of *Re Horley Town FC* where a playing field was found to have been subject to a contract holding gift to the club, i.e. it was held on a trust in favour of the members from time to time. As it had been sold, the surplus proceeds of that sale belonged under the contract to the persons who were members of the club at the time of sale.

It can be seen from the above that, despite what was said in *Re Endacott*, these 'club trusts' are no longer regarded as an exception to the beneficiary principle. They have, in fact, been brought within that principle by means of the way the courts have interpreted them. This is fine where they are being set up from the start, as in the example above because the draftsperson can take all appropriate actions to make sure that the purpose does not appear as part of the trust.

In the case of wills or badly drafted arrangements it is perfectly possible for the purpose of the gift to be mentioned in the trust. For instance, a sum of money may have been left to a club for obtaining and maintaining new club premises. The issue then arises as to what extent this may cause the trusts to offend against the beneficiary principle. The answer to this seems to depend on the contrast between the two cases of *Re Lipinski's Will Trusts* and *Re Grant's Will Trusts*.

In the former, a will contained a bequest in favour of the Hull Judeans Maccabi Association. It was stated that it must be used to acquire and maintain a headquarters for their youth branch. On the face of it, this looks like a trust for a purpose which should fail, but this was held not to be the case. Under the club rules, if the members ever brought the Association to an end the club's property (including the new youth HQ) could be sold and the net proceeds divided among the members. Hence although it appeared to be a gift for a purpose, ultimately, when the purposes of the club ceased, the members would take the property.

In *Re Grant's Will Trusts*, on the other hand, there was a gift of funds to the Chertsey and District Constituency Labour Party for the benefit of the constituency headquarters. The rules of the party provided that if the local party ever ceased to require a headquarters the property was to pass, not to the members, but to the National Executive Committee of the national Labour Party. This restriction was held to prevent the gift being to the members of the Chertsey Constituency Party because they could never apply it for their own use.

There has been criticism of the outcome in *Re Grant* in that perhaps the facts could have been differently interpreted, but this does not alter the basic concept that such trusts will only be regarded as offending the beneficiary principle where, upon disposal of the property, the proceeds cannot reach the hands of the members.

It may be asked why the courts have adopted such a laid back position. In fact, it has been commented that the court was so laid back in *Re Lipinski* that it could have been regarded as almost prone. The answer lies at the start of this chapter, there is nothing wrong with wanting to maintain your cat or dog, or trying to set up a trust for an unincorporated association. It just does not fit very happily into the concept of a trust, which therefore means that the courts have no reasons to justify a harsh application of the rule in situations of genuine difficulties.

FURTHER READING

Primary sources

Barclays Bank v. *Quistclose Investments Limited* [1970] A.C. 567

Conservative and Unionist Central Office v. *Burrell* [1982] 1 WLR 522

Lamb v. *Eames* (1871) 6 Ch App 597

Morice v. *The Bishop of Durham* (1805) 10 Ves 522

Neville Esates v. *Madden* [1961] 3 All ER 769

Pettingall v. *Pettingall* (1842) 11 LJ Ch 176

Pirbright v. *Salwey* (1896) WN 86

Re Astor's Settlement Trusts [1952] Ch 531

Re Endacott [1960] Ch 232

Re Grant's Will Trusts [1979] 3 All ER 359

Re Haines (1952) *The Times*, 7 November 1952

Re Hooper [1932] 1 Ch 38

Re Horley Town FC [2006] EWHC 2386

Re Lipinski's Will Trusts [1976] Ch 235

Re Recher's Will Trusts [1972] 3 WLR 321

Re Thompson [1934] Ch 342

Saunders v. *Vautier* (1841) 4 Beav 115

Perpetuity and Accumulations Act 1964

Secondary sources

Hayton, David, Matthews, Paul and Mitchell, Charles (2006) *Underhill and Hayton: Law of Trusts and Trustees*, 17th edn, LexisNexis Butterworths.

Morris, J.H.C. and Leach, W.B. (1962) *The Rule Against Perpetuities*, 2nd edn, Stevens & Sons.

6

EQUITY AND TRUSTS

Common intention constructive trusts

Lloyds Bank Plc v. *Rosset and Another* [1991] 1 AC 107

Judith Puech, Northumbria University

Trusts often arise in the context of the family home and disputes over its ownership, typically where legal title to the property is in the name of one of the parties to the relationship but the other claims a share in the property by virtue of, for example, their contributions to the purchase price, improvements to the property or the payment of domestic expenses. Obtaining a share may be possible if the partner without legal title can assert a beneficial interest in the property which requires showing that the legal owner holds it upon trust to give effect to that beneficial interest. Apart from the special position of married couples who can invoke the property adjustment provisions of the Matrimonial Causes Act 1973 in the event of their relationship breaking down, and registered civil partners, who can rely on the similar provisions of the Civil Partnership Act 2004, the legal principles applicable to the claim are those of the law of trusts, particularly the law relating to resulting and constructive trusts.

While the 1991 House of Lords decision of *Lloyds Bank Plc* v. *Rosset* is the most significant development of the law of constructive trusts in this area, consideration should be given to the social context in which these trusts have developed. The use of the constructive trust in the context of ownership of the family home initially emerged in response to the situation of the married woman and the question on divorce of ownership of the matrimonial home purchased in the husband's sole name. If she had made a direct contribution to the purchase price then the wife could claim an interest under a resulting trust. However, the home would generally be purchased by means of a mortgage, repaid from the husband's income. The resulting trust fails to recognise anything other than financial contributions to the purchase price, ignoring the value of other contributions made by the wife and the reality of the domestic situation of the parties. Accordingly the constructive trust was developed, particularly so by the House of Lords in *Pettitt* v. *Pettitt* and *Gissing* v. *Gissing* to provide the non-owning spouse with a share in the matrimonial home.

Establishing an interest under a resulting trust is limited to evidence of a direct contribution to the purchase price. A wider range of conduct will give rise to the finding of a constructive trust, but it is important to note that there are essential requirements which must be fulfilled before a party can claim a beneficial interest under such a trust.

The cases of *Pettitt* and *Gissing* established that the constructive trust gives effect to the common intention of the parties as to how the beneficial interests in the property are to be held, the common intention arising from the express oral agreement of the

296

parties as to their respective beneficial interest in the home or in the absence of express discussions, inferred from their conduct.

Despite a relatively simple statement of the law, when each of these differing situations are analysed it will be seen that each is not as simple as first appears, both in terms of interpretation and the ensuant case law, particularly the advent of the 'new model' constructive trust developed by Lord Denning and imposed whenever justice required it (*Cooke* v. *Head*, *Hussey* v. *Palmer*, *Eves* v. *Eves*). Subsequent developments in the Court of Appeal, however, in cases such as *Burns* v. *Burns* and *Grant* v. *Edwards*, saw the rejection of the wide discretionary approach envisaged by Lord Denning and a return to the conventional property based principles espoused in *Gissing*.

While these Court of Appeal decisions served to restore certainty to the law, the House of Lords decision in *Rosset* provides the clearest statement yet of the requirements necessary to establish an interest in the home. What must be shown, however, is dependent upon two fundamentally different factual situations – where an express agreement to share the beneficial interest in the property exists and where there is no such agreement.

Express agreement

In resolving disputes as to ownership of the beneficial interest in the former home, the first question for the judge to ask is whether the parties have come to any agreement, arrangement or understanding that the property is to be shared beneficially. Such agreement must be based on evidence of express discussions between the parties.

On its own, however, the existence of agreement will not establish a constructive trust. In essence the agreement amounts to a declaration of trust, such an express trust being unenforceable for want of writing (section 53(1)(b) Law of Property Act 1925). Accordingly the non-legal owner must show that he or she has acted to his or her detriment in reliance on the agreement in order to render it inequitable for the partner entitled to the legal estate to deny the other's interest, thereby giving rise to a constructive trust to which the formality requirements do not apply (section 53(2)).

Upon dissecting these requirements, a number of difficulties can be seen. Firstly, the agreement must be based on evidence of express discussions – 'an express common intention is one that is communicated between the parties' (*Springette* v. *Defoe*). Lord Bridge gives 'outstanding examples' of cases of the situations in the first category as being those of *Eves* v. *Eves* and *Grant* v. *Edwards* both of which involved excuses by the male partner as to why the property was not to be put in the parties' joint names, the courts considering the representation to raise a clear inference of a common intention that the claimant was to have an interest in the house – 'otherwise no excuse for not putting her name onto the title would have been needed'. Whether such statements can be considered as evidence of genuine common intention is patently questionable.

In *Rosset*, Mrs Rosset's claim that it had been expressly agreed between her and her husband that the property was to be jointly owned was rejected. As Mr Rosset provided the whole purchase price of the property (using money from his family trust) and the cost of its renovation, Mrs Rosset had formidable difficulty in establishing her claim, a difficulty added to by the circumstances of the trustee's stipulation that the property be bought in Mr Rosset's sole name.

As outlined earlier, common intention alone will not establish a constructive trust. The claimant must also show that he or she has acted to his or her detriment in reliance on the agreement. Like proof of the common intention, the requirement of detrimental reliance is not without its difficulties, it being far from certain the type of conduct needed to satisfy the requirement.

The question of detrimental reliance was not analysed in any great depth in *Rosset*, Lord Bridge limiting his comments to the requirement of detrimental reliance once an agreement is found, whereupon it is only necessary for the claimant to show that 'he or she has acted to his or her detriment or significantly altered his or her position in reliance on the agreement'. *Grant* v. *Edwards*, by comparison, addressed the issue in more detail. However, their Lordships propounded different views as the sort of conduct required, ranging from 'conduct on which the woman could not reasonably have been expected to embark unless she was to have a interest in the house', to the 'quid pro quo' – 'whatever the court decides the quid pro quo to have been, it will suffice if the claimant has furnished it' and finally the view of Browne-Wilkinson VC that 'any act done by [the claimant] to her detriment relating to the joint lives of the parties, is sufficient detriment to qualify'. One strand of consistency, however, is that the conduct does not have to be referable to the acquisition of the house.

Lord Bridge agreed that the conduct of each of the women in *Eves* v. *Eves* and *Grant* v. *Edwards* was sufficient to support their claims to an interest in the home, being heavy labouring work to the property by Janet Eves and substantial contributions to the household expenses in the case of Linda Grant. Other examples of sufficient acts of detrimental reliance include the claimant acting as an unpaid business assistant and looking after the house and children, the claimant foregoing a promising political career to work on the defendant's property development projects while he was in prison and a payment of £12,000.00 by the claimant to her partner so that he could pay his ex-wife's mortgage (*Hammond* v. *Mitchell*, *Chan* v. *Leung*, *Stokes* v. *Anderson*).

On a cautionary note, however, Lord Bridge appears to have placed little value on the detrimental acts relied on by Mrs Rosset. Her acts of supervising the builders, going to builders merchants and obtaining materials and undertaking skilful painting and decorating were 'so trifling as to be almost de minimis'. Even if agreement had been established, he doubted whether her contribution was sufficient to support a claim to a constructive trust.

The role of the claimant's conduct in establishing the necessary detrimental reliance is clearly an important consideration. Although confusion surrounds the question of what suffices as detrimental conduct in the first of Lord Bridge's situations, nevertheless, a wide range of conduct is accepted. Where no agreement exists, however, the standard of conduct required is strict, arguably erroneous and the subject of a number of criticisms.

Absence of agreement: inferred common intention

Absence of express agreement may not be fatal to the claim. The court may be persuaded to infer one. Lord Bridge indicated that this will only happen where the conduct leads the court to infer that an agreement must have underpinned what happened. It is necessary to show that there is no real alternative explanation as to what happened other than the fact that there must have been agreement to take a share of the property. Elaborating on the type of conduct which would lead the court to this conclusion, Lord Bridge indicates that direct contributions to the purchase price, or to the mortgage will readily lead the court to infer that an agreement was present. Presumably this is explainable on the basis that no rational person would contribute to the purchase of property in the name of another without either showing a gift to that person (which is generally excluded by the facts) or intending to obtain a benefit for him or herself.

While this rationalisation of the conduct necessary to raise the inference makes sense, it leaves the claimant, very typically the female partner, who has contributed to the household unit in other ways, for example, by looking after the house and children, perhaps giving up her job to do so, in a rather disadvantageous and somewhat unfair position. These non-financial contributions will not provide her with an interest in the home. The law clearly fails to take into account the domestic reality of many relationships, arguably undervaluing the role and contribution of the claimant to the family unit.

It has to be acknowledged, however, that although *Rosset* has restricted the scope of acceptable conduct, this restrictive approach is, as will be seen, rooted in authority.

As noted, conduct is essential to the claim to a constructive trust in two respects. Firstly, it establishes the common intention. Secondly, it provides the detrimental reliance. Its importance cannot be understated therefore. However, what is open to question and criticism is the apparent limitation to direct contributions to the purchase price as the only type of conduct capable of providing the necessary evidence. Previous authorities had established that in determining common intention from conduct the court looks to the expenditure incurred by the parties, in particular expenditure referable to the acquisition of the house – the payer paying towards the purchase price or to the mortgage instalments, including instances where the claimant makes financial contributions to the household expenses so as to enable the mortgage instalments to be paid, such contribution being indirectly referable to the acquisition of the house 'since one way or another it enables the family to pay the mortgage instalments' (*Burns* v. *Burns*).

It is open to interpretation as to whether Lord Bridge intended to rule out these indirect contributions. If so, it clearly works to the detriment and injustice of a claimant who has made such contributions, particularly as it appears inconsistent with the earlier position and authorities. His Lordship referred to the conduct of the female partners in *Eves* v. *Eves* and *Grant* v. *Edwards* as sufficient to support the respective claims because they involved an express representation. On their own, the conduct 'fell far short' of conduct to give rise to a constructive trust. A similar question can be asked in respect of improvements made by the partner to the home and whether they have been ruled out under this categorisation.

Amelioration of the strict approach adopted by *Rosset* is apparent in subsequent decisions and the remarkable ability of the courts to find a common intention from discussions or the rather tenuous existence of a direct contribution (see, for example, *Drake* v. *Whipp*, *Oxley* v. *Hiscock*, *Midland Bank* v. *Cooke*). Further, in the recent case of *Le Foe* v. *Le Foe*, the court held that the wife's indirect contributions entitled the court to infer a common

6

EQUITY AND TRUSTS

intention for the wife to have an interest in the home, the judge believing that in using the words 'direct contributions' Lord Bridge did not mean to exclude such contributions. The issue is plainly one of uncertainty therefore and is compounded by the specific nature of the conduct outlined by Lord Bridge - direct contribution to the purchase price. Such payments traditionally give rise to a presumed resulting trust - a somewhat confused overlap in classification and while it may be considered as a question of semantics, the outcome for a claimant can be rather different under each trust. A proportionate share is awarded under a resulting trust (*Springette* v. *Defoe, Huntingford* v. *Hobbs, Ashe* v. *Mumford*). Under a constructive trust, the courts have adopted a rather more generous approach to the issue of quantification. This can be seen in subsequent cases, such as *Midland Bank Plc* v. *Cooke*, where a wedding gift of £1,100.00 from the groom's parents to be used towards the deposit of the home was considered a direct contribution to the purchase price and accordingly the wife was entitled to a beneficial interest in the property. If the court dealt with the matter on a resulting trust basis, the wife would have been entitled to a small interest proportionate to her direct contribution. However, the court was not bound to deal with the matter on the strict basis of a resulting trust but was free to infer an intention to share the beneficial interest in some different proportions to be assessed by the court undertaking a survey of the whole course of dealing between the parties relevant to their ownership and occupation of the property, taking into consideration all conduct which threw light on the question what shares were intended. This 'broad brush' approach can be seen in *Drake* v. *Whipp* and *Le Foe* v. *Le Foe* where the Court eschewed the straitjacket of the mathematical approach 'in favour of a more holistic approach of looking at the parties' global dealings over the span of their ownership of the property'.

The issue of quantification has been recently reviewed in the Court of Appeal decision of *Oxley* v. *Hiscock* whereupon it was considered that the law had moved on since decisions such as *Springette* v. *Defoe* in approaching the matter on a resulting trust basis. Rather, where under any of Lord Bridge's categories, the court finds a common intention to share the property, then (in the absence of evidence of any discussion between the parties as to the amount of the share each was to have), each is entitled to that share which the court considers 'fair' having regard to the whole course of dealing between them in relation to the property. This included the arrangements which they made to meet the outgoings, such as mortgage contributions, council tax, utilities, house keeping etc.

Recent caselaw suggests that the courts have moved on from the proportionate resulting trust approach. However, the somewhat discretionary approach adopted since *Midland Bank* v. *Cooke* et al., has left the law in a state of uncertainty. *Oxley* adopts an approach based on what is 'fair' which is arguably no more than the court was attempting to do in *Midland Bank* v. *Cooke*. Ironically, a fair division of the sale proceeds gave Mr Hiscock 60% and 40% to Mrs Oxley, the assessment based on their direct contributions to the purchase price and having been treated as contributing equally to the mortgage outgoings - the same outcome as under a resulting trust analysis.

Conclusion

Although *Rosset* set out in very clear terms the principles for determining claims to a beneficial interest in the home, uncertainties in the law remain. Indeed as has been seen particularly in the second of Lord Bridge's categories, *Rosset* gives rise to questions and criticisms of its own and the subsequent effect on quantification cannot be ignored.

In its 2002 discussion paper, the Law Commission considered the current law to be complicated, difficult to apply and not suited to the typical informality of those sharing a home. Several reasons for this criticism were highlighted: the unrealistic exercise of identifying the common intention of the parties; uncertainty as to contributions which count, in particular the questionable status of indirect contributions; the failure of the law to recognise non-financial contributions to the home; the difficulties in the quantification of the share – the decisions being inconsistent and difficult to reconcile; and the uncertainty of the law leading to lengthy, costly litigation.

Despite these criticisms, the Law Commission rejected legislative reform of property law as a viable way forward. Rather, the problem should be addressed by, *inter alia*, those living together being encouraged to make express declarations of trust setting out their respective beneficial entitlements, the courts taking a broader view of the kinds of contributions from which a common intention might be inferred and adopting a broader approach to quantifying the value of the share.

This is undoubtedly a controversial area. There is an underlying tension in the law between, on the one hand, seeking to promote certainty by adhering to the application of the established principles of trust law, and on the other hand the emergence of a more flexible approach, promoting a fairer more just solution, seen in cases such as *Midland Bank* v. *Cooke* and *Le Foe* v. *Le Foe* and seemingly encouraged by the Law Commission. What is clear, however, is that until such time as there is reform in this area, the question of ownership remains as that defined by *Rosset* and the apparent inconsistencies, criticisms, questions and tensions will remain.

FURTHER READING

Primary sources

Ashe v. *Mumford and Others*, *The Times*, 15 November 2000 (C/A)

Buggs v. *Buggs* [2003] EWHC 1538 (Ch)

Burns v. *Burns* [1984] Ch 317

Chan v. *Leung* [2002] EWCA Civ 1075

Cooke v. *Head* [1972] 1 WLR 518

Drake v. *Whipp* [1996] 1 FLR 826

Eves v. *Eves* [1975] 1 WLR 1338

Gissing v. *Gissing* [1971] AC 886

Grant v. *Edwards and Another* [1986] Ch 638

Hammond v. *Mitchell* [1991] 1 WLR 1127

Huntingford v. *Hobbs* [1993] 1 FLR 736

Hussey v. *Palmer* [1972] 1 WLR 1286

Le Foe v. *Le Foe and Woolwich Plc* [2001] 2 FLR 970; EWCA Civ 1870

6

EQUITY AND TRUSTS

Lloyds Bank Plc v. *Rosset and Another* [1991] AC 107

Midland Bank Plc v. *Cooke and Another* [1995] 4 All ER 562

Oxley v. *Hiscock* [2004] EWCA Civ 546

Pettitt v. *Pettitt* [1970] AC 777

Springette v. *Defoe* (1992) 24 HLR 552

Stokes v. *Anderson* [1991] 1 FLR 391

Secondary sources

Adkinson, R. (2004) 'Cohabitee Rights' *NLJ*, 25 June 2004, 952-3.

Edwards, S. (2004) 'Property Rights in the Family Home - Clarity at Last' [2004] *Fam Law*, 34, pages 524-527.

Law Com. No. 278, Sharing Homes: A Discussion Paper (2002), Executive Summary paras 7 and 15.

Rotherham, C. (2004) 'The Property Rights of Unmarried Cohabitees: The Case for Reform' [2004] *Conv*, 268-292.

Thompson, M. (2002) 'An Holistic Approach to Home Ownership' [2002] *Conv*, 273.

Thompson, M. (2003) 'The Obscurity of Common Intention' [2003] *Conv*, 411-424.

Thompson, M. (2004) 'Constructive Trusts, Estoppel and the Family home' [2004] *Conv*, 496.

Breach of fiduciary duty

Bristol and West Building Society v. Mothew [1998] Ch 1

Valerie Humphreys, Birmingham City University

The Court of Appeal in *Bristol and West Building Society* v. *Mothew* was faced with having to rule on the nature and application of elements of fiduciary duties in equity. There were in essence two key components in the case: the scope of the fiduciary duty of confidence, normally considered to have the notion of loyalty at its heart, and the pursuit of a remedy for breach of a fiduciary duty as an alternative to claiming remedies in contract and/or tort.

There is little doubt that the recession and the accompanying slump in the property market in the late 1980s and early 1990s caused many mortgage lenders to suffer substantial losses. As they were often unable to recover their money from the borrowers, in some instances they sought to recover them from the solicitors (or valuers) whom they had consulted. In the absence of fraud, they seemed to be compelled to make their claim in breach of contract and/or negligence, but the rules of causation and remoteness of damage at common law were problematic. Hence they turned to equity and alleged breach of trust and/or fiduciary duty in their search for a remedy.

Background and context

It is important, before looking at the case, to understand how fiduciary duties arise, what purposes they serve, and the advantages which may accrue to a claimant if s/he is able to establish the breach of such a duty.

When lawyers talk about 'fiduciaries' or 'fiduciary duties' it is often unclear exactly what they mean. A useful explanation of the role of a fiduciary is given by Millett LJ in *Mothew*:

> A fiduciary is someone who has undertaken to act for or on behalf of another . . . in circumstances which give rise to a relationship of trust and confidence. The distinguishing obligation of a fiduciary is the obligation of loyalty . . . A fiduciary must act in good faith; he must not make a profit out of his trust; he must not place himself in a position where his duty and his interest may conflict; he may not act for his own benefit or the benefit of a third person without the informed consent of the principal . . . They are the defining characteristics of the fiduciary.

The range of fiduciary duties is centred on the need to protect individuals from outside influences, with the accompanying incentive towards ethical behaviour. The courts have in recent years begun to insist on a distinction between the duties which are owed only by fiduciaries and those which can be owed by fiduciaries and non-fiduciaries alike. As indicated by *Mothew*, it is only the former which should be termed fiduciary duties. Such a

6

EQUITY AND TRUSTS

duty, Millett LJ explains, is characteristic of a fiduciary and gives rise to special conse-quences different to those which follow from breaches of other duties imposed by equity or the common law. In many respects these consequences may be more advantageous for, or remedies more readily awarded to, the claimant. Furthermore, as noted below, not every breach of duty by a fiduciary is a breach of his fiduciary duty. Fiduciary duties are in a sense 'extensions' of trustees' duties, and breach of any of them is liable to attract equit-able remedies.

There are significant consequences which follow from a ruling that a breach of a fiduciary duty has occurred, and practical benefits to claimants from such a ruling. The equitable remedies available for breach of such a duty are generally more extensive and flexible than the usual remedy of damages for breach of contract or for negligence. Remedies in equity, such as rescission, accounting for profits and equitable compensation, may prove of more value to a claimant, and will avoid him/her having to deal with issues of causation and remoteness of damage in contract and/or tort.

One of the leading cases on causation and remoteness in trusts is *Target Holding* v. *Redferns*, in which solicitors paid the lender's money to the borrower (their client) before completion of the sale of the property and before any charge over the property to secure the loan had been taken. In the event no real harm was done as the transaction was ulti-mately completed satisfactorily, but nonetheless the lender sought to recover the full amount of its loss (which arose on the default of the borrowers) from the solicitors. It alleged breach of trust and the majority of the Court of Appeal agreed. However, the House of Lords allowed the solicitors' appeal, on the grounds that a trustee in this situa-tion is liable only to make equitable compensation for the losses caused by the breach. Lord Browne-Wilkinson ruled that while the common law rules on causation and remote-ness do not apply to such a breach, there does have to be '. . . some causal connection between the breach of trust and the loss to the trust estate for which compensation is recoverable . . . '. As the lender had suffered no loss thereby, it was not entitled to com-pensation. It is clear following this case that it is not necessary for a claimant to show, for example, foreseeability, but it remains important to address the issue of causation - the loss suffered must have been caused by the breach. In addition, compensation will be lim-ited to the loss which flows from the breach.

The facts

In *Bristol & West Building Society* v. *Mothew* a solicitor acted in respect of a mortgage transaction for both the lender (the building society) and the borrowers. The lender attached a condition to the grant of the £59,000 loan to the effect that the borrowers should raise the balance of the purchase price without further borrowing. The borrowers failed to comply with this condition in that there was a sum of £3500 outstanding from an earlier mortgage to a previous lender, and this was to be secured by a second charge on the property. The society's standing instructions to solicitors acting for it required them to report to the society prior to completion any proposal by a borrower to create a second mortgage or borrow in order to finance part of the purchase price, along with any other relevant matters which ought to be brought to the attention of the society. The solicitor, who was fully informed of the borrowers' intentions, omitted to inform the lender that the borrowers had not complied with this condition, and, in fact, the solicitor made a misrepresentation to the contrary. It was conceded by the solicitor that he made untrue statements and that his failure to report the borrowers' arrangements for a second mortgage was a breach of his instructions. It was accepted, however, by both parties that the mistake was negligent but not fraudulent. The borrowers defaulted on the mortgage repayments and the house was eventually sold at a loss, leaving insufficient funds to repay the lender. The lender sought to recover the full extent of its loss from the solicitor, alleging breach of contract, negligence and breach of trust. Chadwick J ruled that the solicitor was liable, in effect on all three grounds. The Court of Appeal reversed that decision in part.

There are two significant parts to the Court of Appeal's ruling:

1. In respect of the claim for breach of contract and misrepresentation, both of which were admitted by the solicitor, the Court felt bound by the ruling of Hobhouse LJ in *Downs* v. *Chapell*, though apparently with some reluctance, to hold that it was sufficient to show that the lender had relied on the misrepresentation; it was unnecessary to show that it would have acted differently if it had been given the correct information. In fact, the lender had already conceded that it would have proceeded with the loan even if it had known about the charge. However, the lender had still to establish what, if any, loss was attributable to the solicitor's negligence (some might for example be attributable to a fall in property values) and any damages awarded might not cover the full extent of the lender's losses. In the event that they did not, the only recourse for the lender was to equity.

2. Chadwick J had ruled that the solicitor had obtained the loan by misrepresentation, and that he then held the money on a constructive trust for the lender. By applying it to the purchase of the property, he had committed a breach of trust, and he was therefore liable, as a fiduciary, to restore the money in full, plus interest. The same judge confirmed his view in the case of *Bristol and West Building Society* v. *May, May and Merrimans*. In the course of that latter judgment the judge explained why a constructive trust arose. It arose, he said, because the solicitor had given misleading information to his client; this constituted a breach of fiduciary duty which enabled the court to impose a constructive trust on the property acquired as a result of the breach. He clearly considered himself to be imposing a remedial constructive trust as the appropriate remedy for the breach of fiduciary duty.

After considering Chadwick J's views, the Court of Appeal in *Mothew* held that the solicitor's conduct in providing the plaintiff with the wrong information, although a breach of duty, was neither dishonest nor intentional but was due to an oversight, and was unconnected to the fact that he was also acting for the purchasers; accordingly, a breach of trust, if it had occurred, would be something of which he would be unaware. Millett LJ made it very clear in his judgment that he would not wish to treat such conduct as involving a breach of trust unless compelled by authority to do so; in his judgment no such authority required him to reach that conclusion.

6

EQUITY AND TRUSTS

On the issue of breach of fiduciary duty, Millett LJ, having reviewed the authorities, decided that no such breach had occurred. Accordingly, the Court of Appeal ruled that the solicitor's conduct and subsequent application of the money advanced to complete the purchase was neither a breach of trust nor of fiduciary duty.

The implications of the decision

1. Breach of fiduciary duty

In his discussion of fiduciary duties Millett LJ states very clearly that not every breach of duty by a fiduciary is a breach of a fiduciary duty. He agrees with the words of Ipp J in *Permanent Building Society* v. *Wheeler*:

> It is essential to bear in mind that the existence of a fiduciary relationship does not mean that every duty owed by a fiduciary to the beneficiary is a fiduciary duty. In particular, a trustee's duty to exercise reasonable care, though equitable, is not specifically a fiduciary duty . . .

It is axiomatic that, for example, a trustee who makes an error of judgment does not necessarily commit a breach of fiduciary duty. It follows that if the solicitor had been acting for the lender alone he would not have been accused of such a breach, so was the situation different because he was acting for two principals?

A concomitant of the basic obligation to avoid a conflict of interest and duty is the principle that prohibits a fiduciary from acting, or continuing to act, where there is a conflict between the duties owed to multiple principals. Millett LJ explained that a '. . . fiduciary who acts for two principals with potentially conflicting interests without the informed consent of both is in breach of the obligation of undivided loyalty . . . (this) automatically constitutes a breach of fiduciary duty.' However, this was not, in his Lordship's view, a factor of which the lender could complain – it had made a fully informed decision to retain the solicitor knowing that he was acting for both itself and the borrowers.

It was forcefully argued by counsel in *Mothew* that a solicitor who acts for both lender and borrower in the same transaction has an unrestricted obligation to each client to act in best interests of each, including an obligation to disclose to the lender information about the borrower which is material to the transaction. It is, of course, important when acting for two principals that the interests of each are not allowed to compete and that each is regarded as equal by the fiduciary who must act in good faith towards each, and as if each were a sole principal. However, the courts have ruled, conduct which is in breach of this duty need not be dishonest but it must be intentional; a negligent act or omission which happens to benefit one principal at the expense of the other does not constitute a breach of fiduciary duty, though it may well be a breach of the duty of skill and care. The principle involved here is what Millett LJ termed the 'no inhibition' principle, *viz.* the fiduciary must not be inhibited by the existence of one principal from serving the interests of the other as faithfully and effectively as if he were the sole principal. Furthermore, the fiduciary must not place himself in a position of actual conflict of duty, i.e. where he cannot fulfil his duty to one principal without neglecting his duty to the other – Millett LJ calls this the 'actual conflict' rule. Chadwick J had decided that this rule had been breached by the solicitor; the Court of Appeal disagreed and decided that, in order to constitute a breach of fiduciary duty, conduct must be at the very least intentional (though it need not be dishonest). Unintentional conduct may be a breach of a common law duty of skill and care, but it is not a breach of fiduciary duty.

2. Breach of trust

Clearly once he had received the mortgage advance the solicitor held it on trust for the lender, whose property it remained in equity until it was paid over to the purchase of the house. The solicitor knew that he was a trustee of the money for the lender; but he did not realise that he had misled it. Therefore, Millett LJ ruled, relying on the judgment of Lord Browne-Wilkinson in *Westdeutsche Landesbank Girozentrale v. Islington London Borough Council*, he could not be bound to repay the money to the society so long as he was ignorant of this fact, because it was material to the effect on his conscience. Again, the Court ruled, unintentional conduct may be a breach of a common law duty of skill and care, but it is not a breach of trust.

Conclusion

Mothew is an important case in the challenging area of fiduciary duties. The lucid judgment of Millett LJ provides a very useful account – and a few definitions and explanations – of the limits of these duties and of claims made in respect of them.

It is an undisputable fact that more and more claimants nowadays are seeking to argue that they should be treated as beneficiaries of a fiduciary duty. As has been indicated, there are a number of reasons for this, for example, the range of remedies available is wider than that offered by the law of contract or tort. In addition, while breaches of trust or fiduciary duty must cause the loss complained of, the tests of causation and remoteness are not as onerous as those for negligence or breach of contract; the question which has to be asked is not what position the plaintiff would have been in had the negligence not occurred or if the contract had been performed, but rather whether the loss would have been sustained but for the breach of trust or fiduciary duty. The use of fiduciary liability as a 'long stop' in cases where a sufficient remedy is not available by any other means is common, though is not to be admired (for a full discussion see Hayton). Rulings in equity, and the common law, nowadays should be based on consistent principle and rationality, not on the length of the Chancellor's foot!

FURTHER READING

Primary sources

Bristol and West Building Society v. Mothew [1998] Ch 1

Bristol and West Building Society v. May, May and Merrimans [1996] 2 All ER 801

Downs v. Chappell [1997] 1 WLR 426

Permanent Building Society v. Wheeler [1994] 14 ACSR 109

Target Holdings v. Redferns [1996] AC 421

Westdeutsche Landesbank Girozentrale v. Islington London Borough Council [1996] AC 669

Secondary sources

Barnett, A. (2003) 'The Soliciting Solicitor' Part 1 (2003) 154, *NLJ*, 393.

Burrows, A. (2002) 'We Do This at Common Law and That in Equity' (2002) *OJLS*, 22 (1).

Conaglen, M. (2005) 'The Nature and Function of Fiduciary Loyalty' (2005) *LQR*, 121 (Jul), 452.

Hayton, D. (1997) 'Fiduciaries in Context' in Birks, P., *Privacy and Loyalty*, Clarendon Press, Oxford.

Investment by trustees

Nestlé v. National Westminster Bank
[1993] 1 WLR 1260, [1994] 1 All ER 118

Meryl Thomas, Birmingham City University

Bears don't live on Park Avenue

(Bernard Baruch)

Historical background to investment by trustees

A trust must be effectively managed by the trustees. The trustees cannot behave in relation to the trust as they would were it their own property. Rules of equity have evolved and developed to control the behaviour of the trustees in relation to the management of the trust, and these rules have been supplemented by legislation. Nowhere is this more clearly demonstrated than in the area of trustee investment.

A trustee is under a duty to follow the terms of a trust, and this applies to the investment of the trust fund. Historically the trust deed itself marked the limits of the trustee's powers of investment. If the settlor authorised investments in property of a hazardous nature then the trustee could invest in such; if the settlor prohibited investments, even of the safest kind, then the prohibition bound the trustee. Within these limits a rule developed that the trustee must act like a prudent man of business. The Court of Chancery decided that a prudent man of business would invest in 3% Consolidated Bank Annuities. So in the absence of an express clause to the contrary, this was the investment the trustees should make.

Over a period of time Parliament intervened and increased the range of investments available to the trustee in the absence of an express clause. The Trustee Act 1893, section 1 allowed for 15 types of investment to be made (subject to a contrary intention in the trust deed), and the Trustee Act 1925, section 1 largely reflected section 1 of the 1893 Act, but added three more types. To a modern reader the range of investments in these Acts is surprisingly narrow (and safe), with no allowance being made for the investment in equities (shares). The trustees could principally invest in fixed interest securities and loans secured on land and buildings. Undoubtedly these Acts reflected the investment climate of the day.

The Trustee Investments Act 1961, at the time it was introduced, was revolutionary. It was the first statute to permit the trustees, in the absence of an express clause, to invest in shares and wider forms of investments. The object of the Act was to allow trustees to invest in assets with greater potential for return, without there being any undue risk to the capital. The Act, by the time the current law contained in the Trustee Act 2000 came into effect, seemed stale and complex, with the trust fund having to be valued and divided into narrow range investments (which represented safe investments, such as gilts and government bonds) and wider range investments (namely, equities, provided they fulfilled certain restrictive conditions). Originally the maximum that could be invested in equities was 50% of the fund, but by the Trustee Investments (Division of Fund) Order 1996, this was increased to 75%. It was against this legislative background that the case of *Nestlé* was heard.

Facts of the case

The trust in **Nestlé** took the form of a family settlement. The testator, by his will, gave his widow (W) a life interest in the family home and a tax free annuity of £1,500 for the duration of her widowhood. On W's death the home was to be sold and the proceeds of sale and the capital from the annuity fund would fall into residue. The testator's two sons, G and J, were each entitled to half the income generated from the residue fund for life. The capital of each son's share was to be held on trust for his children, and if he failed to produce any, his share would accrue to the other son. Such trusts were common in the seventeenth to nineteenth centuries, since they enabled landed families to preserve their wealth and power, and they depended very much on the trustees acting fairly between the different classes of beneficiaries and choosing investments which would provide a reasonable income for the life tenant and at the same time maintain the capital value for the remainderman.

In this settlement the National Provincial Bank (later the National Westminster Bank) was appointed trustee, and the trustee was given an express power of investment which allowed the trustee, *inter alia*, to invest in ordinary shares in companies incorporated in the UK.

W died in 1960. J died in 1969. G died in 1972, without any children. The appellant was J's only child, and she became entitled to the whole fund. The value of the fund in 1922 (when the settlement came into existence) was about £50,000 (the equivalent of about £1 million at 1988 values). The value of the fund in 1986 was £269,203. The appellant claimed that, had the fund been managed with proper care, it would have been worth £1.8 million, and she brought an action that the failure to make appropriate investments was a breach of trust. The appellant failed in her action.

Misunderstanding and failure to review the investments

The appellant's main claim against the bank was twofold. Firstly, she claimed the bank misunderstood the true extent of its investment powers in that it believed that the term 'company' in the investment clause was limited to certain types of companies only; and, from 1961 onwards it mistakenly believed that the Trustee Investments Act 1961 governed its powers of investment. Secondly, she claimed that the bank failed to carry out regular reviews of the investment of the annuity fund. The court accepted both these arguments, and added that had the trustee taken legal advice or asked the court for directions there was no doubt that its mistake would have been revealed (since the Trustee Act 2000 section 5 a trustee must obtain and consider advice, unless he concludes that in the circumstances it is unnecessary to do so, see *post*). Despite this, however, the appellant surprisingly was not afforded a remedy by the court. Staughton LJ said, '. . . the misunderstanding of the investment clause and the failure to conduct periodic reviews do not . . . , afford [the plaintiff] a remedy . . . they were not, however, without more, breaches of trust. [The plaintiff] must show that, through one or other or both of those causes, the trustees made decisions which they should not have made or failed to make decisions which they should have made' (pages 133–134). Likewise Dillon LJ referred to Megarry VC in *Cowan* v. *Scargill* where the latter said, '. . . if trustees make a decision upon wholly wrong grounds, and yet it subsequently appears . . . that there are, in fact, good reasons for supporting their decision, then I do not think that they would incur any liability'.

The court set an almost impossibly high standard in **Nestlé** (see *post*, next section), asking the appellant to demonstrate that a loss resulted from the bank *failing to make decisions it should have made*. Staughton LJ made it clear that the Bank's performance was not to be judged with hindsight. It is conceded that investment philosophy during the period of 1921–1959 was certainly very different from that in the latter years of the trust: equities were regarded as risky in the 1920s and 1930s and inflation was low. Hence a portfolio low in equities would not have been unusual. Nevertheless, the appellant adduced evidence that the Barclay de Zoete Wedd (BZW) equity index had risen by 659% between 1922 and 1960, while the equities in the fund had only increased by 419%. The BZW index represents a calculation of the performance of the leading shares. Companies are removed and added to it depending on their performance, and it would be difficult for this trust fund (or any small to medium-sized trust fund) to match or better this index since it was too small. Thus the court refused to accept that any loss should be based on the difference between the value of the trust fund and the value of the shares in the BZW index. A different index, however, for example, one based on the average performance of a broad selection of ordinary shares would not, it is suggested, have presented such a problem, and may have afforded the appellant a stronger argument.

A further point made by the appellant was that the bank's misunderstanding of the extent of its investment powers resulted in it investing the annuity yielding part of the fund only in bank and insurance company shares. Diversification into other sectors of the market was not made, and the appellant claimed she should be compensated for the loss of chance of a gain that might have been made were the equities diversified beyond the bank and insurance shares. The court once again rejected this argument. Dillon LJ said that if the bank had invested the whole of the annuity fund in fixed interest securities, and none in equities for the entire period of 1922–1960, then, on the evidence loss would clearly be proved. In such a case the bank would have to make good to the trust 'fair compensation' (presumably by reference to the loss caused to the trust estate) for failure to follow a proper investment policy. This illustrates the conservative approach of the court to investment principles in a family settlement. It will clearly sanction a trustee investing in a manner that does not generate a high income or capital yield, and one where 'preservation of the trust fund will outweigh success in its advancement' (*per* Leggatt LJ), but it is unclear whether this preservation must be in real or nominal terms.

6

EQUITY AND TRUSTS

The prudent man of business

Undoubtedly linked to the appellant's inability to discharge the burden of proof sufficient to demonstrate a breach of trust was the general duty imposed on the trustee when choosing investments. The standard was formulated by Lindley LJ in *Re Whiteley*, where he said, 'The duty of a trustee . . . is to take such care as an ordinary prudent man would take if he were minded to make an investment for the benefit for other people for whom he felt morally bound to provide.' Dillon LJ in *Nestlé* pointed out that the principle remains applicable irrespective of the width or scope of the investment clause. The idea of prudence stems from nineteenth century case law, and emphasises that trustees should be cautious in their approach to investment, and avoid risk. The problem with this is that it can legitimately sanction inactivity and slothfulness, as it did in *Néstle* and the standard is unrealistically high. It can be argued that the very nature of investment activity attracts risk, albeit that some investments are more risky than others. The standard was altered somewhat by *Bartlett* v. *Barclays Bank*, where it was made clear that risk was allowed, but that the trustees had to avoid investments that were of a hazardous nature. The combined effect of *Bartlett* and *Nestlé* is that the trustees must focus on protection of the trust fund and steady growth.

Hence a claimant, when seeking to prove a breach of trust in relation to investment by the trustees, faces an uphill battle to prove their claim, and, in the absence of severe financial loss to the beneficiaries, it seems that the court will be reluctant to intervene. This reluctance clearly illustrates the court's refusal to review investment decisions made by the trustees, a reluctance which the court exhibits in relation to the exercise of discretions generally by the trustees (see *Gisborne* v. *Gisborne*). At one level in *Nestlé* the appellant failed because she did not adduce the correct type of evidence and the quality of evidence needed to discharge an impossibly high burden of proof, but it is doubtful whether she would have succeeded in her action even if the evidence had been more robust, because of the relationship between evidence and the prudent man of business test.

The Trustee Act 2000

The Trustee Act 2000 was passed as a result of the Law Commission Report No. 260, 'Trustees Powers and Duties' 1999. The Report said that '. . . the law governing the powers and duties of trustees has not kept pace with the evolving economic and social nature of trusts . . .' (para. 1.1). This is illustrated very well in relation to investment by the *Nestlé* case itself.

Section 4 of the Act introduces the 'Standard Investment Criteria' (SIC), and the trustees must have recourse to these whether they are investing under the Act or an express investment clause. The SIC aim at providing a degree of protection for the beneficiaries, given that the Act has introduced a much wider power of investment than under the previous law. (See Section 3 of the Act, which widens the trustee's statutory power of investment and says that the trustee can 'make any kind of investment that he could make were he absolutely entitled to the property'.) Section 4 says that the trustees *must* from time to time review the investments of the trust, and consider whether, in the light of the SIC, the investments ought to be varied. The SIC are not new: they are either 'borrowed' from the Trustee Investments Act 1961, or they codify some of the principles expounded in *Cowan* v. *Scargill*.

The SIC are as follows:

(i) the trustee must consider the suitability to the trust of investments of the same kind as any particular investment proposed to be made or retained and of that particular investment as an investment of that kind, and

(ii) The trustees must also consider the need for diversification of investments of the trust, insofar as is appropriate to the trust in question.

What this means is that if the trustees decide that an investment in shares is a suitable investment, they must first look at the various sectors that are available to invest in, for example, banking, oil etc. (you might like to look at the *Financial Times* for a full list of the companies listed on the UK stock exchange, and the various sectors). If the trustees think that retail companies are a suitable investment for the trust, they must further consider whether an investment in a given company (for example, Marks and Spencer or Next) is suitable. The second aspect of the SIC is the need for diversification of investments, insofar as it is appropriate to the trust in question. The larger the trust the more diversification the trustees can make, and *vice versa*.

Section 1 of the Trustee Act 2000 has, it seems, altered the standard of care from that of a prudent man of business. The object of the section is to increase the range and choice of investments available to invest in, which the prudence test limited. The trustee must now exercise 'such care and skill as is reasonable in all the circumstances', so the standard has moved from prudence to reasonableness. But the test is not one of 'objective' reasonableness, but rather 'subjective' reasonableness in that the 'knowledge and expertise that [the trustee] has or holds himself out as having' is taken into account. Hence, if the trustee acts 'in the course of a business or profession' then 'any special knowledge or experience that it is reasonable to expect of a person acting in the course of that kind of business or profession' is also taken into account. The Act attempts to impose greater responsibility and hence liability on professional trustees (although in practice it may not achieve this since their liability may be limited by an express clause – see *Armitage v. Nurse*), and reflect the decisions prior to the introduction of the Trustee Act 2000 which were commensurate with the idea of greater liability being attached to a professional trustee receiving remuneration for his office (see *Re Waterman's Wills Trusts* and *Barlett v. Barclays Bank Co. Ltd (No. 1)* at page 534). The Court of Appeal in the *Nestlé* ignored this point in that it was not discussed, and therefore no notice was taken of the fact that the trustee in the case was a bank.

This leaves us posing the question, if the provisions of the Trustee Act 2000 had been in force at the time the *Nestlé* was heard, would the outcome of the case have been different? It is clear that the court believed that the bank had failed to appreciate the scope of its investment powers and to review the investments on a regular basis. This behaviour would clearly breach the SIC in the new Act. But the action in *Nestlé* failed because of the appellant's failure to prove loss, not only because the bank had failed to seek advice on the investment clause, had misunderstood the investment clause and had omitted to conduct regular reviews, but also because the trustees made decisions they should not have made or failed to make decisions they should have made. It would seem that the Trustee Act 2000 does nothing to affect this; and that the appellant would still encounter the evidential problem of

6

EQUITY AND TRUSTS

showing that she had suffered a loss as a result of the decisions made by the trustees. Since the standard of care has changed, however, rather than making careful and cautious investment decisions the trustees can take a reasonable risk in order to make a profit.

Duty to act fairly between life tenant and remainderman

This duty still exists in relation to modern-day trusts, and it is a product of the family settlement trust, which we talked about earlier. The duty means that the trustee must act in an even-handed manner between the tenant for life and the remainderman, favouring neither one above the other in the investments he makes, i.e., he should not make investments that generate a high income yield at the expense of capital growth and *vice versa*. The case of *Nestlé* illustrates this principle very clearly. Hoffmann J, at first instance said,

> A trustee must act fairly in making investment decisions which may have different consequences for different classes of beneficiaries . . . They are, for example, entitled to take into account the income needs of the tenant for life or the fact that the tenant for life was a person known to the settlor and a primary object of the trust whereas the remainderman is a remoter relative or stranger. Or course, these cannot be allowed to become the overriding considerations but the concept of fairness between the classes of beneficiaries does not require them to be excluded.

Staughton LJ in *Nestlé* said that it is not always easy to decide what is an equitable balance between the beneficiaries. He said that the personal circumstances of the beneficiaries can be taken into account. If a life tenant is living in penury and the remainderman has ample wealth, then the trustee can take this into account. In *Nestlé* itself one of the dominant considerations for the trustees was the fact that the life tenants (G and J) were living abroad, and that the fund could be invested in such a manner as to exempt them from certain UK taxes. Staughton LJ said that this was a factor that the trustees should bear in mind, but that it would rarely justify more than a modest degree of preference for income paid gross over capital growth. Furthermore, the trustees should bear in mind that the life tenants might return to the UK (as happened in this case) and the tax benefit would then be lost.

Conclusion

Nestlé is bemusing in that both Dillon and Leggatt LJJ were contemptuous in their criticism of the bank's behaviour, and yet they failed to hold the bank liable for any loss occasioned by breach of trust. This is all the more surprising given that the bank was a paid trustee, of whom a higher standard of knowledge and responsibility is expected. It seems that the technical shortcomings of the appellant's evidence and the unduly high standard of prudence thwarted the appellant's case.

FURTHER READING

Primary sources

Armitage v. Nurse [1998] Ch 241

Bartlett v. Barclays Bank [1980] Ch 515

Cowan v. Scargill [1985] Ch 270

Gisborne v. *Gisborne* (1877) 2 App Cas 300

Nestlé v. *National Westminster Bank* [1994] 1 All ER 118

Re Waterman's Wills Trusts [1952] 2 All ER 1054

Re Whiteley (1886) 33 Ch D 347

Secondary sources

Kenny, A. (1993) 'Are a Bank Trustee's Fees Performance Related?' [1993] *Conv*, 63.

Lazarides, M. (1994) 'Banker-Customer: Trustees' [1994] *JIBL*, N64.

Stauch, M. and Watt, G. (1998) 'Is There Liability for Imprudent Trustee Investment?' [1998] *Conv*, 352.

6

Tracing

Foskett v. *McKeown* [2001] 1 AC 102

Caroline Sawyer, Oxford Brookes University

The villain of this piece was dead before the problem was discovered, and the parties to the proceedings were his innocent victims. Timothy Murphy had taken out a life insurance policy for £1 million, for which he had to pay premiums of £10,220 per year. When he died, the policy would pay out either £1 million or, if it was more, the value of the units of investment notionally allocated under the terms of the policy. The proceeds of the policy would belong to Mr Murphy. He settled them on trust for his wife and his mother, subject to a power for Mr Murphy to appoint the proceeds to a class of people including his wife, his mother and his children, but excluding himself. Later he appointed the proceeds as to one-tenth for his wife and the rest for his three children equally.

Five premiums were paid before Mr Murphy died. He paid the first two himself out of his own money. It was not clear where the next one was paid from. The last two were paid by Mr Murphy out of money he had misappropriated from business deals. He had got access to this money by getting involved, with a Mr Deasy, in a building scheme in Portugal. Some 220 prospective purchasers paid Mr Murphy and Mr Deasy for their plots. The arrangement was that the money would be held in a separate account for them until either the development was completed and the plots were transferred to them or the money was repaid with interest. The development was never carried out, and when the money came to be refunded it was found that some of it had been spent, including on the fourth and fifth premiums of Mr Murphy's life insurance policy. It was possible to trace the payments through various bank accounts and show that it was those purchasers' money that had been used.

When Mr Murphy died, £1,000,584.04 was paid out on the life insurance policy. The purchasers of the plots in Portugal claimed to trace their premiums into a share of the policy proceeds, saying that as at least 40% of the premiums had been paid with their money, they were entitled to at least 40% of the proceeds. The trial judge agreed with them. The Court of Appeal held, however, though only by a majority, that they were entitled only to have the money improperly used to pay the premiums back, with interest, out of the policy proceeds. The purchasers appealed claiming the proportionate share of the proceeds, and the children cross-appealed claiming that the purchasers had no interest in the proceeds at all, as they had also successfully claimed proprietary interests in the land in Portugal as a result of the transactions.

The judgments in the case

The leading judgment, given by Lord Millett, is set out last. He considered the case to be 'a textbook example of tracing through mixed substitutions'. The money paid in premiums consisted partly of Mr Murphy's own money and partly of the purchasers' money, and was 'inextricably mixed' so that the purchasers' money was represented by 'an indistinguishable part' of the sum that would become payable by the insurance company on the death of Mr Murphy. Lord Millett looked first of all at how the purchasers' interest would be established, through following, which he distinguished carefully. Following means looking at the same, identified asset; this would not work for the claimants because the identity of the purchasers' money was lost within the bank and the insurance company. Tracing means identifying a new asset which substitutes for an old one. This was more plausible, as the purchasers were claiming on the new asset constituted by the debt owed by the insurance company. If tracing was established it meant that the remedy was to give the purchasers back what was theirs, rather than there being any discretion in the court in finding what they should get.

An important element of the judgment hinges on the analysis of money in a bank account. It is not money at the bank as such, because the money belongs to the bank. What belongs to account holders is the right to claim payment to the value standing to their accounts. Tracing therefore is not of the money but of its value. 'Tracing', says Lord Millett,

> is thus neither a claim nor a remedy. It is merely the process by which a claimant demonstrates what has happened to his property, identifies its proceeds and the persons who have handled or received them, and justifies his claim that the proceeds can properly be regarded as the claimant's property. It enables the claimant to substitute the traceable proceeds for the original asset as the subject matter of his claim. But it does not affect or establish his claim.

For this reason, he said, there was nothing particularly legal or equitable about tracing either, there was no sense in maintaining different rules of tracing in law and equity, and 'one set of tracing rules is enough'.

Lord Millett also discussed the difference between unjust enrichment and tracing. A claimant in unjust enrichment does not have to show that the defendant has the beneficial interest in the claimant's property or its proceeds, but does have to show that the defendant has been unjustly enriched. Such a defendant who has changed his position in reliance on the transaction may have a defence. Conversely a defendant in tracing may not have been enriched at all, but may have paid the full price for the property. However, if he had notice of the claimant's interest in it, he would still have to give it back.

The simplest tracing situation is where property is misappropriated by a trustee who uses it to acquire an alternative item. The beneficiary may then choose whether to have that new property or to sue the trustee in breach of trust; the new asset may be used as security for the money recoverable. The claimant has the choice which to pursue, and the choice will no doubt depend on whether the new property is more valuable than the old. Lord Millett then discussed the more complicated situation where the trust property is only part of the purchase price of the new asset. He considered that it does not matter at what point the mixing of funds takes place. A donee can never obtain a better title than the donor, and a donor who is a trustee can never profit from his trust. Lord Millett

6

EQUITY AND TRUSTS

dismissed the idea that a beneficiary whose trustee mixes funds can never have more than a lien - that is, cannot claim an equitable interest in the new asset. 'In my view the time has come to state unequivocally that English law has no such rule.' In this case, the purchasers could claim a beneficial interest in the funds obtained by the misuse of their equitable property, and because the timing did not matter they need not show that their property had contributed to an increase in the value of the asset in question (the policy proceeds). The children were volunteers, so bound by the equitable interests. The purchasers of the Portuguese plots took a rateable interest in the proceeds of the insurance policy.

It was important, said Lord Millett, to note that the purchasers traced their money firstly into the premiums and then into the insurance money, not both at once. The purchasers had an interest in the policy even before it was realised following Mr Murphy's death. As to the question of whether it mattered who paid which premium, Lord Millett thought not, and that the nearest analogy was with an instalment purchase. The death benefit was the result of the policy being in place and the various premiums paid, and identifying the precise premium which prevented the policy from lapsing was irrelevant. The ownership of the policy should be identifiable at all points from inception to maturity, not only in the light of events. Accordingly Lord Millett agreed with the minority view expressed in the Court of Appeal by Morritt LJ, that the purchasers and the children were entitled to the proceeds of the policy in the proportions that their money and their father's money respectively had paid for the premiums. Moreover, where property was mixed, the overall value of the resulting property would be divided based on the relevant proportions, not on the price of what was put in. In the case of unit-linked policies, he thought the division should be in accordance with the number of units allocated to each premium. The investment element of the sum would be divided with reference to the value at maturity of the units allocated in respect of each premium, and the rest divided rateably in proportion to their contributions to the premiums. However, the precise division of the proceeds had not been argued and he was content for it to be in proportion to the payment of the premiums.

Lord Browne-Wilkinson, who gives the first judgment in the case, had at first been inclined to agree with the Court of Appeal, but explained that he had changed his mind after reading Lord Millett's judgment. He found that there was, however, a question as to whether the purchasers would indeed get a proportionate share of the policy proceeds, because the policy would not have lapsed had the last premiums not been paid, as the payment of the first two was sufficient, given that Mr Murphy died so soon. The children had suggested that the purchasers would be unjustly enriched if they were given a proportionate share of the proceeds rather than merely their money back, because they had not been expecting more than their money back with interest and they would therefore be getting a 'windfall' instead. Lord Browne-Wilkinson said there was nothing unjust about a 'windfall' that came as a consequence of the ownership of property.

Lord Steyn considered first the relative moral claims of the purchasers and the children, but both were innocent parties. He referred to the academic literature on tracing. In particular, he approved of Peter Birks' views that there was no need to distinguish between legal or equitable tracing. Having traced the asset, one could then simply ask what rights a claimant could practically assert. At that point, the question might entail asking whether those rights were equitable or legal, or personal or proprietary. He also approved the judgments of Sir Richard Scott CV and Hobhouse LJ, as he then was, who in the Court of Appeal had analysed the claim of the purchasers to a proportionate share of the proceeds of the policy and found that they were analogous to a claim made by a beneficiary whose trust money had been used to improve the trustee's house: if the wrongfully-made payments had not improved the value (and they had not) then, although there was a claim for the return of the money with interest, there was no claim to a rateable share in the value of the house. The purchasers were, however, not arguing that their money had improved the value of the proceeds, but that they were part of a common fund used to purchase the policy, and that was why they were entitled to a proportionate share in the proceeds. This was the analysis taken in the Court of Appeal by Morritt LJ, which did not impress Lord Steyn. He said: 'The purchasers' money did not 'buy' any part of the death benefit. On the contrary, the stolen moneys were not causally relevant to any benefit received by the children'. Referring to the work of Roy Goode, he said: 'Justice does not support the creation to the prejudice of trade creditors of a new proprietary right in the surrender value of the policy.' Because the purchasers had suffered no loss through the use of their money in the payment of the policy premiums, justice did not require them to have a proportionate share in the proceeds, though they were entitled to the return of their money with interest.

Lord Hope, who also discussed the academic literature on tracing, dealt more fully with the children's claim that the purchasers had no claim at all to the policy proceeds. He found that the establishment of the proprietary claim to the land in Portugal was an entirely separate issue, and there had not been, as the children claimed, an election by the purchasers to take that instead of an interest in the policy proceeds. Lord Hope considered that there was no reason to regard the payments out of the purchasers' money as setting up a claim to a proportionate share but, like Lord Steyn, considered that the purchasers did have the right to claim reimbursement from the proceeds. As to the principal question as to whether the purchasers could claim a proportionate share of the proceeds rather than merely repayment of the sums they had put in, Lord Hope thought this really a question of the equities affecting each party. Because the purchaser could not show that their money contributed to the amount paid to the trustees of the policy, they could not show that they had any proprietary right to a proportionate share of the proceeds. As to the competing equities between the purchasers and the children, this was a contest between two innocent parties: the purchasers had made a small but involuntary contribution; the children had made no contribution at all. Again, the purchasers' argument failed because the payments made out of their money did not increase the fund itself. The children's innocence also meant that an argument for a proportionate share based on unjust enrichment failed. Lord Hope also tried to apply Roman law to the circumstances of this case, using the doctrines of 'commixtio' and 'confusio'. He did not feel that this worked, however, largely because the Romans dealt in physical objects rather than the incorporeal, but also because even if the rules could be applied to a chose in action such as that in issue in this case, he still did not feel that the answer would have been clear to or unanimously held by Roman lawyers.

Lord Hoffmann was inclined to agree with Lord Millett, except on the way that the proportion of the proceeds that belonged to the children was calculated. He thought the calculations

6

EQUITY AND TRUSTS

formulated in the insurance policy itself were unrealistically complex, and should be regarded as something to be used only if the particular event did happen, in order to calculate what should then be paid out. Lord Hoffmann held that although one contingency was the death of Mr Murphy, that death did not of itself affect the proprietary interests in the proceeds.

This case therefore sees the House of Lords finding that the beneficiaries' claim succeeded on the basis of property rights rather than on the basis of a claim that the children would be unjustly enriched if they were to keep all the proceeds save the wrongly-paid premiums, as emphasised by Lord Millett when referring to the beneficiaries' 'hard-nosed property rights' (para. 109). The majority view was that the beneficiaries' money was used together with the deceased's to acquire the policy, so the beneficiaries and the deceased's children (who were volunteers) shared the proceeds. The dissenting minority disagreed, however, that the misapplied money could be traced into the acquisition of the policy, so in their view only the premiums were recoverable by the beneficiaries. The judgment put an end to the distinction between beneficiaries' rights where the property in issue had been acquired using different mixtures of funds. Previously, where their funds were used along with those of other innocent parties, the property acquired would be shared proportionately to what was put in, whereas when the other party was the trustee who had misapplied the funds, a proportionate claim could not be made on the assets acquired. Lord Millett held that in the latter circumstances the beneficiaries could choose whether to claim a proportionate share or satisfaction of the missing money (para. 124). The beneficiaries therefore succeeded in claiming 40% of the proceeds of the policy, rather than merely refunding of the money used to pay two of the premiums.

FURTHER READING

Primary source

Foskett v. *McKeown* [2001] 1 AC 102

Secondary sources

Berg, A. (2001) 'Permitting a Trustee to Retain a Profit' [2001] 117, *LQR*, 366–371.

Birks, P. (1997) 'The Necessity of a Law of Tracing' in Ross Cranston (ed.) *Making Commercial Law: Essays in Honour of Roy Goode*, Oxford University Press.

Goode, R. (1998) 'Proprietary Restitutionary Claims' in Cornish, W., Nolan, R., O'Sullivan, J. and Virgo, G. (eds) *Restitution: Past, Present and Future*, Hart Publishing.

Stevens, J. (2001) 'Vindicating the Proprietary Nature of Tracing' (2001) *Conv*, 94–102.

Knowing receipt

Bank of Credit and Commerce International (Overseas) Ltd and International Credit and Investment Company (Overseas) Ltd v. Chief Labode Onadimaki Akindele
[2001] Ch 437

Caroline Sawyer, Oxford Brookes University

Dubious financial schemes are far from unknown, but the broad scale on which they were carried out by the Bank of Credit and Commerce International during the 1980s was quite unusual. The bank was closed down by the Bank of England in July 1991 following a report by the management company Price Waterhouse showing that it had been committing 'widespread fraud and manipulation'. The case of *BCCI* v. *Akindele* was one of the many individual cases that followed the collapse of the bank. Mr Akindele, a prominent Nigerian businessman, had invested ten million United States dollars with the bank through an investment company. Because of the fraudulent activities of the bank, the money was subject to a constructive trust, and the bank's liquidators claimed that Mr Akindele owed $6,679,226.33 plus interest, as a result of his knowing receipt of trust money (or, originally, alternatively in damages for conspiracy to defraud). The relevant area of law was that of liability for the knowing receipt of trust money, and the two questions to be answered in the case were, firstly, what, in fact, Mr Akindele knew or ought to have known or suspected about the money he received and, secondly, what knowledge was required for a person in receipt of improperly paid trust money to be liable to give it back.

The facts

Mr Akindele had made an agreement in 1985 which recited his desire to invest $10 million in banking shares, with a view to the value of those shares growing and giving him a good return on the investment. It also recited that ICIC would invest the money in shares in BCCI on the terms in the agreement. Those terms said that Mr Akindele would invest $10 million through ICIC in BCCI, and would hold the shares for a minimum of two years. The shares would not be properly transferred to him, as the sellers would sign blank transfers and keep the shares in their own names until the transfer to Mr Akindele, or his nominee. Mr Akindele would definitely continue apparently to hold the shares for two years. Up to five years from when he began to hold the shares, he could decide to sell them, and the ICIC company would sell them at a price that would represent a return to Mr Akindele of 15% on his original investment. It was part of the agreement that the ICIC company could buy the shares itself. Mr Akindele could call for the transfer of the shares to his name, or that of a nominee, during the five-year period, and also were he to hold them for more than five years. If that happened, there would be no further obligations among the parties.

What the liquidators of the bank and the investment company later said was that the agreement was a sham. They said that all parties knew that there was never any intention that Mr Akindele would purchase any BCCI shares. The purpose of the agreement was to provide a cover for the investment company to have the use of $10 million for two years, and for Mr Akindele to have a guarantee of a 15% return on his money. They said the agreement was obviously a sham, since it was so obviously artificial that it was clear that Mr Akindele was never really going to buy the shares, and it was also said that the rate of return of 15% was impossibly high. The claim was therefore that any money made by Mr Akindele from the terms of the agreement arose from dishonest transactions and there-fore, in equity, he could not keep the money.

The facts about Mr Akindele's state of mind were found at trial in the Chancery Division, where Carnwath J had found that there was no evidence that Mr Akindele considered the 1985 agreement to be a sham. There was nothing to indicate that holding the shares for the full five years and having them transferred into his name was not within the range of actions he might take. He had, in fact, spent over $330,000 more in taking up a rights issue of BCCI shares a few months after the agreement was made. An expert called to establish that it was reasonable for Mr Akindele to expect a return of 15% could not con-vince the judge, but he was also unconvinced that Mr Akindele had any conception that the arrangement about the shares was anything other than a way of securing his money at a good rate of interest. In 1985, no-one outside the bank had any reason to doubt that BCCI management was operating with integrity. Mr Akindele did not regard the transac-tion as fraudulent, but rather that he thought it reasonable that he, one of a select group of investors, should be offered such an advantageous deal. 'The interest was very high,' said the judge, 'But he was entitled to assume that the bank were offering it in good faith and for proper reasons'. He therefore dismissed the claim.

The bank and the investment company appealed to the Court of Appeal, where Nourse, Ward and Sedley LLJ considered their claim in 2000. Nourse LJ commented that the claimants' evidence had left the court 'in some doubt as to exactly what went on within the BCCI group' (para. 17), but it was agreed that the transaction was underlaid by frauds. The bank needed to be able to present itself as holding more money than it really did, because otherwise there would be problems with depositors and bank regulators, and with the public in general. The bank therefore arranged to buy its own shares through nomi-nees which included the investment company. It paid for the shares with money loaned to it from other companies within its group. Those loans were entered into the accounts of both the lending and the borrowing companies, but were never intended to be repaid or serviced (servicing a loan means paying the interest on it as it falls due). The bank there-fore appeared to have gained the money paid for its shares, and, although it had also incurred the loan to the investment company, nevertheless this made it appear that it was doing good business. The investment company could enter the loan in its paperwork as an asset, so it too looked financially healthier. The problem for the companies was that if these 'dummy' loans were not repaid or serviced, eventually they would have to be written off in the books. At that point the companies, and the group as a whole, would suddenly suffer an apparent loss. From time to time, therefore, it was necessary to make it look as though the loans were operating normally. Money could not be obtained from ordinary bank depositors, because money obtained that way could not be used to service loans. In 1985, needing some money urgently to achieve that, the investment company made the agreement with Mr Akindele which enabled them to use his $10 million to reduce 'dummy' loans and make it appear that everything was operating normally and properly.

In 1988, Mr Akindele sold his shares under the terms of the 1985 agreement. He was paid $16,679,000, representing his original investment plus a return on the money. Unfortunately BCCI had no buyer for his shares and they did not really have the money to repay him. They raised the money by representing the payment as a temporary overdraft to Mr Akindele from BCCI (Overseas), which was later repaid from a loan account held by another individual with the investment company. The claim in the case was therefore for the 15% return on the original investment, on the basis that the whole arrangement was dishonest and Mr Akindele should not be allowed to keep the proceeds of it.

Nourse LJ in the Court of Appeal emphasised that Carnwath J clearly found that Mr Akindele did not know anything about the frauds which undoubtedly lay beneath the 1985 arrangement (para. 28). He knew what the arrangement was, and saw that it gave him an unusually beneficial return, but did not know it was actually fraudulent. The question about whether Mr Akindele's state of mind meant he was liable to repay the money therefore turned on the exact type of knowledge required to establish liability. For that, the Court considered the existing law.

Nourse LJ discussed how Carnwath J had dealt with the tests set out in *Baden* for the necessary state of knowledge: '(i) actual knowledge, (ii) wilfully shutting one's eyes to the obvious and (iii) wilfully and recklessly failing to make such enquiries as an honest reasonable man would make; (iv) knowledge of circumstances which would indicate the facts to an honest and reasonable man; (v) knowledge of circumstances which will put an honest and reasonable man on inquiry. Nourse LJ said that Carnwath J had wrongly omitted to distinguish between knowledge and dishonesty (para. 38), and that his assumption that dishonesty was an essential prerequisite for liability in knowing receipt was incorrect in law. Nourse LJ also referred to the case of *Belmont Finance Corporation*, which concerned even more complex transactions than the present case, and where it had been confirmed that a genuine but unreasonable belief might be innocent. He also referred particularly to *Eagle Trust Plc* v. *SBC Securities Ltd*, in which Vinelott J had said that *Belmont* meant that liability in knowing receipt required only that a person knew he was receiving trust money which was being misapplied. In *Agip (Africa) Ltd* v. *Jackson*, it was said that fraud in a breach of trust was immaterial; what matters is receipt of property knowing that it is trust property which one should not have. Similarly, in *Polly Peck International Plc* v. *Nadir (No. 2)*, it was held that there could be liability in knowing receipt even where the transaction was not fraudulent.

Looking at the recent cases, Nourse LJ posited the idea that constructive knowledge of the breach of trust ought to be enough (para. 54). This would mean that a person would be regarded as being liable for being in knowing receipt of misapplied trust property not only if they knew of the breach of trust, but also if, even though they honestly believed everything was above board, given the circumstances that they did know about, they ought to have realised the funds were being misapplied. But, as Nourse LJ pointed out, the actual decisions did not turn on that. In *Belmont,* actual knowledge was found; and *Agip* was a case on knowing assistance rather than knowing receipt. *Akindele* was therefore the first case in which that court had to consider directly the question of whether a person had to know of the misapplication of trust funds in order to be liable in knowing receipt.

Nourse LJ relied on the 'seminal judgment' of Megarry VC in *Re Montagu's Settlement Trusts*, where he emphasised the difference between the equitable doctrine of notice and the doctrine of constructive trusts. Again, however, that was a case of knowing assistance rather than knowing receipt. Disputing a suggestion in *Brunei Airlines* v. *Tan* that *Baden* was best forgotten, Nourse LJ did suggest it was, however, better suited to knowing assistance than to knowing receipt. The formulation preferred in this case for the requisite state of mind for knowing receipt was 'that the recipient's state of knowledge should be such as to make it unconscionable for him to retain the benefit of the receipt' (paras 69 and 70). So far as Mr Akindele was concerned, it had been found that he regarded the transaction as being an 'arm's-length business transaction', and that the high interest and artificial agreement were not enough to make an honest person necessarily think there must be something dishonest going on. Mr Akindele had neither actual nor constructive knowledge that his receipt of the interest was traceable to any breach of duty by the officials of BCCI, so he was not liable to return the money.

FURTHER READING

Primary sources

Agip (Africa) Ltd v. *Jackson* [1990] Ch 265

Baden, Delvaux and Lecuit and Others v. *Societe Generale pour Favoriser le Developpment du Commerce et de l'Industrie en France SA* [1993] 1 WLR 509

Bank of Credit and Commerce International (Overseas) Ltd and International Credit and Investment Company (Overseas) Ltd v. *Chief Labode Onadimaki Akindele* [2001] Ch 437

Belmont Finance Corporation [1908] 1 All ER 393

Eagle Trust Plc v. *SBC Securities Ltd* [1993] 1 WLR 484

Polly Peck International Plc v. *Nadir (No. 2)* [1992] 4 All ER 769

Re Montagu's Settlement Trusts [1987] Ch 264

Royal Brunei Airlines Sdn Bhd v. *Tan* [1995] 2 AC 378

Secondary sources

Barkehall Thomas, S. (2001) 'Goodbye Knowing Receipt; Hello Unconscientious Receipt' (2001) 21, *OJLS*, 239-265.

Smith, L. (2000) 'Unjust Enrichment, Property, and the Structure of Trusts' (2000) 116, *LQR*, 412.

Tijo, H. (2001) 'No Stranger to Unconscionability' (2001) *JBL*, 299-311.

LAND LAW
(PROPERTY LAW)

Imagine that you are buying a house. You have chosen the house that you like in the estate agent's window and you have arranged a viewing of the property. If you proceed with the sale what will you actually buy? Will you own the land?

In England and Wales all land is owned by the Crown. What you buy is a legal estate and not the land itself. If you buy the freehold estate it means that you hold the bundle of rights in the land that constitute ownership forever. An estate refers to a period of time and with the freehold estate that period of time is forever. You have a perpetual grant and when you die you can pass your freehold estate to your heirs.

Having bought your freehold estate are you bound by any pre-existing rights that may burden your land? For example, suppose a previous owner of your house granted a neighbour a right to walk across the driveway (this could be an easement). Will this easement bind you so that you must allow your neighbour to walk across your drive-way? What if there is a pre-existing restrictive covenant on your land which prevents you from using the land for any business purposes. Will this freehold covenant bind you so that you are unable to use the house for your computer repair business as you had intended? Discovering what estates and interests bind new purchasers of land is a vital part of land law. Two systems of rules exist depending upon whether the legal estate in the land has been registered at HM Land Registry (registered land) or not (unregistered land). The registered land system is replacing the unregistered land system, which will eventually become obsolete.

So you can see that when you buy a house there are many land law issues to be considered. Do you need a mortgage to buy the house? What rights will the mortgagee have in relation to your house? Are there any pre-existing rights in the land that burden the land and may continue to bind you, for example, easements, freehold covenants, leases and licences? Are you buying the house on your own or with a partner? If you and your partner buy a house together you will be co-owners and the property will be subject to a trust of land. What are the implications of holding the property subject to a trust of land? The cases examined in this section of the book provide a vehicle to help explain these principal areas of land law.

CONTENTS FOR LAND LAW

Unregistered land
Kingsnorth Finance Co Ltd v. *Tizard* [1986] 1 WLR 783   327

Overreaching and overriding interests
Williams & Glyn's Bank Ltd v. *Boland* [1981] AC 487;
City of London Bulding Society v. *Flegg* [1988] AC 54   332

Registered title
Abbey National Building Society v. *Cann* [1990] 2 WLR 832   338

Co-ownership
Kinch v. *Bullard* [1999] 1 WLR 423   344

The lease/licence distinction
Street v. *Mountford* [1985] AC 809   349

Contractual licences
Ashburn Anstalt v. *Arnold and Another* [1988] 2 WLR 706   355

Leases – the remedy of forfeiture
Expert Clothing Service and Sales Ltd v. *Hillgate House Ltd* [1986] Ch 340   359

Mortgages – undue influence
Royal Bank of Scotland v. *Etridge (No. 2)* [2002] 2 AC 773   364

Easements
Payne v. *Inwood* (1996) 74 P&CR 42   369

The enforceability of freehold covenants
Rhone v. *Stephens* [1994] 2 AC 310   374

Unregistered land

Kingsnorth Finance Co Ltd v. *Tizard* [1986] 1 WLR 783

Alistair Speirs, Newcastle University

This case is one of the most useful for understanding and explaining some of the key concepts in unregistered land. Central to the case is the distinction between legal and equitable rights. In unregistered land, legal rights bind the whole world. Equitable rights, by contrast, suffer from a comparative disadvantage in that they can be defeated. Historically, the doctrine of notice defined the circumstances in which equitable rights would be lost: equitable rights were good against all persons except a *bona fide* purchaser of a legal estate for value without notice of the right.

The 1925 legislation and the doctrine of notice

The result (that a purchaser for value of a legal estate, provided that he has no notice of an equitable interest, takes free of it) was an inconvenient one. It could result in either of two unsatisfactory outcomes: that the owner of an equitable interest unwittingly lost that interest or that a purchaser found himself unwittingly bound by an equitable interest of which he had no knowledge. For this reason the 1925 legislation sought to reduce the scope of operation of the doctrine of notice. It did so in three ways.

1. By introducing the Land Charges Register for unregistered land (see the Land Charges Act 1972 (LCA) (replacing the 1925 Act)). 'Commercial' interests such as easements or covenants must, generally, be registered or will be void as against a purchaser. Notice does not play a part (see *Midlands Bank* v. *Green*).

2. By making 'family' interests (interests under a trust) overreachable (see ss.2, 27 Law of Property Act 1925 (LPA)). Such interests are detached from the land and attached to the purchase price at the moment of sale, subject to one proviso: the purchaser must pay at least two trustees. Provided that he does so he need not worry about such equitable interests.

3. By the introduction of registration of title (see the Land Registration Act 2002 (LRA) (replacing the 1925 Act)). The doctrine of notice has no role in registered land. None at all. Ever.

The residual role for notice

Does the doctrine of notice have any role in modern-day land law? The answer is that, although the 1925 legislation did quite a good job in limiting its role, the doctrine still lives, albeit in a much-reduced capacity. It has a residual role in unregistered land in the following circumstances.

1. When 'commercial interests' are not registrable under the LCA 1972. Examples of such interests are covenants and easements created before 1926 (see s.2(5) LCA) and interests gained through an estoppel (see *ER Ives* v. *High*).

2. When 'family' interests are not overreached because the purchaser fails to avoid the proviso above. If a purchaser does not pay two trustees then any such interests will not automatically be detached from the land. Instead the question of whether or not the purchaser is bound is determined by applying the doctrine of notice.

The categories of notice
It is still important, therefore, to be able to identify whether a purchaser can be said to be 'without notice of an equitable interest'. We can identify three subcategories of notice (the substance of which are helpfully set out in s.199 LPA).

1. Actual notice (facts within the knowledge of the purchaser).

2. Constructive notice (facts which the purchaser would have discovered if he had taken reasonable care to inspect both the property itself and its documents of title).

3. Imputed notice (facts which came to the attention of the purchaser's agents (such as a solicitor) during the transaction – or should have done had the agent taken reasonable care).

Tizard, then, deals with this important concept of a purchaser's notice of an equitable interest. Care, however, must be taken because the judge (Judge John Finlay QC, sitting as a judge in the High Court) also refers to the registered land principle of 'actual occupation' (see the entries for *Williams & Glyn's Bank Ltd* v. *Boland* [1981] AC 487 and *City of London Building Society* v. *Flegg*). Title to the property which was the subject matter of *Tizard* was not registered, therefore all references to 'actual occupation' are mere *obiter*.

The facts

The facts of *Tizard* are similar to a significant number of other important cases dealing with a particular three party problem. Mr Tizard was the legal owner of the marital home. His name was on the title deeds and he, therefore, was able to deal with the property. However, the house was bought using both his and his wife's money. This meant that his wife had an interest in the house under a resulting trust. Such a trust arises whenever two or more people contribute to the purchase of an asset (unless a gift is intended) because equity presumes that the parties intend to share ownership of the asset according to their contributions. In *Tizard* the judge held, on the facts, that Mr and Mrs Tizard had contributed to the purchase of the house equally and therefore, in equity, each owned half the property. The position therefore was that Mr Tizard held the house on trust for himself and his wife in equal shares. The ownership of the property can, therefore, be represented diagrammatically as follows:

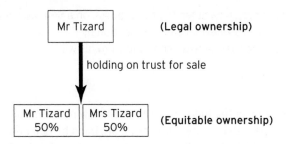

We now need to introduce the third party: the claimant, Kingsnorth Finance Co. Ltd. At a time when Mr Tizard's marriage was breaking down and he had agreed to sell the house and split the proceeds with his wife he, perfidious male, mortgaged the property without his wife's knowledge. Mr Tizard received £66,000 from the claimant in return for granting it a legal mortgage over the house. He then, apparently, emigrated across the Atlantic with the proceeds. The mortgagee, Kingsnorth Finance, sought possession of the house in order to sell it to recoup the sum paid to Mr Tizard for the mortgage. The full position at the time of trial therefore is:

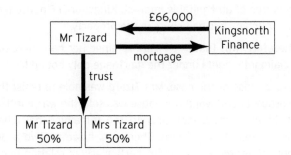

The question for Judge Finlay was whether the mortgagee took free of Mrs Tizard's equitable interest or whether her half share of the equitable ownership was binding upon Kingsnorth. Because a mortgagee is 'a purchaser' and because Mr Tizard was the only trustee (see the second item in 'The residual role for notice' above) the answer was to be found in the doctrine of notice. The case fell squarely into the remaining residual scope which the doctrine has retained post-1925. The question therefore could be narrowed to 'did the claimant purchaser have notice of the wife's equitable interest?'.

The history of the dealings between Mr Tizard and Kingsnorth Finance was, so far as relevant, as follows:

1. Mr Tizard filled in a form in which he indicated that he was single.

2. Kingsnorth Finance instructed a surveyor (Marshall) to inspect the property.

3. At the relevant time Mrs Tizard had moved out of the house to a limited extent. She visited the property every day to give their children meals and sometimes stayed overnight if Mr Tizard was away. Generally, she slept elsewhere but kept most of her clothes at the house.

4. Marshall visited the property, at Mr Tizard's request, on a Sunday. Only Mr Tizard was at the house but Marshall saw evidence of occupation by the children (but not Mrs Tizard). Mr Tizard volunteered that he was separated from his wife.

The decision

On the basis of these facts the judge came to the following conclusions. Firstly, Marshall was the agent of Kingsnorth Finance. As a result, anything he had notice of was automatically imputed to his principal (see 3 under 'The categories of notice' above). Under this principle, since Marshall knew that Mr Tizard was married then Kingsnorth Finance had notice of Mrs Tizard's existence. Taken together, this imputed notice and the declaration by Mr Tizard that he was single put Kingsnorth Finance in the position that they should, reasonably, have enquired whether Mrs Tizard had any interest in the property. Kingsnorth Finance, therefore, had constructive notice of Mrs Tizard's interest in the property (see 2 above).

The result of this analysis was that it was clear that Kingsnorth Finance was not a *bona fide* purchaser of Mr Tizard's legal estate without notice of Mrs Tizard's equitable interest in the property. The element 'lack of notice' was absent. Since only a *bona fide* purchaser without notice takes free of an equitable interest, Kingsnorth Finance did not take free of Mrs Tizard's. It was bound by her half share in the property.

The conclusion, therefore, was that Mrs Tizard retained her half share of the value of the property and the claimant's rights under the mortgage only bound Mr Tizard's share.

That was enough to dispose of the case. Mrs Tizard was able to resist the application for possession of the property and when the house was sold she was entitled to half the proceeds. Kingsnorth Finance could look only to the remaining half share to offset the £66,000 loan which it paid to Mr Tizard. There are, however, two aspects of the case, which, although only *obiter dicta*, are useful, particularly in relation to dealing with problem questions. The first of these relates to constructive notice and the extent to which a purchaser must go in order to satisfy the requirement of reasonable inspection.

Reasonable inspection

As noted above, a purchaser has constructive notice of facts which he ought to have discovered. It is therefore important to know how extensive the purchaser's enquiries and inspections need be. The purchaser will have notice of any fact which falls within the territory delimited by the concept 'reasonable enquiries and inspection'; if the purchaser does discover such facts he has actual notice of them, if not he has constructive notice of them. On this point the judge set the bar for purchasers high. The judge stated that if one of the reasons for an inspection by the purchaser (or his agent) was to discover who was in occupation of the property then a pre-arranged visit may not be sufficient. In order to be safe, therefore, it appears that the purchaser should make a surprise inspection of the property. This, it is submitted, asks too much of purchasers and pushes the concept of reasonable inspection beyond its limits. Judge Finlay, had no need, on the facts of this case, to go so far because Mr Tizard volunteered to Marshall that he had a wife who had moved out.

Under these circumstances Marshall, and therefore Kingsnorth Finance, was put on notice of the existence of a wife who lived at the house until quite recently. It is reasonable to require that a purchaser so informed should make enquiries as to whether the wife has an interest in the property. It does not seem reasonable that a purchaser (or mortgagee) should have constructive notice of a wife's equitable interest merely because he carried out the inspection at a time agreed with the vendor (or mortgagor).

Registered land

The second part of the judgment which contains useful *obiter* is that relating to 'actual occupation'. This is a concept which is important in land, title to which is registered. The concept occupies a role similar to that held by the doctrine of notice in unregistered land but is quite distinct in terms of definition, content and operation. In some circumstances a person with an interest in registered land may lose that interest to a purchaser unless he is in 'actual occupation' in the same way that a person with an interest in unregistered land may lose that interest to a purchaser unless the purchaser has notice of the interest. A more detailed exploration of this registered land concept is to be found in the entry for *City of London Building Society* v. *Flegg*.

Tizard concerned unregistered land, therefore whether Mrs Tizard was or was not in actual occupation for the purpose of the Land Registration Act was entirely irrelevant. However, the most authoritative case in this area (whether the equitable interest of a wife bound a mortgagee), at the time *Tizard* was decided, was *Boland*, a case concerning registered land. The judge drew on *Boland* and considered whether Mrs Tizard could be said to be in 'actual occupation', i.e. had this been registered land would her interest have bound the claimant. Mrs Tizard was not in full-time occupation because she generally slept elsewhere and visited to look after the children. Nonetheless, Judge Finlay had little doubt that she was in 'actual occupation' of the house. *Boland* had decided that a physical presence was necessary but that did not mean, stated Judge Finlay, that a 'continuous and uninterrupted presence' was necessary. As is often the case, the question of whether a person is in actual occupation is one of degree. It can be helpful to note that the degree to which Mrs Tizard was present was considered sufficient, if only in *obiter*.

FURTHER READING

Primary sources

City of London Building Society v. *Flegg* [1988] AC 54

ER Ives Investments Ltd v. *High* [1967] 2 QB 379

Hunt v. *Luck* [1902] 1 Ch 428

Midland Bank Trust Co Ltd v. *Green* [1981] AC 513

Wilkes v. *Spooner* [1911] 2KB 473

Williams & Glyn's Bank Ltd. v. *Boland* [1981] AC 487

7

LAND LAW (PROPERTY LAW)

Williams & Glyn's Bank Ltd v. Boland [1981] AC 487
City of London Building Society v. Flegg [1988] AC 54

Alistair Speirs, Newcastle University

Just as *Tizard* is an enormously helpful case to students tackling a question relating to unregistered land so *Boland* is indispensable to an understanding of the workings of registered land. *Flegg* acts as a refinement to the principles laid down in *Boland*.

Registration of title

The traditional method of proving title was (and still is in relation to unregistered land) a historical one. One established, by searching documents of title, an unbroken chain of transfers ending with the current owner. The law determined how far back it was necessary to go to establish 'good root' of title (now 15 years – see the Law of Property Act 1969 s.23).

This process was inefficient. Each time a property was sold the same investigation of title was required, a wasteful duplication of effort. In order to do away with this process the Land Registration Act 1925 (now replaced entirely by the 2002 Act of the same name (LRA 2002)) introduced a register of title. In respect of registered land one does not need to apply a historical approach to establishing title. One simply asks who does the register record as owner. Furthermore, the register, because it is conclusive (see s.58 LRA 2002), does not merely record ownership of title; registration as owner creates ownership.

The tactic adopted to pursue the goal of shifting land ownership onto the register was a gradual one. Initially only certain (geographical) areas were subject to registration. A property would 'become registered' when it was dealt with (for example, sold) within these areas of compulsory registration. The scope of the scheme was extended until, some 65 years later (1 December 1990), all of England and Wales became subject to compulsory registration. However, a property does not move on to the register until a specified transaction occurs in relation to it (see s.4 LRA 2002). Consequently both registered and unregistered systems run in parallel and the student of land law is required to be able to employ the principles of both.

The guiding principles of the scheme adopted by the LRA 1925 were described by a former Chief Land Registrar as:

1. The mirror principle – the register is designed to reflect all the relevant details relating to ownership of the land and rights in the land which a purchaser, for example, needs to know. As will be seen, the register's mirror is subject to a considerable defect.

2. The curtain principle – interests which a purchaser does not need to know about are kept off the register. The principle of overreaching means that a purchaser does not need to know about 'family' interests in the land (see the explanation, above, under *Tizard*). Interests under a trust are therefore excluded from the register (see s.33 LRA 2002).

3. The insurance principle – the state provides compensation should an error in the register cause loss.

It is the first two of these principles which are called into play by *Boland* and *Flegg*.

The cases

Boland came to the House of Lords as conjoined appeals of two cases, however, the facts of each were materially the same. In each case there was a wife (the principles are entirely independent of gender but these were the facts) who had contributed to the purchase of the matrimonial home and therefore had an equitable interest under a resulting trust, as in *Tizard*. In each case the husband had been created the sole legal owner and had later granted a mortgage to the plaintiff bank in return for a loan. The picture is therefore very similar to that in the unregistered land case *Tizard*:

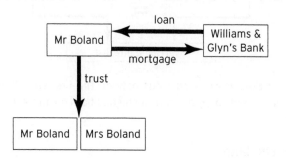

The crack in the mirror

In *Tizard* the question was whether the claimant had notice of Mrs Tizard's right. The doctrine of notice is entirely banished in the realm of registered land. The equivalent question in registered land is whether Mrs Boland had an 'overriding interest' which bound the bank. Overriding interests are third party interests which are not recorded on the register but nevertheless bind a purchaser. They exist in opposition to principle 1 above and can represent a trap to the purchaser. Under the LRA 1925 types of overriding interests were listed in s.70(1) and included such third party rights as easements, leases and, importantly the rights of those in 'actual occupation' (s.70(1)(g)). One of the advances made by the LRA 2002 was to reduce the number and scope of overriding interests in an attempt to reduce the extent of the 'crack in the mirror'. However, rights of those in actual occupation continue to be overriding under Schedule 3(2) of the 2002 Act.

The key ingredients to an overriding interest under s.70(1)(g) were, and now under Schedule 3(2) are (i) an interest in the land (ii) and actual occupation. The full list of ingredients, however, was extended by the 2002 Act and the full recipe can be expressed as shown in the diagram below:

Operation of LRA 2002 Schedule 3(2)

```
              ┌─────────────────────────┐
              │     Interest in land     │
              └─────────────────────────┘
                    +    │
                         ▼
              ┌─────────────────────────┐
              │   Actual occupation by   │
              │     owner of interest    │
              └─────────────────────────┘
                    +    │
                         ▼
              ┌─────────────────────────┐
              │ No enquiry (by purchaser of │
              │ owner of equitable interest) │
              └─────────────────────────┘
                         +
       ┌─────────────────────┐         ┌─────────────────────┐
       │ Occupation by owner  │         │                      │
       │ of interest obvious  │   or    │   Purchaser knows    │
       │ on reasonably careful│         │     of interest      │
       │ inspection by        │         │                      │
       │ purchaser            │         │                      │
       └─────────────────────┘         └─────────────────────┘
                         =
              ┌─────────────────────────┐
              │    Overriding interest   │
              └─────────────────────────┘
```

For the purposes of *Boland* we need focus only on the first two elements. Mrs Boland would have an interest binding on the bank if she had both an interest in the land and was in actual occupation.

An interest in the land

It is important that the third party has a right in the land as opposed to, merely, a personal right (against, for example, the owner or occupier) in relation to the land. A lease is an estate in land; a tenant's rights are attached directly to the land. A license, although possibly superficially similar, is merely a personal right against the occupier of a property. A student who rents a private flat has rights in the flat but a student in university halls has a mere contractual license from the university. A purchaser of the private flat will be bound by the student's right. A purchaser of the university halls cannot be.

In *Boland* the bank argued that the wife's interest, a mere equitable 'minor' interest, was not a right in the land capable of being rendered overriding by the addition of actual occupation. This argument was rejected. Such interests were interests in the land.

Actual occupation

This element can be thought of as occupying a role similar to that of notice in unregistered land. It is, however, quite different in principle; Lord Wilberforce in *Boland* was quite clear: notice has no application, even by analogy, to registered land. The enquiry as to whether a person was in actual occupation is a purely factual one. It focuses upon the presence of the third party and not on what the purchaser or his agent knew or ought to have known.

In *Boland* the bank was able to point to reasonably recent authority which denied that the wife was in occupation on her own account, rather that she was present merely as the 'shadow of her husband'. Lord Wilberforce rightly condemned this doctrine as 'heavily obsolete'. More than one person could be in actual occupation of a property at the same time; the fact that one was dealing with a husband and wife did not mean that their occupation was unified. Mrs Boland was in actual occupation.

A bad result for mortgagees

The result of the case followed from these two findings. At the time the mortgage was granted by Mr Boland, Mrs Boland had an overriding interest: an interest which bound the claimant notwithstanding that it was not protected by entry on the register. Just as in *Tizard* (but for entirely different reasons) the wife's interest bound the mortgagee – her share in the property was not subject to the mortgage.

This was a bad result for mortgagees. Many mortgages had been taken without enquiry of occupiers (wives or otherwise) as to whether they had an equitable interest in the property. Such mortgages did not, following *Boland*, provide the security which had been sought for the loans advanced.

Better results for mortgagees follow

Boland and *Tizard*, however, represented the nadir for mortgagees. There followed a line of cases which softened the blow considerably:

1. In *Paddington BS* v. *Mendelsohn* the court held that where the equitable co-owner knew in advance about the mortgage he or she must be deemed to have intended his or her interest to be subject to the mortgage. This meant that nearly all mortgages granted in order to finance a purchase (as opposed to a mortgage taken out after purchase of the property to raise funds for some other purpose, as in *Boland*) were unaffected.

2. *Abbey National Building Society* v. *Cann* provided two pieces of authority which gave solace to mortgagees.

The first concerned the date on which to test whether the equitable co-owner was in actual occupation. Two dates were in the running. The date the mortgage was created (or in the case of a sale, that the sale was effected) or the (later) date when the register was amended to record the mortgage (or sale). The House of Lords determined that it was the earlier date which was applicable. This avoided a window, between creation of the mortgage and its entry onto the register, during which someone with an equitable interest could go into occupation.

The second concerned the degree of occupation required. Mrs Cann had not been in the property herself but her effects had been moved in 35 minutes before the relevant time. The House accepted that occupation by proxy was possible but held that, on the facts here, the level of occupation was insufficient. What was required was 'a degree of permanence and continuity' and 'acts of a preparatory character carried out by courtesy of the vendor prior to completion' cannot constitute actual occupation.

7

LAND LAW (PROPERTY LAW)

3. In *Lloyds Bank plc* v. *Rosset* both issues (whether the wife had an interest in the property and whether she was in actual occupation) were contested. The Court of Appeal held that she did have an interest in the property and that she was in actual occupation; she had an overriding interest against the bank. The Court of Appeal judgment represents the most authoritative examination of the latter issue because the House of Lords found that it was able to decide the case in favour of the bank on the first issue. It is helpful to set out the four methods by which an equitable interest may be acquired:

(a) under an express trust – this requires signed writing (see s.53(1)(b) LPA 1925);

(b) under a resulting trust – as seen in *Tizard* and *Boland*, the equitable interest is acquired as a result of contributions to the purchase price. The size of the equitable share acquired reflects the share of contributions;

(c) a constructive trust – the elements required here are an agreement (or common intention) to share the beneficial interest plus some act by the claimant of detrimental reliance. The size of share is according to the agreement or intention of the parties;

(d) a proprietary estoppel – this is theoretically distinct from a constructive trust but, as was pointed out in *Oxley* v. *Hiscock*, in the area of equitable co-ownership the analysis is often indistinguishable. A proprietary estoppel arises where the owner encourages the claimant to believe (or fails to discourage her in the belief) that she has an interest in the property plus some act of detrimental reliance by her on the basis of that belief.

In *Rosset* the wife claimed an interest under a constructive trust. Lord Bridge, who gave the only speech, set the test at a high level. He stated that where there was no evidence of an express agreement by the parties (i.e. where there was evidence only of an unspoken agreement or a common intention) the court would look for strong evidence pointing toward the acquisition of an equitable interest. In his view only direct contributions to the purchase price (as opposed to other forms of detrimental reliance such as paying household bills or doing work on a house) would be sufficient. In this case there were no such direct contributions and Mrs Rosset had no interest in the property. The issue of whether she was in actual occupation was therefore immaterial.

4. And so, finally, to *Flegg*. The facts of *Flegg* were similar to *Boland*, but that two couples were involved, rather than one. The purchase of Bleak House was made by a married couple (Mr and Mrs Maxwell-Brown) and the wife's parents (Mr and Mrs Flegg). Both contributed to the purchase but only the former were created legal owners. Unknown to the Fleggs, the Maxwell-Browns mortgaged the property to the claimants. The facts of the case can therefore be represented as follows:

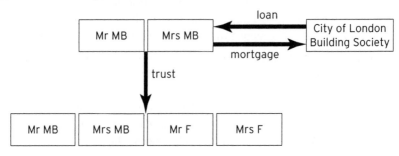

At first sight one might compare this diagram with the equivalent one for *Boland* and draw the conclusion that the same result should apply. The reason the House of Lords held that the Fleggs did not have an overriding interest which bound the Building Society was because of the operation of overreaching. Overreaching causes the interests under a trust to be detached from the land and attached to the purchase monies (or loan in the case of a mortgage) (see s.2 LPA 1925). The reason that this device saved the day for City of London Building Society but not Williams & Glyn's Bank lies in the proviso mentioned under *Tizard* above: the purchaser must pay at least two trustees. Here both Mr and Mrs Maxwell-Brown were trustees. In *Boland* only Mr Boland occupied that position.

Boland raised the spectre of a very large number of defective mortgages. The cases which followed *Boland* gave some comfort to mortgagees. If there were two trustees or the equitable co-owner knew, in advance, of the mortgage then the security was good. Occupation had to be shown to have existed when the mortgage was created and must be more than a fleeting presence. Furthermore, *Rosset* meant that fewer cohabitees than might have been thought had an interest in the property.

FURTHER READING

Primary sources

Abbey National Building Society v. *Cann* [1990] 2 WLR 832

City of London BS v. *Flegg* [1988] AC 487

Eves v. *Eves* [1975] 1 WLR 1519

Hodgson v. *Marks* [1971] Ch 892

Lloyds Bank plc v. *Rosset* [1990] 2WLR 867 (HL); [1989] Ch 350 (CA)

Oxley v. *Hiscock* [2004] EWCA Civ 546; [2004] 3 All ER 703

Paddington BS v. *Mendelsohn* (1985) 50 P&CR 244

Strand Securities v. *Caswell* [1965] Ch 958

Williams and Glyn's Bank v. *Boland* [1981] AC 487

Secondary sources

Freeman, S. (1980) 'Wives, Conveyancers and Justice' (1980) 43, *MLR*, 692.

Rotherham, C. (2004) 'The Property Rights Of Unmarried Cohabitees: The Case For Reform' [2004] *Conv*, 268.

7

LAND LAW (PROPERTY LAW)

Abbey National Building Society v. Cann
[1990] 2 WLR 832

Caroline Sawyer, Oxford Brookes University

Cann came a few years after *Flegg* and was heard at the same time as *Lloyds* v. *Rosset*; judgment in both cases was given on the same day, with cross-references between the two cases. Like both of them, *Cann* strengthens the position of mortgagees. It says that where property is bought with money that is secured by a mortgage, the mortgagee always has priority over the claims of the mortgagor's equitable co-owners.

Priority of co-owners and mortgagees: the background

The problem addressed in *Cann* was the one that arises when the legal owner of mortgaged property fails to keep up the mortgage payments and the mortgagee wants to repossess and sell the house in order to realise their security. The mortgagee can get a possession order against the mortgagor, but if there is someone else living in the house who has an interest in it, removing them may be very difficult if they have not postponed their rights to the mortgagee's rights. The other interest may be a tenancy that the mortgagor has granted, or it may be an equitable share in the property.

Situations like this arise frequently, because the person who buys the legal title to the property needs more money than is available to buy the property or to keep up the mortgage repayments. Prospective mortgagees such as banks and building societies always require mortgagors to tell them of anyone who may be taking an interest in the property, so that they can make sure their interests are postponed, and they always require mortgagors to ask permission before taking tenants or lodgers. But mortgagors do not always tell the mortgagee about the tenant or co-owner, and they do not always tell their tenants or equitable co-owners about the mortgage either. The awkward situation that comes up when the mortgagor defaults on the mortgage payments and the mortgagee tries to repossess the property can be as much of a surprise to the tenant or co-owner as it is to the mortgagee.

If the mortgagee cannot obtain a possession order against everyone living in the house, they cannot sell the house with vacant possession. That would mean the security that the house represented was unlikely to discharge the debt, so the mortgagee's security would be unlikely to guarantee the debt to them as they had expected. The fact that the mortgagor had not performed their side of the mortgage bargain, or had even deliberately deceived the mortgagee, would not affect the rights of the tenant or co-owner, who might well also have been deceived. If this happened frequently, professional mortgagees might become very wary and taking out a mortgage might become very difficult. The social and economic consequences of the mortgage industry not operating properly would be enormous.

Against the idea of defending the rights of mortgagees is that of defending the rights of the third parties – the tenants or co-owners. They may be at risk of losing their home unexpectedly, and may be put at a considerable financial disadvantage. Some old-fashioned tenancies, granted under the Rent Acts, have very advantageous terms which a new tenancy could not replace. A co-owner who loses his interest in land because it has been overreached by a mortgage must look to the legal owners – the mortgagors – for his share of the capital money, but the mortgagors have probably spent it; the mortgagee is probably realising their security because the mortgagors did not have the money to pay their mortgage instalments, and they are probably in considerable debt. If residential tenants or co-owners are frequently dispossessed of their homes, that too can have enormous social and economic consequences. Being evicted is very disruptive and people may find it difficult to keep their jobs and families going; they may also have to be rehoused at public expense.

Establishing priority: the 'registration gap' and the *scintilla temporis*

The legal question of whose interest has priority, where there is a conflict, is in general resolved by looking at the chronological order in which transactions happened, along with the issue of whether the transaction was of a type capable of taking priority over a subsequent transaction. As to establishing the detail of how a property is purchased and mortgaged, before *Cann* went to the House of Lords, the leading case was a Court of Appeal case of the *Church of England Building Society* v. *Piskor*. In that case, the court had to decide whether a mortgagor's tenant had priority over the mortgagee. The tenancy had to have existed before the mortgage was created. The question was whether there was a time-gap between the mortgagor getting his title and that title being mortgaged to the mortgagee. If so, the tenancy could be established in that gap and take priority over the subsequent mortgage.

Thus, in *Piskor*, the court considered the mortgagee's usual requirement that the mortgagor hold a legal title in the property to be mortgaged and held that there was a *scintilla temporis* – a tiny bit of time – between the purchase and the mortgage, and that an interest adverse to the mortgagee could be established, derived from the mortgagor's interest, in that gap. This meant that, when property was bought with the aid of mortgage money, a co-owner, unknown to the mortgagee, who was in occupation would take priority over the mortgagee, unless the interest was overreached by the mortgage (which counts as a 'purchase' within the terms of section 2 of the Law of Property Act 1925) where there were two legal co-owners, as in the case of *Flegg*. A tenant, whose interest could not be overreached, since tenancies are 'commercial' rather than 'family' interests, was also a potential obstacle to the mortgagee realising its security.

The facts in *Cann*

George Cann was buying a house in Mitcham to live in, but was £4,000 short of the purchase price. The shortfall was more than made up by a combination of a contribution to the purchase price by George's mother, Daisy, and a mortgage advance of £25,000 from the Abbey National, which secured the loan by a mortgage on the property on the transfer to George of the legal title. Neither Daisy nor the Abbey National knew of the other's involvement – or, at least, there was no evidence that they did. When George defaulted on the mortgage instalments and the Abbey National tried to repossess the house, Daisy asserted the equitable interest she had acquired by way of resulting trust, by contributing to the purchase price. Daisy referred to the time-gap represented by the *scintilla temporis* between the transfer to George of the legal title and the encumbrance of that title by the mortgage to the Abbey National. She said that, during that time-gap, her equitable interest had become protected by her occupation of the house, and so it took priority as an overriding interest and the Abbey National could not repossess against her.

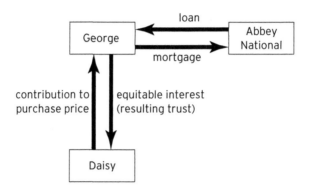

The appeal to the House of Lords was made by Daisy, because she had lost in the Court of Appeal. In the House of Lords, Lord Oliver said that it was 'good conveyancing sense' for the Abbey National to win because the result was then 'just, convenient and certain'. The idea that it was sensible for the mortgagee to win was carried through by the House of Lords, where Daisy finally lost again, on more detailed principles.

The essence of the judgment means that where there is an 'acquisition mortgage' – that is, the mortgage secures the money used to buy the property – the mortgagee's interest will always take priority over any other interest. However, the court had to address and amend several principles of law to achieve that outcome.

Conveyancing in *Cann*

1. Closing the registration gap
The case appeared to be going to turn on whether, on the facts, Daisy was in occupation when the mortgage was made. This meant considering the way that conveyancing worked.

Completion day is the day on which the purchase money is sent. When it is received at the vendor's bank, the deed that transfers the legal estate is completed and the deed is then sent to the purchaser for the purchaser's solicitor to register it. (If the vendor also has a mortgage, it will be paid off by the vendor, usually out of the purchase money received, and there will be a discharge of the vendor's mortgage as well, which will also go to the purchaser's solicitor, or that discharge can be effected electronically.) The purchaser's solicitor will then send all the documents to the Land Registry for registration of the changes to the legal title.

Completion day is still the day on which people move houses. When land titles were unregistered, the making of a deed in relation to unregistered land transferred the title. But, with registered land, the date on which the legal title is transferred is the date when the change of ownership is registered. When the Land Registry receives the registration application, it stamps it with the date of receipt, which then becomes the date used for registration. But that is still a few days after the 'completion' date.

It had been taken previously that the operative date for deciding whether overriding interests were effective was the date of registration. In that situation, a claimant using paragraph (g) of s.70(1) of the LRA 1925 (which dealt with overriding interests, and has now been repealed and replaced by paragraph 2 of Schedule 3 to the Land Registration Act 2002) would almost inevitably have moved in some days previously, on completion day, and therefore established occupation before the time of registration. Actual occupation at the relevant date, which was the date of registration of a purchase, protects the property rights of the occupier against destruction by the purchase. To maintain that the purchase, or mortgage, nevertheless took priority, the House of Lords decided in *Cann*, however, that the mortgage was completed on completion day (although registration is also required to complete a legal mortgage). This meant that the relevant time for establishing actual occupation would therefore be completion day as well, rather than registration day. This still did not apply, however, to the other overriding interests, where the relevant date remained that of registration, as stated in the legislation. This particular point has since been formalised for the Land Registration Act of 2002 (see Schedule 3 para. 2 (c)(i)). Accordingly, the 'registration gap', in which actual occupation might be established by a co-owner to the detriment of a mortgagee or other purchaser, was closed.

2. Abolishing the *scintilla temporis*

However, asserting that the relevant date for Daisy to establish her overriding interest was completion day would still not have been enough, because of the *scintilla temporis*. Daisy's equitable interest would still be established in the momentary gap between the transfer of the legal title to George and his mortgaging it. Daisy would therefore be able to claim an interest in George's new unencumbered title which would override the subsequent encumbrance of the mortgage.

The court decided that, because the Abbey National had provided part of the purchase money, the purchase and the mortgage securing that part of the purchase money were only one transaction and that therefore George never had an unencumbered title. All he ever had was the equity of redemption – the right to pay off the mortgage and reclaim the full, unencumbered legal title. It said, therefore, that Daisy's claim must be subsequent to the mortgage, this result being achieved by the abolition of the *scintilla temporis*.

The overall effect of this judgment was that acquisition mortgages – those securing money used to buy the property from a vendor – would always have priority over all co-owners' equitable interests.

Problems with the judgment in *Cann*

There are some difficulties of legal doctrine inherent in the judgment in *Cann*, besides the decision that the provision of section 70 (1) of the Land Registration Act 1925 that overriding interests were to be applied on the date of registration did not apply to paragraph (g). This is the part of the decision that was regularised by Schedule 3 para. 2 (c)(i) of the Land Registration Act 2002.

First of all, in case it might appear unfair to Daisy to decide that the Abbey National's contribution was all-important and her own contribution of much less consequence, the court also said that she must have known of the existence of the mortgage. However, no evidence of this is mentioned at all. Even were Daisy demonstrably to have known about the mortgage, that is tantamount to importing ideas of notice into registered conveyancing.

Secondly, the idea that all George ever owned was the 'equity of redemption' relies on something that did not survive the 1925 legislation. That effectively abolished the equity of redemption by the provisions of sections 85–87 of the Law of Property Act 1925. Previously, the legal mortgagor had lost his legal title to the property during the mortgage, as it was transferred to the mortgagee as security pending the repayment of the loan (or performance of any other obligation) and the redemption, or release, of the mortgage. During the currency of the mortgage, therefore, the mortgagor had only the right to get the mortgaged property back. After the legal date of redemption, that was an equitable right only. It could, however, be valuable and could be sold – if the mortgaged property was worth £500,000 and could be regained on payment off of a mortgage loan of £150,000, the right to regain the property on payment of £150,000 would be worth £350,000. The 'equity of redemption' was therefore worth £350,000. After 1925, however, the transfer of the legal estate by way of mortgage became impossible. A legal mortgage was carved out of the legal title, which remained with the mortgagor. The value of a property after deduction of the debt secured on it is still called the 'equity', but the concept is really now an equitable right to have the mortgage redeemed: the mortgagor still has the legal title throughout and can mortgage it successively at law. The references to the 'equity of redemption' are not to that post-1925 concept, however, but to a form of property interest that was out of date by the time of the case. The idea of the restructuring of mortgages in the 1925 legislation was exactly to leave the legal estate with the mortgagor, so that he could create further legal mortgages and thus have the opportunity to make the most out of the capital value of his land.

Potential gaps in *Cann*

Cann only solves mortgagees' potential problems with co-owners, not with tenants. A similar practical problem arose in **Barclays Bank v. Zaroovabli** because the Bank had failed to register its mortgage promptly and a statutory tenant asserted a right against it. Though here the Bank had failed to apply to the Land Registry for a period of some years, the same problem could arise in the 'registration gap'. *Cann* and the LRA 2002 amended that only for interests protected by actual occupation (LRA 1925 s.70(1)(g); LRA 2002 Schedule 3, para. 2), not for short legal tenancies (LRA 1925 s.70(1)(k); LRA 2002 Schedule 3, para. 1).

There was also no enquiry as to whether Daisy had paid the deposit, as co-owners who are also relatives often do (because mortgage funds are not available until completion day). Had she done so, she might have established an equitable interest derived from the equitable interest George obtained on exchange of contracts, which could have been protected by actual occupation if she moved in before the moment of completion. This situation remains to be investigated in future cases.

The politics of *Cann*

Cann is most easily explicable as one of the series of cases that aim to protect the position of mortgagees.

So far as the problems of law and equity are concerned, it is worth noting that the problem in *Flegg* also arose at the practical level because the Building Society had failed to register its mortgage; however, the court treated the mortgage as legal, in that the House of Lords allowed it to overreach the resident parents' equitable interests, even though it was only equitable. The relationship with *Rosset* is clear: the cases were heard in series and inter-relating judgments subsequently given by the same court on the same day. *Rosset* is a judgment that has attracted criticism as particularly harsh on co-owners.

So far as the problems of reimporting the doctrine of notice and reinventing the equity of redemption are concerned, *Cann* falls in line with *Paddington Building Society v. Mendelsohn*, where it was held that an equitable co-owner who knows of the likely existence of a mortgage cannot have priority over it, and *Henning*, where the court held that if a mortgage is repaid by alternative mortgage funds, the later mortgagee steps into the shoes of the earlier one so far as priority of the mortgage is concerned.

FURTHER READING

Primary sources

Abbey National Building Society v. Cann [1990] 2 WLR 832

Barclays Bank v. Zaroovabli [1997] Ch 321

Bristol and West Building Society v. Henning [1985] 1 WLR 778

Church of England Building Society v. Piskor [1954] Ch 553

City of London BS v. Flegg [1988] AC 487

Lloyds Bank plc v. Rosset [1990] 2WLR 867

Paddington BS v. Mendelsohn (1985) 50 P&CR 244

Williams and Glyn's Bank v. Boland [1981] AC 487

Secondary sources

Goldberg, G. (1992) 'Vivit ac Vivat Scintilla Temporis' (1992) 108, *LQR*, 380.

Robinson, M. (1997) 'The Mortgagee's Tenant' (1997) 113, *LQR*, 390.

Smith, R. (1990) 'Mortgagees and Trust Beneficiaries' (1990) 106, *LQR*, 545.

7

LAND LAW (PROPERTY LAW)

Kinch v. Bullard [1999] 1 WLR 423

Jan Cookson, Northumbria University

The case of *Kinch* v. *Bullard* concerns co-ownership of property, and serves to clarify the law on severance of a beneficial joint tenancy by service of a written notice under s.36(2) Law of Property Act 1925 (LPA 1925). This subject area could seem narrow, but the case is, in fact, a very interesting illustration of the rules of co-ownership and severance at work.

Two forms of co-ownership and the right of survivorship

Co-ownership arises where two or more people are entitled to ownership rights in the same property *simultaneously*. Their interest exists in the same property at the same time. There are two forms that such ownership may take: that of a 'joint tenancy' or that of a 'tenancy in common'. The essence of the *joint tenancy* form of co-ownership is that the whole property interest is owned by each individual joint tenant. There is no concept of 'shares', of one joint tenant having a separate part of the total interest. Instead, each joint tenant, along with the other joint tenant(s), is seen as owning the totality. By contrast, where a *tenancy in common* exists, each co-owner is entitled to an individual share in the property, one that is separate from that owned by the other co-owner(s). The shares may or may not be of equal proportion and value.

A right of survivorship

A joint tenancy gives rise to a critical outcome: the 'right of survivorship'. On death, a joint tenant's entitlement is simply extinguished. The deceased does not have any distinct share in the property that could pass by will or by intestacy. In consequence the ultimate survivor of joint tenants ends up the sole owner of the whole property interest. It is a gamble. 'Survivor takes all.' By contrast, and consistent with the concept of distinct shares, there is no right of survivorship when a tenant in common dies. Instead, the deceased tenant in common's individual share passes under the terms of his or her will if there was one, or otherwise by intestacy.

Co-ownership and the use of a trust

It is a statutory requirement, under sections 34–36 LPA 1925 (as amended), that co-owned property must be held in trust. Co-owners thus own their property with two different caps on: as trustees who hold the legal estate and as beneficiaries who own the equitable interest.

In *Kinch* v. *Bullard*, for example, the co-owners bought their home in their own names for their own benefit. Since the legal title was transferred to them, they became the trustees of the trust. And since they bought the property for their own use and enjoyment, they were also its beneficiaries.

Joint tenancy and tenancy in common within a trust

The requirement for a trust gives rise to the issue of which of the two forms of co-ownership is applicable to ownership at law, and which to ownership in equity.

1. *Legal estate.* Co-owners must hold the legal estate on a joint tenancy. This is a statutory requirement under s.1(6) LPA 1925.

2. *The equitable interest.* By contrast, the equitable interest under a trust can be co-owned by the beneficiaries either as joint tenants or as tenants in common.

How then, is this decided? Provided what are called 'the four unities' exist, then co-owners have the freedom to specify if they wish to be equitable joint tenants or tenants in common. Should they fail to do so, there are equitable presumptions as to which form will prevail. However, co-owners should, and the majority now do, make an express statement of their choice in the document under which they acquire their interest.

Severance of a joint tenancy in equity

'Severance' is the process by which a co-owner can convert his or her relationship with the other co-owner(s) from that of a joint tenant into that of a tenant in common. Severance cannot occur in relation to the mandatory joint tenancy of the legal estate (s.36(2) LPA 1925). Its significance is therefore in relation to the equitable interest in a property and, of course, it is here that the right to the value and enjoyment of the property lies.

A beneficial joint tenancy can be a very attractive vehicle at the time of purchase of a property, especially to domestic partners. Not least, it obviates the need to make wills leaving the property to each other, since on the first death of a couple who are joint tenants, the whole property interest remains vested in the survivor. However, it can also become undesirable later on, for a number of reasons which, as *Kinch* v. *Bullard* illustrates, include a souring of the joint tenants' relationship.

If a joint tenancy is converted into a tenancy in common, the effect is to avoid the right of survivorship. A severing co-owner will lose the possibility of becoming the sole beneficial owner of the property by outliving the other co-owner(s); but will gain the certainty, firstly, that their death will not automatically 'benefit' another co-owner, and, secondly, that they now hold a distinct share in the property which it will be possible to dispose of by will.

A severing co-owner will obtain one equal portion of the total interest. Where there are two joint tenants, they will both become tenants in common, in equal shares. Where there are more, for example, three, the severing co-owner will hold a one-third share. The severance will not affect the other two co-owners, who will continue as joint tenants and together hold a two-third interest.

Methods of severance

A joint tenancy can be severed:

1. Under s.36(2) LPA 1925 (as amended) by written notice served on all the other joint tenants.
2. At common law under the methods outlined in *Williams* v. *Hensman*, i.e. by
   (i)   an act operating on the joint tenant's share;
   (ii) mutual agreement;
   (iii) mutual conduct.
3. By homicide.

(Note that generally it is not possible to sever by making a will.)

Kinch v. *Bullard* concerns the first of these methods.

Severance by written notice under s.36(2) LPA 1925

Case law prior to *Kinch* v. *Bullard* had clarified the following points:

   (i)   no particular form of notice is required (*Re Draper's Conveyance*);
   (ii) the notice can be given without consent from the other co-owners (*Harris* v. *Goddard*);
   (iii) the notice must express an intention to sever, and for the severance to happen immediately (*Harris* v. *Goddard*).

The issues raised by *Kinch* v. *Bullard* concerned *service* of the notice.

The facts

Mr and Mrs Johnson (H and W) were beneficial joint tenants of the matrimonial home. In 1994 W learnt that she was terminally ill. In 1995 she began divorce proceedings, and had her solicitors prepare a written notice of severance. On Friday, 4 August 1995 the notice was sent by ordinary first class post to the matrimonial home where H and W still lived. That weekend H had a serious heart-attack and was hospitalised on 7 August. Meantime the postman duly delivered the notice through the letter-box at the property. W then destroyed it, having recognised that H's heart-attack meant that she was now likely to outlive him and it would, therefore, be to her advantage if the beneficial joint tenancy remained intact. H died on 15 August without having seen the notice. W died the following January.

The case was brought by H's executors (the Plaintiffs) and W's executors (the Defendants) to determine whether or not there had been severance of the beneficial joint tenancy under s.36(2) LPA 1925.

The arguments

Section 36(2) LPA 1925 provides:

> . . . where . . . any tenant desires to sever the joint tenancy in equity, he shall give to the other joint tenants a notice in writing of such desire.

On the facts, the issue the case raised was whether H had validly been 'given' a notice that he had not actually received. The Plaintiffs relied on s.196 LPA 1925. Section 196 deals with service of notices under the 1925 Act and was relevant because previous case law had established that 'serving' under s.196 meant the same as 'giving' under s.36(2).

Sections 196(3) and 196(4) provide as follows:

(3) Any notice . . . shall be sufficiently served if it is left at the last-known place of abode or business in the United Kingdom of the . . . person to be served . . .

(4) Any notice . . . shall also be sufficiently served, if it is sent by post in a registered letter . . . and if that letter is not returned through the post office undelivered.

The Plaintiffs' case was that W's notice had complied with s.196(3): it had been put by the postman through the letter box of H's last known place of abode, and was therefore validly 'served' or 'given'.

The Defendants' principal arguments raised the following points:

1. *Was ordinary post an acceptable method of service under s.196(3) LPA 1925, or did service have to be by recorded or registered post?*

This point was based on one way of reading together sections 196(3) and 196(4). Neuberger J held there was nothing in the wording of s.196(3) to suggest that the method of delivery mattered. All that was required for effective service under that subsection was proof of delivery to the correct address. Thus ordinary first class post was acceptable, and service took place under s.196(3) when the postman left the notice at the property.

2. *Did effective service require actual receipt of the notice by H?*

Arguably this point had already been determined in an earlier case. *Re 88 Berkeley Road* had held that receipt of notice of severance was *not* needed for effective service. However, because the notice in that case had been sent by recorded delivery, the decision actually concerned s.196(4) (which covers recorded as well as registered post), rather than s.196(3). In any event, in respect of s.196(3) also, Neuberger J decided that there was no requirement for H to have received the notice. The natural meaning of s.196(3) was that service was effective if a notice could be shown to have been left at the last known place of abode or business. Receipt was not necessary. (It maybe worth mentioning here that under s.196(4) service by recorded or registered post is deemed to have occurred even without delivery, unless the notice is actually returned undelivered. By contrast, delivery must be established under s.196(3). Thus, service by ordinary post may be more difficult to prove even though receipt by the addressee isn't needed.)

3. *Was the notice valid given that by the time it was served, W had lost her 'desire' to sever?*

The case hearing proceeded on the assumption that by the time the notice was delivered W had changed her mind and no longer wished to sever the joint tenancy, having recognised she was likely to outlive H. Notwithstanding, it was held that the notice remained valid. Clear words would be needed before s.36(2) could be construed as requiring the court to inquire into a sender's state of mind, and there were none. The function of s.36(2) was to instruct a joint tenant how to sever. Therefore, a notice which complied with that section was effective once it was validly served, irrespective of its sender's state of mind at the time of service. Neuberger J did allow that it might be possible to withdraw a notice, but only if the sender told the addressee she wished to do so before it had been given. This gloss was, however, *obiter* and expressed tentatively.

4. *Was service of the notice effective given that W, whose notice it was, had destroyed it, after delivery but before its receipt by H?*

Neuberger J held service was still good. It accorded with the plain words of s.196(3) that a notice was effective on delivery, notwithstanding that the sender had then prevented the addressee learning of it. In this case, of course, this worked to the benefit of the addressee's estate. Since H had predeceased, severance had to occur for the estate to inherit. However, the judge also expressed the view that in the event of W having been the one who had predeceased, her estate would not have been allowed to assert that service had been effective. The equitable rule that a statute cannot be used as an engine for fraud would have prevented W relying on s.196, given she had taken steps to suppress a notice that she herself had sent.

The decision

Accordingly, the case was decided in favour of the Plaintiffs. W's notice had been effective to sever the beneficial joint tenancy. W and H had become tenants in common, and on H's death his estate became entitled to his one-half share of the property.

Conclusion

The significance of *Kinch* v. *Bullard* lies in its clarification of the law relating to service of a written notice of severance of a beneficial joint tenancy under s.36(2) LPA 1925. It establishes that a notice will be validly served within s.196(3) LPA 1925 if it is delivered to the last known place of abode of the addressee, even though the addressee does not actually receive it. The method of service under s.196(3) can be by ordinary first class post. And an uncommunicated change of mind in the sender before delivery will not be effective to withdraw the notice.

FURTHER READING

Primary sources

Goodman v. *Gallant* [1986] Fam 106

Harris v. *Goddard* [1983] 1 WLR 1203

Re 88 Berkeley Road NW9 [1971] Ch 648

Re Draper's Conveyance [1969] 1 Ch 486

Williams v. *Hensman* [1861] 1 John & H 546

Secondary sources

Percival, M. (1999) 'Severance by written notice – a matter of delivery' [1999] *Conv*, 60.

Tee, L. (1995) 'Severance revisited' [1995] *Conv*, 104.

The lease/licence distinction

Street v. *Mountford* [1985] AC 809

Caroline Sawyer, Oxford Brookes University

The lease/licence distinction and *Street* v. *Mountford* in context

The question of what a lease is has long been an interesting and even contentious issue. Leases began as personal, rather than proprietary, interests, but well before the 1925 legislation they had been accepted as capable of being legal estates in land – the strongest form of property in English law. They also still function as contracts between the landlord and the tenant. But not all arrangements for the temporary use of land are leases. A person may be on another's land without having a property interest in it, for example, the person you invite to tea has your permission, or licence, to be there, but does not have any interest in the land that can survive your withdrawing the permission and asking them to leave. Revoking such a bare licence requires that you give only reasonable notice, so they have time to go. The licensee certainly does not have an interest capable of binding the person who buys the land from you. Alternatively, a permission may be given under a contract, so that money may change hands in return for the permission. The permission may therefore be specifically enforceable, so long as the original owner still has the land. But contractual licences do not bind third parties and are not proprietary, although Lord Denning held that view and so for a while it was the rule. Many rules apply to leases or tenancies (the two are equivalent terms with different social usages – leases are usually longer, and tenancies usually short-term but renewed probably monthly) but not to licences, and the boundary between the two is therefore an important legal issue.

The most important case on the question remains *Street* v. *Mountford*, heard in the House of Lords in 1985. The case gained its immediate social importance from the context of the time, because of its implications for the widespread practices of landlords in the 1980s. A series of Rent Acts, the last of which was passed in 1977, afforded residential tenants considerable protections and advantages which were not available to mere licensees. A tenant could register a 'fair rent' with the local council and it would then be illegal to charge more than that rent, or to charge a premium (a lump sum, also sometimes called a 'fine'). Provisions for security of tenure meant that it was also very difficult to evict a Rent Act tenant. Landlords felt that 'fair rents' were far from fair as, in an environment of housing shortage, market rents were much higher. Since the Rent Acts did not apply to licences, landlords would therefore go to considerable lengths to represent the arrangements under which they received money from residential occupiers of their property as licences rather than leases or tenancies, and the facts of the case law surrounding the question are therefore often both colourful and arcane. *Street* v. *Mountford* was not an isolated case, but the culmination of a lively series of cases on the conflicting rights of landlords and tenants. Unlike most land law cases, the case was front-page news. Although the heat has gone out of the social debate, since the Rent Acts were repealed in 1989 and replaced by a regime allowing for market rents and easy eviction, the case law on what constitutes a lease remains central to this area of law.

Mr Street, Mrs Mountford and the top floor flat

Mr Street owned a house in Boscombe that was divided into flatlets or bedsits. The Mount-fords occupied one of these, and then when it became empty the neighbouring one as well, giving them occupation of a whole floor, including the shower and lavatory, which had previously been shared. In March 1983 Mrs Mountford signed an agreement about the top floor which was headed 'Licence Agreement' and said clearly at the end: 'I understand and accept that a licence in the above form does not and is not intended to give me a tenancy protected under the Rent Acts.' Nevertheless in August 1983 she went to the local council and registered her 'tenancy' for a fair rent under the Rent Acts, provoking Mr Street to ask the county court to declare that the arrangement was a licence and not a tenancy agreement.

The Recorder who heard the case in September 1983 found that Mrs Mountford had exclusive possession of the flat, that she had a 'stake' in the room rather than merely personal possession, and that she and her husband 'behaved as tenants'. The Recorder described the word 'licence' as 'a false label' and found that the substance of the arrangement, as seen from the written agreement, amounted to a tenancy, in large part because Mrs Mountford had exclusive possession of the top floor of the house.

When in April 1984 the landlord appealed to the Court of Appeal, however, Slade LJ found that Mrs Mountford had an exclusive right of occupation, rather than exclusive possession. He placed great weight on the requirement for Mrs Mountford to keep her room tidy and to have her landlord's permission for anyone else to sleep on the premises, and on the statement that the personal permission was not assignable. He also noted that provisions about repair, insurance and quiet possession that he considered usual for leases were absent from this agreement, and considered that the express statement that the arrangement was intended to be a licence and not a lease could be displaced only by showing that the statements in it were inaccurate or even 'a deliberate sham'. The assertion was that the agreement was indeed in reality for exclusive occupation by the Mountfords, and that this amounted to saying that the written agreement was a sham. Slade LJ admitted that if the arrangement was found to be a licence then this would give landlords a way of avoiding the Rent Acts, and thus avoiding the intentions of Parliament. Nevertheless, he held that the weight of legal authority was against Mrs Mountford, that such a thing as exclusive occupation short of a tenancy did exist, and that that was what Mrs Mountford's agreement amounted to. He relied, in particular, on the decision in *Somma* v. *Hazelhurst*, where Cumming-Bruce LJ, citing earlier authority in aid, had taken in effect a view that the parties were free to contract as they wished, even if a court, for example, might disapprove of the bargain. Slade LJ held that the agreement did not 'pull the wool over anyone's eyes' or 'misrepresent the true nature of the agreed transaction', and so Mrs Mountford lost her case. Griffiths LJ agreed with Slade LJ, saying that if the use of that sort of agreement to avoid the Rent Acts became widespread, Parliament might have to legislate to include residential licensees, as well as tenants, within the protection of the Rent Acts.

Mrs Mountford appealed to the House of Lords, who heard the case in the spring of 1985. The judgment was given by Lord Templeman, and is much cited, especially for its occasional imagery. Lord Templeman approached the case by considering the nature of a tenancy, starting with the statutory definition in s.205 of the Law of Property Act 1925, against the mediaeval hinterland of the lease as the basis of a mere personal action. The traditional view, he said, was that 'the traditional distinction between a tenancy and a licence of land lay in the grant of land for a term at a rent with exclusive possession'. Discussing the authorities, he said that 'an occupier who enjoys exclusive possession is not necessarily a tenant', and set out categories of people who would be in that position. They might be fee simple owners, trespassers, mortgagees in possession, objects of the owner's charity or service occupiers. Deciding on the category into which a particular arrangement fell was a matter not only of deciding the facts, including the facts of the parties' intentions, but of deciding what the law was. In particular, there was an underlying issue of freedom of contract – where there was legislation designed to protect residential occupiers from the demands of landlords, could those residential occupiers agree with the landlords not to be caught by the legislation even where they appeared to be in exactly the situation Parliament had intended to deal with? Saying that the intention of the parties was that she should be granted exclusive possession for a term at a rent, Lord Templeman concluded that Mrs Mountford was a tenant, not a licensee, even though the agreement between them clearly stated the contrary to be the case.

Landlords, tenants and freedom of contract

In the course of argument, it was suggested to the court that the existence of the Rent Acts should be ignored in deciding whether or not the arrangement was a lease or a licence. In talking about whether Mr Street had managed to 'drive a coach and horses' through the Rent Acts (Lord Denning had declined to talk about a 'coach and four' in the similar case of *Facchini* v. *Bryson*, preferring to talk about an 'articulated vehicle'), Lord Templeman said that he accepted that the Rent Acts were irrelevant to the construction of the legal effects of the agreement between the parties. However, he said that the ineffectiveness of the Rent Acts in altering the effect of the agreement was 'like the professed intention of the parties'. Here it is the word 'professed', or put forward, that is important. The phrase suggests that the true intention of the parties may lie behind those words, and may be different from what they indicate.

Lord Templeman went on to discuss the case law, taking the approach that the labelling of the arrangement as a licence, even where that was specifically expressed to be the intention of the parties, was irrelevant. What mattered was the actual arrangement itself, in the light of what the common law said about the nature of a lease. Most famously, Lord Templeman said: 'The manufacture of a five-pronged implement for manual digging results in a fork even if the manufacturer, unfamiliar with the English language, insists that he intended to make and has made a spade'.

The first question to consider in deciding whether or not there is a lease is whether there is an intention between the parties to create legal relations and to give the tenant a 'stake' in the land. Often where there is an arrangement between family members or friends, it will be found that there was no intention to create legal relations. This often applies where the arrangement is characterised by generosity – that there is a reduced rent because of the personal relationship. Notably, such a generous arrangement will often mean that the formalities for the creation of a lease are also absent, given that a deed will be required to create a legal lease, even for a very short period, in the absence of a market rent (section 54 (2) Law of Property Act 1925), and for an equitable lease a formal contract would be required.

If an intention is 'professed', then **Street v. Mountford** says that that will not be taken to be conclusive. Considering how Lord Denning had dealt with the earlier case of **Errington v. Errington and Woods**, Lord Templeman said that: 'Words alone do not suffice. Parties cannot turn a tenancy into a licence merely by calling it one.' He considered all the circumstances of the case and found that the parties' conduct indicated that 'what was intended was that the occupier should be granted exclusive possession at a rent for a term with a corresponding interest in the land which created a tenancy'.

The most important aspect of the agreement was that of exclusive possession. As he went through the previous case law on what the requirements of a lease or tenancy were, Lord Templeman returned to the substance of the agreement between Mr Street and Mrs Mountford. Discussing that agreement in the light of **Addiscombe**, he said: 'In the present case it is clear that exclusive possession was granted . . . it is unnecessary to analyse minutely the detailed rights and obligations contained in the agreement'. Exclusive possession is not conclusive – a person may have exclusive possession and still be a licensee – but the circumstances where that applies are very limited. Along with the situation where the occupier is a lodger or service occupier, Lord Templeman approved the exceptional categories mentioned by Lord Denning in **Errington v. Errington and Woods**, and also that of the commercial tenant at will in **Isaac v. Hotel de Paris Ltd**. Otherwise, Lord Templeman found that only agreements that were truly personal in nature and truly created only personal privileges would be contractual licences rather than tenancies, and the way to tell was by looking at whether or not the agreement conferred exclusive possession.

Lord Templeman's focus on the issue of 'exclusive possession for a term at a rent' – a phrase which recurs in his judgment – can be misleading if taken out of context. In **Street v. Mountford**, Lord Templeman was concerned to consider the difference between the contractual tenancy that Mrs Mountford claimed she had and the contractual licence that Mr Street said was the true nature of the arrangement between them, as evidenced by the written agreement. He said that if 'exclusive possession for a term at a rent' did not constitute a tenancy, then the distinction between these became 'wholly unidentifiable'. The recurrent phrase is sometimes taken to mean that these requirements now constitute the requirements for a lease, but it should be taken in its context. Lord Templeman's judgment focused on residential tenancies, and surveys the authorities on how landlords might successfully avoid the operation of the Rent Acts by making licence arrangements with their occupiers. It considers issues of what constitutes exclusive possession in those circumstances, and how far Parliament's legislation on residential tenancies should be undermined by the principle of freedom of contract. In the sort of case that Lord Temple-man was discussing, the payment of money in exchange for the right to occupy the premises is universal, and he does not address directly the issue of whether or not the payment of rent is a necessary requirement of a lease. He said: 'the only intention which is relevant is the intention demonstrated by the agreement to grant exclusive possession for a term at a rent . . . where as in the present case the only circumstances are that residential accommodation is offered and accepted with exclusive possession for a term at a rent, the result is a tenancy'.

Lord Templeman said that the implications of the decision in *Street* v. *Mountford* for future disputes between landlords and residential occupiers were that, save in exceptional circumstances, the only question in relation to a residential occupier would be whether they were a lodger or a tenant. Mrs Mountford was a tenant. Attempts by landlords to represent the occupier as a lodger rather than a tenant did continue for a while, giving rise to further case law at the highest level, especially where exclusive possession was denied to each of several occupiers (see especially *Antoniades* v. *Villiers*; *AG Securities* v. *Vaughan*) until the deregulation of private residential housing in the late 1980s, and added further to the case law on the definition of leases.

Early in his judgment in *Street* v. *Mountford*, Lord Templeman considers section 205 of the Law of Property Act 1925, the 'definition section' of the Act. It defines a 'term of years absolute' (another word for a lease) at paragraph (xxvii) but – because it is not relevant to this case – Lord Templeman does not mention the important provision 'whether or not at a rent'. This provision is important as a matter of principle, however, and it could not logically be otherwise. As a legal estate in land, a lease is a solid form of property. It would be odd if it could not be the subject of a gift. The history of the lease, which Lord Templeman also briefly addresses, is also relevant here. The lease, having been originally a personal arrangement, has developed through the law of contract into one of the two major elements of the law of real property. Leases retain elements of contract as well as property, and especially where they contain covenants as between landlord and tenant, the elements of contract remain very important. The reason for long leases, as where one purchases a flat, having a periodic rent provision, often called 'ground rent', is to ensure that the contractual elements of the lease work easily, since contracts require consideration. This is not the same as a service charge, which is levied to cover real expenses such as repairs. Where a rent provision is included in a lease solely to ensure there are no issues about whether contractual elements operate, the consideration may be purely nominal. Rents of one pound, or historically one shilling, may be found, and, since contract law does not require that consideration be in money to be valid, 'peppercorn' rents really do exist.

Conclusion

Street v. *Mountford* remains the leading case on the definition of a lease, and indicates that the fundamental principle is that of exclusive possession. With a limited range of exceptions, where exclusive possession is granted, the arrangement will be a lease. The question is one of the substance of the arrangement, including the intentions of the parties, and this will be decisive, regardless of what label is put on it.

7

LAND LAW (PROPERTY LAW)

353

FURTHER READING

Primary sources

Addiscombe [1958] 1 QB 513

Antoniades v. *Villiers*; *AG Securities* v. *Vaughan* [1990] 1 AC 417

Errington v. *Errington and Woods* [1952] 1 KB 290

Facchini v. *Bryson* (1952) 159 EG 394

Isaac v. *Hotel de Paris Ltd* [1960] 1 WLR 239

Somma v. *Hazelhurst* [1978] 1 WLR 1014

Secondary sources

Bridge, S. (1996) 'Street v. Mountford: no hiding place' (1996) *Conv*, 344.

Bridge, S. (1997) 'Down to business with *Street* v. *Mountford*' (1997) *Conv*, 137.

Bright, S. (2006) 'Tolerated trespass or a new tenancy?' (2006) 122, *LQR*, 48.

Morgan, J. (2005) 'Exclusive possession, occupation and the 1954 Act' (2005) *Conv*, 255.

Ashburn Anstalt v. Arnold and Another [1988] 2 WLR 706

Patrick Bishop, Swansea University

7

LAND LAW (PROPERTY LAW)

The Court of Appeal in *Ashburn Anstalt* v. *Arnold and Another* (hereafter referred to as *Ashburn*) were called upon to consider two perennial issues in the law of real property; namely, the essential characteristics of a lease (see the entry for *Street* v. *Mountford*) and the extent to which a contractual licence is capable of binding a third party purchaser or any successor in title to the licensor. The latter issue will be the subject of discussion in this case entry.

The distinction between personal and proprietary interests in land

Prior to consideration of the actual decision, students need to be fully cognisant of a fundamental distinction in land law, namely, the difference in nature and effect between proprietary interests and personal rights. In general, a proprietary interest in land is capable of binding third party purchasers and Other successors in title to land (such as those inheriting land under a will or a trustee in bankruptcy). Personal rights, by contrast, are only enforceable between the original contracting parties because of the general contractual principle that the burden of a contract cannot be enforced against a person not a party to the original agreement. The effect of such a principle is also evident in relation to freehold covenants (see the entry on *Rhone* v. *Stephens*). The orthodox position, that a contractual licence merely creates personal rights and is not capable of constituting a proprietary interest in land, is often traced back to the dictum of Vaughan CJ in *Thomas* v. *Sorrell*: 'A disposition or licence properly passeth no interest, nor alters or transfers property in anything . . .'. Rather oddly, the case concerned alcohol licences and was no way concerned with land law, nevertheless the traditional view remained in the ascendancy until 1952.

Any student of law will quickly become familiar with the judicial creativity of Lord Denning, such creativity was apparent in *Errington* v. *Errington*, where his Lordship launched a concerted attack on the orthodox view of contractual licences. A father purchased a house in order to provide accommodation for his son and daughter in law. Title to the house was conveyed to the father but it was agreed that if his son and daughter in law paid all the mortgage instalments he would then transfer the property to them. Unfortunately, the father died and the property was transferred to his widow. Subsequently, the son went to live with his mother while the daughter in law remained in occupation of the house, continuing to pay the mortgage instalments. The mother then attempted to revoke the licence. The Court of Appeal concluded that the daughter in law's licence was not revocable by the mother even though she was not a party to the original agreement. Denning LJ (as he then was) stated that the original agreement gave rise to an 'equity', capable of binding successors in title subject to the doctrine of notice. Consequently, the mother was bound by her daughter in law's contractual licence.

The decision was greeted with considerable criticism, largely on the basis that in reaching such a conclusion, Denning LJ disregarded two seemingly binding authorities. The House of Lords in *King* v. *David Allen* and the Court of Appeal in *Clore* v. *Theatrical Properties* decided that contractual licences are purely personal to the original contracting parties. *King* was concerned with the right to place advertisements on the exterior of a building and *Clore* related to front of house rights in a theatre, as such, Denning LJ considered that such cases could be distinguished from occupational licences.

The principles enunciated above were followed and extended by Lord Denning MR in subsequent decisions, for example, in *DHN Food Distributors* v. *Tower Hamlets LBC* it was opined that a constructive trust would arise in all cases involving contractual licences. However, the departure from orthodoxy did not escape criticism from both academics and the judiciary. For example, in *National Provincial Bank Ltd* v. *Hastings Car Mart Ltd*, Russell LJ, in a dissenting judgment (incidentally Lord Denning MR also heard the appeal), expressed concern that the law had been developed without sufficient regard for established principles of property law and in contradiction of previous authority. However, when the appeal reached the House of Lords (*National Provincial Bank Ltd* v. *Ainsworth*) the court declined to reach a final conclusion on the matter. Thus, the issue remained unresolved until the decision of the Court of Appeal in *Ashburn*.

The facts

The case revolved around an agreement, entered into in February 1973, between Arnold, the defendants, and Matlodge. Arnold had a sub-lease of shop premises and sold it to Matlodge for the purposes of redevelopment. Under the terms of the conveyance, Arnold was entitled to remain in occupation of the property, rent free, as a licensee until the end of September 1973. Thereafter, they were entitled to remain in occupation until one quarter notice was given certifying that vacant occupation was required so that the site could be redeveloped by the freehold owners. The claimants, Ashburn Anstalt, were successors in title to Matlodge, having purchased the freehold in 1985. Less than a month after completion, the claimants informed the defendants in writing that they were required to vacate the premises. The defendants refused, which induced the claimants to bring an action for possession.

The *Ashburn* decision

It was argued by the defendants that the agreement allowing them to occupy the premises amounted to a tenancy or alternatively a contractual licence and in any event they had an overriding interest by virtue of actual occupation under section 70(1)(g) of the Land Registration Act 1925 (see now schedule 3, paragraph 2 of the Land Registration Act 2002).

The court had little difficulty in concluding that the agreement constituted a lease and consequently, despite a lack of registration, the claimants were protected by virtue of their actual occupation. However, Fox LJ, in giving the judgment of the whole court, took the opportunity to express his views on the proprietary status of contractual licences. As such, the views promulgated by the Court of Appeal are necessarily *obiter*, having concluded the agreement in question amounted to a lease it was not strictly necessary for the court to come to any firm conclusion relating to contractual licences. However, the court heard extensive arguments on the issues raised by the *Errington* decision and therefore considered it appropriate to resolve the matter insofar as this could be achieved by *obiter dicta*. Although rather lengthy, its worth quoting in full the following statement of Fox LJ (at page 22), which nicely encapsulates the view of the court:

> Before *Errington* the law appears to have been clear and well understood. It rested on an important and intelligible distinction between contractual obligations which give rise to no estate or interest in the land and proprietary rights which, by definition, did. The far-reaching statement of principle in *Errington* was not supported by authority, not necessary for the decision of the case and *per incurium* in the sense that it was made without reference to authorities which, if they would not have compelled, would surely have persuaded a court to adopt a different *ratio*. Of course, the law must be free to develop. But as a response to problems which had arisen, the *Errington* rule (without more) was neither practically necessary nor theoretically convincing.

Given the often understated rhetoric of the English judiciary, the attack on the principles developed by Lord Denning from *Errington* onwards, is extremely powerful. However, the court did not rule out entirely the possibility that a contractual licence in certain circumstances could result in the creation of a proprietary interest in land via the imposition of a constructive trust.

It was emphasised by Fox LJ that the court will not impose a constructive trust if the evidence is slender, the test in such cases is: 'whether the [third party] has acted in such a way that, as a matter of justice, a trust must be imposed . . .'. This necessarily raises the question: in what circumstances will a constructive trust be imposed in a contractual licence scenario? Some light may be shed on the issue by considering the facts of the *Ashburn* case itself and the earlier Court of Appeal decision in *Binions* v. *Evans*. In *Ashburn*, the conveyance that transferred the land to the third party purchaser stated that the sale was 'subject to' the licence agreement entered into between Ashburn and Matlodge. The court concluded that mere notice of the contractual licence, without more, was insufficient to warrant the imposition of a constructive trust. However, Fox LJ accepted that a constructive trust was justified in *Binions* v. *Evans*. Here the third party purchaser had expressly taken subject to the licence and as a result, paid a reduced purchase price. Thus, in order for the purchaser's conscience to sufficiently be affected, he/she must have purchased the land at less than full value in return for an express undertaking in favour of the licensee. Whether future courts will impose a constructive trust in a wider range of circumstances remains to be seen.

Given that the discussion of contractual licences in *Ashburn* was necessarily *obiter*, the extent to which the pronouncements of the court represent an accurate statement of the law is a matter of debate. The Court of Appeal's decision was criticised and indeed overruled by the House of Lords in *Prudential Assurance Co. Ltd* v. *London Residuary Body*. However, the criticisms did not relate to the courts' discussion of contractual licences and have not undermined the decision's persuasive force. Thus, the Court of Appeal in *Habermann v. Koehler* stated '. . . the decision of this court in *Ashburn Anstalt v. Arnold* governs contractual licences . . .' (at page 323). Furthermore, Sir Christopher Slade in *Lloyd v. Dugdale*, having cited Ashburn, opined: 'Notwithstanding some previous authority suggesting the contrary, a contractual licence is not to be treated as creating a proprietary interest in land so as to bind third parties who acquire the land with notice of it'.

The views promulgated in *Errington* and subsequent decisions of Lord Denning, were described by Browne-Wilkinson V-C (as he then was) in *IDC Group Ltd v. Clarke* as a 'heresy', further, it was hoped that the principles expressed in *Ashburn* would put the 'quietus' to that heresy. Thus, the decision of the Court of Appeal represents a return to the orthodox view, which dominated prior to the intervention of Lord Denning in 1952. The minor uncertainty regarding the circumstances in which a court is prepared to impose a constructive trust notwithstanding, it is now patently clear that a contractual licence is a personal right, enforceable between the original contracting parties only, and in no way represents a proprietary interest in land.

FURTHER READING

Primary sources

Binions v. Evans [1972] Ch 359

Clore v. Theatrical Properties [1936] 3 All ER

DHN Food Distributors v. Tower Hamlets LBC [1976] 1 WLR 852

Errington v. Errington [1952] 1 KB 290

Habermann v. Koehler (1997) 73 P & CR 515

IDC Group Ltd v. Clarke [1992] EGLR 187

King v. David Allen [1916] 2 AC 54

Lloyd v. Dugdale [2002] 2 P & CR 13 p. 167

National Provincial Bank Ltd v. Ainsworth [1965] AC 1175

National Provincial Bank Ltd v. Hastings Car Mart Ltd [1964] Ch 665

Prudential Assurance Co. Ltd v. London Residuary Body [1992] 2 AC 386

Thomas v. Sorrell (1673) Vaugh 330

Secondary sources

Battersby, G. (1991) 'Contractual and Estoppel Licences as Proprietary Interests in Land' [1991] *Conv*, 36.

Hill, J. (1988) 'Lease, Licences and Third Parties' (1988) 52, *MLR*, 226.

Leases – the remedy of forfeiture

Expert Clothing Service and Sales Ltd v. Hillgate House Ltd [1986] Ch 340

Alistair Speirs, Newcastle University

The background

The twin goals of that great raft of legislation enacted in 1925 were to simplify transactions in land and to permit fragmentation of interests in land. The latter goal was, to a great extent, achieved by largely eliminating the doctrine of notice through introduction of the land charges register (see the Land Charges Act 1925 (now 1972)), registration of title of land (the Land Registration Act 1925 (now 2002)) and the device of overreaching beneficial interests under a trust (ss.2 and 27 of the Law of Property Act 1925 (LPA)). The former goal was tackled by simplifying the ways in which land could be held by, for example, permitting legal ownership by joint tenancy only (see ss.1(6), 36(2) LPA) and limiting the types of legal estate which can exist at law (as opposed to in Equity). By s.1(1) LPA the only two legal estates permitted at law were the estate in fee simple absolute in possession and a term of years absolute (the leasehold estate).

Leases – the essentials

A lease is, at its simplest, an estate in land carved out of the fee simple. It derives from a contract by which the holder of the fee simple (the lessor or landlord) grants to the lessee (or tenant) the right to occupy the land for a period of time. In order to create a legal (as opposed to equitable) lease the contract must be contained in a deed (see s.52(1) LPA) unless the term is for three years or less (ss.52(2)(d), 54(2) LPA) in which case no formality is required (not even writing – see the Law of Property (Miscellaneous Provisions) Act 1989 s.2(5)(a)).

The definition of a lease is usually said to include three elements: certainty of term, exclusive possession and rent. The first imposes a requirement that the parties to the contract have defined, at the outset, the term for which the lease is to run. Thus a purported lease which was expressed to terminate at the end of the Second World War was insufficiently certain and therefore void (*Lace* v. *Chantler*). Exclusive possession focuses upon the right of the tenant to exclude everyone (including the landlord) from the land during the period of the lease. As to the third element, rent, there is high judicial authority that payment of rent is an essential characteristic of a lease (Lord Templeman in *Street* v. *Mountford*) but this is not the case (see s.205(i)(xxvii) and *Ashburn Anstalt* v. *Arnold*).

At the heart of a lease, as noted above, is a contract. The parties may include such contractual terms, or covenants, as they wish. Leases are particularly closely regulated forms of contract and, in addition, other obligations are imposed by statute and the common law. Typical obligations imposed by covenants include the landlord's obligation to permit 'quiet enjoyment' of the property by the tenant and the tenant's obligation to pay rent.

Termination of leases

The most obvious way in which a tenancy may come to an end is 'effluxion of time' – the term of the lease simply expires. In addition, in common with other types of contract the parties may agree to vary the contract and bring the lease to a premature end by 'surrender'. Alternatively the lease may be terminated, in the right circumstances, by the unilateral action of the lessor by giving notice to quit. Another method by which the landlord may terminate the lease is by forfeiture.

Forfeiture

Should a tenant breach one of the covenants imposing an obligation upon him then the landlord has a number of potential remedies. Since the breach is a breach of contract the landlord has the usual contractual remedy of damages and, in certain circumstances, Equity's superior remedy of specific performance. In addition, however, where the lease (as is usual) contains a forfeiture clause the landlord may be able, relying upon the tenant's breach of covenant, to terminate the lease. It is fair to characterise the law concerned with forfeiture as being complex; both statute and the common law regulate closely the circumstances in which forfeiture may be applied.

The first trap which the landlord must avoid is waiver of the breach. He will lose the right to forfeiture if he either expressly or impliedly treats the lease as continuing. The most common method by which this may occur impliedly is by demanding or accepting rent (even as a result of a clerical error) from the tenant with knowledge of the tenant's breach.

The procedure which the landlord is required to follow in order to forfeit a lease is set out in s.146 LPA. The aim of the provision is to permit the tenant an opportunity to remedy the breach and avoid forfeiture of the lease. Section 146(1) requires the landlord to serve a notice which:

(a) identifies the breach;

(b) if the breach is capable of being remedied, requires the tenant to remedy the breach; and

(c) requires the tenant to make monetary compensation for the breach.

Of these three requirements it is the second which has been most problematical and which has generated the most litigation.

In addition, s.146(2) provides to the court discretion to give relief from forfeiture where it considers it appropriate to do so in all the circumstances.

The cases on s.146

The question which s.146(1)(b) prompts is: which breaches are 'capable of being remedied'? In order to answer this question it is helpful to distinguish between (i) positive and negative covenants and (ii) complete and continuing breaches. A positive covenant is a promise to do something (for example, to repair) while a negative covenant is a promise not to do (for example, not to use the property for immoral purposes). A complete breach is one that occurs on a once-and-for-all basis, for example, assigning the lease (in breach of a negative covenant not to assign) as opposed to a continuing breach such as a failure to repair the premises.

1. *Scala House & District Property Co. Ltd* v. *Forbes*

The breach of covenant in *Scala*, on the classification system above, was a complete breach of a negative covenant. The lease contained a covenant not to assign or sublet the lease without the consent of the landlord. The defendant tenant intended to run a restaurant in the premises and entered an agreement with third parties by which they would be responsible for managing the restaurant. Unfortunately this agreement amounted, at law, as a result of error by the defendant's solicitor, to a subletting of the premises. The claimant landlord served a s.146 notice upon the defendant requiring, *inter alia*, the defendant to remedy the breach insofar as the breach was capable of remedy.

The decision of the Court of Appeal focused upon the question of whether the breach was 'capable of remedy'. It held that this (complete) breach of this (negative) covenant was not capable of remedy: a breach by unlawful subletting (or assigning) is never capable of remedy.

The tenant, of course, still had that second opportunity to avoid forfeiture provided by s.146(2). Here the court was swayed by a number of factors (that the subletting was unintentional, the result of error, that the landlord had suffered no loss, could not reasonably have withheld consent and would be granted a windfall if the lease was forfeited) to grant relief from forfeiture.

2. *Expert Clothing Service and Sales Ltd* v. *Hillgate House Ltd*

Here the tenant was in breach of two positive covenants: to give notice to the landlord (within one month) of any charge (mortgage) created over the property and to carry out reconstruction work on the premises by a specified date. Both of these were complete breaches because the dates for carrying out the required actions had passed. The landlord served a s.146 notice but, importantly, failed to require the tenant to remedy the breaches, as required by s.146(1)(b). Once again, then, the question for the Court of Appeal was whether the breaches were capable of being remedied. If they were not then there would be no point in the notice requiring remedy. If they were capable of remedy, however, then the notice served by the claimant was defective and invalid.

The court performed a subtle shift in considering the question of remediability. Rather than focus upon whether the *breach* was capable of remedy, Slade LJ stated, the court should consider whether the *harm* done to the landlord was capable of being retrieved. In the case of a positive obligation the answer to this question was, generally, yes. This was true even where the positive obligation had a deadline imposed, for the harm could generally

7

LAND LAW (PROPERTY LAW)

be remedied by doing the required thing, even out of time, and paying compensation to the landlord. In this case, both breaches were remediable and therefore the s.146 notice was invalid.

3. *Savva & Savva* v. *Hussein*

Expert Clothing, since it was concerned with positive covenants, left the question of the remediability of breaches of negative covenants without definitive answer. *Savva* followed *Expert Clothing* and applied the same reasoning to negative covenants.

Here the tenant's breach consisted of failure to abide by a covenant which forbade altering the premises without the landlord's consent. He had erected signs, altered the facia of the premises and installed a flue to ventilate the café. The landlord, as in *Expert Clothing*, served a s.146 notice omitting the requirement to remedy.

Staughton LJ (who gave the leading judgment) was clear. The word 'remedy' in s.146 was not to be interpreted as requiring restoration of the position to that which it would have been if the breach had not occurred. Instead 'remedy' is concerned, with one exception, with removal of the mischief which flowed from the breach. In this case such remedy was possible and the notice was invalid. The one exception relates to covenants prohibiting assignment and subletting; *Scala* had established that such breaches were not capable of remedy.

Conclusion and reform

There has, over the years, been much statutory intervention to protect tenants (particularly residential tenants). The Rent Acts, for instance, provided residential tenants with indefinite security of tenure and the ability to demand a 'fair' (sub-market) rent. The courts have, generally, defended this statutory protection of the tenant. A good example of tenant-friendly decisions is found, for example, in the cases concerning the lease/license distinction (see, for example, *Street* v. *Mountford*). The extension of the concept of remediability of breaches in the cases above can be seen as springing from that same impulse to provide protection to tenants.

The Law Commission's consultation paper 'Termination of Tenancies for Tenant Default' took the view that the law of forfeiture 'is complex, lacks coherence, and can lead to injustice'. The Commission has proposed major changes to the law, contained in the draft Landlord and Tenant (Termination of Tenancies) Bill, which aim to 'simplify, clarify and modernise the current law' and to provide landlords and tenants 'a level playing field'. When enacted the Bill will sweep away the current 'excessively technical and unnecessarily complicated' system.

The doctrine of waiver, identified above as a trap for landlords, would disappear. The new scheme would require the landlord to serve a written 'tenant default notice' setting out details of the breach, the remedial action required and a date for completion of the remedial action. The primary purpose of this notice is to seek compliance by the tenant with his obligations under the tenancy. Only if the notice fails in this primary purpose can the landlord make a 'termination claim'. If the court is satisfied that the tenant is in default, the terms of the legislation will permit the court to make such order as it considers appropriate and proportionate in the circumstances. The 'circumstances' include the conduct of the parties, whether any steps have been taken to remedy the default and the reasonableness of the timescale provided for remedy. The court has a choice of orders, including a termination order (ending the tenancy), a remedial order (staying the termination claim and giving time to the tenant to remedy the breach) and an order for sale (thereby avoiding a potential windfall for the landlord).

The cases examined here illustrate a movement away from an examination of the breach towards a more tenant-friendly examination of the possibility of remedying the harm caused to the landlord by the breach. The proposed legislation seeks to remove much of the technicality of the law on forfeiture. It will permit the tenant the possibility of complying with the terms of the tenancy agreement. Ultimately, however, it will give the landlord the remedy of termination of the lease where that is the appropriate and proportionate response.

FURTHER READING

Primary sources

Ashburn Anstalt v. *Arnold* [1989] 1 Ch 1

Expert Clothing Service and Sales Ltd v. *Hillgate House Ltd* [1986] Ch 340

Lace v. *Chantler* [1944] KB 368

Savva & Savva v. *Hussein* (1997) 73 P&CR 150

Scala House & District Property Co. Ltd v. *Forbes* [1974] QB 575

Street v. *Mountford* [1985] AC 809

Secondary sources

Termination of Tenancies for Tenant Default, 2004 Law Com CP No. 174.

Termination of Tenancies for Tenant Default, 2006, Law Com No. 303.

7

LAND LAW (PROPERTY LAW)

Mortgages - undue influence

Royal Bank of Scotland v. *Etridge (No. 2)*
[2002] 2 AC 773

Patrick Bishop, Swansea University

The central issue before the House of Lords in *Royal Bank of Scotland* v. *Etridge (No. 2)* was the effect of undue influence on a tripartite mortgage agreement, i.e. an agreement involving a mortgagee (usually a bank or other financial institution), a principal debtor/mortgagor and a third party guarantor or surety. The facts of such cases follow a predictable pattern, the principal debtor, almost invariably the husband, will procure the agreement of his wife to charge her interest in a jointly owned home in order to secure his personal debts or the debts of his business. Where the surety's agreement has been obtained by undue influence, the fundamental question becomes: In what circumstances is the surety entitled to have the agreement set aside on the basis that consent was obtained by undue influence, misrepresentation or some other vitiating factor?

The courts in this area are faced with a tension between two competing policy aims. There is an obvious need to protect potentially vulnerable spouses who may be coerced into a disadvantageous agreement. Equally, the courts are acutely aware of the socio-economic importance of mortgages as a means of providing both personal and business finance. An approach which excessively undermines the mortgagee's confidence in the security provided is therefore rightly seen as undesirable. The case law in this area can therefore be analysed as an attempt to find a workable compromise between these competing aims.

The facts

The *Etridge* decision involved eight conjoined appeals; seven of which involved wives who contended the mortgage agreement they had entered into was unenforceable against them on the grounds that their agreement had been obtained by undue influence. The eighth appeal concerned an action in negligence against a solicitor who had provided advice to a wife acting as surety for her husband's debts. The significance of the decision lies more in the general principles promulgated by the House of Lords than the actual decision in each particular appeal.

Background to the *Etridge* decision

This area of land law has been the subject of two House of Lords rulings within an eight year time frame. As such, the decision in *Etridge* can only be fully understood in the context of the earlier decision in *Barclays Bank plc* v. *O'Brien*.

In *O'Brien* a wife signed documents creating a second mortgage on a jointly owned home in order to secure the overdraft of the husband's business. Mr O'Brien misrepresented to his wife the extent of the liability, stating that the overdraft totalled £60,000 when in fact it was £135,000. Mrs O'Brien signed the relevant documents on the bank's premises without reading them, the bank made no effort to reveal the nature of the documentation to her. The official policy of the bank at the time was to explain to a surety in Mrs O'Brien's position the nature and effect of the mortgage and to recommend that independent legal advice be sought. This policy was not adhered to. When the overdraft was exceeded the bank sought possession of the property in order to realise the security provided by the mortgage. Mrs O'Brien argued that as a result of the misrepresentation, the charge, at least as far as it related to her share of the property, was unenforceable by the bank.

The first issue here is one of terminology; much of the case law in this area will refer to 'undue influence,' but as O'Brien, a case concerning misrepresentation, illustrates, the phrase in this context is used in a generic sense to encompass any vitiating factor or equitable wrong on the part of the principal debtor. In essence, the House of Lords agreed with Mrs O'Brien's central assertion on the basis the bank had taken insufficient steps to ensure that the wife knew of the nature and extent of her liability and the consequences of default and therefore were fixed with constructive notice of the undue influence.

In reaching the above conclusion Lord Browne-Wilkinson adopted a classification of undue influence previously employed by the Court of Appeal in *Bank of Credit and Commerce SA v. Aboody* which placed cases of undue influence in either class 1 or class 2, the latter being subdivided into two.

(i) Class 1. A scenario involving proven actual undue influence in which case the complainant is entitled to have the agreement set aside. Such is the case whether the agreement is to the surety's manifest disadvantage or not.

(ii) Class 2(A). This category involved a scenario where the law will presume that undue influence has been exercised because of the nature of the relationship between the parties. Relevant relationships will include solicitor and client, doctor and patient and clergyman and parishioner. Such a presumption can be rebutted if the alleged wrongdoer can prove that no actual undue influence was exercised over the vulnerable party.

(iii) Class 2(B). For present purposes the most important class of undue influence. This category will involve a case where it is shown that a relationship exists whereby the complainant must prove that she placed trust and confidence in the alleged wrongdoer. Where such a relationship of trust and confidence exists, the burden of proof will shift to the alleged wrongdoer to illustrate to the court that undue influence has not occurred. This category is not restricted to married couples but extends to all emotional relationships including non-marital and homosexual partners, siblings and even employer/employee.

In *Barclay's Bank v. O'Brien*, Mrs O'Brien did not attempt to have the agreement set aside against her husband but rather argued that the transaction was unenforceable against her by the mortgagee bank. The issue was resolved by the utilisation of the doctrine of notice in which case the issue is whether the bank had notice of the wife's right to set

7

LAND LAW (PROPERTY LAW)

aside the agreement. Crucially, the fact that the mortgage was created over a matrimonial home, without more, was insufficient to place the bank on enquiry. For this to happen there needs to be something in the nature of the transaction, which alerts the mortgagee that consent to the agreement may not have been freely given. Therefore, in order for a bank to be placed on notice it must be shown that:

(a) on the face of it, the agreement is not to the financial advantage of the wife; and

(b) in a transaction of this kind, there is a substantial risk that in procuring the wife's consent the husband has committed an equitable wrong that would entitle the wife to set the transaction aside.

Where such a situation exists, a bank can ensure that it is not affected by notice of the vitiating factor by insisting, prior to finalising the transaction, that the wife attends a meeting (in the absence of the husband) with a representative of the bank. During the meeting, the wife should be informed of the extent of her liability, the consequences of default and urged to take legal advice.

Far from settling the issue the decision in *O'Brien* generated considerable litigation, for example, the requirement that the agreement is not to the financial advantage of the wife proved to be problematic, particularly when the mortgage was used to secure the debts of a business, which, if successful would benefit both parties to the transaction. Furthermore, the role of the independent legal adviser was an issue in both *Banco Exterior Internacional* v. *Mann* and *Barclays Bank Plc* v. *Thomson*. Given such confusion it was stated by Lord Hobhouse of Woodborough that the purpose of the decision in *Etridge* was to 'settle the law and enable certainty to be re-established.'

The *Etridge* decision

As a starting point, the classification of cases of undue influence promulgated by the court in *O'Brien* was discarded as unhelpful. The initial foundation in cases of this type is that the evidential burden falls on any surety who wishes to set aside any transaction on the grounds of undue influence. In cases of presumed undue influence (as opposed to actual undue influence, for example consent brought about by threats of violence), a surety will be able to establish presumed undue influence if it can be demonstrated that:

(a) the surety placed trust and confidence in the primary borrower so that the latter gained ascendancy of the former; and

(b) the transaction was one which called for an explanation, sometimes referred to as 'manifest disadvantage'.

In relation to the second requirement, it is clear that the mere fact that a wife stands surety for her husband's business debts is not automatically treated as a transaction which calls for an explanation because spousal interests are often inseparably linked.

Once the claimant has satisfied the two-stage test above, the burden then shifts to the party wishing to enforce the agreement to rebut the presumption that undue influence has been exercised. Even where the husband is the source of the undue influence, thereby allowing the wife to set the agreement aside against him, problems invariably arise because the surety/wife has also undertaken obligations to the mortgagee bank. The issue then becomes in what circumstances is the bank tainted by the undue influence and from a practical perspective, what measures must a bank undertake to ensure that its conscience is not affected by the equitable wrong committed by the principal debtor/husband?

In *Etridge*, the House of Lords confirmed that a bank is 'put on enquiry' whenever one person stands surety for the debts of his/her spouse or for the debts of any other person involved in any non-commercial relationship (whether heterosexual or homosexual, platonic or whether or not involving cohabitation) of which the lender is aware. Such relationships become relevant because of the potential that in such relationships, a manipulative influence may be exerted by one party over the other. However, it was made clear that a lender is not placed on enquiry where money is advanced to two persons jointly, for example, where a matrimonial home is charged in order to secure the joint indebtedness of both parties.

The duty of the mortgagee

Whenever a mortgagee is placed on enquiry as discussed above, the mortgagee must take reasonable steps to ensure that the surety is aware of the risks inherent in the transaction. The approach of the court was to lay down a series of practical steps, which if adhered to, will ensure the surety is unable to dispute that she is bound by the agreement. In essence, the procedure will involve the giving of independent advice to the surety in relation to the nature and effect of the transaction. The detailed steps that must be undertaken by the mortgagee are as follows:

1. The mortgagee is required to contact the surety requesting that she nominate a solicitor and that the purpose is to ensure that she cannot dispute the validity of the transaction at some later date.

2. The mortgagee should not proceed any further with the transaction until the surety responds by nominating a solicitor.

3. The mortgagee, with the principal debtor's consent, will provide the nominated solicitor with all relevant information regarding the nature and terms of the agreement and the extent of liability.

4. A face-to-face meeting will then take place between the surety and her solicitor during which the surety is advised. As a minimum, the solicitor must concentrate on explaining the risks involved, for example, loss of home or bankruptcy, and emphasise the voluntary nature of the agreement emphasising that the decision is hers alone.

5. If after receiving all relevant advice the surety/wife wishes to proceed a letter confirming that advice has been proffered will be forwarded to the lender.

If all steps are fully undertaken, then on receiving the confirmation from the advising solicitor, the bank is able to proceed with the transaction safe in the knowledge that the surety/wife will be unable to impugn the agreement should the bank exercise its right of possession and sale.

Given the socio-economic importance of mortgages as a means of securing business and personal finance, the House of Lords were careful not to place too onerous a duty on banks and Other lending institutions. In general, the threshold at which a bank is placed on enquiry is low. However, such an approach certainly has simplicity to recommend it and will ease banking bureaucracy. The solicitor in this context is not considered an agent of the lender and therefore the lender is in no way responsible for the quality of the advice given to the surety. Therefore the net effect of the *Etridge* decision is to transfer the onus to advising solicitors, who face liability and the payment of damages should the advice given prove negligent.

FURTHER READING

Primary sources

Banco Exterior Internacional v. *Mann* [1995] 1 All ER 936

Bank of Credit and Commerce SA v. *Aboody* [1994] 1 AC 180

Barclays Bank plc v. *O'Brien* [1994] 1 AC 180

Barclays Bank plc v. *Thomson* [1997] 4 All ER 816

Secondary sources

McMurtry, L. (2000) 'Unconscionability and Undue Influence: an Interaction' [2000] *Conv*, 594.

Thompson, M.P. (2002) 'Wives, Sureties and Banks' [2002] *Conv*, 174.

Thompson, M.P. (2003) 'Undue Influence before Etridge' [2003] *Conv*, 314.

Payne v. Inwood (1996) 74 P&CR 42

Deborah Rook, Northumbria University

Payne v. *Inwood* is not a ground-breaking case, but it is highly illustrative of a complex area of easements: the acquisition of easements. Students rarely have any difficulty in ascertaining whether a right is capable of being an easement. The essential characteristics of an easement, as established in *Re Ellenborough Park* are relatively easy to understand and apply. However, things become more challenging when one considers whether a right, which is clearly *capable* of being an easement, has, in fact, been validly *acquired*.

The methods of acquiring an easement

There are various methods of acquiring an easement but not all of these methods can be applied in all situations. There are a number of hurdles to jump over in order to successfully apply a given method.

The first hurdle – a grant or a reservation?
The first hurdle being to decide whether the stated facts give rise to a grant of an easement or a reservation of an easement. This distinction is crucial to understanding the acquisition of easements. Easements exist for the benefit of land and therefore there will usually be a close proximity between the two parcels of land. The dominant land will enjoy a benefit over the servient land. A grant of an easement generally arises where a landowner sells part of his land and gives the purchaser an easement over the retained land, for example a right of way across a track on the land retained by the seller. Thus a grant of an easement arises where the land sold (or leased) has the benefit of the easement over the land retained. A reservation of an easement is exactly the opposite. Here the landowner sells part of his land but wants to retain a right over the land being sold, for example a right of way across a driveway sold to the purchaser. Thus a reservation of an easement arises where the land retained by the seller has the benefit of the easement over the land sold (or leased).

The second hurdle – which method applies?
Determining whether facts give rise to a grant or a reservation is crucial because not all of the methods of acquiring an easement apply to a reservation. The methods of acquisition available on a grant of an easement are as follows:

1. Express grant by deed.

2. Section 62, Law of Property Act 1925 (LPA 1925).

369

3. The rule in *Wheeldon* v. *Burrows*.

4. Necessity.

5. Common intention.

However, for a reservation of an easement only an express reservation by deed or an implied reservation by necessity and common intention are available. The rule in *Wheeldon* v. *Burrows* and the part of s.62 LPA 1925 that creates new easements do not apply to reservations of easements.

If there is no express grant/reservation by deed, then it becomes necessary to examine the various methods of impliedly creating an easement to see if any apply. Where the facts concern a possible grant of an easement, it is generally best to rely upon the rule in *Wheeldon* v. *Burrows* or s.62 LPA 1925 rather than using the more precarious methods of necessity and common intention, which generally apply in very limited circumstances such as landlocked property. It is an oversimplification to state that the rule in *Wheeldon* v. *Burrows* and the use of s.62 LPA 1925 are mutually exclusive. However, in most situations, only one of these methods will apply. The difficulty for students is deciding which to apply in any given scenario.

The third hurdle – the rule in *Wheeldon* v. *Burrows* or s.62 LPA 1925?

In most cases the decisive factor is the nature of the occupation of the relevant parcels of land immediately before the easement was created. If the two parcels of land (i.e. the land that becomes the dominant and servient tenements) are owned and occupied by one person immediately before the purported grant of the easement, then the rule in *Wheeldon* v. *Burrows* can be considered. However, if the two parcels of land are occupied by two different persons then s.62 LPA 1925 can be applied. *Payne* v. *Inwood* clarifies this point. The case makes it clear that in order to trigger s.62 LPA 1925 to create a new easement there needs to be diversity of occupation, i.e., different occupiers of the dominant and servient tenement. The case illustrates this point and in doing so emphasises the requisite timing for establishing different occupiers. Diversity of occupation needs to be immediately before the easement was created.

The facts

The background

The two parcels of land at the heart of *Payne* v. *Inwood* were adjoining terraced houses known as number 1 and number 1A. Each house had a yard at the back of it. The yard behind house 1A was accessible from the front of the house by walking through the front door and exiting by the back door into the yard. However, there was another route of access to the yard and this was the source of the dispute. To access the yard behind house 1A it was also possible to walk alongside house 1 and pass through the yard behind house 1. The respondents, the owners of house 1A, argued that they had an easement to use this alternative route of access to their yard. The appellants, the owners of house 1, submitted that the respondents had only a licence which was revocable at will. At first instance the judge decided that an easement had been created by means of s.62 LPA 1925. The Court of Appeal reversed that decision and held that no easement had been granted. The history and chronology of ownership and occupation was crucial to the outcome of this case.

Initially house 1A was owned and occupied by Miss C and house 1 was owned and occupied by another. Miss C enjoyed a licence to use the alternative route of access to her yard. Later house 1 was put up for sale and Miss C purchased it. For one week both houses, 1 and 1A, were owned exclusively by Miss C until the sale of house 1A to Miss W. Miss C later sold house 1 to Mr and Mrs Inwood and house 1A was subsequently purchased by Mr and Mrs Payne.

Creating an easement from a licence

Mr and Mrs Payne submitted that Miss W had acquired an easement under s.62 LPA 1925 when she purchased house 1A. Section 62 is an unusual statutory provision because it serves two very different purposes. On the one hand it acts as a word saving provision and automatically transfers the benefit of existing easements on the sale of the dominant tenement to a new owner. On the other hand it creates new easements from existing licences, and it was this aspect of s.62 LPA which was considered in *Payne* v. *Inwood*. There are a number of prerequisites to the creation of a new easement under s.62. These can be summarised as follows:

(a) There must be a conveyance, for example a transfer or grant of a legal estate by deed; and

(b) There must be diversity of occupation of the two parcels of land immediately prior to the creation of the easement (see the next section below); and

(c) There must be some previous user of a 'right', for example a licence to do what it is that is now claimed as an easement.

Let us use the case of *Goldberg* v. *Edwards* to illustrate these points. In that case, s.62 operated to convert a licence into a legal easement. Goldberg was occupying an annex at the back of the house owned by Edwards. Edwards gave Goldberg permission to walk through the front door of his house to access the annex as an alternative to the outside access. Edwards later granted Goldberg a legal leasehold estate. At this point s.62 converted the licence to walk through the house into an easement. The prerequisites listed above were all satisfied: there was a deed granting a legal estate; there were two different occupiers of the annex and house immediately prior to the grant of the lease; and there was a pre-existing licence to walk through the house.

The need for diversity of occupation

Why did s.62 fail to create an easement in *Payne* v. *Inwood*? Two reasons were given. Firstly, there was no evidence of the use of the access route along the side of house 1 by previous owners of house 1A. Section 62 cannot create new rights where there has been no actual enjoyment of the 'right' by the owner of the dominant tenement over the servient tenement. A new easement cannot be created from nothing. Secondly, there was no diversity of occupation of the two parcels of land just before the transfer of the legal estate to Miss W. Miss C owned and occupied both houses for one week prior to the sale of house 1A to Miss W and this was fatal to the claim.

Payne v. *Inwood* was not the first case to establish the need for diversity of occupation in the use of s.62. The significance of this case was instead its clarification of an ambiguity in the law. The House of Lords' decision in *Sovmots Investments Ltd* v. *Secretary of State for the Environment* is usually cited as authority for the need for diversity of occupation. Lord Wilberforce explained the reasoning for diversity of occupation:

> The reason is that when land is under one ownership one cannot speak in any intelligible sense of rights, or privileges, or easements being exercised over one part for the benefit of another. Whatever the owner does, he does as owner and, until a separation occurs, of ownership or at least of occupation, the condition for the existence of rights, etc., does not exist.

However, while confirming the earlier decision in *Long* v. *Gowlett* on this point, the discussion in *Sovmots* on the need for diversity of occupation was only *obiter dicta*. Following *Sovmots* there was some ambiguity as to whether diversity of occupation was in fact needed to trigger s.62 LPA. The decision in *Payne* v. *Inwood* has now laid that uncertainty to rest.

Continuous and apparent use

There is, however, one exception to the need for diversity of occupation. If the use of the 'right' is continuous and apparent so that it is self-evident that the user attaches to the land that becomes the dominant land, then it does not matter if, prior to the conveyance, the two parcels of land were owned and occupied by one person. This was the decision in *Broomfield* v. *Williams* and was recently confirmed in *P&S Platt Ltd* v. *Crouch*. Both these cases concerned the right to light and in *Payne* v. *Inwood* the court recognised that the right to light is in a special category. It is possible that this exception to the rule of diversity of occupation may be limited to rights to light.

The rule in *Wheeldon* v. *Burrows*

At first instance the court rejected a claim that an easement has been acquired using the rule in *Wheeldon* v. *Burrows*. Why was the claim rejected since there is no need for diversity of occupation under *Wheeldon* v. *Burrows*? In fact the most likely scenario for successfully applying *Wheeldon* v. *Burrows* is where the two parcels of land are owned and occupied by one person just before the purported creation of the easement. In *Payne* v. *Inwood* this was exactly the position. Miss C owned and occupied both houses and then sold one of them to Miss W. Surely this is an ideal scenario for applying *Wheeldon* v. *Burrows*? The answer is 'yes, it is'. However, it does not mean that an easement was created. For an easement to be impliedly granted using the rule in *Wheeldon* v. *Burrows*, a number of rules must first be satisfied. Prior to selling off part of his land, an owner must have used the 'right', for example, a route of access, that is now claimed by the purchaser as an easement. This is not really a 'right' as such because the owner is simply using his own land. But for the purposes of *Wheeldon* v. *Burrows* the use of this 'right' is called a quasi-easement. This is simply a label that is attached to a particular use by the owner of his own land and should not be confused with an actual easement. To convert this quasi-easement into an actual easement, three rules must be considered. The quasi-easement must be:

(a) continuous and apparent;

(b) necessary to the reasonable enjoyment of the land transferred;

(c) used by the owner at the date of the transfer for the benefit of the land sold.

The respondents in *Payne v. Inwood* would have struggled to satisfy the second rule listed above. The case of *Wheeler v. J.J. Saunders* also involved an alternative route of access for the benefit of the land sold to the claimant. In this respect it was very similar to *Payne v. Inwood*. In *Wheeler v. Saunders* the claimant failed to establish an easement. The reason the claim failed was that the claimant already had a route of access onto his land which was suitable and adequate and consequently the court held that an alternative, second route of access was not necessary to the reasonable enjoyment of the land transferred.

Conclusion

The significance of *Payne v. Inwood* lies in its clarification of the law. Here was a clear Court of Appeal endorsement of the House of Lords' *obiter dicta* in *Sovmots* concerning the need for diversity of occupation in the use of s.62 LPA to create a new easement. This endorsement was necessary to end the years of speculation.

FURTHER READING

Primary sources

Broomfield v. Williams [1897] 1 Ch 602

Goldberg v. Edwards [1950] Ch 247

Long v. Gowlett [1923] 2 Ch 177

P&S Platt Ltd v. Crouch [2004] 1 P & CR 18

Re Ellenborough Park [1956] Ch 131

Sovmots Investments Ltd v. Secretary of State for the Environment [1979] AC 144

Wheeldon v. Burrows (1879) 12 ChD 31

Wheeler v. J.J. Saunders [1996] Ch 19

7

LAND LAW (PROPERTY LAW)

The enforceability of freehold covenants

Rhone v. Stephens [1994] 2 AC 310

Deborah Rook, Northumbria University

The rules for the enforceability of freehold covenants

Freehold covenants generally arise when an owner sells part of his land. In order to pre-serve the quality and value of his retained land he may require the purchaser to enter into covenants (promises made by deed). For example, a covenant not to use the land for business purposes or a covenant to contribute to the maintenance costs of a shared driveway. These covenants are enforceable between the original parties by privity of contract, but when either, or both, of the original parties sell their land, can the covenants be enforced by, or against, their successors in title? It is important to appre-ciate that each covenant has a benefit and a burden. The original covenantee enjoys the benefit of the covenant and when he sells his land the benefit must pass to his succes-sor in title for her to be able to enforce the covenant. The original covenantor has the burden of the covenant and when he sells his land the burden must pass to his succes-sor in title for her to be liable under the covenant. A number of rules determine whether the benefit and/or burden have passed in any given instance.

The enforceability of freehold covenants is a complex area of law that is in need of reform. The Court of Appeal recently added its voice to the call for urgent Parliamen-tary intervention (*Thamesmead Town Ltd* v. *Allotey*). It can be a bewildering array of rules to the unprepared law student and the key to understanding how to use the rules is to break them down into a series of questions, each leading to the next. For example, 'is the covenant negative or positive'? 'Has the burden of the covenant passed to the successor in title of the covenantor'? (if so, has it passed at law or in equity?) 'Has the benefit of the covenant passed to the successor in title of the covenantee'? (if the bur-den passes in equity the benefit must also pass in equity). Breaking a problem down into this series of successive questions makes it easier to work through it.

The case of *Rhone* v. *Stephens* concerned a positive covenant, that is, a covenant which requires the expenditure of money. A negative covenant is simply the opposite and requires no money. A covenant not to allow a boundary wall to fall into disrepair is a positive covenant even though it is worded negatively because money is needed to comply with the covenant. When examining the rules for the enforceability of free-hold covenants, it is imperative to appreciate that covenants may be enforced in law or in equity.

Different enforcement rules in law and in equity

Under the common law the burden of a positive covenant cannot pass to a successor in title of the covenantor. This is because a person cannot be made liable upon a contract unless he or she was a party to it. The case of *Austerberry* v. *Oldham Corporation* is clear authority for this rule. But can the burden pass to the successor in title in equity? In the days before the fusion of the jurisdiction of law and equity, the courts of equity in 1848 reached a landmark decision in *Tulk* v. *Moxhay*. This case permitted the burden of a covenant to pass to a successor in title in equity provided that certain conditions were satisfied. Over the years these conditions have become known as the *Tulk* v. *Moxhay* rules and are as follows:

(i) the covenant must be negative;

(ii) the covenantee must retain land at the date of the covenant and the covenant must touch and concern that retained land;

(iii) the original parties must have intended the burden to run with the land;

(iv) general equitable principles apply which nowadays equates to the need for registration of the restrictive covenants either as a Class D(ii) land charge in unregistered land or by the entry of a notice on the charges register if the estate is registered at HM Land Registry.

It is clear from these rules that for the burden to pass in equity the covenant must be a negative covenant (*Haywood* v. *Brunswick Permanent Benefit Building Society*). Therefore if the covenant is negative the burden may pass provided the rules in *Tulk* v. *Moxhay* are satisfied, whereas if the covenant is positive the burden cannot pass at common law or in equity. This can seem somewhat harsh on the unsuspecting covenantee but there are a number of ways of circumventing the fact that the burden of a positive covenant does not pass. One such way comes from the case of *Halsall* v. *Brizell* and is called the doctrine of mutual benefit and burden. It was this doctrine that the court considered in *Rhone* v. *Stephens* and to understand the significance of *Rhone* v. *Stephens* we need first to examine *Halsall* v. *Brizell*.

The doctrine of mutual benefit and burden in *Halsall* v. *Brizell*

This case concerned the enforceability of a positive covenant to contribute to the maintenance of estate roads and sewers. The original covenantor purchased a house and in the conveyance he entered into a positive covenant to pay towards the maintenance costs of the facilities over which he was granted an easement. Therefore, he enjoyed the benefit of the easements to use the facilities, as expressly granted in the conveyance, and in return he accepted the burden of contributing to their maintenance.

But what happened when the original covenantor, who was clearly bound by privity of contract to comply with the positive covenants, sold his house to a third party? Did the burden of the positive covenant pass to the third party? *Austerberry* v. *Oldham Coporation* tells us that the burden cannot pass at common law and the rules in *Tulk* v. *Moxhay* for passing the burden in equity only apply to negative covenants and have no application here. At first sight it would seem that the third party purchaser was not bound by the covenant to contribute to the maintenance of the facilities. But in *Halsall* v. *Brizell*, the court relied on broad principles of justice to the effect that a person cannot take the benefit of a transaction without taking the burden also. The third party purchaser could not enjoy the expressly granted easements to use the estate roads and drains without accepting the burden of contributing to their maintenance.

Rhone v. Stephens

This case clarified a number of points concerning the enforcement of positive covenants and, in particular, the use of the doctrine of mutual benefit and burden. The chief contribution of this case was to clarify two requirements for the application of this doctrine. Firstly, the need for mutuality between the benefit and burden. The burden of spending money must directly relate to whatever benefit is enjoyed. There was a clear relationship of mutuality in *Halsall* v. *Brizell* where the money was to maintain the roads and drains over which the person enjoyed an easement. Secondly, the successors in title must have the opportunity to choose whether or not to take the benefit and thereby to be able to escape the burden (of spending money) if the benefit is rejected.

The facts of the case concerned a large house which had been divided into two separate dwellings, known as Walford House and Walford Cottage. The roof of the house extended over part of the cottage. When the owner of the house sold the cottage he covenanted, on behalf of himself and his successors in title, to keep the roof of the house in good repair (since any disrepair would affect the cottage also). Over time both the house and the cottage were sold and eventually the new owners of the house allowed the roof of the house to fall into disrepair so that water leaked into the bedroom of the cottage.

The difference between enforcing a negative and a positive covenant

The new owners of the cottage wanted to enforce the positive covenant against the successor in title of the original covenantor, but the burden of a positive covenant does not pass at law or in equity. Lord Templeman explained why equity will intervene in the enforcement of the restrictive covenant but not a positive covenant: 'Equity does not contradict the common law by enforcing a restrictive covenant against a successor in title of the covenantor but prevents the successor from exercising a right which he never acquired.'

It is a subtle but vital distinction. In *Tulk* v. *Moxhay*, the restrictive covenant preventing the owner from building on part of Leicester Square in London could be enforced in equity because the owner had never acquired the right to build on that land. The conveyance imposed restrictions depriving the owner of some of the rights which he could otherwise exercise over the land, for example, the right to unrestricted building. Therefore equity can prevent a breach of a negative covenant and thereby treat the land as subject to a restriction, but cannot compel an owner to comply with a positive covenant which would thereby require him or her to spend money when they had not contracted to do so. Lord Templeman explained that, 'Enforcement of a positive covenant lies in contract; a positive covenant compels an owner to exercise his rights. Enforcement of a negative covenant lies in property; a negative covenant deprives the owner of a right over property'. In this respect *Rhone* v. *Stephens* was merely confirming the existing reasoning behind the rule that only the burden of a negative covenant can pass in equity.

The first requirement – the need for mutuality between the benefit and the burden

The cottage owners sought to invoke the doctrine of mutual benefit and burden from *Halsall* v. *Brizell*. It was accepted that the house owners enjoyed the benefit of the right of support, an easement that arises when two adjoining houses share a common wall. It was contended that if the house owners enjoyed the benefit of the right of support they must accept the burden of maintaining the roof. The House of Lords emphatically rejected this line of argument. There was no relationship of reciprocity between the specified benefit and burden. Taking a benefit under a conveyance, for example a right of support, does not make every burden in the conveyance enforceable.

The second requirement – an element of choice

Their Lordships developed a further dimension to the rule in *Halsall* v. *Brizell* by stating that for the application of the doctrine of mutual benefit and burden there must be an element of choice as to whether or not to accept the benefit. If, as with a right of support, there is no choice and the person has to take the benefit, then, according to their Lordships *Halsall* v. *Brizell* has no application. Lord Templeman stated that

> In *Halsall* v. *Brizell* the defendant could, at least in theory, choose between enjoying the right and paying his proportion of the cost or alternatively giving up the right and saving his money. In the present case the owners of Walford House could not in theory or in practice be deprived of the benefit of support if they failed to repair the roof.

Choice plays a pivot role in the more recent case of *Thamesmead Town* v. *Allotey*. This case also concerned the rule in *Halsall* v. *Brizell*. The benefits at stake were rights to use shared roads, sewers, drains and communal landscaped areas on the estate. The burden at issue was to contribute to a service charge for the maintenance of those facilities. Mr Allotey was a successor in title of the original covenantor and he was reluctant to contribute to the costs of maintaining the shared facilities. He argued that the burden of the positive covenants had not passed to him at law or in equity and therefore he did not have to pay the service charge. What is particularly significant here was his claim that he did not want to use the communal gardens. If he never used the garden, he submitted, why should he have to contribute to its maintenance? The court agreed with his submission. It accepted that in cases where a successor in title of the covenantor chooses not to take the benefit of a facility then that person will not have to pay the price of any related burden. Consequently, Mr Allotey was spared the cost of maintaining the communal gardens, but did have to contribute to the maintenance of the shared roads and drains that he used. It seems clear that the courts are keen to limit too liberal an interpretation of the doctrine of mutual benefit and burden and have begun to construe its application narrowly.

7

LAND LAW (PROPERTY LAW)

Conclusion

There have been numerous calls for the reform of the existing law. It is clear that in some circumstances it would be beneficial for positive covenants to be capable of enforcement against successors in title. It is clearly unsatisfactory that there are no direct means of enforcement. Reliance on the indirect means, such as the doctrine of mutual benefit and burden, is invariably inconvenient and unreliable. It is with great interest that we await the Law Commission's consultation paper (2008) and ultimately its report on the law of easements and covenants.

FURTHER READING

Primary sources

Austerberry v. *Oldham Corporation* (1885) 29 Ch D 750

Halsall v. *Brizell* [1957] 1 All ER 371

Haywood v. *Brunswick Permanent Benefit Building Society* (1881) 8 QBD 403

Thamesmead Town v. *Allotey* (2000) 79 P & CR 557

Tulk v. *Moxhay* (1848) 2 Ph 774

Secondary sources

Goo, S.H. (1993) 'Enforcement of Positive Covenants' (1993) *Conv*, 234.

Gravells (1994) 'Enforcement of Positive Covenants Affecting Freehold Land' (1994) 110, *LQR*, 346.

The Law Commission, Report on the Law of Positive and Restrictive Covenants (Law Com No. 127, 1984.

Index

A and Others v. *Secretary of State for the Home Department (No 2)* 60-1
A-G's Reference (No 6 of 1980) 44
Abbey National Building Society v. *Cann* 335, 338-43
acceptance 167, 269-70
  battle of the forms 169
  by performance 170
  communication 169
  mode of 169
  postal acceptance rule 169
acte clair doctrine, EU law 125
actus reus
  attempts 23
  non-fatal offences against the person 13, 14
  theft 17
Adam Opel GmbH v. *Mitras Automotive UK Ltd* 175
Addis v. *Gramophone Co Ltd* 217, 221
Addiscombe 352
Adeneler v. *Ellinikos Organismos Galaktos* 116
administrative action, judicial review *see* judicial review of administrative action
administrative law, use of term 55
advertising, European Union 148
AG Securities v. *Vaughan* 353
AG v. *Guardian Newspapers (No 2)* 79
Agip (Africa) Ltd v. *Jackson* 323, 324
agreement to contract 170
  see also contract terms
Ailsa Craig Fishing Co Ltd v. *Malvern Fishing Co Ltd* 193
Albany International BV v. *SBT* 157
Albert v. *Lavin* 84
Alcock v. *Chief Constable of South Yorkshire Police* 232-3, 235
Allingham v. *The Minister of Agriculture and Fisheries* 95
AMG Group Ltd v. *Morrison* 107
Anns v. *Merton BC* 236
Antoniades v. *Villiers* 353
appropriation *see* theft
Arcaro 120
Armitage v. *Nurse* 313

arrest, powers of, breach of the peace 85
Ashburn Anstalt v. *Arnold and Another* 355, 356-8, 359
Ashe v. *Mumford* 300
assault occasioning actual bodily harm 14
Associated Provincial Picture Houses Ltd v. *Wednesbury Corporation* 95
Aston Cantlow and Wilmcote with Billesley Parochial Church Council v. *Wallbank and Another* 64, 70-4
attempts 21-3
  actus reus, determining existence of 23
  mens rea 23
  objectivist approach 22
  subjective approach 22
Attorney General Reference (No 2 of 1999) 10
Attorney General v. *Fulham Corporation* 95
Attorney-General for Jersey v. *Holley* 28-9, 30
Attwood v. *Lamont* 204
Austerberry v. *Oldham Corporation* 375
Austin and Saxby v. *Commissioner MPC* 87

Baker v. *T E Hopkins & Son Ltd* 251
Balfour v. *Balfour* 172, 179-83
Bank of Credit and Commerce SA v. *Aboody* 365
Barclays Bank plc v. *O'Brien* 364-6
Barclays Bank v. *Quistclose Investments Ltd* 293
Barclays Bank v. *Zaroovabli* 342
Barker v. *Corus UK Ltd* 246-7
Barnett v. *Chelsea and Kensington Hospital Management Committee* 242-3
Barrett v. *MOD* 239
Bartlett v. *Barclays Bank* 312, 313
Battered Woman Syndrome 26, 30
battle of the forms 169
Baumbast and R v. *Home Secretary* 143
Bayer AG v. *Commission* 157
BCCI and International Credit and Investment Company (Overseas) Ltd v. *Chief Labode Onadimaki Akindele* 321-4
Beatty v. *Gillbanks* 89
Becker v. *Finanzamt Münster-Innenstadt* 128
Belmont Finance Corporation 323
Bernini 142

bias, judicial review *see under* judicial review
Bidar 144
Bill of Rights 1689 64
Binions v. *Evans* 357
Blackburn v. *A-G* 99
Boggein v. *Williams* 20
Bond v. *an Adverteerders and Others* v. *Netherlands* 148
Bonnington Castings Ltd v. *Wardlaw* 243
Booth v. *White* 261
Bourhill v. *Young* 15, 231, 256
Bowerman v. *ABTA* 167, 169
Brasserie du Pêcheur v. *Germany* 130, 131
breach of contract
  damages
    aim 217, 219
    assessment 217
    for loss of amenity 220
    Ruxley Electronics 217-21
breach of the peace 89
  definition 84, 85
  developments since *Laporte* 87
  distinction between action to prevent
    imminent breach and action taken to
    prevent breach becoming imminent 87
  Laporte case 86-7
  power of arrest 85
  prevention 84-8
    action short of arrest 85-6
    legitimacy of action 85-7
Brice v. *Brown* 231
Brinkibon Ltd v. *Stahag Stahl und Stahlwaren handelsdesellschagt* 169
Bristol and West Building Society v. *May, May and Merrimans* 305
Bristol and West Building Society v. *Mothew* 303-7
Broomfield v. *Williams* 372
Burmah Oil Co. v. *Lord Advocate* 65
Burns v. *Burns* 297, 299
business efficacy test, contract terms 188, 190

Candler v. *Crane Christmas* 236, 238
Caparo Industries plc v. *Dickman* 225, 229, 236
Carillion Construction v. *Felix (UK) Ltd* 175
Carlgarth, The 265
Carlill v. *Carbolic Smoke Ball Company* 167, 168, 169-70
cartels, EU law *see under* EU law
Cassis de Dijon 132-8, 147, 148

causation 249-53
  chain of 250-1
    broken by intervening act 249-52
    defining *novus actus intervieniens* 250-1
    novus actus intervieniens 249-52
causation, factual 242-8
  but for test 242, 243, 246, 250
  joint and several damages 247
  novus actus interveniens 242
  remoteness 242
Central London Property Trust v. *High Trees House Ltd* 176
Chadwick v. *British Transport Commission* 231
Chan v. *Leung* 298
Chan Wing-Siu and Others v. *R* 49, 50
Chandler v. *DPP* 78
Chappel & Co Ltd v. *Nestle Co Ltd* 173
cheque guarantee cards 168-9, 170
Choithram v. *Pagarani* 285, 287
Christmas v. *General Cleaning Contractors* 266
Church of England Building Society v. *Piskor* 339
City of London Building Society v. *Flegg* 328, 331, 332, 336, 336-7, 343
Civil Partnership Act 2004 296
Civil Procedure Rules 1998 99
Clore v. *Theatrical Properties* 356
Coffey 20
Colegio de Oficiales de la Marina Mercate Espanola 143
Collier v. *P & MJ Wright (Holdings) Ltd* 176
Collins v. *Godefroy* 173
Collins v. *Willcock* 43
Combe v. *Combe* 176
Commercial Plastics Ltd v. *Vincent* 204, 205
Commission v. *Belgium* 142, 143
Commission v. *Belgium (Walloon Waste)* 134
Commission v. *Denmark (Danish Bottles)* 134
Commission v. *France* 143
Commission v. *Germany (Beer Purity)* 136
Commission v. *Greece (Processed Milk)* 137
Commission v. *Ireland (Re Souvenir Jewellery)* 134, 315
Commission v. *Italy* 112, 127
common law implied terms 186
Compensation Act 2006 247
competition
  abuse of dominant position in EU *see under* EU law
  cartels *see under* EU law
consensus in idem 170

consent and offences against the
person 42-6
body adornment 45
boxing and fighting sports 44
contact sports 44-5
definition of consent to injury 42-3
effectiveness of consent 43-4
exemptions to general rule 44-5
freely given consent 43
horseplay 45
informed consent 43-4
public policy or legal justification 45
surgery 44
Conservative and Unionist Central Office v.
Burrell 292
consideration 167, 170, 172-8
definition 172
economic duress 175
must be sufficient or real 173
part payment of existing debt 175-6
promissory estoppel 176, 177
conspiracy 23-4
constitutional law, use of term 55
contemplation principle, murder and joint
enterprise 49
contra preferentem principle 193
contract law 165-222
consideration *see separate entry*
contracts
essential features 167
for future performance 170
requirements for enforceable 170
contracts, freedom of 173
discharge 208-16
exemption clauses *see separate entry*
frustration of contract 208-16
implications and importance of *Davis*
judgments 215
modern legal test 214
radical alteration test 214, 215
intention to create legal relations 179-85
Lord Justice Atkin's speech 181-2, 183
presumptive tests 183-4
introduction 165
misrepresentation 197-201
damages 197, 198
fraudulent 197
innocent 197
offer and acceptance 167-71
agreement 170
see also acceptance; offer

remedies 217-22
restraint clauses 202-7
contract terms 186-91
express terms 186
implied terms 186, 187-90
basis for implication 188
business efficacy test 188, 190
common law 186
employment contracts 190
established usage 188
identifying presumed intention
of parties 189
officious bystander test 187, 189, 190
statutory 186
tenancy agreement 186-90
contractual licences 355-8
contributory negligence 259-61
definition 259
Cooke v. *Head* 297
Costa v. *ENEL* 112
Council of Civil Service Unions v. *Minister
for the Civil Service* 93
Council of Europe, establishment 109
covenants (freehold)
enforceability 374-8
doctrine of mutual benefit and burden
375-6, 377
negative compared with positive covenant
376-7
rules in law and equity 375
negative 374, 375, 376-7
positive 374, 376-7
Cowan v. *Scargill* 311, 312
crime statistics 1
Criminal Attempts Act 1981 21, 22
criminal, recklessness 33-6
objectivist approach 33-4
subjectivist approach 34, 35
Criminal Damage Act 1971 33
criminal law 1-53
consent and offences against the person 42-6
criminal damage, recklessness 33-6
defences, provocation and diminished
responsibility 25-31
gross negligence manslaughter 8-11
inchoate offences 21-4
intoxication defences 37-41
murder, joint enterprise 47-52
murder and intent 3-7
definition, direct versus oblique intent 3-4
direct intent 3

criminal law (*Continued*)
    oblique intent 4-7
  non-fatal offences against the person 12-16
  theft and appropriation 17-20
Criminal Law Act 1977 24
Crossley v. *Faithful & Gould Holdings Ltd* 190
Crown prerogatives 65
Currie v. *Misa* 172

D & C Builders v. *Rees* 176
da Costa en Schaake NV v. *Nederlandse belastingadministratie* 124
Dalton v. *Angus* 269
damage, remoteness of 254-8
damages
  breach of contract
    aim 217, 219
    assessment 217
    for loss of amenity 220
    Ruxley Electronics 217-21
  joint and several 247
dangerous drugs, intoxication defence 40
Dann v. *Hamilton* 260, 261
Davis Contractors v. *Fareham UDC* 209, 212-15
De Agnostini and TV-Shop 138
de Geus en Uitdenbogerd v. *Robert Bosch GmbH* 122
De Peijper 135
Deborah Lawrie-Blum v. *Land Baden-Württemberg* 140-4
declaration of trust 275, 276-7
  when required in writing 277
defences, intoxication *see* intoxication defence
defences to negligence *see* negligence, defences
Defrenne v. *Société Anonyme Belge de Navigation Aerienne (SABENA)* 151-3
demonstrate, right to 89-92
  reasonable use of the highway 90
Denkavit International BV Bundesamt für Finanzen 130
Derry v. *Peek* 238
DG of Fair Trading v. *Proprietary Association of GB Medicaments and Related Classes of Goods No 2* 107
DHN Food Distributors v. *Tower Hamlets LBC* 356
Dicey, A.V.
  Law of Constitution 64
  rule of law *see* rule of law, Dicey's rules
Dillenkofer v. *Germany* 130
diminished responsibility

  as defence to murder 25, 27-8, 31
    requirements 25
direct intent 3
discretionary trusts 280, 281, 282
disease, factual causation 243-8
Docherty v. *Brown* 22
doctrine of implied repeal 64
Donoghue (or Mc'Alister) v. *Stevenson* 225, 227-9
Donoghue v. *Stevenson* 238, 239, 255, 264
Dooley v. *Cammell Laird & Co Ltd* 233
Dori (Faccini) v. *Recreb Sri* 128
Dorset Yacht v. *Home Office* 236
Doughty v. *Turner Manufacturing Co.* 257
Downs v. *Chapell* 305
DPP v. *Camplin* 25, 26, 27, 29, 30
DPP v. *Jones (Margaret)* 89, 91, 92
DPP v. *Majewski* 37-41
DPP v. *Smith* 14
Dr Bonham's Case 65, 104
Drake v. *Whipp* 299, 300
Dulieu v. *White* 231
Duncan v. *Jones* 85
Dunlop v. *Selfridge* 172
duty of care 225-30, 236-41
  assumption of responsibility 239, 240
  Donoghue v. *Stevenson* 225, 227-9
  fairness 236, 238
  foreseeability 236, 238
  gross negligence manslaughter
    see separate entry
  occupiers' liability 265-7
  pre-*Donoghue* 225-6
  proximity 236, 239
  special relationship 238, 239-40

Eagle Trust plc v. *SBC Securities Ltd* 323
easements, acquisition 369-73
  continuous and apparent use 372
  diversity of occupation, need for 370, 371-2
  grant compared with reservation 369-70
  methods 369-70
  pre-requisites 371
  rule in *Wheeldon* v. *Burrows* 370, 372-3
economic duress 175
economic loss, negligently inflicted 236-41
E'Estrange v. *F Graucob Ltd* 193
employees' wages, protection in event of employer's insolvency 127
employment contracts
  contract terms 190
  restraint clauses 202-6

Entick v. *Carrington* 57, 58, 59, 60
Entores v. *Miles Far East Corp* 169
Errington v. *Errington and Woods* 352, 355,
    357, 358
Esso Petroleum Co Ltd v. *Harper's Garage
    (Stourport) Ltd* 202
Esso v. *Mardon Petroleum Co Ltd* 197
*Etablissements Consten SA and Grundig-
    Verkaufs-GmbH* v. *EEC Commission* 156, 157,
    158-9, 160
EU law
    acte clair doctrine 125
    advertising bans 137-8
    competition, abuse of dominant position
        (Article 82) 161-4
    competition law, cartels (Article 81) 156-60
        anti-competitive agreement, sanctions 159
        block exemption regulations (BER) 159-60
        exemption 159-60
        and market integration 158
        prohibition 156-9
        scope, trade between member states 157
        scope, vertical and horizontal
            agreements 157-8
        trademark rights 158-9
    damages, retroactivity in claims 151
    direct effect 112-13, 116
        critique 118-19
        limitations 127-8
        requirements 113
    Directives, failure to implement 130
    effective judicial protection (l'effet utile) 116-21
    equal pay for equal work 151-4
        aim of Article 119 152
        developments since *Defrenne II* 154
        retrospective application 153
        temporal limitation 153
    freedom to provide services 145-50
        issues of public morality 149
        medical treatment 149
        private associations 149
        use of virtual communications 148
    incorporation into UK law 65-6
    indirect effect 116-21
    interpretation in national courts 118
    mergers, control of 164
    preliminary rulings 114, 122-6
        nature of procedure 124
        purpose 122, 123
        when obligation is not an obligation 124-5
    relationship with national law 111

    selling arrangements 136-8
    social policy 151-5
    soft law and interpretation of national law 120
    state liability
        criteria for 129-30
        establishing 128-9
        under *Francovich* 116
        as supranational law 111
        supremacy 112
    treaties
        horizontal direct effect 152, 153
        vertical direct effect 152
    undertaking, meaning of 156-7
Eugen Schmidberger v. *Austria* 134
European Atomic Energy Community 109
European Coal and Steel Community 109
European Communities Act 1972 65-6
European Convention on Human Rights 70
    freedom of assembly and association 89
    freedom of expression 89
    peaceful enjoyment of possessions 73
    summary of rights 73
European Court of Justice
    preliminary rulings 122-6
    relationship with national courts 122-3, 125
European Economic Community 109
European Union
    advertising 148
    citizenship 113
        introduction of concept 143
    customs union 114
    Directives, failure to implement 130
    fidelity principle 118
    free movement of goods 132-9
        Cassis de Dijon 132-8
        Cassis de Dijon, mutual recognition 136
        Cassis de Dijon, Rule of Reason 134
        Cassis de Dijon, ruling 136
        derogations as argued in *Cassis* 135
        derogations of Article 30 134-5
        MEQR 133
        principle of mutual recognition 136
        quantitative restrictions 133
        selling arrangements 136-8
    free movement of workers 140-4
        definition of worker 140-3
        public service derogation 142-3
        role of EU citizenship 143-4
        trainees as workers 142
    insolvency, wage protection for employees 127
    law *see* EU law

European Union (*Continued*)
loyal cooperation 118
market integration, contribution
of competition law 158
single market 114
solidarity principle 118
treaties 109
Lisbon 109
Europemballage and Continental Can v.
Commission 161-4
Evans et al. v. *DPP* 92
Eves v. *Eves* 297, 298, 299
exemption clauses 192-6
conditions for enforcement 192-6
clause covers breach 193-4
clause enforceable in light of UCTA 194-6
clause incorporated into contract 192-3
contra preferentem principle 193
definition 192
reasonableness test 195-7
Expert Clothing Service and Sales Ltd v.
Hillgate House Ltd 361-2
Expo Fabric UK Ltd v. *Naughty Clothing Co* 195
express terms 186

Facchini v. *Bryson* 351
Factortame 112, 119
Fairchild v. *Glenhaven Funeral Services Ltd*
245-6
family home
constructive trusts 296-302
direct contribution to purchase price
296, 299, 300
presumed resulting trusts 300
Farley v. *Skinner* 221
Farrell v. *Merton, Sutton and Wandsworth
Health Authority* 234
fiduciary duty
acting for two principals 306
breach of 303-8
equitable remedies 304
duties 303-4
role of fiduciary 303
Fitch v. *Dewes* 202
flying pickets 85-6
Foakes v. *Beer* 176
Forster & Sons Ltd v. *Suggett* 202
Foskett v. *McKeown* 316-20
Francovich v. *Italy* 114, 116, 119, 129-30
freedom of assembly and association 89
freedom of contract 173

freedom of expression 89
Froom v. *Butcher* 260, 261
frustration of contract 208-16
implications and importance of *Davis*
judgments 215
modern legal test 214
radical alteration test 214, 215

Gebhard 148
George Mitchell (Chesterhall) Ltd v. *Finney
Lock Seeds* 192-6
Ghaidan v. *Godin-Mendoza* 64, 74
Ghosh 20
Gillies v. *Secretary of State for Work
and Pensions (Scotland)* 107
Gisborne v. *Gisborne* 312
Gissing v. *Gissing* 296
Glasbrook Brothers Ltd v. *Glamorgan County
Council* 173
Goldberg v. *Edwards* 371
Goldsoll v. *Goldman* 204
Gomez 18, 19
goods, free movement in EU *see* European
Union, free movement of goods
Gourmet International Products 138
Grant v. *Edwards and Another* 297, 298, 299
Great Peace Shipping v. *Tsavliris Salvage
(International) Ltd* 215
Greer v. *Sketchley Ltd* 205
Gregg v. *Scott* 243-5
Grimaldi v. *Fonds des Maladies
Professionelles* 120
gross negligence manslaughter 8-11
breach of duty 9
defendant's state of mind 10
gross negligence 9-10
risk of death 10-11
when duty of care arises 9
Grzelczyk 144

Habermann v. *Koehler* 358
Hadley v. *Baxendale* 255
Halsall v. *Brizell* 375-6, 377
Hambrook v. *Stokes Bros* 231
Hammond v. *Mitchell* 298
Hancock and Shankland 4
Hanover Insurance Brokers Ltd v. *Schapiro* 206
harassment 13
Harris v. *Goddard* 346
Harrison v. *Duke of Rutland* 90
Harvey v. *Facey* 168

Haughton v. *Smith* 2
Haynes v. *Harwood* 250, 251
Haywood v. *Brunswick Permanent Benefit Building Society* 375
healthcare tourism, European Union 149
Heaven v. *Pender* 226, 228
Hedley Byrne & Co Ltd v. *Heller & Partners Ltd* 200, 201, 236-40
Herbert Morris v. *Saxelby* 203
Hickman v. *Maisey* 90
highway
    reasonable use for demonstration 90
    use incidental to right of passage
Hill v. *Chief Constable of West Yorkshire* 229
Hinks 19, 20
Hinz v. *Berry* 231
Hirji Mulji v. *Cheong Yue SS Co Ltd* 211
Höfner and Elser v. *Macroton GmbH* 156
Hollier v. *Ramblers Motors (AMC) Ltd* 193
Home Counties Dairies Ltd v. *Skilton* 204
Homicide Act 1957
homicide statistics 1
Hotson v. *East Berkshire Health Authority* 244
House of Lords Act 1999 64
Howard Marine & Dredging Co Ltd v. *Ogden & Sons (Excavation) Ltd* 198-201
Hubbard v. *Pitt* 90
Hughes v. *Lord Advocate* 257
Hui Chi-ming v. *R* 49
Human Rights Act 1998 60, 64, 66, 68
    freedom of assembly and association 89
    freedom of expression 89
    impact on judicial review, bias 107-8
    impact on official secrets legislation 80
    and public authorities *see* public authorities and Human Rights Act
Humphries v. *Connor* 85
Hünermund 137
Hunter and Others v. *Canary Wharf Ltd* 268-72
Hunter and Others v. *London Docklands Development Corporation* 268-72
Hunter v. *British Coal Corp* 233
Hunting Act 2004 63, 68
Huntingford v. *Hobbs* 300
husband and wife, agreements between, *Balfour* v. *Balfour* 179-83
Hussey v. *Palmer* 297

IDC Group Ltd v. *Clarke* 358
illness, factual causation 243-8

implied terms 186, 187-90
    basis for implication 188
    business efficacy test 188, 190
    common law 186
    employment contracts 190
    established usage 188
    identifying presumed intention of parties 189
    officious bystander test 187, 189, 190
    statutory 186
    tenancy agreement 186-90
inchoate offences 21-4
    attempts 21-3
        actus reus, determining existence of 23
        mens rea 23
        objectivist approach 22
        subjective approach 22
    conspiracy 23-4
    incitement 24
    meaning of 21
incitement 24
Indemnity Act 1965 65
Inland Revenue Commissioner v. *National Federation of Self-Employed and Small Business Ltd* 99-100, 101
Inland Revenue Commissioners v. *Rossminster* 59, 60
intent and murder 3-7
    direct intent 3
    oblique intent 4-7
        natural consequences test 4-5
intention to create legal relations 179-85
    Lord Justice Atkin's speech 181-2, 183
    presumptive tests 183-4
    social and domestic relationships 183-4
interest of the state, in *Ponting* 78-9, 80
intoxication defence 37-41
    dangerous drugs 40
    involuntary intoxication 38
    mens rea 38
    public policy 39-40
    self-induced intoxication 37
    specific and basic intent, distinguishing 39-40
    voluntary intoxication 37, 38-9
        and mistake 40
invitation to treat, compared with offer 168
IRC v. *Broadway Cottages* 281, 282
Isaac v. *Hotel de Paris Ltd* 352

J A Mont (UK) Ltd v. *Mills* 205, 206
Johnson v. *Unisys Ltd* 190

joint tenancy 344
  converted into tenancy in common 345-8
  description 344
  right of survivorship 344
  severance by written notice under LPA
      1925 346-8
  severance in equity 345-8
    description 345
    methods 346
  within in trust 345
Jolley v. *Sutton London Borough
  Council* 257
Jones v. *Lock* 276
Jones v. *Padavatton* 184
Joseph Constantine Steamship Line v. *Imperial
  Smelting Corp Ltd* 208
judicial review
  bias 104-8
    apparent bias test 105
    impact of Human Rights Act 107-8
    Pinochet case 104, 106, 108
    real possibility test 107
  as legal remedy, factors determining
      applicability 98
  and royal prerogative 94
judicial review of administrative action 93-7
  description 93
  grounds for 94-6
    illegality 95
    irrationality 95
    procedural impropriety 95
    proportionality 96
judicial review proceedings
  standing (locus standi) 98-103
    test for 98-102
    test for, legislation 99
    test for, scope of sufficient interest
        test 99

Keck and Mithouard 136-7
Kempf 141
Khorasandjian v. *Bush* 269, 270, 271
Kinch v. *Bullard* 345, 346-8
King v. *David Allen* 356
Kingsnorth Finance Co Ltd v. *Tizard* 327,
  328-31, 333, 336
Knight v. *Knight* 279
Knightley v. *Johns and Others* 249-52
Kohn 17
Kolpinghuis Nijmegen 120
Kranemann 142

Lamb v. *Eames* 291
land
  registered *see* registered land
  unregistered *see* unregistered land
Land Charges Act 1972 327, 359
Land Charges Register 327, 359
land law 325-78
  co-ownership 344-8
    joint tenancy 344, 345
    joint tenancy, severance in equity 345-8
    joint tenancy converted into tenancy
        in common 345-8
    tenancy in common 344, 345
    use of trust 344-5
  contractual licences 355-8
  distinction between personal and proprietary
      interests 355-6
  easement 325
  easements. acquisition 369-73
    continuous and apparent use 372
    diversity of occupation, need for 370, 371-2
    grant compared with reservation 369-70
    pre-requisites 371
    rule in *Wheeldon* v. *Burrows* 370, 372-3
  equitable interest, acquiring 336
    constructive trust 336
    express trust 336
    proprietory estoppel 336
    resulting trust 336
  equity of redemption, abolition 342
  estate, meaning of term 325
  freehold covenants, enforceability 374-8
    doctrine of mutual benefit and burden
        375-6
    negative compared with positive covenant
        376-7
    rules in law and equity 375
  lease/licence distinction 349-54
    exclusive possession 351, 352-3
  leases *see* leasehold property
  mortgages, undue influence 364-8
    mortgagee's duties 367-8
  overreaching 337, 359
  purchase of property
    completion day 341-2
    summary of considerations 325
  registration of title 332
    compulsory 332
  restrictive covenant 325
  see also registered land; unregistered land
Land Registration Act 1925 332, 333, 341, 359

Land Registration Act 2002 332, 333, 359
Lansing Linde v. *Kerr* 204
Law of Property Act 1925 277, 327, 342
Lawrence v. *Metropolitan Police Commissioner*
18, 19
Le Foe v. *Le Foe and Woolwich plc*
299–300, 301
Le Lievre and Another v. *Gould* 226, 228
lease
   compared with licence 349
   exclusive possession 351, 352–3
leasehold property
   breach of covenant 360–3
      complete 361
      continuing 361
      forfeiture 360–3
   certainty of term 359
   contract 360
   covenants
      breach *see* breach of covenant *above*
      negative 361
      obligations imposed 360
      positive 361
   creation of lease 359
   definition of lease 359
   exclusive possession 351, 352–3, 359
   remedy of forfeiture 360–3
   rent 359
   termination of leases 360
      reform proposals 362–3
Leclerc v. *Au Blé* 135
Leclerc-Siplec 137
legal advice, suspects in police custody 82–3
Letang v. *Ottawa Electric Rly Co* 261
Levin 141
liberty, right to 58, 60–1
licence
   compared with lease 349
   exclusive possession 351, 352–3
Lister v. *Romford Ice and Cold Storage*
Co Ltd 188, 189
Litster 119
Littlewoods Organisation Ltd v. *Harris*
203–5, 206
Liverpool City Council v. *Irwin* 186–90, 190
Lloyd 20
Lloyd v. *Dugdale* 358
Lloyds Bank plc v. *Rosset* 296, 297, 298, 299,
300–1, 336, 338, 343
Locabail (UK) Ltd v. *Bayfield Properties* 105
Luc Tiet Thuan v. *R* 27–8, 29, 31

McFarlane v. *EE Caledonia Ltd* 233, 234
McGhee v. *National Coal Board* 246
McGowan v. *Barr & Co* 226
Mcloughlin v. *O'Brian* 231, 232, 234
McPhail v. *Doulton (In Re Baden's Deed Trusts)*
279–82
McPherson v. *Buick Motor Co* 227
malice aforethought 3
Malik v. *BCCI* 190
Malone v. *Laskey* 269, 270
mandatory order 99
manslaughter
   compared with murder 8
   involuntary
      categories 8
      compared with voluntary 8
      use of word reckless 11
   voluntary, compared with involuntary 8
   see also gross negligence manslaughter
March v. *E & MH Stramare Pty Ltd* 246
Marleasing SA v. *La Comercial Internacional*
de Alimentación SA 117–18, 119, 128
Marshall v. *Southampton & South West*
Hampshire Area Health Authority 113,
118, 128
Martinez Sala 144
Mascall v. *Mascall* 285, 286–7
Mason v. *Provident Clothing & Supply*
Co Ltd 202
Matrimonial Causes Act 1973 296
Matthews 6
medical treatment, within European Union 149
mens rea
   attempts 23
   intoxication defence 38
   murder 3
   non-fatal offences against the person 13, 14
   theft 20
Merritt v. *Merritt* 183
Midland Bank Trust Co Ltd v. *Green* 327
Midland Bank v. *Cooke and Another* 299,
300, 301
Milroy v. *Lord* 275, 285, 286
Minister of Pensions v. *Chennell* 255
Ministère Public v. *Muller* 136
misrepresentation 197–201
   fraudulent 197
   innocent 197
   negligent, damages 197
Misrepresentation Act 1967 197, 201
Moenich v. *Fenestre* 204

Moloney 3, 4, 5
Morice v. The Bishop of Durham 291
Morris v. Murray 262
mortgages, undue influence 364-8
    mortgagee's duties 367-8
Moss v. McLachlan 85-6
Motherwell v. Motherwell 271
Mullen v. Barr & Co 226
murder
    compared with manslaughter 8
    defences
        diminished responsibility 25, 27-8, 31
        provocation 25-31
    and intent 3-7
        definition, direct versus oblique intent 3-4
        direct intent 3
        oblique intent 4-7
    joint enterprise 47-52
        contemplation principle 49
        definition 48
        knowledge that other person is armed 50-1
        scope of 48-9
        withdrawal from 52
    mens rea 3
Murphy v. Brentwood DC 229, 239

National Carriers v. Panalpina (Northern) Ltd
    210, 215
National Coal Board v. England 262
National Provincial Bank Ltd v. Ainsworth 356
National Provincial Bank Ltd v. Hastings
    Car Mart Ltd 356
national security 76
natural law 64, 65
Nedrick 5-6
negligence
    definition 223
    foreseeability 249-52
    see also economic loss, negligently inflicted;
        psychiatric injury, negligently inflicted
negligence, defences 259-63
    illegality 262-3
    volenti non fit injuria 261-2
nemo judex in casua sua 104-8
Nestlé v. National Westminster Bank 310-14
Neville Esates v. Madden 293
New Zealand Shipping Co v. AM Saterthwaite &
    Co 173
Ninni-Orasche 141
non-fatal offences against the person 12-16
    actus reus 13, 14

cause compared with inflict 15
    meaning of inflict 15
    mens rea 13, 14
Nordenfeldt v. Maxim Nordenfeldt 202
novus actus intervieniens 249-52
nuisance, private 268-72
NZ Shipping Co Ltd v. AM Saltherthwaite &
    Co 167

Oberg 143
oblique intent 4
    in murder, natural consequences test 4-5
occupiers' liability 264-7
Occupiers' Liability Act 1957 264
offences against the person, and consent see
        consent and offences against the person
Offences Against the Person Act 1861 12-16
offer 167, 168-9
    communication 168
    compared with invitation to treat 168
Official Secrets Act 1911 76, 79
Official Secrets Act 1989 77, 79, 80
official secrets legislation and the separation
        of powers 76-80
    impact of Human Rights Act 80
officious bystander test, contract terms 187,
    189, 190
overreaching 337, 359
overriding interests (land) 333-7
    actual occupation 333, 334-6
    description 333
    interest in land 333, 334-6
    key ingredients 333-4
    mortgagees' position 335-7
Overseas Medical Supplies Ltd v. Orient
        Transport Services 195
Overseas Tankship (UK) Ltd v. Morts Dock &
        Engineering Co Ltd (The Wagon Mound)
        250-1, 254, 255, 256-7
Owens v. Brimmell 259-60, 261
Oxley v. Hiscock 299, 300, 336

P&S Platt Ltd v. Crouch 372
Paarl Wilson and Co v. Partenreederei Hannah
        Blumenthal 215
PACE 81, 82-3
Paddington Building Society v. Mendelsohn
        335, 343
Page v. Smith 233
Palmer v. Tees Health Authority 234
Paradine v. Jane 209

Parker v. *Clark* 183, 184
Parker v. *Southern Railway Co* 192
Parliament
    binding successors 64, 65
    supremacy *see* supremacy of Parliament
Parliament Act 1911 66-8
Parliament Act 1949 67
Parochial Church Council as public authority
        see Aston Cantlow . . .
Paul v. *Constance* 275-8
Payne v. *Inwood* 369, 370-3
Pennington v. *Waine* 286-8
Percy v. *DPP* 84
Permanent Building Society v. *Wheeler* 306
Perpetuity and Accumulations Act 1964 290
perpetuity period, definition 290
Pettinghall v. *Pettinghall* 291
Pettitt v. *Pettitt* 296
Pharmaceutical Society of Great Britain v. *Boots
    Cash Chemists (Southern) Ltd* 168
Phelps v. *Hillingdon LBC* 239
Photo Production Ltd v. *Securicor
    Transport Ltd* 193
picketing
    flying pickets 85-6
    use of highway 90
Pinnel's Case 175-6
Pinochet case 104, 106, 108
Pioneer Shipping Ltd v. *BTP Tioxide Ltd
    (The Nema)* 215
Pirbright v. *Salwey* 291
Pitts v. *Hunt* 262
police
    detention
        free legal advice 82-3
        PACE requirements 82
    interviews
        Appropriate Adult 83
        tape-recording 83
    powers and the rights of suspects 81-3
    role of custody officer 82
Police and Criminal Evidence Act 1984
        (PACE) 81, 82-3
Polly Peck International plc v. *Nadir* 323
*Poplar Housing and Regeneration Community
    Association Ltd* v. *Donoghue* 72
Porter v. *Magill* 107
postal acceptance rule 169
Printers and Finishers Ltd v. *Holloway* 203
prison tariffs, Home Secretary's powers
        to increase 59

private nuisance 268-72
Procureur du Roi v. *Dassonville* 133
professional qualifications, and freedom
        to provide services in EU 146-9
promissory estoppel 176, 177
property law *see* land law
property purchase
    completion day 341-2
    summary of considerations 325
proportionality and grounds for judicial review
        of administrative action 96
proprietory estoppel 336
provocation
    as defence to murder 25-31
    reasonable man test 25-31
    requirements 1957
Prudential Assurance Co Ltd v. *London
    Residuary Body* 357
psychiatric injury
    as bodily harm 12-16
    negligently inflicted 231-5
        Alcock 232-3, 235
        developments after *Alcock* 233-4
        involuntary participants 233, 234
        law before *Alcock* 231
        rescuers 233, 234
        secondary victims 232-3, 234, 235
psychological harm 13
public authorities
    and Human Rights Act 70-5
    meaning of public authority 72-3
    ultra vires actions 94-5
public interest defence 78, 79, 80
Pupino 120
purposive construction 116

R (Campaign for Nuclar Disarmanent) v. *Prime
    Minister* 102
R (Daly) v. *Secretary of State for the Home
    Department* 96
R (Laporte) v. *Chief Constable of
    Gloucestershire* 86-7
R (on the application of D) v. *DPP* 35
R (on the application of Haw) v. *Secretary of
    State for the Home Department* 92
R (on the application of Heather) v. *Leonard
    Cheshire Foundation* 72
R (on the application of Jackson and Others) v.
    Attorney-General 63, 64, 65, 66, 67, 68
R (Roberts) v. *Parole Board and Another* 61
R v. *Adomako* 8-11

R v. *Ahluwalia* 26, 27, 30
R v. *Aitken* 45
R v. *Allen* 38
R v. *Anderson* 48, 49
R v. *Barnes* 43, 44
R v. *Barnsley Metropolitan Borough Council ex parte Hook* 104
R v. *Bateman* 8, 9
R v. *Becerra and Cooper* 52
R v. *Billinghurst* 45
R v. *Blaue* 44
R v. *Bow Street Metropolitan Stipendiary Magistrate, ex parte Pinochet Ugarte* 104, 106, 108
R v. *Brady* 35
R v. *Brown* 42-3
R v. *Burstow* 12-13, 14, 15
R v. *Byrne* 27
R v. *Castle* 35
R v. *Chan-Fook* 12, 15
R v. *Chief Constable of Devon and Cornwall ex parte CEGB* 84
R v. *Coney* 44
R v. *Dobinson* 10
R v. *Dryden* 26
R v. *English* 47-52
R v. *G and Another* 33-6
R v. *Gittens* 27
R v. *Gough* 105
R v. *Greatrex* 51
R v. *Gregson* 30
R v. *Hatton* 40
R v. *Heard* 39, 40
R v. *Hinks* 17-20
R v. *HM Inspectorate of Pollution, ex parte Greenpeace Ltd* 101
R v. *HM Treasury, ex parte British Telecommunications plc* 130
R v. *Horseferry Magistrates' Court, ex parte Bennett* 60
R v. *Howell* 84
R v. *Humphreys* 26
R v. *Inner West London Coroner, ex parte Dallaglio* 105
R v. *Ireland* 12, 14, 15-16
R v. *James* 29
R v. *Jones* 45
R v. *Karimi* 29
R v. *Kingston* 38
R v. *Konzani* 43-4
R v. *Lattimore and Others* 81-2

R v. *Lawrence* 11
R v. *Lipman* 39
R v. *Misra* 10-11
R v. *Mitchell and King* 52
R v. *Mohammed*
R v. *Morgan James Smith* 25, 26-8, 29
R v. *Morhall* 26, 29
R v. *Morris* 19, 48, 49
R v. *Moses* 29
R v. *O'Flaherty and Others* 51, 52
R v. *O'Grady* 40
R v. *Olugboja* 43
R v. *Paddington and St Marylebone Rent Tribunal* 187
R v. *Parmenter*
R v. *Pigg* 23
R v. *Ponting* 77-9
and interest of the state 78-9
R v. *Powell and Daniels* 47-52
R v. *Rafferty* 49-50
R v. *Rahman and Others* 51
R v. *Richardson and Irwin* 40
R v. *Rowland* 28
R v. *Savage*
R v. *Savage and Parmenter*
R v. *Secretary of State for the Environment, ex parte Friends of the Earth* 102
R v. *Secretary of State for the Environment, ex parte Rose Theatre Trust Co* 101
R v. *Secretary of State for Foreign and Commonwealth Affairs, ex parte Lord Rees-Mogg* 100
R v. *Secretary of State for Foreign and Commonwealth Affairs, ex parte World development Movement Ltd* 99-100, 101
R v. *Secretary of State for the Home Department, ex parte Brind* 96
R v. *Secretary of State for the Home Department, ex parte Pierson* 59, 60
R v. *Secretary of State for Transport, ex parte Factortame Ltd* 66, 130, 131
R v. *Seers* 27
R v. *Seymour* 8
R v. *Shayler* 79, 80
R v. *Sheehan and Moore* 38
R v. *Shivpuri* 21-2, 36
R v. *Somerset County Council ex parte Fewings* 95
R v. *Stone* 10
R v. *Sussex Justices ex parte McCarthy* 104
R v. *Tabassum* 43

R v. *Thornton (No 2)* 26
R v. *Uddin* 51
R v. *Wacker* 9
R v. *Weller* 28
R v. *West London Coroner, ex parte Gray* 10
R v. *Wilson* 43
R v. *Woollin* 3, 6-7
Race Relations Board v. *Applin* 24
radical alteration test 214, 215
Re Adams and the KensingtonVestry 277
Re Astor 291, 292
Re Baden's Deed Trusts No 2 279, 282-3
Re Casey's Patents 173
Re Draper's Conveyance 346
Re Endacott 292-4
Re the European Union and taxpayers, ex parte Smedley 100
Re Gestetner's Settlement 281
Re Grant's Will Trusts 294
Re Gulbenkian's Settlement Trusts 281, 282
Re Haines 291
Re Hooper 291
Re Horley Town FC 294
Re Lipinski's Will Trusts 294
Re M 60
Re Montagu's Settlement Trusts 324
Re Polemis 254, 255, 256, 257
Re R [1991] 44
Re Recher 293
Re Rose 285, 286-7, 288
Re Saxone Shoe Co Ltd's Trust Deed 281
Re Selectmove Ltd 176
Re Thompson 291
Re Waterman's Wills Trusts 313
reckless, use of word in involuntary manslaughter 11
recklessness *see* criminal damage, recklessness
registered land 325
  actual occupation 331
  overriding interests 333-7
    actual occupation 333, 334-6
    description 333
    interest in land 333, 334-6
    key ingredients 333-4
    mortgagees' position 335-7
  priority of co-owners and mortgagees 338-43
    establishing priority 339, 340-1
    postponement of interest 338
    registration gap and *scintilla temporis* 339, 340-1
    tenants 342

property purchase
  completion day 341-2
  registration of change of ownership 341
  transfer of legal title 341
remedies, contract law 217-22
remoteness of damage *see* damage, remoteness of
Rent Acts 349-450, 362
rescuers, psychiatric injury 233, 234
retrospective legislation 64, 65
Rewe-Zentral AG v. *Bundesmonopolverwaltung für Branntwein (Cassis de Dijon)* 132-8
Rhone v. *Stephens* 355, 374, 375, 376, 377
Richards v. *Delbridge* 276
right to demonstrate *see* demonstrate, right to
Road Traffic Act 1988 261
Roberts v. *Chief Constable of Cheshire* 82
Robinson v. *Harman* 217, 219
Rockler 143
Roe v. *Minister of Health* 256
Roles v. *Natan* 264, 265-7
Rothwell v. *Chemical & Insulating Co Ltd and Others* 247-8
Rowe v. *Prance* 278
Royal Bank of Scotland v. *Etridge* 364-8
Royal Brunei Airlines v. *Tan that Baden* 324
royal prerogative, and judicial review 94
Royscot v. *Rogerson* 201
rule of law 57-62
  Dicey's rules 58-61
    absence of arbitary power 58, 59
    every man is subject to the ordinary law of the land 58, 59-60
    liberties are protected by judicial decisions 58, 60-1
  in *Entick* 58
  history 57-8
  today 61
Ruxley Electronics and Construction Ltd v. *Forsyth* 217-21
RW Green Ltd v. *Cade Bros Farm* 195

Säger v. *Dennemeyer* 146-9
St Albans City and District Council v. *International Computers Ltd* 195
St Helen's Smelting Co v. *Tipping* 270
sale of business, contract, restraint clauses 202
Sale of Goods Act 1979 194
SAT Fluggesellschaft v. *Eurocontrol* 157
Saunders v. *Vautier* 292, 293
Savva & Savva v. *Hussein* 362

Scala House & District Property Co Ltd v.
   Forbes 361
Scally v. *Southern Health and Social Services*
   Board 190
Scotland Act 1998 64
Securicor cases 193, 194
separation of powers
  description 76
  and official secrets legislation 76–80
services, freedom to provide *see* EU law,
   freedom to provide services
sexual assault, as crime of basic intent 39
Sexual Offences Act 2003 39
Shadwell v. *Shadwell* 173
Sharp v. *Powell* 255
Shelley v. *Shelley* 277
Shirlaw v. *Southern Foundries (1926) Ltd* 187
shop opening hours 137
Singh (Gurphal) 10
Smith v. *London & South Western Railway Co.*
  254–5
Sotgiu v. *Deutsche Bundespost* 142
South Caribbean Trading Ltd v. *Trafigura BV* 177
Sovmots Investments Ltd v. *Secretary of State*
   for the Environment 372
Spartan Steel v. *Martin* 238
specific and basic intent offences, distinguishing
  39–40
Spring v. *Guardian Assurance plc* 190
Springett v. *Defoe* 297, 300
Spycatcher (AG v. *Guardian Newspapers*
  (No 2)) 79
Srl CILFIT and Lanificio di Gavardo SpA v.
  Ministry of Health 122, 123–5
statutory implied terms 186
Steel and Lush v. *United Kingdom* 84
Steymann 141
Stilk v. *Myrick* 173, 174, 176–7
Stokes v. *Anderson* 298
Street v. *Mountford* 349–53, 359
supervening events 208
Supply of Goods (Implied Terms) Act 1973 195
supremacy of Parliament 63–9
  binding successors 64, 65
  history 63–4
  incorporation of EU law 65–6
  and international law 64, 65
  limitations 64–6
  retrospective legislation 64, 65
Supreme Court Act 1981 99
Swan v. *North British Australasian Co. Ltd* 260

Tamplin Steamship Co Ltd v. *Anglo-Mexican*
  Petroleum Products Co Ltd 211
Tankstation 't Heukske and JBE Boermans 137
Target Holdings v. *Redferns* 304
Taylor v. *Caldwell* 33–5, 210
telephone calls, silent and abusive 12, 13–16
television reception, interference with 268–71
tenancy agreement, contract terms 186–90
tenancy in common 344
  description 344
  within in trust 345
Thamesmead Town Ltd v. *Allotey* 374, 377
The Moorcock 187
theft 17–20
  actus reus, elements of
   appropriation 17
   belonging to another 17
   property 17
  mens rea 20
   dishonesty 20
   intention to permanently deprive 20
Thomas v. *Farr plc* 204
Thomas v. *Sawkins* 85
Thomas v. *Sorrell* 355
Thomas v. *Thomas* 172, 173
Thompson v. *LMSR Co* 193
tort law 223–72
  defences to negligence *see* negligence,
   defences
  introduction 223
  negligently inflicted economic loss 236–41
  negligently inflicted psychiatric injury 231–5
  remoteness of damage *see* damage,
   remoteness of
  see also causation; causation, factual; duty of
   car; negligence; occupier's liability;
   private nuisance
tracing 316–20
treaties 65
Treaty and Act of Union 65
Tremain v. *Pike* 257
trespassers 264
trespassory assemblies 91
Trojani 141
Trustee Act 1893 309
Trustee Act 1925 309
Trustee Act 2000 309, 312–14
Trustee Investments Act 1961 309
trustees
  investments by 309–15
   diversification of investments 313

duty to act fairly between life tenant and
 remainderman 314
in equities, restrictions 310
historical background 309-10
Standard Investment Criteria (SIC) 312-14
standards required, ordinary prudent man
 312, 313
standards required, reasonable 313
obligations 273
trusts
beneficiary principle 291
breach of fiduciary duty 303-8
 acting for two principals 306
 equitable remedies 304
causation, and remoteness 304
certainty of intention 275-8, 291
certainty of objects 275, 279-84
 class ascertainability test 281
 individual ascertainability test 281, 282-3
certainty of subject matter 275
clubs 294
common intention constructive trusts
 296-302
 absence of agreement, inferred common
 intention 298-300
 detrimental reliance 298, 299
 express agreement 297-8
constitution 285-9
 incompletely constituted 285
constructive trusts 300, 336
creation
 express trusts 275-8
 settlor declares himself to be trustee 275-7
 settlor transfers subject matter of trust to
 trustee 275, 277-8
declaration 275, 276-7
 when required in writing 277
definition 273, 291
discretionary 280, 281, 282
express trusts 336
 creation 275-8
 requirements for valid 275
family home
 constructive trusts 296-302
 direct contribution to purchase price 296,
 299, 300
 presumed resulting trusts 300
fixed 280
investments by trustees *see* trustees,
 investments by
knowing receipt of trust money 321-4

non-charitable 290-5
 rule against perpetual trusts 290-1
origins of concept 273
resulting trust 336
tracing 316-20
 compared with unjust enrichment 317
unicorporated associations 292-4
Turk v. *Moxhay* 375, 376

Unfair Contract Terms Act 1977 194
unincorporated associations
 definiton 292
 trusts 292-4
unregistered land 325, 327, 328-31
 doctrine of notice 327-8
 actual notice 328
 categories of notice 328
 commercial interests not registrable under
 LCA 1972 328
 constructive notice 328
 effect of 1925 legislation 327, 359
 family interests not overreached 328
 imputed notice 328
 residual role 327-8
 equitable rights compared with legal
 rights 327
 good root of title 332
 Land Charges Register 327
 purchaser
 notice of equitable interest 328
 reasonable enquiries and inspection 330-1

Van Duyn v. *Home Office* 113
Van Gend en Loos v. *Nederlandse Administratie
 der Belastingen* 111-15, 129
Videan v. *British Transport Commission* 251
Vlassopoulou v. *Ministrium fur Justiz* 146
volenti non fit injuria 261-2
Von Colson and Kamann v. *Land
 Nordrhein-Westfalen* 117-18
Von Colson v. *Land Nordrhein-Westfalen* 128

W v. *Essex CC* 234
Wagner-Miret v. *Fondo de Garantia Salarial* 119
Walter Rau v. *De Smedt* 135
War Charges Validity Act 1925 65
War Damage Act 1965 65
Ward v. *Byham* 174
Watford Electronics Ltd v. *Sanderson
 CFL Ltd* 195
Watson v. *British Boxing Board of Control* 240

Watts v. *Morrow* 221
'Wednesbury unreasonableness' 95
Weld-Blundell v. *Stephens* 254, 256
Westdeutsche Landesbank Girozentrale v. *Islington London Borough Council* 307
Westminster City Council v. *Haw* 92
Wheat v. *E Lacon & Co Ltd* 265
Wheeldon v. *Burrows* 370, 372-3
White and Collins v. *Minister of Health* 95
White v. *Chief Constable of South Yorkshire Police* 233-4
White v. *Jones* 238, 239

Williams & Glyn's Bank Ltd v. *Boland* 328, 331, 332, 333-6, 337
Williams v. *Carwardine* 168
Williams v. *Roffey Brothers & Nicholls (Contractors) Ltd* 173-7
Williams v. *Williams* 174
Wilsher v. *Essex Area Health Authority* 243
Wilson v. *First County Trust* 74
Winterbottom v. *Wright* 225-6
workers, free movement *see* European Union, free movement of workers
Wyatt v. *Kreglinger and Fernau* 202

The essential reference for all students of law

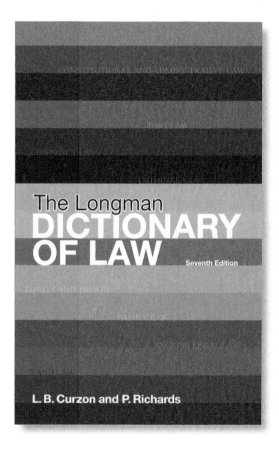

- Fully comprehensive entries on all aspects of English Law
- Clear definitions of specialised legal terminology
- Cross-referenced, giving full references for cases and statutes

The dictionary is fully supported by a companion website which links to additional legal information, and provides updates to definitions.

Available from all good bookshops or order online at:
www.pearsoned.co.uk/law